JOSEPH IN EGYPT

JOSEPH IN EGYPT

A CULTURAL ICON FROM GROTIUS TO GOETHE

BERNHARD LANG

YALE UNIVERSITY PRESS
NEW HEAVEN AND LONDON

Copyright © 2009 Bernhard Lang

All rights reserved. This book may not be reproduced in whole or in part, in any form (beyond that copying permitted by Sections 107 and 108 of the U.S. Copyright Law and except by reviewers for the public press) without written permission from the publishers.

For information about this and other Yale University Press publications, please contact:
U.S. Office: sales.press@yale.edu   www.yalebooks.com
Europe Office: sales @yaleup.co.uk   www.yaleup.co.uk

Set in Arno Pro by IDSUK (DataConnection) Ltd
Printed in Great Britain by TJ International Ltd, Padstow, Cornwall

Library of Congress Cataloging-in-Publication Data

Lang, Bernhard, 1946-
   Joseph in Egypt : a cultural icon from Grotius to Goethe / Bernhard Lang.
      p. cm.
   Includes bibliographical references and index.
   ISBN 978-0-300-15156-5 (ci: alk. paper)
   1. Joseph (Son of Jacob)   I. Title.
   BS580.J6L26 2010
   222'.11092--dc22

                                                                                                               2009013409

A catalogue record for this book is available from the British Library.
10 9 8 7 6 5 4 3 2 1

The paper used for the text pages of this book is FSC certified. FSC (Forest Stewardship Council) is an international network to promote responsible management of the world's forests.

Printed on totally chlorine-free paper.

for
St Mary's College
The University of St Andrews
Scotland

Contents

	List of Figures	viii
I	INTRODUCTION	1
1.	Joseph as a Cultural Icon in Early-Modern Times	3
2.	Joseph in Genesis	17
3.	Post-biblical Traditions	31
II	THE ICON OF PIETY: JOSEPH FOR CHILDREN	55
4.	On Education	57
5.	A Lesson in Godliness – Lavater	65
6.	Starting Life with Joseph – Goethe	84
	Appendix: Joseph Portrayed – Trautmann	100
III	THE ICON OF CHASTITY: THE HANDSOME HEBREW	113
7.	On Sexual Morality	115
8.	Libertine Libido – Mrs Rowe	123
9.	Irresistible Eros – Bodmer	138
10.	The Triumph of Chaste Love – Fielding	153
IV	THE ICON OF LEADERSHIP: JOSEPH THE STATESMAN	177
11.	On Statecraft	179
12.	Civic Humanist – Grotius	186
13.	Competent Courtier – Zesen	204
14.	Hebrew Freemason – Albrecht	228
V	AGAINST THE ICON: RADICAL READINGS	247
15.	On Historical Criticism	249
16.	Despotic Ruler – Morgan	255
17.	Tax Collector – Voltaire	270
VI	THE ICONIC TEXT: A BEAUTIFUL STORY	287
18.	On Literary Criticism	289
19.	A *conte philosophique* – Voltaire	296
20.	The Triumph of Beauty – Chateaubriand	317
	Postscript	336
	Notes	340
	Bibliography	366
	Index	385

Figures

1. *Les Devoirs de la vie domestique*. Par un père de famille. Brussels: Frères 't Serstevens, 1707, frontispiece. 58
2. J.R. Schellenberg, *60 biblische Geschichte des Alten Testaments in Kupfer geätzt*. Winterthur: verlag Heinrich Steiner, 1774, frontispiece. 78
3. J.K. Lavater, *Christliches Handbüchlein für Kinder*. 2nd edn. Zurich: Bürgkli, 1781, frontispiece. 79
4. J.G. Trautmann, *Joseph Sold by his Brothers*, c. 1760. Goethehaus, Frankfurt, Germany. © Freies Deutsches Hochstift, Frankfurter Goethe-Museum. 101
5. Rembrandt, *Joseph Accused before Potiphar*, 1655. Gemäldegalerie der Staatlichen Museen, Berlin. 103
6. B.E. Murillo, *Joseph and his Brothers*, 1670. Wallace Collection, London. By permission of the Trustees of the Wallace Collection, London. 104
7. Melchior Kysel [Küsell], *Icones Biblicae Veteris et Novi Testamenti – Figuren biblischer Historien Alten und Neuen Testaments*. Nürnberg: Büggel, 1680, figure 30. 105
8. B. Breenbergh, *Joseph Distributing Grain in Egypt*, 1645. Belasting & Douane Museum, Rotterdam, The Netherlands. 106
9. Rembrandt, *The Persian*, 1632. Source: Online Catalogue of Spaightwood Galleries, Upton, Mass. The print was sold in 2006. 107
10. J.G. Trautmann, *Joseph Selling Grain in Egypt*, c. 1760. Goethehaus, Frankfurt, Germany. © Freies Deutsches Hochstift, Frankfurter Goethe-Museum. 109
11. Henry Fielding, *The History of the Adventures of Joseph Andrews*. 5th edn. London: A. Millar, 1751, vol. 1, facing p. 30. 163
12. Henry Fielding, *The History of the Adventures of Joseph Andrews* (The Novelist's Magazine, vol. 1). London: Harrison, 1780, facing p. 20. 164
13. Henry Fielding, *The History of the Adventures of Joseph Andrews*. Illustrated with reproductions of the original designs. London: Heinemann, 1903, facing p. 36. 165
14. B. Breenbergh, *Joseph Distributing Grain in Egypt*, 1655. University of Birmingham, Barber Institute of Fine Arts; Birmingham, England. 201
15. Ph. von Zesen, *Assenat*. Amsterdam: Hagen, 1670, frontispiece. 215
16. Ph. von Zesen, *Assenat*. Amsterdam: Hagen, 1670, 111. 217
17. Ph. von Zesen, *Assenat*. Amsterdam: Hagen, 1670, 245. 220
18. Ph. von Zesen, *Assenat*. Amsterdam: Hagen, 1670, 141. 222
19. Emanuel Schikaneder, *Die Zauberflöte. Eine große Oper in zwey Aufzügen*. Music by Wolfgang Amadeus Mozart. Vienna: Alberti, 1791, frontispiece. 237

I

INTRODUCTION

1

Joseph as a Cultural Icon in Early-Modern Times

Blessed Joseph! I would thou hadst more fellows!
    John Bunyan, *The Life and Death of Mr. Badman* (1680)

There is not a more illustrious or beautiful example of virtue for the inspiration of youth in true or fabulous history than the story of the young Joseph as recorded in Genesis chap. xxxix. Not only that instance, but the whole conduct of this life, are such admirable examples of wisdom and virtue as must excite the most perfect esteem and love of his character, more than any fictitious description that ever was yet written.
    William Dodd, *The Beauties of History* (1795)

There is nothing more perfect than the hero of a book.
    Paul Scarron, *The Comical Romance* (1651)[1]

TRADITIONAL LIFE IN SEVENTEENTH- AND EIGHTEENTH-CENTURY EUROPE had its own, distinctive character. Although they lived in a world presumably as chaotic as ours, people had a stronger sense of order that led them to believe in what I suggest calling "imagined structures of stability", implying that neither the structures nor the stability were observable and demonstrable facts of life, but rather were ideals imagined to exist and be relevant. In the early-modern period in Europe, people were generally involved with strong "imagined structures of stability" such as family, church, profession, and social class. Life itself was seen as a closed process: as a sequence of recurrent acts, with events unfolding in variable fashion yet fundamentally unchanging. Action was perceived as repetitious, and no matter how seemingly new a moment might be, it was merely one instant within a continuum governed by traditional ideas, patterns, and paradigms. To step out of the pre-established pattern meant to sin against the universal order and, as a consequence, to be lost to the chaotic powers that loom at the margins of, or beyond, ordered existence. Life, in other words, was fundamentally characterised by assumed stability – the stability of established archetypes that guaranteed an overwhelming sense of comfortable security for all who followed their prescriptions.

A CULTURAL COMMUNITY

In early-modern times, until about 1800, the intellectual elite of the West had a clear understanding of the origins of the cultural system they supported: it was seen as deriving from three ancient peoples – the Hebrews, the Greeks, and the Romans. Life's essential institutions, patterns, and beliefs were all thought to have been established, discovered, or revealed in ancient times. People generally did not believe in cultural progress (a more recent notion) but in the sudden emergence, between the eighth century BCE and the first century CE, of a cultural style encompassing religion, morality, art, and law that was somehow unsurpassable and that should remain the standard for all subsequent ages. (In the twentieth century, the philosopher Karl Jaspers called this period the "axial age" of human history.) The literary legacy of this age – the Bible, ancient Greek literature (especially Homer, Plato, Aristotle, and Plutarch), and Roman writings (Virgil, Cicero, and legal collections) – was held in high esteem and deemed the most fundamental cultural and social resource. To be educated and equipped for life, one had to be familiar with this body of literature: with its prescriptions listed in the Ten Commandments and the sayings of Jesus, with its sacred tales of creation and paradise, with its many heroes and heroines of war and peace.

Much of the literature included in this canon has an oral background that favours, for mnemonic reasons, "heavy" characters, "persons whose deeds are monumental, memorable, and commonly public".[2] Wise Nestor, cunning Odysseus, and the brave Greek soldiers who died in battle at the pass of Thermopylae in 480 BCE, but also sinful Eve, chaste Joseph, and the suffering Christ: all these heroic types counted as "archetypal figures, by divine wisdom providentially inserted into the historical process"[3] to serve as examples of virtue or vice. "The accounts we have of the Old Testament saints were not intended for histories only, barely to inform and divert us, but for precedents to direct us, for ensamples", explains a biblical commentary published in 1720.[4] Tradition frequently emphasises the graphic quality of the example or model, producing, in the words of an eighteenth-century novelist, "a kind of picture in which virtue becomes, as it were, an object of sight".[5] Visual clarity implies easy, quick, and unambiguous comprehension. The exemplar of virtue is designed to evoke an image that may be absorbed instantaneously like a painting that can be "read" at a glance. Once an exemplary figure is evoked, he might be dubbed "a living image of all virtues" (*ille virtutum viva imago*).[6] The exemplar is beheld and admired as an "image" or "icon".

The proper – and often spontaneous – response upon encountering an iconic character was imitation, culminating in the imitation of the saints and especially of Christ, for these embody virtue often in heroic measure and sometimes in perfection. While no one can be obliged to live a life of absolutely perfect holiness or to continually perform heroic deeds, the saints nevertheless provide moral orientation. When early-modern teachers considered which materials to use for educating the young, the answer was easy: the ancient books about the ancient heroes. If there was anything like meaning and purpose in human existence, it was embodied in the ancient heroes and to be found in these very books. When one was looking for consolation in a life of misery, look no further than there. This body of literature catered to all needs one could possibly imagine; it was complete, and therefore, strictly speaking, no new books were needed, no supplements required to add missing episodes to stories or fill gaps in legal collections. But if there was to be new literature, cultural leaders claimed that it should be based on the ancient canon, for only then could it be culturally satisfying, morally useful, and aesthetically pleasing. To be relevant, a new book somehow had to echo and imitate certain stories, characters, or ideas familiar from the canonical corpus, thereby manifesting and renewing the undisputed – and imagined – ideal truth codified in that corpus.

It may be difficult for us in the twenty-first century to picture what life must have been like when to live meant to search for one's place within these "imagined structures of stability" and to be educated meant to be exposed, continuously and intensively, to the classical canon. Yet, even in contemporary life, we can occasionally get a glimpse of the traditional imagined order of being, its implied spirit, and the mentality associated with it. This happens on ritual occasions: when we attend a Sunday service at church which regularly culminates in the sermon, join friends to celebrate an annual holy day such as Christmas, or are present at the annual school prize-giving, with the headmaster invoking lofty ideals of democracy, progress, or the friendship between nations. All of these celebrations are not actual events in the sense of something unexpected and surprising that happens only once (and may therefore upset the calm course of everyday life); instead, they are rituals marked, as theatre theorist Bernard Beckermann suggested, by "iconic presentation". In iconic presentation, "we do not discover anything new; we merely witness a preordained action. In performance the scene has the effect of an unfolding ritual, every step of which is not unexpected".[7] Accordingly, rituals rehearse what people feel and know already. Intellectual rituals – rituals such as the delivery of a sermon to a congregation or the performance of a didactic play before an audience – serve the three functions of storing, reminding, and teaching: storing knowledge that might otherwise get lost, reminding a community of shared values and traditions and thereby strengthening its cohesion, and teaching the young.[8] Whenever we happen to be present when such rituals are performed, we are made aware of a world, now no longer extant, in which *all* of life was under the spell of iconic ceremony.

One iconic character, whose story was frequently told and even staged, was Joseph, the subject of the present study. In the seventeenth and eighteenth centuries, the biblical Joseph epitomised the ideal man: handsome, virtuous, and wise, he was promoted to high office and successfully dealt with an economic crisis that affected the world in which he lived. When reading and writing about Joseph in Egypt, people in early-modern times celebrated the virtue and wisdom embodied in the character of Joseph by reminding themselves of these attributes, strengthening their sense of community and solidarity, and passing on the intellectual treasures of the story to the next generation. Whenever someone wrote or read about Joseph, attended a theatrical performance of the story, or recounted the biblical tale to children, he or she participated in a huge communal intellectual ritual act. That act's central and paradigmatic figure, Joseph, individually or collectively contemplated, served as a cultural icon – an image of canonical status and hieratic quality against which people measured their own moral identity; a picture, moreover, rich enough in graphic detail to be convincing for the intelligent, but simple enough to be readily grasped even by the less able.

A COMMUNITY OF READERS

Reading presented the individual with an ideal opportunity to contemplate Joseph, one for which an archaic, venerable technique was available and widely practised. It had its prototype in the traditional monastic liturgy that required monks and priests to recite selections from the book of Psalms every day, and the whole Psalter every week, as prescribed in the Rule of St Benedict. When using this archaic reading technique, people "did not just read their books through, but lived them through. It was a matter of reminding themselves of ever the same ideas".[9] The typical English household of the eighteenth century, according to Paul Hunter, owned books containing moral advice and guidance on the practice of piety, books that were tirelessly read and re-read, supplying the reader with edification and moral instruction as well as pleasure. "The pleasures of repetition and the comfort of familiarity are seldom given their due in sophisticated literary theory," Hunter notes, "even though we know how important they are for oral audiences (well beyond their function as a mnemonic device for tellers) and for children who love to hear anything – rhyme, phrasing, story line – that they recognise from a previous telling."[10] Repetition and recognition are fundamental to the paradigm. Generally speaking, when reading a book in this archaic mode, people know from the start that there will be few surprises, for they are already familiar with the story, often from childhood, and they remember it from beginning to end. A book became a lifelong friend. In this sense, the humanist Erasmus of Rotterdam in 1501 exhorted his readers to make St Paul their "special friend" and spend much time with his letters: "You must have them always in your pocket. Read them by day, and study them by night, so as to know them by heart."[11] Texts from classical antiquity were also deemed appropriate for continual re-reading; in the words of Alexander Pope's *Essay on Criticism* (1711):

Be Homer's works your study and delight,
Read them by day, and meditate by night.

A literary example is Parson Abraham Adams (in Henry Fielding's novel *Joseph Andrews*, 1742) who never fails to carry with him an edition of the plays of Aeschylus – the ancient Greek playwright – copied out by hand, in the original Greek, and bound in calfskin. When this precious book is accidentally destroyed, he laments the loss of a "dear friend", his "inseparable companion for upwards of thirty years".[12] Often, individuals adopted this archaic mode of intensive reading in their study of the Bible. One example is the French philosopher Jean-Jacques Rousseau. In his memoirs he reports on his daily Bible reading – in bed, before falling asleep: "I have mentioned how I suffered from sleeplessness in my youth. Since then, I had got into the habit of reading every evening in bed until I would feel my eyes growing heavy. Then I would put out the candle and try to doze off for at least a few moments. My usual bedtime reading would be the Bible, and this way I have read the whole of it through at least five or six times."[13]

Rousseau's and Parson Adams's reading technique reflects an intellectual activity practised primarily in pre-modern times, when people of a more traditional mindset focused on a small number of canonical and quasi-canonical texts that they carefully read, re-read, and meditated upon. They absorbed what they read. They looked not for entertainment, but for something infinitely more serious: edification through the establishment of close contact, renewed every day, with the central texts and tenets of European culture. There are, of course, various levels of edification. At the lowest level, edification means pious entertainment based on superficial emotional involvement. At a more intense level, however, edification may be the outcome of an intense emotional as well as intellectual process: when readers come under the spell of a well-told story, they may be deeply touched and emotionally aroused to the point of being ready to change their lives, for instance by emulating – rather than merely imitating – Joseph (or some other hero) and leading a life nourished by the same spiritual resources as the protagonist of the biblical narrative. Identifying with Joseph, they create for themselves a new identity. This may involve adopting the same relationship with God, adopting the same belief in divine guidance, and displaying the same moral courage as their biblical role model. Readers thus may come to inhabit the same religious and moral space as the hero they know only from a book.[14]

In early-modern Europe, the emerging educated middle class, while still committed to the archaic mode of reading, developed a contemporary approach. It had its prototype in the study of the daily newspaper, an invention of the seventeenth century. This new reading technique was essentially a restless activity devoted to the consumption of new articles and books, the collection of information on a wide variety of subjects, and the fast absorption of fresh ideas. The modern reading habit has been characterised as "nomadic": "readers are travellers; they move across lands belonging to someone else, like nomads poaching their way across fields".[15] When based on this technique, reading was an unstructured, multi-focus activity that involved frequent displacement: from one book to the next, from novel to poem, from essay to stage play or epic, without finally settling upon one author or one literary type or one subject, or even one unified set of ideas. Reporting on his studies, Samuel Johnson admitted in 1763 that "I myself have never persisted in any plan for two days together"; this is not a defect, but in his mind becomes a general rule: "A man ought to read just as inclination leads him; for what he reads as a task will do him little good."[16]

Most early-modern readers came to adopt this new style of reading for which specialists have suggested the term "extensive" (as opposed to traditional "intensive" reading). A typical "extensive" reader was Anton Reiser, the semi-fictional titular hero of a German novel published in 1785. During his school-days, Anton "went to a vendor of used books and obtained one novel and one comedy after another, and began reading with a kind of fury", and, it must be added, with much emotional investment in his sentimental reading material, often shedding tears while reading, and entering by turns into the violent, raging passions of anger, fury, and revenge, and the mild emotions of magnanimous forgiveness and all-enveloping compassion.[17] Although "extensive reading" was thus associated with entertainment, the voracious consumption of "light" texts found in novels, newspapers, and magazines, and with nonchalantly passing from one text to the next, it was adopted by its more serious proponents to further their education and sharpen their wits.[18] The example of Samuel Johnson, already mentioned, belongs here. *L'Homme aux quarante écus* (The Man with Forty Crowns, 1768), one of Voltaire's many stories, provides another example of the new, Enlightenment approach to reading. With no more than forty crowns to his name, the hero – the emblematic Everyman – begins his career in poverty. Yet, clever though poor, he knows how to contest the many unreasonable claims that others make on him. He eventually succeeds in accumulating a small fortune, achieving a reasonable level of education and social prestige, as well as a real name – Monsieur André. Naturally, M. André also acquires some books: "How greatly did the mind of Monsieur André expand from the time he procured a library! He lives with his books as with people, and is as careful in his choice of them. What a delight it is to gain instruction, to expand one's knowledge by spending just one crown, without leaving home."[19] Monsieur now has the means to issue dinner invitations, and even the learned figure among his regular, carefully chosen guests. They eat, drink, and spend the night in lively, cheerful conversation – fuelled, no doubt, by their extensive reading.

Voltaire's story ends with an account of one such occasion. Present are M. André, his wife, a Sorbonne theologian, a well-known Jew, a reformed pastor, the secretary of a prince who, as a Christian, belongs to the Orthodox Church, and two philosophers, not forgetting three intelligent young ladies. The animated conversation of this mixed company is not confined to any one subject; instead, it ranges rather freely, always assuming the breadth of reading of all who participate. In fact, books are a favourite subject. The book of Genesis is mentioned, along with the tales of the *Arabian Nights*. Among the classical authors named are Virgil, Horace, and Ovid. The traditional canon, which includes the Bible, is not forgotten among those who read to further their education and promote their social status. Voltaire's story culminates in this advice: "Read; improve your knowledge. Reading alone invigorates the mind. Idle conversation distracts, and gambling makes one stupid."[20]

Writing Joseph

During the seventeenth and eighteenth centuries, much of the literary, intellectual, and political culture of the modern world emerged: the level of literacy increased considerably; reading material became more widely available and its consumption, for many, an obsession; the novel rose to become the most prominent literary genre; the art of the epic, while still practised with virtuosity, declined; the Enlightenment called for rationality in moral and political thought; and new religious and aesthetic sensibilities made themselves felt, announcing Romanticism and new ideals of individualism and personal fulfilment. Many features of this unique cultural climate are echoed in the unprecedented proliferation of literature focused on Joseph.

This literature emerged, as all literature does, from a market in which both authors and readers participated. In Joseph, people recognised their religious, moral, and political ideals. As they heard and read the biblical story anew, exposing themselves to it and absorbing it in the archaic, "intensive" way, a multi-layered mental image was built up – and in the hands of creative authors that image took on a life of its own. To understand why this should be the case we have to remember that in literary history the Joseph story ranks with the *Odyssey* and other ancient legends as a canonical model story that supplied authors with archetypal scenes and plots to imitate, elaborate, and allude to. Invited not least by the gaps and blanks left by the biblical narrator, authors expanded, embellished, reshaped, dramatised, and updated the biblical story to highlight the relevance of Joseph as a cultural icon for their own, seventeenth- or eighteenth-century society. They came to produce an entire library centred on Joseph: novels, stage plays, poems, books for children, operas, and critical treatises, all meant for more or less rapid consumption, for satisfying the appetite of readers (or theatre-goers) who no longer exclusively relied on the intensive reading technique. What readers were looking for in the retold story, and what authors sought to deliver, were new ways of telling the old tale, with a new emphasis put on certain ideas or episodes – a fresh slant – without, however, a change in the story's substance and general message. This acceptance of flexibility in the storyline permitted the introduction of innovative and decidedly modern ideas that belonged, in our terminology, to the new age of the newspaper. But however far authors might depart from the original biblical story, the Bible remained present as an "intertext", to borrow a term from modern literary theory: the parent or referent text of a literary work, directly or subtly alluded to and recognised by readers familiar with it. Just as the use of an intertext provides multiple literary possibilities for the author, so its recognition affords moments of pleasure to the knowing reader.

It would be easy to establish a core list of, say, between one hundred and two hundred examples of rewritten Joseph stories.[21] But how best to approach this huge and, at first sight, intractable body of material? For the present study, a selection has been made of twelve works, written in Latin, German, French, and English, belonging to a variety of literary genres, and spanning a period of 177 years, beginning with the Latin drama *Sophompaneas* by the Dutch lawyer Hugo Grotius (1635), and ending with the German autobiography of Johann Wolfgang Goethe (1811/12). Here is a chronological list of these twelve sources:

Grotius, Hugo	1635	*Sophompaneas*	drama	Latin
Zesen, Philipp von	1670	*Assenat*	historical novel	German
Rowe, Elizabeth Singer	1736	*The History of Joseph*	epic poem	English
Morgan, Thomas	1737/40	*The Moral Philosopher*	treatise	English
Fielding, Henry	1742	*Joseph Andrews*	comic novel	English
Bodmer, Johann Jakob	1753	*Joseph und Zulika*	epic poem	German
Voltaire	1764	*Dictionnaire philosophique*	essay	French

Voltaire	1776	*La Bible enfin expliquée*	commentary	French
Lavater, Johann Kaspar	1771	*Christliches Handbüchlein*	children's bible	German
Albrecht, J. Fr. Ernst	1792/94	*Der keusche Joseph*	dramatised novel	German
Chateaubriand, Fr. R. de	1802	*Génie du Christianisme*	treatise	French
Goethe, Joh. Wolfgang	1811/12	*Dichtung und Wahrheit*	autobiography	German

The early-modern interest in the figure of Joseph is not confined to literature. Several of the textual sources in our list mention paintings or illustrations of scenes from the Joseph story, thus adding a visual dimension to the dominating textuality. Thus Grotius has Joseph's brothers discover and discuss a series of paintings in Joseph's residence, depicting major biographical scenes, Zesen's novel includes etchings, and Goethe refers to a Joseph cycle painted by Frankfurt artists when he was a boy. Artists and illustrators all over Europe loved to render scenes such as *Joseph Sold by his Brothers* into slavery and *Joseph and Potiphar's Wife* (the evil woman seeking to seduce the virtuous young man) either in new compositions or reflecting patterns established in medieval or Renaissance art. Impressive inventories of hundreds of such artists have been compiled, lists that include famous names such as Murillo, Rembrandt, and Angelica Kauffmann.[22] In fact, when visiting even minor galleries of early-modern art, one occasionally encounters *Joseph Selling Grain in Egypt* or *Joseph Revealing himself to his Brothers*. Joseph figures prominently in the visual world of early-modern times. In addition to literary and visual presentations of the Joseph theme, we may also mention musical treatments in the form of operas and oratorios such as Georg Friedrich Händel's *Joseph and his Brethren* (1744) and Etienne-Nicolas Méhul's *Joseph en Egypte* (1807), the latter being among Goethe's favourites.[23]

The selection made, with its emphasis on literature and the neglect of visual and musical creations, no doubt reflects the preferences and academic competence of the author, but care has been taken to cover the three broad categories that can be distinguished in the immense corpus of early-modern writing on our biblical hero: Joseph in teaching, Joseph in literature, and Joseph in critical thinking.

Joseph in Teaching

There is a large group of texts that use the Joseph story in the pedagogical process. Mothers and fathers tell the story to their children at an early age, and educational theorists such as the English philosopher John Locke and the French bishop Fénelon give instruction on how to go about this task. The telling of the biblical story is only the beginning of a child's exposure to Joseph. The next stage is the reading of the story, sometimes facilitated by children's bibles that offer a simplified paraphrase rather than the complete text as found in the Bible. In the eighteenth century, a good children's bible was illustrated, and the present book includes one such illustration, showing the popular – and very dramatic – scene of Joseph being sold by his brothers (see Fig. 7, p. 105). If a boy attended a Jesuit school, as was the case with François-Marie Arouet (later known as Voltaire) in Paris, he might witness the performance of a Joseph play and even take part in it. Piety, endurance, and the readiness to forgive others were major virtues to be learned from the story, irrespective of whether it was retold orally, included in a children's bible, or presented on stage. The Joseph materials selected for the present book to illustrate the theme of "Joseph in teaching" come from German-speaking lands and date from around 1800: a section from a children's bible compiled by the Swiss pastor Johann Kaspar Lavater, then a European celebrity, and sections of the biography of Johann Wolfgang Goethe who as a child of thirteen devoted his first juvenile literary effort to writing his own version of the Joseph story.

We should not think, however, that in early-modern times this story was taught only to children. Adults also were reminded of its message. During the year 1789, when the whole of Europe was holding its breath and following the reports about the French Revolution, Lavater gave twenty-four public lectures in Zurich on Joseph. He also recommended that heads of households assemble everyone, including servants, and tell them the biblical story. The educational role of parents, in early-modern practice, extended far beyond mere responsibility for small children. In middle-class households domestic servants were considered child-like dependent members of the family and therefore entitled to receive biblical instruction, for instance in the context of domestic evening worship conducted by the head of the household. Even the extended household of the court was seen as a community in need of pedagogical attention. How such a wider community could be exposed to the story of Joseph can be seen from the protracted performance of a pious Joseph play, entitled *Comoedie vom Erzvater Joseph* (Joseph the Patriarch, a Drama). It was staged in Dresden in February 1678, when one of Europe's most elegant courts celebrated a family gathering of the house of Wettin (the continuing eminence of which can be measured by its close links with the present-day royalty of both Britain and Belgium). This social event, considered to be the culmination of courtly life in seventeenth-century Germany, involved not only pageants, hunting parties, and sumptuous banquets, but also the performance of a specially written trilogy on Joseph. The description of the event, published later, explains that plays such as the one performed to entertain the guests aim at their edification, exhorting them to a virtuous and godly life and dissuading them from "beastly lust" (*viehischen Begierden*) and all kinds of vices.[24] Apparently neither royalty and courtiers, nor members of the nobility were bored with performances of the moralising Joseph play spread over three days.

Joseph in Literature

In early-modern times, we see a shift from epic and stage play as the foremost literary genres to the novel. Although we consider only one stage play in detail – one written in Latin by the Dutch humanist Hugo Grotius, and subsequently often performed in Dutch translation in Amsterdam – mention is made of other Joseph plays, one of which featured regularly on the stages of theatres where Goethe was director. To present "Joseph" in epic format was rarer, but nevertheless attempted with remarkable success in English by Elizabeth Singer Rowe and in German by Johann Jacob Bodmer, both of whom echo the accomplished art of John Milton. For close readings, three Joseph novels have been selected: *Assenat*, a German baroque novel by Philipp von Zesen (today largely forgotten); *The History of the Adventures of Joseph Andrews* by Joseph Fielding, a classic of English literature still printed and read today; *Der keusche Joseph* (Chaste Joseph), a novel in German by Johann Friedrich Ernst Albrecht (also forgotten, but remarkable for portraying Joseph as a Hebrew Freemason).

These works typically present Joseph as a model to emulate: a model of piety, endurance, forgiveness, and chastity. These core Christian values and attitudes, understood as eternal, unchanging, universally valid, absolutely binding, and providing stability, are clearly taught and shown in action in the epic poems of Rowe and Bodmer, as well as in Fielding's novel (and of course in the report given by Goethe in his autobiography, and in Lavater's book for children). To highlight Joseph's virtue, other essentially evil characters feature in these texts: Joseph's brothers and, more prominently, Potiphar's young wife, a figure dominated by misguided passionate love for the hero. Most often, she is seen simply as someone who fails to control herself, but at least one author, Johann Jakob Bodmer, develops a certain amount of sympathy for her. Did these authors succeed in presenting Joseph as an example of virtue to be imitated? At least some moralists had doubts. Instead of discussing the issue, they would have preferred not to bring up the subject at all, because even moral writing may inspire immorality. A romance about virtue might serve as an aphrodisiac, promote libertinism, and corrupt the reader, because in the reader's mind a virtuous scene may perversely metamorphose into its opposite. This also applied, argued the German jurist Christian Thomasius in 1688, to the biblical Joseph story:

> I bet this is true: amongst one hundred young readers of the passage in the Bible about Joseph and Potiphar's wife, you will hardly find more than one or two who, in their hearts, do not consider Joseph a silly fool – and this, despite the Holy Spirit having inspired the author, and

his reticent non-emotive language. Most would go as far as wishing the same thing could happen to them.[25]

Thomasius has no illusions about the mentality of the young: "They fondly imagine that if it did, they'd certainly get more out of it than Joseph." The libertine temptation was strong.

A further concern discussed in literature relating to Joseph is the new situation of state and politics as it developed in early-modern times. In the works focusing on politics – Grotius's drama and the novels of Zesen and Albrecht – Joseph is clearly represented as the iconic leader, but he is not actually a traditional political figure; instead, the authors present him both as a member of the rising bourgeoisie and as one singled out for political leadership. In fact, these authors portray Joseph's policies as representing a new, improved version of statecraft. Grotius and Zesen commend him enthusiastically, whereas Joseph never attains his triumph in Albrecht's unfinished novel. The large number of early-modern texts on Joseph may be explained as representing the effort of the literary elite to retain the ancient biblical story within the canon of the readers of the modern age and make it accessible to an audience with new literary tastes and an increasing commitment to new ways of reading. The biblical subject matter was still very much on the minds of both authors and readers, but the form was largely innovative, heralding the victory of the novel and its emancipation from traditional subjects. Belonging to two worlds at the same time, tradition and modernity, the one not yet completely established, and the other, though weakened, still far from disappearing, Joseph for a moment could serve as a reassuring emblem of continuity. Joseph emerges as a transitional figure incorporating features from two worlds: the ancient, traditional order shaped, more or less directly, by the unchanging cultural icons of biblical and Graeco-Roman provenance; and the contemporary, emerging world of modernity. Around 1800, after the French Revolution, the intellectual foundations of Western society changed dramatically as the past no longer seemed to offer convincing examples or "icons" to rely on for solving its moral, social, and political problems. Intellectuals became increasingly convinced that one could no longer learn from past history.[26] Having lost their traditional authority the biblical heroes fade, and ultimately vanish from sight.

JOSEPH IN CRITICAL THINKING

Our third, smaller group of sources is committed to a reading of the Joseph story in the interests of historical reconstruction, aesthetic appreciation, and moral evaluation. Here it is no longer the pastor, educator, or poet who speaks, but the historian, biographer, and literary critic. In early-modern times the task of historical research and the study of literature were no longer understood as the mere cultivation of traditional learning; instead, proponents came to adopt the ideals of criticism and independent judgement. Critical thought was first applied to the Joseph story in England and France in the eighteenth century; only later, especially in the nineteenth and twentieth centuries, were they joined – and perhaps surpassed – by German biblical critics. The three critics selected for close study are the English philosopher Thomas Morgan and the two French writers Voltaire and Chateaubriand. While today Morgan is known only to a few historians of deist philosophy, the two French authors are still widely known, though not for their contributions to biblical studies. These three critics, concerned as they were with different aspects of the background and message of the biblical story, all agreed on its high literary merit, but disagreed about almost everything else. Historical research on the Bible led to controversial results: for Morgan, the biblical text veils the evidence that Joseph was a power-hungry historical patriarch of the Israelite people; Voltaire saw him merely as a literary figure echoing a Jewish tax collector working in the service of Egypt. On the moral message, Morgan and Voltaire strongly disagreed: the English philosopher took him to be an icon of despotism, whereas Voltaire appreciated the protagonist's generosity and clemency towards his brothers. Voltaire and Chateaubriand, both practitioners of literary criticism, agreed that Joseph was an eminently iconic figure, though one belonging to the realm of literature rather than to that of political or moral life. Voltaire recognises in "Joseph" the oriental genius of storytelling, while Chateaubriand extols "Joseph" as embodying the literary genius of the Bible and therefore of Christianity. The two eminent French critics teach us that Joseph can be fully rehabilitated in the realm of aesthetics, while disappearing from the company of those archetypal heroes whom Providence wisely inserted into the march of history.

Our account of critical engagement with the Joseph story ends in 1802 with Chateaubriand, but a more recent commentary is included in the present book; written in 2008, it offers a restatement of Voltaire's view of "Joseph" as a *conte philosophique*. Between the two dates, much has happened, and much has been written on Joseph. One event rekindled interest in both the historical study of Joseph and in using the biblical hero as a literary subject: the decipherment of hieroglyphic writing by Jean-François Champollion in 1822. While no records concerning Joseph were found in the ancient hieroglyphic texts, one discovery was seen as coming close: the discovery, around 1900, by pioneers in the fledgling discipline of Egyptology, of Pharaoh Akhenaten whose splendid poetry, promotion of the arts, and attempt to reform ancient polytheism were admired by historians and writers alike. While historians disclaim any relationship between the biblical story and Akhenaten, the mysterious figure of this pagan monotheist fired the imagination and opened up an array of new literary possibilities. Joseph's pharaoh could now be given a name, a philosophy, and a story. In the twentieth century, prominent authors such as Thomas Mann in Germany and Hubert Lampo in the Netherlands recast the biblical hero.[27] Both Mann and Lampo made Joseph the chancellor of Akhenaten's Egypt. In the present book we must refrain from pursuing Mann's portrayal of Joseph's Egyptian reforms that strangely resemble the American president's state-directed economy, the "New Deal" of the 1930s, with Franklin D. Roosevelt becoming the provider for the democratic world. Nor can we consider Lampo's image of Joseph the dictator whose ruthless determination contrasts, unfavourably, with the mildness of Pharaoh Akhenaten: therein lie other fascinating studies.

In this book, I offer for each of the authors from Grotius to Goethe: a summary of the Joseph story as used or interpreted; a brief study of the ancient or modern sources used and exploited by the writer; and elements of an interpretation, based on the life, times, and intellectual world of each author. Of course, this approach is not applied schematically but with some flexibility, to allow for the specific character of each of the works considered. Whenever it seemed best to let original sources speak for themselves, existing translations were edited or fresh translations provided. Care has been taken to make these readable, and I follow Voltaire in his preference for dynamic versions: "Woe to the makers of literal translations, who by rendering every word weaken the meaning! It is indeed by so doing that we can say the letter kills and the spirit gives life."[28] It is intended that each chapter, dedicated to one literary work, should stand on its own, and should be capable of being read independently of the rest of the book. However, I would advise most readers first of all to familiarise themselves with the Bible story, as summarised in Chapter 2, of Joseph in Genesis.

2

Joseph in Genesis

THE BIBLICAL BOOK OF GENESIS BEGINS WITH THE CREATION OF HEAVEN, earth, and humankind; tells of primeval times – human existence in the garden of Eden and banishment from this paradise, the rival brothers Cain and Abel, the great flood that almost extinguished the human race, and so on – in order then to tell the stories of Israel's ancestors, including the patriarch Joseph. What follows is a condensed version of what we learn about Joseph in Genesis:[1]

THE STORY

Once upon a time there was a boy called Joseph. Son of Jacob and Rachel, he has ten elder half-brothers – sons of his father by other wives. His father's favourite, he is given a special, long-sleeved robe[2] to wear, and invites the envy of his brothers, all the more through his imprudence in reporting their misdeeds to his father, and in telling them about his two symbolic dreams: of his brothers' sheaves of grain bowing down to his, and of the sun, moon, and eleven stars making obeisance to him – both revealing him as the born leader and both also manifestly suggestive of his future greatness. Fatefully unaware of the developing fraternal conflict, Jacob sends Joseph to enquire after the welfare of his brothers who are shepherding their father's flocks far from home. He finds them at Dothan. As they see him approaching in the distance, they make plans to kill him, and thus to frustrate for ever the unwelcome future portended by the dreams. The eldest brother, Reuben the reasonable, restrains the others from bloodshed. Instead of killing Joseph, they capture and confine him in a pit, a dry cistern or well, not caring if he should die there. While Joseph languishes in the pit, a caravan of traders draws near; on the suggestion of Judah, the brothers free Joseph from the pit and sell him to the Ishmaelite or Midianite traders for twenty pieces of silver. The caravan proceeds, taking the Hebrew slave to Egypt. As evidence of Joseph's death, the brothers present the boy's bloodstained coat (allegedly found in the wilderness, but in reality taken from the victim and stained with animal blood) to their disconsolate father.

The Egyptian master, a man named Potiphar, to whom the merchants sell the seventeen-year-old boy, finds him to be quick, capable, and trustworthy, and soon appoints him steward of his household. Under Joseph's administration, everything prospers in his master's house, and the blessing of heaven rests visibly upon it. But Joseph, "handsome in form and appearance", attracts the notice of his master's wife. She makes advances towards the irresistibly attractive young man, which he rejects, saying nobly that he will neither betray his master's trust nor sin against God. Further advances are likewise repulsed. In the end, enraged at what she considers a slight received at Joseph's hands, she vengefully brings a false accusation against him before her husband. Joseph, accused of attempted rape, is duly cast into the state prison. There, however, God is still with him. He wins the favour and confidence of the keeper of the prison, who even commits the other prisoners to his charge. Soon afterwards, Pharaoh's chief cupbearer (or butler) and baker offend the king, and they too are placed in custody. Joseph is appointed to wait upon them. He hears from them one morning about their dreams. Unable to interpret these themselves, they recount them to him; and he suggests what they might portend. Three days later, on Pharaoh's birthday, the chief butler, as Joseph foretold, is restored to office, whereas the chief baker is hanged.

For two years, Joseph endures imprisonment (the chief butler having forgotten his promise to mention him to the king) until Pharaoh has two enigmatic dreams: in the first he sees seven beautifully healthy, well-fleshed cows; these are attacked and eaten up by seven lean cows. The second dream repeats the pattern with heads of grain – a stalk with seven ears of grain, plump and full, swallowed up by a stalk with seven thin ears, blasted and wizened by the east wind. In Egypt, much significance is attached to dreams, and Pharaoh is disturbed to find no one able to interpret them. The chief butler, belatedly recalling Joseph's skill in his own case, mentions him to the king. Joseph is sent for; and, having been brought before the king, declares the significance of the ominous dreams – seven years of plenty, to be succeeded by seven years of famine. In view of the future foretold, Joseph suggests the practical measure of making provision for the years of famine by storing up in advance a fifth of the harvest from each of the years of plenty. Pharaoh reacts immediately, shocked by the prospect of the impending crisis but also impressed by Joseph's sage advice. He makes Joseph bearer of the royal seal, investing him with authority over the entire land of Egypt, especially over its well-organised governing bureaucracy, in order to give effect to his proposal. He also confers upon him other marks of royal favour. To mark his admittance into the Egyptian bureaucracy, he bestows upon him an Egyptian name, Zaphnath-paneah, and marries him to Asenath, daughter of Potiphera, priest of the great national temple of the sun-god at On (Heliopolis). At the time of this promotion, Joseph is thirty years old. He embarks without delay on his economic programme: during the seven years of plenty, he amasses grain in the granaries of every city. In the fifth of these years, Asenath bears him two sons who are named Manasseh, in allusion to his "forgetting" of his past troubles, and Ephraim, on account of his "fruitfulness" in the land of his affliction.

When the years of famine set in, Joseph opens the storehouses, and Egyptians come from all over to buy grain. The famine then extends beyond Egypt, to all the earth, becoming particularly severe in Canaan. Jacob gets to hear about the availability of Egyptian grain, so he sends all his sons, with the exception of the youngest, Benjamin, to buy grain in Egypt. On coming into Joseph's presence, the brothers prostrate themselves before him, but do not recognise him; his Egyptian dress and shaven face disguise him. He receives them harshly, and accuses them of being spies, sent to discover "the nakedness of the land" – finding parts of Egypt that might be vulnerable to invasion. The charge throws them off their guard. They seek to disarm his suspicion – in true oriental fashion – by volunteering information about their honourable family, of which Joseph at once takes advantage: desirous, namely, of asserting the truth about Benjamin, he insists that one brother shall be detained in Egypt, while the others go home to fetch their youngest brother. Their conscience bothers them, for they recognise in their misfortunes a nemesis for their treatment (long ago) of Joseph, and Reuben reminds them how he had sought to divert them from their original evil purpose. Joseph understands perfectly well what they are saying, and is much moved by it; he adheres, however, to his terms, and retains Simeon as hostage. Having secretly given orders for each man's payment to be restored and hidden in his baggage, and having given them provisions for the way, he lets the others go, and they return to Canaan. Upon arrival, they recount to their father what has befallen them. The bewildering discovery of the money in their bags adds to both their and his anxiety. Jacob bitterly reproaches them for what they have put him through in depriving him of yet another of his sons.

The famine continues, relentless in its severity, forcing Jacob to send a second time to Egypt for grain. This time the brothers are accompanied by Benjamin; they also take their father's presents with them, to conciliate, if possible, the Egyptian governor. Joseph, seeing Benjamin with his other brothers, and perceiving thus that they have spoken the truth, is prepared to show them friendliness, and invites them to a feast in his house. At this point, Simeon is released. They make ready their gift for Joseph, and when he comes in, he again enquires tenderly for his father, and expresses his satisfaction at seeing Benjamin. The brothers are surprised to find themselves seated at the feast according to their ages, and that Benjamin is honoured with an extra portion, five times as large as any of theirs. They feast and make merry, unaware of impending trouble. The denouement fast approaches. The brothers depart, their sacks once more filled with grain, Joseph this time having privately given orders for his silver goblet – a precious drinking cup that doubles as an instrument of divination – to be hidden in Benjamin's sack. But before they can have gone far, he sends messengers after them, who overtake them and charge them with the theft. Their consciences are clear, and voluntarily they offer to commit any offender to justice. Dismay and despair seize them when the goblet is found in Benjamin's sack. With affected indignation, Joseph reproaches them for what they have done. Judah, replying on behalf of them all, attempts no excuse, for no justification seems possible: a just retribution has repaid them for their earlier crime; they will remain slaves in Egypt. But Joseph presses his advantage home: he will retain only Benjamin. Judah now steps forward, and in a speech of striking beauty, remarkable no less for its grace and persuasive eloquence than for its frankness and generosity, intercedes on Benjamin's behalf. Explaining the whole story from the beginning, including Jacob's earlier loss of a son, he entreats Joseph to have compassion for the feelings of an aged father, begging Joseph to let him remain as a slave in his brother's stead. Overcome by the pathos of Judah's heartfelt appeal, and convinced at last of the genuine change in his brothers' attitude, Joseph discloses himself to them: "I am your brother Joseph, whom you sold into Egypt." His first enquiry is for his father. Stunned by amazement and fear, they cannot answer at first, but he reassures them, and allays their anxiety. In what they have done, after all, they have been the unconscious instruments of Providence, because "God did send me ahead of you to preserve many lives". Joseph also sends an affectionate summons to his father, inviting him to come and settle in Egypt, where he can support him. Upon Jacob's arrival in Egypt, Joseph hastens to meet his father. He presents his father and brothers to Pharaoh who, when he learns that they are shepherds, agrees that they should settle in Goshen.

Meanwhile, Joseph also has to deal with Egyptian economic affairs. As the famine continues in the country, the people first of all use up all their money for grain, then they exchange their cattle, and finally offer themselves and their land. Thus all the land in Egypt, except that belonging to the priests, becomes the property of Pharaoh, and the previous owners become tenants of the king, liable to payment of an annual rent of one-fifth of the produce. The sole exception to this rule is the priests: receiving a fixed revenue in kind from the crown, they have no need to sell their possessions for food.

Jacob lives with Joseph in Egypt for seventeen years (just as Joseph lived the first seventeen years of his life with his father in Canaan). As the time of Jacob's death draws near, Joseph, hearing of his sickness, brings his two sons to see him. The aged patriarch blesses the two boys, against Joseph's wishes giving first place to Ephraim, the younger, in view of the future greatness of the tribe that will descend from him. After Jacob's death, Joseph makes arrangements for his burial. (No other burial in the Bible is accorded so long and detailed an account as this.) His brothers, still haunted by a sense of guilt, fear that he will now exact retribution for their past behaviour, and send accordingly to crave his forgiveness. He replies generously that he does not stand in God's place, to exact vengeance for actions that, however intended, have been overruled by God's providence for good, and assures them that he will continue to look after their welfare. Honoured in Egypt, Joseph lives to the age of one hundred and ten.

Narrative Structure, Date, and Meaning

Two aspects of Joseph's identity form the basis of the narrative: (1) he is the favourite son of his father; (2) he is the most accomplished interpreter of dreams. Each of these definitions reflects a major facet of ancient Hebrew society. The first reminds us of the fact that the ancient Hebrews understood their society as a social formation based on kinship: descent, lineage, and family defined an individual's membership of, and social position in, the community. Much significance was attached to the love between father and son in biblical and, more generally, in ancient Semitic mentality: it occupies the place we in modern times tend to assign to the love between a man and a woman. The relationship of father to son was seen as underpinning the whole of society and as the basis of all wholesome growth and development. This is reflected in the personal name an Israelite was given. Joseph, the protagonist of our story, was Joseph *ben* Jacob, "Joseph, son of Jacob". In addition to being defined by descent, a Hebrew individual could also become distinguished by personal achievement or divine calling (or both) by becoming a warrior, hero, sage, prophet, or king. The two systems of designation – natural by descent, cultural by achievement or calling – could, however, be brought into mutual tension and conflict. In fact, such conflict in this case seems unavoidable, because a hero such as Joseph had to leave his family in order to distinguish himself as the world's most capable interpreter of dreams.

The two key, though opposed, aspects of personal identity, natural and cultural, generate the Joseph story: the protagonist's kinship through his being born into this particular family, and his achievement gained through his efforts to transcend the restrictions imposed by his kinship group. These two notions are given narrative form in two plots: the conflict between elder brothers and the youngest, and the progress of the hero from "rags to riches" or, more accurately, from prisoner to prime minister – from uncertain and difficult beginnings to triumph and glory. The conflict between the brothers, though at the outset an almost deadly enmity, is eventually resolved. The theme of fraternal discord is suspended at the moment of Joseph's being sold into slavery, to be resumed only much later; thus the two plots are intertwined. The resulting structure can be represented as a series of three movements or chains of events:

plot 1	plot 2	plot 1, continued
fraternal conflict (the hero's narrow escape from death)	from rags to riches (initiation tests and the hero's triumph)	fraternal conflict resolved (one episode in the hero's wise rule)

The clear, yet complex and sophisticated narrative structure enables the biblical writer to tell a sustained story with carefully arranged episodes that lead from initial conflict via delaying moments to the final resolution. The two plots include and support each other. The second one – "from rags to riches" – is inserted into the first, "fraternal conflict", to create a narrative that combines organic unity and a high degree of complexity in a manner rarely found in the Bible. Thus the first plot is not told as a continuous story but is suspended at one point. The first half of the first plot serves as the introduction to the second one, for it explains how Joseph became a slave. The second plot is then used as the introduction to the second part of the first plot, for it explains why Joseph's brothers approach their unrecognised brother for help. The two intertwined chains of events are co-ordinated by divine providence. In fact, the story celebrates divine providence, for by saving the life of Joseph, God, as becomes clear at the end, also saves the lives of his brothers.

The Joseph story, even in summarised form as above, strikes us as an outstanding piece of literature: it ranks among the Bible's best-told stories. Six clusters of episodes give narrative substance to its bare bones:

(1) Difficult beginnings: the hero of the story is involved in two conflicts – one with his brothers, who hate him, and one with Potiphar's wife who, after being rejected by the hero, also comes to hate him.
(2) The hero as interpreter of dreams: in jail, the hero demonstrates his superior wisdom by interpreting obscure dreams of important persons, including the king.
(3) The hero's wise counsel to the king and his promotion to high office. Through the interpretation of dreams, the contact between hero and king is established, and the hero is given an important task, a major problem to solve.
(4) The hero, during a time of general famine, provides for his brothers, and eventually reveals his identity to them. Due to the hero's generosity, the fraternal conflict is resolved. The hero invites his brothers and father to move to Egypt, where they settle.
(5) The hero's economic measures applied to the adopted country.
(6) Endings: the end of the life of the hero's father is described in detail – his testament, blessing, and burial. The hero's death is dealt with more briefly.

Prior to being recorded, many of the stories told in the Bible circulated as oral tradition: this is one of the fundamental insights of modern biblical criticism. The story of Joseph is no exception. Its composition of clusters of episodes makes us suspect that what we have here are items from the repertoire of an expert oriental storyteller who, in flexible oral performance, was at liberty to develop and embellish or simply summarise the individual items, or even add new ones. Moreover, the narrator may not include everything, for he could rely on the memory of an audience already well versed in the plot, characters, and other narrative details.

As a coherent narrative, the story of Joseph – like many other biblical stories – seems to have gone through three stages of development: oral, novelistic, and canonical. At the oral stage, it must have been a kind of folk-tale about a hero's progress from promising but problematic beginnings via a period of testing all the way up to ultimate glory in high political office.[3] This folk-tale, when written down around 500 BCE,[4] received a particular twist through the narrator's emphasis on extolling Joseph as the founding father of the Jewish Diaspora in Egypt and as the exemplar of a Jewish leader who helps new immigrants to settle in a country that is as wealthy as it is welcoming to newcomers.

We may call this written form of the story a "Diaspora novella".⁵ Its most distinguishing feature is the suppression of an episode that no doubt stood at the end of the earlier, presumably oral version: the return of Joseph's brothers to Canaan at the end of the seven years of famine. Instead of sending the brothers back home, the Diaspora novelist makes them stay in Egypt. The subsequent third, final stage brought the insertion of the Joseph novella into the long compilation with which the Old Testament begins, a book that starts with accounts of creation and paradise, and tells the story of Israel's ancestors, up until the end of the Jerusalemite monarchy (Genesis to 2 Kings). The Joseph story is used within this canonical narrative to account for the presence of the Israelites in Egypt; it serves as the prologue to the Israelites' exodus from Egypt under their leader Moses. At the canonical level, Joseph, at the end of Genesis, vaguely prefigures King Jehoiachin who, at the end of the second book of Kings, is the most respected foreign personality at the court of the king of Babylon. Each of the three stages of the story – oral, novelistic, and canonical – has left its mark on the text as we read it in the Bible; and each has also obscured, though never completely erased, the meaning the story had at the previous stage.

The Diaspora novella's fourfold message

Recent biblical criticism suggests interpreting the Joseph story in the first place as a Diaspora novella: a story that reflects Jewish life as no longer confined to a Palestinian geographical setting. Read with the Diaspora in mind, many features of the biblical story do indeed appear in a new light and immediately make sense. Its setting in two countries – Palestine and Egypt – reveals that Diaspora Jews think of themselves as belonging to two geographic locations. Some Jews emigrate to Egypt in order to improve their economic circumstances. Those living permanently in Egypt remain in touch with the land of Israel, a land currently suffering under a terrible drought that leads to famine; they send messengers back and forth and even send grain to alleviate the suffering. (Here one can refer to the apostle Paul who, visiting the Christian communities of Greece and Asia Minor, collected money to send to the poor Christians of Jerusalem.) Occasionally, the storyteller alludes to typical Diaspora controversies such as the debate about the rightful place of burial: Jacob, Joseph's father, wants his bones to be interred in the land of his fathers in Israel, in the family's traditional burial ground; Joseph, by contrast, as the more assimilated Diaspora Jew, is ultimately in Egyptian fashion "embalmed and placed in a coffin in Egypt".⁶ But apart from telling a story about life in the Egyptian Diaspora, the biblical author also wishes to impress a particular set of messages on his audience: (1) the foreign country, portrayed in glowing colours, is welcoming to Jews; (2) if you are a newcomer, there will always be someone – a Jewish brother – to help you;

(3) rather than merely living as parasites in a foreign social and economic world, Jews actually contribute something important to the pagan state and may assume leading roles; and, finally, (4) Diaspora Jews form an open rather than a closed society, and in this they differ from those committed to a Judaism based upon the principle of separation and strict adherence to the law of Moses.

This is a story told in praise of Egypt: this must have been the very first impression for the earliest readers and was the most elementary message its author wished to convey. Egypt is seen as a country endowed with rich pastures for flocks and herds, and abundant grain-producing land, promising economic security. In addition, the Egyptians themselves are a friendly and welcoming people. There is a certain memory of Israelites having been slaves in Egypt – indeed Joseph began his life in Egypt as a slave – but these days are gone and almost forgotten.[7] The Egyptians, represented by their Pharaonic leader, are friendly to the Jews, assigning them the best pastures available. Intermarriage does not seem to be much of a problem: Joseph has an Egyptian wife, and his father-in-law is a priest of a polytheistic religion. While the Jews living in Egypt know that this is not the land of their (or their parents') birth, they nevertheless appreciate and indeed love their adopted country. To the Diaspora it is home, not exile: Jews can be happy and fulfil their destiny even when abroad. This attitude can be found in another passage of the book of Genesis. The account of paradise mentions four rivers in the garden of Eden; these can be identified as the Nile in Egypt, the little rivulet in Jerusalem, and the Euphrates and the Tigris in Mesopotamia.[8] Dating from the same period as the Joseph story, the note on the geography of paradise is quite telling: the four rivers enclose the Jewish people, at home and abroad. Wherever Jews live – in Egypt near the Nile (here called Pishon), in Jerusalem, or in Mesopotamia by the Tigris or the Euphrates – is paradise. In losing the original paradise, the Jews have rediscovered paradise almost everywhere! Thus the book of Genesis extols Egypt as the ideal, paradise-like country for the Jews to settle in, a friendly land, welcoming to incomers. Not all the Diaspora Jews have felt this way, however. The book of Exodus depicts Egypt as the house of slavery, so that an exodus, a mass emigration to the land of Israel, was called for. The book of Esther, set in Persia, also emphasises that the Jews were surrounded by enemies. Whereas the Jews of the Joseph story have no enemies, the book of Esther records large numbers of them: over seventy-five thousand.[9] The Joseph story presents a rather idealised view of Diaspora existence, a view not justified by the experience of all.

Are you a new Jewish immigrant in Egypt? You can rely on the help of Jews who are already well established there: this is the author's second message. In the idealised view, the life of the Jewish Diaspora is marked by a unique though often fragile and endangered virtue: that of social solidarity. Solidarity, in ancient as in modern societies, takes two forms, depending upon whether it functions in the context of the kinship group or in the context of the wider, mostly urban society. Since both types figure in our story, we can explain them with reference to it. In the land of Israel, Joseph's father Jacob is the revered patriarch who dominates his family, i.e. his sons. There is no essential, hierarchical difference between Jacob and his sons, for they are all united in one organic unit, the family. Mutual solidarity is expected within the kinship group. By selling him into slavery, Joseph's brothers commit a heinous crime against the family. In Egypt, solidarity takes a different form. Here the essential unit is not the kinship group but the association comprising a wealthy and influential patron surrounded by less influential and sometimes poor clients. Patron and client exchange services, but the underpinning ideology means that the patron is his client's benefactor and, in times of need, his actual saviour. The entire political system can be thought of along these lines: the king or, as in the Joseph story, the prime minister can be considered the patron, and the citizens, his clients. In the story, Joseph acts as a wealthy and influential patron who welcomes and cares for newly arrived immigrants, helping them to find food, shelter, and eventually even land to settle. He intercedes with the state's central administration, and on his recommendation, the immigrants are granted permission to stay and are allotted land for pasture. In return – one should not miss this point – they are asked to take care of the king's livestock.

The novelist's particular wish here is to depict Joseph and the new immigrants as being doubly united, embracing both kinds of solidarity. As a patron, Joseph grants solidarity in a hierarchical political and economic system; as a kinsman, he offers to restore the broken social bonds of kinship. The novelist's insistence on kinship solidarity must be seen as essential to his message. All Jews, he insists, trace their ancestry to Jacob, Joseph's father, as is clear from Jacob's second name, Israel. Therefore all Jews, especially when living in a foreign environment, are brothers and must uphold the idea of kinship solidarity. This sense of mutual belonging should overrule all conflicts, disputes, and differences that families might harbour. Thus the Joseph tale, as a moralising story, celebrates solidarity and extols it as the chief virtue displayed by Diaspora Jews.

Apart from recommending this essential part of Diaspora existence, the Joseph story also reflects the hopes, dreams, and illusions of Jewish life in Egypt.

Living as a minority amongst other ethnic groups posed a challenge to which some Jews, including the author of the Joseph story, responded by asserting their intellectual superiority and pointing out the contribution they were making to the community as benefactors. Jewish superiority and benefaction are key ingredients in the biblical story; indeed, they function as another essential message no reader can miss. Joseph, the lowly imprisoned Hebrew slave, listens to the dreams told by others, and offers his interpretation. He understands that one of his fellow inmates' dreams betokens the prisoner's release and rehabilitation, and that another inmate's dream signifies his execution, both of which come true. Thus Joseph establishes his fame as an unrivalled interpreter of dreams. His masterpiece, however, is his divination of the future from the dreams of Pharaoh. In addition to being the unrivalled master of oneiromancy, Joseph also becomes the perfect administrator, and by organising the storage of grain during the years of abundance, he saves Egypt from ultimate starvation. In this role, Joseph acts as an exemplary benefactor. The idea realised in this story is that of reciprocity: in the foreign country, the Diaspora Jews are given land, a home, and protection; in return, they offer their services to others, both on a personal level (as demonstrated by Joseph interpreting the dreams of his fellow prisoners), and on a public level (as is evident in Joseph's administration). The Jews are portrayed as the benefactors of the pagan society and state. Though immigrants in a foreign land, they are the best of neighbours and the best of citizens. Indeed, the entire social and economic system of Egypt would break down without them. Thus, they come to form an important, indeed a necessary and indispensable group within Egyptian society.

The idea of a member of the Diaspora having a brilliant career finds its fullest and most daring expression in the figure of Joseph. In inventing this figure, the novelist created the literary type of the "Diaspora hero", a Jew providing the ideal role model for all Jews living beyond Palestine. The Jewish novella writers loved characters who achieved promotion in a pagan court; thus, Ahikar became chief cupbearer, keeper of the signet, and chief fiscal administrator in Assyria, Daniel a high-ranking administrator at the Babylonian court, Esther the wife of the Persian king, and Mordecai (also in the book of Esther) the bearer of the royal signet ring.[10] According to early Jewish propaganda, two rulers of Ptolemaic Egypt appointed some particularly trustworthy Jews to high courtly or military office, committing, as Josephus affirms, "the whole kingdom to Jews".[11] None of these claims seems to be based on historical reality. Whether in fact certain Diaspora Jews were ever promoted to high office within the pagan state is difficult to say. Only one possibly genuine historical instance is known: in the fifth century BCE the Jew Nehemiah may have held the office of cupbearer at the Persian court of Susa. According to his autobiographical account: "I was cupbearer to the king. [...] I carried the wine and gave it to the king."[12] The cupbearer or wine taster was a trusted member of the king's entourage, responsible for the king's nutriment reaching him free of poisoning. The Greek historian Xenophon mentions this office, describing it as follows: "Now it is a well-known fact that the cupbearers, when they proffer the cup, draw off some of it with a ladle, pour it into their left hand, and swallow it down – so that, if they should put poison in it, they may not profit by it."[13] Attested throughout centuries of Persian history and legend, the cupbearer was a favourite and trusted youthful official. His responsibilities and his influence extended far beyond mere service at the royal table;

accordingly, Herodotus calls this office "a position of no small honour".[14] Some historians, including Ernest Renan, have doubted the historicity of Nehemiah's claim to have held a position at the imperial court of Persia, comparing him to "persons in our own day willing to claim close relations with a king or with the President of the Republic because they have obtained a letter from some subordinate local official", while others go so far as to consider him an entirely fictional character.[15] Today, historians tend to accept Nehemiah's claim to have been one of the important personalities if not at the Persian court, then at least somewhere within the imperial administration. A Jew in such a high office may have helped to lend the Joseph story at least a modicum of credibility.

As a fictional Diaspora hero, Joseph is superior in intelligence and thus achieves royal acknowledgement and promotion to high office; at the same time he maintains strong bonds of solidarity with the Jewish community for which he obtains privileges from the adopted pagan state and acts as a patron in time of need. In all of this Joseph pre-eminently represents the Israelite people: his father Jacob, given the honorific name Israel, was the people's eponymous ancestor; Joseph, as Jacob's favourite son, represents the people in a new setting – amidst the Diaspora. Joseph stands for the disparate young Israel that flourishes beyond Palestine. No doubt, the Joseph novella was prompted by the cultural circumstances of the Egyptian Diaspora, and gave the Jewish community an identity, a founding father, and a founding myth. If biblical criticism is correct in assigning to Genesis a date later than the book of Exodus, Joseph may be considered the last and ultimate hero of our canonical compilation of traditional Hebrew legends, a man portrayed as the abiding model for Jewish – and indeed human – existence.

To understand this fourth and final message of the biblical story, we must consider its alternative, for as an emblematic figurehead of Judaism, Joseph vies with Moses. Our biblical storyteller seems to have preferred his own hero, whose governorship was a blessing to Egypt, to Moses, who, having killed an Egyptian, fled out of Egypt and who insisted on separating the Hebrews from all the other nations of the ancient world. Moses stands for separation, law, and priestly religion in a barren desert setting where existence is reduced to its essentials; Joseph for openness, reconciliation, friendship, and benefaction in a country known for its treasures and luxury, its lush pastures and fat cattle, its abundant supply of enriching waters and fish, and its legendary harvests; in short, a land where people peacefully "sit by the meat pots and eat bread to the full".[16] Instead of an exodus from Egypt, the novella tells the story of an exodus in reverse – out of Palestine and into Egypt.

A comparison between the Moses and the Joseph stories reveals further dimensions of these alternative founding fathers and their respective varieties of Judaism. The very literary types chosen for the telling of the two stories – legend and folk-tale – seem to carry a message. To decode this message, we can rely on elements of interpretation suggested by Max Lüthi, who, as an expert in European folklore, highlights the difference between folk-tale (*Märchen*) and legend (*Sage*), arguing that each is the result of a distinctive intellectual effort and expresses a particular worldview or, more precisely, its own unique perception of the place of the human individual within society, accompanied by a specific view of the supernatural.[17] The worldview of the legend represents *parochialism*. Accordingly, the world of the legend is determined by a restricted geographical horizon and inhabited by a group with clear boundaries and a well-defined identity. Its inhabitants act within these boundaries, and in so doing they associate with members of the same community. Beyond the present world lies the realm of the supernatural that occasionally manifests itself in spectacular, miraculous ways, inspiring awe and fascination; the sacred and the profane are clearly distinguished. The worldview of the folk-tale, by contrast, is that of *universalism*. The folk-tale's lack of geographical and ethnic specificity allows for its protagonist to be sent out into the wide world where he interacts, potentially, with everyone. The folk-tale hero is usually portrayed as an isolated individual who breaks away from his home, never to return; far away from his homeland, the loner whose life began as a wanderer finds a secure place, possibly a leading position in a foreign kingdom. The folk-tale thus inspires trust and confidence. The hero's trust is bolstered by his occasional reliance on supernatural helpers. The supernatural is part and parcel of a unified world in which it enjoys a calm and quiet presence and therefore is hardly noticed as something special. The legend juxtaposes a profane and a sacred world, whereas the folk-tale knows of no distinction between the two. The holistic worldview of the folk-tale thus contrasts sharply with the differentiated perception characteristic of the legend. Lüthi concludes his interpretation by pointing out that each of the two genres is animated by a distinctive mood that affects its respective audience or readership: the legend by a serious, sombre, portentous atmosphere, and the folk-tale by a bright, playful, and cheerful one, in which all questions are forgotten because there are only answers.

Although Lüthi's binary typology of traditional European oral lore cannot be applied in every detail to biblical literature, it does help to reveal certain features of biblical stories that might otherwise go undetected. From a Lüthian perspective, the story of Moses appears as a national legend. It describes a situation of intense human suffering, presents its hero as a visionary, someone chosen as a prophet and mediator between the human and divine realms, and reports on several dramatic miraculous divine interventions, culminating in the drowning of Pharaoh's chariots in the sea and in God's giving of the law on Mount Sinai, an act that binds God and the Hebrews together in a foundational covenant. Moses in this story remains surrounded and supported by his people, the Israelites; although divinely chosen, he is first and foremost one of them, a member of the community. This legend, ultimately, has the people as its theme, and not Moses as an individual; and the chosen ones are seen to be permanently and intimately bound to God, who becomes their Lord. The legend, finally, claims to be true in the sense that the characters existed and the events reported actually happened, albeit in the distant past. In the Joseph story, told in the form of a folk-tale, the situation is different. Its protagonist has many characteristics of the cumulative portrait of the male fairy-tale hero established by Lüthi: as the central figure, he is never overshadowed by others, though the youngest child of his parents; his evil brothers are envious and seek to do him harm; he leaves his family, making his way into the wide world, never to return; he enjoys the favour and support when needed of invisible powers that come to him freely, guiding him through the dangerous, unknown world and protecting him wherever he goes; living in a world he can ultimately trust (though never fully understand), he never has any doubts about these friendly powers and cheerfully takes their intervention for granted; there is in no sense a permanent contact or a contract between the hero and the supernatural agents; without actually knowing it, he always does just the right thing, and ultimately secures success, wealth, and happiness for himself. Unlike the protagonist of the legend who closely and consistently identifies with his people, Joseph during much of the story remains a socially isolated figure: one who acts on his own. As a result, he is in a better position to relate to others, in fact to almost everyone he encounters. The fairy-tale hero's universal openness – a virtue he himself is hardly aware of – makes him into an eminently social and accessible person.

The folk-tale, as interpreted by Lüthi, presents the individual as an uprooted and lonely person, as one pushed out by family and country and thrown into an unknown and unknowable world; yet it inspires in those who listen to it a sense of trust, inviting them to share in its optimistic vision of an ultimately beneficent world in which even the rootless can find their place. The tale of Joseph embodies many characteristics of the folk-tale, and, like such tales, refrains from claiming belief in the historicity of the events narrated or of its hero and those he interacts with. Instead, it invites even today's reader to share a vision that is not only poetic and pleasing, but also intellectually and emotionally satisfying.

In offering a modern, twenty-first-century interpretation of the Joseph story, I do not wish to suggest that this is how readers in the seventeenth and eighteenth centuries understood it. But while we must be wary of imposing interpretations of ancient texts suggested by scholars in the twenty-first century upon readers and authors of earlier ages, it nevertheless makes sense to indicate how the Joseph story may be understood today. The way we understand the Bible now will help us to measure both our distance from, and our cultural solidarity with, authors who, like Grotius and Goethe, lived in a crucial period of Western intellectual and literary history and contributed much to its cultural development.

3

Post-biblical Traditions

A WONDERFUL STORY LIKE THE ONE ABOUT JOSEPH COULD NOT FAIL TO have many echoes in later writing. In Judaism, Christianity, and Islam, a rich Joseph tradition developed, diversifying as it grew, and leaving its mark on folklore, poetry, and many other forms of literature, including novels, stage plays, sermons, and learned commentary. A mere catalogue of the relevant ancient, medieval, and modern sources in Hebrew, Arabic, Latin, and modern languages would fill a volume, and even then could not hope to be representative, let alone complete. But although the richness of the Joseph tradition precludes even the attempt to offer a comprehensive survey, the very nature of the early-modern adaptations of, and commentaries on, the Joseph story forces us to take a closer look at some of the post-biblical Joseph materials. The reason for this is simple: all of the seventeenth- and eighteenth-century authors were familiar with or at least aware of alternative versions of the Joseph story, versions composed either in early post-biblical times or as late as the sixteenth century. In their writing, Grotius, Zesen, Fielding, Mrs Rowe (and others) often echo not only the biblical text, but also those later traditions which they exploit for details, embellishments, and names. So our task involves sketching the repertoire upon which they were drawing.

In what follows I offer brief summaries of three versions or clusters of variations of the story, designating them, for the sake of convenience, by adjectives that indicate their provenance: Jewish, Islamic, and Christian. Each of the summaries is followed by brief details of authorship, date, modern interpretation, and the like. The three versions are presented in chronological order; accordingly, we begin with the Jewish versions.

JEWISH VERSIONS

In the centuries around the time of Christ, two distinct forms of Jewish culture developed: Hebrew- and Aramaic-speaking Judaism with its centre in

Jerusalem, and Greek-speaking Diaspora Judaism which, although widely scattered around the Mediterranean basin, flourished especially in Alexandria in Egypt. Because Joseph was a Hebrew living in Egypt, Alexandrian Jews had a natural liking for him, and, unsurprisingly, they frequently told his story. Embellishing and developing it according to Hellenistic taste, they created versions that were as aesthetically pleasing as they were intellectually pertinent. The best-known ancient Jewish versions, told in the *Testaments of the Twelve Patriarchs*, the *Story of Aseneth*, and Philo's *On Joseph*, all reflect the Jewish culture of Alexandria. This is also true of two accounts of Joseph included in ancient Jewish historical works: the *Jewish Antiquities* by Josephus[1] and *On the Jews* by Artapanus. Some of these writings merit a closer look, both for their extraordinary literary quality and the impact they made on subsequent, including early-modern, versions of the biblical story. Two preferred themes of Hellenistic culture dominate – politics and love – and both are adapted to suit Jewish concerns. We will begin with Joseph the statesman.

> According to the historian Artapanus (*c.* 200 BCE), Joseph, a young man excelling in wisdom, obtained knowledge of his brothers' plot against him.[2] With the help of friends among the neighbouring Arabs, he managed to save his life by escaping to Egypt. There he was recommended to the king, became governor of the country, and not only stored grain during the seven years of plenty, but also introduced major reforms. Hitherto the Egyptians had farmed the land in a disorganised, haphazard manner; but Joseph devised a system of marking out the boundaries of arable land. He also made much barren land cultivable and allotted some of it to the priests. Moreover, Joseph invented and prescribed standard measurements. Artapanus also seems to have attributed to Joseph social reform that aimed at preventing the exploitation of the lower classes by the more powerful. On account of all these reforms, Joseph was greatly loved by the Egyptians.

Joseph the founder and legislator does not have an exact precedent in the Bible, though it was possible to derive the notion from a passage that refers to Joseph as a man appointed by Pharaoh "to instruct both his princes and himself, and to teach his elders wisdom".[3] Joseph, moreover, according to the Bible, redefined the economic status of the priests and fixed the taxes to be paid by the peasants. Apparently, these hints sufficed to fire the imagination of Artapanus, leading him to portray Joseph as an archaic cultural hero who, following Greek tradition, acts as "first inventor" (*prôtos heuretês*). As a statesman, he embodies the Greek ideal of a ruler who, endowed with extraordinary vision, devises practical measures, establishes political institutions, and reorganises the state. In the

Greek tradition, similar reforms were attributed to Solon who in 594 BCE arbitrated between the social classes of Athens and gave the city its first constitution. Inspiration for some of the details in Artapanus's portrayal of Joseph no doubt also came from legends about King Sesostris whom tradition considered one of the founders of ancient Egyptian political institutions.[4]

More in tune with the biblical account, but also focusing on politics, is a book known as *The Life of the Statesman, or On Joseph,* commonly referred to as *On Joseph*.[5] Its author, Philo (c. 10 BCE–CE 54), an educated, Greek-speaking Jew living in Alexandria, wrote what one might call a philosophical exposition of the Joseph story. To us, it appears a somewhat strange mixture of exegetical commentary on the text of Genesis and a more systematic treatise on the character and ethics of the ideal statesman. The exegetical link is most evident in Philo's description of the three stages of Joseph's education for his political office.

> The first stage of Joseph's career is that of the shepherd, deemed the ideal early training ground for overseeing others – managing sheep rather than people. Joseph undergoes this experience in Canaan, where he grows up with his brothers. The second stage is reached once the future statesman is appointed to the position of steward in a major household. This happens in Egypt, where his master was quick to realise the capabilities of his slave. He immediately frees him from slavery and makes him a full citizen. As his master's steward, Joseph rules over all the household slaves and oversees all matters pertaining to the proper management of the estate. He also shows single-minded determination in resisting his mistress's temptations and remaining faithful to his master. The household, understood as a small-scale state, prepares Joseph for the next step. The third and final stage is reached once Joseph interprets the dreams of the king of Egypt and is immediately appointed governor. Now he can apply all he has learned, and indeed his skills are in great demand during the ensuing crisis – the seven difficult years of dearth.

In much of his treatise, Philo disregards exegetical detail; instead, he focuses on the philosophical portrayal of the ideal statesman with little recourse to Scripture.

> While Joseph enjoys in effect the role of a king, Pharaoh retaining only a nominal royal position, the statesman in normal circumstances stands more properly between the monarch and the people. He has to take great care to remain independent of both. The statesman must speak to the king

> with neither fear nor flattery; he must also stay fearless even if a tyrant should threaten him with death. Equally, he must never let himself become dependent upon those who, as is well known, will try to influence or dominate him. But he must refrain from being insensitive to the wishes of the people, and especially to the laws and customs of the country and its cities. Though he may improve existing customs by promoting good order, established laws must stay in force. In dealing with the people, it is most important to act selflessly for the common good, and not for one's own advantage and profit. Politics must never be for personal gain, but for the common good, for the statesman is above all a "father" who cares for the members of his household. In two respects in particular, the statesman must stand far above others. First, he must be committed to an ethic of restraint, especially sexual restraint; his rigid traditional morality must transcend the lax mores of others, for instance many Egyptians. (Philo, the Roman citizen, is here echoing upper-class Roman sentiments about the laxity of Egyptian morals.)[6] Second, he must be much more far-sighted, intelligent, and discriminating than normal people can aspire to be. In times of prosperity and peace, he has to prepare for times of war and times of economic problems, and he has to do so without disclosing his policy to others. Moreover, he must be an interpreter of people's daydreams – their aspirations, ideologies, and wishes. As a statesman-philosopher, he must be able to discriminate between that which is good, honourable, useful, and reasonable, and that which is bad, disgraceful, pernicious, unlawful, and selfish.

Unfortunately, we know very little about Philo's life, but we do know of his involvement with local politics in Alexandria in Egypt, the largest Jewish community outside Palestine. In CE 38, Alexandria saw riots against the Jewish minority living there. Jews were not only ridiculed, but also beaten, stabbed, dragged through the city, set on fire, and their bodies left to rot. Apparently, the Roman prefect stood by and watched, doing nothing to stop the violence. In CE 40, Philo led a delegation of Alexandrian Jews to Rome, to plead their cause before the emperor. We have no way of telling whether Philo wrote the treatise before or after the events of the years 38 and 40; if linked to these events, Philo's book could be interpreted as an injunction to upper-class Alexandrian Jews to assume political responsibility. Another possibility might be that Philo wrote the book for his politically ambitious nephew Tiberius Julius Alexander who became Roman procurator of Judaea from CE 46 to 48, during a time of famine that plagued Judaea as well as other parts of the eastern Mediterranean (with the exception of Egypt). In this case, Philo might have been seeking to remind his nephew, an apostate from Judaism, of his Jewish roots by holding up

Joseph as an example of the ideal statesman, the impeccable governor and provider for his people. All of this must remain speculative, however. At any rate, Philo's *On Joseph* shows that in first-century Alexandria some Jews could realistically aspire to some form of political career. In fact, the later career of Philo's nephew (most likely after Philo's death) is amazing: we find him as prefect of Egypt in CE 66–70, then as a military adviser participating in the Roman war against Judaea, and eventually as praetorial prefect in Rome, the second most powerful position after the emperor himself.[7] In ancient times no other man of Jewish descent held such an important imperial office.

While the accounts of Artapanus and Philo reflect Hellenistic political philosophy, the version presented in the *Testaments of the Twelve Patriarchs*, written in Greek presumably some time in the second or first century BCE, echoes the style and romantic interest of Hellenistic novel-writing. But rather than adopting a narrative form, the Jewish author gave his work the more didactic form of twelve speeches imagined to have been delivered in turn on the deathbed of the sons of Jacob, as an exhortation to their own children. In his speech, Joseph gives a relatively detailed account of his early days in Egypt; others, especially Reuben, Simeon, Naphtali, Gad, and Benjamin, refer to their involvement with the selling of Joseph or to their reactions to their brother either in their early days in Palestine or later as they travelled to Egypt. Most of the "Joseph" material appears of course in Joseph's own testament; the others offer only a few scattered remarks. From all this one can reconstruct some of the features of the Joseph story as told by preachers in the Greek-speaking synagogue. It runs approximately as follows:[8]

> The story begins with a kind of theoretical preamble. The human soul does not have a fixed, immutable moral quality; its moral direction – towards good or evil – must be chosen by the individual and stabilised by constant practice. Good and evil powers compete for influence; Beliar (the devil) is very active, as are God's angels. Beliar most often takes advantage of envy or erotic attraction, seeking to make these feelings escalate so as to prompt evil acts. Beliar is at work amongst Joseph's brothers, so they proceed with their evil plan: they arrest him, take away his beautiful coat, replacing it with a loincloth, then confine him in a dry cistern, far away from home. They do not listen to his pleas for mercy. Eventually, Judah and Gad sell him for thirty pieces of gold; secretly, they keep ten pieces for themselves, and the rest they share with their brothers.[9] Despite their assertion that Joseph is dead, Jacob knows otherwise, for he sees Joseph in mysterious visions as a living person. Benjamin has similar visions of his absent brother.[10]

> Brought to Egypt as a slave, Joseph first works in the household of a merchant. But a noble lady from Memphis, who has heard of the beautiful young Hebrew, comes to see him. She persuades her husband to buy the Hebrew for whatever sum the merchant claims. So Joseph comes to work as a slave in the household of Potiphar, one of Pharaoh's chief officers. His wife – the noble lady – falls in love with him. At first, she kisses and embraces him, pretending he is like a son to her. Soon, it becomes clear what she wants: inflamed with lust, she wishes to lure him into her bed. When begging and pleading fail, she comes up with ever new approaches – threats of punishment if he does not comply, all kinds of promises if he should give in. Seeing that Joseph is a resolutely pious Hebrew, she even promises to abandon idol worship for him. Eventually, she goes as far as offering marriage after her own husband has been poisoned. She also threatens, "If you will not lie with me, I shall hang myself, or else throw myself off a cliff." Joseph realises that an evil spirit – the spirit of Beliar – has assumed complete control of her. One day, having enlisted the help of magicians,[11] she sends a servant to him with a bowl of delicious food. Through an angelic vision granted by God, Joseph realises that the food is enchanted: mixed with magical substances, the concoction is designed to break his resistance and inflame him with love for her. Joseph will not touch it. He resists as firmly as ever, so all her advances fail. Finally, she goes to see Joseph, arms, breasts, and legs seductively uncovered to show off her beauty, for she is indeed very beautiful; but again, Joseph will have none of it. In desperation she grabs hold of him by his clothes, trying to force him to lie with her. He manages to shake her off, but leaves his garment behind, and runs away naked. Enraged, she keeps the garment as evidence against him. Upon her husband's return the next day, Joseph is whipped and thrown into prison.
>
> Still she does not give up. She keeps sending word to Joseph, saying, "Please fulfil my desire. I shall release you up out of your darkness." She also goes in person, in the dead of night, to his prison cell to listen as he prays. But Joseph does not yield, for God protects him from all her designs. On his deathbed, Joseph tells his children his story, exhorting them to strict self-control and purity, patience and prayer. Self-control, loved by God, will triumph over all temptations.

What our summary cannot convey properly is the fact that the *Testaments of the Twelve Patriarchs* blend romance-like amplification of the biblical tale with moral advice and exhortation to virtue. The first draws upon Hellenistic storytelling, whereas the latter is largely inspired by a Jewish variety of Hellenistic popular philosophy.[12] The major ingredient of this philosophy was Stoicism, and no ancient reader could have missed the Stoic note on which Joseph ends his exhortation. Stoic philosophy originated around 300 BCE as a development of the wisdom that had been taught in the schools of Egypt and the Middle East for more than two millennia; newly recounted in Greek and rethought to suit an evolving cultural world, it became the most popular philosophy of the centuries immediately before and after Christ. Stoicism made a lasting impact on later moral discourse, even down to our own day. Hellenistic Jews applied the Stoic ethics of self-control specifically to restraining not just irregular sexual acts but also the desire for them.[13] The *Testaments* are an important early source for understanding what came to be a specifically Western concept of sexuality: sin in a sexual context, according to this notion, happens in the mind, and not in the act; in order to behave properly, a man has to control – and actually eliminate – desire, not just refrain from touching a woman.[14] The *Testaments* hold up Joseph as a paradigm not only of chastity; many other virtues, including humility, patience, endurance, and compassion in his dealings with others, are also highlighted. "Pattern your life", Benjamin tells his children (and all readers of the *Testaments*), "after the good and pious man Joseph."[15]

A similar, and more clearly romantic, elaboration of the Joseph tale is a work entitled *The Marriage and Conversion of Aseneth* (also known as *Joseph and Aseneth*), presumably written some time between the second century BCE and the first century CE, when Hellenistic Judaism flourished in Alexandria. In the early-modern period it was largely known in Latin, as an abridged account included in the *Speculum historiale*, an encyclopaedic universal history compiled by the French Dominican scholar Vincent of Beauvais (c. 1250). Under the heading "*Ex historia Asseneth*" (From the Story of Aseneth), he told the tale as follows:[16]

> During one of his tours of inspection in Egypt, Joseph visits the city of Heliopolis. There he is cordially received and entertained by the governor Potiphar and his wife. He also meets this couple's daughter Aseneth, a girl of extraordinary beauty who, living in social exclusion in an isolated tower, grows up without ever meeting any men. When she is told by her parents to greet Joseph with a kiss, Joseph refuses to accept the greeting, explaining that he is not allowed to be touched by a woman who worships idols. To compensate for this rejection, Joseph blesses her. Distressed, Aseneth retires to her quarters, destroys all her idols, and fasts. On her eighth day of fasting, she is visited by an angel who strangely resembles Joseph; he tells her to exchange her black sackcloth for a white garment, for her name is now entered in the heavenly book of life, from which it can

never be erased. The angel also announces her forthcoming marriage to Joseph. After having given his blessing to both Aseneth and her seven maids, the angel vanishes. As Joseph returns to Potiphar's house, he declares his intention of marrying Aseneth, and is granted Pharaoh's permission to do so. The entire population of Egypt is granted a whole week's holiday to celebrate the wedding of the happy couple.

In the second year of the famine, Joseph's father Jacob and all his sons and their families immigrate to Egypt. Jacob, described as a prince and hero who, despite his old age, is still strong, healthy, and handsome, receives Aseneth with a kiss and blesses his Egyptian daughter-in-law.

One day, the twenty-nine-year-old son of Pharaoh happens to see Aseneth, and is immediately inflamed with love. In order to make Aseneth his wife, he secures the help of two of Joseph's brothers – Dan and Gad – in staging a rebellion against his own father and against Joseph. After an attempt to enter Pharaoh's chamber fails, the prince and his fifty armed men manage to surprise Joseph and Aseneth while they are travelling. But the prince fails to capture Aseneth, for Joseph and his men quickly take up arms to protect her. In the ensuing battle, most of the rebels are killed, and Pharaoh's son is badly wounded. The Hebrews attempt to save his life, but although they carefully wash and bandage his wounds, the Egyptian prince dies after three days. Pharaoh, inconsolably stricken with grief, also dies. He leaves the crown to Joseph, for his second son and heir is still an infant. Once the crown prince has grown up, Joseph will relinquish his position as vice-regent, and the prince will assume full rule over Egypt.

The *Historia Asseneth* develops the brief indication in Genesis that Joseph married an Egyptian girl. As is to be expected, Joseph's good looks are matched by those of Aseneth, and, predictably, she has to convert to the monotheistic faith of Joseph. The emphasis on her beauty echoes an aspect characteristic of late-ancient Graeco-Roman romances, while the conversion episode aligns the marriage with orthodox Jewish practice. As in much of post-biblical storytelling (including accounts in the New Testament), an angel is introduced to symbolise God's immediate intervention. The rebellion of Pharaoh's (unnamed) son adds an unexpected twist. This addition fills the long and otherwise uneventful period of Joseph's governorship over Egypt; it also echoes the ancient notion, well known from Homer's *Iliad*, that war and strife are frequently caused by a man's sudden desire for a beautiful woman. But unlike Helena, the beautiful wife of the king of Sparta, the Egyptian upper-class lady Aseneth was never captured and abducted. The *Iliad* celebrates armed contest in a heroic setting; the Jewish novel, by contrast, teaches a lesson to Jewish men of the Diaspora: they may indeed marry a pagan girl, provided she abandons her lifeless idols and comes to worship the living God.

Looking back at the Jewish sources summarised here, we can see that their essential message corresponds to the two pillars of Judaism: monotheism and strict morality; the Aseneth tale stands for monotheism (for it is to Jewish monotheism that Aseneth converts), whereas the *Testaments of the Twelve Patriarchs* and Philo's treatise emphasise strict morality. These texts elaborate and embellish certain aspects of the Genesis story of Joseph and thus point the way for further elaboration and embellishment. The Hellenistic versions above all demonstrate their authors' enthusiasm for the Joseph figure, an enthusiasm that proved to be contagious. Among those who, through contact with Jewish lore and literature, came to share such interest in the story were Muhammad and his followers.

Islamic versions

The Qur'an, revealed (as tradition has it) to the prophet Muhammad by Allah in the early seventh century CE, includes a fine version of the Joseph story. It is the only relatively long, complete, and coherent narrative section of the Qur'an, the suras of which often appear, at least to the non-initiated reader, to be disjointed and difficult to follow. The Qur'an itself seems to acknowledge the privileged status of the "Yûsuf" chapter by calling it "the best of all tales".[17] The account approximately follows the biblical version, but includes several interesting variations and embroidery.

> At the very beginning, Yûsuf reports his dreams exclusively to his father, not to his brothers, so as not to provoke their resentment. Later, having been thrown into the cistern, Yûsuf receives a divine revelation: Allah assures him that some day in the future he, Yûsuf, will be able to confront his brothers with their crime. Or, again, after buying the Hebrew slave, Yûsuf's owner suggests to his wife that they might eventually adopt the boy as their son. The most conspicuous difference between the biblical and Qur'anic versions can be found in the treatment of what happens at the house of Yûsuf's Egyptian master (both this master and his wife remain anonymous). Here Yûsuf's mistress is given a very prominent role. Yûsuf feels a certain initial attraction to her, but through divine intervention (we are not told how) he finds the strength to resist. After an unsuccessful attempt to seduce the Hebrew, the woman accuses him of making improper advances, but her

> accusation is not accepted by her husband. Another member of the household suggests that if Yûsuf's shirt is torn in front, then he truly did attempt to violate her; but if it is torn behind, the evidence suggests rather that she ran after him. The forthcoming evidence exculpates Yûsuf, and the master chides his wife (without, apparently, making too much of the matter). In the episode following, the storyteller clearly enjoys recounting a comic scene: Yûsuf's mistress invites some women of the city to a gathering, displaying to them the much-discussed object of her passion. Being distracted by the beauty of Yûsuf, they all cut their hands with the sharp knives provided them for peeling fruit; such is the punishment for their salacious curiosity. Nevertheless, the women all agree: "This is no ordinary mortal! This is none other than an honourable angel."[18] Since Yûsuf stays on in the household, his mistress continues her advances, though to no avail. Eventually, we find Yûsuf in prison (why, we are not told). Much later, after Yûsuf has been brought before the king to interpret his dreams, the matter of seduction will surface again, at which point the former mistress repents and publicly admits her fault. What follows – the interpretation of dreams, Yûsuf's rise to power, his unexpected meeting with his brothers – corresponds to the biblical tale. The political side of the story – how Joseph handles the years of plenty and the years of dearth – remains undeveloped; by contrast, Yûsuf's meeting with his brothers is reported at length. The story ends with the immigration of Jacob and his family to Egypt. As his father and mother pay him homage by prostrating themselves before him, Yûsuf reminds them of the prophetic vision Allah had granted him when he was a boy.

The Yûsuf story as told in the Qur'an resonates with the life of Muhammad himself: both Yûsuf and Muhammad are holy men who have received revelations early in life, face adversity and trials through the actions of others, but are eventually confirmed in their mission.[19] Nothing in this analogy should surprise us, for Muhammad sees himself as the last of a series of holy men, all of whom had to fight for acknowledgement by the society in which they lived. It is impossible for the prophet to speak about a holy man of a past age without also thinking of himself, his own divine mission and difficult career; in short, of the typical biographical pattern of dishonour in their own country shared by prophets of all ages. Muhammad goes as far as putting an autobiographical report into Yûsuf's mouth that does not actually fit in with the story; but it chimes perfectly well with the Arabian prophet's own experience:

I have forsaken the creed of a people who do not believe in Allah, and who moreover are unbelievers in the world to come. But I follow the creed of my fathers, Ibrahim and Isaac and Jacob. Never could we attribute any partners whatever to Allah – that comes of the grace of Allah to us and to mankind, yet most men are not grateful.[20]

The prophet, having forsaken Arabian polytheism, has decided to follow the religion of the patriarchs of old – from Abraham to Jacob; a religion that does not associate any partners with God (as for instance in Christianity's Trinitarian teaching). Instead of gratefully accepting this message, many of Muhammad's contemporaries "ungratefully" reject the prophet and his mission. As for the seductress, the prophet portrays her as any good oriental storyteller would do; she strikes us as someone who might appear in the stories of the *Arabian Nights*. But only briefly does the storyteller gain the upper hand; the prophet quickly returns to his true purpose by making her realise her fault and repent – in this, she is presented to the prophet's audience as a role model for all to follow. Just as Muhammad somehow identifies with Yûsuf himself, so the Egyptian woman is given the paradigmatic role of the prophet's idealised audience – the role of sinners who sooner or later come to realise their fault, recognise the prophet's authority, and sincerely repent.

Although Yûsuf's mistress is a loser in the Qur'anic tale, she nevertheless is given much prominence, so that she impresses herself on the reader as a more vivid personality than the saintly figure of Joseph. Readers are likely to develop some degree of sympathy for her. The Qur'anic image of Yûsuf's mistress has inspired later Muslim authors, especially Persian ones, to develop her personality further by giving her a name – Zulaikha (Zuleika) – and making her the protagonist of a more elaborate love story. The best-known versions, in epic form, are by the two Persian poets Firdussi (940–1020)[21] and Jâmi (1414–1492). The latter transformed the Qur'anic legend into a long romance with many dramatic episodes, complete with a happy ending. What follows is a brief summary of Jâmi's *Yûsuf and Zuleika*:[22]

> A king's fair daughter, Zuleika, has several dreams in which the figure of a handsome young man appears. One of the dreams implies that he is Grand Vizier in Egypt. She prevails upon her father to send a marriage embassy to the vizier, but to her horror comes to realise that the vizier approached is not the man she has seen in her dreams. Nevertheless, Zuleika marries the vizier, though he is a eunuch – an emasculated priest of an Egyptian temple. One day, Zuleika sees a handsome young man offered for sale at the slave market, and she persuades her husband to

purchase the boy for adoption. Having obtained him, she indulges him as an adopted son, showering him with fine clothes and maternal affection until a new passion is kindled within her. She falls ill, consumed with distress. As she confides her secret to her nurse, her confidante devises a plan to unite the two. But all attempts fail. Eventually, Zuleika accuses the slave of seduction and he is thrown into prison, but soon released on the evidence of his torn shirt; a member of Zuleika's household – identified as a baby that normally lacks the ability to speak – had explained how to examine the garment properly and draw the relevant conclusions. After some time, however, Yûsuf is returned to prison, where Zuleika often visits him to declare her love. As before, Yûsuf remains unresponsive. What follows is the familiar story of Yûsuf's release from prison, his interpretation of the royal dreams, and his rise to the office of Grand Vizier. One day, he is approached by a beggar woman in whom he recognises Zuleika, now a poor widow who long ago has repented of her lying. She is still in love with Yûsuf, however. Yûsuf receives her into his house where, nursed back to health, she regains her former beauty. Yûsuf forgives her, and the two are at last happily united in marriage.

Although Zuleika, as in the Qur'an, is portrayed as a sinner (for she lied about Yûsuf), her love for Yûsuf as such is never denounced as sinful. Instead, the author depicts her as a woman who goes through all the agonies of unrequited love in order to see, after a lengthy delay, all her hopes fulfilled, for, so one must conclude, true love can overcome all obstacles. To demonstrate this, the oriental poets even made Zuleika the protagonist who, on the scale of importance, ranks above Yûsuf. Versions of the Persian Zuleika romance filtered into the folklore of the Islamic world,[23] and by the eighteenth century, European writers became aware of "Yûsuf and Zuleika". The episode of the talking infant in Zuleika's home so amused Voltaire that he could not help retelling it, with relish, in his *Dictionnaire philosophique*. Goethe, when writing his *West-Eastern Divan*, includes "Jussuph und Suleika" in his list of the great pairs of lovers in Eastern literature.[24]

Elements of Muslim versions of the Joseph tale entered, and even dominate, the account given in the *General estoria* (General History), a universal history begun in 1272 at the court of the Castilian King Alfonso el Sabio. This book and the circumstances of its compilation merit a closer look.

In thirteenth-century Spain, Fernando III (1199–1252) conquered the Muslim kingdoms of Córdoba, Murcia, Jaén, and Sevilla, thus virtually completing the Reconquest, the re-establishment of Christian political control over a peninsula that had been under Arab rule for several centuries.

Fernando the warrior king was followed on the throne of Castile by his son Alfonso el Sabio (Alfonso the Learned, 1221–1284). Before his father's death he had taken part in the Reconquest and never later gave up military ambition, but his tastes lay more in the peaceful art of promoting cultural life. He surrounded himself with writers and scholars, and actively participated in the composition of poetry and works of history. Cultural life flourished, and although the Muslims had been thrown out of the country, Alfonso showed interest in their culture, seeking to appropriate and learn from their rich literature. Among the works he compiled with the assistance of other scholars is the *General estoria*. Left incomplete, this first attempt to write a universal history in a vernacular language – Castilian rather than Latin – was to cover the period from the creation of the world to the birth of Anna and Joachim, parents of the Virgin Mary. The *General estoria* gives ample space to Joseph: more than eighty pages in the English translation.[25]

The *General estoria* tells the story of Joseph with palpable delight and a flair for the exotic. Were it not explicitly framed as a true account based on all available sources, the modern reader would compare it to the *Arabian Nights*.

> In keeping with the oriental notion that history is primarily about the rule and deeds of monarchs, the story of Joseph is told as an extended episode during the reign of Pharaoh Nicrao. A great warrior, this pharaoh conquered many lands, and on one of his military expeditions he came as far as Spain, where he was no less successful in his exploits than elsewhere. His period is presented as the golden age of ancient Egypt. "This pharaoh was a great man," we are told, "very handsome and intelligent, a doer of good to everyone. He cancelled the taxes for three years, ordered his treasury opened, and divided it among his nobles (*ricos omnes*), and those of his household, and his people. They all loved him because of this, and thanked him very much, and prayed to God for him."[26] The career of Joseph – his boyhood in Canaan, the hatred of his brothers, his being sold to merchants, his entering into the service of Phutiphar (as he is called here), the attempted seduction by Zulayme, the imprisonment, the interpretation of Pharaoh's dreams, the elevation to high office, the seven years of famine, the arrival of his brothers, and his reconciliation with them – is all told in more or less the same way as it is in the Bible. A few episodes are added to embellish the account, however. Before elevating him to high office, Pharaoh Nicrao tests Joseph's abilities by assigning him the task of building a city in a swampy area of the Nile delta. By draining the swamp, Joseph masters the task, completing it within a short period of time. Having thus demonstrated his capabilities,

> Joseph can be made governor of Egypt. Another unexpected detail is the identity of Joseph's Egyptian spouse: after Phutiphar's early death, Joseph marries his widow Zulayme and promises her never to mention the unpleasant incident of the attempted seduction. To complete the story, mention must be made of Joseph's missionary zeal and success. Under Joseph's influence, his friend Pharaoh Nicrao came to abandon belief in the pagan idols of Egypt; he converted to belief "in our Lord God, as Joseph believed and taught him", though he felt obliged to keep it secret to prevent rebellion.[27]

Occasionally, one gets the impression that the story of Joseph is told in order to highlight the character of the Egyptian king, a figure left undeveloped in the Bible. The Egyptian king's portrait as someone who grants tax exemptions and gives gifts to his nobles seems to have been meant as an idealised depiction of Alfonso who financially supported the rise of the noble houses.[28] The narrator here assimilates ancient Egyptian society to that of medieval Castile where the *ricos omnes* (literally, "rich men"),[29] with their vassals and banners, were socially almost on the same level as the king.[30]

The *General estoria*'s long section on Joseph includes remarkable digressions on cultural and natural history: on the flooding of Egypt by the Nile, on crocodiles and dolphins, on why the Libyans dislike shepherds, on the gentile kings who ruled various parts of the world at the time of Joseph, on the first breeding of mules, on the introduction of weights and measures in Greece, and on the story of Prometheus who was believed to have been a contemporary of Joseph. Like the entire work, these digressions reflect the enthusiasm for encyclopaedic and historical knowledge, derived from a great variety of sources, including the work of the Hellenistic historian Diodorus Siculus. The *General estoria*'s portrait of Joseph's pharaoh seems to mirror the figure of Sesostris, one of the early kings of Egypt whom Diodorus extols as a great warrior who subdued much of the ancient world.[31] Other works exploited are Peter Comestor's *Historia scholastica* (a twelfth-century Latin work of history, written in France) and Abu Ubaid al-Bakti's *Book of Roads and Kingdoms* (a work by an important eleventh-century Arabic historian and geographer who lived in Spain). Since all the sources used are unquestioningly treated as equally reliable, contradictory information is sometimes awkwardly juxtaposed, resulting in clumsy and illogical presentation.[32] Nevertheless, the *General estoria* appears as a celebration of Joseph and his time, and is remarkable as a synthesis of materials deriving from classical, Christian, and Muslim sources.

The bold embellishment found in Alfonso's *General estoria* announces a similar, and even bolder development of the Joseph story by the Renaissance humanists. But in order to understand the humanists, we have to insert a note on ancient literature, for they not only admired it but also sought to blend it with the biblical story.

CHRISTIAN VERSIONS

The Christian repertoire of Joseph traditions includes the ancient Jewish versions, and even some of the Islamic elaborations were known to and appreciated by many Christians. Nevertheless, Christians did make their own significant contribution to the growth and development of the Joseph corpus – by adapting the biblical story to classical taste and style.

In late antiquity, Greek and Latin poetry still stood under the spell of Homer and Virgil, the epic poets *par excellence*. Despite the waning of classical culture and its supporting pagan religion – the religion of gods and goddesses, mythic tales and songs, temples and sacred groves, mysteries celebrated in secret, priestly sacrifices of bulls and pigs and sheep, and colourful pageants performed before large crowds – these early poets were not forgotten; in fact, they were still studied in Christian schools of higher education. This generally meant the study of classical literature, rhetoric, and the basics of jurisprudence. One who enjoyed such an education was Romanos the Melodist (*c.* 485–555). Born in Syria and possibly of Jewish descent, he became a famous religious poet based in Constantinople, the capital of the eastern part of the Roman Empire. His metrical homilies (so-called *kontakia*), sung to the congregation, fascinated them, and encouraged some (much less successful) imitators. Two of Romanos's *kontakia* feature the life of Joseph whose feast is celebrated by the Orthodox Church on the Monday of Holy Week, the week before Easter:

> One, an epic of forty stanzas, traces the entire career of Jacob's favourite son, from his earliest dreams to his reunion with his aged father in Egypt. The second work is more narrowly focused on Joseph the "chaste youth" in his encounter with the passionate Egyptian woman. Joseph is presented as God's holy warrior, protected by the "impenetrable armour of virtue".[33] He is also an athlete, competing in a match in which each thrust and parry must be delivered with masterly precision, because (according to the refrain), "the eye that never sleeps sees everything". The basic plot comes from Genesis, but Romanos pulls out all his rhetorical stops to capture and keep the attention of his congregation – and to ensure that they will not miss his Lenten message of eternal vigilance in the face of sexual temptation. The struggle is set in a cosmic context reminiscent of Homer:

> The devil came to bolster the Egyptian woman: he would escort the adulterous bride. "Be hard," he said. "Use yourself as a hook, tempered and tested. Prepare the bait, land the youth," he said. "Braid the locks of your hair into a snare for him. Adorn your face with cosmetics: scarlet lips, beguiling eyes. Coil chains of gleaming gold around your neck; drape your body in precious silks. Apply your most potent perfumes – they soften any young man – for the struggle will be titanic and Olympic. You must attack with lust. He will defend himself with purity. You must not be defeated; we cannot be mocked. For he is sure to say, "I will not do what you desire, because the eye that never sleeps sees everything."[34]
>
> These blandishments fail, of course, but the battle continues; eventually, Romanos concludes this *kontakion* with an appeal for assistance in the face of temptation and forbidden desires.

While the "sung sermon" of Romanos is not quite an epic, it comes close to being one, and those who have read Homer or Virgil will easily recognise the epic tradition upon which the singing homilist draws. But the world of epic poetry had vanished even before the days of Romanos, and during the Middle Ages no serious attempt was made to revive it. The revival came only with the Renaissance, when, in the fifteenth century, humanists rediscovered classical literature and celebrated first Virgil's *Aeneid*, and later also Homer's *Iliad* and *Odyssey*, as the greatest literary achievements of ancient times. Central to literary education, these epics were once again studied either in the original Greek and Latin or in modern vernacular translations. Also admired and studied were certain works of ancient playwrights, especially Seneca, whose *Phaedra* ranked as the unsurpassed model of an ancient tragedy.

The Renaissance, a cultural movement that originated in Italy and culminated in the first half of the sixteenth century, established a new kind of scholar: the humanist. Humanists rediscovered the literature of the Greeks and Romans, considering it the quintessential expression of human civilisation. Whoever wanted to produce new literary texts first of all had to study the works of Cicero, Seneca, and Virgil, to name but a few. Joseph was a familiar figure to the humanists, and occasionally they retold the biblical story in the form of ancient drama and epic, always endeavouring to incorporate episodes or stock characters borrowed from Seneca, Virgil, or other ancient playwrights. Thus Pandolfo Collenuccio (1444–1504) in his Italian *Comedia di Iacob e Ioseph* gave Potiphar's wife not only a Latin name – he called her Beronica – but also a servant and confidante, Sidonia, in keeping with ancient poetic practice.³⁵ The most accomplished humanist version of the Joseph story, however, is not an Italian stage play but a Latin epic, written by Girolamo Fracastoro (1483–1553). Today Fracastoro is chiefly remembered as the author of a long medical treatise in poetic form that gave the name "syphilis" to the venereal disease. He came close to understanding that certain diseases are caused by the self-propagating, transmissible agents ("germs") we now term bacteria and viruses. Church historians know Fracastoro as a devout Catholic who also wrote theological books.³⁶ In 1546–1547, when serving as the Council of Trent's official doctor, Fracastoro persuaded Pope Paul III to move the meeting from Trent to Bologna because of the dangerous petechial fever that had broken out in Trent. But besides being an important medical scholar, Fracastoro was also an outstanding humanist poet. The language of choice for his poetry was Latin, and, like other humanists, he sought to revive the poetic power of Virgil. It was with Virgil in mind that he wrote his Latin hexameter epic on Joseph. Although apparently death prevented the author from finishing his poem, the two extant cantos are impressive for their use of *inventio*, the "discovery" of ancient literary material applied and imitated in the creation of a poem. Here is the story Fracastoro tells in his "Joseph":³⁷

> After an invocation of the divine Muses, the poet proceeds to explain how Pluto, god of the Netherworld, sows the spirit of discord and envy in the hearts of Joseph's brothers. Soon this spirit overwhelms the brothers, filling them with hatred – "they gather daily more disdain, / sharpen their envy, give their rage the rein".³⁸ On one occasion when Joseph meets them far from home, they are quick to take him prisoner and plot to kill him. First they throw him into a pit; there, Joseph prays to God, and God sends an angelic messenger to visit and comfort the distressed boy. Eventually his brothers sell him to a caravan of Arab merchants who take him to Egypt. There, he is given as a gift to Potiphar, who is in charge of the royal army. In Potiphar's house he soon becomes the chief steward. Pluto again intervenes by sending one of his infernal spirits to sow the seeds of love for Joseph in the heart of Iëmpsar, Potiphar's wife; and likewise, the seed of love for Iëmpsar in the heart of Joseph. Further, Iëmpsar's nurse, Iphicles – or rather, the infernal spirit disguised as Iphicles – tries to bring the two together. Iphicles reports to Iëmpsar what Joseph (allegedly) told her – of his secret love for Iëmpsar; and Iëmpsar at once confesses her own secret love for the Hebrew to Iphicles. The nurse gives her a magic potion, explaining that it is the potion of decision: if someone is undecided in any matter, it would help one to make up one's mind. With Joseph, Iphicles has no chance, for his

vigilant guardian angel scares her away as she enters the chamber of his Bible-reading protégé.

The demon's magic potion, a powerful aphrodisiac, makes Iëmpsar burn with love for Joseph. Feeling no longer in control of herself, but under the spell of some higher power, she resolves to reveal her desire for Joseph. When Joseph arrives, summoned by Iëmpsar's maid Ephren, he is greeted with the declaration that she knows all about his passion for her. Taken aback by her ardent kisses and protestations of love, Joseph curtly explains that he will have none of this and must stay faithful to his master, and promptly leaves. Iphicles (still a demon in human guise) later finds Iëmpsar in low spirits, indeed ready to commit suicide. On Iphicles's advice, Iëmpsar performs sacred rites, imploring the gods to help her win the attention of Joseph. On a day designated by Iphicles as auspicious for the matter, Iëmpsar again receives Joseph, inviting him to join her in bed. Joseph refuses. He also tells her that the advice she claims to have received from Iphicles cannot have been given by her nurse; instead, one of the Furies must have been deceiving her. As he speaks, the demon, infuriated at being discovered, enters the chamber and throws one of the snakes she is carrying at Joseph. Since the Hebrew is inviolable, protected by his guardian angel, the snake bites Iëmpsar instead and spits venom into her wounds. Horrified, Joseph flees. Iëmpsar, seized by madness, cries for help and accuses Joseph of attempted rape. Iphicles, hurriedly approaching, confirms the accusation made by her mistress. Potiphar puts Joseph in fetters and sends him to prison. At night, Joseph is visited and comforted by his guardian angel. The warder soon takes pity on Joseph, removes his chains, and befriends him. Eventually, after having interpreted the dreams of two fellow prisoners, Joseph similarly assists the king of Egypt and is made vice-regent of the country, to guide it successfully through the fourteen-year cycle of feast and famine.

An oracle, given to the high priest of Heliopolis by the sun-god Apollo, declares that his beautiful daughter will not be given to an Egyptian man in marriage; she is destined to marry a foreigner. Both the high priest and the king come to believe that the foreigner in question can only be Joseph. At the end of the seven years of plenty, as the entire population celebrates its well-being, the king gives the young lady to Joseph in marriage to fill the land with further rejoicing.

After the marriage has been duly celebrated, the years of dearth begin. Joseph, well prepared for this period, opens his granaries and sells grain, both to Egyptians and foreigners. Among the latter are Joseph's brothers. As they carry their merchandise home, they realise that the Egyptian governor has apparently taken pity on them; in fact, as they report to Jacob, "all of us have seen him shed a tear in secret". Returning to Egypt and accompanied this time by their brother Benjamin, they are again well received by the vice-regent, are invited to bathe, and are shown round the palace, where they admire murals that depict scenes from Hebrew history – Abraham about to sacrifice Isaac, but prevented from doing so by an angel; Jacob as he swears his love for Rachel. After some time, the vice-regent invites them to a banquet. (Here Fracastoro's original text breaks off. The continuation is by Francesco Luisini [1524–1568], a younger contemporary of Fracastoro.)

When Joseph finally reveals his identity to his brothers, he invites both them and their father Jacob to settle in Egypt. Called to take to the road in a dream, Jacob soon arrives, and in due course dies there. Erinys, one of the infernal spirits, then takes the form of Leah, mother of some of Joseph's half-brothers, and appears in their dreams. She warns them about Joseph, telling them that now, after his father's death, he is planning to take revenge and kill them. But the brothers prefer to approach Joseph directly and ask him for forgiveness, which is granted to them; he assures them of his brotherly affection. The story ends with Joseph's death and burial.

Fracastoro retells the biblical story in the form of an ancient epic. The epic form is indicated, from the very beginning, by the invocation of the Muses, and the use of poetic lines in Latin hexameters. When a detail is not to be found in the Bible, Fracastoro's most likely source is Virgil's *Aeneid*.[39] Another important source is Seneca's drama *Phaedra*. To humanists such as Fracastoro, Dido and Aeneas, and Phaedra and Hippolytus were known as archetypal couples whom fate prevented from finally uniting in wedlock, leaving at least one partner – the woman – in sorrow, if not in anger (see below, Chapter 8). Imitating and borrowing from ancient sources lies at the very heart of the humanist programme of literature. Good literature had to echo the work of the ancient masters. Fracastoro made Joseph the counterpart of Aeneas, because both were expelled and exiled from their home country, and each became the founder of a nation – the Latin nation in Italy, the Hebrew nation in Egypt. And each of the two resisted the temptations of a beautiful foreign woman. The sacred oracle of Apollo which announces that the Heliopolitan priest's daughter will marry a foreigner (i.e. Joseph) takes up a theme known from Virgil in whose epic a similar oracle is pronounced for the daughter of the king of Latium.[40] Among the most conspicuous features Fracastoro borrows from his ancient sources are the role of the nurse (found in Seneca's *Phaedra*) and the portrayal of Potiphar's wife as an essentially virtuous woman who, compelled to love Joseph by demonic ruse, is a hapless victim rather than a genuine lustful seductress (analogous to Dido in Virgil's epic). Like Virgil and all epic poets of antiquity, Fracastoro emphasises divine providence and makes the intervention of supernatural beings – a demon and an angel – part of the plot. In order to do this effectively, he relies on numerous ancient sources, two of which I have explained, and there are doubtless others. The angel who visits Joseph in the pit into which he was thrown, for instance, seems to echo a passage from the biblical book of Wisdom.[41] Only a learned humanist who was also an accomplished poet could realise the ambitious project of presenting a biblical story in the form of a Virgilian epic.

Even though Fracastoro never finished his "Joseph", it nevertheless ranks aesthetically as the most ambitious and accomplished rendering of the biblical tale. As we shall see in later chapters, Fracastoro's epic did not remain without echo in the seventeenth and eighteenth centuries. Its quality was recognised by Joshua Sylvester who in 1620 translated it into English, and by Elizabeth Singer Rowe who imitated it in her own early eighteenth-century epic account (see below, Chapter 8). Some of the details Fracastoro invented found their way into other literature as well – the birthday oracle that revealed the identity of Joseph's future wife and the nurse who supports and advises Joseph's mistress. If we listen carefully enough to the great literary symphony, we can still discern Fracastoro's own, distinctive voice.

Concluding comments (based on an observation of Tolstoy)

Perhaps the best way to understand and come to terms with the complex reception history of the biblical Joseph story is by drawing upon an insight that was first expressed, clearly and polemically, by Leo Tolstoy (1828–1910). This Russian writer, best known today as the author of the novel *War and Peace*, in his later years also published books and tracts that aimed at renewing society, morality, true Christianity, and the arts. He increasingly distanced himself from the refined literary culture to which he himself had contributed so much, envisioning a radical break with the past. Once the decadent culture of the European elite, with its major institutions – theatres, orchestras, art galleries, and literary productions – had been abolished or drastically reformed, one would see the re-emergence of vital popular life guided by a sense of morality and simplicity, and nourished by a new generation of artists committed to the ideals of clarity and brevity. While Tolstoy's "puritanism" no longer strikes us as particularly relevant, at least one of his insights merits attention: his distinction between refined and non-refined forms of art.

Commenting on modern novels from Cervantes's *Don Quixote* to Dickens's *David Copperfield*, he notes that they are characterised by the exclusiveness of the emotions they convey, the superfluity of specific details of time and place, and, above all, the poverty of their content.[42] These works are limited in their appeal, because they are tied to a particular place and time, and accessible only to a small literary elite. Their limitations mean that they compare unfavourably with examples of universal ancient art such as – and this is Tolstoy's foremost example – the story of Joseph. That Joseph's brothers, being envious, sold him into slavery; that Potiphar's wife tried to seduce the youth; that the young man attained a high position, took pity on his brothers, and so on – these are all incidents and feelings accessible to a Russian peasant, to a Chinese, to an African, to a child, to an old man, to an educated or a non-educated person; and it is written with such economy, is so free of superfluous details, that the story can be transferred to any other milieu and still be understandable and moving for everyone. "In the narrative of Joseph," Tolstoy explains,

> there was no need to describe in detail, as is done nowadays, Joseph's blood-stained garment, Jacob's dwelling and clothes, and the pose and attire of Potiphar's wife when, straightening a bracelet on her left arm, she said, "Come to me", and so on, because the feeling contained in this story is so strong that all details except the most necessary ones – for instance, that Joseph went into the next room to weep – all details are superfluous and would only hinder the conveying of the feeling, and therefore this story is accessible to all people, it touches people in all nations, ranks, ages, has come down to our time, and will live on for thousands of years. But take the details from the best novels of our time, and what will remain?[43]

Exuberant description, supposedly the hallmark of realism, for Tolstoy is nothing but "artistic provincialism". The Russian author prefers the compact biblical prose style with its paucity of qualifying adjectives and metaphorical descriptions, its lack of references to the interior lives and thoughts of characters, their physical appearance, their personal choices and moral qualities. He would prefer, in other words, a style notable for terseness and economy.

Let us disregard Tolstoy's attack on modern literature and just focus on the valid distinction he made between two literary styles – one simple and unadorned, unencumbered by detail and description, and one complex, developed, and refined, with a preference for excessively studied accessories of time and place and fashion. What happened in the reception of the Joseph story in post-biblical times can be described as the re-creation of a simple biblical tale in the complex, developed style. This occurred first in Hellenistic Judaism with such works as *Joseph and Aseneth* and Philo's *On Joseph*. In fact, all subsequent elaborations and embellishments are inspired by, or derived from, the Hellenistic versions. Why should these have been so influential? To find the answer, we have to consider briefly the cultural situation in which they originated.

The encounter between Judaism and Hellenism in the period between c. 300 BCE and c. CE 200 created a unique intellectual situation, because it allowed some people to grow up in two cultural traditions, each of which they equally, or almost equally, valued. When Jewish intellectuals turned from the study of Greek literature to the reading of the canonical texts of their ancestral tradition, the peculiar style of the latter struck them: a style marked by extreme economy of words, complete absence of epithets, rarity of adjectives, elliptic mode of storytelling, and sudden and unmotivated transitions. Biblical literature appeared somehow too bald, unpolished, and "barbarian" to be taken seriously as refined literature. Lacking stylistic elegance, it was considered primitive, rudimentary, and provincial (rather than having universal appeal, as Tolstoy would have it). "There is an incompatibility to be overcome when the western sensibility confronts the undiluted text of Scripture", notes the literary critic Harold Fisch.[44] The biblical text, he explains, is "too naked". Jewish writers who had adopted the Greek language and absorbed certain elements of non-Jewish culture sought to remedy the deficiencies of their ancestral literature by covering its nakedness. Or, to put it differently, they saw scriptural stories as hollow outlines, requiring to be fleshed out with details, refined and developed. They realised that this could not be done, or could only be inadequately accomplished, by translating biblical books into Greek. In addition to producing translations, they also, and to better literary effect, retold and elaborated the story of Joseph to make it palatable and attractive to new literary tastes. Taking Hellenistic writers as their models, they brought a fresh tradition of vocabulary, style, and storytelling to their task. This tradition prompted a new sensibility for romance, elaborate description, modes of amplification, interest in secondary figures, and, not least, an attempt to moderate the harshness of moral judgement implied in traditional biblical narrative. To improve the biblical text they introduced "a certain opacity to reduce its glare, a certain smoothness to mitigate the harshness of its contours, a mode of amplification to arrest the suddenness of its transitions, and a certain ease of manner to reduce the severity of its moral judgements".[45]

Once Hellenistic Jewish authors had created models for elaborating and embellishing the Joseph story, it was easy for later authors to continue their work by producing ever fresh and innovative versions. In so doing, they stayed within the stylistic paradigm established by Jewish Hellenistic authors, but sought to cater to new tastes and to express novel ideas. Despite the richness of this post-biblical literature, four major themes in the retold Joseph story can be discerned that attract the greatest literary attention: the woman, the protagonist's virtue, the statesman, and the Demon.

As a story, the biblical account suffers from the defect of giving women a minor role in the life of the protagonist; this at least seems to be how post-biblical writers felt about it. Accordingly, they take great care to balance the story of the main male character with that of a female equivalent. This can be done by fleshing out Potiphar's wife as a character with typical human foibles. The Qur'an makes the first step in this direction; later Islamic versions and Fracastoro's humanist retelling of the story are entirely committed to the idea of transforming Potiphar's wife into a more believable figure. This is why she must be given a name (Zuleika or Iëmpsar), and it is also why she is given a supporting cast, most notably a nurse as a confidante, for she must have an entourage within which to flourish and interact – and to display her suffering from unrequited love. Another way of giving the tale a female dimension is to amplify the brief biblical reference to Joseph's spouse Aseneth, making it into a full-blown story; this was successfully done in the Jewish romance *Joseph and Aseneth*. But apart from adding some female interest, the male hero also needed some literary attention. In this respect, however, our post-biblical authors were much less willing to add new dimensions to the canonical portrait of Joseph. All sources in one way or another emphasise Joseph's virtue and intelligence. The *Testament of Joseph* (part of the *Testaments of the Twelve Patriarchs*) puts the Stoic doctrine of constancy in the protagonist's mouth. Artapanus and Philo portray Joseph as a statesman, a position for which he is eminently qualified on account of his wisdom and moral fibre. The Qur'an portrays Joseph as a prophetic figure. The most daring idea comes from the Persian poet who, forgetting Aseneth, depicts a Yûsuf who eventually marries his former, now repentant, mistress and seductress. While these elaborations are significant, they are less successful than those that focus on Zuleika and Aseneth. The third trend, already evident in the Jewish version (the *Testaments*) but completely developed in the humanist one, is the addition of a supernatural framework to the story. Whereas the biblical tale refers only to God as the hidden guiding force of events, later versions reflect the conviction that both the evil brothers and the lustful woman acted under the inspiration of the dark powers of hell. Thus the life of the hero becomes the battlefield where superhuman cosmic powers meet to wage war; in this way, Joseph's eventful life assumes even greater significance than it is given in Genesis.

The four themes – the woman, the protagonist's virtue, the statesman, and the Demon – are all taken up by early-modern writers. And, as we shall see in later chapters, one subject, clearly present in Genesis and in the Jewish tradition (albeit only in Artapanus and Philo) but neglected by the Islamic and humanist traditions, may even assume centre stage: that of Joseph the statesman.

II

THE ICON OF PIETY: JOSEPH FOR CHILDREN

4

On Education

IN WESTERN EUROPE IN THE SEVENTEENTH AND EIGHTEENTH CENTURIES, the education of middle- and upper-class children usually began around the age of three with informal, playful forms of instruction. More formal education, by parents, private tutors, or schoolmasters dominated the child's life from six or seven to fourteen. Childhood ended at fourteen, and educators considered the fifteenth year as the time of transition to youth,[1] when education began to focus upon a young man's future profession and employment, while girls were prepared for marriage and future household responsibilities. The most basic tool of education was the story. Children love stories; they listen with pleasure when they are told and even – perhaps especially – retold. The best teacher, according to Enlightenment pedagogy, is the one who knows the best stories and excels in telling them. Such a teacher can be a living person or a book, especially one that is written for a juvenile readership. Children should be given stories to read, for these capture their interest, exercise their imagination, and it is from them that they learn the groundwork of social, moral, and religious life. In eighteenth-century storybooks for children, heroes and anti-heroes (often children) figure prominently. The stories are generally fictitious – constructed to present a certain moral notion in attractive narrative form. The heroes or heroines exemplify the virtuous life.[2] But despite the enthusiasm with which early-modern educators invented moral fiction, most of them were convinced of the superior quality of biblical stories. In fact, the Bible formed the backbone of much of the education children received. In what follows, we will briefly look at how children were educated in French-, English-, and German-speaking lands.

FRANCE AND FRENCH-SPEAKING SWITZERLAND

The ideal teacher here was the father, as visualised in the frontispiece of a 1707 French manual of education (Fig. 1). While the father lectures with the book

Fig. 1. *Father Lecturing to the Children.* Mother and father, in the eighteenth century seen as the primary agents of education, are shown here teaching their children in the parlour. The two servants busy in the background are evidence of the upper middle-class setting of the idyllic scene of parental instruction. – Anonymous artist, 1707.

open in front of him on the desk, mother sits close by. The main addressees of the instruction are a girl and a boy, presumably six or seven years old. Three smaller children, boys and girls not yet distinguished by dress, also listen, including one who is just beginning to walk with the aid of a walking frame. "The first and foremost task of fathers and mothers is to work incessantly at educating their children well", explains the anonymous *père de famille*, author of the manual.³ This setting in the parlour of the family home, while no doubt idealised, did have its equivalents in reality, if we are to trust the report Claude Fleury included in his "Grand catéchisme historique" (1679):

> One of my acquaintances is sufficiently knowledgeable about religion without ever having learned by heart one of the standard catechisms, and without having had any other teacher in his childhood than his own father. When the boy was three, this good man would spend his evenings after work with the child, taking him on his knee and telling him, in his own words, stories such as the sacrifice of Abraham, the history of Joseph and similar ones, while showing him the relevant illustrations in a picture book. Repeating these stories was a favourite pastime in the family. At the age of six or seven, when the child began to know a little Latin, his father made him read the gospel and the easiest books of the Old Testament, always taking care to explain difficult passages. Great respect and an equal affection for the Holy Bible and for everything that has to do with religion remained with him for the rest of his life.⁴

Fleury, with a sense of regret, concludes his report as follows: "I know quite well that there are not very many fathers and mothers who would bother to do this. Most of them find it more convenient to send their daughters to a convent school, and their sons to college, or to pay for a tutor."⁵ It should be from one's parents that one first hears of Joseph.

Fleury and the diligent father may have relied on the advice given earlier by Frédéric Rivet (1617–1666), a Huguenot educational practitioner and theorist. To get religious education off to a good start, he wrote in 1654, one should refrain from making five-year-old children learn long prayers or catechisms by heart; all of this may instil hatred of religion rather than the love of it. Instead, one should tell children stories, especially biblical ones. One should tell them how God created the world, how Adam and Eve came into being, committed a sin, and had to leave paradise. The stories of Noah and the deluge, and Abraham should also be included, and "all that is so well told (*disertement recité*) about Joseph, Moses, David, briefly: everything that pertains to the sacred history".⁶ Rivet's advice relied on educational experience and, possibly, on family tradition. Both Frédéric Rivet and his father André were employed as tutors by the house of Orange in the Netherlands; Frédéric was responsible for the education of the prince of Orange (b. 1650) who later became William III, king of England, Scotland, and Ireland.

While we cannot be sure of the exact lines of influence, it is interesting to see that Rivet's ideas were shortly to reappear in the work of major Catholic educational theorists such as Bishop Fénelon (1651–1715) and Charles Rollin (1661–1741). Both insist on the early telling of biblical stories, mention Joseph, and give advice on how to go about the job. "Enliven your stories by couching them in vivid and familiar language. Make your characters talk. Children with a lively imagination will feel that they see and hear them," Fénelon writes. To which the bishop adds:

> For example, tell the story of Joseph. Make his brothers speak brutally, and Jacob like a loving and afflicted father. Make Joseph himself speak; let him take pleasure, when he is a ruler in Egypt, in hiding himself from his brothers so as to frighten them, and afterwards revealing himself to them. This homely presentation, together with the great interest of the story itself, will entrance the child, provided that you do not overload him with tales of this kind, but let him long for them and even promise them as rewards if he is good. Never treat these stories as lessons, and do not force the child to repeat them.[7]

According to Charles Rollin's treatise *De la Manière d'enseigner et d'étudier les belles-lettres* (1726/28), the key to successful biblical teaching is the thought-provoking dialogue between tutor and pupil. The tutor should never fail to ask the child questions to make him or her reflect on the stories.[8] When reading about Joseph being sold by his brothers, calumniated by Potiphar's wife, and sent to jail, the teacher should pretend to be astonished, asking whether this is God's way of rewarding his faithful servants. Equally, when seeing how Joseph is eventually elevated to high rank, the child must be led, by question and answer, to understand how despite the obstacles that people put in his way, Joseph was undeterred, and these obstacles proved to be the very means by which his career was advanced – which is, Rollin adds, "the usual method of divine providence" (*ordinairement la conduite de la Providence*).[9] And why not invite other boys and girls to join the family and have them participate in a test of scriptural knowledge? "Which advantage is furnished by good company?" would be one of the questions asked, and one possible answer would have been: divine blessing, as can be seen from the fact that Joseph's very presence in Potiphar's house made this household flourish.[10] To facilitate teaching of the Bible, Rollin included in his treatise a summary of the Joseph story, complete with theological commentary.

Efforts such as these must have left their mark on children, as can be shown at least in the case of little Marie-Angélique. In 1759, then barely six years old, Marie-Angélique Diderot, daughter of the famous French man of letters, called the Joseph story her best tale (*le meilleur de ses contes*), and her father, amused, mentioned it in a letter written to a friend.[11] Actually, Marie-Angélique's mother did not like her use of the term *conte*, for to her it sounded as if her daughter had no grasp of the difference between Scripture and fairy tales.

Britain

A child's reading of the Bible, English theorists insisted, should begin with a selection of easy stories. According to the Puritan divine Richard Baxter, reading biblical stories serves well to introduce children to "Scripture history"; moreover, "it entices them to delight in reading the Bible".[12] While Baxter in *A Christian Directory* (1673) does not recommend any particular stories for children, the philosopher John Locke gives a list, apparently inspired by Frédéric Rivet, whose book on education he owned.[13] "There are some parts of the Scripture", he explains in *Some Thoughts Concerning Education* (1693), "which may be proper to be put into the hands of a child to engage him to read; such as are the story of Joseph and his brethren, of David and Goliath, of David and Jonathan, etc. and others."[14] Locke adds that biblical reading should be for moral instruction in the first place, and he indicates one such lesson – that one should treat others just as one would like to be treated by them, clearly a rule one may ponder when reading the Joseph story. Locke's advice to focus on uninterrupted stories reflects not only his insight into child psychology, but also his critical stance on catechetical indoctrination and his view that Scripture was a collection of discrete aphorisms ultimately to be used to support an abstract system of doctrinal assertions.[15] The aphoristic fallacy was promoted by the traditional preference for using the book of Proverbs and the sayings of Jesus Sirach as early reading matter for children;[16] it is also supported, as Locke observes, by the insertion of cumbersome chapter and verse numbers that impair the flow of what is told. Only by disregarding such devices can one follow storylines or arguments and come to grasp the true meaning of a passage.[17] Children, of course, should read and understand stories rather than biblical aphorisms.

Whether Locke's advice was heeded by many is hard to tell. In the household of the Wesleys, it certainly was not. "He was five years old on the 10th of February", reports Susanna Wesley about her son Samuel in 1732. "The next day he began to learn; and, as soon as he knew the letters, began at the first chapter of Genesis."[18] In due course, towards the end of Genesis, he would read the Joseph story. At least middle-class children such as Samuel and his better-known brothers John and Charles Wesley (founders of Methodism) seem to have begun their biblical reading with Genesis, and from there moved on to Exodus, following the Scriptures as printed in the Bible.

Did the approach taken by Susanna Wesley make the children especially fond of the story of Joseph? We cannot tell. But whatever method was used in instruction, some children came to develop a particular attachment to Joseph. An example is the Scottish geologist, journalist, and writer Hugh Miller (1802–1856). This son of a shipmaster grew up with his widowed mother in a remote parish, where he received his first formal instruction at the local "dame school". Biblical knowledge, though emphasised at school, did not mean much to the boy, until, at the age of six, he discovered biblical stories for himself. One day, he reports in his autobiography, "my mind awoke to the meaning of that most delightful of all narratives – the story of Joseph".[19] This was apparently the first story Miller found, read, and re-read all by himself, rather than under the guidance of the schoolmistress. This discovery – "was there ever such a discovery made before", he exclaims – prompted the boy's interest in reading, and he gives a long list of his early favourite stories: Samson and the Philistines, David and Goliath, Jack the Giant-Killer, and Sindbad the Sailor, to name but a few. Thus well prepared, he soon turned to more complex literature such as *The Pilgrim's Progress* by John Bunyan and the *Odyssey*.

German lands

Although both parents were supposed to contribute to a child's upbringing and education, formal responsibility, until the age of fourteen, generally rested with the father, as is clearly stated in the *Allgemeines Landrecht* of Prussia (1794):

> Rights and duties of parents and children
> § 74. Directing the child's education is mainly the task of the father.
> § 75. He must primarily make sure that the child receives the necessary instruction concerning religion and beneficial knowledge according to his status and circumstances.
> § 111. Until he completes his fourteenth year, the son must submit absolutely to the directions of the father.[20]

The early phase of the educational process, from three to about fourteen, was meant to shape children morally and to teach them reading, writing, and languages. At their Frankfurt home in the mid-eighteenth century, the two Goethe children Wolfgang and Cornelia were taught Latin, French, and Italian, as well as a little English and Greek. The Bible also figured prominently in both the domestic and school curricula of boys and girls, especially when their parents were Lutherans (as in the Goethe family) or Calvinists. Despite the father's legal responsibility, mothers had a prominent share in biblical education. In a family with several children, Bible study under maternal guidance could produce idyllic scenes such as the following from Weimar, Germany, vividly reported by Caroline Herder: on Christmas Day of 1788, the four children assemble around the table for a study session.[21] August (twelve) works on the translation of a Greek fable, and Adelbert (nine) contributes a verse he has translated from the Greek New Testament. Later, a children's bible is opened, and each of the children selects a passage for reading to the others: Adelbert reads Elijah's translation to heaven, Luise (seven and a half) the story of the boy Samuel sleeping in the temple and being called by the Lord, and Emil (five and a half) the Israelites' passage through the Red Sea. Little Emil starts his reading with enthusiasm, but when he falters in the middle of a sentence, his mother helps him to master the longer, difficult words.

Some Lutheran schoolmasters would read and explain one chapter each day, generally starting with the book of Genesis and ending with the book of Revelation.[22] But more complex and sophisticated curricula were also devised, using bibles specially designed to be read by children, typically illustrated books that offered selections of stories from both testaments.[23] The most detailed as well as most successful biblical curriculum for children was set out by the Lutheran schoolmaster Johann Hübner (1668–1731) in a children's bible for use both at home and in school. First published in 1714 and subsequently reprinted many times, and from 1731 with illustrations, this was an anthology of fifty-two stories retold from the Old Testament, and fifty-two stories from the New Testament.[24] If the author's advice of teaching one or two stories per week was heeded, uninterrupted by holidays, Hübner's book provided the complete course material for either one or two years. Hübner takes great care to present the Bible stories in their original form, but equal care is taken to make them accessible. The wording stays relatively close to Luther's translation, though some of the more difficult words are avoided or replaced. To aid the didactic process, the Joseph story is broken down into five episodes, each forming a lesson that was meant to serve as study material for a whole week. Accordingly, the child is supposed to master the Joseph story in five weeks. Each weekly lesson is accompanied by four items meant to facilitate teaching: a one-page illustration capturing the event recounted in the episode, up to thirty-five study questions (one for each sentence of the story!), a short poem summing up the moral message, and a Latin poem as an exercise for the more advanced pupil. As one can imagine, not all educators were as pedantic as Hübner, but his influence was nevertheless pervasive. It can be detected, for instance, in the children's bible written by Johann Kaspar Lavater, discussed below, in Chapter 5, though this Swiss pastor attenuates Hübner's didactic pedantry by omitting the study questions and the Latin poem (he did, however, follow his model by including a German one).

Did German children come to love the Joseph story, as some of their educators claimed? Sophie, a south German girl who in the 1730s spent each morning studying biblical and devotional books under her mother's guidance,[25] provides the answer. "As a girl of six, I shed tears over this story [of Joseph]", Sophie wrote to her fiancé in 1753. "And, as my late mama told me, I once kissed one of my sisters, saying: I want to behave like Joseph, I want to kiss and cry" – referring to Joseph when he made himself known to his brothers.[26] The tears Sophie shed were of course tears of emotion, like those shed by Joseph in Genesis. When writing the letter, the story clearly still resonated with twenty-one-year-old Sophie, for she sees herself, playfully, as Asenath who would eventually marry Joseph (alias fiancé Christoph Martin) – though in reality, the relationship between the two correspondents was soon to end. But both Sophie Gutermann (later La Roche, 1731–1807) and Christoph Martin Wieland (1733–1813) subsequently became respected authors of then widely read novels.

Probably the most famous child to whom the Joseph story appealed, however, was none other than Wolfgang Goethe, to whom we owe a charming autobiographical account. The story of how Goethe recalled his juvenile enthusiasm for Joseph, and how as a teenager he made the biblical hero the subject of his first literary effort, will be told in Chapter 6.

5

A Lesson in Godliness – Lavater

"The story of Joseph is the most fascinating, most entertaining, most instructive story one can think of. It is impossible to invent anything that would surpass its simple beginning, its slow, yet perceptible progress, its wonderful development, and its great impact."[1] Thus wrote Johann Kaspar Lavater, Swiss Reformed pastor, writer, and educator, and sometime friend of Goethe. In describing it as "the most important story of ancient times",[2] Lavater most likely expressed a conviction he had held for at least a quarter of a century: his interest in the story can be documented over a period of twenty-six years of his adult life, in fact his entire career as an author of religious books.

In the eighteenth century, Zurich, though not the capital city of the Helvetic Republic, was the centre of Switzerland's cultural and intellectual life. From amongst its citizens born around 1740, at least three became well-known figures outside their own country: Johann Heinrich Füßli (Fuseli, 1741–1825), painter and friend of William Blake; Johann Heinrich Pestalozzi (1746–1827), the famous educational theorist; and Pastor Lavater (1741–1801). In their youth, the three met as members of the Helvetic Society, a debating club that boasted a membership of about a dozen young men aged between sixteen and twenty. This club was known for its rigorous spartan morality, with which its members terrorised the city.[3] Of the three, only Lavater stayed in Zurich throughout his lifetime, but like the others his fame resonated throughout the German-speaking countries. A prolific author, he wrote widely discussed books on meeting again in life after death (a favourite subject of his time) and, with the young Goethe serving as his assistant, huge controversial tomes on physiognomy, a work that seeks to discern the moral and intellectual character of people by analysing their facial features. One scene from Lavater's life has been immortalised by Goethe, who includes in his autobiography a vivid account of a journey through the Rhineland.[4] Goethe stresses the very different character of the three travel companions of 1774: Lavater, the physiognomist and pious pastor, an amiable person of gentle manners; Johann Bernhard Basedow, an educational theorist intent on promoting his books for parents and schools, a self-centred man who, to the annoyance of Goethe, incessantly smoked his stinking pipe; and finally, Goethe himself, at twenty-five an impressionable author who had just begun to publish.

Though chiefly remembered today as the author of his scientifically untenable ideas on physiognomy and for his failed attempt to convert his acquaintances (including Goethe and the Jewish philosopher Moses Mendelssohn) to belief in Christ, Lavater was also a noted religious educator. Early evidence of his pedagogical interest is an essay he co-authored with Pestalozzi. Entitled "Etwas für die, welche sich verheuraten wollen" (Some thoughts for those who want to get married) and printed in the 22 May 1766 number of *Der Erinnerer*, it deals with the self-education of a man's future spouse. Her general education is presupposed, but if she is to be the true intellectual equal of her husband and an able educator of her children, she should share his interest in at least some of the books admired by him. Lavater and his friend include a list of required reading in their essay:

> Spalding's *Destiny of Man*, Crugot's *The Christian in Loneliness*, and the sermons of these two authors; Rousseau's and Ballexerd's writings on education; Fénelon's *Adventures of Telemachus*, and his treatise *The Education of Girls*; Montaigne's *Essays*; Charron, *On Wisdom*; Toussaint's *Manners*; Theophrast's and La Bruyère's *Characters*, and so on.[5]

Reading these books, the authors hope, would help a woman to develop an open mind and lively spirit, fitting her for her roles as her husband's intellectual partner and educator of the children their marriage would be blessed with. No doubt Lavater was thinking here of Anna Schinz, the woman he married on 3 June 1766, a mere twelve days after the essay's publication. At the time of writing the essay Lavater may not have paid much attention to the fact that one of the authors listed, Fénelon, recommends the Joseph story in *De l'éducation des filles* (The Education of Girls, 1687) as a basic text for a child's education. Within a few years, however, Lavater came to share this conviction, as is evident from his own publications. Here is a brief chronology of Lavater's writing on Joseph:

1768   Johann Jacob Hess compiles an anthology of biblical stories, retold for children; Lavater contributes the Joseph story. The publication is delayed until 1772.

1771   Publication of Lavater's own *Christliches Handbüchlein für Kinder* (Christian Manual for Children). The Old Testament is represented by two retold stories: Abraham's dialogue with God and the life of Joseph.

1774   Publication of an Old Testament picture book for children. Sixty etchings, by Johann Rudolf Schellenberg, which visualise scenes from the Old Testament, have brief legends, contributed by Lavater, printed below the plates. The Joseph story has seven illustrations.
1789   Lavater delivers a series of twenty-three lectures, for adults, on the Joseph story. The first lecture is given on 8 January, the final one on 17 December.
1794   Lavater delivers another public lecture on Joseph, on 12 February. He edits the complete series for publication, dedicating the book to Countess Augusta Bernstorff-Stolberg in Copenhagen: *Vier und zwanzig kurze Vorlesungen über die Geschichte Josephs* (Twenty-Four Short Lectures on the Story of Joseph).

In what follows, we will focus on how Lavater told the story to children, using his version of 1771 as the main text.

Lavater's "Joseph": a summary[6]

Once upon a time there was a boy by the name of Joseph. His father Jacob loved him very much because he was a good, obedient child. He was quite unlike his ten elder brothers – unrestrained, boisterous fellows, in their godlessness ever intent on misdeeds. They hated the boy and sought to get rid of him. This they did by throwing him into a deep pit from which he could not escape. In tears, he implored them, appealing to their sense of mercy – to no avail. But he did not despair: "Now that my brothers on earth show no mercy toward me," he thought, "then my Father in heaven will have mercy. Even if all humans should forsake me, God will be with me, and he will know how to comfort me and to send his blessing." As foreign merchants were passing by, the evil brothers approached them and sold Joseph to them. – *It won't be too difficult for you, my dear child, to imagine how poor Joseph cried and entreated his brothers not to sell him to these strangers. O how wicked it is to treat a human being like an animal, and sell him for money! But in vain did he implore.* – So he had to travel with these strangers to a foreign country, where he did not know a single person. He had to leave behind his old, dear father without saying goodbye, without hope of ever seeing him again. Now he was alone; there was no one left to look after his well-being and happiness – except for God. But for him, God was enough. The merchants brought Joseph to Egypt and sold him to a good Egyptian master who used him as a domestic servant. Yet Joseph remained cheerful, thanking the good Lord for having brought him to this master and for arranging things to his advantage. For who other than God was to be thanked for the boy's being so able and intelligent that he enjoyed his master's trust? Thus Joseph remained a godly boy, his thoughts always being directed to God. He loved to say his prayers. Of God he expected ever the best. He never did anything that was not right and good. He remained steadfast even when the wife of his master sought to distract him from his duties and to entice him unto her company. "As long as I trust in God and obey him, I will fare well; but as soon as I forsake God, he will also forsake me," he said to himself. Joseph would rather have had his hand cut off, or his eye plucked out, than be seduced to sin.

Falsely accused by his master's wife, the innocent boy was thrown into prison. Yet even there he did not despair. – *No, dear child, God never forgets and forsakes anyone, least of all those who put their trust in him. Whoever suffers for the sake of his virtue cannot be unhappy at the bottom of his heart, contrary to what we may think.* – Joseph said to himself, "It is because I wanted to obey God that I am in fetters. God knows that I am in prison and why I am here." Perhaps he would have to spend the rest of his life in chains – but not even this thought prevented him from being cheerful. In his heart he knew that God would not forget him. And indeed, one day, the warden of the jail decided to remove his shackles and made him supervisor of the prisoners. So now he could move freely and talk to his fellow inmates. Learning of the dreams of two fellow prisoners, he offered an interpretation, using the gift with which God had endowed him. It turned out that he had understood the dreams correctly. As Joseph had predicted, one prisoner was hanged, while the other was restored to high office at court.

For a further two years the innocent boy had to stay in prison, where his only joy lay in thinking of God and caring for his fellow prisoners. – *People can be robbed of everything, except God and a clear conscience.* – Encouraged by these thoughts, it was with quiet resignation that Joseph waited for his release. And it came, for when Pharaoh had strange dreams that no one could interpret for him, the Hebrew youth was remembered at court and summoned, and, inspired by God, he succeeded in deducing the true meaning. The dreams announced a sequence of seven years of agricultural abundance, followed by another seven years of dearth. To deal with this situation, Pharaoh appointed Joseph his prime minister, entrusting him with all authority to guide Egypt through these difficult times. During the lean years, Joseph could supply grain to the whole of Egypt, and even to those who came from abroad, from the huge granaries he had wisely filled during the years of plenty.

One day it happened that his ten brothers also travelled to Egypt to beg for grain. Joseph immediately recognised them, but they did not know him. Speaking to them through an interpreter, Joseph treated them harshly. He gave them many sacks of grain, but they had to leave one of their number – Simon – as a hostage in Egypt. Simon would be free again, Joseph promised, as soon as they came back to Egypt in the company of another of their brothers – Benjamin, the youngest. The brothers were dumbfounded. Overwhelmed by the inner voice of their conscience, they began to realise that the time had come for the punishment of their crime. Their hearts were pounding, and they were stung with remorse. – *Our conscience may be silenced for some time and kept quiet, but sooner or later it awakes, making us think with pain, shame and fear of punishment of an earlier, perhaps long forgotten sin.* – Thinking that Joseph would not understand them, they said to each other: "Verily, we have sinned against our brother. When he implored us, we shut our ears and hardened our hearts – and now we are punished with affliction. God has seen the crime we have committed against our godly brother. But from now on, and for the rest of our lives, we will stay away from all wrong." Joseph had not forgotten his native tongue and so understood them very well. He realised that God had touched their hearts. Nevertheless, Joseph wanted to test their sincerity. He told them to travel back home to Canaan and to return with their youngest brother, Benjamin. And so it happened. After some time, they returned to Egypt, again begging for grain. And again, Joseph gave them grain as he had promised, but once again he treated them harshly, making them look like thieves who had stolen Joseph's own cup. Why was Joseph so unkind? "Far be it from me to take revenge on them for the crime they committed against me," Joseph said to himself. "Very soon I will reveal myself to them as their brother, and I will treat them with a loving heart for the rest of my life. Every day I will treat them kindly, and never mention what happened in the past. Yet for one more time, they must feel that God is just and that their fear and trembling are well deserved. As long as they live, this impression will last, so they will learn to abstain from committing any crime and evil." – *This is what Joseph seems to have thought. Considered in isolation, Joseph's treatment of his brothers may seem cruel and an act of revenge. But, my dear child, do not forget this: if someone who on many occasions has proven his honesty and godliness should appear to do something that is not right, then one should not accuse him too quickly of injustice. Unless you are very sure of that accusation (for every human being is fallible), you should acknowledge his good intention.*

To cut a long story short: Joseph eventually revealed himself to his brothers in a tearful scene of mutual recognition and embracing. "Look at me," he said, "I am Joseph, the one whom you sold into Egypt. But do not be afraid, and do not think that I am angry with you. It was God who made this happen, so that you could survive the great famine. God, who knows what will happen in the future, the good Lord who rewards all those who put their trust in him and who heed his commandments, he made you come here." Reconciled with his brothers, Joseph made his whole family, including his old father, come to Egypt and stay there, providing them generously with all they needed. Great was the joy of both father and son when meeting and embracing after so many years.

When Jacob died, Joseph had him buried in Canaan, as his father had wished, for a good, obedient child will cheerfully and diligently obey his parents even after their death. Hardly was the funeral over, when Joseph's brothers visited him again, asking for forgiveness, but Joseph assured them he had no wish for revenge. Eventually, Joseph also died, at the patriarchal age of one hundred and ten years.

> Could God forsake his little child,
> though ever loving, meek and mild?
> When others evil do intend –
> he's there to shelter and befriend.
>
> My steadfast trust in God I'll show
> when through hard trials I shall go.
> Others will I forgive and love,
> I always trust in God above.
>
> I know some day God will repay
> my trust, make clear to me the way –
> as Joseph was, from fearful past
> to joy and life fulfilled at last.

In the critical edition of the *Christliches Handbüchlein für Kinder*, the Joseph story fills thirty-six pages – a text too long to reproduce in our study. But even from our summary that seeks to retain the flavour of Lavater's prose and (in the last passage) verse, the essential character of the story emerges very clearly. For his young readers, Lavater has a *religious* and a *moral* message, and both are conveyed by the use of a particular educational tool: that of teaching by example – through the figure of Joseph. Religion, morality, and *exemplum* invite further comment, as does the – occasionally poor – literary quality of the Swiss pastor's text. We will begin with Lavater's religious teaching.

Personal piety

The Swiss pastor was not the first to produce a children's version of the Joseph story. In fact, he used a model, the *Biblische Historien* (Biblical Histories). Compiled by Johann Hübner and first published in 1714, this was Germany's most popular Lutheran children's bible. Lavater often followed this book, but also departed from it in characteristic ways. "God does not forsake the godly, even though they may be struck by misfortune", reads Hübner's summary of the story's religious message.[7] Lavater agrees, though he aims at teaching a more comprehensive religious attitude, one that is supposed to shape one's spiritual life more thoroughly – at a deeper level and more permanently. What Lavater seeks to teach through the Joseph story is, quite simply, friendship with God. If the child had already studied the *Christliches Handbüchlein*'s first biblical story, the one placed immediately before that of Joseph, he or she would be well prepared. Much shorter than the Joseph story, "Abraham's Dialogue with God"[8] shows the patriarch as God's partner, as a man whose word counts with God. "As friend associates with friend, thus did God intimately associate with Abraham. [...] Indeed, God's friendship with this godly person was so intimate that whenever he was about to do something important on earth he would reveal it to him."[9] The Joseph story continues in this vein, showing that not only the patriarch Abraham but also every believer can become God's friend. In his preface to the *Christliches Handbüchlein für Kinder* Lavater states his argument as follows:

> You wish to attain happiness, but can it be attained without help? By no means. However, there is someone who can offer help, who can and will provide it. This he has proved from the beginning of the world. Whoever seeks happiness from him and in him; whoever trustfully expects everything that is good and nothing else from him, while heeding whatever he commands and prohibits, he will learn by experience that the invisible God is his father, his friend, his blessing and bliss.[10]

This characterisation of God sounds natural and straightforward to us; nevertheless, it represents an innovation in eighteenth-century children's bibles.[11] The Bible, especially the Old Testament, presents God in two apparently conflicting roles – that of the wise, paternal, benign and loving governor of the universe, and that of the severe judge and wrathful warrior, intent on punishing whoever infringes his commandments. The two roles seem to have been shaped in two different institutional settings within ancient society: the angry deity was characteristic of the military class and reflected its aggressive, warlike spirit; by contrast, the notion of divine mercy was more deeply rooted in the mind of the scribes who sought to keep social life running smoothly by wise counsel and efficient administration.[12] Scribe and warrior have determined political life for thousands of years, and it is no surprise to learn that their diverse mentalities have left their mark on religion. Many of the psalms celebrate God's compassion and love, while divine wrath and punishment are the hallmark of most of the prophetic books. Accordingly, in early modern times, theologians listed "merciful" and "angry" among God's main attributes, and it was often reference to his wrath and anger that dominated preaching. In the age of the Enlightenment Christian theologians came to de-emphasise the vengeful side of God and to highlight his gentleness. The smiter of the unrighteous, though not entirely forgotten, gives way to the protector and friend of the pious. God's wrath appears no longer as a habitual attitude but as a "footnote" to his love. Children's bibles of the time echo this shift of emphasis, and Lavater can be numbered among those who represented the new theology. Far from terrorising the young with images of an angry God to inspire fear and trembling, he assures them of his paternal love and friendship. God loves and cares. "When others evil do intend – he's there to shelter and befriend" is one of the rhymes that sum up the religious message of the Genesis story. The kind of piety inspired by the new benign image of God taught by Lavater is well known to historians of religion; their label for it is "personal piety" or "personal religion".[13] These expressions are used to designate a specific, easily recognised attitude in which the individual sees himself standing in close personal relationship to the divine, confidently expecting help and guidance in his personal life and affairs. The individual matters to God, and God cares about each individual personally and deeply. In one of his books, Lavater himself illustrates this kind of piety with several pages of excerpts from the book of Psalms. "The Lord is my shepherd, I shall not want. – Even though I walk through the valley of the shadow of death, I will fear no evil, for you are with me" (Psalm 23) is just one of the many passages he quotes. The psalmist, Lavater explains, "speaks with the deity of his ancestors not only as a subject speaks with his royal lord, but often also as a child talks with his father".[14] In this way, the psalmist expresses his conviction that "God acts as God *for him alone*. The psalmist is completely sure of God's existence, the attention he is accorded by him, and the interest God has in his personal well-being".[15] The psalmist "venerates the God of Israel as his personal God".[16] And so does Joseph – and his story is told to demonstrate how trust in the personal God works in practice, how it must be maintained in times of misfortune, and how it eventually leads to unexpected success.

In Lavater's time, some European intellectuals – including Goethe – were inclined to believe in the impersonal "god of the philosophers" equated with nature, as taught by Spinoza, rather than in Lavater's God of the Psalms. Arguing against Spinozism, Lavater insists that "the God presented by the Bible is not the god of the philosophers of our time. He is not merely an infinite, inscrutable, unthinkable – I know not what. At the same time and in as much as he reveals himself, he is also a visible, concrete and freely acting being."[17] In fact, many of Lavater's contemporaries felt as he did, so personal piety was a very popular attitude. "The wellspring of his energy is an unshakable faith in God and in the help emanating directly from Him, which manifests itself in never-ceasing providence and unfailing rescue from all distress and every evil."[18] This is how Goethe characterises one of his acquaintances. In the late nineteenth century, Edwin Starbuck, one of the first psychologists of religion, collected statements such as this: "I have the sense of a presence, strong, and at the same time soothing, which hovers over me. Sometimes it seems to enwrap me with sustaining arms. God is a personal being, who knows and cares for his creatures."[19] Personal piety has a long history, the early phases of which arose in the biblical world; but in addition to inspiring historical research, it also invites psychological analysis. Modern empirical research suggests that the feeling of security and divine guidance develops early in childhood. Later in life it emerges most vividly in situations of stress and trouble. Expressions of personal piety may be coloured by specific popular and ecclesiastical traditions and prevailing taste; its essence, however, remains the same throughout history, for it responds to the same human need. In Lavater's day, the relationship between personal piety and human need was captured well by the Romantic poet Novalis: "Without a friend in heaven – who could endure this life on earth?"[20]

If we take a look at Lavater's *Kurze Vorlesungen* of 1789, a text that addresses adult Christians, we find the same emphasis on belief in the personal God as the individual's guide and protector, the same trust in divine providence, and the same focus on the godly life as one that must ultimately lead to success. Some distinctive features in the *Kurze Vorlesungen*, however, reveal Lavater's more mature theology.

As biographical research on Lavater shows, the Swiss pastor's early writing and career are marked by an almost deistic philosophy centred on God and moral teaching, with little emphasis on Christ as God's son and messenger.[21] The *Christliches Handbüchlein für Kinder* (1771) is very much indebted to this focus. Subsequently, Christ assumed a more important role in Lavater's own theology and spiritual life, a life still dominated by writing, but increasingly by the pastoral responsibilities he had, from 1775, at various Reformed churches in Zurich. It is not surprising to find evidence of this shift in his *Kurze Vorlesungen*. While not making this the central focus of his presentation, Lavater now follows established Christian tradition in pointing out that Joseph and Jesus had similar careers: humble beginnings, times of testing and suffering, and eventual ascent to glory. In theological jargon, this parallelism was expressed by saying that Joseph somehow "prefigures" or announces the person of Christ, or that Joseph was a "type" of Christ.[22] This typological reading, much practised by the church fathers of late antiquity, had lost popularity among theologians in early-modern times. Bishop Joseph Hall (1574–1656), for instance, declared that Joseph, rather than being a type of Christ, actually must be seen as a type – or model – of every Christian believer.[23] Although Lavater knew that the "typological" reading of the Old Testament had fallen out of favour with many of his fellow theologians, he believed in the essential validity of the approach. "The story of Joseph foreshadows that of Jesus, for it confirms it without touching it. (It does not *prefigure* it, a misleading term.) It shows the same deity, and the same humanity, the same course of providence with friends and foes of God and virtue, the same silence of God in the beginning, the same speaking of God at the right moment, the same temporary defeat of godly virtue, and, in the end, the same reward for patient and trustful waiting that overcomes the world."[24] This approach inspired Lavater to move from the emotional episode of Joseph's self-revelation to his brothers to speaking of Christ's self-revelation at the judgment that the pastor seems to place immediately after one's death. Interestingly, it is not the forgiving Christ who parallels the forgiving Joseph, as one might expect. Instead, Lavater preaches here a stern warning of judgment, for Christ might reveal himself to the one standing before him by saying: "I am Jesus, the one whom you have persecuted, sold, denied and betrayed" – and then condemn him to punishment. But how blissful it would be, Lavater exclaims, to hear from the mouth of the Saviour not this thundering word of rejection, but rather this acknowledgement of one's Christian love, faith, and hope: "I am Jesus whom you have loved, even though you have not seen me; whom you have venerated in faith, whom you have served in love, for whom you have sacrificed yourself in hope! I know your works and your faithfulness, your patience and your diligence. You have been faithful over a little, I will set you over much; enter into the joy of your lord!"[25]

The full import of this passage can only be appreciated once we realise that heaven and the admission to heavenly bliss after death represent major emphases of Lavater's theology. In fact, Lavater's most noted theological work, published between 1768 and 1778, was a popular book on heaven: *Aussichten in die Ewigkeit* (Prospects of Eternity).[26] This book's message is, quite simply, that whoever is admitted to heaven will also enjoy the renewed companionship of his loved ones – his friends, his spouse and children. In his preface to *Kurze Vorlesungen*, Lavater actually alludes to his favourite teaching about heavenly bliss: "It is soothing consolation in all situations of life's darkness, and especially at the loss of the most delightful of all creatures, that you may draw from this story. By silent contemplation, you will not fail to ascend to the luminous higher regions of hope, where the bliss of meeting again beckons enticingly – oh, the bliss of meeting again without separation."[27]

Moral instruction

The moral message implied in the Joseph story and highlighted by Lavater is one of obedience, duty, filial piety, forgiveness, and familial solidarity, all perfectly exemplified by Joseph. If the storyline for a moment obscures Joseph's righteousness, Lavater is quick to defend and explain: treating his brothers harshly, playing evil tricks on them, and making them fear for their lives must not be misunderstood as Joseph's (mild) revenge; instead, Lavater would have his readers believe, his harshness is nothing but a pedagogical measure to test the extent and sincerity of his brothers' repentance. Joseph's virtues are understood as belonging to a fixed set of normative attitudes. These are to guide one's life irrespective of any circumstances; they must not be abandoned even in the face of adversity. Moral rules are absolutely binding and inflexible. Valid and applicable in all countries and times, they have to be respected by both the free man and the slave, under both favourable and unfavourable circumstances, admitting of no exceptions, modifications, or mitigations (as argued by modern "situation ethicists" and "moral relativists"). Accordingly, no possibility is conceded that moral standards in biblical times might differ from standards valid in eighteenth-century Zurich. God sees all behaviour, and he will eventually reward the virtuous and punish the unrighteous. Moreover, since a sense of morality is naturally present in the human heart, those who have sinned will some day be reminded of their crime by the inner voice of conscience. In his description of the sense of guilt experienced by Joseph's brothers, the Swiss pastor follows Hübner. "Conscience lies dormant for a while, but at the appropriate moment, it wakens and speaks", explains Hübner, and Lavater echoes this idea in similar words.[28]

Lavater's moral message culminates in the notion of suffering for the sake of truth. When the young patriarch is falsely accused by his master's wife, he suffers in silence, knowing that God is aware of his innocence. Suffering, understood as a testimony to truth and righteousness, is valued highly. "Suffering for truth's sake / is fortitude to highest victory" reads a passage in Milton's *Paradise Lost*, and Lavater would agree.[29]

All of this is quite straightforward in the story and needs no repetition: the morality taught by Lavater does not differ from the one shared and promoted by all Enlightenment moralists. The only virtue Lavater avoids highlighting and recommending is Joseph's otherwise proverbial chastity, exemplified by resistance on the part of the protagonist to seduction by his master's wife. Hübner has no problem with the seduction episode and reproduces it in full, complete with the lustful wife's words "sleep with me" and an illustration showing her in bed. While Lavater generally follows the biblical text as closely as Hübner, he felt that he should depart from it in the case of this delicate scene. How should he go about telling a story whose erotic details are embarrassing, but whose moral message – resistance to seduction – provides a pedagogical opportunity? In Lavater's biblical commentaries we can discern a strategy that pays close attention to the age of the readers whom the pastor addresses. In the picture bible of 1774, a book for *small children* experiencing the sacred stories for the first time, the seduction scene is omitted for it would be completely beyond the grasp of the intended audience. For *schoolchildren* below the age of puberty, Lavater devises cautious (and, to us, somewhat comical) paraphrases that eliminate the erotic element from the seduction scene. In the first version of his retelling (presumably dating from 1768), Lavater sought to stay close to the biblical text. The seductress, he writes euphemistically (and to us, comically), "wished that Joseph, instead of her husband and without his knowledge, should keep her company, enjoying himself in her presence".[30] In the *Christliches Handbüchlein* (1771), Lavater tries another, even more circumspect version. Studiously avoiding any reference to the advances of Potiphar's wife, he suggests, quite ingeniously, that Joseph's attention to his master's wife would prevent him from attending to his domestic duties, and this would be his sin.[31] It is only when speaking to *adults*, in his 1794 *Vier und zwanzig kurze Vorlesungen über die Geschichte Josephs* (Twenty-Four Short Lectures on the Story of Joseph), that Lavater abandons all caution. Everyone loves Joseph, Lavater writes, including Potiphar's wife:

> But her love lacks purity and nobility. It does not fit into the proper order of things, for she is forgetful of her primary duty: the one pledged to her own husband. Urging the steward to an act of adulterous love, she seeks to seduce him to unfaithfulness. By fear of God, by avoidance, by flight he resists. In vain she cajoles and presses him; in vain she seeks to entice him in all manner of ways. In vain she promises him fine presents. In vain, too, she opens her gown, revealing to him her most alluring views. All in vain.[32]

Here we can see that the Swiss pastor, far from being prudish, could even go beyond the biblical text by embroidering the seductress's erotic self-presentation. As a matter of course, such explicitness would have no place in the *Christliches Handbüchlein für Kinder*. Lavater was a conscientious educator, a man who had definite ideas about what was fitting and proper.

Pedagogical method

To understand how Lavater told, and moralised, the story of Joseph for children, we must first turn to his pictorial Old Testament, a book he created in close collaboration with Johann Rudolf Schellenberg, then a well-known Swiss engraver. The volume *60 biblische Geschichten des Alten Testaments* (60 Biblical Scenes from the Old Testament, 1774) contains sixty copper etchings, each depicting a biblical scene.[33] Accompanied by a legend of a few lines (by Lavater), each etching fills a full page. Seven illustrations depict episodes from the Joseph story. The illustrations were meant mainly for very young children, whose parents were beginning to explain bible stories to them. The frontispiece depicts a domestic scene: sitting in a comfortable chair, a mother points to a picture in the book open on her knee, showing it to the four attentive children who cluster round her, watching and listening as she explains (Fig. 2). It is clear from this frontispiece what Lavater and the engraver had in mind when designing the illustrations: the pictures were the focus of the children's attention, whereas the text is meant to help the mother find appropriate words of explanation. Older, more advanced children would no longer simply watch and listen, but would actually read the story – most likely under parental guidance. This can be seen from another frontispiece – that of Lavater's *Christliches Handbüchlein für Kinder*: a mother, the child on her lap and two older ones looking on read a story together, while the father listens contentedly and watches the scene with approval (Fig. 3). The book – no doubt the *Christliches Handbüchlein für Kinder* – is held jointly by the mother and the little boy (aged about six) to indicate that he can already read. Apart from the frontispiece, this book does not include any illustrations. The emphasis now is on reading, though still guided by the mother.

Lavater's belief in the value of religious instruction is also evident in the dedicatory letter of the *Vier und zwanzig kurze Vorlesungen* addressed to Countess Augusta Bernstorff-Stolberg in Copenhagen, one of his many correspondents. In the preface to his Joseph lectures he evokes an ideal scene in an upper-class patriarchal household that unites everyone, from husband to child to servant, within the protective frame of a community that is both economic and spiritual. Within this scheme, the mother and mistress assumes a quasi-priestly role, acting as spiritual guide and teacher responsible for moral order in the home. Here we get the first glimpse of a development, soon to be in full swing, of the Victorian ideal of the mother-centred Christian home.[34] Lavater invites Countess Bernstorff-Stolberg to assemble her considerable household – her husband, family members, and many servants and attendants – to read to them from his book. This would be particularly appropriate for Sunday mornings, when staying at their summer residence in Bernstorff.[35] All those who own a

Fig. 2. *Mother Explains the Bible.* The mother points to a picture in the book open on her knee, showing it to the four attentive children who cluster round her. The illustration serves as the frontispiece of a picture bible for Swiss children. – Johann Rudolf Schellenberg, 1774.

Fig. 3. *Reading under Mother's Guidance.* Holding a small child on her lap, the mother listens to an older boy and girl reading, watched with approval by the father. This frontispiece to a religious manual for Swiss children suggests that the book – J.K. Lavater's *Christliches Handbüchlein für Kinder* (Christian Manual for Children) – should be used by young readers under parental guidance and supervision. – Johann Rudolf Schellenberg, 1771.

copy of the Joseph lectures – especially fathers and mothers – are invited to do likewise. By exposing one's family and servants to the biblical story and by recommending Joseph as a model to emulate, one may inculcate the proper social order and prevent it from dissolving. In other words, Lavater considers the biblical story the perfect antidote to the destabilising forces of the French Revolution, intended as it is to promote traditional order in both the home and wider society. To stem the tide of the Revolution and its assault on the social hierarchy, one must hold up the example of Joseph acting as the faithful steward of his master. "Take Joseph as your model", Lavater exhorts all servants. "His wisdom and faithfulness, his prudence and his concern for his master's well-being must guide your behaviour. It must be your purpose to promote, to the best of your ability, the order and prosperity of the household into which divine providence has placed you."[36] The appeal to providence serves to inculcate and sanction the clear distinction between superior and inferior, master and servant, nobility and common folk. The Swiss pastor's lesson is not only one of godliness, but also one that seeks to support a social structure that had lost its stability and unquestioned status. If read and understood properly, the story of Joseph could do much to prevent anarchy and chaos, the two evils feared most by Lavater and all enemies of the Revolution.

The countess and her husband belonged to a kind of secret society that flourished at the Danish court; unlike other societies during the Enlightenment, this one claimed to be enlightened not by pure reason, but by the spirit of Christ who could be contacted through arcane procedures. Lavater's interest in the occult is well known, as is his journey to Copenhagen in 1773, from which he returned unconvinced of these high claims. It may well be that he dedicated the *Vier und zwanzig kurze Vorlesungen* to the countess to instruct her in a more sober kind of empirical theology – one that does not rely on any arcane and doubtful procedures, but on the evidence of divine providence in our everyday lives, and in the historically accurate biography of Joseph. Lavater emphatically believed in, and asserted, the historical nature of this biblical narrative: "Who could dare to think, or even stand up and assert in public: this story is pure fiction?"[37] With the help of his lectures, Lavater sought to teach the countess what he considered one of the most elementary lessons of religion, a lesson as relevant to adults as it is to children.

Lavater was confident of the efficacy of the form in which his religious and moral message – "the truth" – had to be taught: "These truths have to be made vivid and are to be brought before the child's eyes in real examples (*wahre Beyspiele*) and applied to specific cases; if a child is not completely brutish and without a human heart, then these truths will automatically become important and dear to him."[38] In other words: the "real examples" serve best to convey the essential religious teaching. Like all educators of the eighteenth century (and beyond), Lavater believed in the pedagogical force of the *exemplum*, the "example", i.e. the short, entertaining story told to bring home a moral, religious, or philosophical message. The pedagogical use of biblical narratives was only a special application of the more general idea of teaching through stories. Lavater fashioned his *Christliches Handbüchlein für Kinder* in tune with these Enlightenment ideas. He selected biblical stories such as the tale of Joseph for their narrative and moral quality, and adapted them to bring them within the reach of his young readers. In so doing he followed established tradition, using Hübner's *Biblische Historien* (Biblical Histories) as his model. Lavater followed Hübner's approach in breaking biblical stories into short episodes each of which is given a separate title, such as "Joseph sold by his brothers" and "Joseph in Potiphar's house", to name only the first two of nine episodes distinguished by Lavater (but not indicated in our summary given above). He also followed his model in using rhymed verses, though Lavater has only one poem at the end of the whole story instead of Hübner's many poems inserted after each episode. Lavater's genius is most visible when he departs from his model. Hübner's text is somewhat heavy going, for he tried to stay very close to the individual verses of Luther's rendering of the text of Genesis, numbering each of his sentences as we are used to in standard translations of the Bible. While this procedure may have prepared children for reading the full biblical text, the division into numbered verses restricts the flow and spirit of a well-told narrative. Lavater departed from this model by offering a continuous text, uninterrupted by verse numbers. He also preferred a natural, modern idiom to the archaisms of the Zurich Bible, the translation used by the Reformed communities in Switzerland. Needless to say, Lavater nevertheless learned much from Hübner. But even while following Hübner, he sought to improve upon him. Whereas Hübner inserted moralising comments after each of the five episodes that he distinguished, Lavater incorporated them into the actual narrative to indicate that morality, rather than being a mere afterthought, flows naturally from the story itself.

Did Lavater actually succeed in his endeavour to interest children in his retold "Story of Joseph"? The answer must be in the affirmative. This is the kind of story Goethe would have loved at the ages of thirteen and fourteen, when he enthusiastically read Moser's *Daniel in der Löwengrube* (Daniel in the Lions' Den) and penned his own – lost – version of the Joseph tale (see below, Chapter 6). In all probability most children who came to read Lavater's "Story of Joseph" would have liked it. If we are trying to imagine what young Goethe's "Joseph" looked like, we might come up with something closely resembling Lavater's version. But to say that eighteenth-century children no doubt loved the Swiss pastor's storytelling is not to imply that he produced a literary masterpiece. Unfortunately, we have no contemporary responses to

Lavater's *Christliches Handbüchlein für Kinder*, but early critics did evaluate one of Lavater's similar publications – the 1772 book of Bible history that tells the Joseph story in more or less the same words as in the *Christliches Handbüchlein für Kinder*. These critics, while admiring Lavater's prose, felt uneasy about certain features of his presentation of biblical stories. In a letter, Johann Gottfried Herder expressed his displeasure with the departure from the simplicity of the biblical wording, which he saw as spoiling the true oriental spirit: "Our time has adopted a very strange prejudice against what counts as oriental nonsense, as if by conspiracy: a passage that children or even adults cannot immediately repeat in clear language is said not to be understood by them, and therefore should be substituted – by dull paraphrase, cold definition, and philosophical maxim. Inevitably, the entire spirit tends to evaporate, just as in the chemist's destructive analysis."[39]

While there is little "oriental nonsense" that needs elucidation in the Joseph story, and Lavater does not substitute anything by "cold definition", his repeated insertion of moralising and pious thoughts does change the tone of the story, lessening its impact and interrupting its narrative flow. Treating his young readers as simpletons unable to understand and draw their own conclusions, Lavater never stops telling them how to feel and what to think. This feature is also criticised by another who comments upon Lavater's trite poetry:

> As for the little poems appended [to the stories], I wish they would disappear from the book. They have no other aim than to tell the children how they should feel, and this amounts to telling people what they should see or smell. It is by practice that one has to sharpen their minds. Held up in the proper light and viewed from the proper perspective, every object will be clearly recognised, and the correct attitude follows automatically – much better than by teaching through maxims presented in the form of dull rhymes to be memorised.[40]

In other words, not telling but showing is what a good author should be doing; too much telling spoils and trivialises the message. What this critic objected to in 1772 might well be applied to some of the moralising passages Lavater inserted into the story. Time and again, the Swiss pastor interrupts the flow of the narration by directly addressing the reader – the "dear child" – offering an explanation or a pious gloss that even less able children could work out for themselves.[41] These and similar passages, though dear to Lavater, are – to us – not very convincing, and – again to us – obtrusive rather than necessary. By describing Joseph not only as an exemplary youngster who never feels neglected by God, but also as a somewhat boring and bloodless child-saint who is above making mistakes or having his faith in God challenged, our pious author spoils both the drama and the suspense of the elegantly told biblical tale. Lavater's Joseph, instead of being the hero of an adventure story, is a paragon of moral perfection. Lavater's genius as a moralist is unfortunately not matched by his abilities as a children's author.

But we should not end on a negative note. I am far from suggesting that Lavater's critics should be allowed to triumph over the Swiss pastor and dismiss his book as problematic and ultimately irrelevant. Instead, we should acknowledge and defend our author's love of children and his concern for their moral well-being, his enthusiasm for biblical storytelling, his indefatigable search for weighty meaning in every detail, and his preference for ethical substance, duly explained, over aesthetic canons of taste – all are befitting for a religious educator who is also one of the most amiable and interesting characters of his age.

6

Starting Life with Joseph – Goethe

In his famous autobiography entitled *Aus meinem Leben: Dichtung und Wahrheit* (*From My Life: Poetry and Truth*), Goethe (1749–1832) recounts the story of his boyhood in the German city of Frankfurt am Main. Wolfgang (as the boy was known) was born and brought up in a spacious and elegant frame house on a street called Hirschgraben. This house – still extant as a museum and memorial – was owned by his father, Councillor Johann Caspar Goethe. Following the early years at kindergarten and primary school, Councillor Goethe's two children – Wolfgang, born 1749, and Cornelia, born one year later – never attended regular schools, but from April 1756 were instructed either by their father or by tutors at home. Latin, French, English, music, and drawing were all taught, but Wolfgang's real passion was for studying Hebrew and the Bible. In his autobiography, Goethe asserts that it was his juvenile Bible studies that gave a focus to his otherwise "haphazard life and fragmentary education", and he refers to the peace and happiness he derived from them.[1] Wolfgang's interest in the Bible had a clear focus: the story of the patriarch Joseph. In two particular episodes, Goethe demonstrates his boyish fascination with this biblical figure. The first episode concerns a cycle of paintings of Joseph by Johann Georg Trautmann, then the foremost painter in Frankfurt and a friend of Councillor Goethe.

Joseph in Portraiture

The background to the story is the war waged between Prussia and Austria from 1756 to 1763, the so-called Seven Years War. On 2 January 1759, French troops, allied with Austria, arrived in the free imperial town of Frankfurt. Taking it by surprise, they forced the city council to submit to occupation, took up lodgings in the citizens' own homes, and stayed there until the end of the war. From 25 January 1759 well into the summer of 1761, Councillor Goethe was obliged to put up Royal Lieutenant François de Théas-Thoranc in his house. Having moved in and taken over much of the house, the French officer and gentleman noted their mutual interest in art. In his autobiography Goethe recalls how, when the rooms were divided between the new resident and the poet's family, his father had mentioned a room full of paintings. Although it was night-time, the officer immediately asked to see the pictures, at least cursorily by candlelight. More than satisfied, he complimented Councillor Goethe, and upon learning that most of the painters were still alive and resident in and around Frankfurt, Count Thoranc declared his interest in meeting them forthwith to arrange for some work to be done for him.[2]

Within a few days, Frankfurt's best-known painters – Hirt, Schütz, Trautmann, Nothnagel, and Juncker, along with Seekatz from Darmstadt – were summoned in and set to work. Since the artists were to work under the count's immediate supervision, the councillor's son – ten-year-old Wolfgang – had to surrender his pretty, well-lit room in the attic, so that it could be converted into a gallery and studio. Once this was in place and the artists had begun to work, Wolfgang spent much time watching them. This probably involved visiting Trautmann and the other Frankfurt painters in their own, nearby studios, while Seekatz apparently worked in the new attic studio.[3] Wolfgang was already familiar to the local artists, so they did not mind him being around. The count, too, had taken a liking to the boy, permitting him to be present when projects were discussed and preliminary sketches presented. Wolfgang was even allowed to express his opinion, a privilege he never failed to make use of.

Goethe mentions his enthusiasm for the Joseph story for the first time in his autobiography when describing his interest and participation in the production of paintings for Count Thoranc, perhaps in 1760 or possibly as early as 1759. His boyish love for them is presumably best understood as a reflection of his own fresh discovery of the biblical story. Inspiration probably came first from Johann Heinrich Thym, one of his tutors. Between 1756 and 1765 – for nine years – Thym was Wolfgang and Cornelia's main tutor, teaching them writing, mathematics, geography, and history; presumably also natural science and religion. According to Elizabeth Menzel, the major authority on Wolfgang's education, it was Thym who inspired the boy to start reading for himself, and she lists the works whose authors and titles can be found in the autobiography: a German verse adaptation of Fénelon's *Télémaque*, a translation of Defoe's *Robinson Crusoe*, Schnabel's *Die Insel Felsenburg* (The Island Felsenburg), and a book of travel adventures entitled *Lord Ansons Reise um die Welt* (Lord Anson's Trip around the World).[4] The very fact that even in his sixtieth year the poet could remember these titles shows his deep affection for them; they must be considered among his favourite books. As a kind of biblical adventure story, the tale of Joseph can no doubt be added to the reading list of a boy of his time at the age of ten or eleven. Goethe's autobiography is tantalisingly brief at this point, but clear enough: he wrote a long composition describing twelve pictures illustrating the story of Joseph. "And several of these were actually painted", Goethe remembers.[5] Thym may have helped the boy to write his description of a cycle of twelve pictures illustrating the Joseph story. Wolfgang watched one of the painters – Seekatz – produce a series of twelve paintings illustrating the twelve months of the year, so why not adopt the same pattern – a series of twelve – to illustrate the Bible story? Help also came from two illustrated bibles in the family library: a folio bible with etchings by Matthaeus Merian and the Augsburg children's bible edited by Abraham Kyburz, books that Wolfgang and Cornelia often looked at.[6] Scenes from the story of Joseph figure prominently among Merian's etchings. Here Wolfgang saw Joseph as he was raised from a pit by his brothers only to be sold to travelling merchants. Further scenes showed Joseph running away from his Egyptian master's wife when she sought to seduce him; as he was brought before Pharaoh to interpret his dreams; and in a chariot drawn by four horses, applauded by the Egyptians as their prime minister. Also depicted were Joseph's brothers as they left their father's house for Egypt to buy food, and their arrival before their unrecognised brother Joseph. A final etching depicts Joseph and his brothers dining in grand surroundings, attended by several servants.

The boy's love of the Joseph story did receive acknowledgement and support as some of his suggestions were actually followed by Johann Georg Trautmann, a fact noted in Goethe's autobiography.[7] Seven of the sequence are still extant.[8] The following scenes are depicted: Joseph explaining his dreams to his family; Joseph sold into slavery; Jacob receiving Joseph's bloodstained coat; Joseph and Potiphar's wife; Joseph being called out of prison; Joseph selling grain; Joseph being approached by his brothers. Although it is impossible to detect any influence by Wolfgang on the paintings, they are nevertheless important, at least because they must have heightened his interest in, if not engendered enthusiasm for, the biblical story.

But there may be another reason, one that I venture to suggest despite its hypothetical nature. It seems possible, if not likely, that the largest and most prominent of these paintings, *Joseph Selling Grain in Egypt*, was meant to portray Count Thoranc, benefactor of the city of Frankfurt, as Joseph (see the Appendix to this chapter). And it may well be that the boy was aware of this intention. To investigate this possibility, let us proceed step by step, beginning with this question: how did Wolfgang feel about the French gentleman who, despite his father's reluctance, shared the family home? For the boy, the uninvited guest made a big difference: the stranger's presence brought more life, more interest, and amusement into the house; it served to open his young eyes to a new, wider, more colourful world. Naturally, the boy would also compare the guest and his father. From the mature poet's account in his autobiography one gets the impression that Wolfgang's father and the French gentleman had much in common. Both were art lovers, and both had a tendency to ill humour.[9] Councillor Goethe seems to have suffered immeasurably from not being master in his own house, and he avoided seeing the count as much as he could. Exactly what the count suffered from is less clear, but if we are to trust surviving records, his hypochondriac tendency was due to the fact that he remained at a lowly military rank, and, despite many petitions, failed to earn promotion. Goethe's autobiography does not give a full literary portrait of Count Thoranc, but speaks of him with unique objectivity and indeed admiration. Goethe remembers him as a "benevolent" gentleman of extraordinary character, a man who went out of his way not to offend the family burdened by his presence.[10] For Wolfgang, the count appeared a powerful, competent administrator who mastered his daily tribunal with Solomonic wit and wisdom. In the context of Goethe's autobiography, Thoranc actually contrasts favourably with the poet's father. Wolfgang did not share his father's antipathy to the unwelcome lodger; instead, he loved him for the little presents he gave to him and his sister, and he admired his handling of the steady stream of strangers who came to the house to seek his decision or take orders. While in reality, Count Thoranc was but a minor figure in the hierarchy of command, to the boy he must have seemed to exude power and glory. For him, the count was a man of undisputed status, authority, and public influence, something Wolfgang missed in his father who, despite his qualifications, had never held any public office. One does not have to be a trained psychologist to understand that all boys somehow identify with their father and wish to become equally accomplished. From this perspective, it is easy to discern the role the French gentleman played for the boy: unconsciously, the count seems to have served as a second father figure, a model for Wolfgang to emulate. In the same measure as he admired the count and excused his presence in the parental home, Wolfgang resented the fact that his father did little to welcome the guest. When writing his autobiography in later life, Goethe might still not have fully grasped the impact the count had made on his impressionable young soul, but his report includes enough detail to permit the interpretation I am tentatively suggesting.

To support this reading, we may also invoke the story "Der neue Paris. Ein Knabenmärchen" (The New Paris: A Boyhood Fairy Tale), included in Goethe's autobiography.[11] This story, reminiscent of the *Arabian Nights*, is a tale Wolfgang made up as a boy to entertain his peers. In the context of the autobiography, it serves to illustrate the precocious talent of the writer. Wolfgang tells in this story how, intrigued by a locked door in a wall surrounding a Frankfurt garden, he was ushered through it by a mysterious old man who subsequently showed him round, introducing him to a magic world of military toys, soldiers made of tin, and three fine ladies with whom he engages in dance and dialogue. The venerable old man of Wolfgang's story seems to echo the figure of Thoranc who opened the boy's eyes to a social world that was quite unfamiliar to him. Both the reference to soldiers and the mysterious man's Catholic gesture of making the sign of the cross can be understood as pointing to Thoranc who was both a soldier and a Catholic, that is someone holding beliefs different from those of Wolfgang's Lutheran family. Moreover, Wolfgang in this story takes the old man, for a moment, for a Jew, apparently because of his beard and long, wide, odd-looking garment. Is it taking the argument too far to suggest that this identification, however fleeting, reflects the Joseph-like position Thoranc enjoyed as royal governor of Frankfurt?

One day, presumably early in 1761, the Joseph paintings were packed up and sent from Frankfurt to their destination – the count's brother's castle in France. Shortly thereafter, Goethe's father arranged for the count to take lodgings elsewhere in town, and reclaimed his family home. New tenants arrived, this time worthy friends of the family rather than French military personnel. Count Thoranc was called back to France soon afterwards. Goethe, when writing his memoirs in 1808, assumed that the count died as a governor in the French West Indies (St Domingo), but in fact he died in France in 1794, possibly killed during the French Revolution. For young Wolfgang, the episode came to an end when the paintings left the house. The attic was cleaned and returned to its previous occupant – Wolfgang. However, the episode was not quite over. "I was lodged again in my garret," Goethe reports, "where the ghosts of all those pictures sometimes hovered before me; but then I tried to banish them by working and studying."[12] By studying the Joseph story!

Joseph in early writing

Wolfgang not only studied the biblical text of Genesis, he also began to write his own, imaginative version of the Joseph story, demonstrating once again his early fascination with the Joseph story. In *Dichtung und Wahrheit*, Goethe refers to his account as his first major literary effort. But instead of including a summary of the plot of his own "Joseph" (a text no longer extant), he merely recounts how he went about its writing. Using Goethe's autobiography, a few surviving letters from 1766 and 1767, and a mild dose of imagination, we can reconstruct the complete history of Wolfgang's writing of "Joseph" in all four of its dramatic phases: the build-up of enthusiasm for the subject, the actual writing, feeling the pride of juvenile authorship, and the eventual disillusionment. A chronological table of events may be constructed as follows:

Year	Wolfgang's age	Events
1759	10 years old	Artists begin to paint for Count Thoranc; Wolfgang's attic is used as a studio
1760	11 years old	W. suggests the painting of a Joseph cycle; Trautmann paints it
1761	12 years old	Spring: *Joseph* paintings are sent to France; W. returns to his attic
		Summer: W. takes lessons in Yiddish
1762	13 years old	Summer: W. takes Hebrew lessons, consults a biblical commentary
		September: W.'s father buys a biblical commentary
		W. starts to work on his "Joseph"
1763	14 years old	Moser's *Daniel in der Löwen-Grube* is published in the spring, and read by W.
		W. writes his "Joseph", and has it bound
1764	15 years old	W. continues to work on poetic renderings of biblical subjects (until 1767)
1765	16 years old	30 September: W. leaves for Leipzig, to study; plans to have "Joseph" printed in Halle
1766	17 years old	
1767	18 years old	11 May: W. is disillusioned with his "Joseph"
		12 October: W. reports that he has burnt his "Joseph"

It may have been in the early 1760s that the boy first felt, as he was later to record in his autobiography, that "the artless tale [of Joseph] is extremely charming, but it seems too short, and one feels called upon to elaborate it".[13] So one day – presumably in 1762 – he decided to do just that. And he did so, as he reports, all by himself in his "leisure hours", and not under the guidance of his tutor.[14] Why does Goethe emphasise the fact that he wrote his "Joseph" during his leisure hours? Presumably to stress that this was his project alone, and not something produced under his tutor's guidance, as most likely had been the case when he wrote the essay describing the twelve paintings. Tutor Thym, we must assume, had helped with the first steps, but now, two years later, the young author was on his own.

The boy's writing was accompanied by intensive Bible study and interest in all things Jewish. He not only explored Frankfurt's Jewish quarter, but also persuaded his father to pay for some tuition in Yiddish.[15] By the summer of 1762, however, another tutor had entered Wolfgang's life – Dr Johann Georg Albrecht. A friend of the family and director of Frankfurt's prestigious high school, he served first as Wolfgang's Hebrew tutor. Hebrew, along with Latin and Greek, was taught at the high school. In his autobiography, Goethe lovingly recalls how he went to take lessons with Dr Albrecht, the two sitting together in the teacher's library discussing the Hebrew alphabet and biblical passages. Wolfgang apparently mastered some elementary Hebrew and developed a considerable interest in the book of Genesis, so Dr Albrecht lent him a copy of a commentary – the German translation of a learned work by English divines. Wolfgang took his biblical studies very seriously, and his father appreciated the boy's dedication. Presumably on the recommendation of Dr Albrecht, Councillor Goethe bought the same biblical commentary for himself – or for the pupil eager to study the section on Joseph.[16]

The phase of actual writing seems to have begun some time in 1762. The autobiography reports early difficulties not with the subject but with the form in which to present it: "I had long been wanting to treat the story of Joseph, but the proper form for it eluded me, mainly because I was unskilled in any metre suitable for such a work".[17] Wolfgang read two books that treated the stories of a hero in verse – the German adaptation of Fénelon's *Télémaque* by Benjamin Neukirch and Klopstock's *Der Messias* ("The Messiah"). Both books were written in German verse, using two prosodic types: the *Messias* in unrhymed hexameters imitating the style of Homer, and *Télémaque* in Alexandrine verses, that is iambic lines each with six feet. One can understand the boy's fascination with verse making – and his frustration in trying to imitate these exacting models. Here are some lines from the *Messias* that young Wolfgang and his sister had found in Klopstock's book and which they loved reciting by heart (to the dismay of their father):

Help me! I suffer the pain of vengeful, eternal extinction!
Formerly, I could hate you, with horrible, glowing hatred!
But I can't anymore! This too is grievous affliction![18]

To imitate Klopstock or Neukirch meant writing in a highly rhythmic but possibly monotonous, stilted prose. The solution came to the boy when he discovered that what he had in mind could be done differently – in a short hexameter poem followed by a long text in simple, non-rhythmical prose. This pattern was found in a book published in Frankfurt in the spring of 1763. As the title suggests, *Daniel in der Löwen-Grube* (Daniel in the Lions' Den) is a biblical novel; the author, the then well-known political publicist Friedrich Carl von Moser (1723–1798), rewrote one of the legends of the prophet Daniel who, as the Bible records, served the Persian King Darius as a leading courtier and administrator, fell from grace and was thrown to the animals but, being miraculously protected, was thus vindicated. Moser elaborates the court intrigue that led to Daniel's being thrown into the den, and, by putting long-winded and somewhat tedious, repetitive prayers into the mouth of the protagonist, he manages to fill 144 printed pages. The following prayer, uttered by Daniel in anticipation of being punished by King Darius, gives an idea of Moser's language:

> So I lie prostrate before thee, O Lord, I, thy creature, thy servant. Today, wailing was my song, tears were my prayer. Thou who seest in secret, thou alone knowest the meaning of this day, the strangest day of my life. Is it the last one – ? but, no, O Lord, it is enough for me to know that thou knowest. Thine is the power, thine is the glory, from thee alone is our salvation. Thou art the strength of my life; of whom shall I be afraid? My heart speaks unto thee, I put my trust in your power, thy promises I have as an anchor for my soul. Thou, God of my fathers, thou immutable God of thy people, thou, our only defence: from childhood thou hast guided me wonderfully, marvellous will be thy protection, glorious will be thy salvation. But, O Lord: they have made their decision, thou hast permitted it, I leave it to thee. Thou canst and thou wilt defend thy name. O that only thy will be done, O that only thy name be hallowed! As thou, O Lord, wouldst; as thou in thy wisdom hast decided. My soul misgives me: not for much longer will I worship thee in this world. Thy will be done, thou only, thou ever-lasting Lord of my life, to whom I offer it in sacrifice. [. . .]. [19]

Not much visible action is reported in the story, and the pious protagonist remains a rather pale and bloodless figure. Read today, Moser's book appears as a curious blend of a baroque celebration of the courtier who serves the state with self-effacing, blameless loyalty, and a recommendation of the pietistic believer whose only job is to trust in God and accept his fate with humility, with the expectation of being ultimately vindicated by divine intervention. Seemingly effortlessly, Moser thus blends sentimental piety and politics in a biblical setting, and, despite his verbosity, did not fail to impress at least some contemporaries. One of these was Karl Philipp von Moritz, a German writer who mentions Moser's *Daniel* as one of the books read and re-read by the hero of his autobiographical novel *Anton Reiser* (1785) when he was eleven. Anton is brought up as a very godly boy, and his father supplies him with appropriate reading matter. "Carl von Moser's *Daniel in der Löwen-Grube*, a work of poetic prose, came into his hands; he read it several times from beginning to end, and when his father, as was his habit, would read to him, it was from this book."[20] Anton planned, Moritz tells us, to use *Daniel* as a literary model for writing about the great military leaders of classical antiquity, but he never realised this project.[21]

Had Moser's book not been mentioned by Goethe and Moritz, it would certainly be forgotten, for its literary merit is minimal. Wolfgang, of course, felt differently about the biblical novel, as did Anton in Moritz's novel. From the mature poet's account we learn nothing about his discovery as a boy of his model text. How did the little book come to Wolfgang's attention? One can only guess. Is it too bold to suggest that it came directly from Moser, through mutual acquaintances? Katharina von Klettenberg, a close friend of Moser and a friend and relative of Wolfgang's mother, may have brought it into the house. Wolfgang's mother may have considered it appropriate reading for her children. Whatever the answer may be, we should appreciate Wolfgang's clever idea of using it as a model for his "Joseph". Once *Daniel in der Löwen-Grube* had come into his possession, he read it with boyish enthusiasm, adopted it as his canon of literary taste, and sought to imitate it. The only thing he had to do – and apparently he managed it to his satisfaction – was, as he himself explains, "to differentiate and enlarge upon the characters [of the Joseph story] and to make a new, independent work out of the old story by inserting intermediate actions and episodes".[22] This, unfortunately, is all Goethe divulges about his earliest literary effort.

Once he had Moser's text to emulate, Wolfgang started to write. We may assume that he followed his pattern closely, especially when it came to composing long prayers. What facilitated the juvenile author's work was that he could turn, for the production of a clean copy, to his father's secretary. This man, Johann Balthasar David Clauer, was a family relative who in earlier years had earned a doctoral degree in law, but when his mental capacities declined as a result of illness he became a dependant in the Goethe household. Councillor Goethe used him for simple jobs such as taking down dictation or copying texts, for he could write fast and had a legible hand. Imitating his father, and feeling that he had an important job to do, the young poet dictated his ever-growing Joseph story to Clauer's pen. "Never before had I undertaken so large a work", Goethe reports, "as that biblical epic in prose. Things were fairly quiet just then, so that nothing diverted my attention from Palestine and Egypt. So my manuscript expanded daily, helped by the fact that the narrative, which I recited to myself, as it were into thin air, kept appearing on paper, section after section, and only a few pages occasionally needed to be copied again" – by the secretary.[23]

Once Wolfgang was sure that his "Joseph" was finished, he felt all the pride of juvenile authorship. By adding some poetry of his own – also dictated to Clauer – Wolfgang compiled a real book that he gave the title of *Vermischte*

Gedichte (Miscellaneous Poems).[24] The poems he added were rhymed in form and religious in content, written in imitation of printed texts that were set to music and performed as Sunday church concerts. Proud as he was of his accomplishment, he hastened to one of the local bookbinders and had his *Vermischte Gedichte* bound into a fine quarto volume, for presentation to his father. Like much writing by children, the main purpose of Wolfgang's *Vermischte Gedichte* was to please his parents.

Wolfgang led a carefree early life, though not one without structure and purpose imposed by his father. Councillor Goethe, while appreciating the boy's initiative in producing verse and prose, made sure that Wolfgang received a formal education in preparation for the study of law, the subject in which he himself was an expert and that he wished his son also to study. The Councillor, though having acquired the degree of doctor of law, never worked in the legal profession, nor did he manage to be chosen for office in the administration of the city of Frankfurt. So he devoted much of his time to educating his children, hoping that Wolfgang would eventually embark on a successful public career. The Councillor began to tutor his boy in jurisprudence, teaching him legal definitions with the use of a little catechism-type book of questions and answers; the second stage involved an introduction to the *Corpus juris*, the Latin collection of legal sources.[25] Dr Albrecht also furthered Wolfgang's education: what had begun with Hebrew lessons was extended to other subjects, but Hebrew was apparently dropped from the curriculum, most likely to be replaced by Latin.[26] By the summer of 1765, Wolfgang's basic education was judged to have reached the level required for university entrance, and on 30 September 1765, he left Frankfurt to find board and lodgings in Leipzig to take up the study of jurisprudence.

During all these years of intensive preparation for university, and during his early years in Leipzig, Wolfgang continued his biblical writing so promisingly inaugurated with "Joseph". Apart from his studies, writing was his favourite occupation, and we have reason to believe that he took it more seriously than his career-related studies. Writing developed into a passion, and, in the event of conflict, he would neglect everything else. Examples, mostly fragmentary, of Wolfgang's early literary endeavours survive. In a cycle of poems entitled "Belsazar", Wolfgang treats an episode from the book of Daniel, the same biblical book that had provided the subject of Moser's *Daniel in der Löwen-Grube*.[27] Another poem, a piece with 160 rhymed lines entitled "Poetic Thoughts on Christ's Descent to Hell", deals, in impressively orthodox fashion, with the Last Judgment, understood as the great day of Christ's vengeance and triumph over his enemies, the sinners.[28] A third, much shorter piece of only six lines, is a religious poem Wolfgang inscribed on a blank page in his mother's book of devotions, on the very day of his departure for university.[29]

Joseph in Flames

When Wolfgang settled in Leipzig to begin his studies, he did not abandon his biblical writing. In fact, he took all of his manuscripts with him, hoping to revise and eventually publish some of them. He entertained high hopes. Some of the poems, he mused, "deserved to be set to music and performed for the edification of the congregation".[30] And "Joseph" could make a real book, to be published by the Orphanage at Halle, the famous pietistic foundation that, besides providing a home for orphans, also printed religious tracts. The best-selling title of the Orphanage was *Güldnes Schatz-Kästlein der Kinder Gottes* (The Golden Treasury of God's Children), a copy of which Wolfgang had inscribed with the farewell poem for his mother. Karl Heinrich von Bogatzky, the author, actually lived in Halle, and our young student thought of sending his "Joseph" to him for publication.[31]

More details can be found in the letters Wolfgang exchanged with his sister Cornelia, with whom he stayed in close contact. In October 1766 he mentions to his sister his plan to write a drama to be entitled "Pharaos Thronfolger", a title that translates as "Pharaoh's Successor". Although encouraged by the fellow students in whom he confided, to whom he presumably described the plot of his envisaged project, he could not bring himself to begin. A few months later, in May 1767, Goethe explains to Cornelia:

> You are eager to know more about my tragedies, but I must tell you that thus far I have written no more than outlines. To do the actual writing is impossible, I feel much too weak for such a job. [...] The outline of Pharaoh's Successor is replete with the tragic, and the killing of the first-born in Egypt by the angel is the subject. I would send it [the outline] to you if it were written legibly enough, so that you could decipher it for yourself, or Horn [one of Goethe's boyhood friends] might make a copy.[32]

For some time, Wolfgang must have toyed with the idea, but finally he dropped the project, never having written a line. "To do the actual writing is impossible, I feel much too weak for such a job." Laconic as they are, these words reveal the sorrows of the young writer who was becoming increasingly disillusioned with his juvenile scribblings. Neglecting his legal studies, he eagerly attended the lectures of Christian Fürchtegott Gellert who, besides being a well-known writer of poetry, novels, and stage plays, taught moral philosophy and the history and theory of literature. Wolfgang also took Gellert's tutorials in practical composition, but the master "treated my verses as a mere dreary adjunct and, worse than that, even my prose found little favour in his eyes, for in my old way I would always make a little novel of it, preferably in epistolary form".[33] Receiving little encouragement from his teacher, Wolfgang lost his earlier self-assurance and became somewhat depressed. It dawned on him that Gellert was right and that he still had a lot to learn. No one is born a writer, and even the greatest talent has to be developed. Although Gellert did not recognise Wolfgang's abilities, one of his fellow students did. This was Ernst Wolfgang Behrisch. Eleven years older than Wolfgang and serving as his friendly critic, Behrisch seems to have had considerable influence on the young poet. Behrisch appreciated the love poetry Wolfgang composed as a student, but apparently ridiculed his juvenile prose. Soon, Wolfgang came to share his friend's opinion. By May 1767, when Wolfgang had been studying for a little more than a year, he no longer had any confidence in the literary merit of his "Joseph". "If in the year 62 [actually, 1763] someone had told me about my Joseph, what I am telling myself now, I would have been terribly frustrated and would never again have touched a pen", he wrote to Cornelia.[34] Five months later he came to the conclusion that all of his juvenile writing was utterly worthless.

Two reports survive of the final stage of the young writer's crisis – one in a letter to his sister, and one included in the mature poet's autobiography. The two accounts merit being set side by side:

Letter to Cornelia, 12 October 1767	*Dichtung und Wahrheit*
There was no way for Belshazzar, Isabel, Ruth, Selima, etc. etc. to atone for their juvenile sins other than by an ordeal of fire. Joseph was given the same sentence because of the many prayers he said during his life. For a long time I had considered giving it as a present to the Orphanage [of Halle], to Bogatzky, who might have printed it. It is an edifying book, and Joseph has nothing to do but pray. Here we have often laughed at the simplicity of the child who could write so pious a work. But I should not write too much about the child, for it is not even four years since "Joseph" was born.	This uncertainty of taste and judgment disturbed me more every day, until at last I grew desperate. Of my youthful works, I had taken along the ones I considered the best, partly hoping to win some fame, partly to have a surer test for my progress. But I found myself in the painful situation one is placed in when what is required is a total change of mind and renunciation of everything one has previously loved and esteemed. After some time and many struggles, I was seized with such great scorn for all my finished and unfinished works that one day I burned them all, poetry and prose, sketches, and drafts, in the kitchen fireplace. The smoke filled the whole house and caused our good old landlady no little fear and terror.[35]

Wolfgang's mood is best conveyed by what Goethe wrote in his autobiography, but the letter is more valuable for its details. Here we learn that it was without much regret that the student took leave of "Belshazzar, Isabel, Ruth, Selima, etc." With "Joseph", things were different. Conveying a strong sense of disillusionment, he recalls his hopes of having the manuscript published. He also states, without ambiguity, that it was in the flames of the kitchen fireplace that his childhood perished. As the smoke filled the whole house, a new writer was born – one still very unsure of himself, and one who had to face the daunting task of making a fresh start.

By ironic coincidence, at the same time as Wolfgang gave up the idea of having his "Joseph" printed, his hoped-for editor Bogatzky published a book on the Christian courtier that includes a chapter on the biblical patriarch.[36] Entitled *Der gottselige und christliche Hofmann* (The Devout Christian Courtier, 1767), it sought to demonstrate that life at court, at least at one of the many small princely courts in Germany, was easily compatible with the highest standards of virtue and prayerful godliness. The pietistic author extolled the exemplary life of a recently deceased friend of his, a man who combined his (otherwise unremarkable) courtly career with a life devoted to his wife and family, to daily prayers, regular Bible reading, and sending edifying letters to like-minded correspondents. In Bogatzky's book, Joseph and Daniel figure as the supreme biblical models recommended to courtiers, and the typical pietistic typology is not missing: the late gentleman was another Joseph or Daniel. Unlike Moser's *Daniel in der Löwen-Grube*, Bogatzky's book lacks any serious political perspective: it is only after office hours that the hero's godliness can unfold properly. Wolfgang's prayerful Joseph (despite his later misgivings) would no doubt have won the approval of Bogatzky.

If Wolfgang had continued with his biblical writing, especially by realising the "Belshazzar" project, he would have made a step in the right direction – away from a merely pious story to one full of dramatic scenes. But the moment had not yet arrived, for Wolfgang lacked an adequate model for his writing. With the benefit of hindsight, we can tell why Wolfgang – instinctively – did well to abandon his biblical projects altogether. Moser's *Daniel* was an inadequate exemplar: poorly written, it was simply third-rate literature and, to put it bluntly, pious trash. Wolfgang needed a better literary model, and found it in Shakespeare. It may well be that the anthology *The Beauties of Shakespeare* (compiled by William Dodd, 1752), a book Wolfgang discovered in March 1766, contributed to the crisis of his early student days. He even contemplated writing his own version of *Romeo and Juliet*. But the time had not come for this – he felt too weak to begin serious work on, let alone complete, his literary projects. Shakespeare, moreover, although having come into view, was not yet fully appreciated by our young poet.

In order to progress, Wolfgang had to give up studying in Leipzig. Exhausted after a haemorrhage due to tuberculosis, he left the city in September 1768, a sick and irritated young man who had not taken a single examination. He continued his studies in Strasbourg in 1770, and there he found his new master. On the recommendation of Johann Gottfried Herder, whom he met and befriended there, he rediscovered Shakespeare, and under his guidance regained his creative energy – pride, power, and confidence in his own abilities, instead of gnawing uncertainty and a sense of failure. Now the spell of Moser was broken. Soon, and not without the encouragement of his sister, he began to work on his early masterpiece, the drama *Götz von Berlichingen* (1771), a piece that no longer reflected Moser but in the spirit of "Sturm und Drang" echoed the genius of Shakespeare. Having abandoned Moser's pietistic ideal of the protagonist's humility and acceptance of his fate, Goethe wrote about a hero who asserts his own rights and represents the ideals of independence and freedom.

Epilogue

As Goethe embarked on a double career as a member of the court of Weimar and a writer, "Joseph" and Moser were forgotten. It was only in 1809–1811, when writing the early chapters of his autobiography, that he returned to the subject. He mentions the Joseph scenes that were painted in his childhood home (though he fails to refer to Trautmann as the artist) and describes the enthusiasm with which he wrote the Joseph novel. He even indicates, though a little vaguely, the influence Moser's *Daniel in der Löwen-Grube* had on him. What he omitted, though, was the thoroughly pietistic flavour his Joseph novel must have had, and he says nothing about how his parents reacted to his work. His father apparently loved his son's dedication to writing and studying, appreciating the fact that "Joseph" was written spontaneously, and not as part of the schooling he received from his father or his teachers. When writing *Dichtung und Wahrheit* as a sexagenarian, Goethe did not regret that the juvenile exercise was no longer extant; from the vantage point of the accomplished author, he knew its deficiencies all too well. He had sought to embellish the biblical story by including new scenes and episodes, not realising that such episodes cannot be derived from pure imagination: "I did not reflect – and indeed no youngster can – that substance (*ein Gehalt*) was also required, and that this can only come from our perception of actual experience."[37] Goethe was far from condemning the biblical subject he had chosen for his major juvenile literary effort; what it lacked, he now knew, was the "substance" (*Gehalt*). But what is meant by "substance"? I take it to mean what we would nowadays call a message or central idea – the making of some telling general point that, according to Goethe, would be drawn from one's experience of life.[38]

Goethe made that general point in his autobiography, inserting a lengthy summary of the book of Genesis and recounting in his characteristically elegant prose the whole story from paradise to the great patriarchal figures. This is how he ends his précis:

> Before these family scenes blend into a history of the Israelite nation, one final figure is shown to us that is especially attractive to hopeful, imaginative youth: Joseph, child of the most passionate conjugal love. He strikes us as being calm and clear-minded, and he prophesies personal distinctions that will elevate him above his family. Plunged into misadventure by his brothers, he remains steadfast and upright in slavery, resists the most perilous temptations, saves himself by soothsaying, and rises to merited high honours. First he shows himself to be helpful and useful to a great kingdom, then to his own family. He resembles his great-grandfather Abraham in equanimity and grandeur, his grandfather Isaac in quietness and devotion. The business sense inherited from his father is now exercised on a grand scale: it is no longer a question of appropriating a father-in-law's herds, but of knowing how to acquire nations, along with all their possessions, for a king.[39]

This summary of the story of Joseph, written from the perspective of the sixty-year-old poet, cannot be taken as reflecting young Wolfgang's ideas about Joseph. The last two sentences in particular – where Joseph's personality is seen as being derived from his ancestors – betray the autobiographer's mature thoughts on the subject. It is well known that, in his later days, Goethe sometimes made reference to his character as being made up of traits he had inherited from his own parents and forefathers. It may be appropriate to quote Goethe's well-known jingle:

> I have my stature from papa,
> My way of life so stable;
> My cheerful bent from dear mama,
> And delight in tale and fable.
> With fair maids ancestors made bold,
> I still can sense that itching;
> An ancestress loved fine stones and gold,
> My limbs too feel such twitching.[40]

The general point the mature poet now saw in the biblical tale was that Joseph, the young genius, not only embodies all the talents and virtues of his ancestors, but even succeeds in transcending his forefathers' restricted realm by acting on a wider stage – that of a kingdom. This would be an inspirational message of hope, conveyed by a biblical figure who is, in the mature poet's own words, "especially attractive to hopeful, imaginative youth".[41]

From our tentative reconstruction, the Joseph story emerges as the favourite biblical narrative of an eighteenth-century boy of ten to fifteen years of age. What makes Goethe's account particularly attractive is the fact that he honours his beginnings by revealing how as a boy he used the biblical story as the subject of his first sustained literary effort. The biblical story fired his imagination and led him to discover his literary talent – a latent talent, to be sure, and not one that would announce his later genius. As we have seen, Wolfgang soon came to reject both the subject and the way he wrote about it, for he had to free himself from the constraints of biblical imitation, indeed from the limitations imposed on him by his milieu and his boyish enthusiasm. Nevertheless, even late in life he acknowledged that writing his own "Joseph" constituted his most elementary literary training. He also acknowledged that a relatively unimportant adaptation of a Bible story – Moser's *Daniel in der Löwen-Grube* – served as his first literary model. In brief: the Bible and Bible-related literature shaped the first, embryonic stage of Goethe's writing.

In fact, Joseph also accompanied Goethe during his later career, as can be seen from the list of the operas performed at the princely theatres of Weimar and Halle under his directorship. This list includes a piece entitled *Joseph in Ägypten* (Joseph in Egypt), a blend of opera and religious oratorio set to music by Etienne-Nicolas Méhul. First staged in Paris in 1807, it highlights the reconciliation between Joseph and his brothers, and between Jacob and his sons. Successful throughout Europe, it appealed to an audience that, weary of war and political upheaval, was yearning for the restoration of peace. Between 1812 and 1816 Goethe had it performed ten times.[42] In 1816 especially, after the end of the Napoleonic wars and the establishment of a new political order by the Vienna Congress of 1814/15, it resonated with a sense of European renewal and reconciliation and could serve as both a plea for peace and a celebration of universal reconciliation. This sentiment was not foreign to Goethe, who hated revolutions and rejected war as a political expedient. After one of the performances, on Saturday, 6 April 1816, he entered a laconic, yet telling note of approval and satisfaction in his diary: "Joseph in Egypt. Very good performance."[43] Goethe may have consigned his youthful outpourings on Joseph to the fire, but in later life he never came to reject the educational, moral, and religious qualities of his first favourite.

APPENDIX:

JOSEPH PORTRAYED – TRAUTMANN

After the Joseph paintings left Wolfgang Goethe's attic studio in 1761, they were shipped to France, where they stayed for more than a century. In 1876 they were discovered in Mouans Castle (municipality of Mouans-Sartoux, southern France) by the dedicated Goethe scholar Martin Schubart, and eventually in part acquired by and in part loaned to the Goethe Museum of Frankfurt, and displayed in the restored home of the Goethe family. Today, the cycle of seven Joseph paintings can be seen in Wolfgang's very attic room. The artist, Johann Georg Trautmann (1713–1769), though an able painter, is now largely forgotten, and were it not for the Goethe connection, art historians would spend little time doing research on him. Even the Goethe connection has led to little more than an annotated catalogue of the cycle.[1]

The relevant question in the context of our study is this: does anything in these paintings suggest that Wolfgang did indeed have some influence on them, as he claimed in his autobiography? The most recent and most detailed study on Trautmann to date, by Gerhard Kölsch, indicates that this is unlikely, and, to state the result of my research at the outset, I fully agree. Although Wolfgang may have been the first to suggest the subject of the paintings, they apparently rely on established iconographic models, and not on the imagination, however fertile, of the boy. But what exactly, then, were the models Trautmann relied on? The answer is that we cannot be sure, because we know very little about the artist and have no contemporary documents that would give us a clue. Nevertheless, a review of seventeenth-century Joseph paintings leads to plausible results in the case of the two most important paintings of the cycle. Stated briefly, the result is as follows: Trautmann's painting *Joseph Sold by his Brothers* echoes Murillo's painting *Joseph and his Brothers* (1670), and Trautmann's *Joseph Selling Grain in Egypt* reflects a scene from Breenbergh's *Joseph Distributing Grain in Egypt* (1655).

Joseph Sold by his Brothers

In Trautmann's painting *Joseph Sold by his Brothers* (Fig. 4) we see a fertile spot in an arid landscape: trees with foliage, grass covering the ground, hints of a flock of sheep calmly grazing to the left, to the right the rim of a stone-built superstructure of a cistern or a well. At the cistern, in the shade and shelter of the trees five bearded, turban-wearing merchants take a rest with their camels. The long neck of one of the beasts of burden stretches upward, as it reaches towards the tree's green leaves. In the centre, in front of the tree, stands a

Fig. 4. *Joseph Sold by his Brothers*. While one of the brothers receives payment from a foreign merchant, young Joseph raises up his right hand in a gesture of pleading and desperation. Whether the young Joseph echoes Wolfgang Goethe remains a matter of speculation. The artist blends conventional biblical iconography with Murillo's *Joseph and His Brothers*, 1670 (below, Fig. 6). – Johann Georg Trautmann, *c.* 1760.

well-dressed merchant with a purse fixed to his belt. With his right hand, he puts coins into the open hand of the leader of the shepherds, recognisable by the long shepherd's crook on which he is leaning. Standing behind their leader, two other merchants watch the monetary transaction. The one on the left shades his eyes from the sun, to better witness completion of the transaction. Both the giver and the receiver of the coins hold their right arm horizontally outstretched, apparently still arguing, negotiating the price. To the left of the hagglers, the beardless boy being sold is restrained at the shoulder by one of the shepherds, while another shepherd, to the left, raises his hand to warn and scold the child. Like the merchants' leader, the boy is exposed to full sunlight, highlighting his fine garment, his pleading gesture, and his sorrowful face. Pressing his left hand to his heart, he looks up at his merciless brother who is ready to hand him over to his new master. This imposing figure, made taller by a high white turban, provides a strong contrast with the small, bareheaded boy – his slave. Almost twice as tall as the enslaved child, the master appears a majestic, intimidating figure.

"A caravan of Ishmaelites coming from Gilead, with their camels bearing gum, balm, and myrrh, on their way to carry it down to Egypt" encounters the shepherds, who then sell the boy "for twenty shekels of silver": this is the biblical scene visualised by Trautmann.[2] As is clear to many observers, Trautmann was imitating the famous style of Rembrandt. He "rembrandticised", as Goethe remembers in his autobiography.[3] While we could leave it at that, art historians love to raise the question of whether the artist has invented the general pattern of his painting or has referred to someone else's work. The painting's central figure – the boy Joseph – is perhaps best interpreted as a blend of two figures Trautmann found elsewhere: a Joseph figure by Murillo and, surprisingly, Rembrandt's depiction of Potiphar's wife in *Joseph Accused before Potiphar* (1655; Fig. 5). Bartolomé Esteban Murillo in *Joseph and his Brothers* (1670; Fig. 6) depicts Joseph at the moment of his most acute suffering: when he is brutally seized by his brothers prior to being thrown into the pit. The helpless boy, stripped of his robe and wearing nothing but a shirt, his bare legs dangling, is grasped violently by the two brothers who are dragging him towards the round opening of a cistern, into which he is about to be cast on the end of a rope held by a third brother. The scene is framed by Joseph's other brothers who crowd around and watch the cruel scene intently, the demeanour of these figures variously demonstrating the collective nature of the heinous crime. The turban-wearing figure who stands to the right in the foreground with his back towards the viewer, apparently the leader of the group, echoes Joseph's bare shoulders, but with him it denotes naked brutality; in strong contrast with Joseph, he is shown in a self-confident posture, holding a stick in his left hand and the victim's multi-coloured robe in his right hand. The accompanying dog underlines his leadership position. Clearly, Murillo depicted an episode different from that painted by Trautmann. Nevertheless, the two paintings are remarkably similar in some details: the two brothers at the far left of both paintings, one leaning forward and one standing behind, and Trautmann's pathetic figure of Joseph which unmistakably echoes the helpless victim of the Murillo painting in both gesture and attitude. The boy's right hand, opened in a gesture of desperation, is rendered identically by the two artists, as if Trautmann were quoting the earlier depiction.

For a number of other features in his painting, Trautmann apparently relied on pictures found in illustrated bibles, engravings closely resembling the one shown in *Joseph Sold by his Brothers* (1680; Fig. 7). The setting of the scene under a huge oak tree; the presence of camels; the bearded, turban-wearing leader of the merchants, captured in the act of paying for the new slave, as the central figure – all these details in the etching are reminiscent of Trautmann's painting. Whatever its exact and presumably eclectic iconographic sources may

Fig. 5. *Joseph Accused before Potiphar*. Having failed to seduce her servant, Potiphar's wife accuses him of attempted rape. Joseph raises his hand in protest. The gesture and attitude of the woman captured the attention of J.G. Trautmann who imitated it in his figure of Joseph (*Joseph Sold by his Brothers*, above, Fig. 4). – Rembrandt, 1655.

Fig. 6. *Joseph and his Brothers.* Joseph is brutally seized by his brothers prior to being thrown into the pit. Some of the features of this painting, including the very figure of the defenceless boy, served Trautmann as a model for his own *Joseph Sold by his Brothers* (above, Fig. 4). – Bartolomé Esteban Murillo, 1670.

be, the Frankfurt artist's painting stands firmly within the seventeenth- and eighteenth-century tradition of biblical illustration.

Count Thoranc, according to the family tradition of the French owners of the painting, pointed to the boy Joseph, explaining: "C'est Goethe."[4] Much has been made of this tradition by those seeking to find early portraits of the famous poet. And, if that tradition were correct, would one not be justified in saying that Trautmann presumably predicted Wolfgang Goethe's future career? Now, at the moment of painting, he is just a little boy, but later he will be as important as Joseph? Could this be the key to understanding the secret message embodied in Trautmann's cycle of Joseph paintings? For a moment, this interpretation may sound plausible, but upon scrutiny, the hypothesis falters on several counts. First, around 1760, could anyone have been able to predict Wolfgang Goethe's future success as one of Germany's most important writers? Second, is it likely that the very small figure that lacks all specific features was modelled on Wolfgang? As we have seen, Trautmann's actual model was a figure he had copied from a Murillo painting. The Thoranc family tradition reported by Martin Schubart in 1896 seems to be based on a misunderstanding. The art historian Ludwig Bamberger around 1900 heard a tradition similar to the one

Fig. 7. *Joseph Sold by his Brothers.* Rescued from the pit into which he had been thrown, Joseph is sold to foreign merchants whose turbaned leader seals the transaction with his payment. The illustration was included in a widely circulated book of bible illustrations. – Melchior Küsell, 1680.

previously picked up by Martin Schubart, when visiting Mouans castle, still home to some of Thoranc's paintings. However, the words "C'est Goethe" were attached this time to a genre painting entitled *Boy with a Clay Pipe and Girl with a Cat*. Bamberger was informed that, according to a tradition passed on by Thoranc's daughter, Wolfgang was the boy depicted watching a girl playing with a cat: in this case both Goethe children may have been used as models by the artist, Johann Conrad Seekatz.[5] The dictum "C'est Goethe" – or rather: "C'est Wolfgang" – may thus originally have applied to the boy in *Seekatz's* picture. Later it became erroneously attached to Trautmann's *Joseph Sold by his Brothers*; hence there is no reason to identify the little boy in the latter painting with Wolfgang. The boy Joseph in Trautmann's painting does not provide the key to understanding the cycle of paintings. A more promising candidate for understanding this cycle is another of Trautmann's works: *Joseph Selling Grain in Egypt*.

Joseph Selling Grain in Egypt

Since Trautmann's *Joseph Selling Grain in Egypt* echoes an earlier painting showing the same scene, it is appropriate to begin with a consideration of the model he found among the works of the Amsterdam painter Bartholomeus Breenbergh (1598–1657). The relevant piece, dating from 1644, survived into the twentieth century but was destroyed during the bombing of Dresden in 1945. The picture still exists, however, in the form of an etching made by the artist himself: *Joseph Distributing Grain in Egypt* (1645, Fig. 8).

The middle ground of Breenbergh's etching is crowded with people and activity, while the upper left section is dedicated to Joseph who keeps a watchful eye on the proceedings. Wearing a long robe and a feathered turban and leaning on a stick, he echoes a pictorial source that is unrelated to the Joseph tradition: Rembrandt's *Persian* (1632; Fig. 9), used here to present an oriental man of impressive dignity and authority. Joseph stands, shaded from the sun, on a raised platform from where he supervises the selling of grain from the store, a massive stone structure that towers above him. The servants bring loaded sacks and baskets out of the store, descending a staircase and passing by a desk on the platform at which a scribe notes details in a record book. On close inspection of the picture one can discern a central triangular structure that involves three figures in eye contact: Joseph looks at a young mother who, accompanied by her husband (who covers his eyes with both hands), her old mother, and a small child, kneels on the ground and offers her last piece of

Fig. 8. *Joseph Distributing Grain in Egypt.* Standing on the platform of a granary, Joseph supervises the selling of grain. With an authoritative gesture he tells a servant to give alms to a mother who looks up to him, imploring for mercy. – Bartholomeus Breenbergh, 1645.

STARTING LIFE WITH JOSEPH – GOETHE 107

Fig. 9. *The Persian.* – Wearing a turban crowned with a feather, a mantilla thrown over his shoulders, and a short, belted cloak, this gentleman, like many of Rembrandt's orientals, seems to be a European in foreign garb. A contemporary of Rembrandt, the Dutch painter Breenbergh used the Persian gentleman as model for Joseph in his etching *Joseph Distributing Grain in Egypt*, though he transforms the oriental into a taller, more dignified figure. – Rembrandt, 1632.

jewellery. With a sweeping gesture of his right arm, Joseph instructs a servant to give a huge basket of provisions to the famished family; in acknowledgement of the order given to him, the servant glances up at Joseph. By thus ordering the servant, Joseph allows the poor family to bypass the stone desk below, where a man hands over money from his open purse while the accountant watches intently. This customer has to pay, but the poor woman apparently may keep her necklace. The money gathered in, though only from those who can afford it, is deposited in an open chest placed in front of the desk. On the far left, a man is shown tying up his sack of grain with rope; in a moment, he will lift his hat and staff and leave with his newly acquired precious stores.

Breenbergh's etching reminds us of the fact that the Dutch, in the seventeenth century, were Europe's foremost merchants. Amsterdam, where the artist lived, was then the most powerful merchant city in all Europe. Breenbergh's etching no doubt echoes contemporary Dutch economic life and the two pillars on which it rested: the mercantile system based on the exchange of goods, and the mitigating system of the distribution of alms. The artist thus captures both the spirit of capitalism and the spirit of charity. He assigns the capitalist role to the accountants sitting at the two desks shown in the picture; Joseph, standing aloft, supervises the accountants and prevents them from taking money or valuables from the poor; he embodies the spirit of charity in the same way that the imploring mother represents the needy. Breenbergh thus added a dimension that was absent from the biblical story. The years of dearth involve all Egyptians in economic and financial transactions, in buying and selling: the exchange of grain for money, animals, land, and even people. The notion of almsgiving is foreign to the biblical account. When Joseph returns the money paid by his brothers, hiding it in their sacks, the recipients do not accept the gift gratefully, but feel somehow cheated: the financial transaction thus negated, they remain indebted to the seller. In his etching, Breenbergh transcends this harsh economic regime by modelling Joseph after the Dutch magistrates who were in charge of the poor. The scene thus seems to reflect the efficient system of poor relief of which the Dutch Republic was justifiably proud.[6]

Throughout the seventeenth and eighteenth centuries Breenbergh's etching was frequently copied, and it also found its way into series of biblical illustrations including the *Icones Biblicae* (1680) of the Augsburg artist Melchior Küsell.[7] Although we have no knowledge of Trautmann's immediate pictorial source, the most likely assumption is that he used Breenbergh's originals or works derived from them for his *Joseph Selling Grain in Egypt*, the central piece of his Joseph cycle (Fig. 10). In its present location in the Goethe Museum, the painting fills the greater part of one wall. Its very size – 224 cm high and 134 cm wide – defines its key position, relegating the other paintings to the periphery.

Fig. 10. *Joseph Selling Grain in Egypt.* Standing in a pavilion, Joseph supervises the selling of grain to the starving Egyptians. The governor of Egypt apparently bears the features of Count Thoranc, the artist's patron, who from 1759 to 1762 served as a French military lieutenant in the occupied city of Frankfurt, Germany. – Johann Georg Trautmann, *c.* 1760.

An elegant garden pavilion, an ornamented stone building on a raised platform, enables the artist to dispose many human figures on several levels. Down below, people crowd around a bearded accountant sitting behind a round stone desk. Holding a book in his left hand, he is about to write down the value of a piece of jewellery handed over by someone approaching his desk from his right. Amongst others who press towards the desk a distraught mother stands out. With a desperate gesture of petition, she points at her hungry child sitting on the ground in front of the desk. At her feet, we can see an open purse and some coins. Is there enough money to buy food for herself and the child? To the right, a broad flight of stairs leads up to the second level – the baroque pavilion. Set into a niche there is the statue of an elegant, long-robed female deity – this must be Isis in her role as Demeter the grain goddess, responsible for Egypt's agricultural wealth. Very popular in Egypt and loved by the people, she is honoured as the divine dispenser of all blessing and fertility. An awning provides pleasant shade, yet one majestic figure steps out into full sunlight. Dominating the entire painting, this imposing gentleman clad in a long, wide-sleeved robe and turban is Joseph, the kingdom's chief administrator and royal deputy. He is accompanied by a bearded dignitary and next to him is a man seated at a desk. Behind, but highlighting his majesty, a soldier stands in the shadows armed with shield and halberd – Joseph's bodyguard. Leaning in leisurely fashion on a walking stick, and with his right arm akimbo, Joseph looks down as if from a gallery, approvingly watching his accountants below, as they "gather up all the money that is found in Egypt and in the land of Canaan, in exchange for the grain that they buy".[8]

Trautmann thus depicts accountants, clients and money, but the commodity sold – grain, according to the biblical story – is hardly to be seen. Only on the right side, shaded behind the flight of stairs, can we discern men loading sacks on to a donkey. The structure largely hidden behind the trees must be the storehouse for the grain being purchased.

No wider landscape is included in Trautmann's picture, with the exception of a few trees to the right of the pavilion. One of the trees is outlined against the clear sky, displaying a stag-headed crown with some dead branches, thus indicating the lean years in Egypt during which all vegetation suffered from drought. Also discernible, on the right, is a marginal yet distinct architectural element: the spire of a distant tower. It looks like a church spire, and here Trautmann may be giving us a glimpse of Frankfurt rather than of Egypt in biblical times. Indeed, while Trautmann renders at least some of his figures in oriental garb, the overall atmosphere of his painting is rather modern, reflecting eighteenth-century European architecture and fashion. Modern features are so prominent in this painting that it takes some effort to see it as depicting a scene set in Egypt in distant biblical times. It may be helpful to remember that eighteenth-century biblical illustrators rarely give their paintings the exotic, Eastern quality that we would expect today. Nevertheless, Trautmann – even more than Breenbergh – seems to be studiously avoiding any exotic details in his work, thereby deliberately indicating a contemporary meaning and message. The key to this message can only be the figure of Joseph himself, and we may be justified in seeing him as a thinly disguised Count Thoranc. "C'est Goethe": if we have to take Count Thoranc's words (as explained above) with a pinch of salt, we can be much more confident in coining our own phrase to assert "C'est Thoranc" when explaining this painting, the central piece of the entire Joseph cycle. Although Goethe's father and many other inhabitants of Frankfurt resented the presence of the French, Thoranc's rule had numerous beneficent aspects. A man of sharp intelligence, he was also a far-sighted administrator who, acting as a quasi-governor, modernised the old imperial city by introducing such useful things as house numbers, lighting and cleaning of the streets, regular collection of rubbish, and the surveillance of prostitutes; he also founded an anatomical institute for the training of military doctors.[9] Modern historians agree that despite his relatively short stay in Frankfurt (four years) and despite the city council's antagonism, he did make a contribution to the development of the city, and can indeed be called a foreign benefactor. A temporary resident in this occupied Lutheran city, many of whose inhabitants were well versed in the Bible, Count Thoranc could easily be construed as a Joseph-like figure – a foreign governor and benefactor appointed by the king. As a patron of the arts, Thoranc supported the painters of Frankfurt, and one of them – Trautmann – created the Joseph cycle's central piece to honour the French gentleman. Trautmann's visual homage to Count Thoranc is as remarkable as Goethe's later literary account, and the two combine to form a monument erected to the memory of a singular French gentleman who arrived in Frankfurt as an unwelcome foreign intruder but who turned out, during his brief residence there, to be an undisputed benefactor.

III

THE ICON OF CHASTITY: THE HANDSOME HEBREW

7

On Sexual Morality

In early-modern times, the majority of Europeans, supported by both state and church, insisted on a strict domestic order characterised by marital fidelity. By contrast, a significant minority had only contempt for bourgeois morality; it practised and indeed advertised free love. The detractors from the commonly accepted domestic values came to be known as "libertines". Understood as both a theory and a way of life, libertinism seems to have originated among the French upper classes in the seventeenth century, but quickly spread to other parts of Europe, especially to England. A moral war raged between the conservative and the libertine factions.

The libertine challenge and the moralists' response

The iconic libertine was John Wilmot, Earl of Rochester (1647–1680). From around 1665, under Charles II, "the merry monarch", he dominated social life at the royal court of London for about fifteen years, his life being marked by vivacious conversation, carousing, love affairs, erotic pleasure, and frivolity. In 1680, at the age of thirty-three, the Earl of Rochester was dying from venereal disease and the effects of alcoholism. Shortly before his death, Gilbert Burnet, one of England's leading divines, sought to bring him back into the Christian fold. While the details of Burnet's report on Rochester's deathbed conversion are controversial, it does include a remarkable statement of the libertine view of life.[1] Libertine philosophy welcomes passion as being natural, because it seems unreasonable to imagine that we were given appetites only for these to be restrained and curbed. Accordingly, we should seek to gratify all our natural appetites, especially those for wine and women. However, the theory of libertinism, as transcribed by Burnet, was a mild version of the real thing. True libertines like Rochester would not be satisfied with mere aristocratic excess in the indulging of physical passions; they would add the full range of practical jokes and transgressions typical of young unmarried men who do not shun acts of violence to demonstrate their defiance of law and order. Further, they would propagate their ideas in elegant erotic poetry and novels, such as the compositions that Burnet urged Rochester on his deathbed to have destroyed.[2]

Despite his early death (and alleged deathbed conversion), many young upper-class contemporaries considered Rochester's carefree libertine life a model to emulate. They were especially attracted to the idea of free love. Aristocratic husbands, explains historian Jenny Uglow, came to assume "a natural right to have mistresses, making no secret of their *amours* or their bastards. And although female chastity – for reasons of property, not propriety – was considered imperative until an heir was born, after that high-born women soon claimed equal rights."[3] This was all the more possible since adultery, in eighteenth-century England, was not a crime punishable by the public authorities – a scandal for contemporary moralists.[4] But in spite of the permissibility of certain adulterous relationships, one type remained beyond the bounds even of the libertine moral order: the relationship between an upper-class woman and a lower-class male, especially a mere domestic servant. Cases of such "Mrs Potiphar" relationships are on record, and some of them ended up in court; in one such instance, a landowner sought divorce from his unfaithful wife.[5]

Most members of the European middle classes were shocked to think that this elite culture of loose manners might spread downwards, becoming the fashion of the town for women as much as for men.[6] Moralists did not hesitate for a moment to condemn libertinism. They had believed from time immemorial in the existence of an essential and unchanging moral code that regulated who might sleep with whom in society, household, and family, summed up in the commandment: "Thou shalt not commit adultery." They also quoted St Paul: "Now the works of the flesh are obvious: fornication, impurity, licentiousness [...] and things like these. I am warning you, as I warned you before: those who do such things will not inherit the kingdom of God."[7] By committing the sin of adultery or other forms of sexual immorality, the sinner is excluded from life everlasting in heaven and damned to everlasting torment in hell, or, as the *Historia Iosephi* (1654) puts it, "he leaves the state of grace and salvation, in order to fall into the state of damnation".[8] In addition to quoting St Paul's warning, the author of this seventeenth-century moral treatise, like many of his predecessors and followers, included the Joseph story in his armoury for the fight against libertinism: despite the young man's vulnerability, the Hebrew youth displayed exemplary virtue in his resistance to seduction. "Chaste" is the epithet traditionally attached to his name. We meet chaste Joseph in the poetry of Elizabeth Singer Rowe and Johann Jakob Bodmer as well as in the prose of Henry Fielding. Each of these authors constructs the seduction episode differently, and each comments on it from a different perspective.

Mrs Rowe

Rowe's long poem about Joseph and Sabrina, embellished with scenes, characters, and extraneous episodes borrowed from ancient epic poetry, is set in biblical times. Her Joseph, a stalwart and virtuous Stoic, simply cannot be seduced, while the less restrained Sabrina is portrayed as being driven by strong sexual desires, depicted here as demonic forces. Since she is unable to control them, her doom is inevitable, and her end can be nothing but eternal suffering in hell. Mrs Rowe's *History of Joseph* is to be understood in terms of traditional Stoic–Christian morality. Her moral canons are firm and unswerving, and admit of no qualification. She echoes the sentiments of the early-modern conservative Christians of all persuasions, be they Puritan, Anglican, Presbyterian, or Catholic. These sentiments were based upon the Stoic view of sexuality that was received into Judaism and Christianity in late antiquity.

In the two centuries leading up to our era, philosophers of the Stoic school developed a new concept of sexuality. Whereas according to the archaic domestic code, the family is the unit of sexuality, the Stoic thinkers considered the individual's soul the location where sexuality happens. They saw the human soul as being filled with desires – essentially those of passionate love and vengeful anger and hate. These desires are not deemed natural; instead, they overstep the limits set by nature. Left to themselves, people become sick with passion. Accordingly, there must be therapy for desire.[9] This self-therapy can only be learned from a special kind of medical practitioner – the philosopher who not only promotes the idea of the true sage as a person in full control of his passions but who also offers personal guidance through his teaching and advice. While the sexual impulse has of course always existed, the Stoic focus on erotic fantasies and mental struggles relating to these was innovative at the time. Moreover, it was not just a fashionable ascetic trend soon to be replaced by other ethical ideas; instead, it was a founding event, for it stated how Christians in the West were to feel not only about "sex" (the physical reproductive act), but about "sexuality", understood as an individual matter involving desires, fantasies, and pleasures which is nevertheless regulated by cultural norms. The Stoic discovery has led historians to speak of the birth of a new moral world, indeed "the birth of sexuality" (an expression coined by Michel Foucault) as a sentiment comparable to our own, modern sense of sexuality.

The ideal person, according to this view, is in full control of himself. Morally inadequate, sinful persons, by contrast, are unable to control their desires. Of all desires that upset the equilibrium of one's soul, love is the most violent, indeed the deadliest enemy of virtue and order. This passion must not only be moderated and restrained, but be banished from the soul to the point of complete eradication. The result is serene equanimity: freedom from all disturbance, an equilibrium that can no longer be upset; not even by exposure to erotic situations. "While the sight of someone else's wife in the nude might have an erotic effect on the ordinary man," explains John Rist, "it would have no such effect on the sage."[10] The wise man, one who has mastered the Stoic way of life, "is far more in control of his pleasures than the ordinary mortal".[11] Hellenistic Jews, the New Testament, and early Christian authors all adopted the Stoic perspective. It came to shape Christian teaching and educational practice, and quickly developed into the moral orthodoxy of traditional Western civilisation.[12] Shaped by Stoic and Christian values, this morality can be presented in the form of the ideal biography of those who adopt it. Originally, people appear as animal-like brutes: subject to uncontrolled sexual impulses, they seek more or less immediate and promiscuous gratification, without blushes or hesitation. Although at times latent and dormant, these impulses are easily aroused by an erotic situation, generally by visual exposure to a person of the opposite sex who, consciously or unconsciously, displays his or her body. While some remain at this deplorable stage of nature, indulging in erotic fantasies and forever seeking sexual contact, others begin to control their impulses. They subject themselves to a therapy of desire, possibly through the influence of their parents and teachers or by listening to a sermon or a philosopher's public lecture. They may seek the guidance of a spiritual adviser to help them control their erotic fantasies and restrain their sexual appetites. The attitude they have to learn is that of a warrior who fights against an enemy; this enemy, of course, is not without, but within the human person, residing either in the soul or in the body. Many, and presumably the majority, of those committed to the Western code of sexual conduct remain at this stage that involves them in a lifelong struggle against impure thoughts or wishes. They seek to control their passions by the superior power of reason. Although at times they will be successful, they may also learn that "the spirit is willing, but the flesh is weak". Others, however, a small ascetic elite, will reach the final, ideal stage of moral development: the eradication of all desire. Those who have attained this exceptional state are immune even to strong erotic provocation.

Christians like Mrs Rowe subscribed to the Stoic perspective, though they gave it a religious twist. As Rowe's friend Isaac Watts explains, the love an individual has for God forms an essential factor in the struggle against the passions; the love of God, he insists, "rules and manages, awakens or suppresses all the other passions of the soul".[13] It awakens all sentiments of virtue and suppresses all irregular desires. As a result, the true believer, exemplified by Joseph, is simply immune to the lures of libertinism.

Johann Jakob Bodmer

Bodmer in *Joseph und Zulika* follows Mrs Rowe in giving his story an ancient biblical setting and in using epic poetry as his literary form. But he frames the seduction episode differently. Unlike Mrs Rowe, he focuses on Zulika (as he calls Potiphar's wife), making her the leading character and portraying her as struggling against her desires and sexual fantasies. Bodmer takes great care to exonerate Zulika by placing most, if not all, of the blame on the unhappy and compelling circumstances that surrounded her, carefully contrived by infernal powers that planned to destroy her virtue. Compared with Zulika, Bodmer's Joseph remains a relatively pale, contrived Stoic virtuoso. The contrast between Rowe's *History of Joseph* and Bodmer's *Joseph und Zulika* reflects the difference between two distinct cultural situations and mentalities: Rowe in early eighteenth-century England fought a righteous war against libertinism and its overt advocacy of the legitimacy of sexual pleasure outside marriage, while in Switzerland Bodmer, though far from being a libertine, does not condemn erotic passion. Bodmer belongs to those who see it as an irresistible force that may defy human control and lead to confusion. While Rowe presents Sabrina as a sinner and an evil figure to be condemned by the reader, Bodmer invites his audience to understand, and sympathise with, a bemused Zulika.

In order to properly understand Bodmer's approach to sexual morality, we have to consider the extent to which he was influenced by English poetry, especially that of John Milton and Alexander Pope whom he counted among his favourite writers. Following these two in their appreciation of the emotions, Bodmer placed such concerns at the heart of his poetic theory: good poetry, he asserted, must speak to, and stir up, the emotions. The story of Joseph as told by Rowe implies that men and women can be in full control of their desires. In Bodmer's epic poetry, this assumption is withheld. Rather than following the traditional Stoic–Christian view that regards passions as driven by the human will, he moves towards a perspective of passions as more autonomous phenomena. Although present in the philosophy of Aristotle and rediscovered in the eighteenth century, this perspective remained rudimentary and undeveloped, coming to fruition only in the century that followed.[14] At the end of the nineteenth century emotions would come to be regarded as autonomous, independent of conscious control, and pertaining to the body (rather than to the soul or spirit). Emotions came to be construed as bodily agitations and the nervous activities associated with them. As such, they stood outside moral responsibility. While Bodmer did not theorise about these matters, he clearly moves towards this position, distancing his thought from that of Rowe, and heralding a new conception of psychology.

Mrs Rowe and – as we shall see – Fielding comment on, and fight against, the libertinism that plagued their society. For them, London, whether named or not in the stories they tell, is steeped in immorality. Bodmer's Zurich, by contrast, does not seem to be similarly tainted. True, an evil city does appear in Bodmer's epic: Sodom, where Dison seeks to seduce the innocent Sunith. But this story, only briefly alluded to in *Joseph und Zulika*, remains peripheral to the main plot. In *Joseph und Zulika* Bodmer shows little interest in the libertine problem; instead, he seeks to lay bare a female soul that is tormented by desire. Moral instruction is not his primary aim; instead, he explores the agonies of unrequited love.

Henry Fielding

Fielding adapts the biblical story for use in an eighteenth-century setting. In *The History of the Adventures of Joseph Andrews*, no one is portrayed as a particularly sinful figure: neither Joseph's upper-class mistress, nor the other two women who seek to seduce the titular hero. Fielding carefully avoids addressing what contemporary moralists would have described and stigmatised as mental adultery. According to conservative eighteenth-century Christian morality, a married woman, even before approaching a man she is not married to, has "already, by her wanton looks and unchaste desires, committed adultery with him in her heart".[15] By presenting each of the three women who seek to seduce Joseph Andrews as unmarried, Fielding steers clear of implicit moral judgement; by so doing, he is free to give his seductresses comical roles. Accordingly, the seduction scenes, although repeated, lose the prominence they have in the works of Mrs Rowe and Bodmer. In Fielding's novel, the biblical seduction scene metamorphoses into a plurality of comical episodes that highlight the dangers to which a young, unmarried, and innocent man can be exposed in city and countryside alike.

Fielding's protagonist reflects the "servant problem" of eighteenth-century London. Imitating his betters, he takes the liberty of indulging in the pleasures of city life, including theatre-going.[16] He also asserts his masculinity by loving a woman – Fanny – thereby violating the rule that domestic servants in demeanour should remain child-like and asexual.[17] Although depending on his earnings as a servant, Joseph is ultimately intent on leaving service to marry and set up his own household. All of this amounts to blurring the class distinction between servant and master. Servants were beginning to think of themselves as equal to those who used to be their betters.

Joseph Andrews, though a livelier and more rounded figure than the equivalent in Rowe and Bodmer, is every bit as immune to seduction. The passionate, though chaste, love he feels for a young woman, Fanny, give him strength to resist. Borrowing from the *Ethiopian Story* by Heliodorus, the author offers a graphic illustration of the self-disciplined love between a man and a woman. Fielding's novel celebrates the chaste love that must lead to marriage and the establishment of a new household. But we also recognise that this love is underlain by the Stoic ethic of restraint, enlisted to promote modern ideas of household and family. Restraint, however, is not the dominant note of Fielding's vision of love. He defines love as "a kind and benevolent disposition which is gratified by contributing to the happiness of others". Such altruistic and pure love "may be heightened and sweetened by the assistance of amorous desires", but cannot be reduced to sexual appetite alone.[18] In keeping with the idea of erotic desire as a secondary element of love, Fielding departs from the traditional portrayal of the female seducer as a demonic and sinful being; instead, he sees her as a weak, misguided, and essentially comic figure. That which is comic may be irritating or deplorable, but in the final analysis is not evil. Fielding's novel thus heralds a new, romantic idea of love, one that is still with us today.

We may feel enthusiastic about romantic love, but we should not forget to consider its more prosaic setting in social history. In north-western Europe in early-modern times the partners met relatively late, in their late teens and early twenties. Following marriage, couples typically pooled their resources to create simple ("nuclear") households of their own, which meant that most residences housed just one married couple. A typical couple had two to four surviving children, so that the average household comprised four to six persons. And a typical couple would be devoted to the ideal of marital fidelity.

While to those living in Britain, the Low Countries, much of Scandinavia, northern France, and the German-speaking countries this description of the family seems obvious and familiar (for it has not changed much in more recent times), social historians know that it constitutes an anomaly – a situation that may have arisen just once in history.[19] Elsewhere at that time, in southern and eastern Europe, marriages were typically arranged by extended families, and brides were brought, aged seven to ten, to live with the new husband's extended household. In north-western Europe, the situation was markedly different. From as early as the Middle Ages, both women and men played a major role in selecting their own partners. Late-marriage households were more "modern": more egalitarian and less patriarchal than extended-family households. Women had more influence within the home. Partners in late-marriage households were also more enterprising, more mobile, more prone to leave the agricultural sector of the economy and move to the urban centres, seeking to make a living as wage earners or merchants. However, the nuclear families established by late marriages were less stable and more vulnerable than the extended families of other communities. The marriage bond, unsupported by an extended group, placed all the responsibility for its functioning on the partners themselves. Economically, it was more difficult for family elders to plan for or ensure the household's survival. Without a stable marital bond it was impossible to face an uncertain future, and that bond had to be maintained by the mutual support of husband and wife and reinforced by strict sexual morality prescribing monogamy and proscribing extramarital relationships. The relevant rules were actually quite long established, but in late medieval and early-modern times they were increasingly insisted upon first by the lay population and subsequently by the formal tightening of discipline in Catholic and Protestant doctrine.[20] It is to the same moral cause that Fielding's novel so entertainingly contributes.

8

Libertine Libido – Mrs Rowe

ELIZABETH SINGER (1674–1737), LATER KNOWN AS MRS ROWE, DAUGHTER of a well-to-do English family, was educated to lead a life of leisure.[1] Well-bred and elegant, she attracted the attention of many of the high-ranking and fashionable people of her day. She largely devoted her life to languages, literature, and writing. She studied Italian, published poems, and translated a few sections of Tasso's *Gerusalemme liberata* into fine English verse. In her youth, between 1690 and 1715, she spent much time in London where she associated with other young people who called her Philomela, and she contributed poems under this lyrical name to a weekly journal, the *Athenian Mercury*. After the death of her husband Thomas Rowe in 1715, she retired to her estate in Frome in Somerset, and only sporadically continued her literary production. Not until the last decade of her life, between 1728 and 1737, did she resume writing, three books being published: *Friendship in Death: In Twenty Letters from the Dead to the Living* (1728, often reprinted); *Letters Moral and Entertaining* (3 vols, 1729–1733); and *The History of Joseph* (1736). While Rowe's epistolary fiction was highly original, her *Joseph* echoed the style of Milton and imitated, as we shall see, the *Maiden's Blush*, an epic version of the Joseph story by the seventeenth-century poet Joshua Sylvester. Both her epistolary fiction and *Joseph* seek to teach the same moral lesson, as they celebrate chastity and marital fidelity while presenting libertine desires as sinful, evil and disruptive of one's inner harmony.

SUMMARY OF *THE HISTORY OF JOSEPH*[2]

Books 1 to 3

After an invocation of the Holy Spirit (the biblical equivalent of the Muses), a Miltonian epic-type prologue sets the stage: the infernal powers meet to contrive schemes for harming, or even destroying, the

Hebrew race. An earlier attempt in this direction failed when God intervened just in time to prevent Abraham from killing his son Isaac. The demonic convention supports the plan of the demon Mithra to fill the breast of the pagan prince Shechem with desire for Jacob's daughter Dinah, and thereby provoke war between the Hebrews and the Canaanites, a conflict that should end with the extinction of at least one branch of the Hebrew race. At first, things seem to go well for the infernals. Dinah – the attractive half-sister of Joseph – and her companions are invited to a party held in the palace of Hamor, prince of the Hivites and father of Shechem, where they enjoy a feast of oriental splendour. Enchanted by Dinah's beauty, Shechem makes advances to her. She flatly refuses to hear his protestations of love, so he takes her by force. The feast continues unabated, but Dinah's brothers hear of what has happened, and the next day they invade the palace seeking revenge. Many are killed, including the culprit, whom they find in the company of their unfortunate sister. To the joy of her family, the Hebrew princess is then freed, but her father fears retaliation that might extinguish his race. He implores the help of the Hebrew God to stop vengeance being wreaked. A sacred dread seizes the Hivites, so the Hebrews survive unharmed. The second plot hatched by the demonic powers is directed against Joseph himself: the archdemon Moloch successfully sows discord among the sons of Jacob, and in no time Joseph's brothers seek to kill him. Joseph's guardian angel Gabriel intervenes; he visits Joseph during his confinement in the pit, and assures him not only of his survival, but also of his destiny for greatness. The angel continues to watch over his protégé. Unfortunately for the infernals, the brothers do not actually kill Joseph, selling him instead into presumed obscurity in Egypt.

Books 4 to 8

In Egypt, Joseph is bought by a captain of the royal guard, who takes him to his palace and shows him off to his wife Sabrina. She feels the first stirrings of love for the young man. Seeing that her mistress is in a state of confusion, the maid Cyrena tells her the story of Semiramis to amuse and divert her: once upon a time in Mesopotamia, a peasant found an abandoned baby girl hidden under a beautifully embroidered mantle. He brought the child to his master, an overseer of royal lands and flocks. As the girl, Semiramis, grew up, her beauty did not escape Menon, commander of the king's army, and he took her in marriage. He was then called up, but the couple decided to stay together, even during the war.

Disguised as a male warrior, complete with helmet and javelin, she joined the army. She fought bravely, and one day actually discovered a way to enter a besieged town. As they celebrated victory, Menon, proud of his brave soldier in disguise, revealed her true identity to his lord, King Ninus. Inevitably, the king then fell in love with the woman, and asked Menon to give her up. Neither Menon nor Semiramis wished to comply with the king's wishes. Menon found himself in an increasingly difficult situation. Intimidated by the king, Menon in despair committed suicide, and soon Semiramis became the king's spouse. One night, the restless ghost of Menon appeared to the monarch, foretelling his sudden death. King Ninus duly died, and rule over the country fell to Queen Semiramis. After having built a mausoleum as a royal sepulchre, she dedicated herself to building walls, planting pleasure gardens, and adding many magnificent buildings to the city of Babylon.

When Sabrina finally discloses her passion to the slave Joseph she is firmly rejected. Disconsolate and despairing, she confides her love to Iphicle, her nurse and confidante, who promises to support her mistress using her own magical resources. To explain how, Sabrina is told a second story:

Once upon a time, Gebirus, a wealthy Chaldean, travelled to Egypt to marry Charoba, queen of Egypt. Gebirus was accompanied by Chemis, a handsome young man whose adventures in Egypt were even more memorable than the story of his Chaldean master. An amphibian goddess, normally resident in the Nile, met and fell in love with Chemis; after this she regularly left her watery abode to meet her lover. In reward for the love he freely gave the goddess, Chemis was taught a magic spell otherwise known only to the gods – "this celestial spell / which ev'ry good procures, and can each ill repel".[3] Handed down through the maternal line, knowledge of the spell had been inherited by Iphicle, and she now divulges it to her mistress, hoping that it will take immediate effect and break Joseph's resistance. According to Iphicle, Joseph is actually in love with Sabrina, though he does not dare to admit it. So the magic spell is used, apparently to consecrate a love potion – but to no avail.

Undeterred by this failure, Sabrina remembers the magician and necromancer Harpinus whose still more powerful magic might help. (The name Harpinus – echoing that of the Harpies, ugly and rapacious mythical creatures, half bird, half woman – suggests a hybrid being, half human, half demon.) So Sabrina sends the nurse off to see him. Iphicle accompanies Harpinus to his gloomy underground vault, where his

> kitchen, lit by incandescent blue sulphur burning in urns, is stuffed with magic-making equipment. "The wizard here employs his mighty spells, and great events by divination tells."[4] Harpinus charts the planets, utters arcane spells, performs secret rites to initiate the lovers' union, and promises speedy success. Yet, despite his best efforts, Joseph still does not yield to Sabrina's ever bolder advances. Enraged, she accuses him of having attempted to violate her. While Joseph suffers his undeserved fate in prison (where his guardian angel Gabriel offers consolation), she comes to repent. Her remorse makes her ill. On her deathbed, she admits her despicable crime and, acknowledging the sacredness of the virtue that she had so despised, brings this episode to its sorrowful end.
>
> Joseph, once freed from prison, is promoted to the office of vice-regent, but feels the lack of a wife. One of Pharaoh's daughters has fallen in love with an Ethiopian prince and wishes to marry him. Pharaoh, however, does not grant her wish, because he had planned to give the princess to Joseph in marriage. As for Joseph, he has fallen in love with Asenah, a young Egyptian priestess of Isis, but this marriage seems equally impossible, because Pharaoh has other plans for Joseph. Moreover, Asenah serves as a virgin priestess who, bound by an oath of chastity, is not allowed to marry. At this point, at the very end of the epic, the dark powers of hell make a brief reappearance as they help the two sets of lovers to their desired but seemingly unattainable unions. As Asenah's father, a priest, consults the oracle of the Egyptian gods (who are in reality denizens of hell), the latter release Asenah from her vow, declaring that she is truly destined to be Joseph's spouse. The demonic powers believe – unreasonably, as it turns out – that Asenah will soon corrupt the purity of Joseph's religion. Although the marriage of the two couples is more implied than told, the reader knows that this episode brings the story to a happy ending.

Rowe's poem reflects two seventeenth-century traditions: a *literary* tradition that followed Milton in valuing the poetic canons established by classical authors such as Virgil and Horace, but which also readily drew upon the Bible, especially the Old Testament, for inspiration and aesthetic effect; and a *moral* tradition that looked to Puritan authors such as John Bunyan for the defence of traditional moral standards and for guidance in a society whose elite tended towards libertinism and laxness. From her early days as a poet in the 1690s, Mrs Rowe (then Elizabeth Singer) and some of her contemporaries felt that during the preceding generation – the generation of the Earl of Rochester and Aphra Behn – English poetry, for all its outward beauty, had lost its moral vigour. For the reading public, poetry and immoral libertinism had become closely linked. To rescue poetry from its tainted reputation, the creation of a new literary culture was called for, one that should draw upon the Bible, especially the Old Testament, because of its appeal as a source both of poetical language and of ethical inspiration.[5] In what follows, I will comment on these two traditions and consider how Rowe followed them in creating her *History of Joseph*.

Sources

In the seventeenth and eighteenth centuries, many writers felt that all good literature should imitate that of the ancients, and that the epic was its noblest form. To create a modern epic, one should select a "great" subject of public or national significance, focus on a hero and his noble sentiments, make God and angels intervene in human affairs, give the text an authentically ancient flavour by invoking the Muses to assist the poet, and use certain literary devices such as abrupt beginnings (plunging *in medias res*, with deferred explanations), dialogue between the hero or heroine and a companion such as a nurse or a servant, and similes that embellish and extend the description of events or characters. Finally, the story has to be presented in clear and forceful language, arranged in poetic verses, rhymed or unrhymed. All of these devices were used by Milton whose *Paradise Lost* (1667) ranks as one of the classics of English literature. *Paradise Lost* is the story of how Adam and Eve – here presented as the primeval lovers – were seduced by the devil in paradise and subsequently banished from God's garden to live and work in a fallen world.

Paradise Lost was greeted with enthusiasm, and even outside Britain Milton was hailed as "the Christian Homer".[6] The general admiration for *Paradise Lost* provoked imitation. Milton himself wrote two more biblical epics: *Paradise Regained* and *Samson Agonistes*, and many copied him throughout Europe. Should one also tell the story of Joseph in epic form? asked the Scottish novelist Samuel Pratt. "What an exquisite piece might the genius of Milton make of it," he exclaimed, adding that, if written, the result might be "superior to the now unrivalled *Paradise Lost*".[7] Pratt apparently felt unequal to the task and never tried his hand at it. Writing in 1777, he did not know that one generation earlier, an epic version of Joseph had already been published by Elizabeth Rowe. Her general inspiration to write a biblical epic came from Milton, but we know some of the literary sources she read, absorbed, and exploited to lend substance to her poem and sharpen its focus: a woman who unlawfully falls in love with the young Hebrew slave. These sources were either oriental or classical, and the blend of the two creates the unique atmosphere of the *History of Joseph*.

To give her story an oriental feel, Rowe inserted two stories. She used the *Library of History* of Diodorus of Sicily for her first oriental story, that of

Semiramis, a favourite tale often echoed in the literature of the seventeenth and eighteenth centuries.[8] The second, *Charoba, Queen of Egypt*, by the Arab writer Murtada ibn Nafif, was known to Rowe through a seventeenth-century version in English.[9] One character in this story is Chemis, Iphicle's ancestor who loved a beautiful and powerful nymph of the Nile. Rowe recounts these tales to enliven her own story and, by including the elements of magic and erotic orientalism relished by her readers in this Puritan age, to heighten its Eastern atmosphere.

The classical sources echoed in Rowe's treatment of the biblical story of Joseph were not the fruit of her own reading of Latin literature. Instead, she relied on *The Maiden's Blush* by Joshua Sylvester (1620), a poem she found in "an old folio" of Sylvester's poetic works, a book her biographer calls her favourite reading.[10] But just as Rowe depended on Sylvester, Sylvester depended upon Fracastoro, for rather than being an original work, the *Maiden's Blush* is a fine poetic translation of Girolamo Fracastoro's Latin epic (see above, Chapter 3). Via the *Maiden's Blush*, Rowe's poem thus reflects not only Fracastoro's epic version of the biblical seduction episode, but also the ancient sources the Italian humanist had exploited. These were chiefly two works: Virgil's *Aeneid* and Seneca's *Phaedra*, both of which included stories of a woman's unrequited love for a young man.

Virgil's *Aeneid* tells the epic tale of Aeneas, prince of the royal house of Troy, destined by divine will to rule over the people. Aeneas fights against the Greeks in the Trojan War. When the city is taken by the enemy, he builds a fleet and sets sail to establish a new home for his people in Italy beyond the seas. The voyage is long and perilous, and their fleet is wrecked on the coast of Africa. In the newly founded city of Carthage, he is befriended by the widowed and beautiful Queen Dido, who like Aeneas had fled her native land in search of a new home. Dido develops an uncontrollable passion for the handsome prince Aeneas, a passion that is ultimately consummated (*Aeneid*, book IV).

The episode culminates in two antithetical scenes: Aeneas, reminded by the god Mercury of his task to seek a home for his people in Italy, not in Africa, abruptly decides to leave Carthage; Dido, confused and heartbroken, performs nocturnal rites (learned from a foreign priestess) around a specially constructed pyre – in the hope of bringing back the loved one or, failing this, to cut the bond of love. Aeneas resolutely sets sail, and in the morning Dido sees his ships vanish over the horizon. In a long speech Dido laments her fate and swears eternal enmity between Carthage and Rome. Then she tells an old nurse – the woman who had nursed her late husband – to make final arrangements for the pyre to be ignited. As the nurse leaves, Dido mounts the pyre, lifts Aeneas's sword, and commits suicide.

Unlike Dido and Aeneas, the two protagonists of Seneca's stage play *Phaedra*, the second ancient source, are closely related: Phaedra is the stepmother of Hippolytus. Phaedra, spouse of the Athenian king Theseus, and her stepson are left alone in the palace as the ruler is absent for several years. Phaedra falls in love with Hippolytus, a young man bristling with carefree energy who loves hunting but spurns the hustle and bustle of urban life as well as any association with the female sex. His extreme desire for chastity and independence inevitably thwarts Phaedra's designs, and eventually leads to disaster.

Phaedra takes her nurse into her confidence, but will not see sense and decides that death alone can end her distress. Encountering Hippolytus with her nurse, she feels emboldened to declare her passionate love for the young man. Hippolytus spurns her advances and draws his sword in alarm, before fleeing in horror when Phaedra welcomes death by his hand. The nurse, quickly summing up the situation, decides that "crime must be veiled with crime" (*scelere velandum est scelus*),[11] and loudly accuses Hippolytus of rape. Phaedra's husband Theseus unexpectedly returns home at this most inopportune moment, learns of the alleged crime, and immediately demands revenge. The god Neptune grants his son Theseus his wish. Hippolytus is tragically killed when fleeing the country, dragged to his death by horses bolting in panic from a sea monster. Phaedra herself then dies, committing suicide after confessing her lie, and having witnessed the body of her beloved Hippolytus being borne home.

The two ancient sources – Virgil's *Aeneid* and Seneca's *Phaedra* – did not translate easily and without adaptation into Fracastoro's epic retelling of the biblical seduction episode. Much had to be adapted and changed, but the nucleus remained: the woman madly in love with a young man and in her strategies supported by her maid or nurse; the man resistant and unwilling to comply with the woman's demands. From Fracastoro's poem, known to her through Sylvester's English version, Rowe borrowed not only the main plot for her *History of Joseph*, but also the name Iphicle for the nurse of Potiphar's wife. She changes other names, but the roles remain: Potiphar's wife is no longer called Iëmpsar but Sabrina, the maid Ephren is renamed Cyrena, and Joseph's guardian angel, anonymous in Sylvester, is now identified as Gabriel. The figure of Harpinus, the professional magician, derives from the Dido episode in the *Aeneid* (though Virgil does not name him). From Seneca comes the close co-operation between the heroine and her nurse (a stock figure of ancient drama) as well as the nurse's fateful suggestion that Joseph be accused of attempted rape. Much of the epic atmosphere of Virgil and Seneca survives in the *History of Joseph*.

THE MESSAGE

In order to understand the moral message of the *History of Joseph*, we must take a look at the kind of life led by the social class to which Mrs Rowe belonged, and at the cultural trends and fashions that marked English society around 1700. Elizabeth Singer was born into a privileged landowning family with an assured income. Servants would have taken care of all the essential work, and as an adult she would have had no duties other than being a partner to her husband, with whom she lived in London until his death in 1715, when she was forty-one. The couple had no children, and she never remarried. The life of women of her class was one of leisure and entertainment, spent in the company of friends and family. To escape boredom, they indulged in such pursuits as painting, playing a musical instrument, exchanging letters and writing poetry, playing quadrille (a card game), reading, visiting friends and country seats, spending time with their favourite dog, dressing fashionably, and being seen regularly at social events such as theatre performances, dances, and dinner parties. They would also go to church and occasionally read a religious book. Although filled with many little activities, such an existence might be deemed uneventful and even, by those who cared to think about it, meaningless. In order to enhance their life, lead it with enthusiasm, and make it more worthwhile, members of the leisured class had two options before them: either to retire from fashionable society and reject its empty pursuits, or to intensify their social life, seeking to enjoy its pleasures in the fullest measure possible.

The temptation to go one way or the other had always been present, as can be seen from the long history of ascetic retreat to the monastery or convent, and the equally long history of the prodigal sons who, as in Christ's parable, left their paternal homes with their inheritance to squander on prostitutes and high living. How many people decide on such an extreme lifestyle depends on the ebb or flow of cultural fashions. In England in the seventeenth century, some members of the leisured class experienced what one might call a "libertine moment" or, as its alternative and exact opposite, a "Pascalian" one. Some of those who found themselves caught up in a libertine moment actually decided to make the pursuit of pleasure their central concern.

Like all religious people, Rowe rejected and condemned libertinism. A "Pascalian moment" had not only confirmed her in her unswerving moral strictness, but prompted her withdrawal from city life and its social pleasures. Living on her small country estate in Somerset, she cultivated friendship mainly with the devout, and wrote and published religious tracts. One of her favourite authors was of course Blaise Pascal, whose *Pensées* she frequently quotes in her work, both in the original French and in her own translation. After the French philosopher's death in 1662, Pascal's notes written in preparation for an apologetic work were published posthumously under the title *Pensées*, becoming a favourite book of all who fled from an empty life of distractions (*divertissement*) to an existence focused on and rooted in God. Replete with psychological observations and brilliantly presented, Pascal's well-reasoned "thoughts" were as spiritually attractive as they were emotionally pertinent. This book, Mrs Rowe states in one of her letters, has "given my thoughts a situation superior to all earthly things. In reading that book, I lose every care, and grow independent on all below the skies: the trifling hopes and fears of human life vanish before a more important interest, while I yield to the evidence of these just reflections."[12] As a writer, Mrs Rowe joined Pascal in his battle against emptiness and especially against its most pronounced form, libertinism. In a poem entitled "A Description of Hell, in Imitation of Milton" (first published in 1709), she includes the atheist, libertine, wanton beauty, and fool in her list of the principal denizens of the place of eternal damnation.[13] There can be no doubt about the sincerity of her fight against libertinism, a moral disease that continued to threaten the authority of Christian teaching and undermine traditional mores.

In early-modern England, the biblical Joseph story was well known and frequently used in moral instruction. One example of this can be found in *The Life and Death of Mr. Badman* (1680), a Puritan devotional book by John Bunyan. In commenting on adultery as one of the sins of young Mr Badman, the author brings up the story of Joseph, describing Potiphar's wife as a woman driven by "whorish affections" and "unclean desire"; Joseph, by contrast, although "a young man, full of strength, and therefore the more in danger to be taken", resisted "her daily temptation, her daily solicitation, her daily provocation heartily, violently, and constantly".[14] Bunyan takes great care to point out that sexual sin is not merely a physical act; it has its roots in the poisoned heart and mind of the sinner. More graphically, the evil person, having committed "spiritual adultery with the devil", is, as it were, pregnant with sin, and must some day give birth to it.[15] Long before being acted out, the sin already exists. Another author who used the Joseph story for moral instruction is Daniel Baker. His poem "Joseph" (1697) depicts Joseph as a Stoic hero who has gained control of himself by banishing all passion and lust from his heart, while Potiphar's young wife, although at first striving to disengage her heart from her new object of love, eventually gives in and decides to follow her desires.[16] In Baker's poem, a virtuous young man devoted to traditional moral norms meets a woman inclined to follow libertine principles. As might be expected, contemporary preachers and moral commentators did not fail to issue a call for a return to moral strictness. They singled out masquerades for special disapproval – the fashionable Venetian-style evening events, those highlights of the London social calendar at which male and female participants donned fancy dress and masks to conceal their faces, spoke with dissembled voices, and generally engaged in mirth and frolic. Such occasions permitted people to reinvent themselves, adopting a different and potentially promiscuous persona such as shepherdess, Blue Domino or turban-wearing oriental. Real identities being disguised, normal social order was deemed to be suspended. "Touching, embracing, fondling, impromptu dancing, and other forms of bodily contact ordinarily taboo between strangers in public – all were allowed. [...] The libertinage of the masquerade was its most notorious popular association, and the idea that mass disguising inevitably resulted in licentiousness one of the stock assumptions of the century," a modern historian explains.[17] The evening of masquerade, to friend and foe alike, "seemed a kind of collective foreplay – the Dionysiac preliminary to indiscriminate acts of love".[18] Debauchery, then, was never far off, and the story was told of a man who stood upon a chair to deliver a sermon in praise of adultery.[19] In a real sermon entitled "A Persuasive to Chastity" (1748), preached before King George II in London, Edward Cobden attacked adultery and pointed out the evil influence of masquerades.[20] The two sexes, he claims, have come to vie with each other "in disregarding all rules of decency and violating the sanctions of the marriage contract". The preacher commends "the example of Joseph's faithful conduct" as "a dissuasive from the sins of immodesty which are risen, perhaps, to a greater height, and spread to a wider extent than was ever known in former ages".

Like Bunyan, Baker, and Cobden, Mrs Rowe also invokes the example of Joseph to counter libertinism. When Bunyan exclaimed "blessed Joseph! I would thou hadst more fellows!" Rowe would certainly have joined him.[21] Yet, she spends more time focusing on female figures than on the male protagonist. At the beginning of her poem she tells the story of Dinah, Joseph's beautiful half-sister. Lured into the palace of Hamor, a pagan prince, Dinah resists the advances of Shechem, who nevertheless takes her by force. We may see in this episode a first warning of the difficulty of protecting one's virtue in urban life. It is noteworthy for exemplifying two typical moral types: the young woman who strives to maintain her purity, and the young man who cannot control his desires. As the *History of Joseph* continues, the same pattern is repeated, though with reversed gender roles: Joseph is the young man who defends his purity, and Sabrina the lustful woman who cannot control her desires.

Before proceeding to the dramatic clash between Stoic Joseph and libertine Sabrina, Rowe digresses to tell the story of another oriental woman: Semiramis. At first sight, it is very loosely connected to the main plot and seems to be inserted for no other reason than to create suspense. One could apparently omit it from the poem without losing anything. It is not made clear why Cyrena, Sabrina's maid, should choose to tell the tale of Semiramis, rather than any other entertaining story. The Semiramis tale is supposedly introduced merely to divert Sabrina, yet it seems to carry a relevant, if somewhat obscure, message. Sabrina apparently understood – or rather misunderstood – the story as demonstrating the conquering power of love. Although this is not made explicit by the poet, the story seems to imply to Sabrina that love is irresistible – a lesson she wishes to believe. With some determination and ingenuity, any lover worth his salt will go through thick and thin in order to be united with his beloved. Had she thought a little further, however, Sabrina would have learned a different lesson by realising that Menon, Semiramis' first lover, took the ultimate revenge on King Ninus. And although love may indeed be irresistible, its illegitimate forms are inevitably destructive. Unlike the men in the story, Semiramis is "true to love, and virtue's strictest laws".[22] By presenting her as a paragon of faithfulness, Elizabeth Rowe creates in the oriental heroine a female counterpart to Joseph.[23] In fact, the stories of these two characters are remarkably similar: both Joseph and Semiramis start their careers as outcasts (in prison and as an exposed infant, respectively), demonstrate determined respect for the marriage bond, and eventually rule over their countries. To alert the reader of her epic to this parallelism, Rowe introduces the foundling girl as being abandoned on "a mossy bed, o'er that a rich embroider'd mantle spread" – a mantle reminiscent of Joseph's "coat of many colours".[24] Like the Joseph story, that of Semiramis entails an account of embattled chastity: Joseph and Semiramis both suffer harassment by social superiors. Both behave virtuously throughout, and yet neither is able to prevent a third party from misconstruing the situation in which they have been placed. In the end, both use their eminence to substantially alter the societies they come to control. Sabrina's maid, in telling this story, wants to warn her mistress of her potentially unhappy fate and discourage her from further involvement with Joseph. Iphicle, the artful nurse, takes the opposite view. Cyrena and Iphicle thus impersonate the oscillations of their mistress's resolve between the strict dictates of reason and the urgent appeal of passion.

Rowe's *History of Joseph*, then, has a clear moral message: driven by strong sexual desire, the pagans Shechem, Ninus, and Sabrina inevitably prepare their own downfall and destruction. By setting up Joseph as a model, Rowe celebrates biblical – and, by implication, Puritan – sexual restraint. The fact that she also holds up Semiramis as a worthy example implies a wider, more ecumenical perspective: even pagans may be truly virtuous. Virtue is always endangered by all kinds of destructive passions, "but the most fatal is forbidden love".[25] Convinced of the essential goodness of human nature and, accordingly, of the soul's power to overcome evil inclinations,[26] Rowe creates an idealised narrative space

> where vice and wanton beauty quit the field,
> and guilty loves to steadfast virtue yield.[27]

The moral status of Sabrina remains ambivalent, because it is not made clear whether the passion she feels for Joseph is spontaneous, or whether it arises from the evil inspiration of the demon Mithra, who in the story also fills

Shechem's breast with "mad desire" for Dinah. In the end, Sabrina recognises her sin and repents, thus admitting responsibility for her evil deeds – her attempt to seduce Joseph and lying to her husband. Hers is a typical case of deathbed repentance, a subject then much debated in England.[28] There is one biblical precedent: one of the thieves crucified together with Jesus sincerely repents and is promised reunion with Christ in paradise, immediately following death. While some took this to imply the effectiveness of last-minute repentance, others warned against basing any bold conclusions on a singular and very particular case. Theological hardliners, when considering the issue, would either never admit the validity of deathbed repentance, or grant it only when preceded by the conspicuous exercise of Christian virtue. The less extreme view, however, insisted only on sincerity. In the words of Bishop Gilbert Burnet: "If the mind of a sinner, even on a death-bed, be truly renewed and turned to God, so great is His mercy that He will receive him even in that extremity."[29] Gilbert Burnet's defence of such deathbed repentance is included in the pamphlet in which he records the real or alleged conversion of the famous libertine John Wilmot, Earl of Rochester.

Sabrina repents at the hour of her death. Will she be saved from eternal damnation? Burnet, no doubt, would favour this outcome, if only to prevent the dark forces of hell from celebrating their victory. But Mrs Rowe, a strict nonconformist,[30] would not side with the Anglican bishop's soft approach. The last words she puts into the mouth of Sabrina merit quoting:

> The world, the boundless universe I'd give,
> My first unblemish'd honour to retrieve:
> 'Tis vainly wish'd! – to some strange realms below,
> Some dark uncomfortable coasts I go.[31]

This is also Mrs Rowe's last word on the matter. Just as virtue will eventually be rewarded, there is equally no escape from eternal punishment: this is her stark warning to all sinners. Her righteous war against libertinism allows no liberal, compromising stance like that of Bishop Burnet.

The *History of Joseph* is certainly Rowe's poetic masterpiece, but it is not her most complex defence of the orthodox Western code of sexual morality. In her *Letters Moral and Entertaining* (1728) she sheds the mask of biblical and oriental disguise in order to instil morality more directly. Now she creates a complex fictional world in a contemporary English setting, surprising – or delighting – her readers with its moral simplicity.[32] The main ingredients are as follows: the stories (all told in letters of confession) start with a romantic plot; a hero or heroine struggles with temptation (thus making the narrative more sophisticated and realistic than the *History of Joseph*); complications ensue, in some cases leading to sinful acts; regularly and predictably there is a more or less dramatic conversion that brings the story to an abrupt conclusion; the conversion may be perfected by the convert's retreat to the peaceful atmosphere of the countryside. All the stories, variations on essentially the same theme, make a telling and ineluctable moral point. In other words, they start like novels and end like sermons. An example is the letter "To Belinda, from Sylvia, to inform her of the reasons of her sudden retreat into the country". Here Mrs Rowe tells the story of an eighteen-year-old woman with a country or small-town background who experiences the city as a dangerous place where virtue and control of desire are difficult to maintain. We meet Sylvia, her fictional character, in London as part of the entourage of a noble French family. As a guest of the family she not only enjoyed the privilege of bed and board, but also became the conversation partner of Monsieur le comte de R., a well-bred, charming, but married aristocrat. An innocent friendship developed. Soon, she was to discover a particular affection for him in her heart, and fell in love with him – without telling anyone, including the *comte*. Although it remained a secret inclination, her equanimity was gone, and she began to experience a severe emotional crisis. Increasingly uneasy with herself, she is tormented by "all the fantastic effects of spleen, vapours, caprice".[33] Jealous of the comte's wife, she came to feel terribly guilty of a "criminal affection, forbid[den] by earth and heaven".[34] Sylvia, alone in the city, is in a dangerous position, in a situation comparable to that of Joseph in Potiphar's house. Unlike Joseph, though, she is not the object of desire, but rather the one who, yielding to her "criminal affection", might possibly seduce a man. In order to escape from her "guilty love", she left the city, for fear her reputation and ultimately her virtue would be compromised. In the loneliness of the country, her passion subsided and her peace of mind returned. Happy to have survived the trial of the city without harm, she is "almost in a state of insensibility with regard to mortal things"; this is how she describes the new, Stoic state of her soul to her friend Belinda.[35]

Sylvia's inner peace did not last very long, however. A year after she fled to the country, the comte comes to visit her brother. She realises that her "criminal passion for Monsieur le comte" had not been "perfectly extinguished", as she had thought.[36] Instead, his presence once again throws her into confusion. "My soul was full of anxiety to think how I should bear this inner struggle for seven or eight days while the comte intended to stay."[37] Whereas earlier, the comte had never suspected Sylvia's secret "guilty passion" for him, he now not only becomes aware of it, but apparently feels a similar affection for her.[38] She tells her friend Belinda how the story ends: upon realising the situation, the comte immediately cuts short his visit and leaves the morning after his arrival. The comte, Sylvia muses, "certainly left us so suddenly to free me from such a criminal perplexity, or to stifle the same kindling guilt in his own breast. The last was what my brother believed."[39] But while consciously feeling relieved by the departure, Sylvia nevertheless yields to her repressed feelings, and falls ill. To her correspondent, she complains: "Why was I formed with these soft inclinations, this fatal propensity to love! How happy are you who, amidst the gayest advantages of youth and fortune, can act with such a graceful regularity, and govern your passions with an absolute command, free from those tender emotions which interrupt the felicity of my life!"[40]

Sylvia's story must be seen against the background of a society that subjected its women to a very strict code of conduct that prescribed reserve and modesty. In courtship, it was deemed immoral for a young woman to allow herself to feel love for a suitor until he had asked for her hand in marriage.[41] Another complementary rule forbade unmarried women to develop any interest in, or emotional attachment to, married men. A woman, moreover, who failed to control her desires was seen as committing the dual crime of immodesty and sin. Rowe's story presupposes the Stoic-biblical notion of sexuality: although never having touched the comte, Sylvia has already committed adultery in her heart. Rowe echoes the eighteenth-century idea, expressed for instance by the biblical commentator Matthew Henry, that Potiphar's wife, even before approaching Joseph, had "already, by her wanton looks and unchaste desires, committed adultery with him in her heart".[42] Henry defines sexual fantasies as "adulterous thoughts and dispositions which never proceed to the act of adultery or fornication", and yet, as "heart adultery", defile the soul.[43] Libertinism, for sensitive religious people such as Rowe, begins in the human heart; once the inner purity is destroyed, outward acts of sin inevitably follow. In order not to let this happen, Sylvia retires to the country where she regains her inner peace. Sylvia knows that adherence to strict morality is not fashionable in her day where libertinism reigns; but she tells her friend Belinda that she wants to stay true to biblical standards of moral behaviour. "I sometimes read the Bible, in contempt of all modern refinements, and hope to form my life on that antiquated scheme."[44] If we compare the *History of Joseph* with the letter to Belinda, we realise that the figure of Sylvia blends the role of Joseph (the young man in danger) with that of Sabrina (the lustful woman). In the story of Sylvia, Rowe's protagonist is not a saintly figure like Joseph who cannot be assailed by temptation; she is a believable character who, though feeling a growing "criminal affection" for a married man, successfully fights against her libertine desires. In both stories the crime is the same, and it is described in much the same words: criminal affection, guilty passion, and guilty love in "To Belinda, from Sylvia"; criminal passion, guilty love, forbidden love, unlawful love in the *History of Joseph*. This vocabulary resounds throughout much of Rowe's writing, because as a moralist she is preoccupied with describing illicit love in an endless variety of fictional settings.

Interestingly, Sylvia's sudden, firm and irrevocable decision to quench the flame of her libertine desires was aided by a French novel of impeccable morality, Madeleine de Scudéry's heroic romance *Artamène, ou le grand Cyrus*. The very thought of this novel heightened Sylvia's awareness of her sinful inclination. "It awakened my remorse, and gave me an exquisite sense of the injustice of my secret inclinations", she confides to her friend Belinda.[45] Here we get a glimpse of one of Rowe's most cherished convictions: that the reading of moral stories, including her *History of Joseph*, promotes Christian morality. Giving her readers thus a chance to gain insight into their sinful state, Rowe helps them triumph over sin and potentially gain everlasting bliss in heaven.

Today, for all their literary brilliance, most of Mrs Rowe's moral stories seem a little dull and dusty. Her letter "To Belinda, from Sylvia" strikes us as a curious blend of a young person's neurotic scrupulosity and mature insight into the problems of a society plagued by libertinism. If Sylvia's attitude were to prevail, all social life would be ruined. But in the eighteenth century, readers thought otherwise. Elizabeth Singer Rowe was seen as a worthy imitator of the biblical prophets propounding a stern moral message. One of her admirers, Jane Turell, addressed Mrs Rowe in a poem:

> Inspired by virtue you could safely stand
> The fair reprover of a guilty land.
> You vie with the famed prophetess of old,
> Burn with her fire, in the same cause grow bold. [. . .]
> A woman's pen strikes the cursed serpent's head,
> And lays the monster gasping, if not dead.[46]

Even allowing for poetic exaggeration, the poem, published in Boston in 1735, conveys something of the moral authority Mrs Rowe enjoyed well beyond the confines of England.

9

Irresistible Eros – Bodmer

JOHANN JACOB BODMER (1698–1783), ONE OF THE MOST PRODUCTIVE and influential Swiss writers of his time, is today mainly known as a literary critic whose writing contributed to the development that led to the movements of sensibility, the *Sturm und Drang* (storm and stress) movement of the 1770s and 1780s, and Romanticism. For inspiration, Bodmer looked to English literature, which he read and commented on with great enthusiasm.[1] He translated Milton's *Paradise Lost* into German, both in prose and poetic form, and in his critical writing defended Milton against some of his continental detractors. He countered Voltaire's criticism that *Paradise Lost* diminishes its biblical model by the addition of angels, devils, and other supernatural agents. According to Bodmer, these figures, rather than being foreign to the ethos of biblical simplicity, are artistically genuine, convincing, and perfectly justifiable. While they may have violated contemporary Enlightenment canons of philosophical correctness, they arouse, touch, and stimulate the reader, as should all good literature.

But Bodmer not only translated Milton and celebrated him in critical writing; he also wanted to be a German Milton and produce epic poetry comparable to *Paradise Lost*. In this vein, he wrote and published several epic poems on the patriarchs of the biblical book of Genesis: on Noah, the deluge, Jacob, Jacob's daughter Dinah, and Joseph. Having come across Elizabeth Singer Rowe's *History of Joseph*, he quickly penned his own version of the story, and published it as *Joseph und Zulika* (1753). Here is a summary of the story as Bodmer tells it:[2]

JOSEPH AND ZULIKA

After a day's work for his Egyptian master, the Hebrew slave relaxes by taking a stroll on the roof of Potiphar's palace. In a nearby branch of the

Nile, three young women are cooling off, bathing and disporting themselves in the water. Joseph enjoys the scene, but an invisible angel makes sure no impure thoughts cross the young man's mind regarding the three naked and beautiful young Graces. While the guardian angel Simri hovers near Joseph, an evil figure, the fallen spirit Chemosh, roams around the girls. As the two spirits meet, they discuss Joseph's character. Is he a man of perfect virtue, as Simri asserts? No, argues Chemosh, and is granted permission to test Joseph's virtue with real temptation – the unsurpassable, seductive beauty of Zulika, his master's young wife.

In the next scene we see Potiphar dining in the company of his servants, including Joseph. Separated from his spouse, who generally leads a life of her own in the palace's female quarters, Potiphar feels lonely. To remedy this situation, he decides to grace the meal with her presence, and calls for her. To contribute to the festive atmosphere thus occasioned, Joseph takes his harp to sing the enchanting "Song of the Virtuous Virgin". This is the tragic story of Sunith, a young girl driven by an insatiable desire to see the city of Sodom. *En route*, she is abducted by Dison and taken to the city, a place of dubious repute, as it turns out. Sunith, a paragon of virtue, withstands Dison's advances and stoutly defends her virginity. Moreover, she is able to tame the flame of his lust and to teach him the dignity and chastity of true love. Eventually, the two leave the city again, Dison wishing to restore the girl to her parents. However, they are overtaken by a band of robbers. Wounded by a poisoned arrow, Dison dies in the virgin's arms. She also dies, for she has tried to suck the poison from his wounds. Sunith's father finds the couple, hears the dying girl's story, buries them in the same grave, and departs after sorrowfully strewing flowers over it.

Zulika, immediately struck by the young man's good looks and beautiful voice, is moved to tears by the heart-rending tale. Once retired to her quarters and alone (for her husband has been called away on an urgent mission), Zulika cannot sleep. Her agitated mind is full of the tormenting presence of the Hebrew. When eventually she does fall asleep, her soul stays awake. She has a strange dream in which she sees Joseph as the spirit of the sun. As this spirit's golden rays touch the surface of the Nile and warm the waters, a plant emerges from the depths. Kissed by the sun, it develops buds that open to form golden, sweetly scented flowers. (This dream, left unexplained, suggests that Zulika feels as if she were dead when away from the invigorating presence of the young man. He alone can impart strength to her weak soul.

More boldly interpreted in Freudian terms, the dream seems to indicate the as yet subconscious wish of Zulika to be physically united with Joseph, and to give birth to his child.)

The next day Zulika chances upon Joseph as he sleeps, enjoying his siesta in the shade of an acanthus bower in the palace garden. Overcome by the desire to touch him, she tiptoes up and manages to press a tender kiss on the innocent sleeper's lips. Back in the palace, she realises the depth of her love for the Hebrew, burns with desire, and confides her passion – and sorrow – to Myris, her nurse and confidante. At first, Zulika is taken aback by Myris's advice that the lovers' union be speeded up by the use of magic. She would rather die than openly confess her love. At this moment, the goddess Isis appears in the form of Zulika's mother to encourage the young woman to admit her love to Joseph and live with this little imperfection in her otherwise unblemished character. Accordingly, Zulika goes to meet the unsuspecting Hebrew, whom she tries to seduce. While unveiling her head and uncovering her shoulders to reveal her charms – enhanced by the girdle of Venus that she has donned especially for the occasion – she confides her feelings for him. Joseph, shocked, rejects her advances forthwith. In a long speech he seeks to explain the philosophy of beauty. Beauty, he tells her, is from heaven, but can only retain its value when it remains united to virtue. Although prepared to countenance a bond of chaste friendship with his master's wife, he would never yield to erotic wishes. Finally sensing that her self-control is gaining the upper hand over her lustful craving, Zulika gives in, and once more retires to her quarters.

Her regained balance is of short duration. Concerned about her mistress's mental state, Myris speaks with Joseph, seeking to turn his heart – to no avail. Still, Joseph is willing to enter the female quarters of the palace to play the harp and sing for Zulika in order to soothe her spirits. Initially, Joseph's harmonious melodies effectively perform this task. Choosing an appropriate song, he seeks to tell Zulika more about the Hebrew philosophy of love and beauty. But Chemosh, who never fails to be present on such occasions, prevents Zulika from hearing. Again he succeeds in firing the lust in her heart. Overwhelmed by desire, Zulika throws herself upon the harpist, holding him tightly and kissing him. Joseph disengages himself with equal violence from her embrace. The harp falls to the ground. He runs away, leaving his outer garment in her hands. While Zulika, hair dishevelled, dress torn, and deeply hurt, is sitting in sorrow on the floor, Potiphar enters. Questioned about what

> happened, Zulika remains silent. The answer – a lie – comes from Myris: Joseph sought to rape her, but fled when he realised that Myris was approaching. The rest of the story is quickly told: Joseph fails to convince his master of his innocence and is sent to prison where he suffers in silence. Since the angel Simri cures Zulika's heart of impure wishes, both her peace of mind and her marriage are restored. Chemosh, the evil one to blame for all the woe, is banished to the Libyan desert.

Much of the literary work done in Bodmer's home in early 1753 centred on themes borrowed from Mrs Rowe. We meet two men sitting in the same study: an older one, aged fifty-five, imitating and improving Rowe's *History of Joseph* by writing *Joseph und Zulika* in German hexameters; and a young man, aged nineteen, who, in writing *Briefe von Verstorbenen an hinterlassene Freunde* (Letters by the Departed to Surviving Friends), sought to imitate Rowe's *Friendship in Death: In Twenty Letters from the Dead to the Living* (1728; German translation 1734).[3] The older man was of course Bodmer himself, and the young man none other than Christoph Martin Wieland (1733–1813) who subsequently became an author of more distinction than Bodmer, not least due to his later residence in Weimar and his association with Goethe. Wieland, as it were apprenticed to Bodmer, began his literary career as a writer of epic poetry and letters, but later turned to writing novels, some of which came to be recognised as classics of German literature. Before living as a guest in Bodmer's house (October 1752 to June 1754), Wieland had already written some remarkable poetry, but it was in Zurich, under Bodmer, that he received formal training in the art of writing and the craft of literary criticism. One of the first lessons Wieland learned from his admired master was the exploitation of other authors' work for literary devices, themes, episodes, plots, and poetic expressions, an art in which Bodmer excelled. In what follows we will first look at how Bodmer relied on Rowe's *History of Joseph* and other sources, and then how the master himself and his apprentice Wieland understood the newly created epic poem *Joseph und Zulika*.

Sources

Although Bodmer was a creative author, he nevertheless was frequently dependent on literary models that he sought to imitate. Imitation and adaptation of existing works or parts of works were his primary poetic techniques. Fortunately we know how Bodmer felt in this case about his main source, the *History of Joseph*. Immediately upon reading this epic poem, Bodmer published a short review, explaining his ambivalent attitude towards it.[4] He does not comment on the moral message of the English poem, and apparently had no difficulty accepting its validity (though in his own epic of Joseph, written later, he avoided Rowe's strict moral message). What prompted his critical comment was the poetic merit of the *History of Joseph*. In his criticism Bodmer distinguishes sharply between Rowe's use of language and the composition of her poem. The critic is full of praise for her skilful verses and diction; she "has good poetic taste" (*ist von gutem poetischem Geschmack*) and talent.[5] On the other hand, in his opinion she is less good at constructing an epic plot.

For Rowe, an epic poem may have various loosely connected episodes, can include borrowed and inserted stories, and generally cracks on at a fast pace. This is how beginners go about writing, Bodmer counters: mistrusting their own genius, they tend to integrate as much extraneous material as possible; as a consequence, they neglect poetic elaboration and fine tuning, the result being more a dense outline or skeleton than a real epic that should move with studied deliberation. The key to producing a more successful epic would have been less action and fewer events, and more art – circumstantial narration with finely elaborated detail, and a plot progressing at an almost processional pace. According to Bodmer, the story Rowe tells could actually furnish sufficient material for several small epic poems. By describing "the character [of the protagonists], how they feel, what their intentions are, all down to the most trifling detail", she could have evoked "more passion" (*mehr Affekt*) and thereby made a greater emotional impact.[6] The hallmark of a good epic, according to Bodmer, is its ability to touch one's heart and stir one's emotions, and in this Mrs Rowe failed. For all its brevity, Bodmer's critical essay announces a major development in European literature: the movement away from the calm and playful classicism still represented by Mrs Rowe, towards a new appreciation of passion and sensibility commonly associated with the emergence of the novel and, eventually, the age of Romanticism.

Bodmer never imitated his literary models without changing something. In telling his epic tale, he narrows the focus of Rowe's *History of Joseph* to the seduction scene by cutting out most of the rest. He also uses different names for his characters: Joseph must of course be Joseph, but Potiphar's young wife changes from Sabrina to Zulika (inspired by Jûsuf-and-Zuleikya traditions in the Islamic world) and the nurse from Iphicle to Myris. Relying on a variety of biblical passages and echoing scenes he is familiar with from classical sources, Bodmer carefully reworks Rowe's epic. A few examples will demonstrate this. The opening scene amalgamates two biblical episodes – King David watching Bathsheba bathing from the roof of his palace and the prologue of the book of Job in which Satan receives divine permission to test the integrity of Job.[7] The evil spirit allowed to test Joseph is Chemosh; he is given the name of a pagan god that appears in the Bible and resembles the evil spirit who in the book of

Tobit spoils Sarah's marriage but is eventually banished to Egypt by the angel Raphael.[8] In one of his earlier epics, Bodmer uses the same name – "Chemosh, the beast-like spirit" – for Satan.[9] As a place of banishment, Egypt is of course not viable in Bodmer's epic, but neighbouring Libya, where Dido's rejected suitor Iarbas lived, qualifies nicely for the role.

Bodmer's creative use of a variety of sources is particularly evident in the banqueting scene during which Potiphar's young wife sees Joseph for the first time. Joseph is called in to sing to his own accompaniment on the harp. According to the Bible, upper-class Hebrew boys were taught to play the harp or lyre; this was the case with David,[10] so why should it not equally have applied to Joseph? But the banquet setting is clearly classical rather than biblical. Just consider the following passage in *Leucippe and Clitophon*, a Greek novel dating from late antiquity:

> After the meal was over, a young slave – one of my father's servants – came in with a lute ready tuned. First he played it with his hands alone, sweeping over the strings and producing a subdued tone by twanging them with his fingers; then he struck the strings with the plectrum, and having played a short prelude he sang in concert with the music. The subject of his song was the chiding of Apollo as Daphne fled from him; his pursuit, and how he all but caught her; and then how the maid became a tree, and how Apollo made for himself a crown out of its leaves. This story, as he sang it, at last set my heart more fiercely ablaze: for love stories are the very fuel of desire. However much a man may school himself to continence, by the force of example he is stimulated to imitate it.[11]

Bodmer follows the ancient tradition of having the harp or lute played after the feast, and a love song performed, though he departs from his model by having his harpist sing a song of chaste, rather than lustful love. It may well be that Bodmer actually knew *Leucippe and Clitophon*; in the modern period, he was not the only reader who enjoyed Achilles Tatius's Latin romance. The song performed by Joseph replaces Rowe's two inserted tales, and Bodmer gives it a better fit to make it less intrusive. Joseph's "Song of the Virtuous Virgin", performed to entertain Potiphar and Zulika, echoes a story Bodmer had written as an episode in his own *Die Sündflut* (The Deluge, 1751). The story of Noah's daughter Sunith – a girl who falls in love with and converts a young man of Sodom, but dies young, much to her father's grief – forms an elaborately told episode that precedes the account of the deluge.[12] *Die Sündflut* presents Noah as a prophet who preaches repentance to the immoral citizens of Sodom, while his daughter Sunith, in love with a young man from this city, converts at least this one person. In a later scene, Bodmer has Joseph again play the harp, this time not for mere entertainment but to alleviate Zulika's depression, another biblical motif taken from the story of David at the court of King Saul.[13]

Two more classical – Homeric – items used by Bodmer may be mentioned: the deity in human disguise and the "girdle of Venus". Isis in the form of Zulika's mother echoes Athena who often takes the form and voice of Mentor, Odysseus' friend who looks after the hero's son and palace during his absence. The girdle that Zulika wears at the instigation of Chemosh in order to facilitate her attempt to seduce Joseph appears in the *Iliad* as "a curiously embroidered girdle into which all her [Venus's] charms have been wrought – love, desire, and that sweet flattery which steals the judgment even of the most prudent"; more prosaically, it was a piece of provocative female underwear.[14]

By using such allusions and additions Bodmer enhanced Rowe's *History of Joseph*, adding narrative detail and slowing down the pace of the account to compose a delightful epic, written in more or less elegant unrhymed hexameter verses, in imitation of the art of Homer and Virgil. How did Bodmer mean it to be understood?

Characterising Joseph and Zulika

The story of Joseph and Mrs Potiphar (or Zulika, as Bodmer named her) is well known to all of Bodmer's original readers: Zulika falls in love with Joseph and seeks to seduce him; Joseph, upon having successfully defended his chastity, is falsely accused and punished by being sent to prison. Thus the plot does not surprise the audience. Instead of focusing on the events and the outcome (all known in advance), the author makes the characterisation of the two protagonists his main concern. While Bodmer himself does not explain how he went about his self-appointed task of characterisation, he appears to have discussed the matter with Wieland, his young apprentice. Wieland wrote down his master's thoughts (no doubt adding his own reflections) in three short essays, probably at Bodmer's request. Bodmer had these essays published, anonymously, in 1753 and 1754.[15]

Joseph is portrayed as the perfect Stoic virtuoso who cannot be lured into seduction. The perfect harmony of his soul, explicitly invoked by the author, cannot be upset.[16] Wieland takes great care to explain that the presence of Simri, Joseph's guardian angel, does not reduce the human protagonist to a mere puppet (with almost visible strings), as argued by his fictitious correspondent. Simri helps the Hebrew slave only through negative assistance, i.e. by preventing the evil spirit from obfuscating Joseph's powers of reason. He does not increase Joseph's intellectual abilities or virtue by secret influence; this is neither necessary nor even possible, because his superior mental powers are in such harmonious equilibrium. Thus Joseph's ability to distinguish between carnal desire and true love, like his firm resistance to the lure of sex, is due to his own, human capacities. An exemplary figure, he demonstrates exemplary conduct even under stress. But an alternative interpretation is also suggested: the fact that Joseph does not succumb even for a moment may be explained psychologically by the shock and surprise he experiences when confronted with Zulika's totally unexpected demand; the enormity of her request renders him incapable of responding, so succumbing to temptation never enters the question.[17] While all of this somehow makes sense, Wieland knows well enough, and admits, that Bodmer depicts Joseph as having almost superhuman qualities, and thus as someone who does not easily solicit imitation by the reader. So why not invent an episode which highlights Joseph's humanity by showing him to be in love with Zulika? Here is Wieland's response:

> For someone less than a Joseph, but madly in love with a Zulika, and overwhelmed by her complete armoury of lust, it would be a sublime feat then to check himself, mindful of virtue and religion, and also to manage to bring his beautiful foe to reason. A true Joseph, however, must be greater than such a man. Moreover, he must not simply be shown to be involved in a struggle between reason and romantic love, a struggle that, in the eyes of the frivolous, would be merely comical.[18]

One of Joseph's roles, barely developed by Bodmer, is that of teacher and moral guide. This role is indicated in the inserted episode of Sunith and Dison. Bodmer sketches here a typically romantic situation: the virtuous virgin succeeds in converting the libertine rake; tragically, however, as they flee from Sodom, the city of sin, they are killed by robbers. Despite its brevity, the episode does have a moral message: it celebrates female virtue and the power of a young woman to save a man's soul. Joseph, by contrast, even though he tries to convert Zulika, fails in the attempt. But why should he fail? The answer lies in the character of Zulika.

Unlike the soul of Joseph, Zulika's soul is easily disturbed. Nevertheless, for a short while, with the help of Joseph's music, the harmony of her soul can be restored. At first sight, it seems to make sense to understand Zulika as someone whose soul is not amenable to full stoical control. Yet this does not ring true. The test to which Joseph is exposed would only work if Zulika is a lady not only of exceptional beauty, but also well educated, witty, of fine manners and refined taste, and, not least, of superior moral fibre. She must be depicted as an attractive partner in every sense imaginable, not as a woman defined merely by physical beauty and a lustful temperament. In characterising Zulika, Bodmer changes from the *Stoic paradigm* used for the portrayal of Joseph to the *paradigm of sensibility*. Unlike the Stoic paradigm, that of sensibility allows the hero or heroine of a story to be guided by feeling, desire, and passion: emotions that are appreciated rather than merely fought against and suppressed. Bodmer seems to agree with Alexander Pope's *Essay on Man* (1733):

> In lazy apathy let Stoics boast
> Their virtue fixed; 'tis fixed as in a frost,
> Contracted all, retiring to the breast;
> But strength of mind is exercise, not rest:
> The rising tempest puts in act the soul,
> Parts it may ravage, but preserves the whole.
> On life's vast ocean diversely we sail,
> Reason the card, but passion is the gale.[19]

Bodmer uses two supporting figures to enhance the portrayal of Zulika: Myris (the nurse) and Chemosh (the evil spirit). Interestingly, Wieland does not comment on the role of the nurse who could justifiably be blamed for much of Zulika's crime. When Zulika confides in Myris, the nurse is quick to suggest a strategy for uniting the lovers; and at the end, the fabrication about Joseph's attempted rape is entirely hers – just as in Seneca's *Phaedra*. In keeping with early-modern literary theory, Wieland and Bodmer see Myris in the same way as they would see any servant or maid: as a minor, purely functional character whose contribution to the plot ought not to be considered in any serious interpretation; this would also be in agreement with the classical notion that in an epic, the protagonist must be an influential, upper-class person. Today, we might be prepared to see the nurse as Zulika's *alter ego*, part of the complete persona of the heroine.

The evil spirit Chemosh does not initiate the love that develops in Zulika's heart; he merely fans the flames already kindled. True, the evil spirit does contribute to what happens, but some responsibility for her desires remains with Zulika herself. She cannot be exonerated completely. As long as a soul remains innocent, Wieland explains, the evil angel has no power over it; but once it has lost its purity, it is accessible to demonic rule.[20]

A close reading of Wieland's text suggests that although the author defended the presence of supernatural agents in Bodmer's epic, he actually read them as being allegorical, thus reducing them to inner, psychological realities, and not forces working on the human mind from outside. An almost imperceptible, yet real, sense of the physical absence of divine agents seems to surface in some passages of Bodmer's work as interpreted by his student Wieland. One example is those passages that refer to Eros. Although he never mentions the playful child god of love by name, Bodmer does weave references to Eros's arrows into his poetry, describing the lover as someone wounded by them.[21] In one passage, he draws on the notion of a plurality of love-inspiring deities, or rather devilish imps; echoing Milton, he portrays them as tiny winged Erinyes who, like an invisible swarm of fireflies, buzz with their burning torches around Zulika's head, alight on her chin and rosy cheeks, dance in her golden locks, and invade her warm, beautiful bosom.[22] Whenever an ancient epic (or romance) deals with the subject of love, Eros is not far from the poet's mind. By the modern age, however, Eros had degenerated to a purely ornamental imaginary figure, a mere poetic device; no one actually believed in him. The presence of the two spirits Chemosh and Simri is merely owed to the protocol of epic poetry, and not to what the modern author really believed: all epic poetry sets human action in a wider context of cosmic dimensions, for behind all we perceive as our own actions the ancient epic sees the manipulating deeds of the gods or, in the case of the biblical epic, the drama of the battle between good and evil spirits. But precisely this worldview was increasingly losing its hold on the educated elite of the eighteenth century. Despite their commitment to the Christian perspective, Bodmer and Wieland also shared the basic secular values of the Enlightenment and believed in the full responsibility of everyone for his or her own actions. Cosmic intrigues, though poetically acceptable, were irrelevant to everyday living. Wieland in his defence of Bodmer's *Joseph und Zulika* seems to suggest that the author comes close to denying any influence of Chemosh and Simri on the protagonists. In his discussion, Wieland uses the expression "psychological", a neologism of his time, with remarkable frequency. When they inspire "evil fantasies", these spirits pervert the human imagination not by direct intervention, but through the normal "laws of human psychology" (*psychologische Gesetze*).[23] In the final analysis, this means that good and evil spirits have no independent function at all. They do not really direct human affairs; instead, as poetic descriptions, they are merely allegories for exclusively human thoughts and dispositions.

Bodmer characterises his two protagonists with great skill, highlighting the fact that each follows the dictates of a different psychological and moral system: Joseph that of a Christianised, pious version of Stoicism, and Zulika that of a pagan sensibility. Interestingly, we find the same two kinds of characterisation in Mrs Rowe's *History of Joseph*. How are we to understand the juxtaposition, in the English and in the German epic, of male Stoicism and female sensibility?

One possible key to understanding Bodmer's (and Rowe's) approach may be Virgil's story of Aeneas and Dido, in ancient literature the foremost example of a failed love affair. Here, as in Bodmer's poem, the protagonists may be seen as being portrayed on the basis of two completely different psychologies. Aeneas, the male hero, sacrifices the prospect or reality of love for a higher good – his divinely ordained mission – thereby passing the test of initiation that makes him worthy to proceed and found the Roman state. He appears as a truly Stoic character: one who, ultimately, is in complete control of his emotional life. Dido, by contrast, represents the world of sentiment. While Dido, in the eyes of Virgil, was a flawed character, at least some of the ancients sympathised with her; the teacher who taught – or told – Augustine "to weep for Dido because she killed herself for love" being one such example.[24] Was it only in Dido's North Africa, where Augustine grew up, that the ancient romance allowed people to mingle their tears with those of its heroine? It is hard for the modern reader not to feel emotionally involved with Virgil's masterfully told Carthaginian episode. Looking to Dido for his model, Bodmer does not present his heroine just as a frustrated wife; writing in an age of increasing sensibility, he strove to create a well-rounded female character that is quite unlike the Stoic Joseph.

If an ancient story can be read as juxtaposing two psychologies, why should Bodmer not be allowed to use the same pattern for *Joseph und Zulika*? As a matter of fact, the two psychologies appear side by side in an eighteenth-century treatise on literary theory closely associated with Bodmer: in Johann Georg Sulzer's *Allgemeine Theorie der schönen Künste* (A General Theory of the Fine Arts, 4 vols, 1771–1774). Bodmer's close friend not only recommends *Joseph und Zulika* for its literary quality and moral teaching, but also hails Bodmer as the "German Homer" whom his contemporaries have – regrettably – failed to recognise.[25] In his treatise, Sulzer juxtaposes the Stoic and sentimental psychologies as two different ways of reaching the ultimate goal of poetry: evoking "the sublime" (*das Erhabene*).

> There is something sublime about the lofty attitude that keeps the mind unruffled and calm in all eventualities, even in the face of mighty storms of danger and misfortune. The opposite attitude, however, the one marked by violent passions, may produce a similar reaction in us. In the case of the quiet magnanimity of the superior attitude we admire the strength of the soul that remains calm even when most severely challenged. But when strong passions produce effects more powerful than we could ever anticipate, then their overwhelming nature equally invites our admiration.[26]

In other words: in the light of Sulzer's poetics, Joseph appears as the sublime hero who embodies Stoic virtue, while Zulika equally invites admiration as the sublime heroine ruled by strong passions. They live in separate moral worlds: the one in an elevated, ideal space inhabited by immaculate, perfect souls; the other in a lower, more worldly domain of passion, suffering, and sadness.

Bodmer's characterisations of Joseph and Zulika are based on what he believed to be sound rules of poetic theory. Yet problems remain.

A "NOVELISED" EPIC AND ITS DISCONTENTS

A certain imbalance between Bodmer's depictions of the characters of Joseph and of Zulika no doubt strikes all readers. Joseph, while a paragon of virtue, remains a relatively pale figure in the story (as if perfection defied description, or rendered it superfluous), whereas in portraying Zulika, Bodmer has exploited all possibilities of epic elaboration, and one wonders whether *The Story of Zulika* would have been a more appropriate title. Zulika, like Sabrina in Mrs Rowe's epic poem, appears as a colourful version of Virgil's Dido, a woman like herself "wildly and fatally in love, impulsive and romantic",[27] who at once attracts our interest, if not our admiration (see above, Chapter 8). In the terminology of E.M. Forster's literary criticism, Zulika is a "round" character who comes across like a real human being, a dynamic individual with ambitions, faults, regrets, and eventual disappointments.[28] By contrast Joseph is a "flat" and static figure, lacking depth and constructed round a single quality: in Joseph's case, the virtue of saintliness. Normally, round characters are central and carry the plot, whereas flat ones occupy secondary, minor positions. Eighteenth-century poetic theory was well aware of the problem. According to Sulzer, whose work we have invoked, it is infinitely more difficult to present a completely virtuous, Stoic hero in an attractive way than to portray someone stirred up by violent passions.[29] Moreover, from a modern, twenty-first-century perspective, one might question the viability of an epic poem in which the two protagonists are characterised on the basis of two different psychological systems: Stoicism and sensibility. Neither Bodmer nor Wieland (nor Mrs Rowe) seems to have fully understood that Mrs Potiphar is a more interesting and rewarding character to develop than Joseph, whose spotless sainthood does not make him an easily believable literary figure.

In calling Zulika a more believable figure than Joseph, we are responding – willy-nilly, it seems – to an aesthetic code pertaining not to the epic but to the modern novel. This code prescribes for the protagonist a complex personality, with a blend of good and more problematic features. The hero, moreover, should not be portrayed as a rigid and unresponsive mature character, but as one who is still evolving and developing, someone who learns from life. In the eighteenth century, the novel not only established itself as the leading literary genre, it also began – as Mikhail Bakhtin has observed – to breathe its spirit into all other literary forms of expression, including drama and epic poetry. "A lengthy battle for the novelisation of the other genres began, a battle to drag them into a zone of contact with reality", i.e. with credible reality as perceived and described by novelists such as Henry Fielding in England and Jean-Jacques Rousseau in France.[30] Writers came to prefer mutable and complex personalities; as a consequence, traditional literary forms with their unchanging, simple characters were either completely displaced by the new genre or, alternatively, became increasingly "novelised". In keeping with the new era, Zulika, as a well-rounded female character, would have been more at home in a romantic novel than in a (novelised) biblical epic.

Accordingly, *Joseph und Zulika* can be read as a true epic, but also as a novel (disguised in epic form). Read as an epic, it is the story of Joseph, a man whose virtue is put to the test. The evil spirit initiates the test by inspiring a beautiful woman with love for Joseph; she tempts the young man with her offer of love but is rejected, and thus the hero's virtue is established as unassailable. The problem with treating this tale as an epic is that in the telling the temptress and her psychology get a little too much attention, and in the end love is banished all too easily from her heart. These inconsistencies can be avoided in the second possible interpretation. Read as a novel, *Joseph und Zulika* tells the story of a young woman who, despite being married, falls in love with a young man. She does not refrain from revealing this love. Rejected, she suffers even more, and goes as far as having young Joseph punished. Eventually, she becomes resigned to her fate and forgets the episode. The second interpretation would take the story as prefiguring a notion that was soon to become characteristic of German novels in the age of *Sturm und Drang* (1770s): the idea that love, a natural force, cannot be willed or coerced; defying rational control, it works out its own and sometimes fateful dynamics. Read as a novel in epic disguise, Bodmer's *Joseph und Zulika* appears as a story about the irresistible and disturbing power of Eros.

The full implications of Bodmer's approach become visible not in his own poetry, but in that of one of his French contemporaries: *La Christiade ou Le Paradis reconquis, pour servir de suite au Paradis perdu de Milton* (Christiad, or Paradise Regained, a Sequel to Milton's Paradise Lost, 1753), by Abbé Jacques-François La Baume Desdossat.[31] Taking the Joseph story's scene of attempted seduction as prefiguring an event in the life of Christ, Desdossat invented a New Testament setting for the incident. His Mrs Potiphar is none other than Mary Magdalene, a woman of noble blood, beautiful, elegant, wealthy, well educated, of refined manners, and with a unique sensibility. Her only weakness is that she has a passion for men, and cannot decide which of her several lovers she should eventually marry. Incited by the devil (who appears in human form, in the guise of a handsome youth), she seeks to catch the attention of Jesus and include him among her lovers, and makes elaborate preparations to seduce him. Readers, critics, and state censors were scandalised by the (alleged) libertinism of *La Christiade*, denouncing it as a pernicious novel, and the Parliament of Paris had it burnt in 1756. The book did not disappear, however. Voltaire owned a copy and in 1772 published an essay on the scandalous passage "that makes every Christian's hair stand on end".[32]

Scandals like this contributed to the increasingly critical attitude towards, and indeed the impending crisis of, epic poetry. Friedrich Gottlieb Klopstock's *Messias* (1748–1773), another New Testament equivalent of Milton's *Paradise Lost*, was hailed by Bodmer with enthusiasm, but did not fare well with others.[33] It became the last biblical epic to be remembered, but no longer read, after initial publication. The decline of biblical epic poetry is reflected in the early literary career of Wieland. While living in Zurich, the young Wieland wrote one biblical epic himself: *Der geprüfte Abraham* (Abraham Tested, 1753). Written during his literary apprenticeship with Bodmer, in his master's style, and no doubt at his suggestion, it served well to prove his ability. Like his defence of Bodmer's *Joseph und Zulika*, it shows Wieland's closeness to and admiration for his patron. But soon, Wieland was having the doubts and second thoughts that were symptomatic of a period of cultural crisis. In a letter sent in December 1761 to a German correspondent, he expresses his dissatisfaction with biblical poetry – that of his former master, and his own. "Is it not improper and detrimental to religion", he reflects, "to translate the sacred stories into mere fairy tales in an oriental setting? – as seems to be the case with some of the epic poems of our master Bodmer and my own *Der geprüfte Abraham*".[34] Towards the end of the eighteenth century, critical opinion became even more pronounced. When he wrote his *Lives of the English Poets* (1779–1781), Samuel Johnson seized the first opportunity – publication of a biblical epic written by Abraham Cowley – to denounce the genre as essentially "frivolous and vain":

> Sacred history has been always read with submissive reverence, and an imagination over-awed and controlled. We have been accustomed to acquiesce in the nakedness and simplicity of the authentic narrative, and to repose on its veracity with such humble confidence and curiosity. We go with the historian as he goes, and stop with him when he stops. All amplification is frivolous and vain: all addition to that which is already sufficient for the purposes of religion seems not only useless, but in some degree profane.[35]

Johnson's passage thus pronounces a pious epitaph on biblical epic poetry. As a viable literary form, the biblical epic – and *all* epic poetry – declined after the eighteenth century, for the up and coming literary type was now the novel, a genre committed to prose and realism. The age of the epic had come to an end: very much in keeping with the aristocratic culture to which it belonged.

In Bodmer's time, however, the triumph of the novel was not yet complete. Latent conflict between the novel and the epic still characterised the situation of literature. The novel was the new, "modern" genre, marked by contemporary settings, realism, psychological explanation of the motives for human action, and the absence of divine intervention. Authors wrote novels for an increasingly wide and expanding readership. But despite the novel's success, some authors like Bodmer still considered the epic with its ancient setting, poetic diction (often rhymed), and supernatural apparatus the noblest and most sophisticated literary genre. It enjoyed the privilege of an ancient pedigree, for it echoed the art of Homer and Virgil. The epic, for Bodmer, ranked as the "masterpiece of poetry" (*Meister-Stück der Poesie*).[36] Apart from presupposing a thorough knowledge of classical literature, it challenged the writer to develop very special skills. Novel and epic thus represented not just two different literary genres, but two different approaches to reality and indeed two different worlds: one traditional and of venerable antiquity, and one innovative and contemporary. The former is represented by Rowe's *History of Joseph* and Bodmer's *Joseph und Zulika*, the latter by a book Bodmer included in the reading list he published in 1746 for the benefit of intelligent and receptive young ladies:[37] Henry Fielding's *Joseph Andrews*.

10

The Triumph of Chaste Love – Fielding

Henry Fielding (1707–1754) ranks as one of his generation's foremost English writers. He started professional life as a playwright and manager of a theatre, then became a successful lawyer, began writing novels, and ended his career as a justice of the peace and magistrate. For most of his life he lived in and around London. Historians emphasise his contribution to the reform of England's legal system and to the creation of a modern police force. *The History of the Adventures of Joseph Andrews* (1742), the first comic novel in English and the first biblical novella recast in a modern setting, inaugurated Fielding's career as a writer. His later, much longer novel *Tom Jones* (1749), generally considered his masterpiece, still finds many readers today.

Fielding's literary career marks the transition from the age of the theatre (the late sixteenth and the seventeenth centuries, dominated by Shakespeare and Molière) to the age of the novel (the eighteenth and nineteenth centuries, with Swift, Rousseau, Goethe, Dickens and Dostoevsky). Together with his contemporary Samuel Richardson (1689–1761), Fielding created the modern English novel and established its reputation as the leading form of literary expression that was to surpass the theatre in impact and popularity. Both Richardson and Fielding must be considered moralists: writers who sought to foster virtue and social responsibility by characterising good men and women as well as exposing vanity and hypocrisy. The didactic aim of *Joseph Andrews* is particularly evident; as we shall see, this novel's titular hero Joseph echoes the figure of the biblical patriarch as well as some of his trials and triumphs. We will begin with a condensed account of *The History of the Adventures of Joseph Andrews and of His Friend Mr Abraham Adams*, as the full title reads.[1]

Joseph Andrews: a summary

> The setting is England, the time around 1700. After the death of his father, a member of the landed gentry, Mr Wilson leaves his home town

for London. There the young gentleman – he is only sixteen – indulges in a life of leisure, squandering his property by spending on fashionable clothing, parties, drinking, and, most especially, women. He also gets involved with a society of freethinkers and libertines who are convinced that belief in God is nonsense for there is no evidence for God's existence. Owing to his vanity and dissolute lifestyle, the pleasure-seeking rake one day finds himself deserted by his friends and in the debtors' prison. But if a man who at heart is virtuous lacks money, it will somehow find him. It comes in this instance from Harriet Hearty, daughter of a London acquaintance. Taking pity on him, she sends him money, allowing him to regain his freedom. The two marry, and after some engagement in business, they decide to disentangle themselves from the vain and vicious affairs of the world. This is achieved by retiring to the country, to Somerset, where they raise their children in an idyllic environment. Unfortunately, however, their infant son is abducted by "wicked travelling people whom they call gypsies", to their great sorrow.[2] Despite this unfortunate incident, Mr Wilson and his wife Harriet continue to lead a quiet life of rural bliss, marked by simplicity, mutual love, hospitality to guests, and charity to their neighbours.

The stolen infant does not stay long with the gypsies; he ends up in the care of Gaffar and Gammar Andrews, a humble couple who already have one child, Pamela. Both Pamela and Joseph (for this is the name they give their adopted son) in time enter the service of the Booby family, influential members of the nobility. Pamela, having successfully resisted her master's unwelcome advances, impresses the young Squire Booby and eventually marries him. By the age of ten, Joseph is a footman for another branch of the Booby clan, initially working in the stables caring for Sir Thomas Booby's horses. From infancy he has known Fanny Goodwill, a girl of equally humble background, just two years younger than he, and their childhood friendship develops into deeply felt love. Fanny also enters service in the Booby household. One day, however, beautiful Fanny loses her job, due to the jealousy of Lady Booby's maid. In order to stay near Joseph, she finds work on a farm and thus remains in the parish. At seventeen Joseph becomes a personal manservant to Lady Booby, an office to which he is promoted on account of his good looks. Lady Booby, accompanied by Joseph and her maid Mrs Slipslop, stays more often at her London residence than at Booby Hall in Somerset; this is especially true after the death of Sir Thomas. Now a widow, Lady Booby seeks to console herself, consolation mostly being sought from none other than Joseph.

In the city, where social mores are less strict than elsewhere, Lady Booby invites the young man into her bedroom where she, almost nude, seeks to seduce the boy. Her memorable discourse about kissing as a prelude to other things remains unapplied, for her dear "Joey" resists temptation by pretending not to understand what his mistress is after. He also has to spurn the advances of Mrs Slipslop. When the latter falsely accuses him of having made one of the other servant girls pregnant, Lady Booby sends him packing. He not only leaves the Booby residence, he also leaves the city – not, as one might suppose, to go home to his parents, but to go back to his (now former) mistress's parish, in search of Fanny. During his wanderings, he falls into the hands of a band of highwaymen who rob him of what little he has and leave him, stripped and beaten, for dead by the roadside. Fortunately, a coach passes. Although most of the passengers are against picking up the unfortunate victim, the postilion gives him a coat, his only outer garment, and takes him on board. At the coach's first stop, a country inn called the Dragon, the nineteen-year-old chambermaid Betty takes pity on the badly bruised and shivering Joseph, and nurses him at the inn. When Joseph begins to recover, she enters his room one night, and not only to offer him a warming pan: she also seeks to join him in bed. As before, the young man resists. He gets up, pushes her out of the room, and locks the door. Disappointed but in a state of arousal, Betty immediately sleeps with her lustful master, the proprietor of the inn, who has been waiting for such an opportunity. Both adulterers are duly punished by the innkeeper's garrulous wife who brings the episode smartly to a close by dismissing Betty from the inn; at this point, Betty vanishes from the story.

Continuing on his way to Somerset, Joseph chances upon his mentor and friend, the country parson Abraham Adams, a jolly, good-natured man. Adams is travelling in the opposite direction, to London, to find a publisher for his sermons, but at an inn realises that, through an oversight, he has left his manuscript at home. Ever intent on assisting those in need, he decides to give up the idea of going to the city; instead, he accompanies Joseph to help him find Fanny. By chance, Joseph and Adams get separated as they travel. Alone on the road, the good parson happens to turn up just in time to come to the rescue of a young lady as a ruffian tries to ravish her; once the miscreant is turned away and disappears from the scene, Adams realises that it is none other than Fanny whom he has helped. Like Joseph, Fanny excels in chastity, and always manages (often with the help of others) to defend her virginity against the assaults of lustful men. Soon after Adams has met Fanny, the two are joined by Joseph, and they continue together on their frequently interrupted journey home to Somerset.

Lady Booby eventually returns from London to Booby Hall, her country seat, and learns of Joseph and Fanny's return to the parish. She approaches a lawyer to help her to persuade Fanny to move on. As for Joseph, she hesitates. Mrs Slipslop, her confidante, forgoes her own ambitions; instead, she encourages her mistress to marry Joseph. Lady Booby, still lusting for the handsome young man, considers the idea, but rejects it; it seems preferable to have Joseph sent to jail. In the end, all her nefarious schemes fail. As it happens, Joseph and Fanny become profoundly confused upon learning that they are actually brother and sister, making their marriage impossible. They plan to stay together in an eternal bond of chaste love. But soon the truth is revealed: Joseph is not the blood brother of Fanny; he is the son of Mr Wilson. To everyone's surprise, Fanny turns out to be Pamela's sister.

After these astonishing disclosures, Squire Booby, husband to Joseph's supposed sister Pamela, brings order to the situation: he rescues Joseph and Fanny from their legal impasse, reconciles Joseph to Lady Booby, and buys Joseph a new suit. Lady Booby invites everyone concerned – including Joseph, Fanny, and also Adams – to Booby Hall for a celebration. As it is getting late, every guest is assigned a chamber for the night. That night develops into one of confusion, mistaken identities, and much embarrassment (if not hilarity). Beau Didapper, a friend of the family, wishing to visit Fanny in her bedroom, by mistake enters Mrs Slipslop's room, and the two enjoy an embrace – she thinking it is Joseph, he mistaking her for Fanny. As the truth dawns, Slipslop cries for help, accusing him of rape, and Adams, quick as ever to arrive on the scene, lets the culprit escape but treats Slipslop, instead of Didapper, to a blow of his fist. Upon returning to his room, the parson by mistake enters Fanny's bedroom and falls soundly asleep lying next to her, to be surprised, next morning, by Joseph entering the chamber to greet his sweetheart. Until Joseph learns what has happened, he is ready to punish even his beloved mentor for any impropriety.

At the end of this comedy of love, errors, surprises, and revelations, Joseph Wilson and Fanny Andrews get married, and live happily ever after – not in the city, but in the countryside, on their own estate near that of his father. As for Lady Booby, she returns to London, where a young captain helps her forget all about Joseph.

Sources

Authors may generally be said to construct their work on the basis of two different methods. According to the first, they "invent" what they write – the characters, the place and plot – independently, drawing upon their rich and fertile imagination; at any rate, this is how most people envisage the mechanism underlying creative writing, and there is certainly some truth in this perception. The second method, emphasised more by specialist researchers in literature than by the general reader, consists of "reusing" and "adapting" what they find, as more or less ready building blocks, in the vast repertoire of earlier literature – persons, plots, scenarios, descriptions, ideas, and the like. A literary work that relies predominantly on the second method appears as a mosaic of quotations, allusions, echoes, and borrowings. Fielding has certainly used both methods in the writing of *Joseph Andrews*, and he has done so to good effect. In the following initial approach to his novel, we will look at his sources. While some of these are well concealed, others are obvious or even indicated by the author himself.

Fielding took inspiration from four main sources: *An Ethiopian Story*, also known as *The Adventures of Theagenes and Chariclea* by the ancient writer Heliodorus (third or fourth century CE); the novel *Pamela, or Virtue Rewarded* (1740) by Samuel Richardson; the biblical book of Genesis; and *Le Roman comique*, a French novel by Paul Scarron, dating from the seventeenth century (1651–1657). All the main features of *Joseph Andrews* can be explained as deriving from these four texts.

The *Ethiopian Story* is the longest and perhaps most influential of the ancient romances that have come down to us. This book began to fascinate English audiences in the sixteenth century, and in 1717 a new translation was published in London.[3] It is from Heliodorus that Fielding derived the overall plot of *Joseph Andrews*. Both Heliodorus and, imitating him, Fielding tell the story of two young, exceptionally beautiful, chaste, and pious lovers who are separated, united, and again separated (and so on) in a rapid succession of adventurous travel episodes. The story is developed as a series of carefully designed phases:

the love of hero and heroine
the journey of the lovers
arrival at the destination
the marriage.

The second phase – the lovers' journey which takes up most of the story – includes dramatic scenes such as abductions, the intervention of the lovers' guide and mentor (a role admirably played by Adams), and unexpected mishaps. Whatever befalls the loving pairs Theagenes and Chariclea (in Heliodorus) and Joseph and Fanny (in Fielding), while seemingly hindering them from reaching their goal, does in truth bring them closer and closer to it. Hero and heroine are treated as characters of equal status and are given comparable roles, any implied chivalric superiority on the part of the hero being avoided. This feature, prominent in Fielding's novel, is inherited from Heliodorus. "What is especially surprising to the reader of the modern romantic novel", comments David Konstan, "is the extent to which the actions and reactions of the hero and heroine in the Greek novel are alike. Both tend to be represented as victims, both give way to tears, lamentations, and despair, sometimes in language that is all but identical. Correspondingly, the novels eschew episodes in which the hero intervenes actively to save the heroine. There are no scenes in which the valiant lover comes to the rescue of his lady."[4] In addition to the general structure, one can also find details Fielding has borrowed from his ancient model. Just as Chariclea is happily recognised, at the very end, as an Ethiopian princess, Joseph at long last is acknowledged as the son of Mr Wilson, a member of the English gentry. In both cases, the recognition relies upon certain bodily features that reflect something their mothers saw or thought about while pregnant: the physiognomy and colouring of a portrayed white goddess in the case of fair Chariclea, and strawberries that caused Joseph Andrews to be born with a strawberry birthmark.[5]

When reading Heliodorus, Fielding was no doubt reminded of the fact that much of the earlier ancient literature, including the Bible and Homer, gives readers little guidance in their inevitable attempts to visualise its heroes and heroines, say Jesus in the Gospels or Penelope in the *Odyssey*. Nothing is revealed about hair, skin tone, eyes or any remarkable physical features of these figures; they have names, but not faces; we learn nothing about their typical gestures and manner of speaking; nor are we told much about their clothing. Heliodorus, like other writers in late antiquity, departs from this tradition by actually describing characters. Fielding follows him, and his portrait of Joseph Andrews merits close analysis:

> Mr. Joseph Andrews was now in the one and twentieth year of his age. He was of the highest degree of middle stature. His limbs were put together with great elegance and no less strength. His legs and thighs were formed in the exactest proportion. His shoulders were broad and brawny; but yet his arms hung so easily that he had all the symptoms of strength without the least clumsiness. His hair was of a nut-brown colour, and was displayed in wanton ringlets down his back. His forehead was high, his eyes dark and as full of sweetness as of fire. His nose a little inclined to the

Roman. His teeth white and even. His lips full, red, and soft. His beard was only rough on his chin and upper lip; but his cheeks, in which his blood glowed, were overspread with a thick down. His countenance had a tenderness joined with a sensibility inexpressible. Add to this the most perfect neatness in his dress, and an air which, to those who have not seen many noblemen, would give an idea of nobility.[6]

We can almost see Joseph Andrews standing in front of us. But whereas the contours of his body are sketched only in outline, his head and face are awarded detailed description. Several elements here echo other literary portraits Fielding must have known and used for his description. The hero's eyes "as full of sweetness as of fire" no doubt echo Heliodorus's reference to Theagenes's eyes that "sparkled like fire, and at once carried sweetness and terror".[7] Joseph's "broad and brawny" shoulders reflect the "shoulders largely spread" of Theagenes and, it must be added, Adam's "shoulders broad" in Milton's *Paradise Lost*.[8] Adam's "fair large front" (in Milton) corresponds to "his forehead was high" in Fielding's portrait of Joseph. From Milton, but this time from the description of Eve and not Adam, come the "wanton ringlets" characteristic of Joseph's hair. The "thick down" on Joseph's cheeks is again from Heliodorus. Fielding, in other words, developed his portrait of Joseph from elements he found in Heliodorus's novel and in Milton's *Paradise Lost*. The literary portrait of Joseph Andrews, in other words, is the skilful composition of a *poeta doctus*.

For several of his characters, Fielding resorted to sources other than Heliodorus. The very name of the titular "Joseph Andrews" makes the novel a counterpart to *Pamela, or Virtue Rewarded*, Samuel Richardson's famous novel whose protagonist is "Pamela Andrews". The triple theme of chastity, rejection of erotic advances, and eventual marriage is clearly borrowed from Richardson, though transferred from a heroine (Pamela) to a hero (Joseph). Some of the characters present in Richardson's novel reappear in the work of Fielding: Pamela as Joseph's sister, Mr B. as Pamela's husband Squire Booby. Those who turn from Richardson's novel to *Joseph Andrews* find themselves in a narrative world with which they are already familiar. Fielding had of course not only read Richardson and Heliodorus; he often relied on a source with which many of his contemporary readers were thoroughly familiar – the Bible. After having read just a few pages of the novel, the reader realises that the eponymous hero's character, as well as his first name – Joseph – has biblical connotations. In fact, a close reading reveals that all the leading characters of *Joseph Andrews* have their counterparts, and indeed models, in the book of Genesis. The clergyman Abraham Adams echoes his namesake Abraham, for he too is called by God into service, and is held up as someone who exemplifies true faith in divine providence. Like his biblical namesake, the parson appears as a dedicated and compassionate father. When for a moment he believes he has lost one of his little sons, he seems to be being tested by God just as the biblical Abraham was tested when he was asked to sacrifice his son Isaac. The patriarch Jacob finds his equivalent in Mr Wilson, for Jacob, like Wilson, lost a son only to find him again very much later. Potiphar's wife is given more than one equivalent: Lady Booby, Mrs Slipslop, and the chambermaid Betty all seek to seduce the novel's titular hero. At the end of the novel, after having slept with Beau Didapper, Mrs Slipslop falsely accuses her lover of rape, thus again echoing the biblical episode. Joseph Wilson alias Joseph Andrews is patterned on the biblical Joseph; of this the seduction scenes provide the clearest evidence. Fielding is quite explicit in this case, for he has the protagonist write to his sister Pamela: "I hope I shall copy your example, and that of Joseph, my namesake, and maintain my virtue against all temptations."[9] The letter-writer assumes that the relevant biblical story is as well known to his sister as to himself, and Fielding is confident that any further explanation is equally unnecessary for the reader. By implication, Fielding suggests that the Andrews children grew up with the Joseph story, and this would be in keeping with contemporary English practice (see above, Chapter 4).

We should not misunderstand Fielding's use of biblical figures, however; the writer has no intention of reproducing the scriptural account; nor does the scriptural text serve as the authoritatively invoked basis of moral instruction. In fact, Fielding adapts the biblical model to his purposes, for instance by emphasising that Joseph Andrews, unlike the biblical Joseph, demonstrates fidelity not to a man (his master Potiphar) but to a woman (his childhood sweetheart, Fanny). The biblical model, moreover, always stays discreetly in the background; never actually controlling the course of the novel, it is more subtly present as a hidden intertext.

The fourth source to be mentioned is Paul Scarron's *Le Roman comique*, a novel available to Fielding in an English translation of 1712.[10] Fielding's tantalisingly brief reference to Scarron[11] in *Joseph Andrews* disguises rather than reveals the fact that for literary style, burlesque episodes typically set in an inn, and the general comic atmosphere he is indebted to the seventeenth-century French author. Like Scarron, Fielding tells two stories at the same time: the serious, on-going narrative concerning the two lovers, and the discontinuous sequence of light-hearted burlesque episodes. In both threads of the story, the voice of the narrator is heard clearly, never missing an opportunity to contribute to the humorous atmosphere. This is how Scarron's book begins:

> Bright Phoebus had already performed about half his career; and his chariot having passed the meridian, and got on the declivity of the sky, rolled on swifter than he desired. [. . .] To speak more like a man, and in

plainer terms, it was betwixt five and six of the clock, when a cart came into the market place of Mans.[12]

Fielding imitates Scarron's ironic use of ancient mythological motifs as follows:

> Now Thetis the good housewife began to put on the pot in order to regale the good man Phoebus, after his daily labours were over. In vulgar language, it was in the evening when Joseph attended his lady's orders.[13]

Scarron can be credited with inventing this ironic juxtaposition of sublime mythological references and mundane scenes of contemporary domesticity to alert the reader that an important, though thoroughly comical, episode is about to follow.

Fielding, again in imitation of Scarron, divides his novel into short chapters with humorous headings such as "Chapter VII. A scene of roasting, very nicely adapted to the present taste and times" and "Chapter VIII. Which some readers will think too short, and others too long".[14] Of the narrator's many dry-humoured interjections, it suffices to quote but one: when Joseph is accidentally stranded with an unpaid bill at the Dragon, the narrator remarks that "as we cannot therefore at present get Mr. Joseph out of the inn, we shall leave him in it, and carry our reader on".[15] Fielding borrowed all of these techniques directly from Scarron. Following and no doubt surpassing the style of *Le Roman comique*, Fielding created a novel that masks – while commending – its moral message with a unique lightness of touch.

Scenes of seduction

Fielding was not only a *poeta doctus*, widely read and able to draw upon a vast body of literature; he was also a skilful storyteller who created a firm narrative based on an ideological structure designed to accommodate and give coherent meaning to the many literary materials borrowed from other sources, both ancient and modern. The figure of the seductress, a person or persons echoing archetypal Mrs Potiphar, is vital to his story. In comical writing, the equivalent of this biblical character no longer functions as a real threat to the young man she attempts to seduce; here, the seducer and, no less, the party to be seduced are portrayed as essentially comical figures interacting in a situation that mixes the erotic and the funny at the expense of the original gravity of the scene. One example – of many[16] – can be found in Scarron's *Roman comique*. At a country wedding, Madame Bouvillon seeks to seduce a young man named Le Destin, a scene Scarron uses for satirical development by describing how she reveals to him "near the third part of her bosom" and invites the trembling man to give her a back massage.[17] Eventually, the two are interrupted: when Madame answers the knock at the door the messenger flings it open and she gets hit in her face. A similar atmosphere of farce pervades the corresponding scenes in Fielding's novel.

In *Joseph Andrews*, the seductress is represented by three characters: Lady Booby, Mrs Slipslop, and Betty. A master of his craft, Fielding combines repetition with variation. The triptych of seduction is almost symmetrical: in the first scene, Lady Booby is in bed and, taking the young man's hand, asks Joseph to join her; in the second, middle scene, there is no bed in sight; instead, Slipslop, sharing a drink with Joseph, almost throws herself on him, though is prevented from doing so. Betty, the third seductress, enters Joseph's chamber when he is in bed. A brief look at each of the three scenes is in order.

The noble widow lusts for Joseph, though well aware of the fact that any amorous gesture towards the servant would be inappropriate and beneath her. Fielding was no doubt acquainted with the elaboration of the underlying biblical scene in Josephus's *Jewish Antiquities* where Mrs Potiphar tells Joseph that "she was forced, though she were his mistress, to condescend beneath her dignity";[18] Fielding echoes the sentence by putting it into the mouth of Joseph Andrews: "I should think your ladyship condescended a great deal below yourself".[19] Discarding any such scruples along with half her attire, she unashamedly summons Joseph to her bedside: "The lady being in bed, called Joseph to her, bade him sit down, and, having accidentally laid her hand on his [. . ., she] raised herself a little in her bed, and discovered one of the whitest necks that ever was seen; at which Joseph blushed."[20] This scene is intended to be an unambiguous description of what Fielding and early readers would have identified not only as provocative, but also as sinful, immoral behaviour.

It is instructive to see how the novel's illustrators handled the matter. The earliest illustration showing Lady Booby and her servant in conversation pictures her in bed, shoulders and bosom bared, holding the hand of reluctant Joseph (Fig. 11). No viewer can miss the stark contrast between the hesitant, fully liveried servant and the almost naked woman who seeks to kindle the young man's desire by flagrantly displaying her charms. Unnoticed in the background, Mrs Slipslop views the scene, wringing her hands in desperation, horrified at the prospect of Lady Booby, rather than herself, winning Joseph's favour.

A later illustrator, in a more artistically executed engraving, avoids visualising the bedroom episode. He replaced it with another scene, decorously set in the parlour, where Lady Booby sits on a chair, wearing a long society gown, a fine apron (purely ornamental), and a *dormeuse*: a cap with ribbons to adorn her up-swept hair. She berates her servant as he again refuses to comply with her wishes (Fig. 12). "Your virtue! Intolerable confidence!" she exclaims.

Fig. 11. *Lady Booby Seeks to Seduce Her Servant* – to no avail. The maid Mrs Slipslop, who witnesses the bedroom scene, is shocked, because she herself lusts for the handsome servant Joseph. – James Hulett, 1743, for Henry Fielding, *The History of the Adventures of Joseph Andrews*.

Fig. 12. *Lady Booby, Angry with Her Servant.* Speaking a second time of love to reluctant Joseph makes her ladyship angry and leads to the dismissal of her servant. – James Heath, 1780, for Henry Fielding, *The History of the Adventures of Joseph Andrews.*

"Have you the assurance to pretend that, when a lady demeans herself to throw aside the rules of decency, in order to honour you with the highest favour in her power, your virtue should resist her inclination?"[21] Lady Booby's charms are left to the reader's as well as to Joseph's imagination. Joseph, good-looking and elegantly dressed, is standing, as befits a servant, turned away from her. The artist has expertly captured Joseph's new interest in conspicuously fine clothing, as indicated by Fielding: liveried as a typical footman in an upper-class household, he wears a well-fitted velvet coat, white shirt, waistcoat, knee breeches, stockings, and buckled shoes, all of which convey and celebrate his new-found status. Equally well rendered is his bearing through which the young man, though outwardly corrupted by the manners of the city, defends his inner purity. Interestingly, a later and equally well-executed illustration reverts to the bedroom scene (Fig. 13). This engraving looks like a synthesis of the other two: the lady, half undressed in bed, echoes the first illustration, while Joseph, though seated, closely replicates the liveried and prudent servant of the second. The illustrator makes use here (as in the first

Fig. 13. *Lady Booby Seeks to Seduce Her Servant* – but Joseph, though sitting on her bed, turns away, apparently unimpressed by her charms. The scene, set in an elegant bedroom, echoes earlier illustrations of the episode (see above, Figs 11 and 12). – Charles Warren, 1799, for Henry Fielding, *The History of the Adventures of Joseph Andrews*.

illustration) of a well-established artistic device: artists often place a clothed servant in their depictions of nude, seductive women. The dressed figure serves to contrast with and highlight the female nude, emphasising the erotic element. In looking at Lady Booby, viewers could satisfy their sexual curiosity; turning their attention to the servant who, though sitting, turns away from her, they can appreciate Fielding's moral message.

Nevertheless, the message of the first seduction episode was not clear to all early readers. One anonymous reviewer expressed his misgivings. "We are told that the chief end of these pieces is the extirpation of vice, and the promotion of virtue", he comments in 1751 on the English novel.[22] In general, he reflects, novels for the most part perform well in this respect. "But we fear this grand rule has in some places been too much disregarded", the critic adds, offering *Joseph Andrews* as an example:

> As the works of Mr. Fielding are in everybody's hands, there ought not to be a line in them which should cause the modestest lady a single blush in the perusal. This delicacy of style and sentiment has been quite neglected in some dialogues between the wanton Lady Booby and most innocent Joseph Andrews; and more particularly so in one chapter, which must occur to the remembrance of every reader conversant with these works.[23]

The erotic scenes in the novel, while perhaps the most memorable, are also felt to be the most offensive. While at first sight this criticism seems to be a straightforward moral critique, a second reading reveals a rather paradoxical and ambivalent attitude: moralising polemic goes hand in hand with an intense, though often covert, interest in, and enjoyment of, erotic incidents and narratives. Secret curiosity is combined with equally strong moral censure, titillation with edification. Doubtless Fielding shared this paradoxical attitude with other eighteenth-century authors. By teaching virtue while secretly deriving a certain scandalised delight in erotic transgression, he created a work that "could be praised from the pulpit and yet attacked as pornography, a work that gratified the reading public with the combined attractions of a sermon and a striptease".[24]

The second seduction scene, the one involving Mrs Slipslop, repeats the challenge for the hero, cast this time in comical guise. After having been rejected by Joseph, Slipslop runs to her mistress to complain about the unwilling servant. Joseph, according to the lady's maid, is a young man of dubious character, known among the servants as a man renowned for his sexual prowess. There is not one of the servant girls with whom Joseph does not wish to sleep, and one of them he has actually made pregnant. "He is so lewd a rascal that if your ladyship keeps him much longer, you will not have one virgin in your house except myself", the maid declares.[25] Fielding is using here the cliché of the servant as an unreliable, morally deficient person, a cliché matched by its equally prominent counterpart of the good, trusted, and loyal servant. His immediate inspiration no doubt came from a passage found in Philo of Alexandria. In Philo's *On Joseph*, Potiphar's wife accuses her servant not only of the attempt to rape her, but of general sexual misbehaviour. "Not content with simply taking his fellow-serving-women," she tells her husband, "so utterly lewd and lascivious is he that he even attempted to force himself upon me – his mistress!"[26] Both Potiphar's wife, in Philo's retelling of the biblical episode, and Mrs Slipslop, in Fielding's novel, present Joseph's alleged misbehaviour as the culmination of the servant's immorality, demonstrated in word and deed.

The third seduction episode centres on the figure of Betty, the chambermaid. On his way home from London to Somerset, Joseph Andrews is robbed by highwaymen. Betty, chambermaid of an inn, takes pity on him, nurses him, but also shows erotic interest in the handsome, though uncooperative, young man. The episode appears to echo elements of two passages from ancient literature, one from Apuleius and one from Homer. Apuleius writes of a man named Socrates (not to be confused with the famous philosopher of the same name), a poor traveller who, after being robbed of everything he has, ends up in an inn where Meroe, the attractive innkeeper, takes pity on him.[27] She treats him kindly but then, aroused by lust, welcomes him into her bed, and they make love. Since the relationship proves disastrous, Socrates one day secretly takes to the road to escape from her. But Fielding's Betty also has her counterpart in the Homeric nymph Calypso. Homer's *Odyssey* tells the story of Odysseus, king of Ithaca, who after ten years of wandering returns home from the Trojan War to rejoin his faithful wife, Penelope. One of the most elaborate, and idyllic, episodes tells of the shipwrecked protagonist's fate.[28] Rescued on a remote island by Calypso, the hero is lovingly nursed by this beautiful nymph, and subsequently spends several years in her care. She hopes one day to marry him, promises him immortality, and tries by many tricks to make him forget his home. Will the Greek hero yield to these wiles and spend the rest of his life in Calypso's cave on the island of Ogygia? No, he does not, for he remembers his beloved country, his people, and his wife, and he longs to return to them. He passes much time pensively sitting on the shore, sadly considering his fate. Eventually, the gods decide that the yearning Odysseus should be allowed to make his way home, and they send Hermes as a messenger to fair Calypso, ordering her to let him go. Calypso, enraged, curses the gods, calling them unjust, cruel, heartless, and envious of her, for jealousy denying her the happiness she longs for. However, having calmed down and having bethought herself, the nymph decides to be reasonable and to give in. Hurrying down to the sea, she finds Odysseus nostalgically looking out upon the barren ocean, moaning and heartbroken with sorrow. She takes pity on him and tells him of her decision to let him go home. Following her advice, Odysseus fells trees and builds a raft in preparation for the journey. Four days later, the raft, complete with mast and sail, is seaworthy. Supplied with ample provisions, Odysseus takes leave of the sorrowful nymph and sets sail. While Fielding's Betty incident is much less developed than Homer's Calypso episode, it is clear enough that Betty is a Calypso figure, translated from the divine and heroic world to the more prosaic realm of everyday eighteenth-century England. Those of his readers who recognise Fielding's sources, whether obscure or obvious, cannot help but enjoy these allusions and admire the skill with which our author adapts and interweaves them.

A consideration of the way the seduction scenes are built into the storyline of *Joseph Andrews* can help us discern the novel's essential structure. The scenes of seduction are differentiated by geographical location and by the social class to which the seductress belongs. When Lady Booby (upper class) and Mrs Slipslop (one step down the social ladder) try to seduce the boy, this happens in the city, but when Betty (one step down again) indulges in the same behaviour the setting is a country inn, located somewhere between the city and the country parish to which Joseph is travelling. The spatial dimension plays an important role in Fielding's art, for the author assigns a moral significance to the topographical continuum that stretches from the Boobys' stables in the rural parish to Lady Booby's bedroom in her London mansion, and, in reverse, from the London bedroom to Parson Adams's country church. This geographical continuum is divided up to form a tripartite system consisting of city, road, and country.

The city – always meaning London – has a bad image, for the novel treats it as "a world full of bustle, noise, hatred, envy, and ingratitude".[29] Moreover, it is a place of vice: loose morals, prostitution, gambling, drinking, ridiculing of the church, and of wasted lives. Once he is in London, even Joseph Andrews begins to adopt urban ways: he dresses fashionably (as was notorious among domestic servants of the well-to-do in London),[30] patronises the theatre, and behaves with less than total devotion when attending church services. Fashionable dress becomes important to him, and not only because he loves finery; no doubt he also wants to display his newly acquired social status, indicating his belonging, by association, to the higher ranks of society (see above, Figs 11 and 12). But Joseph did not completely and unreservedly identify with urban ways of life. "London is a bad place," he reflected in a letter sent to his sister, "and there is so little good fellowship that next-door neighbours don't know one another."[31] Since London behaviour corrupts the moral life, Fielding is at pains to stress that Joseph managed to retain his purity: "If he was outwardly a pretty fellow, his morals remained entirely uncorrupted."[32] The countryside, by contrast, stands for virtue, purity, and harmony, for a life lived under the guidance of the church. It does not come as a surprise that London was the place where Mr Wilson, as if in an initiation ritual, first became involved with all kinds of dubious women. Whereas he was sucked ever deeper into city life and increasingly controlled by loose women, his son Joseph later manages to disengage himself from the city by resisting its lures. When Lady Booby and her attendant unsuccessfully seek to put an end to Joseph's innocence, his resistance serves as an exit strategy that enables him to escape. His righteous refusal also shapes his personality; as someone who survives city life without being corrupted by it, he becomes a more mature person, indeed a sage whose wisdom is honed by experience.[33] In this respect, he is morally superior even to Parson Adams who, as someone never exposed to the city and its temptations, remains a childlike, essentially comical, though a thoroughly benevolent and amiable character. The presentation of the city as a place of temptation and trial and concomitant maturation prevents us from understanding Fielding's novel simply as a traditional comedy that functions with immutable, fixed characters. *Joseph Andrews*, an embryonic *Bildungsroman*, prefigures the novel of apprenticeship and moral formation, a genre which was to develop in the late eighteenth century, and of which *Wilhelm Meisters Lehrjahre* (Wilhelm Meister's Apprenticeship, 1795/96), by Goethe, is the foremost example.

After leaving the city, Joseph cannot immediately enter the countryside, the desired goal of his pilgrimage; he has to take to the road, the hybrid space that links the two realms without belonging to either. Here he is exposed to further trials.

The space between the city and the countryside proper, represented by the road, the coach, and Betty's Dragon Inn, is still in one sense and direction linked to the city and therefore to sin, crime, and moral confusion. Joseph is robbed by a gang of highwaymen – a realistic detail echoing the insecurity of the roads in eighteenth-century England.[34] Some of the problematic, sinful nature of the city is imported into the countryside by the coach carrying travellers from the city. The postilion alone, by giving his coat to the injured Joseph, prevents the coach from being a mere extension of the evil city and establishes its ambiguous, intermediate character as both welcoming and unfriendly at the same time. The Dragon Inn shares this dual ambience. Betty, the good-natured chambermaid at the inn, is not a complete sinner; moved by pity, she cares for the wounded, naked, and penniless Joseph, defending him against the inn's avaricious and uncharitable landlady and landlord. She takes an amorous interest in Joseph, but is duly locked out of his room. To make up for her disappointment, Betty invites seduction by her master, the landlord of the inn, thereby converting the Dragon into a place of adultery. In other words: the inn is a space with ambiguous status, a place neither completely wicked nor completely good. Parson Adams, in conversation with a host in a different locality, points out the mixed nature of the area through which they are travelling; when he meets some good honest folk, he is "glad to find some Christians left in the kingdom, for that he almost began to suspect that he was sojourning in a country inhabited only by Jews and Turks", i.e. by people not adhering to Christian morals and manners.[35] It is only in the countryside – ironically, symbolised by a village dominated by the country seat of the Booby family – that one can escape from vice and sin and develop the essential goodness inherent in human nature (a doctrine in which Fielding firmly believes).[36] The countryside, under the firm but kindly control of Parson Abraham Adams and his wise teaching, provides the ideal setting for a virtuous and charitable life. Somerset, for Fielding, was apparently an idyllic, almost mythical region; there he was born and spent the first three years of his life. There, in Somerset, everyone can imitate, as Parson Adams affirms, "the manner in which the people had lived in the Golden Age".[37] This Golden Age is staged in the novel's comical climax at Booby Hall, when Parson Adams can sleep with Fanny in one bed (never laying a finger on her, of course), and Beau Didapper succeeds in entering Slipslop's bed to satisfy his lustful desires and yet escapes punishment. Situated in an area apparently steeped in rural innocence, Booby Hall is not a place of sin and concomitant tragedy but a place of hilarity and comical confusion. The countryside alone, it seems, can provide the truly appropriate setting for the comedy, because only there can we be reconciled with the imperfections inherent in our human nature. In comedy, Hayden White explains, "hope is held out for the temporary triumph of man over his world by the prospect of occasional reconciliations of the forces at play in the social and natural worlds. Such reconciliations are symbolized in the festive occasions which the comic writer traditionally uses to terminate his dramatic accounts of change and transformation."[38] The night-time farce, as comic reconciliation, represents society "as being purer, saner, and healthier" than ever before.[39]

Joseph's symbolic journey from the city to the country parish of Parson Adams invites comparison with the great Puritan classic, *The Pilgrim's Progress*, by John Bunyan (1678, 1684), a book much read in Fielding's time. The first volume of Bunyan's novel recounts the lonely travels of its hero, a man named Christian, from the City of Destruction through an often inimical world to his true home, the Celestial City. The second volume repeats the story with a different set of characters and with a slightly different ending. Now it is Christian's wife Christiana, her maid Mercy, and her four sons who repeat the journey, though their adventures are less dramatic than those of Christian. Punctuated by prolonged stays at inns, Christiana's journey proceeds relatively smoothly, and her sons are even able to pick up wives along the way. At the end when, all by herself, Christiana crosses the river beyond which lie the celestial fields and eventually the heavenly Jerusalem, her children and their families stay behind in what seems to be a country parish where they become useful and honourable residents. Although the parish is not described by Bunyan, the context requires it to be thought of as rural rather than urban, for it is positioned somewhere between the City of Destruction and the Celestial City in a space too small to permit the presence of another urban community. Thus the plot of Bunyan's second volume implies the same tripartite topography as depicted in *Joseph Andrews*: the evil city, road and inns as intermediate space, and the country parish as the idealised locality for virtuous Christian living. The wayfaring of Fielding's heroes symbolises an underlying intention: it is a moral pilgrimage made from the vanity and corruption of the Great City to the simplicity and innate goodness of the country. In this respect Fielding, despite the slapstick comedy and mock-heroics, reminds us more of Bunyan than of Cervantes whose name he puts on the title page of his novel ("written in imitation of the manner of Cervantes").[40] Bunyan and Fielding as well as their numerous readers not only lived in the same early-modern England, but also inhabited the same morally symbolic space.

In addition to their connotations of chaos and harmony respectively, city and countryside have their individual metaphysical properties. They are amenable to different supernatural influences. The city, strictly speaking, is the realm not of God but of the devil, represented by the pagan deity Fortuna. This goddess deals with people apparently at random, for one day they may rise, succeed in establishing themselves in good positions, and gain a fortune; another day, they may lose everything and end up in the poorhouse. Caprice and inconsistency being her characteristics, people are left, willy-nilly, to suffer her whims. Symbolic of the dealings of Fortuna – or pure chance – is Mr Wilson's buying of a lottery ticket and selling it for next to nothing, only to learn later that it has won. The countryside, by contrast, is controlled by divine Providence, a power that leads and guides people towards marriage and settling down in quiet and cosy domesticity, far away from noisy, bustling, chaotic London.

At the end of the novel, Fielding offers a portrayal of Fanny reclining undressed in her bridal bed, waiting for Joseph to join her:

> She was soon undressed; for she had no jewels to deposit in their caskets, nor fine laces to fold with the nicest exactness. Undressing to her was properly discovering, not putting off ornaments; for as all her charms were the gifts of nature, she could divest herself of none. How, reader, shall I give thee an adequate idea of this lovely young creature? The

bloom of roses and lilies might a little illustrate her complexion, or their smell her sweetness; but to comprehend her entirely, conceive youth, health, bloom, neatness, and innocence in her bridal bed, conceive all these in their utmost perfection, and you may place the charming Fanny's picture before your eyes.[41]

The author of this passage studiously, and successfully, avoids all lascivious vulgarity by using abstract, rather than descriptive, terms: youth, health, bloom, neatness, innocence, perfection, and, to make up for the lack of descriptive detail, appeals to the reader's imagination. He even mentions the lily, the traditional symbol of virginal purity. The "roses and lilies" echo the biblical Song of Songs. Fielding thus moves from Lady Booby's seductive, sinful, and vulgar display to a very different kind of undress: that of the simple and chaste Fanny who in her innocent nuptial state seems to merge with Solomon's beloved bride in the Song of Songs, or indeed with the beautiful reclining Venus as painted by Renaissance artists such as Giorgione and Titian.[42] This idyllic scene far surpasses its vulgar equivalent, consigning the latter to oblivion.

The moral message

"It is a judicious and moral novel, full of wit and pleasing qualities, without the least stain of libertinage either of mind or of heart. It makes us love virtue", wrote a 1743 reviewer in appreciation of *Joseph Andrews*.[43] To teach the love of virtue, Fielding uses a seemingly simple narrative pattern: the biographical continuum leading from young adulthood to maturity and marriage. This pattern, while easy to understand, is complicated by the fact that Fielding uses it twice over, encoding the novel's moral message in the careers of both Mr Wilson and Joseph Andrews (alias Joseph Wilson, for it is eventually discovered that Mr Wilson is his father).

Mr Wilson tells his story as that of a typical libertine rake who in his youth moves to London where he spends his fortune on gambling and prostitutes. He ends up in the debtors' prison from which he is rescued by Harriet Hearty (a scene that echoes Fielding's own experience of being rescued from the same confinement by the charitable intervention of his sister Catharine).[44] The notion of a benefactress rescuing a man from prison was so dear to Fielding that he used it not only in *Joseph Andrews* but again in *Amelia*, a novel published ten years later (1752). The story of William Booth, told in *Amelia*, parallels that of Mr Wilson: failing as a gentleman farmer, he moves with his wife Amelia and family to London to make a living there. Corrupted by the city, he turns to gambling, and in prison succumbs to seduction by his fellow prisoner, Miss Matthews. Two accounts of rescue from successive prison terms form the substance of the story. First, it is Miss Matthews who pays for Booth's release; but when he finds himself in jail a second time, it is Amelia who comes to his rescue. She asserts her unfailing love for her husband and welcomes him back into her London home; as a haven free from the threats of city life, it may be termed an allegorical representation of the country, the only space where the story can have its appropriate ending.[45] After Booth's second release and his conversion to true Christianity, the family decides to leave London. This decision is facilitated by the discovery that Amelia had been cheated out of her inheritance. Once finances allow, the family retires to a country estate, to live there happily ever after. Thus, thanks to Amelia's strong moral character – and helped along by her inheritance – the couple at last find contentment in the countryside.

Eighteenth-century readers and modern biographers of Fielding agree that the twin stories of Mr Wilson and William Booth are eminently autobiographical accounts, reflecting as they do Fielding's own early life.[46] In his younger years Fielding, then a writer of comedies and political satires, could have been described as a mild version of a London libertine: a generally amiable person, but with a strong sexual appetite that he frequently indulged, and a leaning towards freethinking and irreverence towards the political and religious establishment. Around 1735, however, in his late twenties, he began to change from having libertine leanings to being a morally conscientious Christian believer. He later married and settled down. This development did not involve an abrupt change or conversion; Fielding simply grew up. If in his youth he was drawn to the company of rakes and freethinkers, the mature Fielding increasingly cultivated the friendship of learned clergymen, one of whom was Edward Young, immortalised as the amiable Parson Adams in the novel.[47] We also find him owning and reading religious books such as the three volumes of Isaac Barrow's theological works, no doubt at the suggestion of his friends among the clergy.[48]

In the works of Isaac Barrow (1633–1677), Fielding found one sermon particularly fascinating. Entitled "On Being Imitators of Christ", it explained to an audience of Cambridge students in 1661 that God has never failed to exalt individuals of sublime character whom he continually assists with gifts of his grace. Their constancy in faith and good works in times of adversity makes them models of piety and moral behaviour, for us to imitate and emulate. True, we may detect a certain distance between these giants of virtue and ourselves, but since the capacities of all are essentially alike, imitation is possible and indeed called for. Scripture offers numerous examples of virtuous men, one of them being Joseph, whose resistance to the assaults of sexual temptation makes him an outstanding exemplar. Barrow briefly evokes how Joseph rejects "the solicitations of an imperious mistress, advantaged by opportunities of privacy and solitude", and points out that his "refusal was attended with extreme danger and all the mischiefs which the disdain of a furious lust disappointed, of an outrageous jealousy provoked, of a loving master's confidence abused, could produce".[49] Referring to anyone who considers this example, Barrow asks, "how can he be ignorant of his duty in the like case?"[50] Apparently, the students of Cambridge, young men generally far away from their parental homes and supervision, needed to be reminded of Joseph the chaste. The preacher was palpably enchanted with the models provided by Scripture. Examples, he explains at length, are the very best media for teaching, clearly superior to precepts and abstract principles. "Piety abstractly viewed in precepts" is "an airy project, a name, a notion; but it, being seen in example, will prove a matter substantial, true, and feasible".[51] A good example, in fact, is "like a picture exposed to sense, having the parts orderly disposed and completely united, suitably clothed and dressed up in its circumstances, contained in a narrow compass, and perceptible by one glance, so easily insinuating itself into the fancy, and durably resting therein".[52] A good example, moreover, allows us to see at once "the thing done, the quality of the actor, the manner of doing, the minute seasons, measures, and adjuncts of the action".[53] An example lends a mere precept "a goodly corpulency, a life, a motion; renders it conspicuous, specious, and active".[54]

Isaac Barrow, a genius who reportedly spoke eight languages, was a mathematician of note (who relinquished his Cambridge chair in favour of none other than Isaac Newton), and a powerful preacher who died aged only forty-four. His sermons, published posthumously, were widely read. One reader, Henry Fielding, must have strongly and spontaneously agreed with the notion that the best way to teach is by presenting a moral example in full narrative detail. Inspired – or at least supported – by his reading of Barrow's sermon, Fielding's interest in the figure of Joseph was kindled. He decided to write the fictitious story of a modern Joseph – Joseph Andrews, boldly transposing the biblical figure from Egypt to England, and from ancient times to his own eighteenth century. If by this transposition Joseph lost the aura of a biblical saint, he gained in vivacity for a new, eighteenth-century audience that needed a model "easily insinuating itself into the fancy, and durably resting therein", to use the words of the preacher.

The details of Fielding's praise of chastity derive from two sources that the author cleverly combines: the Genesis story of Joseph, and the ancient romance of Chariclea and Theagenes. The message of chastity is reproduced, almost one to one, from the romance: the lovers, united by the bond of chaste friendship, go through ordeals in an essentially chaotic and alien world that provides no framework of stability. The couple's love, and nothing else, is fundamentally stable, reliable, and certain. Their mutual fidelity is highlighted through the contrapuntal function of the secondary characters. These unsuccessfully seek to force on Joseph a one-sided relationship that involves, in the case of Lady Booby, inequality in power and status. Through the two types of character – the chaste protagonists and the temptresses – the novel contrasts uncontrolled carnal passion with fidelity and socially sanctioned desire. Commenting on the seduction theme of ancient romances, David Konstan asserts that "the whole business is rather a sordid domestic drama, in contrast with which the primary romance seems the more exalted and spiritual, with its almost religious commitment to a chaste conjugal love".[55] Fielding, a careful reader of ancient stories, recognised what Konstan calls "the moral centre of the Greek novel"[56] and appropriated it for his own storytelling by placing the true, chaste love between Joseph and Fanny – the main theme of his narrative – in the midst of scenes of attempted seduction. As a matter of course, true love eventually celebrates its triumph.

Fielding's recommendation of chastity is firmly set against the background of a society in which loose manners were common. In a satirical yet apt description of behaviour, the author has Lady Booby characterise the libertine morality of her age. "I am out of patience," cries the Lady; "did ever mortal hear of a man's virtue? Did ever the greatest, or the gravest men pretend to any of this kind? Will magistrates who punish lewdness, or parsons who preach against it, make any scruple of committing it? And can a boy, a stripling, have the confidence to talk of his virtue?"[57] The implication is that virtue (meaning sexual restraint), though generally expected of women, is quite unheard of among men; lustful Lady Booby, in other words, accepts and seeks to take advantage of a double-standard morality.[58] But in Fielding's generation, moralists sought to tighten the rules by urging men also to embrace the ideal of chastity. The "character of male chastity", our author declares in the opening chapter of *Joseph Andrews*, is "doubtless as desirable and becoming in one part of the human species as in the other".[59] Or, as Fielding has Joseph explain in a letter: "Mr. Adams has often told me that chastity is as great a virtue in a man as in a woman."[60] Accordingly, the chaste male should no longer be regarded as un-masculine and somehow effeminate. Early eighteenth-century English moralists even debated about kissing in public, and – successfully, it seems – advocated more puritanical rules regarding the etiquette of social kissing.[61] By invoking the biblical precedent of Joseph, Fielding upholds the ideal of chastity for men. The result would be a more civilised, morally responsible form of masculinity. Chastity, moreover, helps preserve social peace and harmony, for extramarital affairs, Fielding feels, are "a catastrophe, common enough, and comical enough too perhaps, in modern history, yet often fatal to the repose and well-being of families, and the subject of many tragedies, both in life and on the stage".[62]

Fielding not only holds up the virtue of male chastity, he also seeks to define the role a woman may have in the life of a virtuous man. This role is highly ambivalent, for on the one hand, a woman may endanger a man's moral life when behaving as a seductress; on the other, she may promote a man's moral perfection and indeed support his entire existence. Under the influence of the city, women may become, if not evil, then at least lustful, dominated by a strong sexual appetite; often they ruin an innocent man. Such was the experience of Mr Wilson, when as a young gentleman he came to London. The same fate would have befallen Joseph, had it not been for Fanny, who, as a steadfast source of moral force and direction in Joseph's life, gave him the courage to resist the advances of Lady Booby, Mrs Slipslop, and Betty. Chambermaid Betty, actually, is morally half-way on the side of divine providence, because in taking in the naked and starving Joseph, she acted as the instrument of God.

Where virtue and charity begin, the domination of evil ends. While Harriet and Amelia (not to forget Betty) reflect God's visible and dramatic intervention in moments of extreme distress, Fanny stands for the more subtle, unobtrusive, quiet and beneficent presence of Providence in a man's life. She is there, implicitly, from the very start, and her hidden presence prevents Joseph Andrews from succumbing to temptation. (At this point it may be remembered that the Bible itself distinguishes between two types of divine intervention: as Saviour, God stages dramatic, often miraculous events to rescue his friends from danger; as the one who presides over nature and human life, he blesses all of his creation, enabling it to stay intact and healthy.) Whether they rescue a man in highly visible dramatic fashion, or are just a benign presence underpinning men's moral lives, women have a redemptive quality, and Fielding's masterpiece *Joseph Andrews* patently celebrates this notion, while never imposing it on the reader through dry didactic pedantry.

In his life of Mr Wilson, Fielding tells a realistic (though fictionalised) account of his own early years. The life of Joseph Andrews also seems to be autobiographical, though in a more complex and subtle sense. In the figure of his hero, Fielding reinvented himself as an ideal character, a young man never driven by lust or assailed by temptation, but from the start deeply committed to chaste love. In Joseph Andrews, Fielding portrays his ideal self: the self he came to assume in the same measure as he abandoned the libertine ways of his earlier years. In addition to being a literary masterpiece, *Joseph Andrews* also embodies the new moral creed chosen by the author and open to adoption within wider contemporary society.

IV
THE ICON OF LEADERSHIP: JOSEPH THE STATESMAN

11

On Statecraft

Early-modern European society consisted of three groups, then commonly termed estates, ranks, or orders: the lower, middle, and upper classes. On a map, we might locate them in the countryside, the town, and at a royal or princely residence. We may visualise them in abstract fashion as forming a huge pyramid consisting of three superimposed layers, each layer being smaller in area and depth than the one below. The lowest class of peasants, agricultural workers, servants, and craftsmen, constituting the majority of the population, forms the foundation of the structure and reaches about two-thirds of its height. The next, relatively thin layer, representing the middle class, is made up of merchants, lawyers, and scholars, membership being based on economic success, university education, and urban residence. Finally, the upper class, the smallest group, standing at the peak of the pyramid, comprises royalty and the high nobility; to this privileged class of rulers and military leaders one belonged by virtue of birth.

While we are inclined to think of a pyramid as an ancient symbol of immutability, the social pyramid of the early-modern European population was not at all static.[1] The urban middle class recruited new members from the rural sector, grew in numbers, and in some cities established city councils and autonomous government. The emergence in the early-modern period of the middle class constitutes the major phenomenon in social history before the advent of industrialisation in the nineteenth century. Throughout Western Europe, the middle class gained in importance at the expense of the nobility which it often rivalled for positions in the state administration. Members of this class felt themselves to be culturally superior to the rural peasantry, and were often justified in thinking themselves better educated than many members of the nobility. In the period following the Peace of Westphalia (1648), German cities appear as centres of education and learning, the cultural life of even small towns being strongly influenced by public libraries and theatres, and on occasion by a remarkably rich music scene.[2] Many of the intelligentsia felt that they should be consulted and employed by those in power. They wished to enter the service of the upper class, working as secretaries or privy councillors, even seeking promotion to positions of responsibility in fiscal or military matters or in the administration of justice. Administrators or civil servants, despite having existed since ancient times, became the hallmark of the modern bureaucratic state that, from its beginnings in the sixteenth century, grew and gained momentum in the seventeenth and eighteenth centuries. This hallmark was present irrespective of whether the state emerged in modern times as a parliamentary monarchy (as in Great Britain), as an absolute monarchy (as in France, Prussia, and many German princely states), or as a republic (as in the Netherlands and the United States of America). Unlike the nobility who formerly were trained in the chivalrous pursuits of knighthood – horsemanship, tournaments, warfare, and hunting – the new administrators were schooled in writing, the compiling of reports, record-keeping, and above all in the legal profession: all were typically drawn from the urban elite of the emergent bourgeoisie and from a nobility willing to adapt to the new requirements. Within society, these professionals formed a new group, the "nobility of letters" (*nobilitas literaria*). Most boasted a university degree, and had included in their studies the new discipline of public law (*ius publicum*). In all European countries, the new political class reorganised political life, and in some during the sixteenth, seventeenth, and eighteenth centuries (and beyond) this amounted to actual domination by important first ministers: Olivares in Spain, Oxenstierna in Sweden, Richelieu and Mazarin in France, Burghley and Robert Walpole in England, Kaunitz and Metternich in Austria.[3] Later, Stein and Bismarck were to hold similar positions in Prussia and Prussian-led Germany.

The rise of the administrator went hand in hand with the development of ethical ideals and the adoption of role models for this new profession concerned with the state and public affairs. In the early-modern period, people looked to biblical and ancient literature for guidance in politics as in any other sphere of life. One of the role models for the ideal monarch was King Cyrus of Persia as portrayed in Xenophon's *Education of Cyrus*, a book much admired by the humanists. But where to look for the ideal adviser to the king? The answer was found in the story of Joseph as told in the book of Genesis. Humanists and theologians came to insist on a political reading of the biblical story: for them, Joseph was not just a pious private individual, a youth of exemplary moral strength; he was also an eminently political character. Following the Renaissance rediscovery of Philo of Alexandria's *De Josepho*, secular and religious leaders alike considered Joseph to be a model politician who rose above all petty selfishness, even when working in the service of a foreign and pagan state.[4] Without Joseph, Pharaoh would not have been able to govern Egypt when famine struck. Seventeenth-century European monarchs and republican rulers increasingly felt the need for the advice, support, and expertise of specially trained and competent ministers – exactly like Pharaoh, who in time of crisis entrusted the care of his country's economy to Joseph. The example of Joseph encouraged the notion that the specific national identity and background of an adviser was irrelevant, and that in fact sometimes a foreigner might be the better choice for such an office, as happened in the biblical story. Thus Germans were often found at the courts of Sweden and Russia, Frenchmen in the service of German princes, and so on. Since this favouring of foreign nationals often meant their comet-like rise to influential and elevated positions, the system not only prompted envy and court intrigues, but also attracted adventurers, impostors, swindlers, alchemists who promised to make gold, and all sorts of dubious individuals some of whom did succeed in duping the princes.[5]

To demonstrate how early-modern authors used the figure of Joseph to depict their ideal of a statesman, I have selected three authors: Hugo Grotius, Philipp von Zesen, and Johann Friedrich Ernst Albrecht, who in the seventeenth and eighteenth centuries wrote about Joseph the statesman in the form of a stage play (Grotius), a historical novel (Zesen) and a topical political novel (Albrecht). As we shall see, the ideal characters projected by the three authors differ in many respects, shaped as they were by humanistic, bourgeois, or Masonic ideas. An echo of three distinct cultural periods may be discerned here, allowing for some simplification: the age of humanism that ended during the Thirty Years War (1618–1648), the subsequent age of the lawyers in the seventeenth and eighteenth centuries, and the brief flourishing of Freemasonry that dominated European cultural life during the final decades of the eighteenth century.

The humanist

In the early seventeenth century, humanists such as the Dutchman Hugo Grotius were enthusiastic readers of ancient Greek and Roman literature. Classical literature including Cicero's *De officiis* (On Moral Duty) and Livy's *Ab urbe condita* (The History of the Roman Republic) not only supported the idea of republicanism, but also offered a role to the learned elite. Instead of just being subjects, such citizens should act as leaders. In the figure of Cicero, the humanists met a statesman who, though an author of philosophical books, nevertheless was convinced of the greater relevance of active political involvement. They came to agree with Cicero's essential idea: although theory and practice, philosophy and politics should be closely linked, on the scale of importance the active life of the man of politics ranks far above the theoretical life of the mere thinker. The new learned elite of Renaissance Italy discovered a new task and indeed a mission, and in this spirit they offered their services as lawyers and diplomats to princes, regional assemblies, or city councils. Even Niccolò Machiavelli, known for his belief in the authoritarian rule of the prince (*Il principe*, 1513), eventually came under the spell of the republican ideal. After immersing himself in the work of Livy, this great Florentine political theorist began to modify his earlier conviction and came to appreciate a more democratic, republican form of government. The idea of the city-republic vied with that of the tyrant state, and in the end the republic became the humanists' leading political paradigm. Cicero, as defender of republican freedom, became the model emulated by the humanists: not Caesar, whose cult flourished at the Italian tyrants' courts.[6] Thinkers such as Hugo Grotius and many others eventually adopted this way of thinking, giving it new currency beyond Italy, especially in the Dutch Republic.

In his stage play *Sophompaneas* Grotius offers a favourable portrait of Joseph as an exemplary statesman – a kind of Hebrew Cicero. He is seen as an eminently learned man, one who echoes humanistic ideals both in public and family life. He is also a successful leader committed to new ideals of government and the state. He reforms the state and its institutions, promotes higher education, and guides the economy through difficult times. Moreover, he promotes the ideals of toleration of other religions (Hebrew monotheism in polytheistic Egypt) and clemency towards political rebels (who seek to gain control of one of Joseph's storage strongholds): Renaissance ideals conspicuously absent from the autocratic rule of Cardinal Richelieu in France. Although Grotius was an exceptionally well-qualified member of this class of administrators, political circumstances prevented him from participating actively in political life. But whereas fate denied him active leadership, the Muses inspired Grotius to express his political ideals and ambitions in the form of a biblical play.

The lawyer

During much of its history, political life in Western Europe was characterised by two distinct levels of power: regional and global. In the Middle Ages, regional power was generally in the hands of the landed nobility, feudal lords, dukes, and petty princes, while global power was concentrated in the hands of a few major princes or kings and, ultimately, in the hands of the emperor. The influence of those holding global power was not generally impressive; in fact, it was often negligible, for it was the local lords who actually held sway, and they paid little attention to the higher ranks of the political hierarchy. The early-modern period saw a change in this system, a change that ultimately led to the creation of the absolute state that placed practically all political power into the hands of a monarch, while diminishing the influence of the petty courts, local princes, feudal lords, and, more generally, the nobility. The broad distinction between local and global political power remained visible, but the main locus of power was shifting, often dramatically, from local to global. The new system, devised or supported by political theorists such as Jean Bodin (1530–1596) and Veit Ludwig von Seckendorff (1626–1692), aimed at strengthening the higher echelons of the social hierarchy – princes, prince bishops, and kings – and at weakening the influence and privileges of all the small subsidiary powers, especially the nobility. The one, absolute monarch, rather than the many petty princes, should wield the power: ruler not of a medieval fiefdom, but of the emerging modern state.

The early-modern shift in the distribution of power from nobility to prince also involved a change in the economic system of production, distribution, and consumption. The old feudal system, ultimately no longer viable and therefore declared defunct, involved the exploitation of the peasantry by the lower ranks of local landed nobility. The income gained by these lords from their subjects was used primarily for consumption and for maintaining a life of leisure at court or castle. The early-modern view of economic administration differed fundamentally, for rather than merely exploiting his subjects, the monarch should now act as a responsible, loving "father" of the people. This new system sought to support the economic life of the cities and agricultural production in the countryside, but equally to consider the requirements of public welfare. The idea was to create a flourishing commonwealth, not just a flourishing courtly elite.

To accomplish these changes, the prince needed trusted advisers who, rather than merely securing the prince's personal advantage, actually served the state and promoted public welfare. The need for wise counsel at princely courts began to be felt as early as the sixteenth century. "Most princes", reports Thomas More in his novel *Utopia* (1516), "apply themselves to warlike pursuits [...] rather than to the useful arts of peace. They are generally more set on acquiring new kingdoms rightly or wrongly, than on governing well those that they already have."[7] But how best to develop these useful arts of peace? By the seventeenth century, it was increasingly felt that the solution lay in the employment of ministers, counsellors, and administrators. If the crown was to be successful in the management and supervision of armies, churches, parliaments, prisons, schools, universities, hospitals, publishing houses, and trade centres, the help of expert administrators and the creation of a bureaucratic apparatus seemed indispensable. Although the king might continue to "rule", his administrators and civil servants actually "ran" the country. As a consequence, royal rule gradually became symbolic, while a powerful professional political class arose.

As David Hume explained in 1741, "almost all the princes of Europe are at present governed by their ministers, and have been so for near two centuries".[8] But in order not to lose control completely, a prince would typically elevate one man to the status of "favourite" at court or, more formally, appoint a first minister, and it was through him that he exercised his power.[9] According to Richelieu (1585–1642), the appointment of a first minister whose power is not limited by that of others is indispensable; only an all-powerful first minister can guarantee the efficiency of a government.[10] Ideally, first minister and administrators shared the idea that public affairs are essentially governed by law and legal tradition, and that the man of politics must be trained in jurisprudence. This belief dominated much of intellectual life in the seventeenth and eighteenth centuries, a period one could with good reason call the age of the lawyers.[11]

One of the literary supporters and indeed apologists of the absolute state was the German writer Philipp von Zesen, whose novel *Assenat* extols Joseph as an administrator admired by the people and honoured by the king, his integrity doubted by none. For Zesen, Joseph is the ancient prototype of the ideal statesman, the righteous man who serves king and country to the satisfaction of both. Zesen's novel includes a programme for the control and policing of the population. It appears as a fictionalised manual of political instruction, a blend of novel and political treatise, a textbook set in a narrative frame.

The Mason

In turning from Philipp von Zesen to Johann Friedrich Ernst Albrecht, we enter the political universe of the late Enlightenment. There is still the optimistic practice of "the useful arts of peace", echoed in Albrecht's portrayal of Joseph's efforts to modernise the Egyptian economy and inculcate a modern work ethic. But the position of the counsellor has become ambiguous; or rather, his problematic position, long recognised, has become more acute. "The councillors of kings", More mused in his *Utopia*, "are so wise that they need no advice from others – or at least so it seems to themselves. At the same time they accept and even applaud the most absurd statements of men whose favour they seek for the sake of standing well with the prince."[12] By the late eighteenth century, the issue at stake was no longer finding the ideal adviser to the prince, but rather the creation of a rational basis for his decisions by placing him within a network of enlightened men, effectively imposing restraint. A man of politics, if he wished to hold to Enlightenment ideals, could no longer simply rely on his own resources; instead, he must look to others for advice, support, and possibly even criticism. He must look to men who stand outside the power structure and therefore have a clearer vision. Accordingly,

Albrecht's enthusiasm for Joseph being somewhat attenuated, Joseph is given an Egyptian sage as a secret adviser, a man named Molais who is permitted to be critical of what the statesman does and how he behaves.

Albrecht favours a system built on co-operation between those in power and an educated elite of advisers and experts; their privileged meeting space is the Masonic lodge, defined as the home of political ideals that transcend individual limitations and personal preferences. The lodge exemplifies a place where ideas may freely be exchanged, advice can be given, and friendly criticism articulated. This political scenario heralds a diversification of political roles, a progressive division of political labour: Joseph appears as the political leader, the man in power, responsible for making decisions about and co-ordinating whatever measures are necessary. Molais represents moral authority, and there is even a third role vaguely indicated: that of the expert in technical matters such as innovative technologies (developed in underground laboratories) and the storage of information. All three of these roles – the man in control, the moralist, and the technical expert – remain united in Grotius's and Zesen's images of Joseph: he is a man of all-round competence. But now, in the late eighteenth century, it is increasingly difficult to find any one person capable of performing all these tasks. Despite this modification of the biblical account and his creation of an eighteenth-century composite image of Joseph the statesman, for Albrecht the ideal model to imitate is still Joseph, mainly on account of the initiation fantasy that introduces him to the rational mysteries of ancient Egypt and that binds him into the Masonic brotherhood.

12

Civic Humanist – Grotius

THE BIOGRAPHY OF HUGO GROTIUS (HUGO DE GROOT, 1583–1645) IS ONE of the most moving stories one can tell of a scholar's and failed statesman's career in early-modern times.[1] Grotius was born and grew up in the fledgling Dutch Republic, founded just two years before his birth. The Dutch Republic originated as a result of a clash of two political systems: the kingdom of Spain, part of the Habsburg empire, to which the Netherlands traditionally belonged, and the proud northern Dutch cities whose elite believed in "civic humanism": the republican ideals of self-government, independence, and the leadership of humanists. Grotius's life was marked by another fateful clash: between ideal and reality. The ideal to which he aspired was that of serving his country as a lawyer and a political leader within its republican institutions. His splendid early political career came to an abrupt end in 1618, when, at the age of thirty-four, he found himself not only embroiled in conflicts between opposing political factions, but undeservedly incarcerated in Lovestein Castle. Two years later, in 1621, his wife managed to smuggle the small man out of prison in a chest normally used to carry books into his quarters – one of the most treasured anecdotes of Dutch cultural history. But regained freedom, for Grotius, meant nothing but exile and poverty, for all his belongings had been confiscated. Grotius spent the rest of his life in exile, first in Paris, then in Germany, and then again in Paris. Excluded from political life and essentially unhappy, Grotius found consolation in his studies. In exile in France he compiled his major work, the long treatise *De iure belli ac pacis* (The Law of War and Peace, 1625), a book on which Grotius's reputation as a legal theorist rests until this very day.

For more than a decade while in exile, Grotius strove to be rehabilitated in the Dutch Republic. The vanity of his hope became most evident when he returned to Rotterdam in 1631, only to learn that he would be imprisoned once more if he did not leave the country within a few days. Again, Grotius fled, this time to Germany, where he lived in various places in and near

Hamburg and in Frankfurt. Although he still entertained hopes of repatriation to the Dutch Republic, in his early fifties it began to dawn on him that he should forget his native country and consider a different career. Contacting diplomats of several continental countries, he explored the possibility of entering a foreign country's diplomatic service. Contacts with Sweden proved to be promising. At last, in 1634, after much hesitation, he accepted the Swedish crown's request that he should serve as Swedish ambassador to France. Although this new position freed Grotius from financial cares and inspired new confidence, it did not bring him the political influence he had hoped for. He also suffered from the disrespect shown to him by the Dutch ambassadors to France. Again, he found consolation in writing. This time, he focused on the subject of peace between, and indeed ecclesiastical union of, Catholics and Protestants, much to the dismay of many Protestants, who accused him of supporting the Catholic Church and the Pope. In 1645, he was recalled from Paris to Stockholm, to discover that he had no friends left in the capital city of Sweden. Feeling thus further estranged and unwilling to settle in Stockholm permanently, Grotius again lost his job. As he left Stockholm for another exile in Germany, he died in Rostock following an unpleasant crossing of the Baltic Sea.

Among the many books Grotius published during his long years of exile, one rather small one deserves our attention: his drama *Sophompaneas* (1635). In presenting what happens to one protagonist (Sophompaneas) on one single day (the day he is approached by his brothers) in one place (the protagonist's residence), Grotius's drama follows the standard prescription in contemporary poetic theory.

Sophompaneas: A summary[2]

> Sophompaneas, the hero of the play, is vice-regent of Egypt, second in command after Pharaoh. As the day dawns, Sophompaneas reflects on the daily agenda of a busy administrator. There is famine in the land – this is the second year without a harvest, and the population is getting restless, though Sophompaneas in his wisdom has stored the surplus from the earlier years of plenty in state granaries. The granaries must be supervised and opened to feed the masses, and irregularities have to be dealt with. In addition, he has to decide what to do with a group of Hebrew visitors. Though unaware that Sophompaneas is their brother – the boy whom they, long ago, sold into slavery – they have come to the governor's court to beg for grain. Sophompaneas took Benjamin, the youngest of the Hebrews, hostage, putting the boy under suspicion of theft: he is alleged

to have stolen the vice-regent's ceremonial chalice. Sophompaneas does this to test the brothers: to find out whether there is love and solidarity among them or whether, as in the past, they are ready to sacrifice selfishly the life of one of their kin. In the morning Judah, one of the Hebrew visitors, speaks with Sophompaneas, pleading for his brother. For the time being, Sophompaneas leaves the matter undecided. He has another, more pressing matter to deal with – an Egyptian city whose administration reportedly has fallen into the hands of rebels. The avaricious administrators of Coptos had turned more and more of the citizens into beggars who subsequently staged a rebellion: now it seems they have managed to gain control of the city and its state granary. The vice-regent reacts quickly by sending the military to Coptos. They are instructed to re-establish the exclusive authority of the state. The governor also gives orders to feed the poor and to punish the guilty, stressing, however, that capital punishment must be avoided.

While the Hebrews await the vice-regent's decision, they study the mural paintings in the gallery around Sophompaneas's palace. Memorable scenes from his career are depicted – his being accused of seduction, his imprisonment, his interpretation of various dreams that foretold the future, including the dreams of Pharaoh. The correct interpretation of these dreams led to Sophompaneas's promotion to his present powerful position in the state of Egypt. One of the murals shows how Sophompaneas reorganised Egyptian society by dividing the populace into three classes, assigning a particular task to each. The first has to cultivate the ground, produce food, and engage in elementary crafts such as pottery. The second class comprises the warriors, shown armed, practising military manoeuvres and building a camp. The priests, the third class, offer sacrifices on altars and study the movements of the stars. Eventually, Sophompaneas calls the brothers in. He interrogates Judah, asking especially about his father Jacob. As the interview develops, it transpires that the vice-regent actually knows the Hebrew language. Finally, Sophompaneas reveals that he too is a son of Jacob – none other than Joseph, their brother. "Look at me, my brothers – it is I, Joseph! The Egyptians gave me another name. [. . .] I love you as a brother. [. . .] My cheeks are streaming with tears of joy, and my words are stifled by sobs of happiness."[3] Judah, terrified, begs Joseph's forgiveness for the mischief he did long ago, selling Joseph into slavery. Joseph reassures his brothers of his forgiveness and of the goodwill he has towards them. "To pardon your guilt is so easy, for I love you as a

> brother does his brothers. [...] My life is sweeter since I have been assured of my brothers' affection."[4] He invites them all to settle in Egypt, and suggests that they bring their father Jacob from Syria to be with them. In the final scene, Sophompaneas asks Pharaoh for favours on behalf of his brothers: to grant them pastures in Egypt, freedom of movement in the land, and autonomy in matters of religion. Pharaoh grants all of these requests in a solemn oath.

Sophompaneas gives Egypt a social constitution, improves its rule of law and order by implementing new legislation, and ably handles a revolt – all evidence of his wise and beneficent rule; all evidence, moreover, of Grotius's political thinking. As we will see, the portrait Grotius paints of Sophompaneas not only permitted its author to teach lessons in political theory; it also echoes his own political experience first in the Dutch Republic where he enjoyed a splendid though tragically interrupted political career, and then in France where as an exile he witnessed the ascent and rule of Cardinal Richelieu. Both Grotius's Dutch patriotism and his critical attitude to Richelieu are reflected in his drama.

A LESSON IN STATECRAFT: EGYPT AS ANOTHER DUTCH REPUBLIC

Joseph, as a supreme statesman, devised a new political and social structure, a constitution, for Egypt. According to Grotius's drama, Egypt in Joseph's time was not ruled exclusively by the king; instead, it was a form of republic in which the crown co-operated with several institutions to govern the state. Sophompaneas instructs the Egyptians "to divide themselves into three classes, and to each of these he attributed specific professions whose number he increased by new inventions".[5] "The first group consists of husbandmen and craftsmen who serve our primary needs. These he shows how to lift irrigation water from powerful, foaming streams by the constant rotation of a paddle-wheel" – an echo of the Dutch interest in hydraulic machinery.[6] Also in this first social group are those who "grind grain with their feet and knead clay with their hands", a detail Grotius takes from the account of Herodotus who reports that the Egyptians customarily do things the opposite way to what one would expect – kneading clay with one's feet, and grinding grain by hand.[7] Here Grotius is attempting to give his play some relevant local colour, a feature not otherwise characteristic of his drama. The military make up the second class, men who in peacetime train for battle and practise the use of weapons. The third class of Egyptian men, the priests, enjoy the privilege of being supported by the royal treasury. In addition to offering sacrifices to the gods, they devote themselves to scholarship, studying astronomy and "investigating God's works throughout the universe as far as nature extends".[8]

Of these three, the military class most closely reflects not ancient realities but ideals of Grotius's own time and society. Preoccupied with order, method, and dignity even in warfare, humanists and political leaders preferred well-exercised troops stationed in fixed garrisons to the marauding, foraging, and raiding gangs typical of Germany's Thirty Years War. While there was a trend towards establishing standing armies all over Europe, it was in the Dutch Republic of the 1590s that a model army was successfully set up. Grotius portrays a standing army of well-trained, virtuous Egyptians that, as we learn elsewhere in the play, even in combat remains disciplined. Grotius's Egyptian military class seems to blend the expertise and force of this ideal army with the benign restraint of the *ad hoc* civil militia of Holland; but like many of his contemporaries, Grotius is conscious of the fact that a militia, in whatever manner it may be exercised, remains inferior to a well-disciplined standing army like that of the Dutch Republic and that of Sophompaneas's Egypt.[9]

The portrait Grotius paints of ancient Egyptian society is a typical product of humanist antiquarianism characterised by a vast knowledge of ancient sources and bold speculations on the continuity between ancient Mediterranean and barbarian cultures. Diodorus Siculus, one of Grotius's ancient authorities, reveals that Egyptian society was composed of three classes named after their occupations: priests (the most highly educated), warriors, and those who render the most menial services to the state – cowherds, swineherds, tradesmen, interpreters, and pilots.[10] The income of the priests and the warriors was not subject to taxation. In his *Liber de antiquitate reipublicae Batavicae* (The Antiquity of the Batavian Republic, 1610) Grotius notes that the ancient Egyptian system matches that of the ancient society of Gaul with its three classes of druids, knights, and commoners.[11] This was also the ancient Batavian system, and Grotius sees it reflected in the parliaments of the Dutch Republic in which the various estates are represented. All of this amounted to saying, briefly, that the Dutch and the ancient Egyptian societies shared an essential structure. Guided by the patristic notion of Joseph the reformer of Egyptian society,[12] Grotius is bold enough to make his Sophompaneas the genius who first devised the system. Joseph, in other words, is one of the most important legislators of human history.

Grotius's assimilation of Egypt to the Dutch Republic does not stop there. The humanist depicts Egypt as a country controlled by a network of relatively independent powerful cities, echoing the political situation of both Italy and the Netherlands, the two most urbanised countries of seventeenth-century Europe.[13] Two Egyptian cities are named – Memphis where Sophompaneas resides, and Coptos where the rebels rule. While there is no direct reference to the representation of the three classes of citizens in Egyptian urban parliaments, Grotius does indicate that the cities have self-governing bodies that seem to involve these groups. As soon as the rebellious city of Coptos is brought under control with the help of the army, it can return to normal life. The citizens are barred from repeating their experiments with government that range, in quick succession, from monarchy to aristocracy to the rule of the mob; instead, Coptos is to be governed by "a civil administration" (*civile regimen*) of magistrates – like any city of the Dutch Republic. Sophompaneas gives orders to "install a civil administration, made up of the none-too-wealthy".[14] These magistrates are members of the same class as Grotius himself – typically those who lack the ambition of the wealthy to accumulate ever more riches, and who equally are free from the envy characteristic of the poor. "What holds society together is the middle class (*medium genus*) – less prone to luxury and free from sordid baseness."[15] The original source of this notion is the biblical book of Proverbs, where the wise man's prayer is for moderation in economic life:

> Give me neither poverty nor riches; feed me with the food that is needful for me, lest I be full and deny you and say, "Who is the Lord?" or lest I be poor and steal and profane the name of my God.[16]

Since human attitudes do not change, Grotius feels free to project the biblical – and his own – view rather boldly on to ancient Egypt. In fact, our author speaks of Coptos as if it were a Dutch town where acceptable standards of urban middle-class self-government have to be reinstated. As we can see, the Egypt of Sophompaneas is envisaged as sharing important organisational features with the Dutch Republic. Sophompaneas alias Joseph perfectly embodies Grotius's republican ideals. It is instructive to study the historical background of Dutch republicanism.

Unlike a monarchy with its distinction and distance between king and subjects, ruler and the ruled, the republican ideal promoted the participation of all citizens in government; usually, this meant that citizens should form parliaments, deliver public speeches, elect magistrates, and closely circumscribe the authority of their non-hereditary rulers. In early-modern Europe, republican ideals originated and first flourished in Florence and Venice, where humanists first exchanged the ideal of secluded study for the Ciceronian ideal of the learned statesman who is active in political life. The resulting civic humanism of these cities ultimately influenced the whole of Europe; as one of the most powerful contemporary political concepts it brought about the modern notion of the state and thus helped shape the modern world. Leading scholars such as Hans Baron – who coined the expression "civic humanism" – contend that it continued to inspire Europe's intellectual elite to promote republican and democratic ideals well into the nineteenth century.[17] All of Europe was impressed by Venice, the free city-state ruled jointly by none other than its own citizens, nobility, and prince, and whose ships dominated the Mediterranean.[18] The spectacular wealth Venice gained by trade contributed to its fame. The seventeenth-century intellectual elite of the Netherlands, including Grotius, was eminently receptive to this ideal of civic humanism, not least because the geographical location of the Netherlands was perceived to be similar to that of Venice – another free republic by the sea. Amsterdam was indeed the Venice of the North.

Humanists thrived on explaining their political ideals with reference not to modern but to ancient, mostly classical, examples. Ancient Rome and Athens were considered important cities that during certain periods embodied the republican ideals dear to humanists such as Grotius. But rather than selecting Italy or Greece as the setting for his drama, Grotius opted for Egypt. This choice was obviously guided by his biblical model, but there is a deeper, more relevant reason: Grotius seems to have felt that even in a Pharaonic monarchy, a leader informed by the ideals of civic humanism and given enough power would make a difference. And this is precisely the lesson he sets out to teach in *Sophompaneas*.

Another lesson in statecraft: Sophompaneas and Richelieu compared

Shortly after Grotius had settled as an exile in Paris, French political life came under the domination of Cardinal Richelieu, first minister under King Louis XIII. Richelieu controlled the nation's politics so comprehensively that historians still refer today to the period between 1624 (Richelieu's ascent to power) and 1642 (the cardinal's death) not simply as the age of Louis XIII, but as the age of Louis *and Richelieu*. Grotius and Richelieu, born in 1583 and 1584 respectively and thus almost the same age, were both steeped in humanistic learning. Richelieu was particularly impressed with Grotius's expertise in international commercial law, and he readily embraced Grotius's notion that international trade should be free, and that the sea does not belong to any nation in particular, as argued in *Mare liberum* (The Free Sea, 1609). Backed up by ideas of natural law, this doctrine opposed the Spanish-Habsburg claim to much of the ocean by right of conquest and papal privilege. It also lent support to the international maritime activities of both France and the Dutch Republic. It does not come as a surprise, then, that Richelieu interviewed Grotius first in April 1525 and again in May 1626.[19] In the second interview the cardinal sought to secure Grotius's services as a legal consultant on matters pertaining to maritime trade and the establishment of French trade companies. Grotius wrote at least one memorandum for Richelieu, but he refrained from getting further involved with French politics for fear of appearing disloyal to the Dutch Republic: Grotius, in the 1620s, still considered himself a statesman destined for a political career in his home country.

But Dutch patriotism does not fully account for Grotius's wariness and dislike of Richelieu. The explanation can be found in the fact that the two believed in fundamentally incompatible political philosophies: Grotius, the internationalist, understood natural law (*ius naturae*) to be binding upon all nations, princes, and members of the governing and counselling bodies, whereas Richelieu, the parochialist, relied for his politics on *raison d'état*, the Machiavellian notion that the selfish interest of the state overrules all other considerations. "International law and *raison d'état* stand in natural opposition to each other", explains the historian Friedrich Meinecke: assigning to itself as much legal force as possible, international law wishes to restrict the sway of *raison d'état*; *raison d'état*, however, opposes any such restriction, and has recourse to international law only when it happens to serve its own, egotistical ends.[20] When it came to realising the twin political aims of the internal centralisation of France, and the maximisation of its international influence, the cardinal ruthlessly placed the interests of the state above all considerations of existing law and morality. In *Sophompaneas*, Grotius portrays the protagonist, a man committed to natural law, as the exact opposite of Richelieu. In the preface to his play, Grotius openly distinguishes between two types of politician (*vir in imperio versans* "the man active in political life"):[21] the exemplar of virtue and upright leadership, personified by Sophompaneas, and the man "made up of cunning, deviousness and perfidy, and hardened in his contempt of God and all laws".[22] Although Grotius does not reveal of whom he is thinking here, it is clear enough that the cunning man is none other than Richelieu. Read with the cardinal in mind, a number of features of *Sophompaneas* appear in a new light.

One such feature of the play is the concern with religious tolerance, a subject of much debate in seventeenth-century French politics. In Sophompaneas's Egypt, minorities such as the Hebrews enjoy the natural right to freely exercise their religion. Pharaoh himself guaranteed this right: "I swear to mighty God who rules all things [...] that the Hebrews will always be free to practise their rites."[23] For seventeenth-century readers, it was not difficult to see that Grotius was implicitly commenting here on the situation of the Huguenots – the French Calvinist believers – under the rule of Richelieu. In the royal Edict of Nantes (1598), the Huguenots had been granted the free exercise of their religion, and Richelieu never openly opposed it. However, he began to undermine Huguenot privileges. As a group that boasted its own army, it appeared to him to be a state within the state and therefore a potential threat to royal authority. Seeking to integrate it more fully into the increasingly centralised state,

Richelieu began to destroy the Huguenot army. In 1628, he succeeded in conquering the Huguenot stronghold of La Rochelle. While refraining from further harassment of the Huguenots, Richelieu signalled that they were to be converted to the Catholic faith: a situation Grotius felt most uneasy about, not least because the French apparently suggested – unsuccessfully – that Grotius himself should convert from his Calvinism to Catholicism.[24]

Another, equally topical subject much debated in the age of Richelieu concerned revenge and clemency. The biblical story of Joseph could be read as a narrative argument in favour of moderation and indeed of clemency. Sophompaneas pardons his brothers unhesitatingly; he harbours no desire for revenge. In the very first scene of the play, Sophompaneas banishes all thought from his mind of how his brothers in their hatred plotted his death, turned him into a commodity to be bartered, and finally consigned him to slavery; all of this he is prepared to forget and forgive, for he was "born a mild man" (*ad lenitatem natus*).[25] For Grotius, the desire to inflict revenge on others is inconsistent with natural reason, for "the less successfully anyone uses reason, the more he is inclined to revenge".[26] "Vengeance", he explains, "is disapproved of not only by Christian writers but by philosophers in general" – by Seneca, for instance.[27] The fact that both the teachings of the Bible and pagan philosophers seek to discourage people from taking revenge is of great importance to Grotius, for it places the conciliatory attitude within the sphere of natural law. Once it was established that the idea of non-retaliation belongs to natural law, and not only to the revealed law of the Bible, non-retaliation must become part of the humanist's essential message. Grotius would ban retribution from personal life. Joseph, through his pardoning of his brothers, is upheld as an example of someone who has risen above all primitive and unethical, vengeful behaviour. But Grotius would ban retribution not only from personal life, but also from international politics where it might lead to war and atrocious behaviour towards those who are defeated.

To make his point, Grotius had first of all to portray Sophompaneas as supreme commander of the Egyptian army. In so doing, he departs dramatically from the biblical story of Joseph that is generally understood as being free from any reference to military force. In his textual notes on the book of Genesis, however, Grotius claims to have found a hint at Joseph's status as the commander of the Egyptian army: "And the king said to Joseph, I am Pharaoh, and without your command no man shall move hand or foot in all the land of Egypt."[28] The implication is, Grotius asserts, that no one is to use arms ("move hand") or set out on a military campaign ("move foot") without explicit orders from Joseph. In Grotius's play we hear of a revolt that broke out in one of Egypt's provinces. Sophompaneas gives precise orders regarding the reconquest of Coptos. The army is sent out not to kill but, acting as a police force, to restore law and order. A massacre in the conquered city will thereby be avoided; as many lives as possible are to be spared. Also to be spared are the possessions of the citizens; so looting the city is equally prohibited. Sophompaneas, in addition to imposing restraint, promises honourable soldiers generous rewards from the royal treasury. Among the disobedient, Sophompaneas distinguishes various groups, and each group is to be dealt with differently: the dungeon awaits officials who have abused their authority; permanent penal servitude in mines rewards those who have enriched themselves at the expense of others, while clemency must be shown to those "who only sinned as much as they were compelled to by hunger".[29] No one is singled out for capital punishment.

As is to be expected, Sophompaneas respects all the rules Grotius had outlined in his treatise *De iure belli ac pacis* when waging the "just war" against the rebellious city. These rules essentially recommend moderation: "If the conqueror is to do nothing unlawful, he must first make sure that he puts none to death, unless by some crime he deserves it; also, that he takes nothing from anyone except as a legitimate penalty. And within the limit of how far considerations of security allow one to go, it is always honourable to incline towards clemency and generosity. Sometimes, depending on the circumstances, such conduct is required by rule of custom."[30] These rules reflect ancient thought on the matter. When describing how a military commander should deal with the guilty, Grotius follows Cicero's timeless advice: "When victory is won, we should spare those who have not been blood-thirsty and barbarous in their warfare."[31] "It is a great man's duty in times of trouble to single out the guilty for punishment, while sparing the many."[32] "We should take care that punishment shall not be disproportional to the offence."[33] In general, the statesman "should do as doctors do in their practice: in cases of slight illness they give mild treatment".[34] Sophompaneas, in other words, heeds the advice Cicero gives in his treatise *De officiis* and thus again embodies the virtues of civic humanism. He also follows established Dutch military practice. When Groningen was attacked by the republican army in 1594 and capitulated, only a few contingents were allowed into the city, and these were quartered in specially assigned confiscated premises. No pillage or retribution of any sort was tolerated.[35]

In Richelieu's France, rebels were dealt with differently and, as Richelieu would have argued, for good reasons. The cardinal sought to transform France from its medieval inheritance as a cluster of loosely associated but essentially independent lands (approximately sixteen in number) to a modern state, centred on a royal bureaucracy and efficiently controlled by the king or rather his first minister, Richelieu. Rebellions against the increasingly dominant central power were a problem that often confronted Richelieu, for his policy of enhancing the role of the central government did not meet with general approval. As one can imagine, the lesson of subjection was not easily learned by the traditional feudal authorities, and armed rebellion, in the countryside and in individual towns, was frequent, as were attempts to assassinate Richelieu. Equally frequent were the victories of Richelieu's quickly deployed troops. Richelieu was well aware of the classical tradition of royal clemency, practised by ancient rulers and recommended by authors such as Grotius. But Richelieu had no use for clemency in his political theory and practice: mildness, leniency, and forgiveness might well function in the personal life of Christian believers (and the cardinal thought of himself as one of them), but as soon as the authority of the state was at stake, there was no place for it. In his secret political testament written for Louis XIII, he explains. "Your majesty must be prevented from indulging in inappropriate clemency (*fausse clémence*), which is more dangerous than cruelty [...] In judging crimes against the state it is essential to banish pity."[36] To forgive enemies of the state would be harmful and irresponsible. Although occasionally making concessions in practice, Richelieu when dealing with rebels generally followed this rule.

When two young men – Gaston, brother of the king, aged twenty-four; Henri, duc de Montmorency, aged thirty-seven – rose in armed revolt against Richelieu's harsh regime in 1632, the rebels were quickly defeated. While Gaston was pardoned by the king, Henri was not, despite considerable intercession made on his behalf. Richelieu insisted on the death penalty. Historians have described the pathetic scene that preceded the execution: Monsieur de Charlus, captain of the king's guards, who had removed the duke's decorations and marshal's baton in order to return them to Louis XIII, took the opportunity to try to soften the unrelenting king. "Ah sire," he cried, throwing himself at the king's feet, all around also falling on their knees in tears, "will not Your Majesty pardon Monsieur de Montmorency, whose ancestors served your predecessors so well? Grant him pardon, sire!" "Nay," said King Louis, "no pardon shall be granted him, and he needs must die."[37] Unlike King Louis and, behind him, the cardinal, Sophompaneas insists that one should spare the lives even of rebels. Under the mask of Sophompaneas, Grotius seems to go as far as abolishing the death penalty in favour of penal servitude or even the granting of pardon.

Shortly after Grotius had published *Sophompaneas* (1637), the question of clemency received much attention in French literature, ironically but understandably from authors who were patronised by Richelieu. One of them, Pierre Corneille, then France's leading dramatist, was familiar with the ancient philosopher Seneca's treatise *De clementia* (On Mercy). Mercy or clemency, a virtue particularly becoming and useful to rulers, is defined as "restraining the mind from vengeance when it has the power to take it" (*clementia est temperantia animi in potestate ulciscendi*).[38] Seneca added that "the man for whom vengeance is easy, by disregarding it, gains assured praise for clemency".[39] Seneca had written this work for his pupil the Emperor Nero, whom he advises to practise the Stoic virtue of clemency by being merciful to his subjects. The emperor is exhorted to eschew retributive sentiments such as indignation and hatred that lead to acts of vengeance. Particularly impressive is Seneca's account of how Emperor Augustus, after an attempted assassination, met his opponent Cinna to pardon him and to offer him a major position in the imperial government. The enemy became a friend.

This anecdote, while historically doubtful, is the subject of Pierre Corneille's drama *Cinna ou la clémence d'Auguste* (Cinna or the Mercy of Augustus, 1642). Not only in the Rome of Nero but also in Richelieu's France is the appeal to the ruler's mercy appropriate. Instead of a first minister who had the enemies of the state executed, one would wish to have someone like Augustus who, in Corneille's stage play, offered his friendship to his would-be assassin: "Let us be friends, Cinna" (*Soyons amis, Cinna*).[40] The one who offers his friendship not only forgives and shows compassion, but also asserts his absolute power – he is the one who makes the rules.

Like Corneille, René de Ceriziers, a priest associated with the royal court, also wished to promote a climate of reconciliation and clemency in French politics. He no doubt knew Corneille's *Cinna*, though his own writing is independent. In a book entitled *Joseph ou la providence divine* (Joseph or Divine Providence, 1642), Father Ceriziers, who believed in the biblical story's unique moral message, makes much of Joseph's readiness to forgive others, and he develops the theme in a moral exhortation: those who use their power to take revenge are devils rather than humans, and those who forgive and refrain from humiliating others will experience incomparable inner joy.[41] In his imaginative retelling of the story of Joseph, Ceriziers adds a scene of reconciliation not found in the Bible: the Egyptian vice-regent not only forgives his brothers, but also generously pardons Cyrene – Ceriziers's name for Potiphar's wife.[42] There can be no doubt about Ceriziers's firm commitment to the ideal of clemency as a virtue to be expected from a statesman such as Richelieu. It may not be a coincidence that Ceriziers's book was published in 1642, the year of Richelieu's death, a moment in which the course of French politics could be reconsidered. After a decade of unrest and debate, Cardinal Mazarin, who succeeded Richelieu, fell back upon the methods of his illustrious predecessor. As the works of Ceriziers, Corneille, and of course Grotius all demonstrate, the theme of reconciliation and clemency could not be discussed without reference to such venerable exemplars as Augustus and Joseph.

The Autobiographical Dimension

Literary pursuits were common among humanists, but we should not think of their art as being separate from their lives. This is certainly true of Grotius, who wrote *Sophompaneas* at a crucial period of his life, in fact during a period of crisis. The crisis began in 1631 when he left France for Rotterdam to negotiate his political rehabilitation in person. But he was told, in no uncertain terms, that he was *persona non grata*. To avoid another term in prison, he quickly left the Netherlands for Germany, unsure what to do with his life. It had dawned on him that his hopes of being rehabilitated in the Dutch Republic had to be abandoned for good. He considered entering the service of a prince or of a state – any, other than the Dutch Republic or France.

Between 1631 and 1634, in his phase of reorientation, making new contacts, hesitation, and negotiation, Grotius "spent a great deal of time lost in thought, at times sinking into lethargy, and at the same time suffering from digestive disorders".[43] What bothered him were fundamental political questions: does it befit a humanist to work for a state other than his own? Is it right for a country to use a foreigner in its diplomatic service? In the seventeenth century, two contradictory answers were given. The first answer was that of Grotius, partisan of the independence of the Netherlands from Habsburg Spain. In the past, and in his own writing, Grotius defended the rule that in the Dutch Republic, no "*homo externus*" (man from outside) should be appointed to public office – every councillor, fiscal officer, sheriff, or bailiff had to be a native of the fatherland.[44] In other words, he upheld the patriotic law that the Dutch should be ruled only by the Dutch, and, in particular, not by Spanish authorities. Grotius apparently thought of this rule as a general one: a public office should only be held by a native and full citizen of the state in question. Grotius's civic humanism implied staunch patriotism. The second answer, contradicting that of Grotius, thought of the humanist as someone standing above national interests; as a legal expert who spoke Latin, the language of international law and diplomacy, he could offer his services to any legitimate ruler. In fact, many states employed foreign nationals as their diplomats and representatives at foreign courts. Of the 120 diplomats in the service of Sweden in the seventeenth century, only around 40 per cent were Swedes; the rest were foreigners.[45]

When pondering the issue, Grotius seems to have come to regard the biblical Joseph as a reassuring precedent offering orientation and guidance. Appointed by Pharaoh, Joseph the Hebrew worked for the Egyptian state; following his example, the Dutch humanist might also work for the Swedish crown. The biblical story helped Grotius make up his mind on a fundamental point. Now he could accept the offer of work with the Swedish government as ambassador to France. In a letter dated 13 July 1734, he informed the Dutch authorities that he would enter the diplomatic service of Sweden, adding that he hoped to be of use to his country even in this situation.[46] While Grotius now firmly believed in his new mission, he was far from forgetting his Dutch patriotism.

If this line of reasoning is valid, it may well be that writing and publishing *Sophompaneas* in 1635 helped Grotius to come to terms with his new job and his fresh biographical perspective. By considering Joseph's career and writing the play, he came to accept that someone could work for a foreign government and still somehow support his native country.

At a deeper level, there was another, religious lesson to be learned from the biblical story: that concerning the hidden ways of providence. Grotius, by immersing himself in the book of Genesis, came to share Joseph's belief in "God who has created everything, who watches closely and alertly over all things, who loses sight of nothing and disposes his ordinance from afar".[47] It is this God, the God of Joseph, who, Grotius believed, secretly watched over and directed his own life, although God's purposes may at times remain hidden. Moreover, this was the God to whom he believed he owed his reversal of fortune through being called to a new political office.

While our interpretation of the autobiographical dimension of *Sophompaneas* is both cautious and straightforward, the same cannot be said of the claim that Grotius actually identified with Joseph, seeing himself as another Joseph who, being called to serve a foreign state as a diplomat, could hope to become one of Europe's political leaders. In a slightly attenuated form, this idea can be found in Joost van den Vondel. When this friend of Grotius translated his Latin play into Dutch, he noted the autobiographical dimension: "At times, it seemed to me as if Joseph had come alive in the dramatist [Grotius], or else as if the dramatist had walked the very path of Joseph."[48] Doesn't *Sophompaneas* tell Grotius's own story? Wasn't there a certain coincidence between the life of the Dutch humanist and that of the biblical figure? Does not each of the three successive phases of Joseph's life have a more or less close equivalent in Grotius's biography: the splendid early career of the uniquely gifted young man, the long years of misery spent abroad and in prison, and the great reversal of fate through the invitation to serve a foreign state in an honourable position? Are the analogies between Joseph and Hugo the key to understanding *Sophompaneas*?[49] It is certainly worthwhile to test the idea by scrutinising both the play and Grotius's letters. The result is meagre, however. "The Egyptians are a difficult people and often only grudgingly give way, even to their native rulers", says Sophompaneas;[50] the biblical Joseph never said anything of the kind, so Grotius seems to be referring here to his own political experience. The play celebrates Sophompaneas's "happy household, ruled by the inseparable bond of a couple joined in mutual fidelity", his undivided devotion to his wife, and "the bond of marriage, the holiest covenant": in the biblical account, none of this can be found; again, we may suggest that Grotius is speaking of his own marriage – the only stable relationship he enjoyed in his life.[51] Later, once in the service of the Swedes, Grotius referred to Sweden as his Egypt. In a letter of 1639 he reminds his son Dirk not to forget Sweden and the benefits received from this country: "Note what is written in *Sophompaneas*: 'Let Egypt be your fatherland, for it deserves our esteem', indeed, Sweden is our fatherland. It is to this country that we have to dedicate our lives; accordingly, it is our right to expect to be honoured by Sweden."[52]

None of this amounts to much, and one should not build too much on it. The equation "Sophompaneas = Grotius" occasionally comes into view and is playfully used, but it is far from providing the key to understanding the drama and revealing its message. Grotius was too much of a realist to anticipate an outstanding political career like Joseph's in the diplomatic service. Moreover, as Henk Nellen explains, his sense of humility would have prevented Grotius from taking the equation too seriously.[53] Nevertheless, *Sophompaneas* does have an autobiographical dimension, one that we may summarise by saying that rather than identifying with Joseph, Grotius was willing to learn from the biblical precedent.

While it is an exaggeration to claim that Sophompaneas was none other than Grotius himself, masked as a Hebrew humanist in the service of the state of Egypt, there is some truth in the idea that the biblical figure resonated with his life. It would be misleading, however, to read the play exclusively as an autobiographical document. In addition to being shaped by, and echoing, some of its author's biography, his feelings and beliefs, it is a didactic play aimed at imparting to the audience the very essence of his ideal state and its political leadership based on the notion of civic humanism. But who would take any notice of a humanist's drama written in Latin? In order to find the answer, we have to look at cultural life in seventeenth-century Amsterdam.

Joseph in Amsterdam

Amsterdam, in the mid-seventeenth century, was much more than simply the metropolis of the Dutch Republic. One of Europe's most populous cities, with 150,000 inhabitants, its unparalleled economic and commercial prosperity had made it the empress of European capitals. Wealth attracted humanists, printers, writers, and artists, so cultural life there flourished.

Even today, few have to be reminded of the fact that Amsterdam, during its Golden Age, was the city of painters, Rembrandt (1606–1669) being the most famous of them. Unsurprisingly in Bible-reading Dutch society, the tale of Joseph was one of the most popular Bible stories and was frequently depicted in art. The corpus of Rembrandt's drawings alone lists around fifty items concerning Joseph,[54] and he was not the only Dutch artist interested in our biblical hero. Dutch portrayals of Joseph range from the young dreamer to the old patriarch. Two works stand out as particularly memorable: *Joseph Accused before Potiphar* (1655; see Fig. 5, p. 103) by Rembrandt, and *Joseph Distributing Grain in Egypt* (1655; Fig. 14) by the Amsterdam painter Bartholomeus Breenbergh (1598–1657). Rembrandt's scene is set in a bedroom, echoing, it seems, the Dutch artist's interest in portraying domestic life. Potiphar's wife, fully dressed, stands beside her bed as she accuses Joseph of attempted rape.

Fig. 14. *Joseph Distributing Grain in Egypt*. Standing at the head of the granary staircase, Joseph supervises the selling of grain, while a female figure in the foreground hires a donkey from a shepherd boy. The painting ranks as one of the masterpieces of Dutch art in its golden age. – Bartholomeus Breenbergh, 1655.

Breenbergh's painting takes us from the private space of the bedroom into the public realm: the marketplace where Joseph, now vice-regent of Egypt, supervises the distribution of grain. In this large painting, Breenbergh developed an earlier etching on the subject (above, Fig. 8, p. 106).[55] In the latter, the artist's focus is on Joseph as he grants free grain to a poor mother kneeling in the dust; in the painting, it is on the fine lady in the left foreground, who places coins into the hands of a shepherd boy – either as alms or, more likely, in payment for hiring his donkey to transport the grain that she was buying. Both paintings no doubt spoke to their viewers: Rembrandt teaches a lesson of sexual morality, while Breenbergh echoes civic pride in commerce and efficient public institutions. Some who took a closer look at the bedroom scene (art historians; authors with an interest in eroticism) came to believe that Rembrandt, apart from teaching a moral message, was also venting his anger against Geertje Dircx, his former lover who, after being dismissed from the painter's household, went to court to accuse him of seduction and breach of promise.[56] In this painting, they argue, the artist is presenting his own version of the incident by portraying himself as innocent Joseph and Geertje as lustful and revengeful Mrs Potiphar; her thwarted lust may even be read into her gesture of pointing at Joseph's garment, draped perhaps symbolically over the bedpost.[57] But this connotation doubtless remained undetected by most contemporary viewers, who simply saw the painting as a celebration of Joseph's virtue that they, as citizens of Amsterdam, sought to emulate, in private as well as public life.

In addition to being the city of painters, Amsterdam in the seventeenth century was one of Europe's most prominent cities of the stage. In 1638, Marie de Médicis – the exiled mother of Louis XIII – visited Amsterdam; in her honour and for public entertainment, the best actors of the period staged impressive mythological scenes, ballets, and historical re-enactments by the River Amstel – performances all repeated indoors, in the Schouwburg, Amsterdam's famous public theatre.[58] Built in 1637 on the initiative of an orphanage (which owned the theatre) and encouraged by the city council, the Schouwburg offered the city's – and perhaps Europe's – most sophisticated entertainment, patronised by the educated and the well-to-do. Amsterdam remained until 1658 the only Dutch city where performances could be put on in a permanent theatre; elsewhere, halls had to be rented. From 1655, the Schouwburg broke with the time-honoured tradition of allowing only men to perform (with young boys taking the female roles) by admitting women, and we know the name of the first actress ever to appear on its stage: the young, beautiful, highly talented but illiterate Adriana Noozeman van den Bergh (1635–1661).

Joost van den Vondel (1587–1679), a playwright writing for the Schouwburg, is still recognised as one of the foremost Dutch poets. He translated Grotius's

Sophompaneas into Dutch and had it printed in 1635, the same year as the original Latin edition; it was reprinted several times in the seventeenth century, retitled *Joseph at Court*.[59] It was through this play, performed in Dutch, that Grotius's political philosophy was most widely disseminated in the seventeenth century. While historians speculate about some earlier performances of Grotius's play, we know for certain that at the Schouwburg it was first staged on 25 October 1638, in Vondel's translation. Subsequently, it became one of the theatre's most popular plays. Its success led Vondel to write two more plays about Joseph: *Joseph in Dothan* and *Joseph in Egypt*.[60] Both were staged at the Schouwburg, with Adriana Noozeman in the role of Jempsar, Potiphar's wife, in *Joseph in Egypt*. Grotius's play often formed a finale to Vondel's own Joseph plays. In 1654, for example, all three were performed no fewer than twenty-three times – on successive nights, sometimes even on the same night. Until 1672, when the theatre was closed for renovation, the Vondel–Grotius trilogy still attracted large crowds to Amsterdam's Schouwburg, no doubt thanks to the well-loved story, its hope-inspiring political message, and, not least, the spectacular costumes designed to highlight its oriental setting.

Amsterdam then was not only a city of art and theatre, but also a safe haven for marginalised religious groups fleeing persecution throughout Europe. Expatriates from France and England were particularly numerous. The philosopher Spinoza extolled Amsterdam as a city where "men of every race and sect live in complete harmony"; members of all religions and sects were accepted and even protected by the civil authorities, "provided that they injure no one".[61] A price had to be paid for this tolerance, however: the banning of everything in cultural life that could upset public peace and harmony. With the year 1672 – twenty-seven years after the death of Grotius – our story must end, because when the Schouwburg was reopened in 1677, its Calvinist regents banned all biblical plays from the stage, for fear of profaning God's word and causing offence.[62] Amsterdam's Golden Age was drawing to a close.

13

Competent Courtier – Zesen

Throughout Germany, the end of the Thirty Years War in 1648 brought a new phase of political thought and practice, aimed at the renewal of political and economic life. The new class of legal experts began to reform the state, producing, eventually, the system of princely absolutism. Not only were the new political ideas propagated in the form of treatises on politics, economics, and reform of the courts: they also became the subject of novels, poems, stage plays, and other forms of *belles-lettres*. Hans Jakob Christoph von Grimmelshausen (1621–1676) and Philipp von Zesen (1619–1689), Germany's foremost writers of the seventeenth century, both supported the new political ideas, and some of their work comes close to being informal propaganda. Unsurprisingly, both Grimmelshausen and Zesen used the biblical figure of Joseph in their imaginative writing for political purposes, though in different ways. Published in 1666, Grimmelshausen's *Des vortrefflich keuschen Josephs in Egypten Lebensbeschreibung* (Life of Joseph the Perfectly Chaste in Egypt) had little political content; but when it was republished in 1670, Grimmelshausen added a second part, an imaginative biography of Musai, Joseph's faithful servant who ultimately became steward of his household. Musai serves as spokesman for Grimmelshausen's political and economic ideas. Zesen's Joseph novel, also published in 1670, makes no attempt to disguise its political message; in fact, this slant is announced in its very title: *Assenat, das ist derselben und des Josefs heilige Stahts-, Lieb- und Lebens-geschicht* (Assenat: The Sacred Story of Politics, Love and Life of Assenat and Joseph, 1670).[1] At its most basic level, the political message implied in the story is the same as that already explained by Zesen in an earlier novel, *Adriatische Rosemund* (Rosemund of Venice, 1645): the German lands must not be ruled by a class that can boast mere noble descent; instead, rulers should have acquired a high level of education, irrespective of their humble, bourgeois, or noble background. Competence, not traditional inherited privilege, has to be the basis of any political office.[2] Zesen, like all of Germany's learned elite, believed in a new humanism as a force that would promote peace and enable culture to flourish as never before.

Zesen, born near Dessau and son of a German Lutheran pastor, is remembered today for his poetry and novels, and for his creation of a new literary style characterised by the avoidance of foreign words (French and Latin words had tended to crop up frequently in German baroque texts), and for relinquishing mannered, convoluted, turgid prose in preference for short, well-trimmed, lucid sentences, in the seventeenth century the recommended style at court. Zesen consistently avoids complex subordinate clauses, and, for the benefit of the reader, makes a point of repeating the main thoughts and key words. Zesen never led a fully settled life but moved from city to city; around 1670, we find him in Amsterdam, where he wrote *Assenat* and had the first edition of the novel illustrated and printed.[3] It does not come as a surprise that Zesen was familiar with Grotius's *Sophompaneas*, apparently having consulted a printed copy; he refers to two passages from it in the notes appended to *Assenat*.[4] Zesen may actually have attended a performance of Grotius's *Sophompaneas*, a Dutch version of which was until 1672 part of the repertoire of the Schouwburg (subsequently being banned from the stage, like all other biblical plays). Zesen was perfectly at home in Dutch, and translated several Dutch books into German, notably a bestselling popular medical manual.[5] *Assenat*, of course, was written in German. Reprinted several times, the novel found a wide readership, astonishingly so for a text a little too long at seven books (close to 600 pages in the modern edition), and somewhat too learned for truly popular appeal. The story Zesen tells, however, is fascinating.

Zesen's *Assenat*: a summary

Potiphar, supervisor of the royal kitchen and chief justice of the kingdom, belongs among the most important personalities at the court of Memphis during the reign of Pharaoh Nephrem. Potiphar has two wives: by the older one, Toote, he has a beautiful daughter; the younger one, Sephira, is without child. When Assenat, the beautiful daughter, was born, a mysterious oracle was received from the sun-god:

For twenty Niles no love she'll know
While she grows up in sacred space.
Then with a stranger she will go,
And thus improve her social place.
Listen, O Egypt, and obey,
And always honour what they say.[6]

To comply with the oracle, it is decided that Assenat should not grow up in her parents' home; instead, she is sent to be nursed and cared for in the Sun Palace of Heliopolis, the city of the Egyptian priests. There she lives in the company of other young women, for no males are allowed to pass through the gates of the Sun Palace.

One day, when a caravan of slave traders enters Memphis, the capital of Egypt, the streets of the city resound with the voices of people praying to the gods of Egypt – to Mompht, God of the Nile, but also to the Ram-God, to Osiris, Isis, Knef, and Anubis. Some beat their chests and scratch their arms and shoulders until they bleed, while others inscribe their prayers on waxen tablets that they attach to the knees of idols. Joseph, a Hebrew slave brought into the city by merchants, is quick to understand what people are praying for: that the Nile should flood and fertilise Egypt's fields, yet abstain from rising too high, for this would devastate the cultivable land. The Egyptians also seek to exorcise Typhon, the evil demon, whose aim it is to obstruct the divine blessing. While the Egyptians wail and groan in their superstitious ways, the young slave calmly addresses his God – the one, true deity – in a simple prayer, asking for protection and to be delivered from slavery. As the Egyptians notice and start talking about this handsome slave, Sephira, struck by his youthful beauty, manages to have Joseph bought for Potiphar's household. Treated not like a servant but as a son, he wears the attire of a young man of noble birth, is instructed in hieroglyphic writing, and soon becomes his master's trusted steward – managing the entire household. Joseph is befriended by Nitocris, daughter of Pharaoh Nephrem and confidante of Assenat. Nitocris asks Joseph about the meaning of Assenat's birthday oracle for which the Egyptian magicians had offered many conflicting interpretations, and she is immediately convinced that Joseph has at last given the correct, though hitherto unknown, explanation: after the Nile has risen twenty times, i.e. when she is twenty-one, Assenat will be married to a high-ranking man of foreign origin; the couple will rule over all Egyptians. While Joseph has no idea who this foreigner might be, Nitocris is sure that the mysterious stranger must be none other than Joseph himself, but keeps this insight to herself. She also makes it her business to find out about Joseph's family and background, all of which information is freely given by a Hebrew boy who happens to work in the kitchen of the royal palace. So she is the only Egyptian who knows that Joseph is the son of Jacob, a Hebrew prince, and that he was sold into slavery by his ten stepbrothers.

Three strange dreams – those of Nitocris, her servant girl Samesse, and Assenat – foretell complications in Joseph's career, notably his removal from Potiphar's household and his imprisonment.

Eighteen-year-old Sephira develops increasingly tender feelings for Joseph, and even enters his bedroom, pretending that it is motherly affection that she, as a childless woman, feels towards him, her quasi-adopted son. Joseph responds by telling her to pray for a child; as an expert in the medicinal properties of plants, he also prescribes a special herbal medicine to promote conception. To avoid arousing suspicion, she treats her husband with much tenderness and devotion, with kisses and endearing words; but inwardly her affections are reserved for Joseph, the true object of her desire. She holds Potiphar in her arms, while lusting after Joseph in her heart. By visits to his bedroom, flirtatious glances, and all manner of secretive signs, she seeks to signal her love to Joseph; yet the young man does not seem to understand. So Sephira changes her approach and resorts to a more direct strategy – that of seduction. She begins by openly declaring her love to Joseph and asking him to respond to her desires. This first overt approach turns out to be a complete failure, for not only does Joseph reject her advances; the scene also has a witness. Nitocris, who happens to be in the adjacent room when Sephira speaks to Joseph, has secretly listened, and later reveals her knowledge to Sephira, seeking to dissuade her from her evil intention. But Sephira persists and invents ever more desperate strategies to break Joseph's resistance. Her second attempt involves pretending to faint in his presence so that Joseph must touch her to revive her. Her third act of attempted seduction is accompanied by a dramatic change from begging to threatening Joseph with punishment if he does not comply. At her fourth attempt, she promises to marry him once her husband has been poisoned and eliminated. The fifth attempt involves the giving of food with an aphrodisiac secretly mixed in – but Joseph, who realises that the food is contaminated, eats some in her presence, declaring that an attendant angel is rendering the magic ingredients ineffective. The sixth time Sephira approaches Joseph she declares that without him, she no longer wants to live and is considering suicide. Joseph's response remains the same throughout – he rejects her advances, telling her that he will neither commit such a crime against his master nor compromise his own virtue.

Sephira's advances culminate in a seventh attempt at seduction. Once her husband has left the house to attend the rituals of a holy day, she perfumes her bed and orders Joseph to serve her in her chamber. Fully decked with precious jewellery and wearing a seductive gown that reveals her shapely bosom, she receives him and asks him to sleep with her. Horrified, Joseph flees. Thus deserted, Sephira can no longer hide her true identity – that of a lustful demon. Anger, hatred, and thirst for revenge flash from her eyes. Peals of thunder and flashes of lightning issue from her mouth. Fiery breath ascends from her nostrils. Her hair, completely dishevelled, falls across her face, now disfigured by scars. As Joseph makes good his escape, Sephira screams for her maids. Beside herself with rage, she accuses Joseph of attempted rape. Upon his return home, Potiphar consigns Joseph to jail – conveniently next door to his residence. Even now Sephira approaches the window of his cell, promising to free him if only he will relent and respond to her love. As is to be expected, Joseph remains unassailable in his virtue, preferring to be a God-fearing, innocent prisoner rather than sinful slave to a lustful woman's desires.

Nitocris, upon learning what happened, sends money to the prison warder, ordering him to free Joseph both from his chains and from forced labour in the prison workhouse. She also writes to the jailer to warn him of Sephira's plan to have Joseph poisoned, a plan betrayed to her by one of Sephira's maids. Freed from other responsibilities, Joseph uses his stay in prison to study the art of astrology under the tutelage of a Chaldean fellow prisoner. He is also given an honorary job: to serve the king's cupbearer and the royal baker, two prominent state prisoners. As the king has been having strange dreams that seem to defy explanation, Joseph is recommended to him as an expert interpreter by two members of his court: Nitocris and the cupbearer whom he has restored to office. Joseph explains to the king that there will be a series of seven years of plenty, followed by seven years of dearth in the Egyptian economy, and suggests that a national disaster can be avoided only by taking immediate economic and political measures. Pharaoh Nephrem, convinced of Joseph's outstanding abilities as a steward, at once appoints him governor of Egypt in order to deal with the matter.

Meanwhile, Sephira has died of frustration, just deserts for her crime against Joseph. Potiphar, now living in Heliopolis near his daughter Assenat, has been promoted to the position of chief overseer of the Egyptian priesthood. Potiphar knows of Joseph's false accusation and innocence; in fact, he is proud that his former steward has been made vice-regent of the country. On his inspection tour of Egypt and the granaries he has built, Joseph visits Potiphar's home in Heliopolis, and Assenat immediately falls in love with him. Joseph indicates that he cannot accept even a social kiss from someone who venerates idols. Assenat retires to her quarters, destroys her idols, and fasts and prays for a whole week. Eventually, she is visited by an angel who blesses her and tells her to change her clothes from black to white, in celebration of her new status as a believer in the one true God, the God of the Hebrew governor. Under Joseph's instruction, Potiphar also secretly accepts the teaching of the governor; although personally convinced of the truth of the Hebrew religion, he feels that the Egyptians are not yet ready to be converted to it. Soon, we see the celebration of the marriage of Joseph and Assenat as well as the marriage of Nitocris to the crown prince of Libya.

Joseph at once takes up his political task. He has granaries built, some as simple storehouses, some as impressive buildings in the manner of the Pyramids. During the years of plenty, he uses all state funds available to buy surplus grain from the Egyptian farmers, and when the lean years arrive, as announced in Pharaoh Nephrem's dream, he sells it again so that none has to suffer hunger. Assenat supplements Joseph's management of food distribution by giving alms to the poor of the country, so that not one of them is in want of anything. Apart from dispensing alms and presiding over her husband's household, she educates her two sons Ephraim and Manasseh. She also studies arcane Hebrew scriptures, especially the book of Enoch, and develops her skills as a healer. Many suffering from sickness seek her help, and she freely, and to good effect, dispenses her herbal remedies. When Joseph's brothers first come to him to beg for grain, they are unaware of the Egyptian vice-regent's true identity, but eventually Joseph reveals himself to his brothers and assures them of his forgiveness and brotherly affection. At Pharaoh's invitation, Joseph's entire clan – his father Jacob, his brothers and their families – immigrates to Egypt and is granted land for settlement. While the Hebrews settle peacefully, others – Arabians and Africans – attack Egypt to ransack grain stores there, for their countries too are suffering from an increasingly acute shortage of food. Joseph's troops push the invaders back, but everyone is dealt with kindly, for Joseph, ever disposed to diplomacy and mildness, grants them the privilege of buying grain from the Egyptian state granaries.

Not long after this successful outcome, however, another, quite unexpected event challenges the public peace in Egypt. One of Pharaoh Nephrem's sons not only falls in love with the beautiful Assenat and plans to kill Joseph so as to be able to marry her; he also plots to kill his father and succeed him on the throne. With the help of two of Joseph's brothers he manages to abduct Assenat, but is badly wounded in battle, and the rebellion fails. The episode ends with the death of the rebellious prince. Shortly after this, King Nephrem also dies, and Joseph, in addition to the position he already has, assumes full royal rule. (Only much later, when Nephrem's second son has grown up, does Joseph relinquish the crown of Egypt.) As the seven lean years end, the country once more is regularly inundated by the fertile floods of the River Nile. Egyptian agriculture flourishes again, and Joseph divides the land among the population, claiming no more than one-fifth of the produce as a royal tax. To promote the well-being of Egypt, Joseph not only looks after the Egyptians' material needs; he also promotes intellectual life by establishing, in the priestly city of Heliopolis, an academy of higher learning – of astrology and other arcane sciences, including the secret arts of physiognomy and palmistry.

The final years of Joseph's governance are marked by the death of his father Jacob, of several of his brothers, and of Assenat. Never having fully recovered from the shock of her abduction and becoming increasingly weak, Assenat dies in the twentieth year of her marriage, at the age of forty-one. Joseph honours her memory not by indulging in an immoderate demonstration of grief, but by never marrying again. When he reaches old age, Joseph retires from government, but continues to influence political life by giving wise counsel. His final accomplishment is the draining of the Nile delta marshes and odorous swamps by means of a system of specially devised canals. As a result, Egypt gains new cultivable land, giving it a broader economic basis. Joseph's last days are overshadowed by sad news received from a distant relative living in Uz: Job is lamenting the sudden death of all his sons and daughters, and has been visited by yet further calamities. Joseph himself finally dies at the age of one hundred and ten, sixty-one years after the death of his dear wife Assenat. The memory of both Joseph and Assenat is assured a firm place in Egyptian religion, for superstitious as the Egyptians have remained, they count them among their deities and worship them under the names of Apis and Isis.

Poeta doctus

Like every author writing a historical novel, Zesen has researched his subject thoroughly in the interest of giving his story a local feel. The Nile is there, crocodiles are mentioned along with pagan rites, the names of deities such as

Isis and Osiris, the cities of Memphis and Heliopolis, and much more. In passing, reference is made to the Pyramids. Today we would expect the historical novelist to give his or her writing as much local colour as possible, but not to reveal the sources used and the authorities relied upon for ancient names, foreign customs and manners, and facts of geography and climate. Zesen and some of his contemporaries felt differently. Revealing one's scholarly sources was quite common and not considered particularly pedantic; instead it was appreciated, for it corresponded to the ideal of the *poeta doctus*, the poet-scholar. According to the notion of the *poeta doctus*, a good novel might well include a substantial number of geographic, ethnographic, or antiquarian facts, possibly presented in learned digressions. While Zesen thought of his novel as a book to be read for entertainment and religious edification, he also used it as a means of displaying antiquarian learning and disseminating knowledge. For him, the art of novel-writing required, besides imagination, a heavy dose of learning, and he would willingly share it with his readers.

In order to evoke the exotic world of ancient Egypt in biblical times and to edify his readers, Zesen resorts to a twofold strategy. In the main text of the novel, he inserts instructive asides such as a discussion on the snow-melt from African mountains that feeds the Nile, descriptions of Egyptian antiquities, including the Pyramids, and reflections on the (quasi-) scientific status of astrology (a horoscope may serve as a warning, but not as a revelation of what is inevitable – a reinterpretation of astrology typical of the seventeenth century).[7] Further learned material appears in the many notes and bibliographical references placed at the end of the book. These aphoristic notes contain passages in Latin and Greek, and even a few words printed in Hebrew characters. All of this makes the novel look somewhat like an academic book written by a professional and published by a modern university press. The subject index (a feature of many seventeenth-century novels)[8] contributes to this impression – notes and index together filling close to 40 per cent of the book. The notes explain and expand upon ancient customs and antiquities, pagan deities, plants and animals and other items of natural history, and refer to ancient sources such as the *Histories* by Herodotus.

Zesen's notes also reveal the main sources for his story: the book of Genesis, the *Story of Aseneth*, the *Testaments of the Twelve Patriarchs*, the Jewish historian Josephus, not forgetting Grimmelshausen's *Des vortrefflich keuschen Josephs in Egypten Lebensbeschreibung* (1666) which Zesen pillaged for a number of ideas and episodes (and came close to plagiarising). In the case of the *Testaments of the Twelve Patriarchs*, one could reconstruct practically its entire section on Joseph from Zesen's long quotations. In the opening chapters of *Assenat* in particular, Zesen relies on the *Testaments*: the protagonist's arrival in Egypt as a slave, the interest of Potiphar's wife in the boy, her eventual purchase of him for her household, the night-time visit she pays to him under the pretence of parental care for a quasi-son, the series of attempts to seduce Joseph, her sending of messages to the prisoner, even such a minor detail as the reference to Potiphar's concubine (who has no role in the plot) – all of this can be found in the *Testaments*, and much of it in Grimmelshausen's earlier treatment of the subject. Zesen is especially proud of his use of the *Story of Aseneth*, one source that his rival Grimmelshausen had missed in his research. In addition to utilising sources on Joseph, Zesen exploited ancient literature to embellish his presentation; the oracle announcing that Assenat would eventually marry a stranger, for example, echoes a similar prophecy found in Virgil's *Aeneid*.[9] This is not to say that Zesen merely reproduced or paraphrased the sources on which he relied. The figure of Nitocris,[10] Joseph's friend at the royal court, for example, is his own invention; knowing more than the other characters, she contributes to the narrative coherence of the first part of the novel.

Zesen apparently thought that the time was ripe for presenting biblical stories based on the *poeta doctus* concept, and he had good reason for this. Typical products of baroque learning such as the Jesuit Athanasius Kircher's *Oedipus Aegyptiacus* (Rome, 1652/54) and Samuel Bochart's *Hierozoicon* (1663), a very learned manual on the animals mentioned in the Bible, had just been published and invited exploitation. Zesen made extensive use of these two works, duly referencing them in his notes.

How did Zesen's contemporaries feel about the biblical fiction of our *poeta doctus*? And how might a reader respond to it in the twenty-first century? The popular appeal of *Assenat* continued beyond the book's first edition in 1670.[11] In 1672 and 1679, two further editions followed, complete with notes and index. Subsequently, several abridged versions (without notes) were produced in German (1679) and Danish (six editions, 1711–1776). The novel was a success, and apparently no one felt uncomfortable with its support of the absolute state, its preference for the monarchy, and its programme of control and policing of the population. Zesen's readers seem to have liked the idea of a fictionalised manual of political instruction, a blend of novel and political treatise, a textbook set in a narrative frame. The omission of the notes in some of the later editions mentioned signals a problem, however: the *poeta doctus* concept was in crisis.

This crisis is evident in the voices of three early critics of *Assenat*, all authors of novels themselves: Grimmelshausen (1672), Joachim Meier (1697), and Joseph von Eichendorff (1851). Zesen, they argued, failed to live up to his promise to write a novel, since he never actually delivered. His plot is meagre. In a good novel one expects a lighter touch, more entertainment than instruction, and, above all, a more complex story. Joachim Meier disparaged Zesen as an author whose "inventions are poor and clumsy (*elend und pöbelhaft*), never offering diversions, charming scenes, or complications".[12] Meier's own recipe for a biblical novel comes close to that of the nineteenth-century genre of Sir Walter Scott's historical novel: invent your own plot, use some historical characters (especially for minor roles), emphasise historical colour in speech, manners, and costume, allude to contemporary events, and never spurn suspense and intrigue. The biblical story, for Zesen, is merely the pretext for the bombastic display of learning: rather than writing a novel, he assembles from other books a museum of Egyptian antiquities, argued Eichendorff; a meagre plot, short sentences, and long, superfluous notes: this was how he summarised his verdict.[13] But even as a work of antiquarian scholarship Zesen's work is of questionable merit. According to Grimmelshausen, Zesen has consistently misunderstood his sources (including his, Grimmelshausen's, own novel): he has not fully grasped the difference between the scriptural text (always deemed historically reliable and of unquestionable authority) and post-biblical embellishments. Grimmelshausen considered both the *Story of Aseneth* and the *Testaments of the Twelve Patriarchs* rabbinical fiction rather than reliable historical sources; they may be exploited by a modern author, but it is completely unwarranted to imbue them with special authority.[14] Zesen mistook Jewish novels for history, and thus failed as a *poeta doctus*.

Such criticism reveals the impending crisis of the *poeta doctus* idea rather than informing readers about the literary quality of the novel. Zesen's *Assenat* merits another, more sympathetic reading, though it must be admitted that the first three books of *Assenat*, which bring the story up as far as Joseph's stay in prison, are stronger and better written than the remaining four. The lighter touch of the novel's early chapters eventually gives way to didactic gravity, a change presumably intended by the author. However, there is a strong underlying und unifying theme throughout that can be analysed in terms of excess and restraint.

A World of Excess and Restraint

In his preface to the novel, Zesen tells his readers to start with the learned notes and only then to turn to the narrative, thereby admitting that he offers two books within one cover – an encyclopaedic description of ancient Egypt followed by a didactic novel. The reader who has mastered the book's scholarly appendices is in a position not only to follow the narrative in detail but also to consider interpretive issues or, more precisely, work out the underlying philosophy. This philosophy is present from the book's first page, though never made explicit either in the novel or in the notes. To understand it, we have to turn to the novel itself where it is presented in narrative form, and seek to understand it in the context of the cultural world of the seventeenth century.

The story begins with the description of a pagan ritual performed in the city of Memphis when the deities to whom Egypt owes its fertility are addressed. An entire list of deities is invoked. Some are given epithets: mild Isis, nourisher and provider; Horus the fertile; Mompht, the black god who makes the Nile rise. Generally, the gods succeed in monitoring the rising of the Nile, controlling the flooding and the fertilising of the fields with mud brought from afar. This is apparently possible because the pantheon includes both members who are prone to excess, and others who are opposed to excess. Multi-breasted Isis, as depicted in the novel's frontispiece, stands for excessive fertility (Fig. 15).[15] We are not told precisely who her opponent is, but Zesen seems to assign this role to Typhon, also known as Seth, the excessively evil god, prone to anger and aggression, always intent on obstructing the divine blessing; he is most happy when fertility is replaced by sterility. A myth tells how Typhon murdered his brother Osiris. Mompht also seems to be prone to excess, for he has a companion responsible for restraining him; this is Ompht, god of life-giving mud, who moderates the rising of the Nile, preventing the river from rising too much and thereby destroying, rather than gently overflowing, the alluvial fields.

In general, the gods regulate the course of nature well, securing excellent harvests and permitting a stable agricultural economy. From time to time, however, the system gets out of balance. Occasionally the Nile carries too much sediment, prompting excess fertility and, consequently, an excessive harvest. This may happen several years in succession. The Nile is then exhausted: no flooding at all takes place, so no harvest is possible, for the land stays dry and infertile, unable to bring forth fruit and grain. In consequence of such anarchy, human and animal life are endangered, because the people do not normally store surplus food. Typhon, god of sterility, triumphs over the gods of fertility. Such a crisis can be predicted, however, and measures can be taken to prevent the population from suffering too much from the consequences of nature's excess and exhaustion.

Zesen was fascinated by the notions of excess and restraint. He applies the idea not only to the realm of nature, but also to the human realm, making it a leitmotif in his novel. His general idea, hard to miss in its pages, is this: excess is always an evil thing; it leads invariably to its opposite – deficiency, infertility, disaster, and, ultimately, death. Nature, including human nature, is apparently always prone to excess; to prevent disaster, nature, including the natural appetites of people, must be restrained. Culture, for Zesen, seems to imply the need for taming, calming, and restricting that which tends to excess. One can read the entire novel as a story of excess, its catastrophic consequences, and the attempt to temper it, to impose limits and structure on that which is wild

Fig. 15. *The Wedding of Joseph and Assenat.* The wedding ceremony is presided over by the multi-breasted goddess Isis or Natura, Egypt's fertility goddess. Her presence announces the years of plenty predicted by Joseph. – Christian von Hagen for Philipp von Zesen's novel *Assenat*, 1670.

and exuberant. The hero who conquers and controls excess is of course Joseph, who, from the very beginning, unfailingly imposes order and fends off all that endangers it. Put differently and more succinctly: the challenge Zesen's Joseph is confronted with is not famine but excess. Accordingly, Zesen portrays him not as a saviour who successfully pulls a country's entire population through a period of famine; but as a hero who restrains excess, defeating nature by cultural means. And he manages to do so because he has solved the problem of excess within himself, his own person, by learning how to exercise restraint (e.g. of sexual desire) and by placing communal concerns above personal ones (e.g. by being loyal to his master Potiphar, rather than giving in to Sephira's desires).

It is not accidental that Joseph's first task at Potiphar's court was to lay out a large pleasure garden; its geometric design – in the form of a series of concentric circles – is described in the text and visualised in an illustration (Fig. 16). Both text and illustration highlight its cosmic character, for it includes signs of the zodiac that symbolise the ordered universe. The typical baroque garden with its French geometric layout reflects the idea that a clear pattern has to be imposed on nature; without such imposition, wilderness would exist, uninhabitable by humans. Geometry, it may be remembered, was an obsession of seventeenth-century education; its study was patronised in the princely courts in the hope that its promotion would produce both able, clear-thinking administrators and a stable, ordered society. Geometrically designed palaces and gardens, graceful minuet dances, and the Cartesian philosophy with its preference for clear-cut concepts over fuzzy notions all reflect the same spirit, symbolising the baroque norms of the ordered world.[16]

Once order, synonymous with usefulness, but also with beauty, harmony, and truth, had been imposed on the world around us, seventeenth-century thinkers felt that the structured, tamed environment would in turn influence people, contributing to the clarity of their thought, behaviour, and even physical beauty. That human beauty could be derived from merely looking at another beautiful person, or the artistic representation of such a person, was a widely held notion in the seventeenth and eighteenth centuries. Zesen, echoing Grimmelshausen, refers to this idea in explaining Joseph's extraordinary good looks. Beauty, Zesen explains, was endemic in Joseph's family. There is scriptural warrant for this assumption, for both Joseph and his mother Rachel are said to be "beautiful in form and appearance".[17] Via his mother Rachel (favourite wife of his father Jacob) and his grandmother Rebekah, he inherited beauty from his great-grandparents Sarah and Abraham, both very handsome people. Abraham's good looks apparently derived from the fact that his father Terah was a mason who carved idols – beautiful statues and images of gods and goddesses. Simply through living near them and repeatedly looking at them, Terah's wife came

Fig. 16. *Joseph's Garden.* Joseph, portrayed as a turban-wearing oriental gentleman, gives instructions to the workers who are laying out an ornamental garden. The geometric design, typical of baroque gardens, reflects the ideal of nature completely subjugated to human reason. – Christian von Hagen for Philipp von Zesen's novel *Assenat*, 1670.

under the spell of their beauty. The beautiful human shapes of the idols not only impressed themselves on her mind but also shaped the child that she carried in her womb.[18] This idea of the child being moulded by what a pregnant women sees or even thinks about occasionally appears in ancient Greek sources. In Heliodorus' *Ethiopian Story* – no doubt Grimmelshausen's, and via Grimmelshausen Zesen's, ultimate source – it provides the key to the heroine's true identity.[19] Persinna, the black queen of Ethiopia, conceived her child Chariclea while looking at a picture of the Greek heroine Andromeda; as a result, Chariclea was born with white skin. Indeed, beautiful Chariclea looked very much like Andromeda as represented in the portrait in the royal bedroom. The notion of the influence of what a mother sees, or thinks about, on her unborn child fascinated people throughout Europe in the seventeenth and eighteenth centuries. In Henry Fielding's novel *Joseph Andrews* (discussed above, in Chapter 10) the true identity of the eponymous hero is established through the strawberry-like birthmark he carries on his chest; this mark was said to derive from the strawberries his mother had craved during pregnancy. While Fielding in his comic novel seems to poke fun at the idea, it received support from then current popular and even medical wisdom.[20] In Zesen's novel, it exemplifies the more general conviction that the environment helps shape people's identity and character.

But let us return to the discussion of excess and its fateful consequences! Sephira, Potiphar's young and seductively beautiful wife, is presented as the very model of sexual excess. Driven by an excess of lust, she is, as a result, infertile – she has no child. The scene in which she is described as a semi-naked seductress who, upon being rejected, almost metamorphoses into an evil, fire-spitting demon, illustrates well the destructive nature of erotic excess. Ultimately, her excess is self-destructive, so she disappears from the novel. Her death is merely noted, not elaborated upon, apparently signalling that death was the natural result of her behaviour or, more properly, her very being that defied reform. Interestingly, she is given a male counterpart towards the end of the novel: Pharaoh's son, who lusts after married Assenat, stages a rebellion, seeks to abduct her, is involved in a battle, and dies of the wounds he has received fighting. Again, excess leads to the ultimate form of sterility – death.

Once he is promoted to high office in the state, Joseph acts as the head of the state's agrarian department. With the help of the Hebrew God, he is able to predict the future and guide the Egyptians first through the years of plenty, and then through the years of dearth, until the normal equilibrium is restored. He introduces large-scale storage of food as a measure to combat the famine that he, in his wisdom, foresees as the natural consequence of nature exhausting itself by superfluous production.

At this point in the story, Assenat enters Joseph's life. Zesen paints a vivid portrait of Assenat, who is the exact opposite of Sephira. Her sexuality is restricted from an early age, for she grows up in the confines of the Sun Palace, to which no male person is admitted; the first man she encounters is Joseph, with whom she duly falls in love and, shortly afterwards, marries. Her bedroom, illustrated in the novel, exemplifies order and restraint: she is shown kneeling beside her bed, in prayer, as two courtiers arrive to conduct her to her wedding ceremony (Fig. 17). The contrast between Sephira's and Assenat's bedrooms is that between chaos and order, excess and restraint, lust and chastity (Fig. 18). The wedding of Joseph and Assenat coincides, and contrasts, with the onset of the years of plenty. The contrast is already made clear in her wedding portrait, used as the novel's frontispiece: Isis or Natura, who presides over the wedding, is depicted as a multi-breasted female idol; Assenat, by contrast, is a normal woman, modestly and unrevealingly dressed. Whereas nature soon brings forth its fruit not only in abundance but in excess, Assenat gives birth to just two sons. During the years of dearth, Assenat displays normal capabilities, though she is determined enough to oppose the destructive forces of hunger and sickness by dispensing both alms and herbal medicine. Zesen takes care not to exaggerate her vitality by keeping it within the limits of credibility. Traumatised by her abduction and the prince's failed rebellion, she is considerably weakened and dies at the age of forty-one; Zesen seems to give her the noble death of an upper-class woman who, dying at a young age, continues to be remembered as a paragon of beauty, rather than as a woman marked by the inevitable signs of advanced age.

The final task Joseph masters in Egypt is replete with symbolism. As in his first professional task in the land of the Nile, Joseph imposes order on nature by acting as a landscape architect, though on a larger scale than when laying out Potiphar's pleasure garden. Again we find the pattern of over-abundance and restriction: the swamps that he dries out represent an excess of water; through a carefully devised system of drainage canals, unwanted water is eliminated, making the land capable of cultivation. Unsurprisingly, the newly created province supplies more grain than any other, so that the episode once more highlights the protagonist as the one who, having triumphed over excess, feeds the country.

At the end of his novel, Zesen indicates that after the death of Joseph the Hebrew population multiplied greatly. "The people of Israel were fruitful and increased greatly; they multiplied and grew exceedingly strong, so that the land was filled with them."[21] Relying once more upon his vast store of knowledge,[22] Zesen offers an explanation for the abnormally high fertility rate: the Hebrew women, by drinking the enriching water of the Nile, became as prone as the alluvial fields to bringing forth fruit in abundance.[23] They gave birth usually not to a single child, but to quadruplets and even octuplets. No wonder, then, that phials of muddy Nile water were sent abroad as a highly prized tonic to

Fig. 17. *In Assenat's Bedroom*. Assenat, distinguished by her bridal veil and crown, is shown in prayer as she kneels beside her bed, waiting to be conducted to her marriage with Joseph: a scene of domestic order, godliness and chastity. – Christian von Hagen, for Philipp von Zesen's novel *Assenat*, 1670.

promote fertility. As a result of their enormous growth rate, the Hebrews built new cities in Egypt which, as every reader of the Bible remembers, caused the Egyptians to feel threatened by the ever-growing foreign population living in their country, hence the measures taken against them. These measures led to the enslavement of the Hebrews and, eventually, to their expulsion from the land of the Nile and to their existence, for an entire generation, in the desert, far away from the fleshpots of Egypt. Zesen refrains from going into the matter fully, but he insinuates that after the death of Joseph, excess could no longer be tempered by the Hebrew governor's wisdom.

That wisdom not only coloured Joseph's political and economic activities; it also emerged in the governance of himself. Throughout the novel, Zesen seeks to highlight one essential characteristic of Joseph's personality: the absence, or mastery, of the irregular and disturbing "passions" that seek to dominate life. This character trait was deemed by the baroque mentality vital for those active in politics and administration of the state. Joseph's control of "passions"[24] is evident in his resistance to Sephira's attempts to seduce him. In their encounter, two moral worlds clash – one characterised by excess and chaos, and one marked by restraint and order. These two antithetical worlds, as we shall see, resonate with seventeenth-century cultural and political life.

A POLITICAL WORLD

Zesen's political philosophy emerges quite clearly as soon as we realise that – despite all his display of antiquarian learning, the oriental setting, and the notions of excess and restraint – in reality he sketches, thinly veiled, the imaginary biography of a seventeenth-century German courtier, complete with unpromising beginnings, court intrigues, crises, and eventual rise to high office under an important monarch. Read in this way, much of the novel's plot reveals its contemporary relevance. In what follows we disregard the biblical and exotic setting and names to highlight the seventeenth-century message of Zesen's novel. For the sake of convenience (and fun), we will call the young protagonist J., and his first employers Lord P. and Lady S. (and so on through the whole story), considering them not as figures from distant times, but as contemporaries of our author and his readers. Reading in this way, we can follow a seventeenth-century "courtier's progress" from the hell of a corrupt minor court via an unjustified stay in prison to service at the royal court where the protagonist, capabilities now duly acknowledged, rises to the office of prime minister. Here is the story in detail.

In the beginning there is a boy – J. – who, due to family conflicts, is forced to leave home and enter service in a minor court. One might suppose that J. owes his position in Lord P.'s house to his innate abilities, but this is a deception. He owes

Fig. 18. *In Sephira's Bedroom.* Potiphar's wife Sephira, naked in bed, calls in her servants as Joseph, innocent, flees the chamber, soon to be falsely accused of attempted rape: a scene of crime and confusion. – Christian von Hagen, for Philipp von Zesen's novel *Assenat*, 1670.

it to S., a noble lady with the power and means to recruit him for service and thus further her interest in J.'s good looks. As a commoner – someone who lacks the privilege of high birth – J. remains forever dependent upon the whims and wishes of his lordly owner. Admiring J.'s beauty is not enough for Lady S.; she wants more – she wants him as a lover. As someone who has no wish to capitalise on his good looks, wishing instead to impress with his intelligence, knowledge, and virtue, J. cannot succeed in Lord P.'s house. This house symbolises all manner of vanities and corruptions that plagued baroque courts throughout Europe: most members of society were dependent on the few who enjoyed the privilege of high birth; high social status was ruthlessly exploited for personal advantage; moral rules were flexible; adultery was normal; aphrodisiacs, sometimes administered in secret, heightened sexual pleasures; rivals could be eliminated through poisoning; lasting friendship was never guaranteed, those initially shown favour being equally likely to be suddenly dropped; false accusation regularly ruined careers and led to unjust imprisonment. People at court were absorbed in their own lives and intrigues; they were not particularly concerned about public welfare. The dominating figure in Lord P.'s household is Lady S.: young, beautiful, and corrupt. Lord P.'s other (apparently his first) wife, T., is completely overshadowed by Lady S.; in fact, the former is hardly ever mentioned; she belongs to a different, more wholesome world. As for Lady S., she displays the features of a dragon-like monster, revealing her true identity as a fire-spitting demonic creature once it is clear that her advances are doomed to failure. In keeping with her demonic nature, she has no children; demons, according to traditional Christian thought, may appear in human form, but their womb remains forever sterile. Since under Lady S.'s rule J. would never be able to thrive, Zesen gives her a sudden death, symbolic of his wish that corruption should be entirely destroyed.

(To return briefly to the novel proper, in its exotic setting: Sephira's demise is never described, but merely alluded to as "Sephira's sudden death".[25] While Zesen took the name of Sephira from an earlier source,[26] the sudden nature of her death clearly echoes a New Testament passage concerning a woman with a similar name. According to this passage an evil woman named Saphira, who had lied to St Peter about her financial situation, was punished by God on the spot: "immediately she fell down at his [Peter's] feet and died".[27] Christians traditionally are horrified at the prospect of a sudden, unexpected death, for this would deprive them of final repentance and thus endanger their chance of entering life everlasting. The mere reference to Sephira's sudden death suffices both to evoke this horror and to condemn her as one so evil that her demise does not merit any further comment. The three words – "Sephira's sudden death" – contrast vividly with the page-long descriptions of the death, embalming, and burial of other leading characters of the story: Assenat, Jacob, and Joseph. For Zesen, it would not have made sense to have Sephira buried with any ritual attention. She must vanish; all of her world must perish with her.)

The house and behaviour of Lady S. have only one function: that of serving as a training ground for a hero; to test those who, like J., can survive the hell of temptation and intimidation without any harm other than being demoted and fired.

Philosophically speaking, J.'s training is well calculated. According to revisionist baroque thought, all human beings are essentially alike, but not all are truly civilised. "Like all men, he consisted of flesh and blood", Zesen asserts of J. in the context of one of the seduction scenes.[28] The latter depict an uncivilised woman confronting a thoroughly civilised man. J.'s resistance to temptation is seen not so much as defying the wishes of someone else (the lustful woman) but as overcoming one's own irregular "passions" (a subject to which we will return). Once J. has demonstrated mastery of himself, he has proved his credentials for joining the royal court.

But before taking his place at court, he has to spend some time in a place of transition: the jail. Though secure in this hybrid space "betwixt and between", our hero is still assaulted by Lady S., but he begins to come under the benign protection of N. who, as a princess, represents the court as well as his future spouse, A., her close friend. The hybrid status of the prison stands out in Zesen's discussion of the false accusation against the prisoner: although the allegation constitutes the reason why J. is jailed, it is never put in writing and therefore is never given formal status; thus the accusation both exists and does not exist.[29] (Zesen implies that in ancient Egypt – as in modern times – an accusation remains incomplete as long as it is not put in writing, duly deposited, and made available to the accused person. Today one would consider Joseph's detainment illegal.) In prison, J. prepares for his future career by broadening his knowledge (he studies astrology) and practising his skills at dream interpretation. Once released from prison because his competence in oneiromancy is again needed at court, he can finally embark on a second career.

J.'s second career – at the royal court of an important country – is very different from his first one. Now his good looks, while never denied, are of little relevance. Equally irrelevant is his being patronised by a person of high rank (N., daughter of the king). The decisive qualities that prompt his promotion at court are his intelligence and professional competence. The royal court at M., with its ecclesiastical extension at H., is symbolic of a new regime recommended by reform-minded seventeenth-century political authors: a regime based not on inherited class, privilege, and rank, but on professional competence, virtue, and dedication to public welfare.[30] It is in this world, in the service of king and state, that J. can finally thrive. Here he can fully realise his political vision, to the benefit of all.

At the domestic level, too, J. is now also properly at home – in his own, well-ordered household. Zesen's illustrator sums up the message well in depicting two contrasting scenes: one in which Lord P.'s wife, naked in bed, calls in her servants as J. runs out of the chamber – a scene of utter confusion (see Fig. 18); and one in which A. is shown as she kneels in prayer beside her bed, waiting to be conducted to her marriage ceremony – an image of order and godliness (see Fig. 17). While these scenes seem to permit a glimpse of what may be called J.'s private life, they actually represent and reveal the essence of two contrasting worlds: the chaotic immoral situation of an unreformed princely court and the calm godliness of a court established according to "modern", rational principles.

Zesen portrays J. as the ideal courtier. As a member of the *nobilitas literaria* he has mastered all the arts, including occult ones such as astrology. As befits a scholar, he uses even his time in prison to further his knowledge of the sciences. Since a courtier must of course have no criminal record, Zesen explains carefully that despite his stay in jail, J. was never formally accused of any crime: although he threw J. in prison, Lord P. only half believed the stories of Lady S., so never submitted a formal bill of accusation.[31] From the perspective of the administration, an unwritten accusation does not count, in keeping with the ancient rule that "what is not on record in writing, does not exist in the world" (*quod non est in actis non est in mundo*). Therefore J.'s stay in prison in no way hampers his political career. Without having first to clear his name, he can be promoted to the position of prime minister, purely on the merit of his success in dream interpretation and his expert advice on preparation for the years of dearth. He is highly respected for his innovative ideas concerning the economy of a country whose prosperity rests on state-directed agricultural production. Throughout the novel, J. maintains his interest in learning, as is evident from the academy which he establishes in H. to support the nobility of letters and their learned pursuits. ("It is at Heliopolis that the most learned of the Egyptians are said to be found", wrote the ancient historian Herodotus, and Zesen picks up and develops this comment.)[32]

In the career of courtier J., political concerns and activities predominate, so there is little time for an idyllic family and domestic life. Once J. and A. are married, A. no longer plays a conspicuous role in the story, and when she does appear, it is for the most part as a public figure who untiringly supports and supplements her husband's political and social responsibilities. Accordingly, we learn little about her personal and domestic life. She even accompanies her husband on his tours of inspection, lending a note of feminine charm to his mission. Moreover, "she fed the hungry and gave water to the thirsty. To those who were ill she gave medicine. Every day during the seven years of dearth she told her husband not to forget the poor, and due to her insistence, they were so well cared for that not one of them was in want of anything."[33] (In fact, one has the impression that the competent pair govern the country very much as a couple, just as A.'s birthday oracle had predicted. He is called the country's saviour, and she, the female equivalent, *Heilandin*.)[34]

In addition to describing courtier J.'s dedication to his political office, Zesen seeks to highlight his mastery of irregular and disturbing "passions", a theme of particular relevance to seventeenth-century authors. For them, the court was an ideal world: well ordered, measured, predictable, and peopled by the civilised elite who doubled as paragons of morality. In such a world, a character like P.'s wife would be the exception rather than the rule. Perfection of self-control as we find it in J., according to Zesen and his contemporaries, underpins the strict rules of etiquette compulsory for all who move in the courtly world. Far from being concealed in his soul, the courtier's inner qualities manifest themselves to others. They are easily recognisable even by those who have little contact with court and political life, evident as they are in even the most trifling details of etiquette, speech, gesture, and bearing: "He never spoke a single word that he had not carefully considered, as if weighing every one. [. . .] Joseph knew how to moderate all his gestures and words – his entire being – in such a skilful way that everyone watched him in amazement and listened to him in awe."[35] In other words: J., in addition to being a man of virtues, embodies the ideal of the polite and polished courtly gentleman, and he serves both as a mirror image and a role model for Zesen's intended readers.

While the extent of a courtier's self-control may fall short of the ideal, state control over public affairs is almost complete, especially when the king's carefully chosen favourites such as our hero are appointed to master difficult situations. The populace, Zesen argues, must never be left without political guidance and supervision. During the seven years of plenty, people might become indolent and neglect their work. "To prevent this, one has to take measures well in advance."[36] So J. establishes, by law, "reviews of life" (*Untersuchungen des Lebens*): once a year each citizen is summoned to appear before a magistrate to give an account of "how he lives, what he does, how he is feeding himself and his family". While this measure is described in very much the same words by Herodotus,[37] Zesen adds, in keeping with political ideas of his own time, that this scrutiny serves "to abolish all misbehaviour, wipe out all sloth, and punish all life led in luxury".[38] At first, people react with scepticism to J.'s policing of the population; but once the years of dearth have arrived, they acknowledge his political competence: "Now they realise how prudently, how wisely he acts. Those who ridiculed him now praise his wisdom. Those who derided him now extol his timely care and provision to the skies. The scoffers now implore his mercy, calling him their preserver, their saviour, their national father."[39]

The notion of control extends far beyond the individual and the state; in its most complete form, it is represented by God's governance of his creation. God sees to it that his established laws are obeyed, irregularities corrected, and the wicked banished from the world. Once God has decided on the course of things, all human obstruction is in vain. (Even Egyptian polytheists acknowledge this fact: "It will happen. Heaven has so decreed. The gods have so decided. Therefore we will submit in silence to that which has been decreed. Let us await the fulfilment of this divine decree in silence. We cannot do anything but keep hushed silence and await the appointed hour.")[40] In Zesen's novel, people not only wait in silence; some of them also know exactly what they are waiting for. Zesen presents God as the one who preordains everything, including the marriage of J. and A., but also reveals his plan, through oracle or dream, to the chosen few – just like a king who confides in an inner circle at court. It is clear that in such a world Fortune, the unpredictable goddess, has no place.

Under the able management of J., public welfare is both ensured and predictable. Zesen, who occasionally lets his authorial persona directly address the reader, does not fail to commend prime minister J. as the civil servant's ultimate role model:

> What else shall we say? Joseph is a true didactic mirror for all statesmen, a model for all active in the service of kings and princes. All statesmen, ministers and governors must look in this noble mirror. Here they can learn how, through dedication to public welfare, they may promote their own well-being; how, through being faithful, they may become rich, and how, in spite of neglecting their personal advantage, they may nevertheless have much profit. Prosperity, welfare, and well-being will automatically accrue to those who follow this model. Their estate will be like a blossoming tree whose leaves do not wither, like a plant that grows and never vanishes.[41]

Zesen's insistence on the infallible connection between selfless dedication to the state and personal success is so complete that the reader almost forgets that at one point in his career J. had to suffer imprisonment. It is hard to find any source that surpasses Zesen's novel in optimism – the optimism typical of a generation of German baroque intellectuals who, in 1648 after thirty years at war, were totally convinced of their ability to bring to society a new prosperity and happiness.

14

Hebrew Freemason – Albrecht

In the late eighteenth century, Germans discovered, in addition to playing cards and drinking beer, a new pastime: the reading of novels. According to one observer, there was a sudden surge of appetite for unpretentious reading matter not only among the gentry and the urban elite of people hungry for education, but also among the lower classes of "domestic servants, simple craftsmen, hawkers, and apprentice boys".[1]

Literary historians, like our observer, remember Johann Friedrich Ernst Albrecht (1752–1814) as one of the first writers in Germany to both inspire and cater to this appetite by producing trivial literature – books without literary ambition, hastily written for commercial success, published anonymously, often about the adventures of criminals and prostitutes, the mysterious apparition of ghosts, and intrigue at the courts of princes. Sex, crime, and courtly life, not forgetting politics, and often a blend of all four, are his main subjects. Some of Albrecht's novels strike us as thinly veiled political propaganda, generally in favour of enlightened France and Frederick the Great, but critical of the despots of Russia. Without doubt the most prolific writer of his age, Albrecht wrote at least eighty novels before, during the last decade of his life, he turned to the writing of popular medical treatises for the lay reader, especially for women.[2] Albrecht's biography reads like the plot of one of his adventure stories. Embarking on a medical career with the military, he began writing novels, became acquainted with the famously attractive actress Sophie Baumer whom he married and accompanied on her tours, was befriended by the writer Friedrich Schiller (who took more interest in Sophie than in Ernst), moved to Altona where in 1796 he assumed directorship of a theatre, was divorced by his wife, and went back to practising as a doctor. Altona, a Danish enclave near Hamburg, enjoyed freedom of the press (unlike the rest of Germany), and attracted liberty-seeking German intellectuals and artists, especially those in favour of the French Revolution and its republican and democratic ideals.

Some of Albrecht's political ideals are reflected in his novel *Der keusche Joseph* (Joseph the Chaste, 1792/94), written in Leipzig in the years before he moved to Hamburg and Altona. The novel also reflects Albrecht's enthusiasm for the theatre. Like many of his novels, *Der keusche Joseph* is presented as if it were a stage play. Each chapter of the "dramatised novel" (as literary historians call the form) begins with an indication of the setting and a list of the "cast" – the interacting characters – followed by the actual text in dialogue form. The "drama" was never meant to be performed; like many of his contemporaries, Albrecht merely adopted the dramatic and dialogue form as a convenient vehicle. It reflects his thinking in terms of "scenes" performed on the stage, which came quite naturally to someone who loved the theatre and who in his writing was occasionally assisted by his actress wife. It also caters to the taste of a readership brought up in a primarily oral culture, who were used to reading novels aloud in the then fashionable reading societies.[3]

ALBRECHT, *DER KEUSCHE JOSEPH*: PLOT SUMMARY[4]

Joseph, hated by his brothers, is sold to Midianite merchants. These merchants, especially their leaders Hira and Odol, befriend Joseph, and stay in close contact with him, even after he has entered service with Potiphar, steward of the royal household of Egypt. Potiphar bought Joseph because it was well known in Egypt that the Hebrews were more faithful, punctual, industrious, and intelligent than native Egyptian servants. Before long, two women fall in love with the handsome Hebrew: Daluka, wife of Potiphar, and Asnath, the unmarried daughter of Potiphera, one of the leading priests of Egypt. The two have quite different reasons for their feelings and wishes. Daluka does not love her husband but has married this ugly old courtier because of his prominent political position; so Daluka is looking for a young lover, and she does not fail to tell Joseph of her love – to no avail. Asnath and Joseph fall in love at first sight, declare their feelings, and immediately join hands as a pledge of future marriage. As Joseph continues to reject Daluka's advances, she accuses him of attempted rape, so Joseph is thrown into prison. Asnath, quite unsure of herself and her feelings, accuses herself of impure thoughts and is also imprisoned, but is released as soon as her innocence is acknowledged.

Meanwhile, Odol and Hira have ingratiated themselves with two important Egyptian priests: Molais and Potiphera, the latter an old sage, the former a young man who, despite his youth, has been promoted to the position of high priest above all other priests in Egypt. As a token of friendship, the priests have initiated Odol and Hira into the Egyptian mysteries, revealing to them their sacred doctrine that is not for the ears of the profane. This esoteric doctrine is essentially one of monotheism: behind the plurality of deities worshipped by the common Egyptians stands one single deity – the one collective soul of all the gods and goddesses and indeed the soul of all creation. About two centuries earlier, a Hebrew sage by the name of Abraham had stayed in Egypt and imparted this esoteric teaching that is now transmitted within the priestly guild. It is also revealed to some non-priests who may be foreigners, individuals who were granted membership in the esoteric brotherhood led by the priests of Egypt. Molais is well aware of Joseph's unique intelligence and character; convinced of his innocence, he uses Joseph's term in prison to instruct him in esoteric lore. Joseph is not only allowed to move freely within the state prison, he is also permitted to pass through secret doors and underground galleries to the vaults where he finds a priestly city, complete with family homes, workshops, record offices, and memorial halls. There are kitchens where rejuvenating elixirs are brewed, workshops in which architectural models are built, and archives where extensive map collections, provincial and economic records, histories of Egypt, and other secret archival material are maintained and stored. There is even a conservation workshop dedicated to the preservation and restoration of old, damaged texts and documents. In one of the subterranean galleries a secret tribunal meets to decide the fate of prisoners, whether they are to be punished or pardoned; the decisions, without fail, are respected by the king. Here, invisible to the eyes of the profane, and unknown to them, the priests work for the benefit and welfare of Egyptian society.

Joseph's first two – apparently brief – nocturnal visits to the subterranean world of the priests have a definite aim, for they serve to initiate him into the Egyptian mysteries. During the first visit, he meets Odol (masked, but recognisable by his voice) in one of the underground galleries. Odol guides him to the priestly tribunal whose members pronounce a death sentence on Masnak, one of Joseph's fellow prisoners. On the second visit, Molais serves as Joseph's guide and instructor. In the gloomy underground vaults the novice is exposed to images of horror, death, and decay, but he also sees delightful images that presage eternal bliss. Other images are of an erotic nature, tempting all his senses. Finally, he finds himself in a gallery of mummies where a long inscription extols the virtues of the brave, deceased warriors and gentle sages, all former benefactors of Egypt. Gradually, it dawns on him that the key common to all of these experiences is the doctrine of life everlasting. A life of self-control and virtue prepares the novice for confronting his own mortality and attaining eternal life. Once the initiation is complete, Joseph, like Odol and Hira, belongs to the secret fraternal order led by the priests. This order comprises the truly enlightened members of society, an elite class conscious of its privileged access to higher knowledge that carefully guards this privilege, for knowledge, too widely disseminated, would severely damage the social order. For if all were enlightened, all would aspire to join the priestly class. Who then would work the land?

After he has interpreted the dreams of two fellow prisoners and subsequently one of Pharaoh that has political and economic implications, Joseph is freed not only from prison, but also from slavery. Pharaoh appoints the former slave to governorship, and he is free to marry Asnath. Daluka is predictably very angry with both Joseph and Asnath whom she seeks to kill with poison, but the attempt fails, for the witch whom she engages administers a potent life-enhancing elixir rather than a bottle of poison. So Daluka herself ends up in prison, is eventually pardoned through Joseph's intervention, but still harbours feelings of revenge.

As governor of Egypt, Joseph stays on friendly terms with the priests and others of the secret fraternal order. He also continues to consult the underground archives. Two projects figure prominently in Joseph's political programme: the extension of arable land and the inculcation of a strict work ethic, for many of the Egyptian commoners are indolent. Joseph's rule is welcomed by most Egyptians. Some have doubts about his character, for Daluka has spread rumours about Joseph's lack of chastity; but all doubts are dissipated in a secret assembly of priests, sages, and magicians, convoked by Molais. Yet after some time, Molais himself feels that Joseph, having become proud of himself and his achievements, is departing from the humility required of all members of the fraternity. So he speaks to him, explaining how and why Joseph has disappointed him. More effective is the plan of Hira and Odol, soon realised, that Joseph should once more assert his virtue by coming to terms with his own past – his family in Canaan. Hira and Odol travel to Asia to meet Joseph's brothers and Jacob, and the brothers realise that they are speaking with the Midianite merchants to whom they long ago sold Joseph. Although the two Midianites learn that the brothers now recognise and regret their sin, the merchants do not tell them about Joseph's political career. Later, when Joseph's brothers travel to Egypt to buy corn, the governor of Egypt first thinks about revenge and has

> them imprisoned. Nevertheless, they are treated well in prison, and Joseph soon decides to show clemency and to forgive them. Eventually he reveals himself to them and celebrates their reunion. (At this point the story breaks off, because the author never wrote or published the concluding fourth volume. So we are neither informed of the fate of Daluka nor do we learn about Jacob's immigration to Egypt. One would anticipate that Daluka would commit suicide, and Joseph and Molais become reconciled as the story's inevitable happy ending.)

Albrecht's novel is suffused with an atmosphere that the foregoing summary cannot convey – that of Freemasonry.[5] Some of the Masonic terms strike the eye even at a first reading: Masons address each other as brother, they are organised in a fraternal order, whatever is deliberated by the Masonic council must not be divulged to non-members.[6] The presence of an officer called the "high priest" signals one development typical of Freemasonry in the late eighteenth century: to the three grades of "apprentice, fellow craft, and master mason", some lodges added higher grades such as "high priest". Molais, the name of the novel's high priest, is presumably meant to be pronounced as a French word, and it has clear Masonic connotations: Jacques de Molay, a man falsely accused of heresy and executed by the French king in 1314, was the last Grand Master of the Knights Templar. Freemasons acknowledge the Templars as somehow belonging to their tradition, and commemorate Molay's fate in their writings; according to Masonic legend, Molay had founded the fraternal order by giving to the members certain secret ritual objects, including a relic of John the Baptist.[7] In the year Albrecht began to publish his novel, the official records of the papal commission dealing with the Templars became available in printed form and through them, in 1792, Jacques de Molay came to the attention of all who were then interested in the Knights Templar, including the Freemasons.[8] Masonic interest in de Molay was thus reignited.

Despite its fragmentary nature, the main message of Albrecht's novel is clear enough: society is composed of two classes – the unenlightened majority who go about their everyday life, and the enlightened minority of specially selected and trained individuals. To the first group one belongs naturally, by virtue of one's birth; to the second, individuals belong by selection and calling by a secret council of sages. A new member joins the secret fraternity through a complex ritual performed in secret, known as "initiation". The fraternity and its initiated members feel themselves to be the rightful leaders of society, including the state as its most powerful institution. In writing his novel, Albrecht did not merely seek to describe and dramatise the functioning of human society in ancient Egypt and biblical times; the world he describes, but thinly disguised, is his own, eighteenth-century society. No contemporary reader would be misled by biblical names such as Hira and Odol,[9] the Egyptian setting, and the period clothing worn by Josef, Daluka, and Molais. Everyone would understand that the secret society joined by Joseph and led by the priests was none other than a Masonic lodge. Membership in this lodge was open not just to Egyptians, but also to foreigners such as Hira and Odol, and Hebrews such as Joseph. As the story develops, the reader comes to understand that the well-being of the state depends on the co-operation of priest and politician, lodge and leader, symbolised by the two young protagonists Molais and Joseph, portrayed as friends and rivals (and again friends, as we may reconstruct the missing end). A close reading of *Der keusche Joseph* reveals the story's two dimensions as a historical novel and a contemporary political pamphlet.

A HISTORICAL NOVEL

An idea, fashionable among the educated of the seventeenth and eighteenth centuries, suggested the existence of two religions: one superstitious, practised by the masses, and one enlightened, adhered to by an elite minority and not divulged to the vulgar. The enlightened religion focused on no more than belief in one God and life after death. This enlightened religion and its minimalist creed were said to be not a recent invention of deist philosophers, but the timeless privilege of those who managed to advance beyond vulgar thought and practice. In ancient times, so it was thought, the enlightened religion was well known to philosophers and priests who transmitted it by secret initiation preceded by prolonged periods of probation. Such initiation procedures, celebrated in secret, also served to unite the enlightened few in a universal brotherhood. These beliefs about ancient times were nourished by the writings of such authors as Ralph Cudworth (1617–1688), William Warburton (1698–1779), and Cornelis de Pauw (1739–1799).[10]

Standard historical accounts of the past tend to highlight the contribution that important political, religious, and cultural leaders and founders such as Moses, Alexander the Great, Jesus, and the Emperor Constantine made to the development of humankind. Eighteenth-century Freemasons disagreed with this "big men" approach to history. For them, the shaping of human history by great leaders is only half the story. Historical leaders, rather than acting as isolated individuals endowed with unusual charisma, intelligence, and wisdom, are only the exponents of that "universal brotherhood" whose members prefer to remain invisible. Behind every historical leader stands a secret, well-organised network of advisers and helpers, all members of the brotherhood. These are the custodians of a tradition of higher wisdom that cannot be divulged to the laity. Only at certain privileged moments in history could this knowledge be applied to shape or reform a society's intellectual, cultural, religious, or political life. What historical sources and learned accounts normally describe is only the foreground of what happened in the past; what went on behind the scenes, though providing the key to a proper understanding, remains concealed and untold. Off-stage, plans were devised, decisions made, leaders manipulated, and events carefully orchestrated. If as a student of the past you come across any major event that served to advance the cause of freedom, dignity, and human understanding, you can be sure that it was staged by a conspiracy of the enlightened. The conspirators may have either co-operated internationally or worked locally through one of their lodges or agents.

Ancient records of the Essenes, a Jewish sect that flourished in New Testament times, fired the Masons' imagination and inspired their own ritual. According to the Jewish historian Josephus, full membership of the sect was attained in successive stages. Candidates, provided with a small hatchet or pick and an apron, had to undergo a one-year probation before being admitted to Essene ablutions. Then followed a two-year period of initiation, leading, after the swearing of the oath of fidelity, to table-fellowship. Only adult men were received as full members, although boys are said to have been trained by them.[11] Ancient reports such as these were taken as evidence for the venerable antiquity of the Masonic order itself, through its self-styled association with the ancient sect.

To permit a glimpse behind the scenes of history, some Freemasons wrote novels. The best-known example is a work entitled *Ausführung des Plans und Zweks Jesu* (The Plans and Aims of Jesus, 12 vols, 1784–1793), written by Karl Friedrich Bahrdt.[12] The plans and aims of Jesus did not originate with the Galilean preacher himself; behind him, Bahrdt asserts, stood the order of the Essenes whose widespread ramifications extended to Babylon and Egypt. The Essenes had set themselves the task of dissuading the Jewish people from their sensuous messianic hopes and leading them to a higher knowledge of spiritual and rational truths. To achieve this aim, they selected two children and nurtured and instructed them in the higher knowledge required to become preachers and teachers. Although the two are well known as John the Baptist and Jesus of Nazareth, traditional accounts of the lives of these two eminent religious leaders failed to see them as being sent and permanently supported by the order of the Essenes. This order utilised hidden caves all over Galilee, as well as in the neighbourhood of Jerusalem: underground galleries where clandestine gatherings and consultations could take place; whenever he mysteriously retired to the desert, it was in fact to these caves that Jesus retreated to receive instructions for his ministry, or for supplies to feed the hungry crowds who followed and listened to him. Albrecht's novel *Der keusche Joseph* is based on the same general idea of a dual system of leadership: behind a great figure, whose story is told in the Bible, stands a secret fraternal order by whom he is selected and trained to further the order's aims; and at some point, the chosen one begins his successful public ministry during which he remains accountable to his anonymous masters and benefactors.

Both Bahrdt and Albrecht wrote long chapters on the training and initiation of their respective heroes. Albrecht's account surprises his readers by offering long descriptions of underground scenarios and initiation tests, and on close inspection we can discover the literary source for these: a French novel entitled *Sethos, histoire ou vie tirée des monumens anecdotes de l'ancienne Egypte* (Sethos: A History or Biography based on Unpublished Records of Ancient Egypt, 1732). Written by the French historian Jean Terrasson, the novel became popular throughout Europe, for it resonated with an educated readership's interest in the exotic world of the East in general and Egypt and its ancient mysteries in particular. To us, it is an important document of early eighteenth-century orientalism. It was available in English under the title *The Life of Sethos* (1732). Germany produced two translations, the first entitled *Abriss der wahren Helden-That, oder, Lebens-Geschichte des Sethos* (Précis of True Heroism, or Biography of Sethos, 1732–1737), and a second one called *Geschichte des egyptischen Königs Sethos* (The History of Sethos, Prince of Egypt, 1778). The second German translation was published in a cultural climate that had already changed since the 1730s. Now the novel resonated more specifically with Masonic sentiments. Not only was the new German translator, the well-known writer Matthias Claudius, a Freemason; his readers, too, were reminded of the similarities between Terrasson's Egyptian mysteries and the secret ceremonies celebrated in Masonic lodges. Perceived as a Masonic novel, Terrasson's book came to inspire some of the features of Mozart's opera *Die Zauberflöte* (The Magic Flute, 1791)[13] and, evidently, Albrecht's *Der keusche Joseph*.

Albrecht's novel imitates Terrasson's *Sethos*, exploiting it for subplots and descriptions of Egyptian customs and manners, as well as priestly institutions such as the subterranean city below the Pyramid of Cheops.[14] Albrecht even borrows names from *Sethos*. Terrasson's evil Queen Daluca becomes Potiphar's wife Daluka, and Sethos's Phoenician friends Saphon and Giscon reappear as the Midianites Odol and Hira. In "Joseph the Chaste", as in *Sethos*, Egypt's intellectual life resides in a secret order dominated by priests, and those who govern the country rely on priestly advice and guidance. There is one main difference between the two works, however, one that can only be understood fully by considering the context in which they were written. In having Sethos trained by a priest and acknowledging the priestly class as the educated elite, Terrasson was thinking of the Catholic priests of his time. Amedes, tutor of Sethos, presumably echoes Fénelon (1651–1715), the famous Catholic priest (later bishop) whom Louis XIV invited to Versailles to educate the dauphin, the young duke of Burgundy. In the preface to his book, Terrasson actually refers to Fénelon's Les Aventures de Télémaque (The Adventures of Telemachus, 1699) as a model didactic novel set in ancient times that he sought to emulate.[15] When Terrasson extols the priestly class, he not only extols Fénelon as a famous educator and member of the Académie Française, then (as now) the leading scientific and literary society of France; he also celebrates another institution, of which he – an ordained priest like Fénelon – was a member: the Collège Royal in Paris, then (as today, now called the Collège de France) France's foremost centre of advanced studies. Albrecht, by contrast, bore no allegiance to the Catholic clergy; the priesthood he celebrates is that of the enlightened philosophers of his day.

The novel's central episode is the initiation of its protagonist Sethos into the priesthood of Egypt, for only an initiated Egyptian is able to exercise the office of king.[16] Amedes, mentor of Sethos, prepares the young man for the initiation trials. Sethos must prove his manly courage through confrontation with the four elements – earth, water, fire, and air – in extreme situations. This is done by penetrating into the interior of the Pyramid of Cheops. The first of these tests, though not explicitly developed in Terrasson's novel, involves the novice's burial, and is famously visualised in the frontispiece of the libretto of Mozart's Die Zauberflöte (Fig. 19).[17] The etching is dominated by a large stone arch resting on pillars. Behind this, a structure with a further, smaller arch is visible, and a door that leads into what must be a subterranean temple. The gloomy space in the foreground is framed by a pyramidal structure on the left (decorated with hieroglyphs), and a huge vase or urn placed on a stone pedestal on the right, both strongly lit from above. The ground here has been dug up, and we can discern fragments of sculpted stones, a spade, a pickaxe, and an hourglass, all indicating that the scene is a graveyard. Just visible, but most important, is the human figure of which we see protruding only the head and the bare left shoulder. This figure looks up to the symbol of a flaming star hanging overhead. This star and flame, a Masonic symbol, represent the light that calls the novice out of his symbolic grave to a new life. The novice is depicted here as having been buried alive, in order to symbolise his death and subsequent resurrection to new life.

Albrecht's description of Joseph's initiation departs radically from that of his literary model. Unlike Sethos (in Terrasson's novel) or Tamino (in Die Zauberflöte), Joseph is never subjected to physical testing. Instead of having to confront the challenge of a demanding and dangerous ordeal, Joseph merely goes through a period of instruction and personal study, which, for Sethos, is only half of the initiation. In his Joseph novel, Albrecht simply omits the dramatic, physically demanding ritual; his hero is exposed to no more than an

Fig. 19. *Underground Egypt.* – A Masonic novice is waking from his symbolic grave, directing his gaze at the symbol of a flaming star hanging overhead. The engraver depicts the Egyptian underworld as a place of death and rebirth in the Masonic tradition; replete with arcane symbolism, it highlights the funerary urn of Jacques de Molay, the last Grand Master of the Knights Templar. – Ignaz Alberti for the opera libretto of Mozart's *Zauberflöte*, 1791.

intellectual diet of instruction, learning, and quiet meditation. Instructed and enlightened, he is well prepared to lead the Egyptian state. But Albrecht's novel does not end at this point; instead, it develops a question of much importance to the secret fraternity: does Joseph, when serving as the Egyptian state's prime minister, follow the ideals and standards in which he has been trained? Or does he neglect the advice of his brothers, members of the secret order?

A key figure of the secret order is Molais, Joseph's Egyptian guide and adviser. In the story he matches Joseph in importance. He represents a type-figure that often appears in eighteenth-century German novels. Known as the "genius" (in Roman religion, a personal guardian spirit) and acting as emissary of the order, this anonymous old man secretly protects, but also meets, directs, advises, and supervises the protagonist; only at the end of the story does he reveal his identity either to the protagonist or the reader.[18] In some cases, one suspects that he may be an angelic being. Albrecht the rationalist adapts this type-figure to his own taste by divesting the genius of his enigmatic nature: instead of portraying him as an old and mysterious sage, he presents him as a young man whose name and status as the high priest of Egypt are never in doubt. Albrecht may be credited with the invention of a new, non-mysterious figure that works behind the scenes but is otherwise well known to both the novel's protagonist and the reader.

For Albrecht and his generation, historical novels involving secret societies and their emissaries provided more than entertainment; they also offered commentary on current affairs. One political statement made in Albrecht's novel is implied in the very fact that the initiate is a Hebrew.

A STORY OF JEWISH EMANCIPATION

By admitting a Hebrew to the Masonic fraternity, Albrecht addresses one specific problem widely discussed in the late eighteenth century throughout Europe: what about the Jews? Should they remain an isolated, underprivileged group as they had been for centuries, or should they be tolerated and respected, and perhaps even granted the same civil rights as everyone else? If Jews had remained on the margins of society, no one would have asked these questions. During the eighteenth century, however, a new type of Jew appeared: one who had acquired Western education and had adjusted his behaviour to conform to the general standards of society. This development first became apparent in England, Holland, and France, but by the 1780s it had become a permanent feature of social life throughout Europe, including Germany.

In Germany, Christian Fürchtegott Gellert (1715–1769) promoted toleration by inventing the literary figure of the noble Jew.[19] He found a prominent follower in Gotthold Ephraim Lessing (1729–1781) in whose dramatic poem

Nathan der Weise (Nathan the Wise, 1779) the central characters, as representatives of Judaism, Christianity, and Islam, discover at long last that they are blood relatives. In *Ernst und Falk* (1778/80), a delightful dialogue between the two titular characters, Lessing celebrates an enlightened ethic and attitude that encourages the wisest of any city or country to transcend parochialism by embracing the cosmopolitan perspective of an idealised Freemasonry. He even touches on the question of whether Jews, or only Christians, could be received into Masonic lodges, and answers that everyone should be able to join.[20] Gellert's and Lessing's recommendation of religious tolerance, peaceful coexistence, and cosmopolitanism clearly resonated with Albrecht. But enlightened thinking expressed in literature was one thing; social reality another. In Germany, Jews were still considered second-class citizens. The major lodges did not admit them as members, though there were a few exceptions, and the problem was articulated in a pamphlet entitled *Werden und können Israeliten zu Freymaurern aufgenommen werden?* (Is it Possible to Receive Israelites into Masonic Lodges?, 1788); the Hamburg-based author answered the titular question in the affirmative.[21] One of the few minor lodges that followed the author's suggestion was the "Einigkeit und Toleranz" lodge (Concord and Tolerance, its name and motto), founded in 1792 in Hamburg.

"Einigkeit und Toleranz" made a point of admitting Jewish members, and the banker Elias Israel and the merchant Jakob Labatt were amongst its leaders.[22] One of the founding members describes the lodge as follows: "This Jewish merchant [presumably Labatt] who lacked neither manners nor academic training assumed leadership of this Masonic club. There were no boring ceremonies, the festive atmosphere spoke to the heart, rules were strict without being pedantic, and lectures on subjects of moral and historical interest were both instructive and entertaining."[23] Membership was open to everyone: "There is no religious discrimination. Turks, Jews, and Christians are all our brothers."[24] Another early source offers a description of the lodge's work: "Its chief concern is to ennoble and enlighten humankind, to liberate from any prejudice that might harm the human race, to deliver the spirit from all fetters that are incompatible with the dignity of the human spirit, and, finally, to practise virtue which we consider a daughter of true wisdom. All of our work is meant to promote these objectives. We will have nothing to do with Rosicrucianism, alchemy, spirit-seeing and other dubious pursuits. Amongst us, all research into the arcane is deemed ridiculous."[25] The lodge existed at least until 1807. Among its activities were the founding of a successful Jewish school for the poor and the establishment of a hospital and a public library. We also know of the lodge's contribution to a monument for Gotthold Ephraim Lessing.

When "Einigkeit und Toleranz" was founded in 1792, its ideas were not new. During his many travels throughout Germany, Albrecht must have been well aware of the Jewish question and the radical solution recommended by some Freemasons. Their practice of religious tolerance and peaceful coexistence became central concerns of his novel about Joseph. *Der keusche Joseph* was intended as a Masonic novel written in support of the same ideas on which "Einigkeit und Toleranz" was based. Just as in the novel Egyptians, Midianites, and a Hebrew belong to the same fraternity, so "Einigkeit und Toleranz" united Christians and Jews on an equal footing.

The novel's emphasis on, and historical interpretation of, monotheism is both instructive and demonstrative of Albrecht's favourable attitude to Judaism. In the late eighteenth century, Freemasons generally believed that monotheism had originated as a secret doctrine of the Egyptian priests, had been revealed to Moses by his Egyptian teachers, and eventually was imposed on the reluctant Hebrews.[26] Albrecht departs from this notion by making the belief in one single God the original property of the Hebrews; it was known to Abraham (long before Moses), and when Abraham sojourned in Egypt, he taught it to the local priests, who subsequently adopted it as the focus of their esoteric religion.[27] Behind this assumption stands the more general idea that Mesopotamia, the home of Abraham, rather than Egypt, was the original cradle of civilisation; historians like Voltaire had little doubt about the temporal priority and original superiority of Babylonian culture; the arts, he asserts, including the veneration of one supreme deity, spread from the land of the Euphrates to that of the Nile[28] – and Abraham may have been its mediator. Albrecht makes sure that the monotheistic deity retains its Israelite aura; thus at one point in the story, Joseph uses the expression "the Eternal" (*der Ewige*) to refer to God; in doing so, he follows the Jewish philosopher and publicist Moses Mendelssohn (1729–1786) who in his biblical translation preferred to render the divine name as "the Eternal" instead of "the Lord".[29] The emphasis on the doctrine of monotheism and its introduction into Egypt by Abraham betray a bias in favour of Judaism.

Given the composite atmosphere of the novel, suffused by both Jewish and Masonic influences, is it going too far to suggest that Albrecht wrote it specifically in support of the admission of Jews to Masonic lodges?

A STORY OF POLITICAL LEADERSHIP

The Masonic fraternity had high expectations of their initiated members. In one passage, Albrecht has Jacob (Joseph's father) sum up what these were:

> Jacob: O strangers, all that you are telling me bears the mark of knowledge and wisdom that are deeper than one would expect from you as Midianites. So I conclude that you must be initiates of an order that is now spreading through the entire world. Its members take notice of every good

idea and activity and are intent on giving it currency in the country in which they happen to live. This great fraternal order, if it continues in this manner, will lead our world to happiness. Although I do not know where this order has its central seat, I nevertheless realise that it does not send its emissaries to someone whom they do not deem worthy to be considered. So be doubly welcome, for you bring me the assurance that I am not deemed unworthy in the eyes of the order.[30]

If only everyone would acknowledge and heed the wisdom of the Masonic fraternity, the world might be led to happiness: this is exactly how the Freemasons felt about their mission, especially during the last two decades of the eighteenth century, the classical period of Masonic activity in Germany. And Albrecht, of course, was a Freemason, though a member with a difference. In his book anonymously published in 1785, entitled *Gespräche Maurerey betreffend* (Dialogues on Freemasonry), he has the chief character, Mr Siebriz, explain how he joined a lodge but subsequently became disillusioned. He had expected to become part of a group of high-minded idealists intent on improving society by exchanging ideas and engaging in socially beneficial activities, but instead he met unworthy people who generally failed to live up to the original Masonic ideals. Masonic leaders enriched themselves by extorting large contributions from members, while the latter, instead of helping others, sought to promote themselves, hoping to gain respectability, improve their status, and perhaps even be considered for an influential political position. Moreover, members rarely trusted one another. Mr Siebriz feels uncomfortable with the irritating difference between ideal and reality; nor does he like the empty and meaningless ceremonial of which his lodge makes so much. Why should any pomp and ceremony be necessary: secret initiations, the wearing of a worker's apron, the handling of a trowel and other symbolic objects displayed on a special carpet? All of these paraphernalia could be dispensed with, and if there had to be any symbolism, it should be displayed for didactic purposes, and not for the sake of mystifying members and non-members alike. Only general and far-reaching reforms could purge the lodges of misuse, mismanagement, and superfluous ceremonies. "A lodge that pursues its work in secret, that avoids all noise, all conspicuous display and all pursuit of praise; where the brothers live in harmony and peace among people who speak of them with respect [...] and where every brother is welcomed as a friend" – such a lodge would indeed make a difference.[31] But alas, it does not exist today. In his novel, Albrecht envisions a situation in which true Masonry existed, one that corresponds to his own ideals. And one that plays an important role in political life.

In order to assess the political role Albrecht's novel assigns to the Masonic movement we must briefly look at the general political situation in the final decades of the eighteenth century. All of the many European monarchies at that time were led by rulers who considered their rule essentially "absolute", independent of the general population, ecclesiastical institutions, or privileges traditionally enjoyed by the nobility. In practice, rulers made many concessions, and in some countries parliaments became increasingly important institutions. In the long run, the absolute state did not work, and the burgeoning and increasingly self-confident bourgeoisie claimed attention and demanded respect for their views when political decisions were being made. The French Revolution with its overthrow and abolition of the monarchy in 1789 demonstrated to everyone in Europe that absolute power could be replaced by something else: the republic. In the aftermath of the French Revolution, European intellectuals discussed whether one should follow the French model or develop other ways of reforming the existing political institutions.

Like the rest of Western Europe, eighteenth-century Germany boasted a large number of intellectuals in the sense sociologists give to this term. From the work of Gerhard Lenski one can extract four basic characteristics of intellectuals:[32]

(1) Intellectuals are required to master a complex body of specialist knowledge and related skills that are essentially intellectual (rather than manual) in nature.
(2) Such specialist knowledge cannot be acquired quickly even by the able; in other words, it is acquired through long years of training, normally at institutions of higher education.
(3) Intellectuals may be engaged in any type of employment, but they are concentrated in teaching, the arts, and church-related activities.
(4) Though intellectuals often have considerable influence over others, they rarely have much formal authority. They are like ministers without portfolio, experts without the power to translate their ideas into public policy.

Set between the unenfranchised masses of the peasantry, of craftsmen and workers on the one hand, and the princes with their power-wielding military, judicial, and bureaucratic apparatus on the other, they formed a third group occupying an intermediate space. This space can be considered hybrid, for it shares some characteristics with its otherwise very different neighbours. With the social space of the masses it shares the lack of political power and influence, and frequently also a sense of dissatisfaction with the state; with the space belonging to the government it shares the knowledge and skills needed for dealing with public affairs. During the eighteenth century, European intellectuals developed two major paradigms for articulating their claim to influence, power, and leadership.[33] The first of these paradigms envisaged their class as the "republic of letters", a kind of intellectual aristocracy that resorted primarily to the printed word to express and disseminate its ideas. The second paradigm, known as the Masonic option, promoted the idea of associations with rules of membership, grades of initiation, and secret meetings. Both movements were convinced that the society and state within which they lived were in urgent need of reform; their evils should be rooted out, their wounds healed, the structures reformed, their life reinvigorated. Yet in their analysis of the evils and in their strategies for improvement they differed radically.

How did the *république des lettres* work in practice? The privileged hybrid space where the men of letters met on equal footing with members of the government and the military comprised the literary salons; there new ideas could be discussed freely and without fear of state censorship. The discussions held in the salons and the ideas made public in printed form, for instance in the many volumes of the famous *Encyclopédie* (1751–1772), were thought to give rise to enlightened public opinion that would eventually reach those in power and influence their policy. In the interests of a fresh and free intellectual climate, philosophers such as Voltaire and Diderot sought to weaken, if not eliminate, all ecclesiastical influence on public life, and they welcomed the expulsion of the Jesuits from France in 1764. Ancient Egypt, Diderot claimed, could serve to illustrate the pernicious influence of a priestly caste on an entire civilisation. In his article "Egypte" in the *Encyclopédie*, Diderot explains that life on the shores of the Nile was far from idyllic, for it was fundamentally flawed by the pervasive influence of the priestly caste.[34] Originally founded to promote philosophy and the sciences, the priestly order soon degenerated into a school of superstition. Priests, moreover, were consumers and not producers, and thus the country was eventually ruined. Sons of priests had to be priests, but others could also join the sacerdotal order, so the latter constituted an ever-increasing part of the population. They were known for their general indolence and aversion to manual work, so priesthood presented an attractive option to many Egyptians. As a result, the effective working population decreased, and the country's prosperity declined. Priestly domination, whether ancient and Egyptian or modern and Jesuit, ruins any country – or so Diderot claims.

Masonic thought and practice differed sharply from those of the *république des lettres*. The Masonic option's key characteristic was its secrecy. A secret fraternal order was supposed to be able to promote its teaching unchallenged by state censorship and public control. Whereas those who thought of themselves as part of the "republic of letters" aimed at influencing political leaders indirectly via public opinion, the Masonic movement curtailed the spread of new ideas. If generally known, they felt, fresh approaches to religion, politics, or cultural life would undermine the existing order, incurring the disapproval of those in power, and thus would obstruct, rather than promote, the changes the fraternity sought to bring about. Interestingly, the German philosopher Immanuel Kant expressed similar opinions when he distinguished between two public realms: that of the state, a realm characterised by order and obedience to the prince and his administration; and that of the scholars in which freedom of speech and enlightened thought are vital.[35] You cannot argue with a prince or a tax official, but you can – and should – debate with your fellow scholars. The Enlightenment, rather than being a movement that shapes all social classes and functions in all social situations, is assigned a precise social and institutional location.

For intellectuals like Albrecht and other Masons, the case of the ancient Egyptian priesthood served as a strong precedent for the functioning and beneficial influence of a secret fraternal order.[36] In "Joseph the Chaste", Albrecht describes a social pyramid in which the space between the broad base of the powerless masses and the topmost governing authorities is occupied by the priestly class. The members of the secret priestly fraternity are linked both to the masses from which they recruit their members, and to the government that they seek to influence, not least by placing members such as Joseph in influential government positions. Albrecht gives the social space between the powerless masses and the state governors a tangible character by locating it under the ground, in the caves and galleries where the priests live and work. The priests, while lacking formal power, have all the knowledge needed to govern the state – they do medical research, study legislation, and keep the records and annals of the state. Knowledge is the true basis of their influence. Albrecht has a clear understanding of the power derived from record-keeping: those who have no access to public records and documents are powerless.[37] Government in Egypt, according to the novel, rests on the close co-operation between king and priesthood. The king, while not bound to accept their advice, respects the priests and the pronouncements of their secret tribunals. The priests, while remaining independent of the royal institutions, never hesitate to offer their expert advice. Though both priests and statesmen (such as Joseph) are working for the benefit and welfare of the people, they do so in different ways. Commenting on this shared aim, Molais says to Joseph: "You can do it in public, while we [priests] must do it in secret."[38] The point is that Masonic influence was essentially indirect, secretive, and discreet, not subject to evidentiary verification. The influence attributed to them was always (as in Albrecht's novel) mysterious and arcane, transmitted in the dark of the subterranean world, or at least far removed from view. Freemasons sought proximity to power, but most of them never held direct office.

The separation of the intellectuals (or priests) from the general populace is equally strict, for not everyone can join the fraternity. For this reason, the fraternal order does not divulge its accumulated knowledge to others.

"Knowledge, kept secret, can be of much advantage for Egypt; but if generally accessible, it would undermine the people's happiness. [...] Nothing can be misused more easily than the enlightenment of the people," explains Molais.[39] Joseph agrees: "I understand that, if everyone wished to join the priesthood, there would not be enough labourers."[40] In other words: the "thinking class" must limit its membership so as not to endanger the services of the "working class", the class that ultimately sustains the entire social pyramid by feeding it. Here we can catch a glimpse of the socially conservative ideology to which Albrecht and presumably most of his Masonic friends were committed. They felt, like many conservative intellectuals of their day in Germany, that enlightened ideas should not be spread indiscriminately throughout society; doing so would risk the kind of destabilisation that led to the destruction of authority and public order in France in 1789. The key to successful intellectual reform is maintenance of the distinction between the masses and the bourgeoisie: between the 80 per cent of the population working mainly in the agrarian sector and the 20 per cent resident in cities and occupied in trade and the professions, including public administration. The masses should be kept in their humble occupations, continue their traditional life, and remain in the care of the pastors, while suitable individuals belonging to the more elevated classes – the urban bourgeoisie – are permitted to become acquainted with the new ways of thinking and acting.[41] In Prussia in 1779, Frederick the Great expressly gave instructions not to over-educate the peasants, for fear they would become unhappy with their status, give up their job of cultivating the land, leave their villages for the town, and upset the economy.[42] Conservative intellectuals like Albrecht supported a restricted, politically responsible form of enlightenment, one that would not disrupt the established social order.

Albrecht's conservatism is apparent in another, quite unexpected feature of his novel. In its preface, Albrecht explains that in ancient times Egypt owed its greatness to Joseph and the priests who had initiated him into their mysteries; but equally, the author hints at the fact that Joseph also contributed to Egypt's eventual decline.[43] How this is meant to be understood remains unclear (for Albrecht never wrote the fourth, concluding volume of his novel), but we may offer a possible interpretation. Albrecht was too much of a realist to idealise the character of the protagonist beyond credibility. In the third volume of the novel, Molais is becoming aware of certain flaws in Joseph's character: he is developing too much of a sense of pride in his accomplishments.[44] Such complacency might well have blinded Joseph to problems that inevitably led to Egypt's decline.

The conservatism of Albrecht's worldview rests on two basic notions: his belief in the paradoxical duality of human nature, composed of both virtue and vice, and his conviction that a state of ultimate, never-ending happiness can never be achieved, even by drastic reform. Albrecht does not belong among the Enlightenment radicals who were convinced of the ultimate goodness of all people and the perfectibility of society through radical reform and, if necessary, by revolution. On the personal level, the conservative view is that people are, paradoxically, both good and evil, naturally inclined to keep order and to love their neighbours, yet always ready for conflict and destruction. In order to promote the good, evil has to be restrained and virtue has to be fostered and supported by education, example, and a favourable social climate. On the political level, the mixture of good and evil is equally evident. Albrecht's novel indicates that having a Joseph – a fully initiated Freemason – in the government of Egypt does not solve Egypt's political problems once and for all. As a friend of the Masonic movement, Albrecht firmly and optimistically believed that the fraternal order could mould people who, once given a chance to be active in appropriate government positions, could work for the general welfare of state and society and even, as was the case with Joseph, guide society through critical times. In an article explicitly addressing this question, Albrecht expresses the hope that there will be "a salutary revolution of opinions and manners, brought about gradually, unnoticed, and in a quiet way".[45] But even such a "revolution" would not produce the ideal state, a state whose problems are permanently resolved to everyone's satisfaction, so that general happiness and stability prevail. For Albrecht and his Masonic friends, history, and the whole of social life, are marked by permanent conflicts and the appearance of ever more problems that leaders must seek to resolve. Solutions, though difficult to work out, are deemed possible. With the help of the Masonic fraternity, the virtuous side of people can be strengthened so that the battle against vice can be waged successfully and the challenges of history can be met with creative responses. Since there will never be an ultimate state of happiness, those united in the secret fraternal order will always be needed, and will constantly be challenged to contribute to solving the world's many problems. This seems to be the ultimate lesson Albrecht's novel seeks to teach.

V
AGAINST THE ICON: RADICAL READINGS

15

On Historical Criticism

IN THE EIGHTEENTH CENTURY EUROPEAN INTELLECTUALS GENERALLY aligned themselves with one of two factions: one group closely associated with the church and its traditional theological learning, and another that promoted freethinking and the values of the Enlightenment. Although some intellectuals wished to avoid conflict by cautiously combining philosophy with Christianity, the general attitude was to pit priest against philosopher, considering the two as born enemies. The two factions disagreed not only about religion as a system of beliefs and liturgical practices; they also differed in their relationship to, and opinion of, civil and ecclesiastical authorities. In England and France (the leading countries in eighteenth-century Europe), the conservative group supported the monarchy and the bishops, whereas the philosophical faction felt oppressed by the church and either ignored or persecuted by the civil authorities. To support its own case, each group invoked the witness of history, which frequently meant ancient and biblical history, for it was in the distant past that the present order was first legitimately laid down, or alternatively, it was then that better models for social and cultural life could be found. Accordingly, much of the intellectual and political debate was about historical facts and interpretations.

Debates about History

When it came to writing history, especially interpretative history with a sweeping global perspective, the priestly and the philosophical perspectives differed considerably.[1] In the debate on the origins of nations and states, the differences were striking: while the philosophical faction described the origins of nations primarily as secular events, those of a religious persuasion thought of the state as divinely instituted. Especially complex and tricky was the question of whether the head of a nation – usually a monarch – took his ultimate legitimacy from the people (or, more precisely, the class of nobles) or directly from God, whose authority he was believed to represent. The answers to these questions were not merely academic; on the contrary, they were immediately relevant to political life, as can be seen from the abolition of the monarchy following the French Revolution of 1789. The conservatives, represented in France by Bishop Bossuet (1627–1704) and in England by Sir Robert Filmer (1588–1653) and Bishop William Warburton (1698–1779), supported the divine right of the monarch exercised alongside powerful ecclesiastical law. Everything that had to do with the priesthood, for them, counted as venerable and noble. They could go so far as to defend pagan priests, for example those of ancient Egypt, as "persons of great eminence", "men of great dignity and authority", "the prime nobility, and heads of the most ancient and honourable families".[2] By contrast, philosophers such as John Locke, Thomas Morgan, and Voltaire all sought to restrain religious influence or even eliminate it from political life. While Locke remained a political theorist, Morgan and Voltaire invoked the witness of history to defend the positions taken in their anti-sacerdotal polemical treatises.

Those who felt comfortable with their own age – the conservatives – sought to integrate biblical and secular history into one single story that culminated, explicitly or implicitly, in the legitimation of the dual governance of society by state and church: by princes, parliaments, and bishops. Those who disagreed – the English freethinkers and the French *philosophes* – contended that before being used as historical evidence, the biblical text should be subjected to critical scrutiny rather than accepted at face value. The "historical and critical use" of biblical records was all the more important since "priests and politicians", focusing "upon the supernatural, fabulous, and incredible part of the story", utilised it "to strengthen and confirm the cursed execrable doctrine of theocracies, hierarchies, church-power, and outward temporal jurisdiction over conscience, and this in order to blind and enslave mankind by subjecting them to an anti-Christian spirituality under pretence of religion, the honour of God, and the salvation of souls".[3] One major task the critical historians set themselves was to challenge the legitimacy of civil and ecclesiastical powers that exaggerated their claims both in theory and practice; these powers should be exposed as oppressive, tyrannical, superstitious, and inimical to freedom.

Early-modern historians paid special attention to the structure of the historical process. While for the conservative thinkers history unrolled as a sacred continuum rooted in biblical revelation, the Enlightenment thinkers perceived it as a discontinuous process in which oppressive and free social and political systems alternated or stood side by side. In the most prosperous times and places, such as the classical Athens of Plato and Aristotle, Augustan Rome, and Renaissance Florence,[4] intellectuals were highly respected and had a recognised role in social, political, and cultural life, a role they were denied at other times and in other places, including early-modern Britain and France. Looking beyond Europe, Voltaire and many of his peers admired China as another example of a country in which intellectuals made an important contribution to social and political life. Chinese society, the Dutch philosopher Isaac Vossius claimed in a treatise published in 1685, was not only the most ancient but also the most praiseworthy in terms of peace, stability, and the cultivation of the arts and sciences.[5] By 1740, freethinkers throughout Europe had discovered their political ideal in books about China, notably in Jean-Baptiste Du Halde's sympathetic account of the history, philosophy, and government of this far-off land. Du Halde's early readers were especially impressed by the fact that this Eastern culture boasted an influential class of respected philosophical writers and a rational religion apparently akin to deism, the natural religion adopted by many as an alternative to the traditional Christian creed. Among the intellectual elite of Europe, "China" became a standard subject of conversation, and indeed inspired a whole philosophical argument. Having appeared in outline in the work of the Confucian philosopher Mencius (c. 300 BCE), this oriental ideal was summarised by Father Du Halde in a substantial chapter.[6] Mencius specifically comments on kings and emperors who not only surround themselves with sages and learned men on whose disinterested advice and services they can rely, but who also consult those sages who prefer not to be directly involved with politics and life at the court. European thinkers cherished their dream, seeing themselves in the role of these influential sages, mandarins, and literati. Just as they decried the tyrannical nature of the Ottoman Empire in the Middle East, these Western writers extolled the virtues of an idealised China whose people, governed by enlightened emperors and guided by a philosophical elite (rather than by priests), were thought to live in contented harmony under the rule of practical reason and tolerance. The (imaginary) political realm of Confucianism represented another oriental world – the good East as opposed to the bad East. Standing in stark contrast to the tyrannical East represented by the sultan of Constantinople and invoked to criticise the mores of contemporary European countries, it symbolised the practical viability of a similar political morality and served as a prototype of, and model for, a new political regime in the West. "China is the only one of all the ancient states that has not been under sacerdotal control", was Voltaire's verdict.[7]

Method

The philosophical faction claimed to have put forward superior arguments – i.e. the truth – because their view of history was based on a novel method. Critical historians considered Pierre Bayle (1647–1706) to be their founding father. Bayle was a Huguenot scholar: a Protestant living in exile in the

Netherlands; the confessional debates made him aware of how partisan opinion could influence one's judgement and distort the facts. His monumental *Dictionnaire historique et critique* (first edition 1697, subsequently enlarged), made available in English translation in the 1730s, served most historians and philosophers of the Enlightenment as a primer in critical thinking. Bayle's original plan had been to correct errors found in other works, but he ended up writing a *Dictionnaire* of more than 2,000 articles, some being short essays while others read like monographs.

Although Bayle never set out to explain his critical method in any systematic fashion, time and again he comments on how a critical historian should go about his job, and the relevant passages constitute the basic canon of historical criticism. This canon may be summed up as follows:[8]

(1) Historical truth can be discovered, though the research that leads to the truth may be difficult to perform.
(2) As a historian you must always have a source for any statement, preferably a contemporary source. Oral tradition alone is worthless.
(3) Since even contemporary reports may be egregiously wrong or biased, be ready to distrust any authority. Examine each fact anew.
(4) Never simply repeat what others have written; the tendency of historians to repeat each other uncritically perpetuates the grossest errors.
(5) Distrust the apologist and the one who is partial and biased.
(6) Be exempt from passions and without partiality towards your own country, religion (including the Bible), and political beliefs – the only state you belong to is the Republic of Letters. In this spirit, point out, rather than excuse or gloss over, evil acts and errors.
(7) Be ready to abandon your own conclusions if you are proven wrong.

Bayle applied these rigorous criteria to both ancient and modern authors, especially to the biographies and teachings of philosophers. To the dismay of some of his early readers, he also included critical articles on biblical figures, his entries on Abraham and David becoming particularly widely known; they are still remembered as early examples of the rigorous moral criticism of biblical figures that used to be celebrated by theological commentators. The biblical criticism of both Morgan and Voltaire – the two authors introduced below and considered in subsequent chapters – is indebted to Bayle's work.[9]

Joseph

While historians today generally ignore the biblical figure of Joseph, this was not the case amongst eighteenth-century writers. Both in Britain and France, historians considered and assessed his life and deeds. Writing historically about Joseph could quite simply mean paraphrasing the story: this is how conservative historians went about their job. Their only additional task was to assign him a date, for which they generally relied on the chronology established by James Ussher, author of an influential historical compendium that famously fixed the creation of the world at 4004 BCE and the birth of Christ at 5 BCE. Accepting Joseph's extremely long lifespan of 110 years as accurate, Ussher suggested dating it as 1745–1635 BCE. The critical school, by contrast, was faced with a more difficult agenda. Applying the criteria of Bayle, they would carefully attempt to separate fact from fiction, evaluate Joseph's deeds as being governed by virtue or vice, assess his contribution to liberty or oppression, and, not least, determine his alliance with either sacerdotal (traditional) or reasonable (deist) religion. Driven by a quest for historical truth, moral excellence, freedom, and the religion of reason, they could not avoid these issues. They felt, in fact, that the biblical text, rather than offering a straightforward and reliable account, actually conceals the historical truth. Like a detective, the critical historian has to search for hints, inconsistencies, and improbabilities in the biblical account, and these, when carefully examined, might finally lead to the hidden truth. Once the historian has found the key, he can produce an account that might differ considerably from anything the unprepared Bible reader would expect.

Bayle in his *Dictionnaire* did not select the figure of Joseph for critical study. But one of Bayle's friends did. This was the English philosopher Anthony Ashley Cooper, Lord Shaftesbury, who between 1698 and 1704 spent much time in Rotterdam where he met and befriended Bayle.[10] The two shared the notion that morality is distinct and independent of religious belief, and held in common a critical attitude to the Bible. Shaftesbury's influential book *Characteristics of Men, Manners, Opinions, Times* (1711) includes a passage in which he writes about Joseph in the style of Bayle, describing Joseph's rule in Egypt as being marred by the granting of unwarranted privileges to the priesthood. A generation after Shaftesbury, the *Characteristics* continued to be widely read, and two readers came to take up the theme of Joseph in their own writings: the English freethinker Thomas Morgan and, in France, Voltaire. Each offered his own historical reconstruction that even today strikes the reader as bold.

Morgan and Voltaire developed their approaches to Joseph as critiques of earlier works deemed by them deficient and uncritical – un-Baylean, we might say – in their historical perspective. Morgan addressed *The Sacred and Prophane History of the World Connected* (1728–1730) by Samuel Shuckford, an immensely learned work on the history of the ancient peoples, including biblical Israel. He accepts Shuckford's chronology (essentially that of Bishop Ussher) and appreciates the wealth of facts presented, but Morgan suggests an alternative interpretation. Originally invited into the land by Joseph, the Hebrews rose to become the ruling class of Egypt; Joseph, a power-craving politician, was the first leader in history to establish a despotic government and to favour the priestly upper class. Morgan studied the biblical record primarily as a moralist, condemning Joseph, and as a political philosopher, tracing in it the origins of despotism and priestly privilege. He insisted that, from the standpoint of the historian, Joseph must be considered the founder of despotism, an alienating political system that still adversely affected England and other parts of Europe. Joseph, in his eyes, belonged among the great though problematic historical personalities of world significance.

Unlike Morgan, who was more of a dilettante, Voltaire must be considered a professional historian, especially of what was then modern history. But he also immersed himself in the historical sources of ancient times, and he came to reject the easy and unquestioning integration of sacred (biblical) and profane (non-biblical) history, exemplified for instance by Bossuet's widely read survey of ancient history, the *Discours sur l'histoire universelle* (1681). Unlike Bossuet, he did not feel justified in assigning a place to the biblical patriarchs within a viable chronology. Hebrew history proper, according to Voltaire's radical vision, only began with King Solomon, and the stories presumed to report on earlier periods are likely to be legends. Voltaire therefore omitted Joseph from his own survey of universal history, *La Philosophie de l'histoire* (1765). This does not imply a lack of interest in Joseph: we can track Voltaire's lifelong fascination with this biblical patriarch. Voltaire came to develop two equally attractive hypotheses about Joseph: he must be seen either as the protagonist of an ancient oriental folk-tale (Chapter 19 below), or as the counterpart of a Jewish tax collector of the second century BCE whose fictionalised biography forms one of the last pieces to be included in the Hebrew Bible (Chapter 17 below).

16

Despotic Ruler – Morgan

Eighteenth-century English historians, when considering ancient times, did not have to begin from scratch. They could rely on, and develop, what earlier historians had already researched, compiled, and analysed – a wealth of huge tomes of baroque antiquarian learning. Part of this learning consisted in establishing a chronology: a framework of dates and names that facilitated orientation and promoted the flow of linear, ordered narration. Although several chronological systems had been devised in the seventeenth century, the one established by James Ussher (1580–1656) was the most influential. Where Joseph is concerned, the substance of Ussher's chronology is as follows:[1]

1745 BCE	birth of Joseph to Jacob and Rachel
1728	Joseph sold by his brothers into Egypt
1716	Joseph in prison
1715	Joseph freed from prison and made governor of Egypt
1708	a seven-year period of famine sets in
1706	Jacob's family emigrates from Canaan to Egypt
1689	Jacob (Joseph's father) dies
1635	Joseph dies

When writing about Joseph, eighteenth-century historians were not generally interested in challenging Ussher's dates and working out alternative systems; instead, they felt that history implied a more important challenge: that of drawing moral and political lessons from history by evaluating its leading personalities. In what follows I will first offer a brief survey of how early-modern authors assessed the character and contribution of Joseph, and then look at the critical work of Thomas Morgan.

Joseph in England

In early-modern times, sacred history – and indeed all of history – served as a store of exemplary characters, of virtuous men and women worthy of imitation. The relevant lessons could be found in the Bible and in the writings of the profane historians of ancient times. The Bible distinguishes carefully between good people and bad people, especially between kings "who did what was evil in the sight of the Lord" and those who "turned to the Lord with all their heart". Profane historians such as Suetonius and the much-admired Greek biographer Plutarch never hesitated to draw lessons from history, to bestow praise or blame, and weigh the character of those responsible for shaping the destiny of nations.[2] Historical narratives were viewed as teaching virtue and good policy by example. Readers expected the narrator to indicate what they ought to think of an important character, and what lessons should be learned from the events that were chronicled. Just as Plutarch in his *Parallel Lives* assessed the character of Alexander the Great and Julius Caesar, so early-modern historians would seek to evaluate the achievements of Joseph and Moses. Joseph, of course, was a man to be imitated, a model of virtue and personal integrity as well as a great political leader – a man, in the words of the biblical commentator Matthew Henry (1706), who "approved himself wise and good, both in his private and public capacity".[3] Joseph's "generosity" towards his brothers is particularly praiseworthy: "his goodness in returning only friendships and benefits for the most provoking injuries; and expressing more tenderness for his mortal enemies, than was usual with others to the best of friends", notes the historian Thomas Hearne.[4]

The first to depart from this view was Anthony Ashley Cooper, third earl of Shaftesbury (1671–1713), today chiefly known as a moralist and a supporter of the philosopher John Toland. What united Shaftesbury and Toland was the philosophy of deism. Originating with Edward Herbert of Cherbury in the seventeenth century, deism advocated a "natural" rather than "revealed" religion, a belief in God without a Christ or Son of God, without authority residing in the Bible, without belief in miracles, and without a church ruled by priests or ministers. Deism served as the secret religious conviction of many members of the Western intellectual elite, attracting such figures as Voltaire, Jean-Jacques Rousseau, Benjamin Franklin, Frederick the Great, Gotthold Ephraim Lessing, Goethe, and Kant; these thinkers refrained from making their private belief public for fear of scandal, censorship, and persecution. The faith of the deists does not imply the traditional notion of Scripture as a document inspired by God, authoritative, infallible, morally perfect, and historically accurate. In fact, their religion, considered by them to be "natural", is completely independent of the Bible. Accordingly, Shaftesbury felt free to express critical views about Joseph in his *Characteristics of Men, Manners, Opinions, Times* (1711). Shaftesbury must have been familiar with Joseph from an early age: John Locke, secretary to his father and responsible for the boy's education, no doubt made him read the biblical story. As Locke explained in *Some Thoughts Concerning Education* (1693), a child should begin his Bible reading with the Joseph story (see above, Chapter 4). However, as Shaftesbury developed his own independent philosophy, he became increasingly critical of his former teacher, and his reassessment of the figure of Joseph reflected his mature thinking as well as his absorption of Pierre Bayle's biblical criticism.[5] Brought as a boy to Egypt, Joseph was, Shaftesbury claimed, educated by Egyptian priests who trained him in sacerdotal wisdom: magic, astrology, divination, and the interpretation of dreams. Shaftesbury's source for this assumption was a note found in an ancient manual of world history; compiled in the third century CE by Marcus Junianus Justinus, it included the following passage:

> Joseph was the youngest of his brothers. Fearing his superior intelligence, his brothers kidnapped him secretly and sold him to foreign merchants. These carried him to Egypt, where he, by virtue of his sharp mind, quickly mastered the magic arts. He found favour with the king, because he was eminently skilled in prodigies, and was the first to establish the science of interpreting dreams.[6]

According to Shaftesbury, ancient Egyptian culture suffered from three evils: cultivation of the occult sciences (apparently all of which originated in this country), superstitious religious practices (more prominent here than anywhere else), and the influence of priests. The worst feature of Egypt was that the priests had managed to bring the country completely under their control. They not only owned one-third of the land, but also "swallowed up the state and monarchy".[7] As chief minister of Egypt, Joseph remained partial to the priests, while through his marriage he further allied himself with them. Moreover, he made sure "that the Crown, to speak in a modern style, offered not to meddle with the church lands".[8] Joseph, in other words, was involved with and actually supported the priesthood: the consequences of this liaison continue down to our own age.

Shaftesbury published his *Characteristics* anonymously, as was usual for most of the works written by deists. In an age of state and church censorship, it was safer not to be known as the author of a potentially subversive book that could be accused of undermining the authority of church or state. Each European country had its own institutions, history, and means of censorship, ranging from strict Geneva and Scotland to relatively lenient Holland.[9] Most countries, including England and France, fell somewhere between the two extremes. In England, after the Glorious Revolution of 1688/89, parliamentary legislation was dominated by a conservative agenda. The Blasphemy Act (1698) affirmed traditional Christian values by making it an offence for any person educated as a Christian, in writing, printing, teaching, or advised speaking, to deny the Trinity to be God, or to deny the veracity of the Christian religion and its sacred Scriptures. Punishment for these offences was fixed as follows: upon first offending, the culprit was to be rendered incapable of holding any civil, military, or ecclesiastical office; as a consequence of a second offending, he should lose all civil rights and suffer three years of imprisonment.[10] While to us this law looks not only conservative but repressive, its meaning for Britain after the Glorious Revolution was different. In England, it meant a big step towards religious freedom, because Unitarians (who believed in God, but not in the Trinity) and atheists (who had no religion at all) could no longer be threatened with the death penalty. But punishment did persist, as is shown by the case of Thomas Woolston (1669–1733). Woolston's *Discourses on the Miracles of Our Saviour* (1727–30) ridiculed basic Christian convictions, and when in his sixth discourse he argued that Christ's empty tomb was nothing but a fraud – because the disciples had stolen Jesus's body – the scandal was complete. Although this vulgar interpretation was put into the mouth of a fictitious Jewish rabbi, people well understood what Woolston meant. Sentenced to prison in 1729 because he was unable to pay an exorbitant fine for blasphemy, Woolston spent the last three years of his life in jail.

Shaftesbury's critique of Joseph remains brief and sketchy, but a generation after him, another English deist philosopher took up the subject and developed it at length. This was Thomas Morgan (*c.* 1680–1743) who insisted that, from the standpoint of the historian, Joseph must be considered the founder of despotism, an alienating political system that still adversely affected Britain and other countries. In Britain, the faction of the royalists actually defended what Morgan called tyranny.

Thomas Morgan

Royalists in early-modern England argued that political authority and property rights exist only by divine institution – because God gave Adam dominion over the creatures. Monarchs were deemed the natural inheritors of Adam's rights. John Locke (1632–1704), one of the most influential philosophers of the modern age, emphatically rejected this assumption. Property belongs to each human individual by nature or by God's great design, as does liberty. State and government are instituted to foster and protect individual liberty and property.[11] If the state fails to accomplish this, it has to be reformed and made fit for its task. The new political philosophy resonated with Enlightenment thinkers throughout Europe. "*Liberty and property* is the watchword of the English. [...] It is the watchword of nature," exclaimed Voltaire.[12] The slogan invited political activists to work towards limiting the privileges and presumptions of church and state, and to restore the natural rights of the individual. It also invited philosophers and historians to write books that explain why and how people lost their rights to the political and ecclesiastical authorities. One of these books, a three-volume treatise entitled *The Moral Philosopher*, offered such an analysis in the form of biblical criticism, surprisingly arguing – as we shall see – that all political evils began with the figure of Joseph.

Although at first few may have known the identity of the author of the *Moral Philosopher*,[13] published anonymously in three volumes between 1737 and 1740, it soon transpired that the writer was Thomas Morgan, a physician living and practising in London, a man who professed to follow the teachings of John Locke.[14] To the writing of his philosophical treatise he brought three unique gifts. The first was freedom. He had been ordained as minister of a dissenting church in 1716, but was dismissed from his ministry. After losing his pastorate, he studied medicine and eventually practised as a doctor. Thus independent of ecclesiastical or sectarian constraints, he absorbed the philosophy of Locke, and came to think and express himself freely on matters of religion without risking censure by the religious authorities. The second gift, inherited from his earlier clerical activity, was Morgan's thorough familiarity with the Bible and with the traditional teachings of Christianity. He brought his Christian learning into dialogue with the ideas of deism – the philosophy he had come to adopt and adapt to suit his own thinking. Morgan's knowledge of, and identification with, the deist sentiment was the third gift that he brought to the task of writing *The Moral Philosopher*.

In fact these three gifts did not suffice. A fourth gift was needed – courage. To defend deism and to promote it in public was a dangerous matter, for it was not known how the state authorities would deal with those who dissented from the Thirty-Nine Articles adopted by the established Church of England in the sixteenth century. While a certain liberalism reigned, important restrictions still persisted. The toleration of nonconformists applied only to those who accepted belief in the Trinity; those who were thought to be undermining Christianity by attacking it in speech or print risked punishment for blasphemy. To deal with this contradictory blend of freedom of expression and a severely limited tolerance of any views not held by the Church of England, intellectuals generally expressed their thoughts only when meeting like-minded men in informal settings such as privately organised debating clubs or in coffee-houses where they could test their novel ideas. Hearing of a "society of moral philosophers", one could be sure that its members assembled "in order to shew the absurdity of the present mode of religion, and establish a new one in its stead", as one contemporary observer noted.[15] Naturally, these societies have not escaped the attention of modern historians, who point out the relevance of these "republics of freethought"[16] for the dissemination of modern ideas such as freedom of expression and democracy, for the growing importance of popular media such as newspapers and periodical publications, and, as a result, for the emergence of public opinion as a significant cultural and political factor. Morgan first presented his controversial views at a "society, or club, of gentlemen in the country who met once a fortnight at a gentleman's house in a pleasant village".[17] While discussing such views in private was apparently safe, publishing them in print was another, more dangerous matter that required one to proceed with circumspection. Some deistic writers concealed their thinking by disguising it or merely alluding to it in such a manner that only the most astute readers would discover the real message.[18] Others expressed their thoughts unambiguously, but preferred not to betray their authorship. Morgan resorted to the second strategy by omitting his name from the title page of *The Moral Philosopher*, and subsequently, in the second and third volumes, by calling himself Philalethes, "Friend of Truth".

In the *Moral Philosopher* Morgan reconstructs and assesses the history of biblical religion from the beginnings recorded in the book of Genesis to his own time, showing how it developed, was distorted, partially or completely reformed and restored, and, in the course of time, again distorted, until its essential truth was rediscovered in deism. Morgan distrusts both the biblical record and later orthodox versions of church history; the former is often "very general and confused, inconsistent with itself, and contradictory to all the remains of profane history".[19] Everything has to be looked at critically, must be corrected and freed from ideological distortions. Morgan discerns three types of agent who contributed to the religious situation: those who were responsible for all religious evils – the priests, distorters, and manipulators; those who managed to bring some light to bear upon the human situation, though not always enough to enlighten humanity sufficiently – some of the prophets and reformers; and those who see the true light and fight against priestly presumption and privilege – people like Jesus, some of his early followers, and of course the deists. Morgan does not reduce history to a simple sequence of distinct stages, starting with an originally pure religion that was corrupted, then slowly ameliorated, and eventually restored to its original purity. He feels that history is a very complex process in which evil and benign forces fight against each other, with alternating victories, or half-victories, being won on both sides at more or less regular intervals. Nevertheless, despite these complexities, religious history is structured, and some of its decisive events can be discerned. One of its key episodes involves the figure of Joseph:[20]

In ancient times, the land of the Nile was a country known and envied for its unique fertility, riches, and flourishing state-controlled economy. It supported a large native population, and through its export of surplus grain it fed others who lived in distant countries. Everywhere in the ancient world its agricultural productivity and wealth were admired, as were its priests, whose food was supplied by the state.[21] Understandably, many inhabitants of the adjacent, more poorly endowed countries looked to Egypt as the land of their yearning, and they dreamt of going to live some day in this paradise. Egypt held allure for many – merchants, travellers, and foreign invaders as well as individuals and families seeking refuge from poverty. The ancient Hebrews were among those who yearned to settle in Egypt. One of their gods – not the Creator, whom they also worshipped, but their national tutelary – was said to have promised them a land full of riches, a country of wealth and well-being. This land was Egypt. Abraham sought to enter Egypt, but his stay was cut short and he had to leave again. Success came only with Joseph, a man craving power and driven by ambition. He succeeded not only in entering the country but also in gaining control of its riches, as Pharaoh's chief minister. The peaceful settlement of the Hebrews in Egypt was his doing and his chief claim to fame among his people.

Joseph's career in Egypt began humbly. Entering the country as a slave, he became steward of Pharaoh's state prison. There he succeeded in drawing attention to himself first by spreading rumours about his master's wife falling in love with him, a clever story presumably made up for the sake of self-promotion.[22] Then by offering several surprisingly accurate dream interpretations, Joseph's fame grew until he was called before Pharaoh to pronounce on two royal dreams concerning seven fat and seven lean cows. He interpreted the dreams as announcing seven successive years of agricultural surplus, to be followed by seven years of drought and famine. To confront this situation adequately, strong leadership was needed, for the country must be prepared for the crisis and guided through the critical period. Pharaoh appointed Joseph as the land's chief administrator. Joseph assumed the role of Egypt's governor, leaving no more than nominal rulership to the king. For fourteen years Joseph was effectively the most powerful person in Egypt. No sooner was he in office than he used his position to reform the Egyptian state after his own taste and ideals, that is to say: to satisfy his own craving for power over others. Three projects were foremost in his mind: to enhance the authority of the state, and thereby his own position, by making all subjects slaves of the king; to establish the priesthood as a power that would remain permanently distinct and independent of the state; and by inducing the Hebrews to immigrate, to indulge in nepotism by awarding the most lucrative political positions to his own relatives.

Through the state-directed economy or, more precisely, through economic manipulation of the state on a grand scale, Joseph succeeded in establishing Pharaoh's – and his own – absolute authority. Joseph exploited the fact that the country had a predominantly agricultural economy, this being particularly amenable to state intervention. In many towns he built state-owned granaries to be filled with surplus grain during the "fat years". Then lean years followed – not naturally (since the Nile will never fail to flood and fertilise the fields of Egypt), but as a consequence of Joseph's policy of storing and withholding seed grain. What the biblical text describes as wise crisis management on the part of the state is in fact nothing other than a clever control measure. During this artificially induced economic crisis – the first on record in human history – specially installed strongholds safeguarded the storehouses against unauthorised depletion. As the famine set in and people began to suffer, the state took charge of any remaining resources of food. Grain was distributed, but only in return for payment to the state, for Joseph claimed that the reserves belonged to the crown. Grain was made available in very limited quantities; as a result, the population could just about survive. Seed grain was withheld for six years, so that famine continued and the power of the state increased every year. Joseph took advantage of the people's deplorable situation by relentless profiteering. So when buying food, the subjects first spent all their money, then they handed over their livestock and landed property in return for rations of grain, and ultimately they sacrificed their personal liberty to serve the state as slaves. By the time seed grain was distributed at the end of the seventh year, the entire population of Egypt had become enslaved.

Not enslaved, however, were the priests to whom Joseph was related through his Egyptian spouse, daughter of the high priest. Unlike the common people the priesthood was granted special privileges. During the years of famine the priests received their food from the state without having to pay for it. Their land was declared inalienable property, permanently and safely beyond the reach of the state authorities. Moreover, they constituted the only class of Egyptians to enjoy true freedom. These measures abolished the priests' former dependence on the state. Earlier, the priesthood had been subordinate to the state and the priests were civil servants, but now the state itself served the priesthood.[23] The priests not only became the wealthiest class of Egyptians, they also became the wisest, for they had the means and the leisure to study chemistry and natural magic. However, they kept this knowledge to themselves. The privileged clergy arrogantly controlled religious affairs, while keeping the masses in ignorance, superstition, and blind obedience.

Given his position as Pharaoh's prime minister, it was not difficult for Joseph to invite his relatives – the Hebrews or Israelites – to move to Egypt and to feed them during the lean years. The favoured position of the immigrants is clearly evident, for the Hebrew shepherds were not only assigned the richest pastures; their leaders were appointed to the best jobs in the state administration. Unlike the native commoners, they retained their livestock and their freedom, and emerged as the leading secular class. Joseph's brothers announced themselves as shepherds and as Pharaoh's "servants". This humble self-designation must not be allowed to mislead us – for we understand that the Hebrews, shortly after having been presented to Pharaoh, became the country's actual political leaders. The number of Hebrews who settled in Egypt can be calculated: they were not just a group of seventy persons, as a superficial reading of the biblical texts seems to suggest; to arrive at the true total, the extended family of each of these men has to be included, so seventy must be multiplied by thirty – they comprised in fact a group of 2,100 people, led by seventy elders.

Joseph did not achieve all the goals he had set for himself and his people. On the one hand, he had firmly established the systematic exploitation of the peasantry by the state; this was his lasting achievement. Reduced to permanent poverty, the peasants toiled for the support of a privileged class of priests and Hebrews. On the other hand, his attempt to make Hebrew domination permanent proved to be a failure. Foreign rule was not to last very long. Even during the lifetime of Joseph, the prime minister's reputation seems to have declined. While Jacob, former patriarch of all the Hebrews, had been given an Egyptian state funeral celebrated with much pomp and circumstance, Joseph's interment remained private and simple. His loss of influence is passed over in silence in the biblical record. We learn no more than the fact that Joseph himself came to realise the impossibility of consolidating and perpetuating Hebrew rule over the Egyptians. Accepting this, Joseph began to make preparations for their subsequent settlement in Palestine by arranging for the transfer of his own body there. After Joseph's death, the Hebrews rapidly lost all their political and economic privileges. Those who had been masters were now slaves. Reduced to this status and considered aliens, their presence was merely tolerated. No longer

> allowed to live anywhere in the country as they had done in the days of Joseph, they were driven back to Goshen, whence they eventually fled Egypt.[24] Nevertheless, Joseph's political achievements earned world-historical significance on two counts. First, he invented the despotic state that treats its citizens as subjects and slaves; second, it was through his initiative that the priests had become established as a class of their own, independent of state control. The priests, and with them their entire religious organisation, became, as it were, a state within a state. When the Israelites – "this grossly stupid, superstitious and Egyptianised people"[25] – left Egypt, the culture they took with them conformed to the Egyptian model, and they never abandoned it. Inherited from Egypt where it had been promoted by Joseph, their religion remained firmly, and deplorably, in priestly hands.

Morgan's sketch of the true history of Joseph reflects the author's dual role as a historian and a practical philosopher: as a historian he reconstructs an episode of ancient Israelite history, based upon all available sources, biblical and extrabiblical, and offers an interpretation; as a practical thinker, he seeks to explain the lesson implied in the episode, a lesson relevant for his own age. In the following analysis, we will distinguish historical reconstruction from contemporary lesson, though the two are closely related and intertwined.

The historical task was facilitated by Samuel Shuckford's *Sacred and Prophane History of the World Connected* (1728–1730).[26] In this manual that accommodated biblical and ancient history within a single chronological frame (essentially that of Bishop Ussher), Morgan found references to ancient sources and descriptions of the Egyptian society and priesthood. Shuckford knows from ancient sources, especially from Manetho's *Aegyptiaca* (c. 280 BCE), that Egypt had not always been an independent country; for a certain period in remote antiquity, it had been ruled by foreign masters who came from Asia – the Shepherds. They ruled for more than five hundred years, but were at last expelled.[27] In terms of chronology, Shuckford places the beginning of this foreign rule some time between Joseph and Moses. The new Egyptian ruler "who did not know Joseph" (Exodus 1: 8) must have been one of these shepherd kings, and it was under them that the Hebrews began to suffer. All of this is interesting, argues Morgan, but fundamentally flawed: Shuckford failed to realise that the Shepherds and the Hebrews were the same people. Read superficially, the book of Genesis seems to present the Hebrews as an innocent nation of shepherds: "What is your occupation?" Pharaoh asks the brothers of Joseph as they arrive to settle in Egypt. "Your servants are shepherds, as our fathers were" is the answer (Genesis 47: 3). While sounding idyllic, this innocent reply conceals a historical message that is easily missed but can be recovered with the help of Manetho's *Aegyptiaca* and an enigmatic reference to all shepherds being "an abomination to the Egyptians" (Genesis 46: 34), an aside that Shuckford admits not understanding.[28] But Morgan does: far from being simple tenders of their livestock, the Shepherds are in fact a class of foreign lords who controlled Egypt. The identification of the Shepherd rulers with the Hebrews is not of Morgan's invention; it can actually be found in Manetho. After some time, Manetho reports, the Shepherds were expelled from the land of the Nile and eventually founded the city of Jerusalem. Using Manetho's account, Morgan reads the story of Joseph as reflecting the period during which Egypt suffered from Hebrew domination. Although not specifically mentioned by Manetho, Joseph must be considered the first in the line of evil foreign rulers.

Under the governorship of Joseph, the Egyptians lost both their property and their liberty: Morgan takes this as the central event included in the biblical account, and it is accepted by him as reliable information. In focusing on property and liberty, our historian relies on a Lockean key to understand political history. As someone who took away a people's property and liberty, Joseph failed in what is for Locke the central task of government: to protect citizens against the loss of their freedom and their belongings. Accordingly, he is a tyrant, someone who wields "despotical power", defined, in the words of John Locke, as "an absolute, arbitrary power one man has over another, to take away his life whenever he pleases".[29] While Joseph did not go as far as killing anyone, he acts as if he had the power to do so. His rule, moreover, was supported by the priestly class of Egypt, and Joseph ensured that neither their liberty nor their property was in any way diminished. Although not indicated by Morgan, it is clear enough that he was relying on the standard eighteenth-century knowledge of ancient Egypt based on classical authors, found in Shuckford's manual. Egypt was considered a land that boasted an important class of priests; ranked high above the common people, they formed Egypt's nobility.[30] The priests not only were experts in ritual; they also acted as advisers to the king and thus participated in political life. Egypt's political system was an absolute monarchy, and far from being free, the citizens could be considered slaves of the ruler. Early-modern writers generally agreed with Aristotle who had declared that the barbarians of Asia are "by nature more slavish in their character than the Greeks" and so "submit to despotic rule (*despotikê archê*) without complaint".[31] Despotism was endemic in the East.

Morgan's revisionist image of Joseph as a "politician" (in the sense this word had in the eighteenth century: a schemer and tactician),[32] founder of despotic rule, and ally of the influential priestly class, contrasted strongly with the image most of his contemporaries had of the biblical patriarch. As a consequence, Morgan's book prompted others to publish, some seeking to refute its image of Joseph as unfounded, others to defend it against its critics.[33] For our purposes, it is more relevant to listen to his critics than his supporters. "For one line of Hebrew history you have twenty of his pure invention", summarised John Chapman in reaction to the *Moral Philosopher*.[34] The longest refutation of Morgan's *Moral Philosopher* is by Samuel Chandler (1693–1766), minister of a nonconformist church in London. Like Morgan, Chandler argues within the framework of the political philosophy of John Locke that sees the chief task of state and government as the protection of the liberties and property of all citizens. Did Joseph violate these rights? And is such a violation conceivable? The answer is easy to find: "Let a prime minister in this kingdom [Britain], who is a Frenchman, or one in France, who is a Britain [*sic*], engross the corn in either of these kingdoms, and create or prolong a famine by such monopolizing, and hinder the farmers hereby from sowing their lands in a good season, and I can easily foresee his fate, without any assistance of the spirit of prophecy."[35] What fate? "The nation, and even his guards themselves", would rise as one man, and tear "the tyrannical foreigner to pieces".[36] To Chandler, Morgan's reconstruction of Joseph's policy seems unfounded and absurd. Joseph, Chandler claims, rather than violating people's rights, actually promoted them, fixing them by the law he established in Egypt. Joseph's law "was in truth a law that at once settled the demands of the crown and the properties and liberties of the people, and that curbed the avarice and ambition of the priests".[37] He moderated the king's claims to the people's property by limiting the taxes to one-fifth of the agrarian produce; the royal administration could never claim more than this. Since the government receives not a fixed sum but a fixed proportion, the state shares the risk inherent in agriculture. As for the priests, Joseph despised them for their idolatry.[38] Although he did not diminish their extensive landed property, he prevented them from extending their lands and increasing their revenues. "What becomes of our philosopher's charge against Joseph, that he divided the whole property of Egypt between the church and the crown?" Chandler asks. The answer is obvious:

> In reality he [Joseph] made no alteration of property. He left the crown and church only what they each had before. He did indeed ease the people of a burthen they could not sustain, took back the estates they rented into his hands because they could not pay these rents, supplied them liberally with food at free-cost, whilst the scarcity lasted. [. . .] and to prevent all future burthens and oppressions of the people, fixed their rents to a fifth part of the produce.[39]

From this analysis, Joseph emerges as the ideal statesman, the protector of liberty and property – the exact opposite of how Morgan saw him in his radical historical analysis.

In addition to writing as a historian, Morgan wrote as a practical philosopher: an author with a message for his own age and country, someone who warns of dangers, points out instances of abuse, voices his dissent on contentious public issues, and presses for reforms. An anonymous pamphlet of fifty-two pages, published in 1743 in defence of Morgan's *Moral Philosopher*, openly acknowledges its political aim: to make "every true-born Englishman" aware of his "natural hereditary right to liberty and property", and to inspire "circumspection enough to discover, and courage and resolution enough to check, the plots and intrigues of any second Joseph".[40] Morgan's discussion of despotism belongs to a debate in which many eighteenth-century thinkers participated: a debate which, though sometimes presented as historical analysis, sought to promote liberty by describing its main enemy, the despotic state.[41] As early as 1616, the Italian philosopher Giulio-Cesare Vanini had claimed that Moses, a clever politician, had by ruse established his despotic rule over the Hebrews.[42] By 1709, Vanini's view of Moses had found its way into a clandestine manuscript that circulated amongst European intellectuals. First printed in 1719, it denounced Moses as an impostor who exploited the ignorance and credulity of the Hebrews to establish the first despotic state in recorded history. Moses, it was suggested, "was less of a father than a tyrant to them" (*il étoit moins leur Père que leur Tyran*).[43] This line of thought was taken up by Morgan, who extended it to Joseph. Even before Moses, Joseph had founded "the same sort of tyranny in church and state".[44] It could be said that most countries, having a monarch, were subjected to despotic rule. But there were degrees of despotism. The English government, David Hume explained, can be described as "a mixture of despotism and liberty", though one in which "liberty predominates".[45] The French were subject to more oppressive despotism because they enjoyed less liberty. Worst off, at least in popular opinion, were those who lived under Ottoman rule, for they were slaves of the sultan. Naturally, oriental despotism was felt to be evil. Oriental-style despotism was an obvious temptation, especially for rulers; accordingly, critics sought to limit the power of European kings and members of the nobility. Although the Western nations had been civilised for a long time, their governments were sometimes still guided by the legacy of oriental despotism. In fact, this legacy was deemed responsible for the failure to abolish torture,[46] to establish freedom of the press and to grant the free exercise of one's religion. Both individuals and institutions often succumbed to despotic temptation, because despotism "is the worst of all temptations; there is no resisting it".[47]

Closely allied to despotism is clericalism, the – unwarranted and detrimental – rule and influence of priests within the political system. In Morgan's England, there was an established Christian Church ruled by a hierarchy of bishops and priests. The critique of the established church, a stock subject of deistical writings, generally highlights two evils: the large sums involved in state support of the clergy, and the unacceptable extent of clerical authority over the religious beliefs and practice of the people. Both parliament and people should realise that "ecclesiastical revenues are ill-bestowed, and that such a fund of national property might be applied to better uses".[48] Religious beliefs, according to Morgan, should not fall under the jurisdiction of anyone, and religion, if it is to be organised at all, might simply take the form of private clubs of like-minded individuals.[49] In other words, there ought not to be an established church that indoctrinates, supervises, and controls its members. Interestingly, Morgan's critic Samuel Chandler seems to be of the same opinion – as might be expected of a Presbyterian minister whose church was tolerated but not established or privileged by the English crown. When pointing out, against Morgan, that Joseph "curbed the avarice and ambition of the priests",[50] Chandler sought to refute Morgan's negative portrayal of the biblical patriarch, while at the same time voicing a veiled, though mild, criticism of contemporary ecclesiastical presumption.

Morgan's supporters and apologists remained unimpressed by Chandler's attempt to hold up Joseph as an example of someone who actively opposed clericalism. One of them, the writer who called himself Mencius Philalethes, defended Morgan's critique of Egyptian priestcraft and restated it in no uncertain terms. The most remarkable feature of Mencius Philalethes's book, however, is the first name adopted by the anonymous author: Mencius, Friend of Truth, insinuating the idea that, as in China (home of the ancient philosopher Mencius), not the clergy but the philosophers should wield moral authority in state and society. Like Morgan's original work, Mencius Philalethes's defence strongly and angrily attacks English clericalism. Both Morgan and the pseudonymous author understood that those who held authority in their country did so by relying on the co-operation of the clergy, and that it was with their compliance that the emergence of freedom of thought was resisted. If we are to believe that Mencius Philalethes was none other than the deistical writer Peter Annet (1693–1769),[51] we know that he was not mistaken in his analysis, as he went on to experience in the 1760s. Charged with blasphemy, Annet spent a month in prison and subsequently was sentenced to forced labour. Upon being pardoned a year later, he worked as a simple schoolteacher, and died in poverty in 1769. To challenge the accepted view of historical truth – to regard Joseph as the founder of the despotic political system – still had its price, for the state continued to rely on the Egyptian, despotic model rather than the liberal and enlightened one of China. For the freethinkers, not Joseph but the Chinese emperor epitomised competent political leadership.

What, then, are we to make of Morgan, historian and freethinker? In the latter role, he is an impressive and remarkable figure, an intrepid advocate of the separation of state and church. As a historian, Morgan did have some influence, and his work was widely known – in Germany to the philosopher Hermann Samuel Reimarus[52] and in New England to John Adams,[53] later to be the second president of the United States. Today, however, the *Moral Philosopher* is forgotten, and Morgan's interpretation of the Joseph figure no longer accepted. Morgan's bold reinterpretation of the book of Genesis and the character of Joseph strikes readers today as an early example of biblical criticism. In fact, Morgan anticipated the basic method of modern historical criticism of the Bible by two centuries. Not satisfied with the biblical account, he suggested an alternative, and in his view more plausible, interpretation. Although biblical criticism came to use this kind of approach consistently, most more recent biblical critics do not concur with Morgan's negative view of the patriarch. Nevertheless, Morgan does have a point. When twentieth-century social scientists imaginatively reconstructed the origins of the city-state, the presumed precursor of the larger state, they resorted to more or less the same kind of argument as Morgan (though without reference to Joseph). Lewis Mumford, for example, posits the existence of a "primitive citadel", a kind of fortress that served a chieftain and warrior as a base for exercising control over others. In his citadel, he kept not only his women and his booty, but also the annual surplus grain not needed by his subjects for immediate consumption. This confiscation and storage, Mumford argues, must have functioned as the "artificial creation of scarcity in the midst of increasing natural abundance".[54] Accordingly, it was by such clever and somewhat devious devices that the chieftain held sway over the life and death of his community. This is, almost exactly, how Morgan felt about the imposition of a political economy he attributed to Joseph. Stripped of their biblical setting, Morgan's ideas still hold some appeal. We are still inclined to study how things like political systems began in order to understand their function, their contribution (or otherwise) to human welfare, and their possible – and often real – corruption. In the beginning, things are apparently simple and amenable to analysis; in more advanced ages like our own we seem doomed to live in a complex world that is governed by forces beyond our control and comprehension.

17

Tax Collector – Voltaire

VOLTAIRE'S UNIQUE HISTORICAL PERSPECTIVE ON THE FIGURE OF JOSEPH emerged from the philosopher's interaction with a French tradition which, by the mid-eighteenth century, included both conservative and critical voices – the former being well known and published, the latter clandestine. Eventually, Voltaire abandoned both of these voices, and in an easily overlooked footnote that he inserted in one of his anonymously published books he suggested a radically new interpretation of Joseph.

JOSEPH IN FRANCE

The Bible, for French conservative thinkers, was held to be a reliable guide to ancient history, both in the facts narrated and in the evaluations made of events and characters. When early Israelite history was discussed, for instance in Bishop Jacques-Bénigne Bossuet's *Discours sur l'histoire universelle* (1681), the task was easy because it only involved paraphrasing and summarising the biblical account. Since Joseph was well known to all readers of Scripture, it sufficed to refer to him briefly, evoking the major stages of his life.[1] More thorough historians and exegetes speculated about the sources used by the biblical author, gave their paraphrases a chronological framework, and also sought to assess Joseph's character. The question of "who wrote the Joseph story" was rarely considered; according to general opinion, it was written by Moses, and Moses must have used a reliable source – either an account passed on orally by Joseph's descendants, or a memoir written by Joseph himself.[2] To fix Joseph chronologically was difficult; seventeenth-century chronologists suggested as his year of entering Egypt 2167 (Paul Pezron), 1769 (Denis Petau) or 1728 BCE (James Ussher) in their elaborate systems based on the figures they found in the Bible and ancient accounts by chronographers.[3] Most scholars did not linger over matters of chronology, and the Jesuits went so far as to discourage chronological studies, declaring that it sufficed to rely on existing scholarship.[4] Some Catholic writers such as Bossuet simply followed the Irish historian James Ussher.

Despite the general French tendency to extol Joseph as a hero and a saint, one French author pointed out certain flaws in the methods, if not the character, of this Hebrew statesman. In particular, Jean Cauvin (John Calvin, 1509–1564) claimed to detect a lack of wisdom in some of Joseph's political measures. This was in keeping with ancient literary practice, for hardly any historical character could be said to be perfect. Calvin painted a sombre picture of the Egyptian peasantry's situation during the great famine. "It was a miserable spectacle," he wrote, "and one that might have softened hearts of iron, to see rich farmers, who previously had kept provision stored in their granaries for others, now begging food. Therefore Joseph might be deemed cruel because he does not give bread gratuitously to those who are poor and exhausted, but robs them of all their cattle, sheep, and donkeys."[5] The reformer came close to accusing Joseph of cruelty and condemning his transactions as unlawful. But Calvin did not pursue this thought at any length. Despite his evident reservations concerning Joseph's politics, he retained the notion that the biblical patriarch, and the Bible as a whole, must somehow stand above criticism. Calvin, moreover, did not get a hearing in Catholic France, and he had to flee in order to establish himself and his reformed church abroad – in Geneva.

By the eighteenth century, however, we do find critical considerations of biblical history in France. Radical eighteenth-century thinkers questioned all established authorities – the Bible, the church, and baroque historiography. If any truth were to be discovered about past events and the lives of political leaders, that truth could only be found by independent study, unconstrained assessment of all available sources, and the use of reason. Passion for antiquarian erudition had to be balanced by sober reasoning. Some French historians and philosophers no longer believed that sacred history, transmitted in the Bible, was reliable and thus superior to the knowledge of profane history, which remained vague and problematic.[6] All our knowledge of the early history of humankind, they claimed, is ultimately derived from inadequate sources.[7] Biblical history was no exception. Critical thinkers no longer believed that the historical accuracy of the Bible was guaranteed by divine revelation. Accordingly, the Bible, including the story of Joseph, could be subjected to thoroughgoing moral and historical criticism.

The first French critic to portray Joseph in a way comparable to the English philosophers Shaftesbury and Morgan (see above, Chapter 16) was Emilie du Châtelet (1706–1749), a noble and elegant lady known as an eminent mathematician and scientist, and, in addition, remembered for her famous liaison with Voltaire. We happen to know that Madame du Châtelet read Bossuet's *Discours sur l'histoire universelle*, and was disappointed; in the margins of the section on the Jews she noted, "One may say much of these people in theology, but they deserve little place in history." The noble lady, Voltaire reports, "could not endure that one should write at length about the obscure dwellers in Palestine and say not a word on the vast empire of China, the most ancient in all the world and without doubt the best governed".[8] During the years from 1735 until 1749 when he stayed at the country estate of his friend and mistress at Cirey-sur-Blaise, Voltaire participated in Emilie's biblical studies. It is reported that every morning at breakfast a chapter of the Bible was read, each of the participants making critical observations according to his or her interests.[9] They consulted Calmet's twenty-three-tome biblical commentary, of which Mme du Châtelet owned a copy, possibly the gift of Dom Augustin Calmet (1672–1757) himself, since, as a family friend, he had written this family's history. Calmet's work, while providing much information, was mildly apologetic in tone, thus inviting Emilie's criticism. The learned lady entrusted her observations to a manuscript entitled *Examens de la Bible*. In her short passage on the tale of Joseph, Mme du Châtelet calls it one of the most touching stories found in the Bible and extols the protagonist's generosity in dealing with his evil brothers. But everything relating to dreams and dream interpretation she considered strange.[10] Her central critique of Joseph is this:

> Joseph is very unfair to the Egyptians. He takes away their money, their animals, and the fifth part of their possessions in perpetuity – chapter 47, verse 14 ff. It is no pleasure to be ruled by the [biblical] patriarchs. The kings of Egypt could be obliged to Joseph, but as for the Egyptian people, he could not have treated them with more severity.[11]

Mme du Châtelet's manuscript was never printed, but circulated in handwritten copies; the major copy was published only recently (2009).

VOLTAIRE, BIBLICAL CRITIC

In 1750, after Mme du Châtelet's premature death in 1749, Voltaire (1694–1778) received an invitation from Frederick the Great, then Europe's most enlightened monarch, to join his court in Berlin and Potsdam. Voltaire accepted. During his years in Prussia (1750–1753), he began to intensify his biblical and church-historical studies. After having fallen out with Frederick, he returned to France, and devoted even more time to reading and researching. He scrutinised his own growing collection of books and consulted specialised collections such as those of the monastery library of Senones in the Vosges, where Augustin Calmet was abbot. In June and early July 1754 the sixty-year-old philosopher, already a famous author, was cordially received at the abbey, and was lodged and entertained there while spending three or four weeks researching in the abbey's wonderful library. Voltaire enjoyed his retreat in what must have appeared to him a scholar's paradise. "I am devoting myself to history in a huge library," he reported to a friend. "The monks find me the pages, lines and quotations I ask for. Dom Calmet, at the age of eighty-three, climbs aloft on a shaky ladder, making one tremble. And he digs out old books for me."[12]

By the early 1750s, Voltaire's essential vision of biblical history had been formed. Although he never produced a coherent account, the elements of his biblical criticism can be assembled from scattered references. Voltaire came to understand that the ancient nations such as the Egyptians, Chaldeans, Greeks, and Hebrews did not keep records from the very beginning of their existence. Accordingly, little reliable information exists about their beginnings. In the traditions they transmit about the past, three successive ages can be discerned: the age of fables, the heroic age, and the historical age, and they may be likened to night, twilight, and the bright light of day.[13] The first few centuries of their national history were full of absurd fables that resemble the *Arabian Nights* where nothing is true. The stories told about the heroic age are not much better, though now a few names, dates, and places are authentic; what we are told is hardly any more reliable than courtly romances. Next comes the historical age, in which, due to the use of written records, the essentials are true though the details were mostly invented by the ancient authors. In *Des Mensonges imprimés* (On Printed Lies, 1750), Voltaire applies this sequence only to the ancient Greeks and Romans in whose traditions the pattern can be readily discerned. It is clear, however, that he took the pattern to be universally valid and therefore equally applicable to the understanding of the traditions transmitted by the biblical people in the collection of books called the Bible: their historiography, like that of the other ancient nations, also moves through the three stages.

All of the Pentateuch – the five books of Moses – reflects the first stage: that of the fictional past, composed of obscure legend and fable. Scrutinising the biblical record, Voltaire had lost any belief in the reliability of the Pentateuch, and specifically of its first part, the book of Genesis, as an authentic record of the early history of humankind, followed by an account of the early story of the Hebrew nation. One question addressed by Voltaire as by other eighteenth-century critics was whether Moses actually did compile the first five books of the Bible, including Genesis, some time during the second millennium BCE, as the Hebrews wandered through the desert towards the promised land. Starting with the seventeenth-century philosophers Thomas Hobbes and Baruch Spinoza,[14] early-modern critics increasingly questioned the validity of this traditional assumption, and Voltaire joined the doubtful. Quite apart from all kinds of inconsistencies that presuppose the biblical author's domicile in Palestine (which Moses never entered), it seemed improbable that a major and lengthy work should have been written during Israel's sojourn in the desert. Books generally originate in centres of habitation, not among desert nomads. To make sense of the book of Genesis one surely had first of all to abandon the notion of Moses being its author or compiler. While there was little hard evidence available to date ancient Israel's sacred literature, Voltaire seems to have considered it a composite work that he vaguely ascribed to Israel's post-exilic period, i.e. to the fifth century BCE.[15] The compiler, he believed, might have been the Jewish scribe Ezra. In his assessment of the person of Moses, Voltaire refrains from being explicit. Although Voltaire's *Philosophie de l'histoire* (1765) echoes the biblical book of Exodus in a chapter dedicated to Moses as the original lawgiver of the Hebrews, Voltaire reports that some critics even doubt his existence as a historical personality, apparently implying that this is his own opinion.[16]

Voltaire felt little inclination to comment extensively on the following two stages: the heroic and historical ages. Much of the story told in the books of Joshua, Judges, and Samuel no doubt reflects the heroic age of which, upon close consideration, not much survives the test of critical scrutiny. Little can be known for certain about the Hebrew people before the days of King Solomon, who boasted a real court and a courtly life reminiscent of Versailles; with him the recording of more or less reliable information about the ancient Jewish nation began. With Solomon, we enter the historical age.

Voltaire, polemicist

Voltaire's view of biblical history does not come as a surprise to twenty-first-century readers who have become accustomed to this by now well-established critical approach. But then, in the eighteenth century, biblical criticism was felt by many to undermine the authority of the church that based its authority upon God's revelation as recorded in the Bible. For Voltaire, such revelation never took place – it was all mere fiction and legend. The only element he found acceptable and reasonable was belief in God as the Creator of the universe and the guarantor of the moral law; but this belief was based on rational insight accessible to the enlightened minds of all ages (including those of the deist philosophers of his own time), and not upon a particular understanding revealed to a politically insignificant people in the Middle East. During this research begun in Berlin, Voltaire discovered the potential of using his growing biblical knowledge for polemical purposes. In numerous anonymous or pseudonymous publications he attacks the Bible as a book marked by contradictions and containing evidence of presumption, stupidity, delusion, and fraud.[17] In keeping with the philosophical spirit of his day, Voltaire's principal targets for ridicule and attack were the church and the source of its authority, the Bible, for which he apparently had only disdain.

Voltaire's earliest polemical reference to the Joseph story can be found in a controversial treatise entitled *Sermon des Cinquante* (The Sermon of the Fifty). Written around 1752, it circulated first in handwritten copies, one of the "clandestine" texts of the Enlightenment, that is, one not to be seen by those who could alert the royal censors to its existence. Voltaire had it printed anonymously in 1762, and, for fear of censorship, never admitted his authorship. "This furious bill of indictment, by far his most daring work, could have earned him the Bastille or even the stake", explains one modern editor of the text.[18] In the guise of a sermon vaguely reminiscent of a Quaker or Unitarian setting (where every member of the group may address the congregation), the treatise surveys the contradictions, cruelties, and impossibilities inherent in the biblical narrative. The passage about Joseph reads as follows:

> The book [of Genesis] declares that Joseph, a child of this vagabond family, is sold into Egypt, and that, foreigner though he is, he is made first minister as a reward for interpreting a dream. What a first minister he was, compelling a whole nation to enslave itself, during a time of famine, to obtain food! What magistrate amongst us would, in time of famine, dare to propose so abominable a bargain, and what nation would accept it? Let's not dwell upon exactly how the seventy members of Joseph's family, who settled in Egypt, could in two hundred and fifteen years increase to six hundred thousand fighting men [...]. The innumerable contradictions – the sure sign of imposture – are not worthy of consideration.[19]

Joseph is depicted as an evil character, and as a hopelessly improbable one; marred by impossibilities, the whole story is flawed to the point of being unreal. In his later work, Voltaire repeats and enlarges both his list of absurdities and his polemical comments. Concerning the enslavement of the Egyptians he adds that "no other case of such behaviour has ever been reported of the minister of any state. In fact, a minister suggesting such a law in England would soon find himself at the gallows."[20] One of the biblical story's major flaws, he notes, is its complete disregard of the Nile's annual inundation of Egypt. It is simply impossible that the Nile should not have burst its banks for seven years in succession. The entire country would have changed for ever, and it would have required containing the river by building a dam at one of the cataracts – and then all of Ethiopia would have become one vast landscape of marshes.[21] The surprising disregard of the actual agricultural situation, Voltaire concludes, leads one to assert that "the entire story of Joseph is just a novel (*un roman*)". Indeed, whatever is improbable in this story – the failure of natural phenomena, the enslavement of an entire population – may be excused by remembering that it is "nothing but fiction" (*n'est qu'une fiction*).[22] In other words: in *belles-lettres*, the author is not constrained by the dictates of realism. So the Joseph story, for Voltaire, is nothing but a novel, though one echoing superb oriental storytelling – a subject to which we will return below, in Chapter 19, when dealing with Voltaire's article "Joseph" in the *Dictionnaire philosophique*. Although this article generally refrains from polemics, Voltaire did not miss the opportunity to issue a moral indictment on Joseph of the kind earlier expressed by Mme du Châtelet, Thomas Morgan, and Shaftesbury (the last-mentioned being his most likely inspiration):[23] "Subsequently, the entire nation enslaves itself in order to have grain – herein apparently lies the origin of despotic power. We must admit that no king had ever struck a better bargain, but equally, the people had little reason to bless the prime minister."[24] "What a minister – he deserves hanging" (*Quel ministre pendable*) reads the verdict Voltaire wrote in the margin of Calmet's commentary.[25]

Today, Voltaire's biblical criticism is remembered mainly for the polemical use its author made of it. However, a closer look at the French philosopher's work reveals that his interest was more complex and extended far beyond polemics. Less well known, but equally important for Voltaire, was the historical study of biblical literature, of which his critical engagement with the figure of Joseph is but one example.

Voltaire, Historian of Joseph

Throughout his career as a writer, the French philosopher never lost his interest in Joseph. The evidence is scattered through his work from 1731 to 1776, from the early *Histoire de Charles XII* to *La Bible enfin expliquée*, published forty-five years later. The relevant sources are as follows:

1731	*Histoire de Charles XII*
1752/62	*Sermon des Cinquante*
1764	*Dictionnaire philosophique*
1765	*La Philosophie de l'histoire*
1776	*La Bible enfin expliquée*

Although he never attempted a synthesis of his thought on Joseph, it can be reconstructed, or rather assembled like the pieces of a jigsaw puzzle, from his various writings. As the pieces of the puzzle fall into place, the following picture emerges: the Joseph story is flawed by absurdities; these can best be explained by the fact that what we have here is not a historical record, but a piece of fiction. Most surprisingly, it also reflects the biography of a real person: one living not in the age of the Hebrew patriarchs but much later, in third-century BCE Hellenistic Egypt.

When studying the history of Russia and the Ottoman Empire, Voltaire's interest in Joseph had been kindled. He was fascinated by the Ottoman episode in the life of Charles XII, the Swedish king who, in 1709–1715, fought as an ally of the sultan against Russia, and was for some time a generously treated prisoner of the Turks. In his *Histoire de Charles XII*, Voltaire also tells us of one grand vizier "Jussuf, that is to say Joseph, whose life story was as singular as that of his predecessor. Born on the frontiers of Moscovy and taken prisoner with his family at six years of age, he had been sold to a janissary. For some time, he served in a seraglio, and eventually became the vice-regent of the very empire in which he had been a slave."[26] One cannot imagine that Voltaire could have written this passage without thinking of the biblical hero of the same name and with a very similar biography: sold into slavery at an early age, working for a long period in a household, and eventually becoming second in command of the empire. Whether fact or fiction, such stories were the stuff of Eastern folklore. But does the biblical Joseph story belong to this folklore? And do folk-tales echo real persons and events? In his *Histoire de Charles XII*, Voltaire neither raises nor answers these questions, but they seem to have remained with him for many years.

The first trace of Voltaire's historical interpretation of the Joseph figure can be found in a brief, elegant account of ancient history, entitled *La Philosophie de l'histoire*, a revisionist work meant to replace Bossuet's *Discours sur l'histoire universelle*. The ancient Jews receive much attention here: Voltaire devotes six chapters to them – more than to the Chaldeans, Indians, or the Chinese. Despite writing all this about the Hebrews and their leader Moses in Egypt, Voltaire fails to mention Joseph. This name appears only much later in the book, when Voltaire sketches the history of the Jews in Graeco-Roman times. The Jews, Voltaire explains, were then in a constant state of subjection, ruled by foreign powers – in Syria by the Seleucid dynasty, in Egypt by the Ptolemies (third century BCE). It was then that "a Jew named Joseph obtained the right to collect the state taxes in Lower Syria and Judaea, which belonged to this Ptolemy. This was the most glorious time for the Jews, for it was then that they built the third part of their city, afterwards called the enclosure, or the wall of the Maccabees, because the latter finished and completed the work."[27]

Who was this Joseph, the man favoured by the king of Egypt? And how does he relate to the Joseph mentioned in the book of Genesis, a figure whose dates Abbot Calmet gave as 1745–1635 BCE? In *La Philosophie de l'histoire*, Voltaire gives no answers. Later, in *La Bible enfin expliquée*, he was slightly more explicit, though tantalisingly brief in his suggestion that the real Joseph, rather than the legendary figure of Genesis, was a tax collector working in the services of Hellenistic Egypt.[28] This casual statement requires some detective work if it is to be fully understood. First of all the reader is misled by Voltaire's attribution of this idea to someone else: to Nicolas-Antoine Boulanger (1722–1759), a minor French Enlightenment philosopher; and further mystified by Voltaire's statement that Boulanger's "rash conjecture" (*conjecture téméraire*) is completely unfounded. What we have here is a typical case of the literary technique known as the "unrefuted objection"; devised by Pierre Bayle and frequently used by Voltaire, the method consists in attributing one's own opinion to someone else, expressing formal dissent from it, but offering no serious arguments against it.[29] This technique is used to communicate one's opinion to the intelligent, while at the same time concealing it from the ignorant and escaping from censorship. Yet even when we are aware that here Voltaire is revealing his own view and that Boulanger has nothing to do with it, the statement remains cryptic and requires further detective work. In what follows, I present the result of my investigation.

The (undisclosed) source on which Voltaire bases his suggestion is the *Jewish Antiquities* of Josephus. In this work we learn of a Jewish tax collector named Joseph. This Joseph controlled Judaea for twenty-two years in the third century BCE, bringing, as Josephus explains, "the Jewish people from poverty and a state of weakness to more splendid opportunities of life".[30] Here is the substance of this passage in the *Jewish Antiquities* that reminded Voltaire rather strangely of the biblical story of Joseph:[31]

> In the time of Ptolemy Euergetes, king of Egypt, Palestine was ruled by the high priest Onias who had to pay tribute to his royal lord. Onias, small-minded and fond of money, refused to pay the tribute on behalf of the Jewish people, and thus roused the anger of the king. Neither Athenion, the king's ambassador who had just arrived in Jerusalem, nor Onias's nephew Joseph could make the high priest change his mind and hand over the money. Joseph son of Tobias, still young but known for his uprightness and dignity, managed to get his uncle's permission to see Ptolemy and get the matter settled. Joseph began his mission by hospitably receiving and entertaining Athenion in Jerusalem and heaping lavish gifts upon him. Later, while Athenion still had no money to bring to his royal lord, he spoke to the king and Queen Cleopatra, praising Joseph and reporting how well he had been entertained. He also indicated that Joseph would soon travel to Egypt. When Joseph arrived in the city of Memphis, he was at once recognised by Athenion, who happened to be with the king. Ptolemy honoured the young man by rising to greet him, and invited him into his chariot. As Ptolemy complained of Onias's refusal to pay taxes, Joseph answered: "Pardon him because of his age; for surely you are not unaware that old people and infants are likely to have

the same level of intelligence. But from the young you will obtain everything, and in us you will find no fault." Pleased with the charm and ready wit of the young man, Ptolemy took a liking to him. He urged him to take up residence in the palace and promised that he should be his guest every day at table. Thus Joseph became one of the king's "friends" (an institution of political significance in the Hellenistic world).

Soon the day came in Alexandria when the king sold the rights to collect taxes in Judaea, Samaria, and Transjordan. Bidders from all over Syria were present and made their offers. Eventually, Joseph came forward, promising the king twice as much as the others, and received the right to farm taxes despite giving no surety. At Joseph's request, the king granted his new tax collector two thousand foot soldiers to enforce payment by citizens who treated him with contempt. When Joseph arrived at the city of Ascalon, he was not only refused taxes, but also insulted. To set an example, he arrested some twenty of their leading men, put them to death, and gave their property to the king. Approving of Joseph's courage and determination, Ptolemy permitted Joseph to proceed, granting him whatever measures he felt necessary. The example of Ascalon worked well, for out of fear almost all the cities opened their gates to Joseph and paid the tribute. The inhabitants of Scythopolis alone refused to receive Joseph – only to meet the same fate as the leaders of Ascalon. Having thus collected large sums of money and made a handsome profit, Joseph used his wealth to ensure that he retained his status. He also sent many gifts of friendship to the king, to Cleopatra, and to all in positions of power at the court of Egypt, to cement his own position.

One day, Joseph accompanied his brother when he went to Alexandria. The aim of the journey was to find a suitable spouse for his brother's daughter, preferably from among the leading Jews of Egypt. When Joseph was dining with the king, a beautiful dancing-girl came into the banqueting hall. Joseph, having fallen in love with her, asked his brother's help in the delicate matter, for Jewish men were forbidden to have sexual relations with foreign women. To prevent Joseph from breaking Jewish law, Joseph's brother had his own daughter disguised and brought her to Joseph by night to sleep with him. In his drunken state Joseph did not realise how matters really were, so he had intercourse with his young niece. After this had happened several times, he fell still more deeply in love with her. Eventually, the truth was revealed, and his brother urged Joseph to marry his daughter. Joseph gladly agreed, married his niece, and they had a son, Hyrcanus. Joseph also had seven other sons, by his older wife.

When Hyrcanus came of age, his father decided to test his wisdom. Joseph sent his son, still a child of thirteen years, on a two-day journey into the wilderness to sow the ground, giving him three hundred yoke of oxen, but keeping back the yoke-harnesses with him. Having arrived at the place to be ploughed, Hyrcanus decided not to go back home for the missing gear but to slaughter a few oxen and cut their hide into straps to be fastened to the yokes. The task completed, Hyrcanus returned home to be praised by his father for his good sense and quick thinking. In fact, Joseph preferred Hyrcanus to his seven other sons. As is to be expected, the privileged child became the object of violent envy on the part of his lazy and ignorant brothers.

Soon, an opportunity arose for the brothers to take revenge on Hyrcanus. When the latter was sent by his father to Alexandria to offer gifts to King Ptolemy on the occasion of the birth of a son, the brothers wrote to tell the king's friends to watch out for Hyrcanus and to do away with him. The plan was to prevent Hyrcanus from bringing a suitable gift to the king and thus to have Joseph judged unfavourably by the royal master. But Hyrcanus outwitted the king's friends by spying on their preparations, and by using his father's Alexandrian estate to buy presents far more splendid and extravagant than any of the king's friends could offer: one hundred slave boys carrying gifts for the king, and one hundred virgins carrying gifts for the queen. When Hyrcanus's brothers heard that he had obtained many favours from the king and was returning with great honour, they went out to meet and kill him. Joseph, who secretly harboured anger over the sum Hyrcanus had spent on the presents, knew about his sons' plans and refrained from interfering. When the brothers met in battle, Hyrcanus killed two of them and many of their men with them, while the rest escaped to their father in Jerusalem. Shortly thereafter, Joseph died.

After Joseph's death, the conflict between Hyrcanus and his brothers flared up again. Hyrcanus soon realised that the majority of the Judaeans, including the high priest, were on the side of his brothers, so he gave up the idea of returning to Jerusalem. Instead, he established himself in Transjordan where he terrorised the local Arab tribes. He built himself a fortress near Essebonits (Heshbon). After seven years, when Transjordan moved from the Egyptian into the Syrian realm of political influence, his position became increasingly precarious. When the Syrian king Antiochus claimed authority over the area, Hyrcanus, fearing that he might be captured and punished, ended his life by committing suicide. All his property was then seized by Antiochus.

In his copy of the *Jewish Antiquities*, still extant, Voltaire marked the relevant passage, writing "Joseph, tax farmer" in the margin.[32] It did not escape him that the biblical account of Joseph and the story about Joseph and Hyrcanus have much in common. The following features immediately come to mind: in both stories, the hero is favoured by the Egyptian king and granted a privileged position in the administration of the Egyptian state; he helps the king of Egypt to assert his authority over his subjects, especially his right to claim taxes; he acts as a protector of the Hebrew people; he is favoured by his father and hated by his brothers; the brothers seek to kill the hero. Though a closer look may reveal more parallels, many differences are immediately evident: the story told by Josephus has two heroes – Joseph and Hyrcanus – rather than one protagonist; the stories are set in very different ages – the biblical story in the distant age of the patriarchs, the other one in the third century BCE; one has a strongly edifying and religious atmosphere about it which the other completely lacks; the brothers of Hyrcanus remain to the end antagonistic to the hero, whereas the biblical Joseph forgives them their wrongdoing. One may actually conclude that while the two accounts have similar elements, the differences are more striking. But how can one account for the undeniable similarities?

Pondering the similarities and differences, Voltaire came up with the following idea: the relationship of the two stories can be explained by thinking of them as the "original" and an "imaginative echo". The original, historical account is the one set in the third century BCE, told by Josephus about Joseph and Hyrcanus. Josephus is a reliable historian who can be trusted. The biblical story, by contrast, is an imaginative story, just a piece of fiction, indeed a novel (*un roman*),[33] inspired by, and in part based on, events that happened and persons who lived in the third century. From this analysis the biblical story emerges as an edifying historical novel, written in the third century to celebrate Hyrcanus and his father Joseph, rather than to inform about the patriarchal age in which it is set. The Pharaoh of the biblical story echoes King Ptolemy III Euergetes, a historically authenticated king who ruled from 247 to 221 BCE.

Voltaire realised that his "late" dating of the Joseph story was not readily convincing. Specialists, Voltaire anticipated, would see two difficulties: first, the ancient Greek translation of the book of Genesis, which includes the Joseph story, is traditionally dated to a period slightly earlier than King Ptolemy Euergetes – to the time of this ruler's predecessor; second, the Samaritans, generally considered a sect that separated from mainstream Judaism in the fourth century BCE, also have a canonical book of Genesis that includes the Joseph story. Voltaire, fully aware of these problems, seeks to solve them. He suggests that the original Hebrew book of Genesis, as it was read in the third century, did not include the Joseph novella. But when was it inserted? Voltaire thinks that third-century Judaism had two forms of the book of Genesis: a longer Egyptian form that included the Joseph tale, and a shorter Palestinian one that lacked the story. Eventually, Palestinian Judaism also adopted the longer version. This must have happened after the Jewish uprising against Seleucid rule in Palestine in the second century BCE, for it was then that King Antiochus Epiphanes (175–164 BCE) ordered all scrolls of the Torah – the Pentateuch that includes the book of Genesis – to be destroyed. "The books of the law" that Antiochus's inspectors found, "they tore to pieces and burned with fire. Anyone found possessing the book of the covenant, or anyone who adhered to the law, was condemned to death by decree of the king."[34] According to Voltaire, all the copies of the book of Genesis then extant in Palestine perished during the crisis of the 160s. Later, following a successful uprising, traditional Judaism was re-established in Palestine, and the Jews there also adopted the longer, Egyptian recension of Genesis. Voltaire, well acquainted with the details of ancient Jewish history, adds that the Samaritans – a Jewish sect that used the Pentateuch as sacred Scripture while not acknowledging the priesthood of Jerusalem – eventually also adopted the longer version of the text. This reference to the Samaritans is necessary for, according to Josephus, this sect was spared by Antiochus,[35] and one would assume that the Samaritans still owned copies of the shorter version of the book of Genesis.

Finally, we have to point out that Voltaire puts on several masks when presenting his historical reconstruction. First of all, his name is missing from the title page of *La Bible enfin expliquée*, for he attributes the work to "plusieurs aumoniers de S.M.L.R.D.P." – several (anonymous) chaplains of his majesty the king of Prussia (or Poland). In the text, rather than making their own points, the "chaplains" frequently refer to both anonymous critics and known authors of previous generations who in fact never published any of the ideas attributed to them but were all vaguely known as having been sceptical about the historical reliability of some biblical stories. The "chaplains" (alias Voltaire himself) attribute the reinterpretation of the Joseph story to Nicolas-Antoine Boulanger, a Paris *philosophe* and writer who died in 1759 without ever having written anything about Joseph. Thus *La Bible enfin expliquée* is presented under the mask of a group of apologists who seek to refute bold Enlightenment biblical readings. But the mask is too easily recognisable as such to mislead the intelligent reader who is quick to understand the ironic style: while pretending to refute attacks on the historical reliability and moral integrity of the Bible, the work actually promotes the new critical approach. This intention is clearly indicated by the title *La Bible enfin expliquée*, a title that suggests new insight rather than an apologetic presentation of traditional interpretations. Voltaire thus presented his own thought in ironic guise as that of others known for holding controversial opinions, in order to evade censorship.

For fear of censorship, Voltaire never published any of his views about Joseph under his own name. The French system of imposing censorship could be unrelenting. Censored authors and printers were typically "bastilled" – sent to the royal jail in Paris, the Bastille. This was the fate of the historian Nicolas Fréret who in his *Mémoire sur l'origine des Français* (On the Origins of the Franks), read to the Académie Royale des Inscriptions in 1714, sought to demonstrate that the Franks were originally a league of South Germanic tribes and not, as the legend then almost universally received had it, a nation of free men who, originating in Greece or Troy, had kept their civilisation intact in the heart of a barbarous country. His view that the Franks had nothing to do with the ancient Greeks excited the indignation of the abbé Vertot, who denounced Fréret to the government as a libeller of the monarchy. As a consequence, Fréret was sent to the Bastille for six months.[36] Historical criticism was a dangerous matter when it touched upon the interests and founding myths of the state. As the century progressed, an increasing number of writers, booksellers, and printers were jailed in the Bastille, often one hundred or more at a time. In 1734, Voltaire's *Lettres philosophiques* was among the books censored and banned.[37] In order to avoid further censorship and possible imprisonment, Voltaire spent most of his life far from Paris, on one side or the other of the Swiss–French border in Les Délices (near Geneva) and Ferney (on the French side). Historical criticism, especially that of Voltaire, whose aim was to undermine the joint authority of Bible and church, was a dangerous matter.

Epilogue

The radical historical criticism of Morgan provoked some controversy but found little approval in the eighteenth century; that of Voltaire was apparently not even noticed – understandably, for it is not stated unambiguously but has to be extracted from just one tantalisingly brief ironic passage. Thus Voltaire's suggestion that the Joseph story echoes real events and people of the third century BCE does not seem to have had a following, either in the eighteenth century or later. Historians generally continued to accept the biblical portrait of Joseph, though the bolder ones – those committed to a critical rather than a merely antiquarian approach to the Bible – eliminated certain miraculous features, in fact everything that smacks of direct divine intervention, as legendary accretions. Among these critical historians belongs Georg Lorenz Bauer (1755–1806).[38] He treats Joseph as a historical figure whose credibility can be supported by what is known about the elevation of individuals of humble or even slave origins to high office in the Ottoman Empire. The only feature to be omitted as implausible from a truly historical account of Joseph is his ability to predict the future by interpreting dreams. Instead of attributing Joseph's career to his supernatural abilities, Bauer credits him merely with natural talents that were further developed by the education he received from the Egyptian priests who adopted him into their class. Priests, Bauer asserts, were the true rulers of Egypt, and even the king often depended upon their services. Once promoted to the office of grand vizier, Joseph confronted a problem that often plagued the lands of the ancient East, decimating their population: famine. He built huge granaries in which he stored one-fifth of each year's national harvest, a measure that even some modern states should consider. (Here Bauer demonstrates the ancient ideal that one should learn something from history, and that the historiographer should apportion praise and blame. While from Morgan and Voltaire to Bauer, historians thought of themselves as moral philosophers, later historians preferred the ideal of a detached, non-partisan account of what happened in the past.)

Unlike Morgan's obsolete reconstruction, Voltaire's position still invites serious consideration, at least in certain respects. His idea that "Joseph" is a fictitious story that belongs to the category of *belles-lettres* is shared today by the majority of scholars, and Voltaire can be given credit for the discovery of pure fiction in the book of Genesis. The fact that he was the first to state this clearly and unambiguously should secure him a note of recognition in the annals of biblical criticism.

However, recent scholarship does not countenance Voltaire's suggestion that the biblical account echoes historical personalities, events, and circumstances that betray its origin in the late third century BCE, when King Ptolemy III Euergetes ruled both Egypt and Palestine. Neither Joseph, son of Tobias, nor Hyrcanus forms the model for the biblical Joseph; instead, the story told by Josephus in the *Jewish Antiquities* bristles with allusions to the biblical story of Joseph, so that it is clearly impossible to argue the case of influence and literary dependence in the other direction. Scholars agree that Josephus, in his account of Joseph, son of Tobias, and Hyrcanus, grandson of Tobias, used a source they term the "Tobiad Romance", a document that tells the story of an influential Jewish family in the Hellenistic period. That this family actually existed is known from a few original letters that have survived, which are either written by Tobias or mention him by name. Tobias (*c.* 250 BCE) was a Jew who headed a military colony in Transjordan; strongly pro-Ptolemaic in political orientation, he defended, with a garrison of Macedonian and Judaean troops, the Ptolemaic territory against Arab tribesmen. Tobias frequently sent gifts of various sorts – including horses, dogs, donkeys, and slave boys – to both the Egyptian monarch Ptolemy II Philadelphus and his all-powerful finance minister Apollonius.[39] As to the historical value of the "Tobiad Romance", specialists disagree. Whereas most recent authors dismiss it as pure fiction written in Jewish support of the Ptolemaic dynasty,[40] Martin Hengel more conservatively treats it as fictionalised history that permits us a glimpse of the Jewish situation in the third century BCE. Hengel sees Joseph son of Tobias as a man whom the Ptolemaic administration acknowledged in the office of *prostasía*, that is, the political representation of the Jewish people *vis-à-vis* the pagan state. Hengel also thinks that Joseph did hold the office of tax farmer from *c.* 240 to 218 BCE.[41] But Hengel also points out certain historical errors in the account, suggesting that it was composed in Alexandria in the second half of the second century BCE, presumably by someone who used a family chronicle of the Tobiads. While the Jewish novel's historical background may be hard to assess, the story as such is vivid and easily understood: it demonstrates the ability and pluck of a successful father-and-son team in rising to economic importance. They act as clients of the Egyptian king and as patrons of the Jewish people. But once the great Egyptian patron fades from the picture and Hyrcanus is eventually thrown back on his own resources in his fortress in Transjordan, the lonely man commits suicide.[42] Whatever else it may be, the story of Joseph and Hyrcanus reflects the same narrative genius we find in the – presumably much older – biblical Joseph novella.

Today, biblical scholarship has not yet reached a consensus on the dating of the Joseph story. Most specialists (including myself) favour a date some time between 500 and 400 BCE. But there is a minority of scholars who join Voltaire in preferring a Hellenistic dating: a date between, roughly, 300 and 100 BCE.[43] One interesting argument comes from Andreas Kunz, who invokes a remarkable Egyptian inscription: the Famine Stela discovered in 1889.[44] Carved in rock by the River Nile, it dates from the Hellenistic period, presumably from around 200 BCE. This inscription suggests to Kunz that its story dates from about the same time as the biblical tale of Joseph. Is this a plausible suggestion?

The Egyptian inscription recounts the following story: Pharaoh Djoser has a dream in which the god Khnum announces that he will provide relief from a severe seven-year famine. In gratitude, Djoser decrees that all revenue from the area should be given to the Khnum temple on Elephantine Island. The (imaginary) seven-year period of dearth and hunger in the land, the divine revelation received by Pharaoh in a dream, and the imposition of taxes to be paid by the people to the (pagan) temple all have close equivalents in the biblical story. The Egyptian text also refers to over-abundant harvests, though these do not precede (as in the Bible) but follow the years of dearth. Clearly, the inscription had a vastly different purpose from that of the biblical narrative: while the latter was meant to edify Jewish readers living in Egypt, the inscribed text constituted an attempt by Egyptian priests to secure tax revenues for their temple, with the help of a fictional aetiology. But despite their different motives, the similarities between the Joseph story and the sparsely told narrative embodied in the Egyptian inscription are striking and call for an explanation. The relationship between the two is far from clear. The two stories may have drawn upon a common Egyptian repertoire of narrative elements. Another strong possibility is that the Famine Stela inscription records – or, more precisely, uses – an existing ancient local legend about a seven-year famine that ended following the intervention of the god Khnum. Such a legend, of unknown date, might have been transmitted from the Egyptians to the Hebrews, who later produced the Joseph story based upon it. Close cultural links over many centuries would have been enhanced by the geographical proximity of a Hebrew community on Elephantine Island, only two kilometres north of Sehel, site of the Famine Stela, near Aswan on the Nile. The Jewish settlement there began as a military colony in the late sixth century BCE and apparently flourished for several centuries. Thus the local Egyptian legend might have found its way into the Hebrew community at any time after *c.* 500 BCE, leaving plenty of time for the alteration and elaboration typical of the oral tradition. Indeed, the very simplicity of the Egyptian text, even allowing for spatial constraints on the Stela, would imply an earlier provenance than that of the other. So despite the temptation to equate these two, the Famine Stela does not help to pinpoint the date of the Joseph story.

VI

THE ICONIC TEXT: A BEAUTIFUL STORY

On Literary Criticism

In early-modern times, three literary types competed for dominance in cultural life: epic poetry, drama, and the novel. Is John Milton, author of the epic poem *Paradise Lost*, the greatest of all poets? How about the dramatists Shakespeare and Racine? Will the art of Cervantes (*Don Quixote*) and John Bunyan (*The Pilgrim's Progress*) gain ground and outdo the others in popularity? The seventeenth century, boasting as it did prolific and successful authors in all three categories, was undecided. The verdict came with the shift of the focus of cultural life from court to city, from aristocracy to urban elite. The aristocrats had promoted epic poetry and drama, literary forms centred on protagonists of noble birth. The novel, by way of contrast, with its preference for more familiar heroes and heroines, catered to bourgeois, middle-class taste, and continues to do so in our own day. By the early eighteenth century, the triumph of the novel was complete.

The first half of the eighteenth century not only saw the rise of the novel as the most successful literary form, but also witnessed new forms of literary criticism. No longer confined to learned books dealing mainly with the literary inheritance of ancient Greece and Rome, criticism was voiced in French *salons* and English societies alike, as well as being published in periodicals. Whenever a new novel appeared, the critics had something to say about its qualities and merits or lack thereof. Both developments – the rise of the novel and new literary criticism, closely linked – started in England and from there spread to the rest of Europe, gaining particular influence in France and Germany. The first accomplished writers of novels in the modern sense were Samuel Richardson and Henry Fielding, and among the foremost literary critics of that first generation were Joseph Addison, who published important critical essays in his periodical the *Spectator*, and Henry Fielding himself. Samuel Johnson soon emerged as the leading English literary critic of his day. Meanwhile, the new art of literary criticism spread to France, notably engaging Voltaire and Diderot, both of whom not only produced critical essays but also wrote fiction – stories and novels. Diderot made sure to include essays on literary criticism in the multi-volume *Encyclopédie* that he edited between 1751 and 1765. All of these early-modern literary critics were intent on establishing what later came to be called a "canon", a collection of the best literary works, both past and present, to be studied and perhaps imitated. While the endeavour never led to any definitive result, it inspired many lively controversies. No one could definitively answer the question as to what constitutes the aesthetic appeal of literature – does it arise from the imitation of the ancients? Is it the result of emotional release or emotional restraint? Are the works of modern authors as good as and perhaps even superior to those of ancient Greek and Latin writers? When we follow the development of literary criticism through the eighteenth and early nineteenth centuries, we can chart the decline of the belief that the classical authors set for all time the standard in stylistic elegance. Critics began to appreciate a wider variety of styles and literary genres. Eventually, both novels (in spite of Voltaire's verdict) and the Bible, especially the books of the Old Testament, came to be considered objects worthy of appreciation and even of praise. It became quite common to point out the unique quality of biblical poetry, especially the Psalms.[1] As for biblical narrative, critics were quick to discover one story that shared all the qualities of good contemporary fictional prose: the story of Joseph.

This story captured the attention of those who read the Bible with an ear for literary quality. An early example is René de Ceriziers (1603–1662), author of historical works and fiction, a priest closely associated with the royal court of France. Starting with Richard Steele early in the eighteenth century, the theme of Joseph gained in popularity over the following century among literary critics in France and Britain as well as in Germany and Switzerland, as a tentative list shows:

1642	René de Ceriziers, French priest and author
1710	Richard Steele, English playwright and essayist
1726	Alexander Pope, English poet[2]
1726/28	Charles Rollin, French priest and writer on education
1730	Samuel Shuckford, English historian[3]
1731	John Husbands, English literary critic
1738	Josiah Hort, archbishop of the Church of Ireland
1740	Thomas Morgan, English philosopher[4]
1753	Joseph Warton, English literary critic[5]
1753	Jean Astruc, French physician and writer
1760	Laurence Sterne, English clergyman and novelist
1760	Friedrich Gottlieb Klopstock, German poet[6]
1763	James Boswell, Scottish writer

1764	Voltaire, French writer and philosopher
1777	Samuel Jackson Pratt, Scottish writer[7]
1794	Johann Kaspar Lavater, Swiss pastor and writer[8]
1802	François-René de Chateaubriand, French writer

These authors comment on a variety of aspects of the Joseph story: some focus on the aesthetic qualities of the entire story or individual scenes, others praise the story's moral significance, while yet again, the emotional impact is selected by some for special comment. Despite the disparity of interest and level of elaboration, the tributes of these authors combine to produce a single picture. It can be summed up in three points: (1) the Joseph story is a well-told narrative comparable to a novel or, alternatively, to an imaginative oriental tale; (2) replete with pathos, it has the capacity to move readers to tears, revealing the depth of the author's psychological insight, and, like best-selling novels, generally speaks to the reader's emotions and sentiments; (3) presenting its protagonist as a role model, the story extols the nobility of one who stands above the mere wish for revenge: this ultimately is its unique and convincing moral message.

Joseph in British criticism

Those who took a closer look at the Joseph story discovered its *aesthetic* appeal. John Husbands, poet and divine, in his essay "Remarks on the Beauties of the Holy Scriptures" (1731) devotes many pages to celebrating passages from the book of Genesis in general and the story of Joseph in particular. "Surely never was any story, from the beginning to the end, contrived more artfully, never was any plot for the stage worked up more justly, never was any plot unfolded more naturally, than this of Joseph," he explains.[9] Some critics leave it at this level, but others go one step further as they compare the Joseph story to a novel. "The wit of man cannot invent a novel more delicate and moving than the whole story of Joseph", preached Josiah Hort (1674–1751), a Church of Ireland archbishop, inadvertently but revealingly implying that the Joseph tale is a novel or may be compared to this genre.[10] In the age of the novel, biblical stories began to be read as one would read a novel. To be able to do this, one must first isolate the story from the sacred context in which it is transmitted. According to James Boswell, for instance, the mere fact that the story is part of the Bible prevents people from appreciating its literary merit and recognising its novel-like quality. "Were the history of Joseph published by some genteel bookseller as an Eastern fragment and circulated amongst the gay world, I am persuaded that those who have any genuine taste might be taken in to admire it exceedingly [. . .] I have a great mind to make the experiment. Were I a man more known and of more consequence, it might do very well."[11] Boswell did not, however, go on to make the experiment.

Several of our critics comment on the *emotional* appeal of the story. A good example again comes from Boswell, who in 1663 confided to his diary: "This forenoon I read the history of Joseph and his brethren, which melted my heart and drew tears from my eyes."[12] Early-modern readers, greatly affected by some literary text or by a scene from a stage play, would shed tears freely at the heart-rending words or episodes. Scenes of sudden recognition of long-lost friends or the reuniting of beloved family members, or those in which the characters' tears flow abundantly, were particularly likely to prompt such emotional outbursts. Perhaps the most radical statement about the Joseph story's emotional quality was made by Richard Steele. An accomplished and successful playwright, he knew that the value of a piece of literature is not, as it were, inherent in its words; what makes literature great and important is that something extraordinary can happen in the encounter with it. This is true of all great literature, including the Joseph story. "At an hour when he is disengaged from all other regard or interests than what arise from" the biblical story, the reader should expose himself to it. By doing so, he will come to realise that "persons of higher consideration in virtue and merit than ourselves" undergo similar adversities to ours; this realisation enables us to bear our own minor sufferings and humiliations with resignation.[13] Steele's analysis does not stay at this cognitive level, however. The reader may become so deeply involved with the story emotionally that he feels quite "overwhelmed with the vicissitudes of joy and sorrow".[14] Identifying with the characters portrayed, he may come to "feel the alternate passion of a father, a brother, and a son, so warm in him, that they will incline him to exert himself (in such of those characters as happen to be his) much above the ordinary course of life".[15] Thus experienced, the story will "touch, comfort, and improve the heart of man".[16] Without using the term, Steele attributes to it a therapeutic effect upon those absorbed in reading; for him, the Joseph story belongs among those that restore the mind "perplexed with anxious cares and passions", bringing it back "to its usual state of tranquillity".[17] Steele echoes here the notion that a novel, like an ancient stage play as understood by Aristotle, has a cathartic force: the power to shake and cleanse, but also to restore and calm the reader's soul.

While Steele located the importance of the Joseph story in its cathartic power, other critics look for a specific *moral* message. As early as the first century CE, the Jewish historian Josephus found such a meaning in Joseph's generosity; the Hebrew, he explains, "had borne no malice against his brothers, and, even more than this, had been generous to them in loading them with presents such as some would not have given even to requite their benefactors".[18] While Josephus moves quickly from forgiveness (implied in the expression "no malice") to generous gift-giving, early-modern authors, impressed with Joseph's attitude, focused more narrowly on the act of forgiving itself. In a published sermon Laurence Sterne highlights the virtue of clemency: Joseph, rather than taking revenge on his brothers, demonstrates generous forgiveness. A closer analysis reveals that Sterne's sermon is a character sketch, a literary genre popular in the eighteenth century: a short account of the qualities, typical attitudes, and behaviour of a particular human type, highlighting its virtues or vices. For his character portrait Sterne selected the virtuous man who forgives others, exemplified by a biblical figure. He briefly explains how Joseph, by "speaking kindly" to his brothers "and seconding all with the tenderest marks of an undisguised forgiveness in falling upon their necks and weeping aloud", created a model fit to be emulated by all who read the story.[19] Joseph's readiness to forgive, he insists, was not a momentary reaction; "it evidently sprung from a settled principle of uncommon generosity in his nature, which was above the temptation of making use of an opportunity for revenge".[20] In both nature and character, Joseph is shown to be exemplary. "In generously forgiving an enemy, he was the truest friend to his own character"; forgiveness, he adds, "flows only from a strength and greatness of soul, conscious of its own force and security, and above the little temptations of resenting every fruitless attempt to interrupt its happiness".[21] Joseph is a man who, having internalised a Stoic and Christian ideal, stands above the pettiness of others. To forgive, for Sterne, "is the most refined and generous pitch of virtue, human nature can arrive at".[22] Sterne echoes – often verbatim – *The Christian Hero* (1701), a book in which the author Richard Steele extols forgiveness as one of the finest qualities required of a true Christian.[23] In *The Christian Hero*, Steele does not mention Joseph, and in his essay on Joseph he does not refer to the theme of forgiveness; it required Sterne, at once preacher and novelist, to bring the two subjects together and determine the true moral message of the biblical story.

Joseph in French criticism

Jean Astruc, still celebrated today as one of the founders of modern biblical criticism, pointed out the unique *aesthetic* quality of the Joseph story, insisting that "antiquity does not offer us anything that is better written, and written so as to touch us more"; the polished style, Astruc explained, reflects the refined culture, manners, and language of the Egyptian royal court where Joseph, author of his biography, spent most of his life.[24] Father Ceriziers, who heads our list of authors, calls the biblical story a comedy, implying that it can be compared to a stage play that begins with harshness and sadness but ends happily.[25] Its very ending corresponds with what Aristotle, then the ultimate authority in French criticism, described as the typical conclusion of a comedy: "the bitterest enemies walk off good friends at the end, with no slaying of any one by any one".[26] Are all comedies works of fiction? Or may a comedy be a true story? Ceriziers seems to support the latter option, but nevertheless he brings up the theme of fiction, suggesting that "Joseph", as a true story, is superior to the fiction of a romance.[27] Only one critic was actually explicit on the fictitious nature of our story: Voltaire. He offers an unusually elaborate structural analysis in his *Dictionnaire philosophique* (1764), echoing standard literary theory of his day, derived from Aristotle: "In this tale everything that constitutes a good epic poem can be found: exposition, conflict, recognition, peripeteia, and the marvellous. Nothing bears more clearly the hallmark of oriental genius."[28] For Voltaire, the Joseph story was pre-eminently an oriental tale, told with the same consummate skill as the *Arabian Nights*. Later, Chateaubriand followed Voltaire in comparing the Joseph story to a body of secular literature, though he treats it as a Hebrew *Odyssey*. These comparisons were not meant to denigrate the Bible story but to imply appreciation. Compared to other works of literature, the Joseph story stands the test and may even emerge as an outstanding, if not superior, specimen of its kind. Despite their agreement at this level, one must not overlook the different underlying agendas against which the two literary critics applied their arguments. For Voltaire's purposes, the purely literary appreciation of biblical texts was a means of subverting their ecclesiastical authority and helping destroy their sacred aura. To Chateaubriand, by contrast, literary beauty was just one aspect of the mystique surrounding everything biblical and Christian.

The *emotional* appeal of the Joseph story is a frequent theme in French criticism. Completely identifying with Joseph, Father Ceriziers could not even think of him without being moved, and he explains how he is affected by his misadventures: he feels personally persecuted by the evil brothers, being thrown with Joseph into the cistern and trembling in fear of attack by the vipers encountered there; he travels to Egypt in Joseph's company, suffers with him in prison, and hails him as he unexpectedly rises to power. The only situation that does not present a personal challenge, the priest prudently adds, is that involving the wiles of Potiphar's wicked wife.[29] While Ceriziers simply chronicles his feelings, others comment on the technical skill demonstrated by the biblical author in accomplishing such affectivity. One such is Charles Rollin, who in *De la manière d'enseigner et d'étudier les belles-lettres* (1726/28) comments on the Joseph story's recognition scene in a remarkable chapter dedicated to scriptural "passages that are tender and touching". He summarises the biblical passage thus in commending it to the attention of teachers and students:

> Nothing is more tender or touching than the wonderful story of Joseph. It is difficult to hold back one's tears when one sees him obliged to turn away or retire in order to wipe away his tears, so moved is he by the presence of Benjamin. Or when, having made himself known to them, he clings to his

dear brother, holding him tightly, weeping with him and, so we are told, with each of the brothers in turn. For a moment no one speaks, and the silence is infinitely more eloquent than any words. Surprise, grief, remembrance of things past, joy, and recognition: all stifle speech. Their depth of feeling can only be conveyed by tears, which express all that cannot be put into words.[30]

According to Rollin, no proper literary education could be complete without the study of such "passages that are tender and touching".

The *moral* message of the biblical story was no doubt taken for granted by all literary critics; less frequent, however, though still notable, is its discussion, which we find for instance in the contributions of Ceriziers and Voltaire. Father Ceriziers makes much of Joseph's readiness to forgive others – apparently a lesson directed at Cardinal Richelieu, who declared that no statesman should indulge in generous acts of clemency towards an enemy of the state (see above, Chapter 12). Writing more than a century later, Voltaire follows Ceriziers in pointing to forgiveness as Joseph's most noble virtue. Christianity, ancient philosophy, and eighteenth-century moralists all agree on the superiority of clemency and forgiveness to the spirit of revenge that animates the final scene of the *Odyssey*, in which the hero kills all the suitors of his wife Penelope. Heroic anger, love of revenge, and a taste for violence and bloodshed may characterise the warrior, but not the philosopher who prefers equanimity, social harmony, and reconciliation. Without its strong recommendation of *pardonner*, "Joseph" would not have been what it was for Voltaire: a delightful didactic tale that he sought to imitate in his own *contes philosophiques*.

19

A conte philosophique – *Voltaire*

IN EIGHTEENTH-CENTURY PARISIAN SOCIETY, THE SALON WAS A NEW institution, a resurrection of the ancient symposium. It centred on a member of the noble class, typically one who possessed a magnetic personality, and usually a woman (*salonnière*), who had the wherewithal to entertain a large circle of friends and guests. Here aristocrats mixed with members of the bourgeoisie, and their conversation, animated and informed by the presence of men of letters, focused on literature, art, and philosophy. News and gossip were shared in an informal way, letters passed around, and new ideas – those of the Enlightenment – freely expressed in an atmosphere of mutual trust, without fear of scandal or censorship.

At Madame du Deffand's literary salon, for instance, guests were welcomed twice a week, from six o'clock onwards, according to contemporary reports.[1] The previous night's theatre performance was among the favourite subjects discussed, but new books also figured prominently and increasingly as the eighteenth century progressed. Retrospectively, we can see that, throughout Europe, the seventeenth century was the classical age of the theatre, boasting Shakespeare, Racine, and Molière; the eighteenth century, by contrast, developed into an age of reading, because many would come to prefer reading a book or an essay to attending a theatre performance. In France, people read novels such as Fénelon's *Aventures de Télémaque* (The Adventures of Telemachus, 1699) and, in translation, Samuel Richardson's *Clarissa Harlowe* (1747). They enthused over the oriental short stories of *Les Mille et Une Nuits* (The Arabian Nights, first translated from Arabic into French by Antoine Galland, 1704–1717), and enjoyed the witty short essays Voltaire published under the title *Dictionnaire philosophique* (Philosophical Dictionary, 1764). This last work, a kind of philosophical diary or notebook in alphabetical order, would have satisfied the taste of Mme du Deffand who once (by letter) confided to Voltaire that she hated books written in a bookish, impersonal style. A conversational style that creates the illusion of personal presence and encounter would be ideal. "A book without a touch of lightness bores me to death."[2]

When the *Dictionnaire* was published, Voltaire lived at Ferney, Lorraine, where he had bought an estate. Although he was far from the capital, he nevertheless participated in Parisian salon life, if only by correspondence with Mme du Deffand to whom he regularly sent his publications. "I enclose one more work, entitled *Dictionnaire philosophique*", Voltaire wrote on 16 October 1765, adding that "the chapters are varied in the manner of Montaigne, and they are not very long. [. . .] And, to my shame, I acknowledge that I generally like small chapters that don't make one's spirits begin to flag."[3]

Voltaire's "Joseph": a translation

Most essays included in the *Dictionnaire philosophique* concern philosophical, theological, and biblical subjects and are generally aimed at debunking traditionally held ideas and beliefs. An exception is the article "Joseph", a piece of literary criticism. Since this is a very short text, we can insert a fresh translation below (rather than merely presenting a summary, as is the case for the other Joseph texts used in other chapters):

> Joseph
>
> The story of Joseph, read simply as literature, is one of the most precious monuments of antiquity that have come down to us. It doubtless served as the model for all oriental writers. It is more touching than Homer's *Odyssey*, for a hero who pardons is more moving than one who seeks revenge. We regard the Arabs as the first to tell these ingenious stories that have passed into all languages; but nowhere have I seen any to match the tale of Joseph. Almost everything in it inspires wonder, and the ending would move one to tears. [It is unique in the genre; the only Hebrew story of its kind, in it alone an act of mercy and munificence is found. According to some scholars it imitates an ancient Arab tale.][4]
>
> But let's look at the story, without being drawn into further discussion. Here is a lad of sixteen whose brothers are envious of him: they sell him to a caravan of Ishmaelite merchants who take him to Egypt, where he is bought by one of the king's eunuchs. This eunuch had a wife, which is not at all surprising: the Kislar-aga, a complete eunuch with everything cut off, has a harem today in Constantinople. They left him eyes and hands, and he lacks none of the natural impulses of the heart. Other eunuchs, having had removed only the two accompaniments of the reproductive organ, still frequently utilise the latter; and

Potiphar, to whom Joseph was sold, may very well have been one of that number.

Potiphar's wife becomes enamoured of the young Joseph who, faithful to his master and benefactor, rejects her advances. Angered by this, she accuses Joseph of wanting to seduce her. This is the old story of Hippolytus and Phaedra, Bellerophon and Stheneboea, Hebrus and Damasippa, Tanis and Peribea, Myrtilus and Hippodamia, Peleus and Demenette. It is hard to know which of these tales is the original, but the ancient Arab authors lend a very ingenious touch to the episode of Joseph and Potiphar's wife. The writer supposes that Potiphar, undecided between what he is told by his wife and by Joseph, is unwilling to accept the tunic (torn by his wife) as evidence of the young man's advances. There had been a child in a cot in the woman's room. Joseph maintains that she tore his tunic and snatched it from him in the child's presence. So Potiphar consults the boy who is very advanced for his age. The child says to Potiphar: "Look and see if the tunic is torn in front or behind: if in front, that is proof that Joseph wanted to take your wife by force; if it is torn at the back, that shows your wife was chasing after him." Thanks to the child's cleverness Potiphar recognises his slave's innocence. The scene is recounted thus in the Qur'an, following an ancient Arab writer. He does not bother to tell us whose child it was who judged with such acumen; if it was this woman's child, Joseph was not the first on whom she had had designs.

Following this, according to Genesis, Joseph is put in prison, and finds himself in the company there of the king of Egypt's cupbearer and baker. These state prisoners both have dreams one night. Joseph interprets their dreams, predicting that in three days the cupbearer will be restored to favour, while the baker will be hanged – which is precisely what comes to pass. Two years later, the king of Egypt also has a dream. His cupbearer tells him of the young Jew in prison who understands dreams better than anyone else in the world. The king sends for the young man, who predicts seven years of plenty and seven years of want.

Let us break off for a moment to consider the prodigious antiquity of dream interpretation. In a dream, Jacob had seen the mysterious ladder with God at the top; in a dream he learned how to increase his flocks – a method that worked only for him. Joseph himself had learned through a dream that he would some day rule over his brothers. A long time before, Abimelech had been warned in a dream that Sarah was Abraham's wife. – But to return to Joseph: no sooner has he explained Pharaoh's dream, than he is made prime minister on the spot. (It is doubtful if today, even in Asia, one could find a king who would bestow such an office in return for explaining a dream.) Pharaoh has Joseph marry a daughter of Potiphar. We are told that this Potiphar is high priest of Heliopolis, so this is not his first master, the eunuch; or if he is, we must conclude that he has another title besides high priest, and that his wife has given birth more than once. Anyway, the famine arrives as predicted by Joseph, who, to earn the king's favour, forces everyone to sell their land to Pharaoh. Subsequently, the entire nation enslaves itself in order to have grain – herein apparently lies the origin of despotic power. We must admit that no king has ever struck a better bargain, but equally, that the people had little reason to bless the prime minister.

Finally, Joseph's father and brothers also need grain, for "the famine oppressed all the earth" [Genesis 47: 13]. It is hardly necessary to recount here how Joseph received his brothers, how he pardoned them and plied them with riches. In this tale everything that constitutes a good epic poem can be found: exposition, conflict, recognition, peripeteia, and the marvellous. Nothing bears more clearly the hallmark of oriental genius.

How good old Jacob, Joseph's father, responded to Pharaoh no doubt strikes a chord with those who can take the hint: "How old are you?" the king asks him. "I am a hundred and thirty," says the old man, "and I have not yet enjoyed one happy day in this brief pilgrimage."[5]

Eighteenth-century readers loved the short essay, the literary form of the modern age. Found in periodicals, books, dictionaries, and encyclopaedias, it was read quickly in a free moment or pondered during an idle hour that was never wasted, for the essay, in addition to promising entertainment, counted as an excellent means of instruction. The article "Joseph" was of this kind.

In Voltaire's time, as today, an essay was understood as a short work characterised by prescribed incompleteness, by informality, and by the personal touch. The rule of incompleteness allows the author to deal with a subject without pretending to treat it exhaustively, with all the details and all the scholarly discussion that the subject may actually require; it also allows him to focus on an aspect that catches his attention, to make just one powerfully argued point, or to draw incomplete and tentative conclusions. Informality is achieved by developing ideas in a loose structure using a sprightly conversational style that employs description, narration, anecdote, and humour to make the point and hold the reader's attention. The personal touch, never missing from a true essay, permits the author to play up his personality, to draw openly on his prejudices, and to express his own aesthetic opinion and moral judgement in a confidential manner. The reader, in other words, feels he or she is listening to an old acquaintance. "Joseph", like most of the entries included in the *Dictionnaire philosophique*, displays all these characteristics of a critical essay about a specific literary work. But Voltaire's "Joseph" is unique in that it lacks the polemical tone so characteristic of many of the biblical entries found in the *Dictionnaire philosophique*. Here the author combines, in true essay fashion, a factual résumé with satirical asides and an assessment of the merits of the novella, and one can only admire the ease with which Voltaire moves from one theme to the other. The effortless combination of the serious with the satirical, the sublime with the farcical, is not just one of Voltaire's literary strategies; as those who knew him have observed, it was his way of life. Moreover, as Roger Pearson reminds us, we should not forget that Voltaire was quite capable of poking fun at something he agrees with or loves, if he happens to see the possibility of a good joke.[6] If we discount the satirical asides, the residue reveals Voltaire's most startling appreciation of the Bible. Nowhere has Voltaire expressed his admiration for a biblical story as unambiguously as here. Fascinated by the oriental setting and the ancient writer's skill, he recognises the story's potential emotional impact, and fully endorses its ethics.

Voltaire's undeniable fascination with the biblical story had many underlying causes and factors, some of which will be explored in what follows. The main reason, however, must be stated at the outset: without using these exact words, Voltaire felt that the biblical tale of Joseph was a precursor, if not prototype, of his own *contes philosophiques*, of which *Candide* is the best known today. Although modern editions often present Voltaire's stories under the general label of "novels", this term is not accurate; they are better described as *contes*, tales or stories. In eighteenth-century French, *le conte* could be a conversational anecdote, a joke, or a short story, usually one based on oral tradition or sharing its characteristics, including that of humour.[7] Three features in particular characterise both Voltaire's twenty-six *contes* and, from more recent times, *Le Petit Prince* (The Little Prince, 1943) by Antoine de Saint-Exupéry, the most popular philosophical tale today. First, in narrative structure and atmosphere, they closely resemble traditional popular storytelling: they are organised as strings of loosely connected, fast-moving, and action-filled episodes, often centring on a young hero whose life is marked by unexpected turns; exotic locations are preferred, awe-inspiring and miraculous incidents abound. Second, all the features typical of the eighteenth-century novel are absent and indeed studiously avoided: length, effusive sentimentality, careful construction, plausible figures, and realism of events, motivations, and places. The third, and most important, feature of Voltaire's *contes* is their didactic intention; as is well known to all readers of Voltaire, a philosophical point is tellingly made through vivid narrative, anecdote, and example rather than through the discussion of abstract definitions, arguments, rules, ideas, and concepts. In what follows, I will comment on each of the three features of the Joseph *conte* as recounted by Voltaire.

"JOSEPH" AS A TRADITIONAL ORIENTAL TALE

In the West, oriental stories have received much attention ever since the fifth century BCE when the Greek writer Herodotus included a few exotic items in his *Histories*. Some who thought about the matter concluded that the telling of tales of adventure and love may have originated among the Persians. The French humanist Claude Saumaise in the seventeenth century claimed to be able to discern the following sequence: the Persians transmitted the art of storytelling to the Arabs, from whom the Spaniards learned it, and the Spaniards in turn passed it to the French and others.[8] Oriental storytelling culminated in the *Arabian Nights*. Introduced to Western readers in Antoine Galland's French translation (1704–1717), the *Arabian Nights* became very popular, inspired imitators, and generally fired the imagination. Interest in the *Arabian Nights* belongs to the wider phenomenon of European enthusiasm for all things oriental, including the drinking of coffee.

For Voltaire, the Orient, from the plain of Baghdad to the highlands of Persia, was an exotic, enchanted world. The Persians, he assures us, devised new forms of social life and more remedies than any other nation for that terrible poison of life, boredom. "People meet in so-called coffee-houses, large halls where they consume this beverage, which has been introduced to us only recently, at the end of the seventeenth century. Some play, others read or listen to the tales of a storyteller. In one corner, a religious man offers instruction for a few coins, and in another entertainers are to be seen expertly plying their trade."[9] (Voltaire may be thinking here of jugglers or snake charmers.) The sultan, assisted by a grand vizier and surrounded by eunuchs, generally ruled his subjects in peace, though on occasion he might also indulge in a little warfare. Voltaire's fascination with storytelling and exotic settings can be discerned in his own literary work, especially those cast in the oriental mode: *Zadig ou la destinée* (*Zadig or the Book of Fate*, 1748); *Le Monde comme il va* (*The World as it Goes*, 1748); *Memnon ou la sagesse humaine* (*Memnon the Philosopher*, 1749); *Le Blanc et le noir* (*The Black and the White*, 1764); *La Princesse de Babylone* (*The Princess of Babylon*, 1768); *Le Taureau blanc* (*The White Bull*, 1774); and *Le Crocheteur borgne* (*The Blind Porter*, 1774). All of these stories betray Voltaire's love of the oriental setting that permitted him to indulge in the improbable, the fantastic, and the marvellous, features to which oriental tales owe their undeniable charm. Some of these stories still belong in the canon of French literature.

Voltaire considered the story of Joseph a work of fiction, an oriental tale comparable to those of the *Arabian Nights*. One passage in particular alerted him to the conventional provenance of this piece of fiction: that in which the bored wife of Joseph's master seeks to seduce the young steward, a theme well known from other literature (especially from Seneca and Racine, both of whom wrote tragedies on Phaedra and Hippolytus).[10] The presumed antiquity of the book of Genesis suggested to Voltaire the idea that the tale of Joseph, itself inspired by ancient Arab folklore, served as a model for all subsequent oriental tales. At the end of his article, Voltaire lists the essential components of a good epic poem that confirm its ancient and oriental origin. Exposition, conflict, recognition, and peripeteia (the sudden change or reversal of fortune) were essential to good drama and all good storytelling as understood by Aristotle and, following him, by the seventeenth- and eighteenth-century literary theorists. In fact, these components constitute the structure of all forms of literature, including popular tales and Voltaire's own stories. The exposition introduces the characters, the conflict provides the elements of interest and suspense in any form of fiction, its resolution – typically the reversal of the expected fate – often takes the form of recognition, or some kind of unexpected discovery, and the denouement brings the story to its conclusion, generally a happy ending. Voltaire extols the scene in which Joseph makes himself known to his brothers; for him, it is the archetypal recognition scene. In *La Bible enfin expliquée*, he explains this more fully than in the *Dictionnaire philosophique*: "This part of the story has always been considered one of the most beautiful in antiquity. Nothing in Homer is as touching. It is the most perfect recognition scene there could possibly be in any language whatsoever."[11] Voltaire adds that staged versions of the Joseph tale never fail to include the scene. Moreover, "almost all our fiction, be it ancient or modern, and endless dramatic works, have been based on scenes of recognition. None are more artless than that of Joseph and his brothers."[12]

Whereas the scene of recognition is an important structural element, recourse to the marvellous serves the storyteller's aims merely as a strategy to alter the natural course of events, or to highlight the hero's or his opponents' extraordinary or supernatural powers and skills. The wondrous, endorsed by Aristotle[13] as a regular feature of traditional storytelling and indeed a hallmark of the *Arabian Nights*, began to lose its previously undisputed status in Voltaire's time, for many writers began to insist on greater realism by banishing from their sentimental novels all bride-snatching giants, imaginary castles, heroes endowed with superhuman powers, magic weapons, and miraculous events. "With modern subjects, the marvellous of old can no longer be treated seriously," reflected Marmontel, one of Voltaire's contemporaries; "and this is a sad loss for epic fiction."[14] Voltaire concurred:

> And now they've banished spirits, fairies too;
> Reason rules, a story must be true.

But the heart grows dull in a world of grey,
Where sense and logic may not brook demur,
And correctness is the order of the day.[15]

The writer who wished to continue to use myth and marvel had only one possible option: to set his story "in times and places where people still believe in miracles".[16] Fond of the wondrous and fantastical, Voltaire instinctively followed this rule by setting many of his tales in the dreamy and distant world of the East. Unlike the novelists of his day, he never spurned the miracle, the flying horse, and the snatched bride. He also appreciated Joseph's far-seeing dreams and admired the Hebrew hero's skill in divination.

The aesthetic appeal alone of the Joseph story would not have satisfied Voltaire and his contemporaries; for them, a good tale had to make a tangible emotional impact. And the extent of that impact could be measured, at least in the mind of eighteenth-century readers. The century of the Enlightenment not only extolled reason, but also lauded sentiment and the outward display of emotion. The shedding of tears served as a measure of literary accomplishment, even for Voltaire himself. Even at the hundredth reading of Jean Racine's *Iphigénie*, Voltaire reports, he could not avoid shedding "tears of admiration and sympathy" (*des larmes d'admiration et d'attendrissement*).[17] But how best to induce tears in one's readers? Well, the most promising strategy appears to be to place emotionally charged scenes in which tears flow abundantly at strategic points in the story itself, so that the reader is infected, for tears are catching. Towards the end of the biblical tale, Joseph weeps more than once – on seeing his younger brother for the first time, on revealing his identity to his brothers, when meeting his father after so many years, and, finally, at his father's funeral. "The ending would draw tears of tenderness" (*La fin peut faire répandre des larmes d'attendrissement*): this is one of the first things Voltaire tells us about the story of Joseph. In the early nineteenth century, Chateaubriand waxed eloquent on the matter: "Joseph weeping at the sight of his ungrateful brothers and of the young and innocent Benjamin; the manner in which he inquires about his father – this adorable simplicity, this mixture of grief and kindness – are all scenes wholly ineffable. The tears naturally start in our eyes, and we are ready to weep like Joseph."[18] Chateaubriand's enthusiasm shows that for many readers, weeping, in a well-told story, was contagious, the readers finding themselves rapidly reduced to tears. Apparently inspired by Voltaire's own reference to tears in the "Joseph" article, Chateaubriand claimed to know that Voltaire himself had shed a tear when reading the passage on Joseph's meeting with his brothers: "As to the famous pathetic words: I am Joseph, everyone knows that they drew tears of admiration from Voltaire himself."[19] Although we cannot be sure whether Voltaire actually did shed tears when reading about Joseph, it is certain that he could readily imagine so doing. Thus, Voltaire's reference to tears in his article on Joseph is meant as a tribute to those who had so perfected the ancient art of storytelling that he himself emulated. Voltaire included emotional scenes in his own stories, no doubt to provoke a similar reaction in his readers. In accordance with the current literary theory, that of Aristotle, he considered the scene of recognition the appropriate moment for the display of emotions, and in fact his own *contes* – especially *Zadig* – are full of such moments. "The moment of meeting, and that of parting, are the two greatest moments of life", Voltaire explains in *Zadig*; and as such, they are worthy of tears.[20]

The biblical Joseph, of course, is also worthy of tears, which makes his biographer a better poet than Homer – if we follow Voltaire's reasoning expressed elsewhere. "Homer has never drawn tears from anyone's eyes. The true poet, I think, is the one who touches the soul and stirs one's emotions. The others are merely people who speak nicely."[21]

"JOSEPH" SUPERIOR TO MODERN NOVELS

The second feature characteristic of Voltaire's *conte philosophique* is that it avoids the length, sentimental effusiveness, and general atmosphere of the eighteenth-century novel. In the preface to *Zadig*, Voltaire commends the *conte* as "interesting, amusing, moral, philosophical, and worthy of the delight of even those who hate reading novels".[22] While in his essay on Joseph, Voltaire does not comment on this matter, he does so in some of his letters. In his correspondence he recommends the biblical story as being superior to modern novels. In 1759 and 1760, Voltaire sought to persuade Mme du Deffand to read the tale of Joseph, but failed. Here is the story of their correspondence.

Mme du Deffand (1696–1780), Voltaire's correspondent and a friend of many years, divided her time between her Parisian *salon* and reading, and she developed a passion for both. She spent two evenings each week in the company of the many friends who attended her *salon*, but her days were dedicated to reading, an occupation that filled her spare time and supplied sustenance for the social gathering. "I read every day, or at night, for six or seven hours, and at the moment I do not have anything to read", she once complained to her friend Voltaire.[23] By then, the marquise could not read by herself any more. Born in 1696, she was then in her mid-sixties – only slightly younger than Voltaire – and almost blind, so that she depended on the companionship of Mademoiselle de Lespinasse who also served as her reader. Madame was particular, not liking everything that was offered, but lately she had discovered English novels and had developed a taste for them. In a letter that reached him some time during the summer of 1759, Voltaire learned about this new passion. She asked him whether he too liked the novels. His answer, dated 17 September 1759, was unambiguous: "Non, Madame."[24] Voltaire did not like sentimental novels.

But to which novels is Voltaire referring? Even though the existing correspondence between Voltaire and Mme du Deffand remains incomplete, a list of titles and authors can be reconstructed. The following books, all mentioned in the letters, were available in French translation, became the first bestselling novels – in Britain and elsewhere – and were much talked about at social gatherings:

Henry Fielding, *The History of Tom Jones, a Foundling* (1749)
Samuel Richardson, *Pamela, or Virtue Rewarded* (1740)
Samuel Richardson, *Clarissa Harlowe, or the History of a Young Lady* (1748)
Samuel Richardson, *The History of Sir Charles Grandison* (1753)

Besides heralding a new age of sentiment and introspection, Richardson's novels have a clear message: since the virtues of women are generally superior to and more refined than those of men, the latter should both accept and adopt the feminine approach. In these novels, moreover, women emerge as well-educated, intelligent beings endowed with a superior aptitude for moral judgement.[25] This message must have resonated with Mme du Deffand who, as a *salonnière*, presided with unquestioned authority over a company of men.

Mme du Deffand sought in her letters to Voltaire to justify her enthusiasm for these books. Although she fails to comment on Richardson's new ideal of psychological introspection (a feature highlighted by modern literary criticism), she does have a point when defending him in terms of morality. *Pamela*, for instance, is the story of a young serving-girl who resists her master's attempts at seduction until, overwhelmed by such unrelenting virtue, he marries her instead. "Monsieur, you have not read English novels. You would not despise them if you knew them. They are too long, I admit, and you make better use of your precious time. But morality, seen in action, has never been treated in a more captivating manner. With such reading one could die of wishing to be perfect, and one is led to believe that nothing could be easier."[26] "I will not say anything more about the English novels. I am sure you will find them too long, and perhaps one can enjoy them only as long as one does not have anything else to do. I take them to be moral treatises in narrative form. They are most interesting and can be very useful. I am speaking of *Pamela*, *Clarissa* and *Grandison*. Richardson, the author, is a man of wit."[27] Richardson had *esprit* – which is what would have been expected not only of an author, but also of the literati who frequented a Parisian salon. His *Clarissa*, then available as a set of ten small volumes, would have kept the avid reader absorbed for several days.

Despite Voltaire's scepticism about sentimental novels, he did give *Clarissa* a try – with a negative result. Voltaire was clearly bored. He summarised his judgement as follows: "I know that some are determined to recommend the trash called novels. But even if these books should indeed inspire some courage and have certain qualities, the little gain you have will not motivate you to sit down and read it again."[28] This judgement turned out to be justified, though not in all cases. A decade after first reading *Clarissa*, Mme du Deffand decided to have it read to her again – but after a few pages became disillusioned and stopped. "I wanted to read *Clarissa* once more," she wrote to one of her correspondents, "but now she bores me to death. So I'll give her up."[29] By contrast, she liked Henry Fielding's *Tom Jones* even when reread; "it charms me from beginning to end", she tells an English correspondent; and explains: "I only like those novels that paint characters, both good and bad. That is where true moral lessons are to be found; and if one can reap any benefit from reading, it is from books like these" – for example the volumes of *Tom Jones*. "They make a very great impression on me."[30]

Why should Voltaire be so negative about these English novels and, more generally, about all novels? What first comes to mind is Voltaire's individual character. While definitely a man of feeling in the sense this term had in the eighteenth century, his sentimentality was much less effusive than that of contemporaries such as Richardson, Diderot, and Rousseau. Unlike them, he had little interest in exploring the agonies of love, nor was he prone to endless psychological introspection. Thus on opening a romantic novel, he would encounter a world that remained foreign to him, a world to which he could not relate. Since he could not enter this invented sentimental world, he failed to appreciate the novel as a new form of art and cultural expression. Culturally, Voltaire still lived in the seventeenth century. Nostalgic for the great culture of the classical theatre that marked that century, he could not acquire a taste for the contemporary English and French culture of the novel. In France, the theatre of Racine, Corneille, and Molière – with their rhymed stage plays – was gradually being displaced by the prose novels of Abbé Prévost (*Manon Lescaut*, 1731), Rousseau (*Julie ou la Nouvelle Eloïse*, 1761; *Emile ou de l'éducation*, 1762), and Bernardin de Saint-Pierre (*Paul et Virginie*, 1788). In England, the cultural hegemony of Shakespeare's theatre began to be superseded by the popular novels of Fielding and Richardson. Most of these novels were love stories, part of someone's (fictitious) biography, among which Rousseau's *Emile*, the narrative of a boy's education, was an exception. These fictional accounts supplied reading matter for individual consumption and served as the subject of conversation in intimate circles; but gone was the powerful command of the world of theatre, gone were the days when the performance of a stage play was a major social event, drawing large crowds to listen and wonder at the words of the actors. In fact, Voltaire not only harboured nostalgic feelings for the theatre: he also continued to write stage plays and remained a lover of the theatre all of his life. He was proud of the private theatres installed on his estates. Moreover, he clung tenaciously to the outmoded, seventeenth-century tradition of rhythmical declamation in the performance, considering it the essence of true, meaningful poetry. Nevertheless, Voltaire's plays were successful: between 1718 and 1778 (the year of his death), the Comédie-Française staged thirty-one of his dramas in close to 1,900 performances.[31] Compared to the stage plays of the seventeenth century, however, those by Voltaire do not strike us as masterpieces of timeless significance; in fact, they are largely forgotten today.

After this digression on Mme du Deffand's penchant for novels and Voltaire's corresponding disapproval, we can return to our main subject – Voltaire and the Bible. In the summer of 1759, the marquise had asked the master for advice on what to read. Although the letter with the question is no longer extant, we do have Voltaire's reply. In two letters, dated 17 September and 13 October 1759, Mme du Deffand was given the advice she was seeking.[32] The negative part of Voltaire's response – his disapproval of novels in general – was summarised and in part quoted above. But Voltaire does offer recommendations. Abstracted from his letters, these can be presented in the form of a list of recommended authors and worthwhile individual works. Voltaire recommended the following:

non-fiction

philosophical literature:	Lucretius, Bolingbroke, Hume; Voltaire, *Histoire d'un bon Bramin* (The Good Brahmin)
polemical literature:	Pascal, *Lettres provinciales* (The Provincial Letters)
historiography:	Voltaire's *Essai sur les moeurs et l'esprit des nations* (Essay on the Manners and the Spirit of Nations)

fiction

tales from antiquity and the East:	the narrative books of the Old Testament, the tales of Joseph, Daniel and Susanna, and Tobit; the book of the prophet Ezekiel; the *Arabian Nights*; Virgil
satirical fiction:	Ariosto, Rabelais; Jonathan Swift, *Tale of a Tub*; Voltaire, *La Pucelle d'Orléans* (The Maid of Orleans)

German authors are notably absent from this list, which is no coincidence, for Voltaire never read anything in German, and what he did know of did not strike him as worthwhile. Extracting Voltaire's recommended reading from his letters and arranging it in the form of a list inevitably distorts the picture. Voltaire's own books, although not given a central place in the letters, appear to have been given undue prominence. Whereas the *Essai sur les moeurs* may be considered one of Voltaire's main works and we can understand why he gave it much weight, the others – *Histoire d'un bon Bramin* and *La Pucelle* – are two short pieces that just happened to be on Voltaire's mind as he wrote. A copy of the *Histoire d'un bon Bramin* actually accompanies Voltaire's letter of 13 October 1759 and is introduced in the following way: "You ask me, Madame, what I think [about the people]. Well, I think they do not deserve anything but contempt, for there is only a very small number of people that dare to think clearly – and you are one of these. But what is our brain good for? For nothing. Read the parable of the good Brahmin, a copy of which I have the honour to enclose. I encourage you to enjoy this short life as much as you can, and not to be afraid of death, for it is nothing."[33] *La Pucelle*, the other short text mentioned, is a satire on Joan of Arc; condemned by French censorship, it was not readily available, and Voltaire offers to send his correspondent a copy of part of it (which he later did). Apart from satire, Voltaire mainly recommends tales from antiquity and the East. He praises the quality of Virgil's *Aeneid*, the stories of the *Arabian Nights*, and – surprisingly – those of the Old Testament. Here he singles out the narrative books:

> I don't write to Paris, Madame, except to you, because your imagination has always been in tune with my heart, but I will not allow you to make me read English novels as long as you do not want to read the Old Testament. Tell me then, if you please: where will you find a more interesting story than that of Joseph becoming the Controller General of Egypt and recognising his brothers? And Daniel who so subtly confuses the two old gentlemen, does he count for nothing? Although Tobit is not so good, it seems superior to me to *Tom Jones* [by Henry Fielding], a novel in which there is nothing of any merit apart from the character of a barber. You ask me what you should read, as the sick ask what they are allowed to eat; but they have to be hungry, and you have little appetite but considerable taste. Happy is he who is hungry enough to devour the Old Testament! Do not mock it. This book is a hundred times more enlightening about the customs of ancient Asia than Homer. Of all memorials of antiquity, it is the most precious.[34]

The Old Testament writings mentioned by Voltaire all belong to the literary type now known as "novellas": short fictional stories of literary beauty. Of the seven novellas found in the Bible Voltaire mentions three – those of Joseph, Daniel, and Tobit. To complete the list, he could have added the stories of Ruth, Judith, Jonah, and Esther.

Voltaire not only supplies a reading list; he also indicates the appropriate attitude for reading with profit and delight: "But, Madame, do you really want to read just as you listen to someone you happen to chat to? To pick up a book the same way as one asks for trivial news? To read a little, and then put the book down? And then take up another one that has nothing to do with the first, in order to proceed to a third without further ado? This would be unsatisfactory, for real enjoyment cannot exist without a certain amount of passion. You must have a subject of real concern, a true thirst for knowledge that keeps your soul in bonds. Such a subject is not easy to find and rarely imposes itself."[35] What Voltaire recommends is focused reading. Once a topic of interest is found, a focus of attention, it captivates the reader and will stay on his or her mind for a long time, obviating boredom. Reading on and around a defined subject makes us aware of things we would simply have overlooked "when reading with our eyes alone".[36] One such topic, Voltaire suggested, could be the customs and manners of a foreign people, and of ancient times, as they are reflected in the Old Testament:

> Trust me and have the historical part of the Old Testament read to you, the complete text. You will see that no other book is more entertaining. I do not mean the edification to be gained from it. I am referring to the fascinating world of the ancient customs, the large number of events each replete with meaning, to the simplicity of the narrative style, and so on. [...] It is this unrivalled simplicity that I value above all. There is not a page that does not provide a subject for a whole day. [...] If you are lucky enough to take pleasure in this book, all boredom will be banished, and you will see that no one can send you anything to rival it.[37]

Mme du Deffand agrees that adopting this attitude might lead to an interest in the Bible, but she prefers to abstain from studying it. "Read according to your method the Old Testament may actually be quite interesting. This I readily admit. But for many years I have instinctively felt that the whole book is based on ignorance and foolishness, and that I do not have to prove this sentiment to be correct by careful study."[38] Voltaire's "non, Madame" concerning the novels is matched by her "non, Monsieur" concerning the Bible: "No, Monsieur, this reading is not for me".[39] In many respects, the two correspondents feel the same way. Their literary tastes are similar, and both of them think ill of religion. It is only with respect to the Bible that they feel differently.

The philosophical point

For all the emotional and aesthetic appeal of the Joseph tale and despite its superiority to modern novels, Voltaire would have looked for more. For him, a good story also had to have a message; it had to appeal philosophically. Indeed, this is the very essence of the *conte philosophique*. Entertaining and never dull, Voltaire's own *contes* not only capture the imagination and appeal to the reader's emotions, they also convey a clear moral message or drive home a philosophical point.

Read philosophically through the eyes of an eighteenth-century thinker, the biblical Joseph story implies at least two interrelated philosophical issues: the fast and unexpected reversal of fate from wealth to poverty and, conversely, from affliction to well-being, these changes somehow being masterminded by Providence; and the triumph of good over evil by the granting of pardon to others, perhaps in thankfulness for goods received through Providence, or on other, more general moral grounds. As we will see, Voltaire considered both philosophical points, though he eventually decided to mention only the second in his dictionary article.

In order to understand what Voltaire thought about Providence and swift changes of fate, a look at one of his own *contes philosophiques* is revealing. *Zadig ou la destinée. Histoire orientale* (Zadig or the Book of Fate. An Oriental Tale, 1748) tells of the life and adventures of a young oriental man. Zadig's life, a never-ending quest for happiness, is haunted by bad luck, because virtue – Zadig's chief characteristic – never guarantees success. Since the world is imperfect, his quest is regularly thwarted, and the hero's brief spells of good luck are followed by bad times. Bad and good days alternate, with unforeseeable and swift reversals of fortune. Obviously Voltaire was fascinated by the ancient idea of *fortuna*, a force seen as capable of making and breaking human lives, of snatching control from the hands of even the wisest. In the life of Zadig, the impact of *fortuna* is pervasive and inescapable. Although Zadig appears to be a hapless victim of fate, there are nevertheless good moments for him, so life is ultimately worth living. Voltaire's story seems to imply two endings – a closed and an open one, indicating that Zadig either ruled the city of Babylon (Baghdad) happily ever after, or continued to endure the ups and downs of life.[40] An oriental flavour pervades the tale, and there is little doubt that he sought to imitate the narrative technique and the general atmosphere of the *Arabian Nights*.[41]

At one point in *Zadig*, an angel named Jesrad appears, just as in the *Arabian Nights* we meet genies and sinister demons. The angel takes human form for some time, accompanying Zadig for part of his travels, but finally leaves and, as all angels do, vanishes from sight, thereby demonstrating his angelic identity. Before leaving, however, he answers one of Zadig's questions. "But why", said Zadig, "is it necessary that there should be crimes and misfortunes, and that these misfortunes should happen to the innocent?" The angel's answer is as follows: "The wicked are always unhappy. They serve as a trial to the small number of the just that are scattered throughout the world. There is no evil that engenders no good (*Il n'y a point de mal dont il ne naisse un bien*)."⁴² Zadig, of course, belongs among the just, as his very name implies; derived from Hebrew *tsaddiq*, it means no less than the just or virtuous one. More remarkable is the angel's summary appraisal of the human predicament: "There is no evil that engenders no good." Contrary to what one may feel when being affected by adversity and evil, the hidden power of Providence – rather than fickle fortune – will eventually put things right by using what appears as evil as an instrument for producing some good. This is also the point of the biblical story of Joseph, where the protagonist himself explains that from the evil intended by his brothers issued the good of their own survival, and that of all Egyptians, during the years of famine.⁴³ What on Joseph's part involved just one evil resulting in one good is for the angel a general rule.

But why is it that in his essay on Joseph Voltaire does not refer to divine providence, the ultimate triumph of the just and virtuous, and the rule that evil may actually be the cause of some good? The answer must be that in 1747, when writing *Zadig*, Voltaire shared, or came close to sharing, the optimism summed up in the angel's dictum. Two decades later, when publishing his *Dictionnaire philosophique*, his youthful optimism was tempered. The reason was not his advancing years, however, but a natural disaster: on All Saints' Day, 1 November 1755, an earthquake destroyed two-thirds of Lisbon, capital city of Portugal, bringing sudden death to some thirty thousand inhabitants. The event was discussed throughout Europe, leading many, including Voltaire, to disillusionment with optimistic views of human life; people became aware of the fact that one cannot count on virtue being ultimately rewarded in this world. Voltaire devoted an entire philosophical tale to the issue: *Candide, ou l'optimisme* (1759). Although the biblical story did not lose its attraction for Voltaire after 1755, he could no longer subscribe to its optimistic message. This is why the dictum "There is no evil that engenders no good" does not figure in Voltaire's essay on Joseph.

Thus Voltaire was left with the second of the two philosophical issues implied in the biblical story: the theme of pardoning offences received. The biblical story, Voltaire explains, "is more touching than Homer's *Odyssey*, for a hero who pardons is more moving than one who seeks revenge. [...] It is unique in its genre – the only Hebrew story of this kind, the only one in which we have an act of generosity and mercy." Odysseus perpetrated a brutal massacre in which all the suitors of his wife Penelope died – "and there was a hideous sound of groaning as our brains were being battered in, and the ground seethed with our blood" (*Odyssey* XXIV, 184–85). Joseph, by contrast, pardoned his brothers, meeting them with unwarranted mercy and mildness. In modern terms, Voltaire compares the bloody carnage of the archaic period of the Greeks with the sentimental and idyllic scene dating from the late period of Hebrew literature. But this contrast is more than a mere factual observation: it implies a moral distinction. Homer lacks an ethical code;[44] the Joseph story implies one. As in Voltaire's own tales, the story of Joseph aims at teaching a philosophical lesson. In fact, the word "pardonner" – in the sense of pardoning, renouncing revenge, showing generosity and mercy – frames the article, being used at the beginning and again at the end, and sums up an important feature of Voltaire's own ethical ideal.

In Voltaire's literary works, acts of mercy and the rejection of revenge play significant roles. Zadig forgives the envious Arimaze for having him condemned to death, and refuses to accept Arimaze's property as compensation. Zadig has as little interest in killing those who were or still are his enemies, as has Joseph. Both oriental stories are marked by the same ethos of mercy, and we can find the same message in other writings by Voltaire. His Don Alvarez in the stage play *Alzire ou les Américains* (Alzire or the Americans, 1736) personifies a noble Christianity that considers all humans as brothers, and fosters an ethos of benefaction and the forgiving of injustice. Alvarez, former governor of Peru, has grown too old to continue in office and has turned over his duties to his son, Gusman, whom he advises to rule in accordance with Christian principles. Only shortly before his own death does Gusman come to see the wisdom of mercy towards others. He spares the lives of two Indian captives and bids them marry. But Voltaire is far from suggesting that willingness to forgive is a specifically Christian or Western virtue. As a reader of the *Arabian Nights*, where the magnanimous ruler who, in imitation of Allah the Lord of mercy, does not seek revenge, is a standard character, he may have felt that an oriental setting for this teaching was quite fitting. Voltaire consistently conveys the same message: revenge and the death penalty are detestable, while "clemency touches the heart" (*clémence touche le coeur*).[45]

In the preface to *Alzire*, Voltaire refers to magnanimity as "a sentiment much commended by the ancient sages and refined by our own religion".[46] While he may not have believed in the superiority of Christian ethical sentiments, he was well aware of the tenets of the faith. In early-modern times, Catholic teaching strongly emphasised the necessity for forgiveness. "By far the most important duty, the highest fulfilment of the love of our neighbours, that we must practise, is to pardon and endure with equanimity all offences that are made against us", reads a passage of the *Roman Catechism*.[47] While the catechism recommends clemency to all believers, Bishop Bossuet, in *Politique tirée des propres paroles de l'Ecriture Sainte* (Politics Drawn from the Very Words of Scripture, 1709), makes it a duty specifically of princes and rulers.[48]

In eighteenth-century France, the Christian rejection of vengeance was felt to be strongly supported by "the ancient sages" and by *Cinna ou la clémence d'Auguste* (Cinna or the Mercy of Augustus, 1642), a drama that Voltaire considered Pierre Corneille's most accomplished play. The concluding scene in which Emperor Augustus offers friendship to his would-be assassin Cinna – "Let us be friends, Cinna" – offers "one of the finest lessons for princes".[49] Voltaire admired the scene, and hinted at it in his story *L'Ingénu*.[50] Diderot, when merely thinking of the incident, began to cry.[51] Both in the Rome of Nero and in Voltaire's France the appeal to the ruler's mercy is appropriate. Instead of a king who orders books to be burnt, who shuts up his enemies in prison or sends them into exile, one would wish to have someone who stood above revenge. All eighteenth-century intellectuals agreed on this. In addition to Voltaire and Diderot, we may also refer to Montesquieu who, in *De l'esprit des lois* (The Spirit of the Laws, 1748), commends clemency as "the distinctive quality of monarchs"; kings, he explains, have much to gain from acts of clemency, because they earn love and glory. Indeed, "it is always a fortunate thing for them to have occasion to exercise it; and one can almost always do so in our countries".[52] Unsurprisingly, the famous *Encyclopédie* of Diderot and d'Alembert condemns revenge as a barbaric act unworthy of civilised humanity, while praising forgiveness. Applying to himself the virtue of moderation, the sage overlooks small offences, and major acts of injustice are answered with contempt; to pardon is deemed "beautiful" (*il est beau de pardonner*).[53]

Voltaire's comparison of the vengeful, man-slaying Odysseus with the meekly forgiving Joseph is in tune with both the Christian and the philosophical sensibilities of the age of Enlightenment. Voltaire was not the only writer of his age sensitive to just this moral message of the biblical story. A similar sentiment was expressed by Laurence Sterne, the famous English novelist and preacher. In February 1764 Voltaire received Sterne's two-volume collection of sermons that he subsequently reviewed rather favourably in the *Gazette littéraire*, and out of which he copied passages for one of his correspondents.[54] Voltaire appreciated the simple, elegant language as well as the emphasis on the goodness, rather than corruptness, of human nature. One of the sermons is on the story of Joseph, and it stresses, as Voltaire did himself, both the theme of forgiveness and the literary merit of the biblical story. Forgiveness, in good Stoic fashion, "flows only from a strength and greatness of soul, conscious of its own force and security, and above the little temptations of resenting every fruitless attempt to interrupt its happiness".[55] Sterne calls the story of Joseph a "masterpiece", "related with the greatest variety of tender and affecting circumstances" (see above, Chapter 17). It is hard to believe that Voltaire read this sermon without remembering his own article sent in July 1763 to the printer in Geneva for publication a year later in his *Dictionnaire philosophique*.

The article "Joseph", written by Voltaire for his *Dictionnaire philosophique*, constitutes a striking piece of evidence for how he felt about the Bible as philosophically relevant literature. As one recent literary critic puts it, each of Voltaire's *contes philosophiques* brings laughter, breeds tolerance, and humanises.[56] This certainly applies to the Joseph story as understood by our author.

Epilogue

As every reader must know from his or her own experience, our emotional attachment to certain books is deeply rooted in our biographies, our enthusiasm for stories loved in childhood being retained even late in life. *The Swiss Family Robinson* (by Johann Rudolf Wyss) was as unforgettable to the novelist and literary critic E.M. Forster as the historical novels of Sir Walter Scott were for many others.[57] Voltaire was no exception. Even in old age – when Voltaire was eighty – he vividly remembered his childhood interests and asked someone to get him a copy of the *Contes de ma mère l'oie* (The Tales of Mother Goose), for he wished to research the use of certain expressions found there. To Jean Pierre Costard, who helped find him a copy, he explained: "As you can see, old age and childhood meet. I love the *Contes de ma mère l'oie* just as I loved them when I was ten."[58] Collected by Charles Perrault, the *Contes de ma mère l'oie* include Little Red Riding Hood, Sleeping Beauty, and Cinderella, stories still known today.[59]

In similar fashion, Voltaire may have formed an early attachment to the Bible story of Joseph. While we cannot be certain when young François-Marie Arouet (alias Voltaire) first heard of or read about Joseph, we do know that the story from Genesis was the subject of several dramatic productions at the Jesuit school in Paris where he received his education between October 1704 and August 1711, from eleven to seventeen years of age. At the Lycée Louis-le-Grand, as in the Jesuit schools all over Europe, the performance of Latin plays was part of the standard curriculum. Besides furthering the boys' spiritual life, it was meant to develop poise, and the skills of memorising and public speaking. The plays were typically performed at school prize-givings each August and to celebrate church festivals. The titles of some of these plays, and even the dates when they were staged, are known: *Josephus Aegypto praefectus* (Joseph, Prefect in Egypt), 3 August 1707; *Josephus venditus* (Joseph Sold), 20 March 1709; *Benjamin captif* (Benjamin in Captivity), 3 June 1709; *Josephus agnoscens fratres* (Joseph Meets his Brothers), 7 August 1709.[60] Father Gabriel Le Jay, resident master of rhetoric at the Lycée Louis-le-Grand, wrote these plays, and François presumably saw all four as a teenage pupil. "What was best about the Jesuit college in Paris, where I was brought up, was the custom of performing plays by the boarders in front of their parents", Voltaire remembered as late as 1761.[61] It is a pity that we cannot be sure if François ever took part in such performances; given his later love of the theatre, one is tempted to assume that this was indeed the case. Interestingly, Father Le Jay, in *Josephus Aegypto praefectus*, highlights the theme of forgiveness: installed in high office, Joseph acts as a true statesman by pardoning Potiphar and all who had insisted on having him imprisoned and killed.[62] Could it be that Voltaire had absorbed the notion of Joseph's clemency as early as his school-days?

In the preface to the printed version of the Joseph trilogy, Father Le Jay reports with a touch of pride that the performances were capable of drawing pious tears from the audience – and this may be more than just a flourish.[63] True, we know nothing about the tears the pupils themselves may have shed on such occasions, but why should they have been different from everyone else? We can be sure on at least one point: eighteenth-century children were able to appreciate the Joseph story (see above, Chapter 4).

After Voltaire had left the Lycée Louis-le-Grand in 1711, there was no chance of forgetting about Joseph. One of the places he frequented between 1712 and 1717 was the Château de Sceaux, on the outskirts of Paris, where the duchesse du Maine presided over a court of almost royal ambition, complete with an entourage of writers, scholars, and, most importantly, men and women who produced theatrical performances, gave readings, and organised all sorts of elegant social events. The Château de Sceaux differed from the royal court at Versailles in that it was closely linked to the *milieu dévot*, the circles that under the direction of bishops and priests sought to promote Christian standards in moral, social, and political life.[64] One Abbé Charles-Claude Genest, resident philosopher and *homme de lettres* at Sceaux, had written an idyllic and sentimental play entitled *Joseph: tragédie, tirée de l'Ecriture Sainte* (Joseph: A Drama from Sacred Scripture). Before being staged at the Comédie-Française in Paris in December 1710 and January 1711,[65] it had already entertained the select circle of the duchesse du Maine. In 1706 – and presumably also subsequently – not only was it read to an audience that included the duchesse, her family and friends, but it was performed at her private theatre at Clagny near Versailles, the duchesse herself taking one of the parts.[66] Voltaire must have seen or read the play, or both, and presumably was as impressed with it as were many others. Sixty years later he still remembered how it had been received, reporting that "it is said to be the least poor of all the plays based on this appealing theme".[67] Despite his slightly ironic words (so characteristic of him), Voltaire apparently shared the enthusiasm felt for the Joseph play staged by the duchesse and her friends.

In the concluding passage of his article on Joseph, Voltaire himself hints at his emotional attachment to the story:

> What good old Jacob, Joseph's father, replies to Pharaoh, will no doubt strike a chord with those who can take the hint: "How old are you?" the king asks him. "I am a hundred and thirty", says the old man, "and I have not yet enjoyed one happy day in this brief pilgrimage."

The hint is a reference to Voltaire's own age – he was seventy when the first edition of the *Dictionnaire philosophique* was published in 1764.[68] Voltaire reveals to the reader that old Jacob is none other than – Voltaire. This little detail is more than just a joke. The key to understanding it arises from a rather peculiar facet of Voltaire's character: he maintained an almost complete silence about what we would call his private life and sentiments, and, while liberally communicating to others the subjects and progress of his other writing, he never talked about writing his *contes*. As has been suggested by specialists, the autobiography that Voltaire never wrote is hidden in his *contes*. In fact, an autobiographical element can be discerned in all of Voltaire's stories, and it was in them that he sought to come to terms with his fears, hopes, and disappointments in life. In some Voltaire himself is the actual, though carefully masked, hero.[69] It is not difficult to understand how he could see himself not only in the figures of Zadig and old Jacob, but also in that of Joseph, for like Joseph he found himself imprisoned early in life, later being promoted to a high position at a princely court (that of Frederick the Great of Prussia). If it is true that the biblical story was familiar to him from his early days, and that it resonated with his own biography, the emotional appeal it seems to have held for him comes as no surprise. While some of the biographical details must remain conjectural, Voltaire's attachment to the story of Joseph is undeniable and may reach far back into his boyhood. Later in life, when consulting Charles Rollin's *De la manière d'enseigner et d'étudier les belles-lettres* (1726–1728), he was reminded of his early familiarity with the story. Voltaire knew and appreciated Rollin's manual,[70] and it may well be that his article in the *Dictionnaire philosophique* owes its inspiration not only to his exposure, as a boy, to the Jesuit theatre at his school, but also to Rollin's manual, which refreshed his memory and guided his pen.

Voltaire never concealed his appreciation of the Joseph story. He expressed it in both his essay and his correspondence. What he wrote to Mme du Deffand is unlikely to have remained unknown in Paris. We may assume that she showed the letters to her guests, and they may have been circulated or read out as after-dinner entertainment at her parties. The marquise was proud of being a confidante of her country's foremost author. So what Voltaire wrote in his personal correspondence was not as private as it might seem at first sight; we may assume that, through written communication, he felt himself to be an active and respected member of the marquise's famous literary *salon*. And, despite Mme du Deffand's stubborn denial of interest, he may after all have succeeded in making the biblical story of Joseph a topic of conversation in at least one fashionable *salon*.

20

The Triumph of Beauty – Chateaubriand

A MAN OF NOBLE DESCENT BORN IN BRITTANY, CHATEAUBRIAND (1768–1848) was living in Paris in 1789 where he witnessed the bloody events of the Revolution. At that time, he earned his living as a hosiery merchant. Unlike other young aristocrats, he decided against a Grand Tour to Italy to complete his education; instead, he considered the New World to be more adventurous and indeed more worthy of his attention. He spent much of 1791 travelling in the English colonies of North America, a time he later remembered as the beginning of his career as a writer, and it is clear that the experience, a kind of initiation trial, marked a new stage in his life: the shift from youth to adulthood, from uncertainty about what to do with his life to his vocation as a writer. The young man returned to France, got married, fought briefly on the side of the Royalists, was wounded, and soon left his native country to join French exiles in Britain where people like him sought to escape political persecution. The years in Britain (1792–1800) were spent in poverty, devoted to frequent visits to the British Library, to studies and writing. The year 1797 saw the publication of his first book, a political treatise on revolutions in history. Organised societies, he explains, start their existence in simple circumstances, grow to become states, gradually become tyrannical, provoke resistance, opposition, and eventual revolutionary destruction, in order then to begin anew. The book ends abruptly, on a decidedly Romantic note: a celebration of life in the wilderness as the author had experienced it when living among – or near – the native peoples of North America. The implication seems to be: at the present moment, things have to start from the beginning, as if in the wilderness. Chateaubriand began to meditate about new political beginnings in France, but his views remained too vague to crystallise into definitive form.

It was while in this situation that Chateaubriand met fellow exiles such as the well-known poet Louis de Fontanes (1757–1821) who believed that French society should not be pushed back to a state of nature; instead, they believed in the regenerative force of Christian ideals. Before their destruction by the

Enlightenment *philosophes*, especially by Voltaire and the Encyclopaedists, these values had been central to French life. If French society were to be restored to its previous glory and greatness, its Christian spirit had to be reinstated, for religion formed the basis, if not the very essence, of its culture. Since the *ancien régime* had been destroyed by the creation of a particular intellectual culture, that of the Enlightenment, the restoration demanded a new intellectual underpinning, one, as Fontanes suggested, based on a sense of beauty and emotional appeal; soon it was given the name of Romanticism. According to Fontanes, intellectuals should be making it their business to reinvigorate Christianity, and they should do this by writing books in support of religion. Fontanes dreamt up a project of a major book that was to extol traditional religious culture by highlighting its aesthetic perfection. Since the emphasis was to be on the beauty of religion rather than on its truth, the author was to be a poet rather than a theologian, for only the former is a natural expert on aesthetic perfection. As Chateaubriand's mentor and indeed most intimate friend among the exiles, Fontanes won over the young aristocrat and helped initiate his "conversion".[1] Whereas in his *Essay on Revolutions* Chateaubriand had still subscribed to anticlerical ideas of the Enlightenment, he now began to feel differently. Within a few months, and possibly prompted by the shock of learning of his mother's death, he rediscovered the lost faith of his childhood. As Chateaubriand was later to summarise: "I became a Christian. Admittedly, I did not yield to any great supernatural light: my conviction came from the heart. I wept, and I believed" (*ma conviction est sortie du coeur; j'ai pleuré et j'ai cru*).[2] Fontanes had both touched the young writer's heart and fired his literary ambition. Seeing himself from a new perspective as being anti-Voltaire, Chateaubriand adopted the revival of religion as his personal cause, and set to work.

Like many others Chateaubriand returned to France in 1800, after Napoleon had begun to bring an end the period of revolutionary horrors and to impose himself as the new leader. Back in Paris, Chateaubriand was encouraged and supported by friends who supplied lodgings, company, and relevant books, enabling him to complete the manuscript and to revise it for publication as *Génie du Christianisme ou Beautés de la religion chrétienne* (The Genius of Christianity, or The Beauty of the Christian Religion, 1802). The author finds beauty everywhere in Christianity: in the grandeur of the dogmatic system, in the heroic lives of the martyrs and saints, in the impressive architecture (and especially in the picturesque ruins) of the cathedrals, in the sound of the church bells calling the faithful to church, in the joyful and dignified celebration of the liturgy, and, not least, in its unsurpassed literature that begins with the Bible and continues to be written down to our own day.

If Christianity was to be restored and rehabilitated, it was important for the educated to overcome the Voltairean contempt for, and denigration of,

Christian literature. Catholics must be given a new sense of the excellence of their literature, including the Bible. They must be taught to be proud of it. In his demonstration of the Bible's literary qualities, Chateaubriand draws upon an intellectual tradition that originated in French literary circles around 1700. It was then that authors such as Claude Fleury, Bishop Fénelon, Charles-Claude Genest, and Charles Rollin all developed an enthusiasm and indeed a nostalgia for the world of the *Iliad*, the *Odyssey* and the Old Testament, a world that was both heroic and pastoral. Homer and the Bible were seen as echoing the same ancient ways. As Fénelon explains in his *Dialogues sur l'éloquence* (Dialogues on Eloquence, 1718), "you must know Homer, Plato, Xenophon and the rest of the ancients; then Scripture will no longer seem strange and surprising: we find more or less the same customs, the same stories, the same images of grandeur, the same liveliness."[3] Chateaubriand, for whom Fénelon was an authority, agrees: "If Jacob and Nestor are not of the same family, both at least belong to the early ages of the world, and you feel that it is but a step from the palace of Pylos to the tents of Israel."[4] Homer and the Bible are quite similar in that they present the fate of their heroes as being governed by divine providence, or, more accurately, as being decreed by either the monotheistic God of the Bible or deities such as Zeus and Pallas Athena. In fact, in both literatures, nothing happens that is not divinely willed and announced and dependent on divine anger or benevolence. Once the manners and beliefs of ancient Greece and ancient Israel had been identified, idealised, and idolised, they were perceived as blending easily to form the basis for the education of the young elite of France, for instance in Fénelon's didactic novel *Les Aventures de Télémaque* (The Adventures of Telemachus, 1699).

For all his agreement with the Fleury group's approach, Chateaubriand nevertheless shifts the emphasis from ethics to aesthetics. Fleury and Genest in particular valued the biblical and Homeric worlds for their common moral atmosphere and a lifestyle that they declared simpler, yet more noble than and superior to, the refined culture and decadent, pleasure-seeking, enervated ways of their French contemporaries.[5] Chateaubriand, by contrast, focuses on the literary quality that distinguished both biblical and Homeric literature. Even the formal difference between the two literatures is almost abolished in Chateaubriand's bold suggestion that the prose style of the adventures of Joseph may be seen as imitating the epic form of Homeric narrative.[6] Of particular relevance to him was the fact that Homer and the book of Genesis sometimes describe similar scenes and even plots, features that invite close reading and comparison.[7] We can understand why Chateaubriand, intent on highlighting the literary merit of Scripture, selected for a close reading a biblical story that had already fascinated Fleury,[8] Genest and Rollin: the story of Joseph.

Chateaubriand on Joseph

By the time Chateaubriand was writing, literary appreciation of the story from Genesis was well established in France through the work of one member of the Fleury group: Abbé Rollin's *De la manière d'enseigner et d'étudier les belles-lettres* (1726–1728; revised edition, 1736). Chateaubriand knew this manual and actually refers to its section on literature.[9] Rollin's recommendation seems to have inspired Chateaubriand to make the Joseph story the cornerstone of his Christian poetics. To think of Rollin as Chateaubriand's secret muse and master makes sense in view of our author's programme for restoring the intellectual world of the *ancien régime*, since Rollin was one of its last important representatives before the Enlightenment began to dominate the literary scene.

Chateaubriand follows Rollin not only in his choice of "Joseph" to demonstrate the Bible's literary quality; he also uses his method of selecting individual passages for close reading (rather than commenting on the story as a whole). All the passages he selects have to do with Joseph's family: his brothers and his father. Chateaubriand uses the Latin Bible, but also resorts to paraphrase, thus creating his own text of three interlinked episodes that tell how, towards the end of the story, Joseph's family is reunited in Egypt, and Joseph is reconciled with his brothers:[10]

> (*First episode.*) Joseph receives his brothers – those who had sold him into slavery – as they come to Egypt a second time to buy grain. This time they are accompanied by Benjamin, the youngest brother, as requested by Joseph. The visitors are still unaware of the Egyptian governor's identity. Joseph, courteously saluting them, asks, "Is the old man, your father of whom you told me, in good health? Is he still alive?" And they answer, "Your servant, our father, is in good health, he is still alive", and, bowing low, they make obeisance to him. And Joseph, lifting up his eyes, sees Benjamin, his brother by the same mother, and says, "Is this your young brother of whom you told me?" And he says, "God be gracious to you, my son." Then, hastily, for tears are welling up as his heart is moved, he retires to his chamber and weeps. Once he has washed his face and composed himself, he comes out again, ordering, "Set bread on the table."
>
> (*Second episode.*) After the banquet that Joseph gives for his brothers, who are still unaware of his identity, they are given grain and take to the road. On Joseph's order, a precious cup had been secretly hidden in Benjamin's sack. The sons of Jacob are followed and stopped by Egyptian soldiers. The missing cup is found. So the group must return to Joseph for questioning. Joseph affects an intention to detain the culprit. Judah offers himself as a hostage in place of Benjamin. He relates

> to Joseph how, before their departure for Egypt, Jacob had said to them: "You know that my wife bore me two sons. One went out, and you said a beast devoured him; and until now he has not returned. If you take this [child, Benjamin] also, and anything happens to him, you will bring down a grey old man with sorrow into the Underworld." Now Joseph can no longer control himself in front of the onlookers, so he commands that they all should leave so that no stranger will be present when they recognise him. He raises his voice in weeping, which the Egyptians and all the house of Pharaoh hear. And he says to his brothers, "I am Joseph; is my father still alive?" Terror-stricken, his brothers cannot answer him. And he speaks mildly to them, "Come nearer to me." And when they have approached he says, "I am Joseph, your brother, whom you sold into Egypt. Do not be afraid; it was not by your counsel that I was sent here, but by the will of God. Hurry now and return to my father." And embracing his brother Benjamin, he weeps; and Benjamin weeps also, as he holds him tightly. And Joseph kisses all his brothers, weeping with each one.
>
> (*Third episode.*) Subsequently, Joseph invites his father and family to Egypt. Jacob is presented to Pharaoh. When asked his age by Pharaoh, old Jacob (Joseph's father) answers: "The days of my pilgrimage are one hundred and thirty years. My days have been few and evil; and they have not attained unto the days of my fathers."

Clearly, Chateaubriand selected these episodes for their emotional, pathetic quality. "Sentiment" is a word he uses repeatedly in his commentary. In the case of the first episode, Chateaubriand lacks words to describe adequately what he feels, and so resorts to a simple staccato listing of what most impresses him: "Joseph weeping at the sight of his ungrateful brothers and of the young and innocent Benjamin; the manner in which he enquires about his father – this adorable simplicity, this mixture of grief and kindness – are all scenes wholly ineffable. The tears naturally start in our eyes, and we are ready to weep like Joseph."[11] The biblical passage arouses in the reader – at least in Chateaubriand himself – a strong emotional response. The more emotion evoked the better: this sums up how Chateaubriand and many of his Romantic contemporaries felt about the matter.

The second episode is no less marked by "sentiment". Chateaubriand draws up a list of features that give the passage its unique emotional and pathetic quality. Among the Hebrew visitors, emotion is at a high pitch. First, they are afraid that, were Benjamin to be taken prisoner, this would bring renewed sorrow to their aged father – and that prospect all of a sudden overwhelms them. Second, their fear is immeasurably aggravated as they learn the identity of the Egyptian governor – Joseph, their brother whom they sold into slavery. They feel guilty and have good cause to fear his retaliation. Joseph's emotion is even more dramatically presented. First, the scene of recognition is carefully staged. Joseph does not begin by saying, "I am your brother". Instead, he says, "I am Joseph", pronouncing the name that he knew would awaken their guilty conscience, and he pronounced it – as Chateaubriand envisages the scene – in a raised voice so that everyone in the house could hear. Then, however, to the brothers who alone are given the explanation, he added in a low tone, "I am Joseph, your brother, whom you sold into Egypt." Joseph's kindly reception implies that he has already forgiven his brothers. He goes on to explain that far from having harmed him, they are, on the contrary, the very cause of his unprecedented political career. "Here are delicacy, simplicity, and generosity, carried to the highest degree."[12] The scene is not only emotional in itself; its pathos is contagious: "As to the pathetic words, 'I am Joseph', everyone knows that they drew tears of admiration from Voltaire."[13] Well, yes, readers of Voltaire's article on Joseph in the *Dictionnaire philosophique* would know that the happy ending of the story can draw tears, but they would also be aware of the fact that Voltaire neither restricted the tears to this precise moment in the story, nor did he reveal whether his own tears fell on the pages of his Bible as he was reading. If Chateaubriand reads too much into Voltaire's text, he does so to unique effect; he uses Voltaire, the enemy of the Bible, to support his own reading. Finally, Joseph embraces and kisses each of his brothers, beginning with Benjamin. Chateaubriand comments that a modern author would not have failed to represent Joseph as choosing first to embrace the most guilty of his brothers, thereby accentuating the theatrical nature of the scene. The Bible is more realistic here, however, and, as Chateaubriand underlines, "more intimately acquainted with the human heart".[14]

A different kind of "sentiment" marks the third episode: sadness in old age. Hebrew melancholy – Chateaubriand writes *tristesse* – is a sentiment cherished by our author and congenial to the Romantic temper.[15] While *tristesse*, for Chateaubriand, is a feeling characteristic of all persons of heightened sensibility, it is also inspired by old age or, more precisely, by the fact that a person of advanced years knows everything – "If old age is so wretched, it is because it knows every thing."[16] In other words: the old man is sad but wise, sadness being the price paid for wisdom. Although Chateaubriand in the passage about Jacob does not define what he means by *tristesse*, he does give a hint when, for no apparent reason, he adds another quotation from the book of Genesis: "Isaac brought Rebecca into the tent of Sarah, his mother, and took her to wife, and he loved her so much that it moderated the sorrow that was occasioned by his mother's death."[17] By juxtaposing the two passages on the very same page, Chateaubriand seems to suggest that the Hebrews, like the Romantics, and especially like himself, were people of deeply felt sentiments – melancholy, sorrow, and love – and that these lend a profundity to their literature. The biblical episodes echo not the mind of "sophists" (the word Chateaubriand uses for philosophers whose work represents sterile, abstract thinking) but that of an author whose writing springs "from the heart and from tears" (*fait avec le coeur et les larmes*).[18] Biblical storytelling, in other words, is deeply rooted in the emotions. Beauty speaks to the emotions, and we respond spontaneously and emotionally to that which is beautiful.

In addition to emphasising the emotional quality of the scenes he selected for analysis, Chateaubriand takes much interest in their *simplicité*, a stylistic feature appreciated and discussed by eighteenth-century literary critics. The "simple" style – first on the scale of simple, middling, and grand – is relaxed, straightforward, marked by purity and economy of expression, and lacking in all superfluous embellishment.[19] Chateaubriand's relevant rules may be stated as follows:[20] (1) Brevity, the hallmark of simplicity, is generally superior to verbosity. It imparts strength, producing a result that is energetic and to the point. If you are looking for a model, you are likely to find it in biblical prose. (2) Avoid description of trivial detail such as someone's nightcap and nightgown. This rule is frequently disregarded in modern novels. (3) Be particularly careful to respect the rule of simplicity when you are intent on saying something significant, for example when rendering a sublime scene or expressing a sublime thought. Translated into more recent linguistic terminology, one might say the "restricted code" of formal address and communication is nobler than the verbose "elaborated code" with its love of detail and effusiveness of sentiment characteristic of the modern novel.[21] A text written in the restricted code favours objectivity over subjectivity, statement of fact more than personal evaluation and commentary, brevity rather than florid, long, lush description.

Two stock quotations exemplify biblical brevity: "God said" near the beginning of the account of creation, and "I am Joseph your brother"; these were frequently quoted in Latin – *Deus dixit*, and *Ego sum Ioseph, frater vester* – to highlight their venerable antiquity. What fascinated literary critics, including Chateaubriand, about these two passages was the effect they had on the readers: they inspired awe and admiration, even to the point of drawing tears.[22] Had the biblical author attributed to God a long and complicated speech to initiate his creation, the passage would have lost its power; the literary beauty and nobility of the words consist precisely in their consummate economy. Because human language cannot even hope to express the magnificent act of creation, it is best to refer to it in very simple, unadorned words. The same is true of *Ego sum Ioseph*. In 1760, the German poet Friedrich Gottlieb Klopstock offered this comment on the passage: "*I am Joseph! Is my father still alive?* Never has a nobler emotion been expressed in fewer words." Klopstock added: "The artist who would render with complete authenticity what Joseph and his brothers felt at this moment could stop painting, and yet his name would be immortal."[23] Chateaubriand agrees: "Here are delicacy, simplicity (*simplicité*), and generosity, all carried to the highest degree."[24] The particular emotional atmosphere created by such passages was termed "sublime", and it was understood that its evocation required great skill and experience in writing. In this context early-modern literary critics regularly refer to *Peri hypsous* (On the Sublime), an ancient treatise rediscovered by sixteenth-century humanists, which in the seventeenth century was translated into English (by Joseph Hall, 1652) and French (by Nicolas Boileau, 1674). This first-century CE Alexandrian treatise attributed to Longinus explains how the ancient Greek authors create an "elevated" or "lofty" atmosphere by depicting affective scenes that involve nature, the gods, and heroic deeds. Longinus's book also includes the following extraordinary passage:

> A similar effect was achieved by the lawgiver of the Jews – no mean genius, for he both clearly understood and appropriately expressed the power of the divine – when he wrote at the very beginning of his laws the following words: "God said" – well, what? – "Let there be light. And there was. Let there be earth. And there was."[25]

From this often-quoted ancient passage authors learned that the sublime could only be expressed succinctly, and that the Bible, at least occasionally, uses an eminently noble style.[26]

Chateaubriand refines and completes his analysis by comparing passages from the story of Joseph with parallel episodes from the *Odyssey* and the *Iliad*. For each of his three Joseph episodes, he adduces a Homeric passage for contrast, and in each case the analysis produces a noteworthy result. The first episode – the one in which Joseph successfully conceals his tears from his brothers – has a parallel in book VIII of the *Odyssey*, for here, too, the hero hides his emotions from his interlocutors in the story but not from the reader, thus making the reader the hero's confidant. Ulysses is seated at the festive board of King Alcinous, while Demodocus sings of the Trojan War and the misfortunes encountered by the Greeks. The memory of the war, prompted by the song, reduces Ulysses to tears, though he seeks to hide them:

> Touched at the song, Ulysses straight resigned
> to soft affliction all his manly mind:
> before his eyes the purple vest he drew,
> industrious to conceal the falling dew.
> But when the music paused, he ceased to shed
> the flowing tear, and raised his drooping head;

and, lifting to the gods a goblet crowned,
he poured a pure libation to the ground.
Transported with the song, the listening train
again with loud applause demand the strain;
again Ulysses veiled his pensive head,
again unmanned, a shower of sorrow shed.[27]

"Perfections of this nature", Chateaubriand acknowledges, "secured for Homer pride of place among the greatest geniuses".[28] Nevertheless, the corresponding Joseph episode is even more touching, because the biblical passage arouses in the reader – at least in Chateaubriand himself – a stronger and more emotional response than the Homeric scene.[29]

Chateaubriand continues his comparative analysis by considering another emotional scene, one where the weeping, no longer concealed, is unrestrained as the hero makes his identity known to a close relative. Ulysses, disguised as a beggar in the house of the kindly swineherd Eumaeus, leaves his hiding place, discards his rags and, restored to his former appearance by a touch of Athena's wand, approaches his son Telemachus. Magnificently attired, he announces himself to his son. Telemachus is not immediately convinced, thinking that Ulysses may be a spectre or ghost – a divine being demanding homage by sacrifice. Ulysses, however, explains that all this is the work of Athena, whereupon the two embrace:

Then, rushing to his arms, he kissed his boy
With the strong raptures of a parent's joy.
Tears bathe his cheek, and tears the ground bedew.
He strained him close, as to his breast he grew.[30]

What we have here is a stock scene of Homeric and indeed all ancient literature: two individuals happen to meet; at first, one or both are unaware of the other's identity; subsequently, recognition dawns. Recognition is the moment when the accumulating evidence of a character's true identity reaches a tipping point and the initial false impression is no longer sustainable. This tipping point is reached by various means, for instance through disclosure by one individual who has already recognised the other, or through one partner's accidental discovery of the other's identity, for example through some specific physical token or mark, or verbal allusion. Such scenes of recognition, loved by the ancient audience for their literary ingenuity and emotional intensity, appear frequently in the work of Homer and the dramatists of ancient Greece. Aristotle comments on them in his *Poetics*, distinguishing various forms of recognition scene, and arguing that some are contrived while others are natural and convincing for the audience. As he arbitrates between Homer and the Bible, Chateaubriand echoes Aristotle's interest in assessing the quality of recognition scenes. While the meeting between the beggar (i.e. Ulysses) and Telemachus has the potential for dramatic pathos, Chateaubriand feels that Homer has actually spoilt it. The scene as such starts well: Ulysses sets out to meet his son and to reveal his identity to him. The sudden introduction of the goddess who restores Ulysses's health and looks and replaces his rags with royal attire makes the scene unnatural, contrived, and somehow lacking in warmth. When the passions of the reader are to be aroused, "all the wonders ought to emanate from human sentiment", and not from divine intervention.[31] Ulysses, making himself known despite his disguise by some natural feature or mark, would have induced more sympathy, and hence been less contrived and more convincing. Homer did much better elsewhere; thus Euryclea, Ulysses's nurse, recognises the hero by an ancient scar, and Laertes, his aged father, by his reference to some pear trees that the good old man had given to Ulysses as a child. "We love to find that the 'destroyer of cities' has a heart like everyone else, and that the simple affections are its basic element."[32] Homer, then, though capable of telling his story well, failed in the case quoted through resorting to artifice in a scene that required only the simplicity and immediacy of everyday life.

In the corresponding biblical episode, Joseph dramatically switches from confronting his brothers as an Egyptian bureaucrat to welcoming them as a brother. No divine intervention spoils the scene here, for it is only humans who interact. Nevertheless, the divine does come into the picture, as Chateaubriand carefully notes. The great counsel of God governs all human affairs even at moments when they seem to be ruled only by human passions and the laws of chance; the revelation of this fact wonderfully surprises the mind. Don't we love the idea that there is a hidden hand incessantly engaged with us? Don't we love to imagine that we play a role in the plans of divine wisdom, that our transient life has a special meaning in the divine design? Scripture, at any rate, "never fails to introduce Providence into the perspective of its pictures".[33] It is important, however, that Providence is not simply an impersonal force at work in human life. "I am here by the will of the Lord", says Joseph. Had he said, "Fortune has favoured me", depriving God of all intimate, personal involvement, the scene would have lost its impact. The universal perspective of divine intent would disappear, the circle would contract, and the pathos would vanish along with the tears.

The biblical episode ends with a simple, unadorned statement – "the only magnificence of style adapted to such occasions":[34] "And he falls upon Benjamin's neck, and kisses him, and weeps; and Benjamin weeps also, as he holds him in his embrace." Homer, by contrast, spoils the simplicity by adding one of his doubtful similes – comparing the sobs of father and son with the cries of an eagle for its young that have just fallen victim to a hunter, thus awkwardly equating the tender tears of gain with the bird's cry of loss.[35] Thus on all counts, the biblical writer's art emerges as superior to that of the Homeric poet.

The third, and final, episode considered by Chateaubriand involves Nestor, the Greek king of Pylos, a man known for his wisdom and his unsurpassed mastery of rhetoric:

> Slow from his seat arose the Pylean sage,
> experienced Nestor, in persuasion skilled;
> words sweet as honey from his lips distilled.
> Two generations now had passed away,
> wise by his rules, and happy by his sway;
> two ages o'er his native realm he reigned,
> and now th' example of the third remained.[36]

Chateaubriand praises the passage for its soft melody and literary perfection, admiring the skilful alliteration using the letter "l" to imitate the mellifluous cadence of the sage's speech: *toû kaì apò glôssês mélitos glykíôn rhéen audê* ("words sweet as honey from his lips distilled"). Whereas the idea of praising the Homeric passage is not his own (having been expressed in Rollin's manual on education),[37] Chateaubriand's comparison of the Greek scene with a corresponding biblical passage is original and unique: old Jacob looks back on his life as short and troubled, marked by hardship and sorrow; old Nestor, by contrast, is presented as someone whose wise and happy rule extends into the third generation. Two kinds of sentiment can be discerned here: the ancient Greek mentality expressing itself in a sequence of pleasing images, inviting us to share its affirmation of the world; and the Hebrew melancholy or *tristesse*. Chateaubriand feels that Hebrew melancholy is superior to the shallow joy inspired by the words of Homer. Again, the triumph of the Joseph story is complete. In fact, the triumph *must* be complete, for Chateaubriand's philosophy requires the interchangeability of beauty and truth. If the Bible is to be set higher on the scale of truth, it must also be higher on the scale of beauty.

Although the triumph of the tale of Joseph is indeed complete, we must remind ourselves that it was not the aim of our Romantic author to extol biblical scenes at the expense of Homer. For Chateaubriand, the *Odyssey* and the *Iliad* remain valuable classical texts; they are brought in only to highlight, by comparative analysis, "some of the innumerable beauties of the sacred Scriptures".[38] Comparing Homer and the Bible, ultimately, means comparing beauty with beauty and literary excellence with literary excellence, revealing mere shades of distinction. Elsewhere, our author refers to the Bible and Homer as his favourite reading, the ultimate literary models for his own writing, calling them "the two grand and eternal models of beauty and truth".[39]

Chateaubriand's comparison of the biblical Joseph story with Homer's *Odyssey* may not in fact be entirely original. At the end of his famous English translation of the *Odyssey* (1726), Alexander Pope inserted a note that provides a precedent, if not a source, for Chateaubriand. Book XVI of the *Odyssey*, he explains,

> in general is very beautiful in the original; the discovery of Ulysses to Telemachus is particularly tender and affecting. It has some resemblance with that of Joseph's discovery of himself to his brethren, and it may not perhaps be disagreeable to see how two such authors describe the same passion:
> I am Joseph, I am your brother Joseph. (Genesis 45: 4)
> I am Ulysses, I, my son, am he!
> And he wept aloud, and he fell on his brother's neck and wept. (Genesis 45: 14)
> He wept abundant, and he wept aloud.[40]

Pope does not stop after pointing out the parallelism. He goes on to compare the literary merit of the two texts thus juxtaposed:

> But it must be owned that Homer falls infinitely short of Moses. He must be a very wicked man that can read the history of Joseph without the utmost touches of compassion and transport. There is a majestic simplicity in the whole relation, and such an affecting portrait of human nature that it overwhelms us with vicissitudes of joy and sorrow. This is a pregnant instance [of] how much the best of heathen writers is inferior to the divine historian, upon a parallel subject, where the two authors endeavour to move the softer passions.[41]

Here we have the substance of what Chateaubriand writes about Homer and Joseph, including the reference to "majestic simplicity", hallmark of the sublime. No doubt Chateaubriand saw Pope's translation of the *Odyssey* during his exile in England, and he could well have been impressed with the work and the literary judgement of his fellow Catholic. We may therefore venture the suggestion that it was precisely this passage found in the work of Pope that inspired Chateaubriand's comparison between Homer and the Bible.

Another source that Chateaubriand consulted, and echoed in his own writing, is the article "Joseph" in Voltaire's *Dictionnaire philosophique*. In this case, we can see how Chateaubriand followed and, more often and more fundamentally, departed from Voltaire. In fact, the tale of Joseph resonated with the worldview and mentality of the two authors in distinctly different ways.

The Joseph story is superior to the *Odyssey*: Voltaire and Chateaubriand agree on this. However, they give different reasons. The Enlightenment philosopher appreciates Joseph as a man of virtue, a generous and forgiving man, while he feels that Ulysses is not an ideal role model – a man who, upon returning to his home and estate, kills those who, previously entertained as guests, had ruined his possessions and made advances to his wife. Voltaire appreciated the Joseph story as a moral tale, a *conte philosophique* very much in tune with his own attitude as well as with his own storytelling. Voltaire apparently loved the ups and downs of Joseph's fate, and he shared in its general optimism, approving of the happy ending of the biblical story. While Chateaubriand appreciated the literary and aesthetic merits of the Joseph story, particularly in isolated emotional scenes, he only very briefly alludes to Joseph's generosity and pays little attention to the overall moral and philosophical message. Apparently, Chateaubriand was not impressed with this success story of a hero who ascends from rags to riches, from slavery to governorship. His lack of enthusiasm for this theme must be seen in the light of "Atala" and "René", the two short novels he included in the original edition of *Génie du Christianisme*. Clearly, the biblical biography is quite unlike Chateaubriand's poignant tales of *Weltschmerz*, and we can infer that he found beauty less in the pathos conveyed by the storyline than in individual, carefully crafted emotional scenes. It is also notable that Chateaubriand does not fail to comment on the somewhat pessimistic words of the old patriarch Joseph, empathising with words that seem to come from a human heart akin to his own: a heart suffering from *tristesse*. Voltaire, who also refers to Jacob's words, may have experienced moments of melancholy, but *tristesse* did not characterise his mood, even in old age. He remained an Enlightenment optimist who believed in progress to the end of his days.

If we look at their biographies as well as their work in general we can see that neither Voltaire nor Chateaubriand was, as it were, naturally susceptible to the beauty of biblical stories. Voltaire generally attacked the Bible as a document of ancient superstition that prevented its modern readers from seeing the world in rational, Enlightenment terms. Chateaubriand, according to what we know of his youth, was apparently more interested in Homer than the book of Genesis, and it was a pocket Homer, and not the Bible, that he carried with him as a soldier fighting during the French Revolution.[42] Yet both of them came to study the Bible and to agree on the literary craft exhibited by its story. They both offer perceptive interpretations of its beauty, interpretations that anticipate interest in "the Bible as literature" by writers who in the twentieth and twenty-first centuries were to rediscover the aesthetic quality of biblical texts and to celebrate the Bible as providing the basis for a spiritual universe in which the whole of Western culture developed and flourished, including its art and literature.

Chateaubriand's literary canon

Once the literary quality of the Bible had been established, the entire history of Western literature could be rewritten. Chateaubriand boldly insists that Christianity never lacked good authors. In fact, it was their religion that enabled Christian writers to vie with and even surpass their pagan predecessors, and in this they had frequently succeeded. To give his revisionist views at least the semblance of plausibility, Chateaubriand offers a new account of literary history.

Literature, according to Chateaubriand, first existed in Hebrew, Greek, and Latin – with the Bible, Homer, and Virgil. After Virgil, literary history continues with the church fathers who nourished Christian readers for many centuries. In modern times, in sixteenth-century Italy literary creativity reached a peak when Torquato Tasso celebrated the first crusade in his epic poem *Gerusalemme liberata* (*Jerusalem Delivered*), but its Golden Age lay in the seventeenth century, when in France Bossuet and Racine dominated ecclesiastical and cultural life, and in England Milton wrote *Paradise Lost*. Chateaubriand celebrates this as the supreme example of Christian poetry, a work of such stature that it vies with ancient Greek and Roman literature which, in the seventeenth century (i.e. before Voltaire), provided the standard for literary achievement. (Chateaubriand would agree with John Dennis who asserted in 1701 that Milton's poetry is superior to that of Virgil, "purely by the advantage of his religion".)[43] Then came the evil century of the Enlightenment, the age of Voltaire and his adepts, an age intent on undermining and eventually destroying the authority of the church. Chateaubriand sees the eighteenth century as a period of cultural decline. While admitting that in his youth he had occasionally admired certain eighteenth-century authors, he was now disillusioned with them. "Even in the greatest of the authors of the age of Voltaire I find passages marked by a poverty of sentiment, thinking, and style."[44] And when brilliant pages do occur, this was due to the impact of Christianity even on unbelieving authors, as exemplified by the most exquisite scenes in Voltaire's stage plays.[45]

Chateaubriand's review of the history of literature is cluttered with a plethora of names of authors and works, even a mere list of which would require several pages. But if we restrict attention to the works that are extensively quoted, commented upon, and recommended, a short list comprising Chateaubriand's essential Christian library emerges. Set out roughly in chronological order and arranged by literary type, it looks like this:

ancient literature:	Homer, Virgil, Bible
church fathers:	Tertullian, John Chrysostom, Augustine
epic poetry:	Dante, *Divina Commedia*; Tasso, *Gerusalemme liberata*; Milton, *Paradise Lost*
theatre:	Racine (especially *Athalie*); Corneille, *Polyeucte*; Voltaire (only two plays: *Zaïre, Alzire*)
novels:	Fénelon, *Les Aventures de Télémaque*; Bernardin de Saint-Pierre, *Paul et Virginie*; Chateaubriand (two short novels, both included in *Génie du Christianisme*: "Atala" and "René")
historians:	Bossuet, Montesquieu, Charles Rollin
orators:	Bossuet, Massillon
philosophers:	La Bruyère; Pascal, *Pensées*

Our author is far from offering a complete analysis of the literature he recommends. He never considers literary works as a whole (as we do today); instead he looks at individual, isolated passages, which he quotes to indicate their literary merit. This anthological approach – the study of literature based on short extracts – not only dominates the section on "Homer and the Bible", it characterises all of Chateaubriand's literary criticism. No invention of his, this method was quite common in the seventeenth, eighteenth, and nineteenth centuries.[46] Is it possible to profit from everything one finds in a printed book? No, says Johann Amos Comenius (1592–1670), and he tells students to select memorable passages from what they read, copy them, and commit them to memory.[47] Are teachers to inflict complete books on their students? No, says practically minded Bishop Fénelon in his reading list for the young duc de Bourgogne,[48] and Charles Rollin's *De la manière d'enseigner et d'étudier les belles-lettres* (1726/28) agrees. Would people read all of Shakespeare? No, they would rely on literary anthologies such as William Dodd's *Beauties of Shakespeare* (1752). In other words, the intelligent approach is to study the best pages from the best authors. Is it too daring to suggest that the anthological approach reflects the same mentality that produced the Romantic appreciation of fragments and aphorisms and, in architecture, the enthusiasm for ruins; that is, for incomplete architectural monuments? Sometimes the anthological approach led to absurd behaviour, as in the case of one of Chateaubriand's acquaintances: this man would cut pages he considered irrelevant out of the books he owned, in order to create a library whose damaged volumes included only beautiful texts within now oversized covers.[49] No less absurd is it, says Bishop Fénelon, when preachers, misconstruing their essential task, teach their audience only on the basis of isolated scriptural passages chosen for their literary appeal, without placing them in the wider context of the biblical story.[50] Those who rely on isolated texts, the bishop warns, risk distorting their meaning and message and preventing the congregation from learning what is necessary for salvation. Nevertheless, the anthological approach prevailed even amongst those who understood its limitations.

Passages were most often selected for the emotional impact they could make – scenes of recognition, love, nature, solitude, or sorrow. Sadness (*tristesse*) and melancholy figure prominently among the feelings discerned, described, and appreciated by Chateaubriand and other Romantic authors. In addition to the anthological method and the emotional focus, a third feature characterises Chateaubriand's literary criticism: the comparative approach, applied to entire groups of texts. When citing the Psalm of Creation (Ps. 104), "a masterpiece", Chateaubriand insists that Horace and Pindar never attained such perfection.[51] To assess literary merit, our author compares not only the Old Testament with the ancient classical authors, but also the speeches of Bossuet and Massillon with those of Demosthenes and Cicero. From his comparative analysis, French literature does not emerge as inferior to that of the ancient world. When looking at Euripides's tragedy *Iphigenia in Tauris* (*c.* 414 BCE) and Jean Racine's *Iphigénie* (1674), he has no hesitation in preferring the latter, arguing that works of modern masters may surpass those of the ancients they sought to imitate. Similarly, in Chateaubriand's discussion of historians, Bishop Bossuet ranks higher than Tacitus. And how is it possible to achieve such perfection? It is all down to their authors' superior religion. Biblical and Christian authors can produce work that is superior to those of pagans and non-believers, because "the Christian religion is so felicitously designed that it is in itself a kind of poetry (*une sorte de poésie*)".[52]

Although Chateaubriand's *Génie du Christianisme* made its author a famous man, not all early readers accepted its argument. Critics frequently objected to the author's apologetic programme on the grounds that it lacks depth and makes Christianity look rather superficial. But such an objection overlooks Chateaubriand's deep roots in Western philosophy, or, more precisely, in the Platonic idea that beauty echoes the divine and the true. According to traditional Western philosophy, that which is true is also beautiful; conversely, that which is beautiful is also true. Thus in any statement, "true" and "beautiful" may be exchanged (*verum et pulchrum convertuntur*).[53] This philosophical doctrine implies that beauty is not just outward splendour, but reveals a deeper, spiritual reality and may therefore be called "the splendour of truth". Romanticism was particularly receptive to this doctrine, which John Keats summed up with admirable brevity:

"Beauty is truth, truth beauty" – that is all
Ye know on earth, and all ye need to know.[54]

Those who share Keats's and Chateaubriand's Romantic enthusiasm may well find some of this twofold splendour in the story of Joseph in Egypt.

Epilogue: Joseph in Paris

In French cultural history, the eighteenth and the nineteenth centuries form two distinct, sharply differentiated periods. The eighteenth century is the era of Voltaire, the Enlightenment, and the Revolution that ended the *ancien régime* and its monarchy. The nineteenth century brought not only the rule of Napoleon and the restoration of law and order, but also Romanticism and its cult of the imagination. One important difference between the two centuries lies in their prevailing attitude to religion: the Age of Reason was not favourable to it, at least not to its established forms and creeds, so anticlericalism reigned; the Age of Imagination, by contrast, led many to rediscover religious sentiment, the church, and the Bible.

That the new century meant the dawn of a new era could not escape notice in Paris in the spring of 1802. On Easter Sunday, Napoleon staged a High Mass in Notre Dame, to celebrate the restoration of the Catholic Church in France, for it was then that the Concordat concluded with the pope in 1801 was to take effect. In this document, the French government recognised the Catholic religion as being that "of the great majority of the French citizens" (*la grande majorité des citoyens français*) and as beneficial for "the maintenance of civil peace" (*le maintien de la tranquillité intérieure*). All bishops and priests had, from then on, to swear an oath to support the government and to avoid anything that would upset peace, law, and order. At the end of each service, a short prayer was to be said for the state: "O Lord, save the republic. O Lord, save the consuls."[55] (Between 1799 and 1804 France was governed by three consuls, with Napoleon chief amongst them – before he became emperor.) Hence in 1802 – after a decade of turmoil, with the church divided into two factions, one supporting the Revolution's Civil Constitution and swearing allegiance to the new state, and the other refusing to do so – churches were opened again and ecclesiastical life began to resume its normal course. After a decade of silence, the church bells were heard again throughout the country.

As peace reigned in the church and in France, a spiritual renewal was called for, to heal at least some of the damage the *philosophes* had done to Christianity's reputation. This renewal could come only from the very class that had brought about and supported the Enlightenment – the intellectual elite of writers and philosophers. From among the new, post-revolutionary elite came a work published in Paris on 14 April 1802, just four days before Napoleon's Easter Mass – Chateaubriand's *Génie du Christianisme*. As understood by the educated, this work fought Enlightenment anticlericalism both by restoring Christianity's intellectual respectability and by presenting it as emotionally appealing. To its early readers, the book confirmed the notion that they were now living in a completely new era, one comparable to that of the Emperor Constantine who, after putting an end to Diocletian's bloody persecution of Christians, made the church the very foundation of the Roman Empire. In thanking the author for a copy of *Génie du Christianisme,* Jean-François de la Harpe hailed Napoleon as the new Constantine. "One can hardly exaggerate the difference between the end of the year 1799, when Paris had a mere three churches functioning, and Easter Sunday in 1802, when the ceremony of Notre Dame was held", he reflected.[56] It was like the difference between the age of anxiety when Christians had to hide and worship in secret in the catacombs, and the age of triumph when Christian worship began to replace pagan sacrifice in Constantine's Roman Empire. *Génie du Christianisme* was an immediate success, becoming the new, post-revolution generation's favourite book and making its author one of the most popular writers of his time.

As church bells rang out across France again in 1802, cultural life was resumed in Paris. There, society during the first decade of the nineteenth century was singularly receptive to all things oriental. Napoleon's successful Egyptian campaign (1789–1799) inspired architects to add Egyptian stylistic features to buildings, and designers to create furniture in the same mode. "Joseph in Egypt" was a natural choice for staging in both theatre and opera.[57] *Omasis, ou Joseph en Egypte,* by Pierre Baour-Lormian, opened at the Théâtre Français on 14 September 1806. Alexandre Duval's *Joseph,* set to music by the well-known composer Etienne-Nicolas Méhul, saw its first performance at the Théâtre Feydeau on 17 February 1807. The audiences at these performances were no doubt charmed by the splendour of orientalising aesthetics, entertained by the love intrigues, and reassured by the message of peace and harmony. Scenes of reconciliation spoke to a society divided and wounded by more than a decade of war, bloodshed, and revolution, and which now needed a new beginning.

Baour-Lormian's stage play and Duval's opera each attracted supporters and friends, and the merits of the two seem to have been a favourite subject of polite conversation in the *salons* of Paris.[58] While both plays focused on the final, reconciliation scene of the biblical story, they differed in detail. To make the simple plot of the biblical story more captivating, Baour-Lormian added intrigue and romantic interest.[59] He introduces sister and brother, Almaïs and Rhamnès. Almaïs, a beautiful Egyptian girl, has been promised to Omasis (alias Joseph) with whom she is deeply, and madly, in love; but her brother seeks to dissuade her: a foreign slave is not exactly the best possible match for an Egyptian princess. Without introducing these elements, it would have been impossible for the playwright to hold the attention of the audience throughout the five acts.

However, Baour-Lormian's play is badly integrated: the love intrigue and the reconciliation plot are juxtaposed rather than intertwined; the first half of the play is dominated by the figure of Almaïs who then, without rhyme or reason, disappears from the limelight to give way to Omasis, his brothers and his aged father. The Almaïs episode was a distinct failure as a prelude to the actual story told. Duval, by contrast, wrote a much shorter piece in three acts, in prose rather than rhymed verse, with a simple and straightforward storyline: beginning shortly before Joseph's father and brothers arrive in Egypt, the opera ends with the final reconciliation of the Hebrews.[60] Duval and Méhul's *Joseph* won the applause of the audiences at the Théâtre Feydeau, if not (apparently) earning the house much income. Duval reports that the modest financial success of his *Joseph* in Paris was amply compensated at the provincial theatres where the piece became popular; rather than contributing to his own income, he adds with a sense of regret, it "filled the pockets of opera directors" in the provinces[61] – presumably, we may add, due to Méhul's music rather than to Duval's libretto. Nevertheless, the piece was very successful, even beyond France. Soon, it was to figure prominently in the repertoire of German opera houses, and Goethe, Germany's most famous director of opera, made it one of his favourites.[62] In German lands, it resonated with Romantic sensibilities. "A truly patriarchal atmosphere and way of life are combined here with a childlike purity of religious devotion", wrote Carl Maria von Weber in 1817. And, the musician added, "The composer here disdains all tinsel and tawdry; truth of expression is his endeavour, and beautiful, moving melody guides his genius."[63]

We do not know whether Chateaubriand took any notice of this Joseph, hero of the stage, as celebrated in Napoleonic Paris; or, if he did, how he felt about it. But we may take his book as a guide. From the perspective of *Génie du Christianisme*, presentations of "Joseph" in the form of stage plays and operas serve an important function: that of reminding the audience of the religious foundation of their culture. These performances were meant to fill the theatres and opera houses of Europe, as well as the hearts of audiences, with beauty and truth, the divine light and splendour that emanate from the Bible alone.

Postscript

This book started, about two decades ago, as a random collection of echoes of the story of Joseph in early-modern literature. Whenever I came across a literary version or adaptation of the Genesis story, or a reference to it in a letter or diary, I made a note and dropped it into a file. Photocopies of letters by Voltaire, a page from James Boswell's diary, notes made during my bedtime reading of Goethe's autobiography and during (yes, during) the preaching of a sermon, and reflections quickly jotted down after visiting an art gallery – all these fed into my file, so that it grew and grew. It became my most valued treasure, although for quite some time I did not know what it all meant and what to think of it. Is the Joseph story primarily a didactic tale for children? What to make of Joseph the Freemason? And who was Monsieur Boulanger to whom Voltaire attributes a complete reinterpretation of the biblical story? "I must find the answer", I decided. "I must solve these riddles."

Clearly, in early-modern times, the figure of Joseph was open to a whole variety of uses and interpretations. While this observation came easily, its interpretation required some effort. Gradually, I came to understand that very special qualities and functions attached to the story of this biblical character: it served as a kind of privileged storage place for traditional wisdom; at the same time, authors used it as a framework or platform for the discussion of new ideas about exemplary human behaviour. This special quality is perhaps best termed "iconic", for an icon, to all with eyes to see, permits a multiplicity of commentaries and readings. Research in specialised bibliographies, manuals of literary and cultural history, and periodicals too numerous to list led to the conclusion that hitherto scholars had not given much thought to Joseph as an iconic figure. This was understandable, for literary historians seem to consider the subject as belonging to biblical studies, while biblical interpreters (generally theologians) feel that the subject, requiring as it does training in the study of literature, is more properly the domain of historians of literature or, more generally, cultural historians. To research and write about Joseph as a cultural icon would require, I concluded, someone who is willing to get involved with the two relevant disciplines: the study of literature and the study of biblical interpretation. Accordingly, a book on the subject would somewhat ambitiously seek to contribute to both these disciplines. Here, I felt, was a challenge I might respond to. I soon also realised that each of the two disciplines presented its own specific challenges.

In contemporary literary studies one is confronted with two basic options: that of studying a literary work as an aesthetic object to be understood and enjoyed in itself, and that of considering it as being rooted in a particular historical, social, and cultural context. In this respect, I happen to belong to those who insist that, with regard to a work of literature, the cultural context forms the primary interpretative framework. This context, found outside the work to be studied, may be visualised as surrounding it, and the interpreter may be pictured as someone exploring an area by going for a walk. If you want to understand, and perhaps appreciate, an author and his or her work, you cannot just stay at home. What I, as the explorer, eventually came to know is both the work analysed and its surroundings. Accordingly, I found myself in the well-known circular situation: documents of literature and art shed light on the cultural situation in which they originated; yet these documents echo, and can only be understood in the light of, that very situation. Joseph the statesman, represented in novels or on the stage, can only be understood against the background of early-modern political life in Europe; conversely, Joseph the statesman helps us understand certain aspects of that very political life. Interpretation inevitably is a circular process: the meaning of cultural artefacts depends upon the whole of the cultural context, but the context can only be accessed through its manifestation in individual sources such as texts. In cultural analysis, as in many fields of research, interpreters can never find an exterior vantage point from which to judge; they cannot but work within this tricky, though ultimately delightful circle. Only long and intensive engagement within this circle will ultimately yield insight.

In addition to making a contribution to the study of early-modern culture, this book is intended to serve biblical studies; or, more exactly, to help fill a rather curious gap in this academic discipline. Biblical studies, as generally practised in university departments of theology, focus on recovering (hypothetically, it must be admitted) what a story, a custom, a book, or an individual passage meant for its original – i.e. oriental, non-Western – audience in the biblical period. Proud of the progress they have made during the last two centuries, biblical scholars celebrate their achievements in philological and historical research as those of an enlightened age that finally understands the ancient text, while all previous ("pre-critical") ages were marked by a certain amount of ignorance, sometimes bordering on tragic misunderstanding.

Theologians, devoted as they are to the agenda of their trade, typically show little interest in exactly how Moses, Abraham, Joseph, or Jesus and their stories were understood – or misunderstood – in, say, the seventeenth century. Yet biblical characters and themes are not to be strictly confined to Holy Scripture; they often take on a manifold life of their own in art, literature, and education, a life of astonishing vitality. Historians of culture and the arts – as well as scholars in other disciplines – have come to appreciate the impact that biblical figures, texts, and themes made on writers, artists, teachers, and their public through the ages. Accordingly, the need for studies that deal with the cultural "reception" and use of the Bible is increasingly evident; but, alas, such studies are rare.

Today, the growing interest in the "reception" and treatment of the Bible in the arts necessitates the establishment of a new field of biblical studies alongside the more traditional philological research in the Old and New Testaments, a discipline provisionally called *the cultural history of biblical interpretation*. In essence it is cultural history done with the Bible in hand. The many ways in which people during the two millennia that separate us from biblical times have interpreted, and been influenced by, the canonical text of the Bible and its apocryphal supplement is as interesting and historically relevant as discerning what it meant for its original audience. The emergent discipline suggests a fresh way of looking at the history of biblical interpretation: while the traditional paradigm compared modern exegetical achievements with past ignorance, the new paradigm more modestly grants all ages the equal privilege of creatively appropriating a biblical text, coming to terms with it and making it uniquely their own. The new paradigm, moreover, no longer allows the philologist and historian to triumph over the preacher, the creative writer, or artist. The Joseph story, used and reused as demonstrated here by early-modern writers, artists, and educators, offers one such exemplary model for study.

One afternoon in the spring of 2008, when chatting over tea with a colleague from the literature department, conversation naturally focused on Joseph, as many times before. "Do you have a title for the book?" she asked. "*Joseph in Egypt: A Cultural Icon from Grotius to Goethe*", I answered, for this title was my favourite of several that I had considered. "Sounds like a celebration of your favourite figure in the Bible." "That may well be the case", I replied. "But this book is to tell the story of how Grotius, Goethe, Fielding, and Voltaire, and many others celebrated *their* favourite character." And as our conversation continued we agreed that the seventeenth and eighteenth centuries may have been the last period in European cultural history to have been characterised by an almost universal knowledge and appreciation of characters found in the Bible. We also agreed that the story of Joseph, as read and rewritten in early-modern times, could indeed serve as a room with a view – a panoramic view over the wide landscape of early-modern culture and its paramount themes: educating children, stemming the tide of libertinism, leading the state in difficult times, applying critical thought, and enjoying literature (as discussed, in this sequence, in the book).

It is a long way from references assembled more or less at random to the initial idea for a book, and, finally, to sustained research and writing. My dense teaching schedule in Scotland and Germany as well as other writing commitments were unfavourable for a while, but eventually, time was found, friends were willing to help, and my own enthusiasm was kindled.

The present book could not have been written without the assistance of librarians in several countries – those of the state and national libraries of Berlin, Hamburg, London, Munich, Paris, and Zurich; the university libraries of St Andrews and Paderborn; the specialised collections of the Herzog-August-Bibliothek in Wolfenbüttel, the Goethehaus in Frankfurt, and the Institut für historische Bildungsforschung (Pestalozzianum) in Zurich. Among many, I single out librarians Edeltrud Büchler, Colin Bovaird, and Ruth Villiger who, in their respective countries, have been most helpful at various stages. Much advice, help, and encouragement also came from Gabriele Dürbeck, Hans-Werner Engels, Bertram Schwarzbach, and Gia Toussaint, friends and specialists in a variety of relevant disciplines including the history of literature, early-modern culture and religion, and the study of art. I am grateful to photographer Adelheid Rutenburges for collecting and editing the illustrations. Finally, I would like to thank my Scottish editor of English for her invaluable assistance with the manuscript and for her help with translations from the French. All of the above were indispensable in helping my Joseph project to emerge, progress, and reach completion. The finished work is dedicated to my colleagues at St Mary's College, University of St Andrews, Scotland, who, like me, search for light and truth in such venerable tales.

Notes

Chapter 1: Joseph as a Cultural Icon in Early-Modern Times

1. Bunyan, *The Life and Death of Mr. Badman*, 55; Dodd, *The Beauties of History*, 298; Scarron, *The Comical Romance*, vol. 1, 16.
2. Ong, *Orality and Literacy*, 70.
3. Curtius, *Europäische Literatur und lateinisches Mittelalter*, 70.
4. Henry, *Commentary on the Whole Bible*, 2203 on Romans 4: 23; the relevant volume of this commentary dates from 1720.
5. Fielding, *The History of Tom Jones*, vol. 1, 7.
6. The stock example of this terminology is "Cato, the living image of all virtues" (*Cato, ille virtutum viva imago*): Seneca, *De tranquillitate animi*, 16: 2. Moos, *Geschichte als Topik*, 340–41, 462, 585–86 lists medieval examples of the "iconic" terminology; he also discusses medieval interest in exemplars of virtue (xxv–xxvi).
7. Beckermann, *Theatrical Presentation*, 48. See Beckermann's insightful chapter "Iconic Presentation" (43–55).
8. Lang, *Sacred Games*, 138–48: "On Intellectual Ritual".
9. Engelsing, *Der Bürger als Leser*, 183.
10. Hunter, *Before Novels*, 235.
11. Erasmus of Rotterdam, "Enchiridion militis christiani" (*Ausgewählte Schriften*, vol. 1, 372).
12. Fielding, *Joseph Andrews*, 155 (book 2, chap. 12).
13. Rousseau, *Les Confessions*, 579–80 (book 11). On daily Bible reading in the early-modern period, see Lang, "Buchreligion", 156–57.
14. The relevance a "hero" may have for the reader is studied in Unger, *On Religious Experience*, 9–32 (a summary of the work of Hjalmar Sundén, with a key example on p. 22); Jauss, *Aesthetic Experience and Literary Hermeneutics*, 152–88.
15. Chartier, *The Order of Books*, 1. Chartier here quotes the French essayist Michel de Certeau.
16. Boswell, *Life of Johnson*, 303–4 (14 July 1763).
17. Moritz, *Anton Reiser*, 171; emotional involvement, 173.
18. Wittmann, "Gibt es eine Leserevolution".
19. Voltaire, *Les Oeuvres complètes*, vol. 66, 395.
20. Ibid., 377.
21. For one such survey, see Fischer, *Handbuch zu Thomas Manns "Josephsromanen"*, 236–73. Fischer's list includes some 110 Joseph titles printed between *c.* 1600 and 1800. My own list, much longer, includes, in addition to many books for children, four authors not mentioned by Fischer but selected for study in the present book: Chateaubriand, Goethe, Morgan, and Voltaire. A remarkable annotated anthology of some early-modern Joseph materials is

McGaha, *The Story of Joseph in Spanish Golden Age Drama*. Four short interpretative essays, in German and French, deserve to be mentioned: Singer, "Joseph in Ägypten. Zur Erzählkunst des 17. und 18. Jahrhunderts"; Stüssel, *In Vertretung. Literarische Mitschriften von Bürokratie zwischen früher Neuzeit und Gegenwart*, 37–67; Brottier, "Joseph le politique", 57–68; and van der Schueren, "La Tragédie biblique à Sceaux: le Joseph de Charles-Claude Genest (1706)".

22. Pigler, *Barockthemen*, vol. 1, 74–94; Fischer, *Handbuch zu Thomas Manns "Josephsromanen"*, 273–91. The relevant iconology and medieval iconography is discussed in Erffa, *Ikonologie der Genesis*, vol. 2, 389–474.
23. Bocian, *Lexikon der biblischen Personen*, 270–73.
24. Tzschimmer, *Durchlauchigste Zusammenkunfft*, vol. 1, 136. For the (anonymous) Joseph play performed at the court of Dresden, see vol. 1, 131–43; 149–53; 157–60.
25. Thomasius in the January 1688 number of his journal *Monatsgespräche* (Thomasius, *Deutsche Schriften*, 124).
26. Koselleck, *Futures Past*, 21–38.
27. Mann, *Joseph and His Brothers*, originally published in German in 1933–1943; Lampo, *Gelöbnis an Rachel*.
28. Voltaire, *Lettres philosophiques*, letter 18 (*Oeuvres complètes* [Moland], vol. 22, 152).

Chapter 2: Joseph in Genesis

1. Genesis 37; 39–48; 50 – twelve chapters.
2. The traditional rendering is "a coat of many colours".
3. For a reconstruction of the orally transmitted Joseph story as a story of a hero's initiation, see Lang, "Joseph the Diviner: Careers of a Biblical Hero".
4. Earlier critical claims that Genesis 37–50 dates from the tenth century BCE have generally been abandoned. The exact date of the Joseph story, however, is still controversial. Today, many agree with Redford, *A Study of the Biblical Story of Joseph*, 242, that a date between 700 and 425 BCE – with a tendency to prefer the fifth century – is most likely. In palaeo-Hebrew inscriptions, the name "Joseph" (YSP) appears first in a seal impression dating from c. 600 BCE: see Avigad, *Hebrew Bullae*, 88 (no. 131). Later, from the third or second century BCE, "Joseph" is among the most common names of Jews: see Horbury and Noy, *Jewish Inscriptions of Graeco-Roman Egypt*, 1; Ilan, *Lexicon of Jewish Names in Late Antiquity*, 150–68, echoing the biblical Joseph story and its canonical standing within Jewish literature.
5. On the Jewish Diaspora novella, in the Bible also represented by the books of Ruth, Esther, Daniel, and Jonah, see Meinhold, "Die Gattung der Josephsgeschichte und des Estherbuches"; Römer, "La Narration, une subversion". Grottanelli, "Biblical Narrative and the Ancient Novel", adduces comparative material from Hellenistic sources.
6. Genesis 50: 12–13.26.
7. Note that here there is an echo of the exodus tradition which, in the canonical sequence of events, is placed *after* the Joseph story. As an independent tale, the Joseph story actually presupposes the story of the Israelites suffering as slaves in Egypt. The Joseph story also echoes the exposition of Moses as an infant – Joseph, according to Genesis 37, is exposed in a pit in the desert.
8. Genesis 2: 10–14.
9. Esther 9: 16.
10. Tobit 1: 21–22 (Ahikar); Esther 8: 3.
11. Letter of Aristeas 38 (Charlesworth, ed., *The Old Testament Pseudepigrapha*, vol. 2, 15); Josephus, *Against Apion* II, 49.
12. Nehemiah 1: 11; 2: 1.
13. Xenophon, *Cyropaedia* I, 3,9.
14. Herodotus, *The Histories* III, 34.

15. Renan, *Oeuvres complètes*, vol. 6, 1043–44.
16. Exodus 16: 3.
17. Lüthi, "The Fairy-Tale Hero"; Lüthi, "Märchen und Sage"; see also Röhrich, *Märchen und Wirklichkeit*, 9–27.

Chapter 3: Post-biblical Traditions

1. Josephus, *Jewish Antiquities* II, 9–200; for an interpretation, see Niehoff, "New Garments for Biblical Joseph", 48–55.
2. Artapanus's work is lost, but survives in the form of a summary transcribed by the church father Eusebius; see Charlesworth (ed.), *The Old Testament Pseudepigrapha*, vol. 2, 897–98.
3. Psalm 105: 22, Vulgate.
4. Diodorus Siculus, *The Library of History* I, 54.
5. Philo, *De Iosepho*, translated in Philo, *The Works*, 435–58.
6. Niehoff, "New Garments for Biblical Joseph", 36–47.
7. On the career of Tiberius Julius Alexander, see Modrzejewski, *The Jews of Egypt*, 185–90; Grabbe, *Judaism from Cyrus to Hadrian*, 438–39.
8. *The Testaments of the Twelve Patriarchs*, in Charlesworth (ed.), *The Old Testament Pseudepigrapha*, vol. 1, 775–828. Conventionally the individual "testaments" are quoted as separate works; the "Testament of Joseph", the main source, can be found on pp. 819–25.
9. Charlesworth (ed.), *The Old Testament Pseudepigrapha*, vol. 1, 815 (Testament of Gad).
10. Ibid., 813, 827 (Testament of Naphtali, Testament of Benjamin).
11. Ibid., 784 (Testament of Reuben).
12. Kee, "The Ethical Dimensions of the Testaments of the XII as a Clue to Provenance"; Pervo, "The Testament of Joseph and Greek Romance".
13. As well as being seen in the *Testaments of the Twelve Patriarchs*, this is evident in Wisdom of Solomon 10: 13–14 and 4 Maccabees 2: 1–4, two passages that also refer to Joseph.
14. Rosen-Zvi, "Bilha the Temptress: *The Testament of Reuben* and *The Birth of Sexuality*". Although he does not specifically comment on the sexual ethics of the *Testaments*, one scholar elucidates the Stoic background of this work: Kee, "The Ethical Dimensions of the Testaments of the XII as a Clue to Provenance".
15. Charlesworth (ed.), *The Old Testament Pseudepigrapha*, vol. 1, 825 (Testament of Benjamin 3:1).
16. Vincent of Beauvais, *Speculum historiale* 118–24 (Burchard, "Der jüdische Asenethroman und seine Nachwirkungen", 593–600 – Latin; McGaha, *Coat of Many Cultures*, 455–59, and *The Story of Joseph in Spanish Golden Age Drama*, 318–22 – English translation of *Speculum historiale* 118–22).
17. Qur'ān, sura 12: 3 (*ahsan al-qasas*). A textual commentary is offered by Premare, *Joseph et Muhammad*; an analysis of some of the traditional sources underlying sura 12 can be found in Speyer, *Die biblischen Erzählungen im Qoran*, 187–224.
18. Qur'an, sura 12: 31.
19. A "biographical" reading of sura 12 was first suggested by Stern, "Muhammad and Joseph: A Study of Koranic Narrative".
20. Qur'an, sura 12: 37–38.
21. Firdussi, *Jussuf und Suleicha. Romantisches Heldengedicht*.
22. A complete (French) translation is: Djâmi, *Youssouf et Zouleikha*. The following are free, abridged renderings of Jâmi's work: Jâmi, "Yusuf and Zulaikha", translated by Griffith and Rogers; Jâmi, *Yusuf und Zulaikha: An Allegorical Romance*, translated by Pendlebury.
23. Weil, *Biblische Legenden der Muselmänner*, 100–25.
24. "Unbekannte sind sich nah: Jussuph und Suleika", in: Goethe, *Werke*. Hamburg edition, vol. 2, 27.
25. Alfonso el Sabio, *General estoria* I, 203–63 (books 8 and 9; McGaha, *Coat of Many Cultures*, 335–54 offers a slightly abridged translation).

26. Alfonso el Sabio, *General estoria* I, 208 (book 8, 5; McGaha, *Coat of Many Cultures*, 339, modified).
27. Alfonso el Sabio, *General estoria* I, 220–21 (book 8, 13; McGaha, *Coat of Many Cultures*, 359).
28. Hillgarth, *The Spanish Kingdoms*, vol. 1, 306. Alfonso's support of some of the nobles did not prevent continuous struggle between him and the Castilian nobility; see ibid., 308–11.
29. In Spanish, *ricos hombres*.
30. Hillgarth, *The Spanish Kingdoms*, vol. 1, 63.
31. Diodorus Siculus, *The Library of History* I, 53–55.
32. For the mentality underlying the *General estoria* and other traditional compilations (such as "gospel harmonies") that conflate disparate sources, see Donner, "Der Redaktor".
33. Romanos, *Hymnes*, vol. 1, 262; translated in Schork, *Sacred Song*, 163.
34. Romanos, *Hymnes*, vol. 1, 268/70; translated ibid., 166.
35. Collenuccio, *Operette morali*, 143–279. For a summary of the play, see Weilen, *Der ägyptische Joseph*, 18–21. As a further example of a humanist Joseph drama we may refer to the Latin play "Joseph" (1544) by the Dutch schoolmaster Macropedius, see Best, *Macropedius*, 136–53.
36. Jedin, "Laientheologie im Zeitalter der Glaubensspaltung: Der Konzilsarzt Fracastoro".
37. Fracastoro, "Joseph". Two free translations are available: Sylvester, "The Maiden's Blush"; Chenneville, "Joseph", in: Fracastoro, *Fracastor's poetische und philosophische Schriften*, 127–64.
38. Sylvester, "The Maiden's Blush", 106 (lines 173–74).
39. Kempkens, *Joseph und Aeneas. Untersuchungen zum "Joseph" des Girolamo Fracastoro*.
40. Virgil, *Aeneid* VII, 81–106.
41. Of Wisdom it was said that "she went down with him [Joseph] into the pit", Wisdom of Solomon 10: 13. One could construe personified Wisdom as an angel.
42. Tolstoy, *What Is Art?*, 133.
43. Ibid., 134.
44. Fisch, "Biblical 'Imitation' in *Joseph Andrews*", 38.
45. Ibid., 39.

Chapter 4: On Education

1. For fifteen as the end of childhood, see Lavater, *Ausgewählte Werke in historisch-kritischer Ausgabe*, vol. 3, 477; Basedow, *Das Methodenbuch für Väter und Mütter*, 231.
2. Pech, "Beispielgeschichten"; Moore, "Gottseliges Bezeugen und frommer Lebenswandel"; Alzheimer-Haller, *Handbuch zur narrativen Volksaufklärung*.
3. Anonymous, *Les Devoirs de la vie domestique*, 38–39.
4. Fleury, "Grand catéchisme historique" [1679] (*Oeuvres de l'Abbé Fleury*, vol. 2, 465).
5. Ibid.
6. Rivet, *De la première education d'un Prince*, 45. On the author, see Rang, "An Unidentified Source of John Locke's *Some Thoughts concerning Education*", 251–52.
7. Fénelon, "De l'Éducation des filles" [1687] (Fénelon, *Oeuvres*, vol. 1, 119; *Fénelon on Education*, 34). For the impact this educational approach made in France, see Latapie, "Enseigner l'histoire sainte".
8. Rollin, *Oeuvres complètes*, vol. 25, 134–41.
9. Ibid., 135.
10. Ibid., 139.
11. Diderot, letter to Grimm, 5 June 1759 (*Correspondance*, vol. 2, 154).
12. Baxter, *The Practical Works*, vol. 1, 479–80. Similarly, vol. 4, 233.
13. Rang, "An Unidentified Source of John Locke's *Some Thoughts concerning Education*". Locke owned the second, 1679 edition of Rivet's treatise; for the reference to Joseph and children's reading of (rather than merely listening to) the stories of Genesis, see Rivet, *De l'éducation des enfans*, 32–33.

14. Locke, *Some Thoughts Concerning Education*, 213 (§ 159).
15. Locke belongs to those seventeenth-century thinkers who wished to move away from indoctrinating children on the basis of a catechism whose questions and set answers had to be learned by rote by the child; see Sommerville, "The Distinction between Indoctrination and Education in England".
16. See the reading list suggested by the humanist Maffeo Vegio, *De educatione liberorum* (1444; translated in Mout, *Die Kultur des Humanismus*, 167–68). In Vegio's list, the Psalms actually figure as the very first book a child should be exposed to, even before reading the book of Proverbs. For the book of Psalms as a primer, see Stichel, *Beiträge zur frühen Geschichte des Psalters*, 641–42.
17. Locke, *A Paraphrase and Notes on the Epistles of St Paul*, vol. 1, 105–7.
18. Wesley, *The Complete Writings*, 371.
19. Miller, *My Schools and Schoolmasters*, 28.
20. Hattenhauer (ed.), *Allgemeines Landrecht für die Preußischen Staaten von 1794*, 385–86.
21. Caroline Herder, letter of 25 December 1788 (Herder, *Italienische Reise*, 284).
22. Pockels, "Schack Fluurs Jugendgeschichte", 122.
23. Bottigheimer, *The Bible for Children*; Peter-Perret, *Biblische Geschichten für die Jugend erzählt*; Adam et al. (eds), *Die Inhalte von Kinderbibeln*.
24. Hübner, *Zweymal zwey und funffzig auserlesene biblische Historien*.
25. La Roche, "Mein Glüke", 97.
26. Sophie Gutermann to Wieland, 30 January 1753 (Wieland, *Briefwechsel*, vol. 1, 128–29).

Chapter 5: A Lesson in Godliness – Lavater

1. Lavater, *Vier und zwanzig kurze Vorlesungen über die Geschichte Josephs*, 1.
2. Ibid., preface (no pagination).
3. Widmann, "Der 'jugendbewegte Pestalozzi'".
4. Goethe, *From My Life*, 451–62.
5. Lavater and Pestalozzi, "Etwas für die, welche sich verheuraten wollen", 181–82. This list is apparently a revised extract from a longer one published in the Zurich periodical *Der Maler der Sitten*, 1746; this longer list can be found, with critical commentary, in Bodmer and Breitinger, *Schriften zur Literatur*, 18–19, 301–5.
6. Summary of the Joseph story as told in *Christliches Handbüchlein für Kinder*. A critical edition of the relevant passage can be found in Lavater, *Ausgewählte Werke in historisch-kritischer Ausgabe*, vol. 3, 528–63.
7. Hübner, *Zweymal zwey und funffzig auserlesene biblische Historien*, 61. Lavater apparently used a Swiss edition of the work, see Lavater, *Ausgewählte Werke*, vol. 3, 447.
8. Genesis 18: 22–33.
9. Lavater, *Christliches Handbüchlein für Kinder*, 523; see James 2: 23 where Abraham is called God's friend.
10. Lavater, *Christliches Handbüchlein für Kinder*, 485.
11. Bottigheimer, *The Bible for Children*, 59–66.
12. Lang, *The Hebrew God*, 68.
13. Ibid., 111–14.
14. Lavater, *Christlicher Religionsunterricht für denkende Jünglinge*, [no place, no printer], 1788, 108.
15. Ibid., 111.
16. Ibid., 112: "Er bethet den Gott Israels als seinen Personal-Gott an."
17. Ibid., 87.
18. Goethe, *From My Life*, 275 (translation modified).
19. Starbuck, *The Psychology of Religion*, 327.
20. Novalis, *Werke, Tagebücher und Briefe*, vol. 1, 181 (Geistliche Lieder).
21. Weigelt, *Johann Kaspar Lavater*, 14–16.

22. This tradition started around CE 200: see Erffa, *Ikonologie der Genesis*, vol. 2, 416–28; Argyle, "Joseph the Patriarch in Patristic Teaching"; Fischer, *Handbuch zu Thomas Manns "Josephsromanen"*, 229–35. It is present in the Vulgate (the church father Jerome's Latin translation of the Bible), which renders Joseph's Egyptian name as *salvator mundi* (Saviour of the World), a title also used for Christ; see Genesis 41: 45; John 4: 42 (Vulgate).
23. Hall, *The Works*, vol. 1, 53, in an essay on Joseph.
24. Lavater, *Vier und zwanzig kurze Vorlesungen über die Geschichte Josephs*, 117.
25. Ibid., 84–85.
26. Lang and McDannell, *Heaven: A History*, 197–99.
27. Lavater, *Vier und zwanzig kurze Vorlesungen über die Geschichte Josephs*, preface.
28. Hübner, *Zweymal zwey und funffzig auserlesene biblische Historien*, 71.
29. John Milton, *Paradise Lost*, XII, 569–70.
30. *Biblische Erzählungen für die Jugend. Altes und Neues Testament*, 54. This children's bible, edited by Johann Jacob Hess, was first published in 1772; the anonymous contributor of the "Geschichte Josephs" (pp. 50–72) is Lavater, who seems to have written the text in 1768.
31. On "Joseph and Potiphar's Wife" as a problematic episode in children's bibles, see Bottigheimer, *The Bible for Children*, 116–27.
32. Lavater, *Vier und zwanzig kurze Vorlesungen über die Geschichte Josephs*, 28–29.
33. Schellenberg, *60 Biblische Geschichte des alten Testaments in Kupfer geätzt*.
34. For the nineteenth century, see McDannell, *The Christian Home in Victorian America*; for the eighteenth-century situation, Straub, *Domestic Affairs*, 26–28.
35. Lavater, *Vier und zwanzig kurze Vorlesungen über die Geschichte Josephs*, preface.
36. Ibid., 26–27.
37. Ibid., 5.
38. Lavater, *Christliches Handbüchlein für Kinder*, 485.
39. Herder to Lavater on 30 October 1772; see Herder, *Briefe*, vol. 2, 259.
40. Quoted in Lavater, *Ausgewählte Werke*, vol. 3, 467.
41. The "dear child" (*liebes Kind*) is addressed four times, see Lavater, *Christliches Handbüchlein für Kinder*, 531, 534, 535, 553.

Chapter 6: Starting Life with Joseph – Goethe

1. Goethe, *From My Life*, 113.
2. Ibid., 73.
3. This fact seems to be implied by Goethe's own report: at one point, both Councillor Goethe and Count Thoranc went up to the attic to look at one of the paintings done by Seekatz; Goethe, *From My Life*, 93. Goethe also reports that the finished paintings were "gradually brought into that room", the attic studio (p. 77), with the implication that they were not actually painted there. See also Kölsch, *Johann Georg Trautmann (1713–1769)*, 206.
4. Goethe, *From My Life*, 38–39; see also Mentzel, *Wolfgang und Cornelia Goethes Lehrer*, 91–117.
5. Goethe, *From My Life*, 77.
6. Ibid., 38. In his autobiography, Goethe mentions only the Merian bible, but the illustrated Augsburg children's bible edited by Abraham Kyburz is listed in the auction catalogue of Councillor Goethe's library, see Schnitzer, *Goethes Josephsbilder – Goethes Josephsdichtung*, 75–76.
7. Goethe, *From My Life*, 77.
8. Discovered in 1876 by the dedicated Goethe scholar Martin Schubart in Mouans Castle (municipality of Mouans-Sartoux, southern France), these paintings could be acquired by, or lent to, the Goethe Museum, Frankfurt, which is their present location. For a catalogue of the paintings, see Kölsch, *Johann Georg Trautmann (1713–1769)*, 279–87.
9. Goethe, *From My Life*, 73–74 (for the poet's father), 75 (for the French gentleman).
10. Ibid., 74.

11. Ibid., 49–59.
12. Ibid., 95.
13. Ibid., 113 (translation modified).
14. Ibid., 115.
15. See the relevant entry in Councillor Goethe's book of expenses: Johann Caspar Goethe, *Liber domesticus 1753–1779*, vol. 2, 98 (Latin) and 349 (German translation). See also Mentzel, *Wolfgang und Cornelia Goethes Lehrer*, 198–209. The Yiddish tutor was Karl Christian Christfreund (b. 1723).
16. Johann Caspar Goethe, *Liber domesticus*, 110 (in translation, 358) – entry of September 1762.
17. Goethe, *From My Life*, 114.
18. Ibid., 70.
19. Moser, *Daniel in der Löwen-Grube*, 45–47, with motifs from traditional prayer language and Psalm 27: 1, 8 (as translated by Luther). The book is listed in the spring 1763 catalogue of the Frankfurt book fair, see *Allgemeines Verzeichnis derer Bücher, welche in der Frankfurter und Leipziger Ostermesse des 1763 Jahres [...] herauskommen*, Leipzig: Weidmann, 1763.
20. Moritz, *Anton Reiser*, 38.
21. Ibid., 152.
22. Goethe, *From My Life*, 114.
23. Ibid. (translation modified).
24. Ibid., 115.
25. Ibid., 117.
26. Mentzel, *Die Lehrer Cornelia und Wolfgang Goethes*, 210–38.
27. Goethe, "Belsazar", in: Fischer-Lamberg (ed.), *Der junge Goethe*, vol. 1, 199–201.
28. The poem can be found ibid., 72–76: "Poetische Gedancken über die Höllenfahrt Christi" (Poetic Thoughts on Christ's Descent into Hell).
29. Ibid., 78. The poem is a rhymed version of a biblical passage (1 Corinthians 11: 24–26).
30. Goethe, *From My Life*, 115.
31. Raabe, "Goethe und Bogatzky – eine Marginalie".
32. Goethe to Cornelia from Leipzig, 11 May 1767 (Fischer-Lamberg, ed., *Der junge Goethe*, vol. 1, 127).
33. Goethe, *From My Life*, 195.
34. Goethe to Cornelia, 11 May 1767 (Fischer-Lamberg, ed., *Der junge Goethe*, vol. 1, 126).
35. Goethe to Cornelia, 12 October 1767 (Fischer-Lamberg, ed., *Der junge Goethe*, vol. 1, 141); Goethe, *From My Life*, 196.
36. Bogatzky, *Der gottselige und christliche Hofmann nach der Heiligen Schrift* [1767], 23–34.
37. Goethe, *From My Life*, 114.
38. This interpretation can be substantiated by the entry on "Gehalt", found in one of the huge volumes listing and analysing the poet's vocabulary: *Goethe-Wörterbuch*, vol. 3, cols. 1276–78.
39. Goethe, *From My Life*, 113 (translation modified).
40. Goethe, "Vom Vater hab ich die Statur", translated by E. H. Zeydel in Goethe, *Goethe the Lyrist*, 163.
41. Goethe, *From My Life*, 113.
42. Grell, *Goethe als Operndirektor*, 170. Méhul's opera and its impact on early eighteenth-century German culture are studied in Meyer, *Carl Maria von Weber and the Search for a German Opera*, 58–69, 184–89.
43. *Goethes Werke*, Weimar edn, 3rd section, vol. 5, 221.

Appendix: Joseph Portrayed – Trautmann

1. Kölsch, *Johann Georg Trautmann (1713–1769)*, 279–87.
2. Genesis 37: 25, 28.

NOTES TO pp. 102–123   347

3. Goethe, *From My Life*, 76.
4. Schubart, *François de Théas Comte de Thoranc*, 21 and 140–41.
5. Bamberger, *Joh. Conrad Seekatz*, 150 (with 148, Fig. 32). The painting, now apparently privately owned, is listed in Emmerling, *Johann Conrad Seekatz*, 110 as no. 216, and considered an allegory of "fire and earth"; it belongs to a series of three paintings that represent the four elements. The other paintings are entitled *Girl with a Fish* and *Boy with a Dove*, standing for "water" and "air".
6. Prak, "The Carrot and the Stick", 164.
7. Kysel [Küsell], *Icones Biblicae Veteris et Novi Testamenti*, illustration no. 36. On the popularity of Breenbergh's etching, see Verdi, *Bartholomeus Breenbergh*, 42–43 and 63–64.
8. Genesis 47: 14.
9. Grotefend, *Der Königsleutnant Graf Thoranc in Frankfurt am Main*, vi–vii.

Chapter 7: On Sexual Morality

1. Burnet, *The Life and Death of John, Earl of Rochester*, 210–11.
2. Turner, *Libertines and Radicals in Early Modern London*; Turner, "The Erotics of the Novel"; Potter, *Honest Sins*, 3–33, are standard texts on the subject.
3. Uglow, *Hogarth*, 378.
4. Fielding, *Amelia*, 375, annotated by Battestin.
5. Meldrum, *Domestic Service and Gender*, 118–21, discusses cases of sexual relationships between "menservants and mistresses".
6. Uglow, *Hogarth*, 378.
7. Galatians 5: 19, 21 (New Revised Standard Version). The passage is quoted in Calixt, "Historia Iosephi", 212.
8. Calixt, "Historia Iosephi", 219.
9. Nussbaum, *The Therapy of Desire*, 316–483.
10. Rist, *Stoic Philosophy*, 45.
11. Ibid.
12. Early key sources on Western sexuality include two ancient Jewish works that refer to Joseph: the *Testaments of the Twelve Patriarchs* and *Fourth Maccabees*; relevant early-Christian texts include the Sermon on the Mount (Matthew 5: 27–28) and Paul's first letter to the Corinthians (1 Corinthians 7). For recent studies, see Aune, "Mastery of the Passions"; Gemünden, "La Culture des passions à l'époque du Nouveau Testament"; Rosen-Zvi, "Bilha the Temptress: *The Testament of Reuben* and *The Birth of Sexuality*"; Ellis, *Paul and Ancient Views of Sexual Desire*.
13. Watts, *Discourses of the Love of God*, vi.
14. Dixon, *From Passions to Emotions*; Newmark, *Passion – Affekt – Gefühl*, 170–72.
15. Henry, *Commentary on the Whole Bible*, 80 (on Genesis 39: 7–12). Originally published in 1706.
16. Fielding, *Joseph Andrews*, 27 (book 1, chap. 4). On the "riots at the play-houses", in which Joseph participated, see Straub, *Domestic Affairs*, 113–19.
17. Straub, *Domestic Affairs*, 43–46, 141–77.
18. Fielding, *The History of Tom Jones*, vol. 1, 270 (book 6, chap. 1).
19. Hartman, *The Household and the Making of History*.
20. Ibid., 58–59.

Chapter 8: Libertine Libido – Mrs Rowe

1. Stecher, *Elizabeth Singer Rowe*, offers a biographical sketch.
2. Rowe, *Works*, vol. 3, 273–343: "The History of Joseph". Of the ten parts or cantos called "books", only books 1 to 8 form the original poem printed in 1736, and the present

summary and subsequent analysis consider only these. Books 9 and 10 were added for the second edition (1737) upon the request of Rowe's friend Lady Hertford. The biography included in early editions of Rowe's works indicates that the *History of Joseph* was written long before its publication, though no date is given; see Rowe, *Works*, vol. 4, 218–19, 323–24.
3. Rowe, "The History of Joseph", book 6 (*Works*, vol. 3, 308).
4. Ibid., 309.
5. See the Isaac Watts, *Horae Lyricae* (1709), for a description of the situation of poetry around 1700. A secondary source is Prescott, *Women, Authorship and Literary Culture*, 141–66.
6. The epithet was used for instance by a Swiss literary critic, see Breitinger, *Critische Dichtkunst* (1740); the passage is anthologised in Bodmer and Breitinger, *Schriften zur Literatur*, 157.
7. Pratt, *The Sublime and Beautiful of Scripture*, 168–69.
8. Diodorus Siculus, *The Library of History* II, 4–20; Frenzel, *Stoffe der Weltliteratur*, 837–40.
9. The Story of Queen Charoba can be found in Lewis and Burstein (eds), *Land of Enchanters*, 134–39.
10. Stecher, *Elizabeth Singer Rowe*, 31. Sylvester's poem can be found in Sylvester, *The Complete Works*, vol. 2, 103–20.
11. Seneca, *Phaedra* 721 (*Seneca's Phaedra*, ed. Boyle, 89).
12. Rowe, *Works*, vol. 4, 190. For other references to Pascal, see vol. 4, 30–31, 68–69, 70–71.
13. Rowe, "A Description of Hell" (*Works*, vol. 3, 63–66). Stecher, *Elizabeth Singer Rowe*, 232, notes the date.
14. Bunyan, *The Life and Death of Mr. Badman*, 19.
15. Ibid.; see also 58.
16. Baker, "Joseph".
17. Castle, *Masquerade and Civilization*, 37–38.
18. Ibid., 38.
19. Fielding, *Amelia*, 425. Masquerades are a major ingredient in this novel.
20. Quoted by Battestin in Fielding, *Amelia*, 417 n. 1.
21. Bunyan, *The Life and Death of Mr. Badman*, 55.
22. Rowe, "The History of Joseph", book 5 (*Works*, vol. 3, 302).
23. David, "The Story of Semiramis".
24. Rowe, "The History of Joseph", book 5 (*Works*, vol. 3, 297). For Joseph's coat, see Genesis 37: 3.
25. Rowe, "The History of Joseph", book 1 (*Works*, vol. 3, 277).
26. In a letter Rowe asserts that she does not entertain "so ill an opinion of human nature, however atheists and freethinkers have degraded it" (*Works*, vol. 4, 270).
27. Rowe, "The History of Joseph", book 1 (*Works*, vol. 3, 274).
28. Walker, "Rochester and the Issue of Deathbed Repentance".
29. Burnet, *The Life and Death of John, Earl of Rochester*, 269.
30. Stecher, *Elizabeth Singer Rowe*, 196 and 213.
31. Rowe, "The History of Joseph", book 8 (*Works*, vol. 3, 321).
32. Richetti, "Mrs Elizabeth Rowe", summarises and comments on some of the relevant stories.
33. Rowe, "To Belinda, from Sylvia" (*Works*, vol. 1, 90).
34. Ibid., 89.
35. Ibid., 93.
36. Ibid., 219.
37. Ibid., 222–23.
38. Ibid., 222.
39. Ibid., 224.
40. Ibid., 219.

41. Richardson, "Advice to Unmarried Ladies", 168.
42. Henry, *Commentary on the Whole Bible*, 80 (on Genesis 39: 7–12).
43. Ibid., 1633 (on Matthew 5: 27–32).
44. Rowe, "To Belinda, from Sylvia" (*Works*, vol. 1, 88).
45. Ibid., 92.
46. Quoted in Staves, *A Literary History of Women's Writing in Britain*, 169.

Chapter 9: Irresistible Eros – Bodmer

1. Vetter, "J.J. Bodmer und die englische Litteratur".
2. Bodmer, *Joseph und Zulika in zween Gesängen*.
3. Starnes, *Christoph Martin Wieland*, vol. 1, 41.
4. Bodmer, "Über der Frau Rowe Joseph". In a note Bodmer explains that the review dates from 1753.
5. Ibid., 122.
6. Ibid., 121.
7. 2 Samuel 11: 2 (David); Job 2: 1–6 (Satan).
8. Tobit 8: 2–3.
9. Bodmer, *Die Sündflut*, 64: "Chemos, der viehische Geist".
10. 1 Samuel 16: 18.
11. Achilles Tatius, *Leucippe and Clitophon* I, 5 (translation of Stephen Gaselee modified).
12. Bodmer, *Die Sündflut*, 4–21, 71–79, and 85–89.
13. 1 Samuel 16: 14–23. In ancient times, the playing of stringed instruments was generally accompanied by singing.
14. Homer, *Iliad* XIV, 214ff. (translated by Samuel Butler).
15. Wieland, *Schriften*, vol. 1, 411–55.
16. Bodmer, *Joseph und Zulika*, 10.
17. Wieland, *Schriften*, vol. 1, 451.
18. Ibid., 454–55.
19. Pope, *An Essay on Man* II, 101–8 (*The Twickenham Edition of the Poems of Alexander Pope*, vol. 3/1, 67–68).
20. Wieland, *Schriften*, vol. 1, 431.
21. There are at least five allusions to the arrows of Eros in Bodmer, *Joseph und Zulika* (14, 29, 30, 41, 49).
22. Ibid., 37; echoing Milton, *Paradise Lost* I, 767–76, and *Paradise Regained* IV, 15–17.
23. Wieland, *Schriften*, vol. 1, 433; for an interpretation, see Singer, "Joseph in Ägypten. Zur Erzählkunst des 17. und 18. Jahrhunderts", 276.
24. Augustine, *Confessions* I, 13, 20.
25. Sulzer, *Gedanken von dem vorzüglichen Werth*, 3.
26. Sulzer, *Allgemeine Theorie der schönen Künste*, vol. 2, 101 ("Erhaben").
27. McLeish, "Dido, Aeneas, and the Concept of *Pietas*", 136–37.
28. Forster, *Aspects of the Novel*, 73–81.
29. Sulzer, *Allgemeine Theorie der schönen Künste*, vol. 2, 494 ("Held").
30. Bakhtin, "Epic and Novel", 39.
31. Kozul, "La Séduction critique", 167–69.
32. Voltaire, *Questions sur l'Encyclopédie*, art. "Marie Magdeleine" (*Oeuvres complètes* [Moland], vol. 20, 32).
33. Auerochs, *Die Entstehung der Kunstreligion*, 119–260: "Poetische Rabbinen. Probleme christlicher Epik um 1750"; esp. 243–60 on Klopstock.
34. Wieland to Justus Friedrich Wilhelm Zachariä, 8 December 1761 (*Wielands Briefwechsel*, vol. 3, 49).

35. Johnson, *Lives of the English Poets*, vol. 1, 49–50 ("Cowley").
36. Bodmer in: Bodmer and Breitinger, *Schriften zur Literatur*, 79. The same idea can be found in Sulzer, *Allgemeine Theorie der schönen Künste*, vol. 2, 503 ("Heldengedicht").
37. Bodmer and Breitinger, *Schriften zur Literatur*, 27 (first published in the Zurich periodical *Der Mahler der Sitten*).

Chapter 10: The Triumph of Chaste Love – Fielding

1. Fielding, *The History of the Adventures of Joseph Andrews and of His Friend Mr. Abraham Adams* [1742]. All references are to Battestin's annotated critical edition.
2. Fielding, *Joseph Andrews*, 224 (book 3, chap. 3).
3. Heliodorus, *The Adventures of Theagenes and Chariclia*. On the impact of Heliodorus on English literature, see Doody, *The True Story of the Novel*, 213–300, and Mentz, *Romance for Sale*; on Heliodorus and Fielding, see Oeftering, *Heliodor und seine Bedeutung für die Litteratur*, 92–101; Rojahn-Deyk, *Henry Fielding*, 125–29; Lynch, *Henry Fielding and the Heliodoran Novel*; Grimm, *Fielding's Tom Jones and the European Novel since Antiquity*.
4. Konstan, *Sexual Symmetry: Love in the Ancient Novel and Related Genres*, 34.
5. For details and a similar incident told in Zesen's novel *Assenat*, see the discussion below, Chapter 13.
6. Fielding, *Joseph Andrews*, 38–39 (book 1, chap. 8).
7. "Madam, reply'd the old woman, I know the youth you mean; broad-chested, and his shoulders largely spread; his neck bold and straight, and rising his head above all about him; in short, the finest person of a man my eyes ever beheld. He whose eyes sparkled like fire, and at once carried sweetness and terror in their look: he with the fine head of hair curling upon his shoulders, and the yellow down upon his chin." Heliodorus, *The Adventures of Theagenes and Chariclia*, vol. 2, 56 (book 7).
8. Milton, *Paradise Lost* IV, 303. See also: 300 (fair large front), 306 (wanton ringlets).
9. Fielding, *Joseph Andrews*, 47 (book 1, chap. 10).
10. Scarron, *The Whole Comical Works* (1712). On the influence of Scarron on Fielding, see Lynch, *Henry Fielding and the Heliodoran Novel*, 41–51.
11. Fielding, *Joseph Andrews*, 187 (book 3, chap. 1).
12. Scarron, *The Comical Romance*, vol. 1, 3 (part 1, chap. 1).
13. Fielding, *Joseph Andrews*, 38 (book 1, chap. 8).
14. Ibid., headings of book 3, chaps 7 and 8.
15. Fielding, *Joseph Andrews*, 95 (book 2, chap. 2).
16. Seduction scenes abound in seventeenth- and eighteenth-century English novels, see Schulz, *Studien zur Verführungsszene*.
17. Scarron, *The Comical Romance*, vol. 1, 233 (part 2, chap. 10).
18. Josephus, *Jewish Antiquities* II, 46, in the translation of William Whiston, 1736 (Josephus, *The Works*, 55).
19. Fielding, *Joseph Andrews*, 40 (book 1, chap. 8).
20. Ibid., 29–30 (book 1, chap. 5).
21. Ibid., 41 (book 1, chap. 8).
22. Anonymous, "An Essay on the New Species of Writing Founded by Mr. Fielding", 207.
23. Ibid.
24. Watt, *The Rise of the Novel*, 173 (on Samuel Richardson's novel *Pamela*).
25. Fielding, *Joseph Andrews*, 35 (book 1, chap. 7).
26. Philo, *De Iosepho* 51. Fielding may have used a bilingual, Greek and Latin, edition: *Philonis opera quae reperiri potuerunt onmia*, 1742.
27. Apuleius, *Metamorphoses* I, 7.
28. Homer, *Odyssey*, canto V.
29. Fielding, *Joseph Andrews*, 224 (book 3, chap. 3).

30. Straub, *Domestic Affairs*, 45; Meldrum, *Domestic Service and Gender*, 55–58.
31. Fielding, *Joseph Andrews*, 32 (book 1, chap. 6).
32. Ibid., 27 (book 1, chap. 4).
33. This aspect of Fielding's novel is highlighted by Taylor, "Joseph as Hero in Joseph Andrews".
34. Fielding, *An Enquiry into the Causes of the Late Increase of Robbers and Related Writings*.
35. Fielding, *Joseph Andrews*, 177 (book 2, chap. 16).
36. Battestin, *The Moral Basis of Fielding's Art*, 55–56.
37. Fielding, *Joseph Andrews*, 229 (book 3, chap. 4).
38. White, *Metahistory*, 9.
39. Ibid.
40. Battestin, *The Moral Basis of Fielding's Art*, 88–89.
41. Fielding, *Joseph Andrews*, 343 (book 5, chap. 16).
42. For the distinction between vulgar nakedness and idealised nudity, see Clark, *The Nude*.
43. Desfontaines, "Review of *Joseph Andrews*", 357.
44. Battestin and Battestin, *Henry Fielding: A Life*, 296, 330–31.
45. Benedict, *Framing Feeling: Sentiment and Style in English Prose Fiction, 1745–1800*, 34.
46. Battestin and Battestin, *Henry Fielding: A Life*, 330.
47. Ibid., 188.
48. Fielding owned the 1741 edition of *The Works of the Learned Isaac Barrow*; see Ribble and Ribble, *Fielding's Library*, 30–31. Battestin, *The Moral Basis of Fielding's Art*, 32–39, comments on the influence of the sermon "Of Being Imitators of Christ" on Fielding.
49. Barrow, "Of Being Imitators of Christ" (*Works*, vol. 3, 14).
50. Ibid.
51. Ibid., 17.
52. Ibid., 13.
53. Ibid.
54. Ibid.
55. Konstan, *Sexual Symmetry*, 97.
56. Ibid., 48.
57. Fielding, *Joseph Andrews*, 41 (book 1, chap. 8).
58. Battestin, *The Moral Basis of Fielding's Art*, 113–18.
59. Fielding, *Joseph Andrews*, 20 (book 1, chap. 1).
60. Ibid., 46 (book 1, chap. 10).
61. Turner, "Adulterous Kisses and the Meanings of Familiarity in Early Modern Britain".
62. Fielding, *Joseph Andrews*, 85 (book 1, chap. 17). For a similar statement, see Fielding, *Amelia*, 414.

Chapter 11: On Statecraft

1. Garber, "Zur Statuskonkurrenz von Adel und gelehrtem Bürgertum".
2. Roeck, *Civic Culture and Everyday Life in Early Modern Germany*, 162.
3. Scott, "The Rise of the First Minister".
4. Brottier, "Joseph le politique", 57–68.
5. Wunder, "Hof und Verwaltung im 17. Jahrhundert"; Droste, "Patrioten ausländischer Herkunft".
6. Baron, *The Crisis of the Early Italian Renaissance*, 66–67; Pocock, *The Machiavellian Moment*, 49–80.
7. More, *Utopia*, 5–6.
8. Hume, "Of Civil Liberty" (*Essays*, 90).
9. Evans, "The Court: A Protean Institution and an Elusive Subject"; Béranger, "Pour une enquête européenne du ministériat au XVIIe siècle"; Kaiser and Pecar, "Reichsfürsten und ihre Favoriten".

10. Richelieu, *Testament politique*, 305–9 (I, 8, 6).
11. On the ascent of the lawyer in early-modern German lands, see Stolleis, *Geschichte des öffentlichen Rechts in Deutschland*, 394–404.
12. More, *Utopia*, 6.

Chapter 12: Civic Humanist – Grotius

1. Nellen, *Hugo de Groot*, is the authoritative biography.
2. Grotius, *Sophompaneas 1635*, edited by Eyffinger, is a bilingual Latin and English edition with full scholarly apparatus. An earlier English translation, in rhyme, was published in 1652: Grotius, *Sophompaneas, or Ioseph*. An interpretative essay is Eyffinger, "The Fourth Man". Sophompaneas, the titular hero's name, is a euphonic version of Joseph's Egyptian title Psonthomphanêch (Genesis 41: 45 in the Greek Bible).
3. Grotius, *Sophompaneas 1635*, lines 956–58.973.1003–4.
4. Ibid., lines 972–73.1023–24.
5. Ibid., lines 784–86.
6. Ibid., lines 786–90.
7. Ibid., lines 791–92; see Herodotus, *The Histories* II, 36, 3.
8. Grotius, *Sophompaneas*, lines 814–15.
9. On professional and civilian armies, see Schama, *The Embarrassment of Riches*, 240–46; Israel, *The Dutch Republic*, 267–71.
10. Diodorus Siculus, *The Library of History* I, 28, 5; see also Herodotus, *The Histories* II, 164.
11. Grotius, *The Antiquity of the Batavian Republic*, 53 (chap. I, 3).
12. Joseph the social legislator is mentioned by Eusebius, who quotes the Jewish historian Artapanus; see above, Chapter 3. Grotius includes Artapanus in his list of sources, see Grotius, *Sophompaneas 1635*, 146.
13. "The Netherlands, with a population of about three million, were richer and more highly urbanized than Europe save perhaps Italy. Nineteen towns contained over ten thousand people (England then had only three or four); five had more than thirty thousand, and one, Antwerp, maybe a hundred thousand." Zagorin, *Rebels and Rulers, 1500–1660*, vol. 2, 88.
14. Grotius, *Sophompaneas 1635*, line 642.
15. Ibid., lines 649–50.
16. Proverbs 30: 8–9. As an aside we may insert here a brief passage from a later work, one that explains the biblical prayer. In the first chapter of Daniel Defoe's *Robinson Crusoe* (1719), the protagonist reports his father's advice to steer a middle course in life, in accordance with Proverbs 30: 8. "He bade me observe it, and I should always find, that the calamities of life were shared among the upper and lower part of mankind; but that the middle station had the fewest disasters, and was not exposed to so many vicissitudes as the higher or lower part of mankind; nay, they were not subjected to so many distempers and uneasinesses, either of body or mind, as those were, who, by vicious living, luxury, and extravagances, on one hand, or by hard labour, want of necessaries, and mean or insufficient diet, on the other hand, bring distempers upon themselves by the natural consequences of their way of living; that the middle station of life was calculated for all kind of virtues, and all kind of enjoyments."
17. On the "Bürgerhumanismus" thesis of Hans Baron, see Baron, *The Crisis of the Early Italian Renaissance*; Witt et al., "Hans Baron's Renaissance Humanism"; Skinner, "Machiavelli's *Discorsi* and the Pre-Humanist Origins of Republican Ideas".
18. Haitsma Mulier, *The Myth of Venice and Dutch Republican Thought*; Conti, "The Mechanisation of Virtue: Republican Rituals in Italian Political Thought".
19. Nellen, *Hugo de Groot*, 276, 328–29; Thomson, "France's Grotian Moment".
20. Meinecke, *Machiavellism*, 208.
21. Grotius, *Sophompaneas 1635*, 132 (dedication, lines 71–72).

22. Ibid., 130 and 132 (dedication, lines 61 and 79–81).
23. Ibid., lines 1192–95.
24. Nellen, *Hugo de Groot*, 273.
25. Grotius, *Sophompaneas 1635*, line 92.
26. Grotius, *De iure belli ac pacis*, 470 (book 2, chap. 20, 5, 3).
27. Ibid., 469 (book 2, chap. 20, 5, 2).
28. Genesis 41: 44 (Vulgate); see Grotius, *Annotata ad Vetus Testamentum* (1644) (*Opera omnia theologica*, vol. 1, 23).
29. Grotius, *Sophompaneas 1635*, lines 666–67.
30. Grotius, *De iure belli ac pacis*, 846 (book 3, chap. 20, 50, 1).
31. Cicero, *De officiis* I, 11.
32. Ibid. I, 24.
33. Ibid. I, 25.
34. Ibid. I, 24. This passage is quoted in Grotius, *De iure belli ac pacis*, 584 (book 2, chap. 24, 5, 4).
35. Israel, *The Dutch Republic*, 268.
36. Richelieu, *Testament politique*, 341–42 (II, 5).
37. Tapié, *France in the Age of Louis XIII and Richelieu*, 309.
38. Seneca, *De clementia* II, 3, 1. See also Adam, *Clementia principis*.
39. Seneca, *De clementia* III, 5, 3.
40. For Corneille's *Cinna* as a political statement, see Pintard, "Autour de *Cinna* et *Polyeucte*".
41. Ceriziers, *The Innocent Lord*, 137.
42. Ibid., 85–87.
43. Eyffinger, in: Grotius, *Sophompaneas 1635*, 73–74.
44. Grotius, *Liber de antiquitate reipublicae Batavicae* (1610); see the bilingual edition: Grotius, *The Antiquity of the Batavian Republic*, 88 (no foreign councillor, etc.), 100 (no *homo externus*). The "patriotic rule" was presumably derived from the Bible's injunction not to appoint a foreign ruler in Israel (Deuteronomy 17: 15), for the Dutch Republic was often seen as being similar to the early Hebrew state.
45. Droste, "Patrioten ausländischer Herkunft", 310.
46. Grotius to the States of Holland, in: Grotius, *Briefwisseling*, vol. 5, 755 (no. 1935).
47. Grotius, *Sophompaneas 1635*, lines 980–82.
48. "[...] liet my zomtijds voorstaen, dat Iosef, of in den treurspeeldere verrezen was, of dat de treurspeelder Iosefs spoor moest bewandelt hebben." Vondel, "Huigh de Groots Iosef of Sofompaneas", preface; see Vondel, *De Werken*, vol. 3, 435.
49. Vollenhoven, "Sophompaneas".
50. Grotius, *Sophompaneas 1635*, lines 51–52.
51. Ibid., lines 153–54, 160, 1119–20.
52. Grotius addresses Dirk in a letter sent to his brother Willem, 19 November 1639 (*Briefwisseling*, vol. 10, 755, no. 4395). Willem was actively involved in the education of Hugo Grotius's children.
53. Nellen, *Hugo de Groot*, 395.
54. Benesch, *The Drawings of Rembrandt*, vol. 6, 438–39 (index).
55. Verdi, *Bartholomeus Breenbergh*.
56. Blankert, *Rembrandt*, 138–41. On Geertje, see Schama, *Rembrandt's Eyes*, 542–49.
57. Mieke Bal explores this and other hidden phallic symbolism in Rembrandt's renderings of Joseph and Mrs Potiphar, see Bal, *Loving Yusuf*, esp. 91–92, 149.
58. Eyffinger in: Grotius, *Sophompaneas 1635*, 115. Much of the information on seventeenth-century Dutch cultural history is from this source.
59. Vondel, *De Werken*, vol. 3, 431–83.
60. A French translation of Vondel's "Joseph in Dothan" can be found in Vondel, *Cinq Tragédies*. See also Parente, *Religious Drama and the Humanist Tradition*, 110–31.

61. Spinoza, *Tractatus theologico-politicus* [1670], 298 (chap. 20).
62. Smits-Veldt, "Die Kanzel des Bürgers".

Chapter 13: Competent Courtier – Zesen

1. Zesen, *Assenat*, edited by Ferdinand van Ingen. There is also a reprint of the original Amsterdam edition, edited by Volker Meid. I quote from van Ingen's edition.
2. Laforge, "Theorien über Hof, Staat und Gesellschaft in Philipp von Zesens *Adriatischer Rosemund*".
3. Ingen, *Philipp von Zesen*, 14.
4. Zesen, *Assenat*, 388 and 417 (in the notes).
5. Zesen, *Schatz der Gesundheit* (Treasury of Health, 1671), included in *Sämtliche Werke*, vol. 3/2.
6. Literally: "If this child is immediately dedicated to me, she will come to rest in the arms of a foreign man and thus be bettered. Twenty Niles, and this will happen. O Egypt, honour the mouth of these two."
7. Zesen, *Assenat* 165–67; Bergengruen, *Nachfolge Christi*, 132–59 and 222.
8. Welzig, "Einige Aspekte barocker Romanregister".
9. Latinus, king of Latium in Italy, receives an oracle that tells him not to give his daughter Lavinia in marriage to one of his own people; she will eventually marry a foreigner – i.e., Aeneas – the future founder of an empire (Virgil, *Aeneid* VII, 81–106). The same Virgilian passage is echoed in Fracastoro's epic on Joseph, see above, Chapter 3.
10. Zesen found the name Nitocris in Herodotus (*The Histories* II, 100) who knew of an Egyptian queen by this very name.
11. Meid, "Nachwort des Herausgebers", 13*–15* and 32*–33*.
12. Quoted in ibid., 30*.
13. Eichendorff, *Geschichte der Poesie*, 441 and 906.
14. Grimmelshausen, *Das wunderbarliche Vogelnest* [1672], 100–102.
15. Breyl, "Assenat und Isis", 723–25. Note also the depiction of Natura as a woman with two sets of breasts in Zesen, *Sämtliche Werke*, vol. 14, 46.
16. Heiss, "Die Liebe des Fürsten zur Geometrie"; Korey, *The Geometry of Power*.
17. Genesis 29: 17; 39: 6.
18. Zesen, *Assenat*, 17–20, based on Grimmelshausen, *Des vortrefflich keuschen Josephs in Egypten Lebensbeschreibung*, 8–9.
19. Heliodorus, *An Ethiopian Story* X, 14 (Reardon, ed., *Collected Ancient Greek Novels*, 569). According to Pliny (*Natural History* VII, 10 [52]), "sense-impressions received at the time of conception" may influence the form of the child. This notion is also present in the story of how the biblical patriarch Jacob caused goats to give birth to young that were speckled and spotted (Genesis 30: 38–40).
20. In the seventeenth and eighteenth centuries many believed in the shaping of the human foetus by the mother's emotional and imaginative life. Dürbeck, *Einbildungskraft und Aufklärung*, 98–104, 156–76, discusses the relevant eighteenth-century sources; Stanzel, in *Telegonie – Fernzeugung*, and "Telegony: Procreation from a Distance", offers a comprehensive cultural history of the idea.
21. Exodus 1: 7.
22. Possible sources: for the alleged fertility-promoting potency of the waters of the Nile for women, see Seneca, *Naturales quaestiones* 3, 25, 11 and Pliny, *Naturalis historia* 7, 33; for the attribution of the Hebrew growth rate to the drinking of Nile water, see Wendelinus, *Admiranda Nili*, 63. Late ancient and medieval export of Nile water as a tonic is mentioned in Schama, *Landscape and Memory*, 265.
23. Zesen, *Assenat*, 363–64.
24. The Neo-Stoic philosopher Justus Lipsius (1557–1606) is generally invoked as the source of this notion; see Ingen, "Grimmelshausen's *Kreuscher Joseph* und sein Leser", 411–16. See also Ort, "Affektenlehre".

25. Zesen, *Assenat*, 171.
26. Ibid., 430 (notes) indicates that he has taken the name from a Dutch Joseph novel by Jacob Cats (1577–1660; date of novel: 1620); for bibliographical detail on Cats, see Singer, "Joseph in Ägypten", 278. Cats was not the first Dutchman to call Potiphar's wife "Sephira"; the name had already been used in the Latin play *Comedia sacra cui titulus est Ioseph* (1536) by the Catholic humanist Cornelius Crocus (c. 1500–1550), see Wimmer, *Jesuitentheater*, 45–60.
27. Acts 5: 10.
28. Zesen, *Assenat*, 150.
29. Ibid., 171.
30. Breuer, "Grimmelshausens politische Argumentation"; Martens, *Der patriotische Minister. Fürstendiener in der Literatur der Aufklärungszeit*.
31. Zesen, *Assenat*, 158–59 and 171.
32. Herodotus, *The Histories* II, 3.
33. Zesen, *Assenat*, 322–23.
34. Ibid., 195.
35. Ibid., 197; for a similar statement, see 71.
36. Ibid., 282.
37. The Egyptian king Amasis "established an admirable custom [...]; this was that every man once a year should declare before the Nomarch, or provincial governor, the source of his livelihood; failure to do this, or inability to prove that the source was an honest one, was punishable by death." Herodotus, *The Histories* II, 177.
38. Zesen, *Assenat*, 282–83.
39. Ibid., 285.
40. Ibid., 95.
41. Ibid., 349.

Chapter 14: Hebrew Freemason – Albrecht

1. Varnhagen von Ense, *Tageblätter*, 731 (diary entry, 8 October 1855). On "the growth of the novel-reading habit" in eighteenth-century Germany, see the chapter thus titled in Ward, *Book Production, Fiction, and the German Reading Public*, 59–91; and Wittmann, "Gibt es eine Leserevolution".
2. Engels, "Zu Leben und Werk von Johann Friedrich Ernst Albrecht". A list of Albrecht's works can be found in Goedeke, *Grundriss zur Geschichte der deutschen Dichtung aus den Quellen*, vol. 5, 501–4.
3. Weintraut, "Islands in an Archipelago: The German Dramatized Novel".
4. Albrecht, *Der keusche Joseph. Dramatisch bearbeitet*.
5. Albrecht was a member of a Masonic lodge in Dresden, see Thiel, *Johann Friedrich Ernst Albrecht (1752–1814)*, 11.
6. Albrecht, *Der keusche Joseph*, vol. 3, 178.
7. Schiffmann, *Die Entstehung der Rittergrade in der Freimaurerei um die Mitte des XVIII. Jahrhunderts*, 178–91.
8. Moldenhawer (ed.), *Prozess gegen den Orden der Tempelherren. Aus den Originalacten*.
9. These two names are derived from Genesis 38: 1 (*vir Odollamitis, nomine Hira*, Vulgate).
10. Cudworth, *The True Intellectual System of the Universe* (1678); Warburton, *The Works*, vol. 1, 289–90; Pauw, *Recherches philosophiques sur les Egyptiens*, vol. 2, 37–41.
11. Josephus, *The Jewish War* II, 120–61.
12. Summarised in Schweitzer, *The Quest of the Historical Jesus*, 37–42.
13. Assmann, *Die Zauberflöte*, 96 and *passim*.
14. The underground world described by Terrasson (and Albrecht) echoes ancient descriptions: Ammianus Marcellinus, XX 15, 30, translated in Horst, *Chaeremon: Egyptian Priest and Stoic Philosopher*, 45, describes the subterranean world of ancient Egypt; Lucian, *Philopseudês*, 34, has a story about an Egyptian priest living underground for twenty-three years.

15. Terrasson, *Sethos*, vol. 1, x.
16. Ibid., 118–54 (book 3).
17. On this etching, see Assmann, *Die Zauberflöte*, 177–78; Brauneis, "Das Frontispiz im Alberti-Libretto von 1791 als Schlüssel zur Mozarts Zauberflöte".
18. Schneider, *Die Freimaurerei*, 196–209; Thalmann, *Der Trivialroman*, 94–115.
19. Martens, "Zur Figur eines edlen Juden im Aufklärungsroman vor Lessing".
20. Lessing, *Werke und Briefe*, vol. 10, 52.
21. Boscamp, *Werden und können Israeliten zu Freymaurern aufgenommen werden?*. The pseudonymous author is Hans Karl von Ecker und Eckhoffen. For a discussion, see Katz, *Jews and Freemasons in Europe*.
22. Grab, *Demokratische Strömungen in Hamburg und Schleswig-Holstein zur Zeit der ersten französischen Republik*, 95–101; Campe, "Beitrag zu Lessings Denkmal von einer Freimaurer=loge besonderer Art".
23. Schütz, *Freie Bekenntnisse eines Veteranen der Maurerei und anderer geheimer Gesellschaften*, 41.
24. Campe, "Beitrag zu Lessings Denkmal", 118.
25. Ibid.
26. Assmann, *Ägyptische Geheimnisse*, 196–201.
27. The idea that all of Egypt's wisdom derived from Abraham and Joseph, but was later corrupted by the priests of Egypt, can be found in Köpke, *Sapientia Dei in Mysterio Crucis Christi abscondita*, 1700, quoted by Ebeling, *Das Geheimnis des Hermes Trismegistos*, 150–51. A general derivation of ancient Egypt's wisdom from the biblical patriarchs is suggested in the article "Aegyptische Weisheit", in Zedler, *Großes vollständiges Universal-Lexikon*, vol. 1, col. 637. These notions are based on ancient sources such as Josephus, *Jewish Antiquities* I, 155 and 166–68, and Eusebius, *Praeparatio evangelica* 9: 17, 8 (Sources chrétiennes vol. 369, 238).
28. Voltaire, *La Philosophie de l'histoire* (*Les Oeuvres complètes*, vol. 59, 125).
29. Albrecht, *Der keusche Joseph*, vol. 1, 120.
30. Ibid., vol. 3, 177.
31. Albrecht, *Gespräche Maurerey betreffend*, 70. In an article published in 1792, Albrecht repeats his idea of creating a new type of civic association, a type that is public, rather than secret, in nature: Albrecht, "Über den Geist unsrer Zeit", 990–1002.
32. Lenski, *Power and Privilege*, 70 and 365.
33. Koselleck, *Kritik und Krise. Ein Beitrag zur Pathogenese der bürgerlichen Welt*.
34. Diderot, "Egyptiens, Philosophie des", in Diderot's *Encyclopédie*.
35. See Kant's famous essay "What Is Enlightenment?" (1784).
36. For an eighteenth-century Masonic study of the ancient Egyptian priesthood, see Born, "Über die Mysterien der Ägyptier", reprinted with an English translation in Eckelmeyer, *The Cultural Context of Mozart's Magic Flute*, vol. 2, 239–475.
37. France was the first state to declare, by law of 25 June 1794, that citizens have a right to access public records.
38. Albrecht, *Der keusche Joseph*, vol. 2, 320: "Du kannst es öffentlich, wir müssen's in der Stille nur."
39. Albrecht, *Der keusche Joseph*, vol. 2, 321.
40. Ibid., 322.
41. Relevant quotations to this effect can be found in Kreuzer, "Gefährliche Lesesucht? Bemerkungen zur politischen Lektürekritik im ausgehenden 18. Jahrhundert", 64–65.
42. Frederick the Great, letter to Freiherr von Zedlitz, 5 September 1779 (Friedrich II. von Preußen, *Pädagogische Schriften und Äußerungen*, 170). A similar argument can be found in Richelieu's *Testament*: the knowledge of letters, if common to all inhabitants of a state, would endanger its commercial and agricultural basis; see Richelieu, *Testament politique*, 204–5 (I, 2, 10).
43. Albrecht, *Der keusche Joseph*, vol. 1, ix.
44. Ibid., vol. 3, 149 and 156.
45. Albrecht, "Über den Geist unsrer Zeit", 984.

Chapter 15: On Historical Criticism

1. On the political dimension of British historiography, see Levine, *The Battle of the Books*, 267–413; Champion, *The Pillars of Priestcraft Shaken*, 25–52; Pocock, *Barbarism and Religion*, vol. 2: *Narratives of Civil Government*. On French historiography, see Grell, *Le Dix-huitième Siècle et l'antiquité en France*, vol. 1, 500–53; Grell, *L'Histoire entre érudition et philosophie*, 165–91.
2. Leland, *The Divine Authority of the Old and New Testaments*, vol. 1, 178.
3. Anonymous, *A Brief Examination*, 98.
4. Voltaire, *Le Siècle de Louis XIV* (*Oeuvres complètes* [Moland], vol. 14, 155–56).
5. Israel, *Enlightenment Contested*, 640–62.
6. Du Halde, *Description of the Empire of China*, vol. 1, 424–41.
7. Voltaire, *La Philosophie de l'histoire* (*Oeuvres complètes*, vol. 59, 119).
8. The relevant passages are listed in Brush, *Montaigne and Bayle*, 254–56.
9. On Voltaire's indebtedness to Bayle, see Devaux, "Bayle, Pierre".
10. Courtines, *Bayle's Relations with England and the English*, 120–34.

Chapter 16: Despotic Ruler – Morgan

1. Usserius, *Annales Veteris et Novi Testamenti*, 7–9; an English translation is Ussher, *The Annals of the World*, 29–33.
2. On early-modern interest in Plutarch, see Hirzel, *Plutarch*, 111–91.
3. Henry, *Commentary on the Whole Bible*, 88 (on Genesis 47). Originally published in 1706.
4. Hearne, *Ductor historicus*, vol. 1, 234. Hearne echoes Josephus, *Jewish Antiquities* II, 195.
5. Shaftesbury met Bayle in Rotterdam; see above, Chapter 15.
6. Justinus, *Historiarum Philippicarum Epitoma* 36, 2; the original author of this work is Pompeius Trogus, but it survives only in Justinus's abridged version. Stern (ed.), *Greek and Latin Authors on Jews and Judaism*, vol. 1, 335.
7. Shaftesbury, *Characteristics*, 359 – "Miscellany II".
8. Ibid., 363.
9. For surveys of censorship in Europe, see Israel, *Radical Enlightenment*, 97–118; Hesse, "Print Culture in the Enlightenment".
10. Nokes, *A History of the Crime of Blasphemy*, 131.
11. Locke, *Two Treatises of Government* [1690], 368–69 (second treatise, §§ 123–24).
12. Voltaire, *Questions sur l'Encyclopédie*, article "Propriété" (*Oeuvres complètes* [Moland], vol. 20, 291).
13. Morgan, *The Moral Philosopher*, ed. Gawlick, 3 vols. This is a one-volume facsimile reprint of the three original volumes; for vol. 1, the editor used the second, corrected edition of 1738 (instead of the first edition of 1737). Gawlick's long introduction summarises Morgan's thought and comments on his particular kind of "deism".
14. Biographical details are known from Chandler, *A Vindication of the History of the Old Testament*, xiii–xiv, 345 and 556–57; Morgan himself calls Locke "my master, and the first guide and director of my understanding", see Morgan, *Physico-Theology*, 74.
15. Goldsmith, "A Description of Various Clubs", 15.
16. Champion, *The Pillars of Priestcraft Shaken*, 7. See also Allen, *The Clubs of Augustan London*, 127–36.
17. Morgan, *The Moral Philosopher*, vol. 1, vii.
18. As a result, the actual teaching of some of the deist writers is still disputed. John Locke seems to have been too cautious to explain his private beliefs (which may have been non-Trinitarian), and leading deists such as Charles Blount and John Toland may have been atheists who merely pretended to believe in God. In the volume *Atheism from the Reformation to the Enlightenment*, edited by Hunter and Wootton, the notion of concealment figures prominently; see especially the contributions by Wootton and Berman.
19. Morgan, *The Moral Philosopher*, vol. 3, 32.

20. Ibid., vol. 1, 239–43; vol. 3, 6–31.
21. Herodotus, *The Histories* II, 37.
22. Morgan, *The Moral Philosopher*, vol. 3, 9.
23. See also ibid., vol. 1, 239.
24. Ibid., vol. 3, 55.
25. Ibid., vol. 1, 254.
26. Morgan refers to Shuckford's handbook: ibid., vol. 3, 76–83. At least through Shuckford, *The Sacred and Prophane History of the World Connected*, vol. 2, 207, Morgan must also have been aware of Shaftesbury's critique of Joseph.
27. Manetho's *Aegyptiaca*, no longer extant, is known only through quotations made from it by several ancient authors such as Josephus. Today historians agree with Manetho that the kingdom of Egypt was once ruled by foreign lords of uncertain origins, the Hyksos (c. 1650–1540 BCE), whose tyrannical yoke the natives eventually shed. However, there is no logical reason to identify the Hyksos with the Hebrews. According to modern scholarship, the identification of the hated Hyksos with the Hebrews reflects the conflict between native Egyptians and Diaspora Jews that began to develop in the third century BCE. See Josephus, *Against Apion* I, 93–105; and Barclay's commentary in Josephus, *Against Apion*, 48–51, 61–65, 341–49.
28. Shuckford, *The Sacred and Prophane History of the World Connected*, vol. 1, 341–43.
29. Locke, *Two Treatises of Government*, 400 (second treatise, § 172).
30. Diodorus Siculus, *The Library of History* I, 73.
31. Aristotle, *Politics* 1285 A (Simpson's translation).
32. Morgan, *The Moral Philosopher*, vol. 3, 10 – "the Hebrew Politician". The eighteenth-century meaning of "politician" may be exemplified by a reference to Henry Fielding's novel *An Apology for the Life of Mrs Shamela Andrews* (1741): through discreet temptation, servant girl Shamela consciously manoeuvres her would-be seducer towards matrimonial captivity; the title page of the novel refers to "all the matchless arts of that young politician"; see Fielding, *Joseph Andrews with Shamela and Related Writings*, ed. H. Goldberg, 272 (facsimile of the title page of *Shamela*).
33. Against Morgan: Chandler, *A Vindication of the History of the Old Testament*; Hallet, *A Rebuke to the Moral Philosopher*; Chapman, *Eusebius*. For Morgan: Mencius Philalethes, *The History of Joseph Consider'd*; Anonymous, *A Review of the Moral and Political Life and Administration of the Patriarch Joseph*.
34. Chapman, *Eusebius*, vol. 2, vi.
35. Chandler, *A Vindication of the History of the Old Testament*, 382.
36. I use the words of another one of Morgan's critics: Hallet, *A Rebuke to the Moral Philosopher*, 7.
37. Chandler, *A Vindication of the History of the Old Testament*, 402.
38. Ibid., 417.
39. Ibid., 435.
40. Anonymous, *A Review of the Moral and Political Life and Administration of the Patriarch Joseph*, 50.
41. Koebner, "Despot and Despotism"; Mandt, "Tyrannis, Despotie"; Forbes, *Hume's Philosophical Politics*, 142–45, 155–57.
42. Vanini, *De admirandis*, 360–61.
43. The anonymous compilation, generally known as *Traité des trois imposteurs*, was in 1719 published as *La Vie et l'esprit de Mr Benoit de Spinosa*; on its origin and influence, see Schwarzbach and Fairbairn, "History and Structure"; Vermij, "The English Deists and the *Traité*"; Israel, *Radical Enlightenment*, 694–703. The passage on Moses can be found in Charles-Daubert, *Le "Traité des trois imposteurs"*, 660–61, quotation 661.
44. Morgan, *The Moral Philosopher*, vol. 3, viii (preface).
45. Hume, *Essays*, 10 – "Of the Liberty of the Press" (1741).
46. It was not until 1772 that torture was abolished in England.

47. Diderot to Sophie Volland, 1 November 1760 (Diderot, *Correspondance*, vol. 3, 212).
48. Morgan, *Physico-Theology*, 268.
49. Ibid., 281.
50. Chandler, *A Vindication of the History of the Old Testament*, 402.
51. The identification of Mencius Philalethes with Peter Annet is made in Weller, *Lexicon Pseudonymorum*, 432.
52. In Germany, Hermann Samuel Reimarus (1694–1768), professor of Hebrew in Hamburg, owned a copy of *The Moral Philosopher*. When writing his – prudently unpublished – defence of deist philosophy, he did not refrain from expressing his own critical view of Joseph along the lines suggested by Morgan. See Reimarus, *Apologie oder Schutzschrift für die Vernünftigen Verehrer Gottes*, vol. 1, 261. The complete set of the three volumes of *The Moral Philosopher* appears in the catalogue of Reimarus's library: see Schetelig, *Auktionskatalog der Bibliothek von Hermann Samuel Reimarus*, vol. 1, 79. For German works seeking to refute Morgan, see van den Berg, "English Deism and Germany".
53. Adams reports that a copy of *The Moral Philosopher* circulated in Worcester, Mass. in 1755; see Adams, *The Works*, vol. 2, 3.
54. Mumford, *The City in History*, 48.

Chapter 17: Tax Collector – Voltaire

1. Bossuet, *Discours sur l'histoire universelle* (*Oeuvres complètes*, vol. 24, 269–70).
2. Richard Simon briefly mentions written or oral traditions Moses used for writing the patriarchal stories of Genesis. Astruc thinks that Joseph wrote his own biography. Simon, *Histoire critique du Vieux Testament*, 47 (book 1, chap. 7); Astruc, *Conjectures sur la Genèse*, 403.
3. The chronological tables established by Petau (1627) and Pezron (1687) are reproduced in Grell, *Le Dix-huitième Siècle et l'antiquité en France*, vol. 2, 1200–4; for Ussher, see above, Chapter 16.
4. See the *Ratio studiorum* (1599), in Pavur (trans.), *The Ratio Studiorum*, 59.
5. Calvin, *Commentaries on the First Book of Moses Called Genesis*, vol. 2, 408. On the subject see Thompson, "The Immoralities of the Patriarchs in the History of Exegesis".
6. This distinction between reliable sacred and unreliable profane records can be found in Bodin, "Methodus ad facilem historiarum cognitionem" (1566/72) (*Oeuvres philosophiques*, ed. Mesnard 114–16).
7. Fréret, "Réflexions générales sur l'étude des anciennes histoires et sur le degré de certitude des différentes preuves historiques" (1724).
8. Voltaire, *Essai sur les moeurs et l'esprit des nations*, vol. 2, 903–4 ("Remarques pour servir de supplement à l'Essai sur les moeurs", 1763).
9. Reported by Grimm (1776), in *Correspondance littéraire, philosophique et critique*, ed. M. Tourneux, vol. 11, 348.
10. Châtelet, *Examens de la Bible*, 190–91.
11. Ibid., 192.
12. Voltaire to Marie Louise Denis, 12 June 1754 (*Oeuvres complètes*, vol. 99, 163 – D 5843).
13. Voltaire, *Des Mensonges imprimés* (*Oeuvres complètes*, vol. 31B, 379–80). Before Voltaire, Giambattista Vico in *Principj di una scienza nuova* (1744) had already described the history of the nations as a sequence of the age of fable, the heroic age, and the human age. It is not known whether Voltaire actually borrowed from Vico. Ultimately, the notion is derived from Censorinus, *De die natali* 21, a Latin work dating from CE 238. Censorinus reports on how Varro, an earlier author, distinguished between the uncertain age (the earliest period), the mythical age, and the historical period.
14. Hobbes, *Leviathan* [1651], 261–61 (chap. 33); Spinoza, *Tractatus theologico-politicus* [1670], 161–67 (chap. 8).

15. Voltaire, "Moïse" (*Oeuvres complètes*, vol. 36, 387); *L'Examen important de milord Bolingbroke* (vol. 62, 186); *Dieu et les hommes* (vol. 69, 361–62, 376–77).
16. Voltaire, *La Philosophie de l'histoire* (*Oeuvres complètes*, vol. 59, 226).
17. The list of Voltaire's work that deals exclusively or mainly with biblical criticism is rather long, and only the first item predates his stay at Senones: *Sermon des Cinquante* (The Sermon of the Fifty, c. 1752); *Dictionnaire philosophique* (Philosophical Dictionary, 1764, includes many entries on biblical figures); *Questions sur les miracles* (Questions concerning Miracles, 1765); *L'Examen important du milord Bolingbroke* (Critical Inquiry by Milord Bolingbroke, 1766); *Les Questions de Zapata* (The Questions of Zapata, 1767); *Dieu et les hommes* (God and Men, 1769); *Questions sur l'Encyclopédie* (Questions on the Encyclopaedia, 1770/72; nine volumes, with many articles on biblical subjects – Voltaire's longest work); *La Bible enfin expliquée* (The Bible, at last Explained, 1776); *Histoire de l'établissement du christianisme* (History of the Establishment of Christianity, 1785, posthumously published). The foremost secondary source on the subject is Schwarzbach, *Voltaire's Old Testament Criticism*.
18. Heuvel, in: Voltaire, *Mélanges*, 1382.
19. Voltaire, *Sermon des Cinquante* (Voltaire, *Mélanges*, 256).
20. Voltaire, *La Bible enfin expliquée, par plusieurs aumoniers de S.M.L.R.D.P.* (*Oeuvres complètes* [Moland], vol. 30, 67 n. 1).
21. Ibid., 66–67 n. 3).
22. Ibid., 67 n. 1).
23. Voltaire refers to Shaftesbury's *Characteristics* in the article "Tout est bien" in the *Dictionnaire philosophique* (*Oeuvres complètes*, vol. 35, 424).
24. Voltaire, *Dictionnaire philosophique*, article "Joseph" (*Oeuvres complètes*, vol. 36, 259).
25. Voltaire, *Corpus des notes marginales*, vol. 2, 48.
26. Voltaire, *Histoire de Charles XII*, book 6 (*Oeuvres complètes*, vol. 4, 424).
27. Voltaire, *La Philosophie de l'histoire*, chap. 42 (*Oeuvres complètes*, vol. 59, 232).
28. Voltaire, *La Bible enfin expliquée* (*Oeuvres complètes* [Moland], vol. 30, 66–67 notes).
29. Shackleton, *Essays on Montesquieu*, 333–34, explains this literary technique.
30. Josephus, *Jewish Antiquities* XII, 224.
31. Ibid., 158–236.
32. Note in the 1735/36 edition of Josephus, see Voltaire, *Corpus des notes marginales*, vol. 4, 592 (no. 792).
33. Voltaire, *La Bible enfin expliquée* (*Oeuvres complètes* [Moland], vol. 30, 67 n. 1).
34. 1 Maccabees 1: 56–57.
35. Josephus, *Jewish Antiquities* XII, 257–64.
36. Simon, *Nicolas Fréret, académicien*, 16–21.
37. For a list of all the books of Voltaire that were censored, see Weil, *Livres interdits, livres persécutés 1720–1770*, 123–31 (nos. 574–622).
38. Bauer, *Handbuch der Geschichte der hebräischen Nation. Erster Theil*, 172–92.
39. For Tobias's two original letters that accompanied these gifts in 257 BCE, see Bagnall and Derow, *Greek Historical Documents: The Hellenistic Period*, 96–98 (no. 54).
40. Gera, *Judaea and Mediterranean Politics*, 36–58 ("The Tobiads: Fiction and History"); Johnson, *Historical Fictions and Hellenistic Jewish Identity*, 76–93.
41. Hengel, *Judaism and Hellenism*, vol. 1, 267–77.
42. See the splendid interpretation offered by Wills, *The Jewish Novel in the Ancient World*, 187–93.
43. Thus Soggin (*Das Buch Genesis*, 435) thinks that many interpretative problems disappear once it is accepted that the Joseph story dates from the Hellenistic or perhaps late Persian period, i.e. the fourth century BCE. Catastini ("Le testimonianze di Manetone"; "Ancora sulla datazione della Storia di Giuseppe") dates the story to early Hellenistic times: the late fourth or early third century BCE, i.e. the time of King Ptolemy I Soter (323–282 BCE). The second half of the second century BCE has also been suggested (Diebner, "Le Roman de Joseph").

NOTES TO pp. 285–297   361

44. Kunz, "Ägypten in der Perspektive Israels". The text of the Famine Stela inscription can be found in Lichtheim, *Ancient Egyptian Literature*, vol. 3, 94–103; and Peust, "Hungersnotstele".

Chapter 18: On Literary Criticism

1. The relevant eighteenth-century literary critics are John Dennis, Claude Fleury, Robert Lowth, and Johann Gottfried Herder.
2. Pope, *The Twickenham Edition of the Poems*, vol. 10, 131.
3. Shuckford, *The Sacred and Prophane History*, vol. 2, 418.
4. Morgan, *The Moral Philosopher*, vol. 3, 14–15.
5. Warton, in *The Adventurer* no. 51 (vol. 1, 303).
6. Klopstock, *Sämmtliche Werke*, vol. 10, 276.
7. Pratt, *The Sublime and Beautiful of Scripture*, 159–89.
8. Lavater, *Vier und zwanzig kurze Vorlesungen über die Geschichte Josephs*, 1.
9. Husbands, "Some Remarks on the Beauties of the Holy Scriptures", 89.
10. Hort, *Sermons on Practical Subjects*, 230; originally published in 1738.
11. Boswell, *London Journal*, 196–97.
12. Ibid., 196.
13. Steele, in *The Tatler* no. 233 (vol. 4, 189).
14. Ibid. (vol. 4, 190).
15. Ibid. (vol. 4, 193).
16. Ibid. (vol. 4, 190).
17. Ibid. (vol. 4, 189).
18. Josephus, *Jewish Antiquities* II, 195.
19. Sterne, "Joseph's History Considered", 114.
20. Ibid., 115.
21. Ibid., 120.
22. Ibid., 120.
23. Steele, *The Christian Hero*, 91–92.
24. Astruc, *Conjectures sur la Genèse*, 403.
25. Ceriziers, *The Innocent Lord*, 139.
26. Aristotle, *Poetics* 1453a.
27. Ceriziers, *The Innocent Lord*, 133.
28. See below, Chapter 19.
29. Ceriziers, *The Innocent Lord*, 132.
30. Rollin, *Oeuvres complètes*, vol. 26, 407.

Chapter 19: A *conte philosophique* – Voltaire

1. Craveri, *Madame du Deffand and Her World*, 2002, 80. Craveri offers a lively sketch of eighteenth-century Parisian social life in the literary salons: "Madame du Deffand's *Salon*" (60–98).
2. Mme du Deffand, letter to Voltaire, 1 October 1759 (Voltaire, *Oeuvres complètes*, vol. 104, 386 – D 8518).
3. Voltaire, letter to Mme du Deffand, 16 October 1765 (*Oeuvres complètes*, vol. 113, 347–48 – D 12939).
4. This passage is found only in the 1765 edition of the *Dictionnaire philosophique*. It remains to be explained why Voltaire omitted it from later editions of this work. A tentative explanation might be that he recalled the fact that other acts of generosity are recorded in the Old Testament: although David had the chance to kill Saul, he spared his life on two occasions (1 Samuel 24 and 26). The parallelism between Joseph's and David's generosity was noted by Voltaire's friend Emilie du Châtelet, *Examens de la Bible*, 191: "Mais le dénouement de cette histoire est très touchant et Joseph y montre beaucoup de générosité. Je

crois que l'action de David envers Saül et celle de Joseph envers ses frères sont les deux seules actions généreuses qui soient rapportées dans tout l'Ancien Testament" (But the denouement of the story is very touching, and Joseph shows much generosity in it. I think that David's behaviour towards Saul, and Joseph's towards his brothers are the only two cases of generosity recorded in all of the Old Testament.) In the eighteenth century, David's clemency was also noted by Karl Philipp Moritz; when reading of it as a boy, he was moved to tears: Moritz, *Anton Reiser*, 20.

5. The French text used is that of the critical edition: Voltaire, *Dictionnaire philosophique*, article "Joseph" (*Les Oeuvres complètes*, vol. 36, 254–61, annotated by Jacqueline Hellegouarc'h).
6. Pearson, *The Fables of Reason*, 15.
7. Katz, "Marmontel and the Voice of Experience", 249–59.
8. Claude Saumaise in the 1640 Latin preface to his bilingual (Greek and Latin) edition of a novel by Achilles Tatius; see Doody, *The True Story of the Novel*, 260.
9. Voltaire, *Essai sur les moeurs et l'esprit des nations*, vol. 2, 773 (chap. 193).
10. For Seneca's *Phaedra*, see above, Chapter 3.
11. Voltaire, *La Bible enfin expliquée* (*Oeuvres complètes* [Moland], vol. 30, 63 n. 2).
12. Ibid. (*Oeuvres complètes* [Moland], vol. 30, 64 n.).
13. Aristotle, *Poetics* 1460a.
14. Marmontel, "Merveilleux", 907a. A fine essay (untitled) on the absence of the "marvellous" or "wondrous" in the realistic eighteenth-century novel is in the *Rambler* no. 4 of 31 March 1750 (vol. 1, 19–25) by Samuel Johnson.
15. Voltaire, "Ce qui plaît aux dames" (*Oeuvres complètes* [Moland], vol. 10, 19), translated in Voltaire, *Candide and Other Stories*, 189.
16. Marmontel, "Merveilleux", 906b.
17. Voltaire, *Irène* (1778), preface (*Oeuvres complètes* [Moland], vol. 7, 333).
18. Chateaubriand, *Génie du Christianisme*, 780 (part 2, book 5, chap. 4).
19. Ibid., 782.
20. Voltaire, *Zadig* (*Les Oeuvres complètes*, vol. 30B, 200).
21. Voltaire, *Questions sur l'Encyclopédie*, article "Epopée" (*Oeuvres complètes* [Moland], vol. 18, 572).
22. Voltaire, *Zadig* (*Oeuvres complètes*, vol. 30B, 113).
23. Mme du Deffand to Voltaire, 20 September 1760 (Voltaire, *Oeuvres complètes*, vol. 106, 139 – D 9248).
24. Voltaire to Mme du Deffand, 17 September 1759 (*Oeuvres complètes*, vol. 104, 359 – D 8484).
25. On the message of Richardson's novels and their impact, see Beebee, *Clarissa on the Continent*; Clery, *The Feminization Debate in Eighteenth-Century England*. Johann David Michaelis (1717–1791), the first to translate Richardson into German, taught oriental languages at the University of Göttingen; upon reading Richardson, he suggested to the Prussian king the establishment of a university for women. Michaelis's petition actually mentions "Pamela"; see Beebee, *Clarissa on the Continent*, 19.
26. Mme du Deffand to Voltaire, 1 October 1759 (Voltaire, *Oeuvres complètes*, vol. 104, 386 – D 8518).
27. Mme du Deffand to Voltaire, 28 October 1759 (ibid., vol. 104, 424 – D 8559).
28. Voltaire, letter of 6 March 1761 (ibid., vol. 107, 93 – D 9669).
29. Mme du Deffand to Walpole, 27 February/4 March 1772 (*The Yale Edition of Horace Walpole's Correspondence*, vol. 5, 196).
30. Mme du Deffand to Walpole, 14 July 1773 (ibid., vol. 5, 383).
31. Joannidès, *La Comédie-française du 1680 à 1900*, xviii–xix.
32. Voltaire to Mme du Deffand, 17 September 1759 and 13 October 1759 (*Oeuvres complètes*, vol. 104, 358–61 – D 8484, and 397–402 – D 8533).
33. Voltaire to Mme du Deffand, 13 October 1759 (ibid., vol. 104, 401 – D 8533).
34. Voltaire to Mme du Deffand, 13 October 1759 (ibid., vol. 104, 397–98 – D 8533).
35. Voltaire to Mme du Deffand, 13 October 1759 (ibid., vol. 104, 398 – D 8533).

36. Voltaire to Mme du Deffand, 13 October 1759 (ibid.).
37. Voltaire to Mme du Deffand, 17 September 1759 (ibid., vol. 104, 360 – D 8484).
38. Mme du Deffand to Voltaire, 28 October 1759 (ibid., vol. 104, 424 – D 8559).
39. Mme du Deffand to Voltaire, 1 October 1759 (Voltaire, ibid., vol. 104, 385 – D 8581).
40. Pearson, *The Fables of Reason*, 86.
41. Trapnell, "Destiny in Voltaire's *Zadig* and *The Arabian Nights*".
42. Voltaire, *Zadig* (*Oeuvres complètes*, vol. 30B, 220).
43. Genesis 50: 20.
44. This is explicitly stated in Voltaire, *Questions sur l'Encyclopédie*, article "Aristote" (*Oeuvres complètes* [Moland], vol. 17, 374).
45. Voltaire, *Histoire de Jenni* (1775) (*Oeuvres complètes* [Moland], vol. 21, 528).
46. Voltaire, *Alzire*, dedicatory letter addressed to Mme du Châtelet (*Oeuvres complètes*, vol. 14, 115).
47. Rodriguez (ed.), *Catechismus Romanus* [1566], 473.
48. Bossuet, *Politique tirée des propres paroles de l'Ecriture Sainte* (*Oeuvres complètes*, vol. 24, 120–23).
49. Voltaire, *Commentaire sur Corneille* (*Oeuvres complètes*, vol. 54, 111).
50. Voltaire, *L'Ingénu* (*Oeuvres complètes*, vol. 63C, 272).
51. Diderot, *Oeuvres complètes*, vol. 25, 324.
52. Montesquieu, *The Spirit of the Laws*, 94–95 (book 6, chap. 21).
53. Jaucourt, "Vengeance". See also the same author's article "Clémence".
54. Lizé, "Voltaire et Les Sermons de m. Yorick".
55. Sterne, "Joseph's History Considered", 120; Sterne paraphrases here Steele, *The Christian Hero*, 92.
56. Pearson, *The Fables of Reason*, 30.
57. Forster, *Aspects of the Novel*, 45.
58. Voltaire to Jean Pierre Costard, 18 December 1775 (*Oeuvres complètes*, vol. 126, 294 – D 19801).
59. The real title of the book is *Histoires ou contes du temps passé* (1697); a critical edition is Perrault, *Contes*, 241–93.
60. Dupont-Ferrier, *Du Collège de Clermont au lycée Louis-Le-Grand (1563–1920)*, vol. 3, 254–57.
61. Voltaire, letter of 2 November 1761 (*Oeuvres complètes*, vol. 108, 86 – D 10126).
62. "Josephus Aegypto praefectus", in: Le Jay, *Bibliotheca rhetorum*, vol. 2, 241–76. On Le Jay's Joseph plays, see Wimmer, *Jesuitentheater*, 434–37; Brottier, "Joseph le politique", 67.
63. "Nec sine piis spectatorum lacrymis." Le Jay, *Bibliotheca rhetorum*, vol. 2, 125.
64. Pomeau, *Voltaire en son temps. Nouvelle édition*, vol. 1, 60–67; the *milieu dévot* is studied by Preyat, "Maître des divertissements ou trouble-fête?"
65. Joannidès, *La Comédie-française de 1680 à 1900*, chronological table for 1710 and 1711 (no pagination).
66. Genest, *Joseph, tragédie tirée de l'Ecriture Sainte*; in the preface (i–ix), Nicolas de Malézieu comments on the success of the play. For commentaries on the play and its critical reception, see Feeß, *Claude Genest. Sein Leben und seine Werke*, 77–78 (with a summary of the play, 60–66); Preyat, *Le Petit Concile de Bossuet*, 414–15; van der Schueren, "La Tragédie biblique à Sceaux".
67. Voltaire, *La Bible enfin expliquée* (*Oeuvres complètes* [Moland], vol. 30, 64 n.).
68. Voltaire's immediate source for this passage is Genesis 47: 9, but his version may echo a passage found in the ninth letter of Montesquieu's *Lettres persanes* (1721) where the following words are put in the mouth of an oriental eunuch: "For fifty years I have been groaning under the burden of sorrows and fears. I can truly say that in the whole course of a long life I have not known one cheerful day, nor one moment's ease." The topos is of course well known and often used. As one more example, we may quote Goethe as recorded by Eckermann (27 January 1824): "In truth, there has been nothing but toil and trouble, and I can affirm that throughout those seventy-five years I have enjoyed not even four weeks of real ease." The words of

Montesquieu and Goethe seem to echo Psalm 90: 10 – "The days of our life are seventy years, or perhaps eighty, if we are strong; even then their span is only toil and trouble."
69. Besterman, *Voltaire*, 435.
70. Voltaire, *Le Temple du goût*, appendix to the 1733 edition (*Oeuvres complètes*, vol. 9, 207).

Chapter 20: The Triumph of Beauty – Chateaubriand

1. On this often-discussed turning point of Chateaubriand's personal convictions, see Fumaroli, *Chateaubriand. Poésie et terreur*, 367–76.
2. Chateaubriand, *Mémoires d'outre-tombe*, vol. 1, 398.
3. Fénelon, *Oeuvres*, vol. 1, 67 – published posthumously, 1718.
4. Chateaubriand, *Génie du Christianisme*, 769. I conjecture "Israël" for "Ismaël".
5. Fleury, *The Manners of the Israelites*, 3: "a certain noble simplicity, superior to all refinement whatever".
6. Chateaubriand, *Génie du Christianisme*, 763.
7. Ibid., 784.
8. For Fleury's enthusiasm for the Joseph story, see *Oeuvres de l'Abbé Fleury*, vol. 2, 465 (see above, Chapter 4); *Discours sur l'histoire ecclésiastique*, 356 and 376.
9. Chateaubriand, *Génie du Christianisme*, 1108, 1113, 1167.
10. Ibid., 780–81 and 784, reflecting the Vulgate text of Genesis 43: 27–31; 44: 27–28; 45: 1–5, 14–15; 47: 9.
11. Chateaubriand, *Génie du Christianisme*, 780.
12. Ibid., 783.
13. Ibid., 782.
14. Ibid., 783.
15. In his novels Chateaubriand describes and explores this feeling with great literary skill. For him, old age is only one of its causes, one less conspicuous than unrequited love. His boldest theory is that such *tristesse* might actually be intrinsic to Christianity: hopes of heaven deprive human life of its meaning and purpose, and thus inspire a certain amount of sadness. If not tempered by devotion to the practical service of state and church, *tristesse* can take over lives, turn people neurotic and morbid, and then "we behold that sinful melancholy that springs up in the midst of our emotions, when these, deprived of any object, burn themselves out in the lonely heart" (ibid., 716).
16. Ibid., 472: "la vieillesse [n'est] si misérable que parce qu'elle sait tout".
17. Genesis 24: 76.
18. Chateaubriand, *Génie du Christianisme*, 781.
19. Jaucourt, "Simplicité"; Marmontel, "Simple".
20. Chateaubriand, *Oeuvres romanesques et voyages*, vol. 1, 18–19 – preface to "Atala".
21. Douglas, *Natural Symbols*, 40–58.
22. Chateaubriand, *Oeuvres romanesques et voyages*, vol. 1, 19.
23. Klopstock, *Sämmtliche Werke*, vol. 10, 276.
24. Chateaubriand, *Génie du Christianisme*, 783.
25. Longinus, *On the Sublime*, 93 (chap. 9: 9); translation modified.
26. Chateaubriand, *Génie du Christianisme*, 763, refers to *Deus dixit*; for a reference to Longinus, see 748. On the influence of Longinus, see Norton, *A History of the Bible as Literature*, vol. 2, 5–8; Till, *Das doppelte Erhabene*.
27. Homer, *Odyssey* VIII, 79–90, translated by Alexander Pope.
28. Chateaubriand, *Génie du Christianisme*, 779.
29. Ibid., 780.
30. Homer, *Odyssey* XVI, 210–13, translated by Alexander Pope.
31. Chateaubriand, *Génie du Christianisme*, 782.
32. Ibid.
33. Ibid., 783.

34. Ibid., 783–84.
35. Chateaubriand does not include the relevant passage from the *Odyssey* in *Génie du Christianisme*. In Pope's translation, the passage reads: "They [father and son] wept abundant, and they wept aloud./As the bold eagle with fierce sorrow stung,/ or parent vulture, mourns her ravished young;/they cry, they scream, their unfledged brood a prey/ to some rude churl, and borne by stealth away" (*Odyssey* XVI, 237–41).
36. Homer, *Iliad* I, 247–52 [330–36], translated by Alexander Pope.
37. Rollin, *Oeuvres complètes*, vol. 25, 432.
38. Chateaubriand, *Génie du Christianisme*, 786.
39. Chateaubriand, *Oeuvres romanesques et voyages*, vol. 1, 18.
40. Pope, *The Twickenham Edition of the Poems*, vol. 10, 131.
41. Ibid.
42. Chateaubriand, *Mémoires d'outre-tombe*, vol. 1, 330.
43. Dennis, *The Critical Works*, vol. 1, 271 (1701).
44. Chateaubriand, *Mémoires d'outre-tombe*, vol. 1, 142.
45. Chateaubriand, *Génie du Christianisme*, 642.
46. Kullmann, *Description*, 106.
47. Comenius, *Pampaedia*, 384.
48. Fénelon, "Letters to the Abbé Fleury", in *Fénelon on Education*, 117–21 (study programmes for 1695 and 1696).
49. Chateaubriand, *Mémoires d'outre-tombe*, vol. 1, 450.
50. Fénelon, *Oeuvres*, vol. 1, 69.
51. Chateaubriand, *Génie du Christianisme*, 726.
52. Ibid., 672.
53. Chateaubriand alludes to the philosophical doctrine of the interchangeability of *verum*, *pulchrum*, and *unum*: "the beautiful is one, and exists absolutely" (*le beau est un, et existe absolument*): *Génie du Christianisme*, 787–88; he also insists, invoking Plato, that beauty is not perishable but eternal (708). On the philosophical background of Chateaubriand's thought, see Bercegol, "De la grâce au grotesque".
54. John Keats, "Ode on a Grecian Urn" (1820).
55. The text can be found in: Mirbt (ed.), *Quellen zur Geschichte des Papsttums*, 235–37.
56. Jean-François de la Harpe, letter of 6 May 1802, quoted by Maurice Regard in Chateaubriand, *Génie du Christianisme*, 1598 n. 4.
57. Bartlet, *Etienne-Nicolas Méhul and Opera*, vol. 2, 575.
58. This is all one may glean from Duval, "Notice sur Joseph", otherwise an unreliable report; see Bartlet, *Etienne-Nicolas Méhul and Opera*, vol. 2, 572–74.
59. Baour-Lormian, *Omasis*.
60. Duval, *Joseph, drame en trois actes*. A summary of this opera can be found in Meyer, *Carl Maria von Weber*, 184–89. Bartlett, *Etienne-Nicolas Méhul and Opera*, vol. 2, 567–79 supplies all available information on the genesis of the piece.
61. Duval, "Notice sur Joseph", 183.
62. Meyer, *Carl Maria von Weber*, 59. For Goethe's love of Méhul's opera, see above, end of Chapter 6.
63. Quoted by Meyer, *Carl Maria von Weber*, 60.

Bibliography

Primary Sources

Achilles Tatius. *Achilles Tatius*. With an English translation by S. Gaselee and E.H. Wormington. The Loeb Classical Library. London: Heinemann, 1969.

Adams, John. *The Works of John Adams, Second President of the United States*. Edited by Charles Francis Adams. 10 vols. Boston: Little, Brown & Co., 1851–1865.

Albrecht, Johann Friedrich Ernst. *Gespräche Maurerey betreffend*. Leipzig: P.G. Kummer, 1785.

———. "Über den Geist unsrer Zeit." Pages 961–1002 in *Exkorporationen* vol. 2, Leipzig: Richter, 1792.

———. *Der keusche Joseph. Dramatisch bearbeitet*. 3 vols. Dresden and Leipzig: C.C. Richter'sche Buchhandlung, 1792 (vols 1 and 2), 1794 (vol. 3).

Alfonso el Sabio. *General estoria*. Edited by Antonio G. Solalinde et al. 2 parts. Madrid: Centro de Estudios historicos, 1930 (part 1); Instituto Miguel de Cervantes, 1957–1961 (parts 2/1 and 2/2).

Annet, Peter. *See* Mencius Philalethes.

[Anonymous.] *Les Devoirs de la vie domestique*. Par un père de famille. Brussels: Fères t'Serstevens, 1707.

———. *A Brief Examination of the Rev. Mr. Warburton's Divine Legation of Moses*. London: T. Cox, 1742. The long preface (Roman pagination) may be by Thomas Morgan, but not the actual text (Arabic pagination).

———. *A Review of the Moral and Political Life and Administration of the Patriarch Joseph*. London: W. Bickerton, 1743.

———. "An Essay on the New Species of Writing Founded by Mr Fielding" (1751). Vol. 1, pages 206–7 in *Literature Criticism from 1400–1800*. Vol. 1—. Edited by Dennis Poupard et al. Detroit, Mich.: Gale, 1984—.

Aristotle. *The Complete Works. The Revised Oxford Translation*. Edited by Jonathan Barnes. Princeton, N.J.: Princeton University Press, 1984.

———. *The Politics of Aristotle*. Translated by Peter L. Ph. Simpson. Chapel Hill: University of North Carolina Press, 1997.

Astruc, Jean. *Conjectures sur la Genèse*. Edited by Pierre Gibert. Paris: Noêsis, 1999.

Avigad, Nahman. *Hebrew Bullae from the Time of Jeremiah*. Jerusalem: Israel Exploration Society, 1986.

Bagnall, Roger S., and Peter Derow. *Greek Historical Documents: The Hellenistic Period*. Chico, Cal.: Scholars Press, 1981.

Baker, Daniel. *Poems upon Several Occasions*. London: Jones, 1697. Pages 142–52: "Joseph. Gen. 39."

Baour-Lormian, Pierre. *Omasis, ou Joseph en Egypte. Tragédie en cinq actes et en vers*. Paris: Vente, 1807.

Barrow, Isaac. *The Works of the Learned Isaac Barrow*. Published by John Tillotson. 3 vols. 5th edn. London: Millar, 1741. Vol. 3, pages 11–20: "Of Being Imitators of Christ." Also included in vol. 2, pages 495–532 of Barrow, *The Theological Works*. Edited by Alexander Napier. 9 vols. Cambridge: Cambridge University Press, 1859.
Basedow, Johann Bernhard. *Das Methodenbuch für Väter und Mütter der Familien und Völker*. With an introduction by Horst M.P. Krause. Vaduz: Topos Verlag, 1979. Reprint of the original 1770 edition.
Bauer, Georg Lorenz. *Handbuch der Geschichte der hebräischen Nation. Erster Theil*. Nürnberg: J.C. Monath, 1800.
Baxter, Richard. *The Practical Works*. 4 vols. London: George Virtue, 1846. Vol. 1 is a complete edition of *A Christian Directory*, 1673.
Benesch, Otto. *The Drawings of Rembrandt: Complete Edition*. Edited and enlarged by Eva Benesch. 6 vols. London: Phaidon Press, 1973.
Bible. *The Holy Bible. New Revised Standard Version*. New York: Oxford University Press, 1989.
Bible. *Holy Bible. English Standard Version*. London: HarperCollins, 2001.
Bodin, Jean. *Oeuvres philosophiques*. Edited by Pierre Mesnard. Paris: Presses Universitaires de France, 1951. Pages 99–475: "Methodus ad facilem historiarum cognitionem", 1566/72.
Bodmer, Johann Jakob. *Joseph und Zulika in zween Gesängen*. Zurich: Orel, 1753.
———. *Die Sündflut. Ein Gedicht in fünf Gesängen*. Zurich: Heidegger, 1753.
———. *Der erkannte Joseph und Der keusche Joseph. Zwei tragische Styke in fynf Aufzygen*. Zurich: Orell, 1754.
———. *Archiv der Schweitzerischen Kritick*. Zurich: Orell, Geßner & Comp. 1768. Pages 119–23: "Über der Frau Rowe Joseph", 1753.
——— and Johann Jakob Breitinger. *Schriften zur Literatur*. Edited by Volker Meid. Stuttgart: Reclam, 1980.
Bogatzky, Carl Heinrich von. *Der gottselige und christliche Hofmann nach der Heiligen Schrift*. Wernigerode: Struck, 1767.
Born, Ignaz von. "Über die Mysterien der Ägyptier." *Journal für Freymaurer* 1 (1784): 15–132. Reprinted with an English translation. Vol. 2, pages 239–475 in Judith A. Eckelmeyer, *The Cultural Context of Mozart's Magic Flute*. 2 vols. Lewiston, NY: Edwin Mellen Press, 1991.
Boscamp, Carl Friedrich von [Hans Karl von Ecker und Eckhoffen]. *Werden und können Israeliten zu Freymaurern aufgenommen werden?*. Hamburg: Hoffmann, 1788.
Bossuet, Jacques-Bénigne. *Oeuvres complètes*. Edited by F. Lachat. 31 vols. Paris: Vivès, 1862–1866.
Boswell, James. *Life of Johnson*. Edited by R.W. Chapman. Oxford: Oxford University Press, 1970.
———. *London Journal 1762–1763*. Edited by Frederick A. Pottle. Edinburgh: Edinburgh University Press, 1991.
Bunyan, John. *The Life and Death of Mr. Badman*. Edited by James F. Forrest and Roger Sharrock. Oxford: Clarendon Press, 1988.
Burchard, Christoph. "Der jüdische Asenethroman und seine Nachwirkungen." Pages 543–667 in *Aufstieg und Niedergang der römischen Welt*. Edited by Wolfgang Haase. Part II, vol. 20/1. Berlin: de Gruyter, 1987.
Burnet, Gilbert. *Lives of Sir Matthew Hale and John, Earl of Rochester*. London: Pickering, 1829. Pages 175–287: *The Life and Death of John, Earl of Rochester* [1680].
Calixt, Georg. "Historia Iosephi, 1654." Vol. 3, pages 210–19 in idem, *Werke in Auswahl*. Edited by Inge Mager. 4 vols. Göttingen: Vandenhoeck & Ruprecht, 1970–1982.
Calvin, John. *Commentaries on the First Book of Moses Called Genesis*. Translated by John King. 2 vols. Grand Rapids, Mich.: Baker, 1979.
Campe, Johann Heinrich. "Beitrag zu Lessings Denkmal von einer Freimaurer=loge besonderer Art." Pages 116–21 in *Schleswigsches ehemals Braunschweigisches Journal*, Mai 1792.
Ceriziers [Cerisiers], René de. *The Innocent Lord; or, The Divine Providence, Being the Incomparable History of Joseph*. Translated by William Lowre. London: Charles Adams, 1655. – Translation of *Joseph ou la providence divine*, 1642.

Chandler, Samuel. *A Vindication of the History of the Old Testament, in Answer to the Misrepresentations and Calumnies of Thomas Morgan*. London: J. Noon, 1741 [1743].

Chapman, John. *Eusebius. Or, The True Christian's Defense against a Late Book Entitul'd The Moral Philosopher*. Cambridge: W. Thurlbourn, 1739; vol. 2: London: W. Innys, 1741.

Charles-Daubert, Françoise, ed. *Le "Traité des trois imposteurs" et "L'Esprit de Spinoza". Philosophie clandestine entre 1678 et 1768*. Oxford: Voltaire Foundation, 1999.

Charlesworth, James H., ed. *The Old Testament Pseudepigrapha*. 2 vols. New York: Doubleday, 1983–1985.

Chateaubriand, François-René de. *Oeuvres romanesques et voyages*. Edited by Maurice Regard. 2 vols. Bibliothèque de la Pléiade. Paris: Gallimard, 1969.

——. *Mémoires d'outre-tombe*. Edited by Maurice Levaillant and Georges Moulinier. 2 vols. Bibliothèque de la Pléiade. Paris: Gallimard, 1951.

——. *Essai sur les révolutions – Génie du Christianisme*. Edited by Maurice Regard. Bibliothèque de la Pléiade. Paris: Gallimard, 1978. Pages 457–1367: *Génie du Christianisme*, 1802.

Châtelet, Emilie du [Gabrielle-Emilie Le Tonnier de Breteuil, marquise du Châtelet]. *Examens de la Bible*. Introduction and critical edition by Bertram E. Schwarzbach. Paris: Honoré Champion, 2009.

Cicero. *De officiis*. With an English translation by Walter Miller. The Loeb Classical Library. London: Heinemann, 1913.

Collenuccio, Pandolfo. *Operette morali. Poesie latine e volgari*. Edited by Alfredo Saviotti. Bari: Laterza, 1929.

Comenius, Johann Amos. *Pampaedia*. Edited by Dimitrij Tschizewskij. Heidelberg: Quelle & Meyer, 1960.

Cudworth, Ralph. *The True Intellectual System of the Universe*. London: Richard Royston, 1678.

Dennis, John. *The Critical Works*. Edited by Edward Niles Hooker. 2 vols. Baltimore: Johns Hopkins University Press, 1939. Vol. 1, pages 197–278: "The Advancement and Reformation of Poetry", 1701.

Desfontaines, Pierre-François Guyot. "Review of *Joseph Andrews* (July 1743)." Pages 357–58 in Henry Fielding, *The History of the Adventures of Joseph Andrews*. Edited by A. Potkay. New York: Pearson Longman, 2008.

Diderot, Denis. "Egyptiens, Philosophie des." Vol. 5, pages 434–38 in *Encyclopédie ou Dictionnaire raisonné des sciences, des arts et des métiers*. Edited by Denis Diderot et al.

——. *Correspondance*. Edited by Georges Roth. 16 vols. Paris: Editions de Minuit, 1955–1970.

——. *Oeuvres complètes*. Edited by H. Dieckmann and J. Varloot. Vol. 1—. Paris: Hermann, 1975—.

—— et al., eds. *Encyclopédie ou Dictionnaire raisonné des sciences, des arts et des métiers*. 35 vols. 1751–1780. Repr. Stuttgart: Frommann Holzboog, 1966–1967.

Djâmi. *Youssouf et Zouleikha*. Translated by Auguste Bricteux. Paris: Paul Geuthner, 1927.

Dodd, William. *The Beauties of History; or, Pictures of Virtue and Vice*. London: Vernor & Hood, 1795.

Du Halde, Jean-Baptiste. *A Description of the Empire of China*. 2 vols. London: T. Gardner, 1738–1741.

Duval, Alexandre. *Joseph. Drame en trois actes, en prose, mêlé de chants*. Paroles de M. Alexandre Duval, musique de M. Méhul. 2nd edn. Paris: Vente, 1809.

——. "Notice sur Joseph." Vol. 6, pages 179–85 in *Oeuvres complètes d'Alexandre Duval*. 9 vols. Paris: Barba, 1822–1823.

Eichendorff, Joseph von. *Geschichte der Poesie*. Edited by Hartwig Schultz. Frankfurt: Deutscher Klassiker Verlag, 1990.

Erasmus of Rotterdam. *Ausgewählte Schriften*. Latin and German. Edited by Werner Welzig. 8 vols. Darmstadt: Wissenschaftliche Buchgesellschaft, 1968. Vol. 1, pages 55–375: "Enchiridion militis christiani."

Fénelon, François de Salignac de La Mothe. *Fénelon on Education*. Translated by H.C. Barnard. Cambridge: Cambridge University Press, 1966.
──. *Oeuvres*. Edited by Jacques le Brun. 2 vols. Bibliothèque de la Pléiade. Paris: Gallimard, 1983–1997. Vol. 1, pages 89–171, 1201–230: "De l'Éducation des filles."
Fielding, Henry. *Joseph Andrews* [1742]. Edited by Martin C. Battestin. Middletown, Conn.: Wesleyan University Press, 1967. All references are to this edition.
──. *The History of Tom Jones*. Edited by Martin C. Battestin and Fredson Bowers. 2 vols. Hanover, NH: Wesleyan University Press, 1975.
──. *Amelia*. Edited by Martin C. Battestin. Oxford: Clarendon Press, 1983.
──. *Joseph Andrews with Shamela and Related Writings*. Edited by Homer Goldberg. New York: Norton, 1987.
──. *An Enquiry into the Causes of the Late Increase of Robbers and Related Writings*. Edited by Malvin R. Zirker, Middletown, Conn.: Wesleyan University Press, 1988.
Firdussi. *Jussuf und Suleicha. Romantisches Heldengedicht*. Translated by Ottokar Schlechta-Wssehrd. Vienna: Gerold, 1889.
Fischer-Lamberg, Hanna, ed. *Der junge Goethe*. New edn. 6 vols. Berlin: de Gruyter, 1963–1974.
Fleury, Claude. *The Manners of the Israelites*. Translated by Charles Cordell. Newcastle: Hodgson, 1736.
──. *Discours sur l'histoire ecclésiastique*. Nouvelle édition. Paris: Hérissant, 1763.
──. *Oeuvres de l'Abbé Fleury*. Edited by Louis-Aimé Martin. 2 vols. Paris: Lefèvre, 1844. Vol. 2, pages 431–639: "Grand catéchisme historique", 1679.
Fracastoro, Girolamo. "Joseph." Vol. 1, pages 51–96 in *Hieronymi Fracastorii, Adami Fumani* [...] *et Nicolai Archii Comitis Carmina*. 2nd edn. 2 vols. Padua: J. Cominus, 1739.
──. *Fracastor's poetische und philosophische Schriften. Zum ersten Mal aus dem Lateinischen ins Deutsche übersetzt*. Hamburg: Cornelsen, 1857. Pages 127–64: "Joseph. Episch-religiöses Gedicht. Zwei Gesänge. Fragment." Translated by Alphons Chenneville.
Fréret, Nicolas. *Mémoires académiques*. Edited by Catherine Volpilhac-Auger. Paris: Fayard, 1996. Pages 73–126: "Réflexions générales sur l'étude des anciennes histoires et sur le degré de certitude des différentes preuves historiques", 1724.
Friedrich II. von Preußen. *Pädagogische Schriften und Äußerungen*. Edited by Jürgen Bona Meyer. Langensalza: Hermann Beyer, 1885.
Genest, Charles-Claude. *Joseph, tragédie tirée de l'Ecriture Sainte*. Rouen: Eustache Herault, 1711.
Goethe, Johann Caspar. *Liber domesticus 1753–1779*. Edited by Helmut Holtzhauer. 2 vols. Berne: Herbert Lang, 1973.
Goethe, Johann Wolfgang von. *Goethes Werke*. Edited on behalf of Großherzogin Sophie von Sachsen. Third Section: Tagebücher. 15 vols. Weimar: Böhlau, 1887–1919. Known as the "Weimar edition".
──. *Goethe the Lyrist. 100 Poems in New Translation*. By Edwin H. Zeydel. 2nd edn. Chapel Hill: University of North Carolina Press, 1955.
──. *Werke*. Edited by Erich Trunz. 14 vols. Munich: Beck, 1981. Known as the "Hamburg edition".
──. *From My Life: Poetry and Truth*. Parts One to Three. Translated by Robert R. Heitner. New York: Suhrkamp, 1987.
Goldsmith, Oliver. "A Description of Various Clubs" [1759]. Vol. 3, pages 6–16 in *The Collected Works of Oliver Goldsmith*. Edited by Arthur Friedman. 5 vols. Oxford: Clarendon Press, 1966.
Grimm, Friedrich Melchior von, et al. *Correspondance littéraire, philosophique et critique par Grimm, Diderot, Meister, etc.* Edited by Maurice Tourneux. 16 vols. Paris: Garnier frères, 1877–1882.
Grimmelshausen, Hans Jacob Christoph von. *Des vortrefflich keuschen Josephs in Egypten Lebensbeschreibung samt des Musai Lebens-Lauff*. Edited by Wolfgang Bender. Tübingen: Niemeyer, 1968.
──. *Das wunderbarliche Vogelnest* [1672]. Edited by Rolf Tarot. Tübingen: Niemeyer, 1970.

Grotius, Hugo. *Sophompaneas, or Ioseph. A Tragedy*. With annotations by Francis Goldsmith. London: John Hardesty, 1652.
——. *Opera omnia theologica*. 3 vols. Amsterdam: Blaeu, 1679; reprint: Stuttgart: Frommann, 1972.
——. *Briefwisseling*. Edited by P.C. Molhuysen. 17 vols. s'Gravenhage: M. Nijhoff, 1928–2001.
——. *Sophompaneas 1635*. Edited by Arthur Eyffinger (De Dichtwerken van Hugo Grotius). Assen: Van Gorcum, 1992. All references are to this bilingual edition.
——. *De iure belli ac pacis*. Edited by B.J.A. de Kanter–van Hettinga Tromp. 2nd edn. Aalen: Scientia, 1993.
——. *The Antiquity of the Batavian Republic*. Edited and translated by Jan Waszink. Assen: Van Gorcum, 2000.
Hall, Joseph. *The Works*. Edited by Peter Hall. 12 vols. Oxford: Talboys, 1837–1839.
Hallet, Joseph. *A Rebuke to the Moral Philosopher*. Printed, with separate title page and pagination, as appendix to idem, *The Immorality of the Moral Philosopher*. 2nd edn. London: J. Noon, 1740.
Hattenhauer, Hans, ed. *Allgemeines Landrecht für die Preußischen Staaten von 1794. Textausgabe*. Frankfurt: Alfred Metzner Verlag, 1970.
Hearne, Thomas. *Ductor historicus: or, A Short System of Universal History*. 2nd edn. 2 vols. London: Childe, 1704–1705.
Heliodorus. *The Adventures of Theagenes and Chariclia: A Romance*. 2 vols. London: E. Curll et al., 1717. The story is also known as *Ethiopica* or *An Ethiopian Story*.
——. "An Ethiopian Story." Translated by J.R. Morgan. Pages 349–588 in *Collected Ancient Greek Novels*. Edited by B.P. Reardon. Berkeley: University of California Press, 1989.
Henry, Matthew. *Commentary on the Whole Bible*. Peabody, Mass.: Hendrickson, 1991.
Herder, Johann Gottfried. *Briefe. Gesamtausgabe*. Edited by Günter Arnold et al. Vol. 1—. Weimar: Böhlau, 1977—.
——. *Italienische Reise. Briefe und Tagebuchaufzeichnungen, 1788–1789*. Edited by Albert Meier and Heide Hollmer. Munich: Beck, 1989.
Hess, Johann Jacob, ed. *Biblische Erzählungen für die Jugend. Altes und Neues Testament*. New, improved edn. Zurich: Orell, Füssli & Compagnie, 1801.
Hobbes, Thomas. *Leviathan* [1651]. Edited by Richard Tuck. Cambridge: Cambridge University Press, 1991.
Horbury, William and David Noy. *Jewish Inscriptions of Graeco-Roman Egypt*. Cambridge: Cambridge University Press, 1992.
Hort, Josiah. *Sermons on Practical Subjects*. London: Davis & Rymers, 1757.
Hübner, Johann. *Zweymal zwey und funffzig auserlesene biblische Historien aus dem Alten und Neuen Testamente*. Edited by Rainer Lachmann and Christine Reents. Hildesheim: Olms, 1989. – Reprint of the 1731 edition.
Hume, David. *Essays, Moral, Political and Literary*. Oxford: Oxford University Press, 1963.
Husbands, John. "Some Remarks on the Beauties of the Holy Scriptures." Pages 23–140 in idem (ed.), *A Miscellany of Poems by Several Hands*, Oxford: Lichfield, 1731. The page numbers are those of the online facsimile included in *Eighteenth Century Collections Online*, Gale Group.
Ilan, Tal. *Lexicon of Jewish Names in Late Antiquity. Part I: Palestine 330 BCE–200 CE*. Tübingen: Mohr Siebeck, 2002.
Jâmi. "Yusuf and Zulaikha." Translated by Ralph T.G. Griffith and Alexander Rogers. Pages 166–229 in *Joseph and Potiphar's Wife in World Literature: An Anthology*. Edited by John D. Yohannan. New York: New Directions Books, 1968.
——. *Yusuf and Zulaikha: An Allegorical Romance*. Translated by David Pendlebury. London: Octagon Press, 1980.
Jaucourt, Louis de. "Clémence." Vol. 3, pages 521–22 in *Encyclopédie*. Edited by Denis Diderot et al.
——. "Simplicité." Vol. 15, page 205 in *Encyclopédie*. Edited by Denis Diderot et al.
——. "Vengeance." Vol. 17, page 4 in *Encyclopédie*. Edited by Denis Diderot et al.

Johnson, Samuel. *Lives of the English Poets*. Edited by George Birkbeck Hill. 3 vols. Oxford: Clarendon Press, 1905.
——. *The Rambler*. 3 vols. Edited by W. J. Bate and Albrecht B. Strauss (The Yale Edition of the Works of Samuel Johnson, vols 3–5). New Haven, Conn.: Yale University Press, 1969.
Josephus. *The Works of Josephus*. Translated by William Whiston. Peabody, Mass.: Hendrickson, 1987. Originally published in 1736.
——. *Against Apion*. Translation and commentary by John M.G. Barclay. Leiden: Brill, 2007.
Klopstock, Friedrich Gottlieb. *Sämmtliche Werke*. 10 vols. Leipzig: Göschen, 1854–1855. Vol. 10, pages 273–77: "Beurtheilung einiger Gemälde aus der heiligen Geschichte" (1760).
Köpke, Balthasar. *Sapientia Dei in Mysterio Crucis Christi abscondita. Die wahre Theologia Mystica oder Ascetica*. Halle: Waisenhaus, 1700.
Kysel [Küsell], Melchior. *Icones Biblicae Veteris et Novi Testamenti. Figuren biblischer Historien Alten und Neuen Testaments*. Nürnberg: Leonhard Buggel, 1680.
Lampo, Hubert. *Gelöbnis an Rachel*. Translated by Paul Wimmer. Vienna: Österreichische Verlagsanstalt, 1976.
La Roche, Sophie von. "Mein Glüke." *Magazin für Frauenzimmer* 1 (February 1782): 92–101.
Lavater, Johann Caspar. *Ausgewählte Werke in historisch-kritischer Ausgabe*. Vol. 1—. Zurich: Verlag Neue Zürcher Zeitung, 2001—. Vol. 3, pages 431–673: "Christliches Handbüchlein für Kinder", [1771] edited by Martin Ernst Hirzel.
——. *Christlicher Religionsunterricht für denkende Jünglinge*. [no place, no printer]. 1788.
——. *Vier und zwanzig kurze Vorlesungen über die Geschichte Josephs, des Sohnes Israels*. Zurich: Ziegler & Ulrich, 1794.
—— and Johann Heinrich Pestalozzi. "Etwas für die, welche sich verheuraten wollen." Pages 177–84 in *Der Erinnerer* 2, no. 21 (22 May 1766).
Le Jay, Gabriel-François. *Bibliotheca rhetorum. Praecepta et exempla*. 2 vols. Paris: Grégoire Dupuis, 1725.
Leland, John. *The Divine Authority of the Old and New Testaments Asserted*. 2 vols. London: R. Hett, 1739–1740.
Lessing, Gotthold Ephraim. *Werke und Briefe*. Edited by Wilfried Barner. 12 vols. Frankfurt: Deutscher Klassiker Verlag, 1985–2003.
Lewis, Bernard and Stanley Burstein, eds. *Land of Enchanters: Egyptian Short Stories from the Earliest Times to the Present Day*. Princeton, N.J.: Wiener, 2001.
Lichtheim, Miriam. *Ancient Egyptian Literature*. 3 vols. Berkeley: University of California Press, 1973–1980.
Locke, John. *Two Treatises of Government*. Edited by Peter Laslett. 2nd edn. Cambridge: Cambridge University Press, 1967.
——. *A Paraphrase and Notes on the Epistles of St Paul*. Edited by Arthur W. Wainwright. 2 vols. Oxford: Clarendon Press, 1987.
——. *Some Thoughts Concerning Education* [1693]. Edited by John W. Yolton and Jean S. Yolton. Oxford: Clarendon Press, 1989.
Longinus. *On the Sublime*. Edited with introduction and commentary by D.A. Russell. Oxford: Clarendon Press, 1964.
Lowth, Robert. *De sacra poesi Hebraeorum praelectiones*. Edited by Johann David Michaelis. 2nd edn. Göttingen: J.D. Dietrich, 1770.
McGaha, Michael. *Coat of Many Cultures: The Story of Joseph in Spanish Literature, 1200–1492*. Selected, translated, and introduced by M. McGaha. Philadelphia: Jewish Publication Society, 1997.
——. *The Story of Joseph in Spanish Golden Age Drama*. Selected, translated, and introduced by M. McGaha. Lewisburg: Bucknell University Press, 1998.
Mann, Thomas. *Joseph and his Brothers*. Translated by John E. Woods. New York: Knopf, 2005.
Marmontel, Jean-François. "Merveilleux." Vol. 20, pages 906–8 in *Encyclopédie*. Edited by Denis Diderot et al.

———. "Simple." Vol. 5, pages 144–46 in Marmontel, *Oeuvres complètes*. 7 vols. Geneva: Slatkine, 1968.
Mencius Philalethes [Peter Annet]. *The History of Joseph Consider'd. Or, The Moral Philosopher Vindicated against Mr Samuel Chandler's Defence of the Prime Ministry and Character of Joseph.* London: M. Cooper, 1744.
Miller, Hugh. *My Schools and Schoolmasters* [1854]. Edinburgh: Nimma, Hay & Mitchell, 1907.
Mirbt, Carl, ed. *Quellen zur Geschichte des Papsttums.* Freiburg: Mohr, 1897.
Moldenhawer, Daniel Gotthilf, ed. *Prozess gegen den Orden der Tempelherren. Aus den Originalacten der päpstlichen Commission in Frankreich.* Hamburg: Bohn, 1792.
Montesquieu, Charles de Secondat de. *The Spirit of the Laws.* Edited and translated by Anne M. Cohler et al. Cambridge: Cambridge University Press, 1989.
More, Thomas. *Utopia.* Translated by H.V.S. Ogden. New York: Appleton-Century-Crofts, 1949.
Morgan, Thomas. *The Moral Philosopher.* 3 vols. London 1738–1740. Reprint edited by Günter Gawlick. Stuttgart: Frommann-Holzboog, 1969.
———. *Physico-Theology: or, A Philosophical-Moral Disquisition.* London: T. Cox, 1741.
Moritz, Karl Philipp. *Anton Reiser. Ein psychologischer Roman.* Edited by Christof Wingertszahn. Tübingen: Niemeyer, 2006.
Moser, Friedrich Carl von. *Daniel in der Löwen-Grube. In sechs Gesängen.* Frankfurt: Verlag Johann Christian Gebhard, 1763.
Mout, Nicolette, ed. *Die Kultur des Humanismus. Reden, Briefe, Traktate, Gespräche von Petrarca bis Kepler.* Munich: Beck, 1998. Pages 165–73: Maffeo Vegio, *De educatione liberorum*, 1444, chap. 15.
Novalis [Friedrich von Hardenberg]. *Werke, Tagebücher und Briefe.* Edited by Hans-Joachim Mähl and Richard Samuel. 3 vols. Munich: Hanser, 1978–1987.
Pauw, Corneille de. *Recherches philosophiques sur les Egyptiens et les Chinois.* 2 vols. Amsterdam: B. Ulam, 1773.
Pavur, Claude, translator. *The Ratio Studiorum: The Official Plan for Jesuit Education.* St Louis, Mo.: Institute of Jesuit Sources, 2005. A bilingual edition.
Perrault, Charles. *Contes.* Edited by Marc Soriano. Paris: Flammarion, 1989. Pages 241–93: *Histoires ou contes du temps passé*, 1697.
Peust, Carsten. "Hungersnotstele." Vol. 1, pages 208–17 in *Texte aus der Umwelt des Alten Testaments. Neue Folge.* Edited by Bernd Janowski et al. Gütersloh: Gütersloher Verlagshaus, 2004—.
Philo of Alexandria. *Philonis opera quae reperiri potuerunt omnia.* Edited by Thomas Mangey. 2 vols. London: Bowyer, 1742.
———. *The Works of Philo. Complete and Unabridged.* Translated by C.D. Yonge. Peabody, Mass.: Hendrickson, 1993. Pages 435–58: "On Joseph."
Pockels, Carl Friedrich. "Schack Fluurs Jugendgeschichte. Erstes Stück." *Magazin zur Erfahrungsseelenkunde* 4/2 (1786): 96–127.
Pope, Alexander. *The Twickenham Edition of the Poems of Alexander Pope.* Edited by John Butt. 11 vols. London: Methuen, 1939–1969.
Pratt, Samuel Jackson. *The Sublime and the Beautiful of Scripture, Being Essays on Select Passages.* London: Murray, 1777. Published under the pseudonym Courtney Melmoth.
Reimarus, Hermann Samuel. *Apologie oder Schutzschrift für die Vernünftigen Verehrer Gottes.* Edited by Gerhard Alexander. 2 vols. Frankfurt: Insel Verlag, 1972.
Renan, Ernest. *Oeuvres complètes.* Edited by Henriette Psichari. 10 vols. Paris: Calmann-Lévy, 1947–1961.
Ribble, Frederick G., and Anne G. Ribble. *Fielding's Library: An Annotated Catalogue.* Charlottesville: The Bibliographical Society of the University of Virginia, 1996.
Richardson, Samuel. "Advice to Unmarried Ladies." Vol. 2, pages 164–71 in *The Rambler in Three Volumes.* 15th edn. London: J. Johnson et al., 1806. From *The Rambler* 97 (19 February 1751).
Richelieu, Cardinal de. *Testament politique.* Critical edition by Louis André. Paris: Laffont, 1947.

Rivet, Frédéric. *De la première éducation d'un Prince, depuis sa naissance jusqu'a l'aage de sept ans.* Rotterdam: Leers, 1654.

——. *De l'éducation des enfans, et particulièrement celle des princes.* Amsterdam: Elsevier, 1679.

Rodriguez, Pedro, ed. *Catechismus Romanus* [1566]. Vatican City: Libreria Editrice Vaticana, 1999.

Rollin, Charles. *Oeuvres complètes.* Edited by Antoine Jean Letronne. 30 vols. Paris: Firmin Didot, 1821–1825. Vols. 25–28: *Traité des études, ou De la manière d'enseigner et d'étudier les belles-lettres*, 1726–1728.

Romanos Melodos. *Hymnes.* Edited by José Grosdidier de Matons. Vol. 1. Sources chrétiennes 99. Paris: Cerf, 1964.

Rousseau, Jean-Jacques. *Les Confessions. Autres textes autobiographiques.* Edited by Bernard Gagnebin and Marcel Raymond. Bibliothèque de la Pléiade. Paris: Gallimard, 1959.

Rowe, Elizabeth Singer. *The Works of Mrs Elizabeth Rowe in Four Volumes.* London: John and Arthur Arch, 1796. Vol. 1, pages 88–93 and 219–27: "To Belinda, from Sylvia" (two letters); vol. 3, pages 273–334: "The History of Joseph."

Scarron, Paul. *The Whole Comical Works.* 3rd edn. Translated by Thomas Brown, John Savage, and others. London: Nicholson, 1712. We quote from the following edition: *The Comical Romance and Other Tales.* Translated by Thomas Brown et al. 2 vols. London: Lawrence & Bullen, 1892.

Schellenberg, Johann Rudolf. *60 Biblische Geschichte des alten Testaments in Kupfer geätzt.* Winterthur: Verlag Heinrich Steiner, 1774.

Schetelig, Johann Andreas Gottfried. *Auktionskatalog der Bibliothek von Hermann Samuel Reimarus. Redigiert von Johann Andreas Gottfried Schetelig (1769, 1770).* Edited by Reimarus-Kommission der Joachim-Jungius-Gesellschaft. 2 vols. Hamburg: Joachim-Jungius-Gesellschaft, 1978–1980.

Schork, R.J. *Sacred Song from the Byzantine Pulpit: Romanos the Melodist.* Gainesville, Fla.: University Press of Florida, 1995.

Schütz, Friedrich Wilhelm von. *Freie Bekenntnisse eines Veteranen der Maurerei und anderer geheimer Gesellschaften.* Leipzig: Lauffer, 1824.

Seneca. *Seneca's Phaedra: Introduction, Text, Translation and Notes.* Edited by A.J. Boyle. Liverpool: Francis Cairns, 1987.

Shaftesbury, Anthony Ashley Cooper, Third Earl of. *Characteristics of Men, Manners, Opinions, Times* [1711]. Edited by Lawrence E. Klein. Cambridge: Cambridge University Press, 1999.

Shuckford, Samuel. *The Sacred and Prophane History of the World Connected.* 3 vols. London: Knaplock, 1728–1730.

Simon, Richard. *Histoire critique du Vieux Testament.* Nouvelle édition. Rotterdam: Reinier Leers, 1685.

Spinoza, Baruch. *Tractatus theologico-politicus* [1670]. Translated by Samuel Shirley. Leiden: Brill, 1989.

Steele, Richard. *The Christian Hero.* 2nd edn. London: Tonson, 1701.

——. [Untitled essay on Joseph.] *The Tatler* 233 (5 October 1710) = Vol. 4, pages 189–93 in *The Tatler.* Edited by George A. Aitken. London: Duckworth, 1899.

Stern, Menahem, ed. *Greek and Latin Authors on Jews and Judaism.* 3 vols. Jerusalem: Israel Academy of Sciences and Humanities, 1976–1984.

Sterne, Laurence. *The Sermons of Laurence Sterne.* Edited by Melvyn New (The Florida Edition of the Works of Laurence Sterne, vol. 4). Gainesville, Fla., 1996. Pages 113–22: "Joseph's History Considered. Forgiveness of Injuries"; pages 390–98: "Search the Scriptures".

Sulzer, Johann Georg. *Gedanken von dem vorzüglichen Werth der epischen Gedichte des Herrn Bodmers.* Berlin [no publisher], 1754.

——. *Allgemeine Theorie der schönen Künste.* 2nd edn, 5 vols. Leipzig: Weidmann, 1792.

Sylvester, Joshuah. *The Complete Works.* Edited by Alexander B. Grosart. 2 vols. Edinburgh: Edinburgh University Press, 1880. Vol. 2, pages 103–20: "The Maiden's Blush; or, Joseph, Mirror of Modestie, Map of Pietie, Maze of Destinie [. . .]. From the Latine of Fracastorius."

Terrasson, Jean. *Sethos, histoire ou vie tirée des monumens anecdotes de l'ancienne Egypte.* 2 vols. Amsterdam: Aux dépens de la Compagnie, 1732.

Thomasius, Christian. *Deutsche Schriften*. Selected and edited by Peter von Düffel. Stuttgart: Reclam, 1970.
Tzschimmer, Gabriel. *Durchlauchigste Zusammenkunfft. Oder: Historische Erzehlung* [...]. 2 vols. Nürnberg: Johann Hoffmann, 1680.
Usserius, Jacobus (James Ussher). *Annales Veteris et Novi Testamenti*, Paris: L. Billaine/J. du Puis, 1673.
Ussher, James. *The Annals of the World*. Edited by Larry Pierce and Marion Pierce. Green Forest, Ariz. 2003.
Vanini, Giulio Cesare. *De admirandis naturae reginae deaeque mortalium arcanis*. Paris: A. Perier, 1616. Repr., Galatina: Congedo Editore, 1985.
Varnhagen von Ense, Karl August. *Tageblätter*. Edited by Konrad Feilchenfeldt. Frankfurt: Deutscher Klassiker-Verlag, 1994.
——. *Les Oeuvres complètes de Voltaire*. Vol. 1—. Geneva: Institut et Musée Voltaire, 1968–1971; Oxford: Voltaire Foundation, 1971—. Vol. 4: *Histoire de Charles XII*; vol. 36, pages 254–61: article "Joseph" of the *Dictionnaire philosophique*, 1764; vol. 59: *La Philosophie de l'histoire*. Known as the "Oxford edition".
Voltaire. *Oeuvres complètes*. Edited by Louis Moland. 52 vols. Paris: Garnier frères, 1875–1883. Vol. 30, pages 1–316: "La Bible enfin expliquée, par plusieurs aumoniers de S.M.L.R.D.P." [1776] Referred to as Voltaire, *Oeuvres complètes* (Moland).
——. *Mélanges*. Edited by Jacques van Heuvel. Bibliothèque de la Pléiade. Paris: Gallimard, 1961. Pages 253–70: "Sermon des Cinquante."
——. *Essai sur les moeurs et l'esprit des nations*. Edited by René Pomeau. 2 vols. Paris: Garnier frères, 1963.
——. *Corpus des notes marginales de Voltaire*. Vol. 1—. Berlin: Akademie Verlag, 1979–1994 (vols 1–5); Oxford: Voltaire Foundation, 2006— (vol. 6—).
——. *Candide and Other Stories*. Translated by Roger Pearson. Oxford: Oxford University Press, 1990.
Vondel, Joost van den. *De Werken*. 11 vols. Amsterdam: Maatschappij voor goede en goedkoope lectuur, 1927–1940. Vol. 3, pages 431–83: "Huigh de Groots Iosef of Sofompaneas. Vertaalt", 1635.
——. *Cinq Tragédies*. Translated by Jean Stals. Paris: Didier, 1969. Pages 121–96: "Joseph à Dothan."
Walpole, Horace. *The Yale Edition of Horace Walpole's Correspondence*. Edited by W.S. Lewis. 48 vols. New Haven, Conn.: Yale University Press, 1937–1983.
Warburton, William. *The Works*. 7 vols. London: John Nichols, 1788–1794. Vols 1–3: *The Divine Legation of Moses*.
Warton, Joseph. "Translation of a Manuscript of Longinus, Lately Discovered." *The Adventurer* 51 (1 May 1753); 57 (22 May 1753) = Vol. 1, pages 301–6 and 337–42 in *The Adventurer*. 2 vols. London: J. Payne, 1753.
Watts, Isaac. *Discourses of the Love of God and the Use and Abuse of the Passions in Religion*. London: Clark, 1729.
Weil, Gustav. *Biblische Legenden der Muselmänner*. Frankfurt: Literarische Anstalt, 1845.
Wendelinus, Marcus Fridericus. *Admiranda Nili. Commentatione philologica, geographica, historica, physica et hieroglyphica ex CCCXVIII autoribus... illustrata*. Cambridge: Roger Daniel, 1648.
Wesley, Susanna. *The Complete Writings*. Edited by Charles Wallace. New York: Oxford University Press, 1997.
Wieland, Christoph Martin. *Wielands Briefwechsel*. Vol. 1—. Berlin: Akademie Verlag, 1963—.
——. *Schriften zur deutschen Sprache und Literatur*. Edited by Jan Philipp Reemtsma. 3 vols. Frankfurt: Insel Verlag, 2005.
Yohannan, John D., ed. *Joseph and Potiphar's Wife in World Literature: An Anthology of the Story of the Chaste Youth and the Lustful Stepmother*. New York: New Directions Books, 1968.
Zedler, Johann Heinrich. *Großes vollständiges Universal-Lexikon*. 64 vols, 4 supplementary vols. Halle and Leipzig: Johann Heinrich Zedler, 1732–1754.

Zesen, Philipp von. *Sämtliche Werke*. Edited by Ferdinand van Ingen. Vol. 1—. Berlin: de Gruyter, 1970—. – Vol. 7: *Assenat*, [1670] 1990. All references are to this edition.
———. *Assenat 1670*. Edited by Volker Meid. Tübingen: Niemeyer, 1967. Reprint of the original Amsterdam edition.

SECONDARY SOURCES

Adam, Gottfried, Rainer Lachmann, and Regine Schindler, eds. *Die Inhalte von Kinderbibeln. Kriterien ihrer Auswahl*. Göttingen: V & R Unipress, 2008.
Adam, Traute. *Clementia principis. Der Einfluss hellenistischer Fürstenspiegel auf den Versuch einer rechtlichen Fundierung des Principats bei Seneca*. Stuttgart: Klett, 1970.
Allen, Robert J. *The Clubs of Augustan London*. Cambridge, Mass.: Harvard University Press, 1933.
Alzheimer-Haller, Heidrun. *Handbuch zur narrativen Volksaufklärung. Moralische Geschichten 1780–1848*. Berlin: de Gruyter, 2004.
Argyle, A.W. "Joseph the Patriarch in Patristic Teaching." *The Expository Times* 67 (1956): 199–201.
Assmann, Jan. *Ägyptische Geheimnisse*. Munich: Fink, 2004.
———. *Die Zauberflöte. Oper und Mysterium*. Munich: Hanser, 2005.
Auerochs, Bernd. *Die Entstehung der Kunstreligion*. Göttingen: Vandenhoeck & Ruprecht, 2006.
Aune, David C. "Mastery of the Passions: Philo, 4 Maccabees and Earliest Christianity." Pages 125–58 in *Hellenization Revisited: Shaping a Christian Response within the Greco-Roman World*. Edited by Wendy E. Helleman. Lanham, Md.: University Press of America, 1994.
Bakhtin, Mikhail M. "Epic and Novel." Pages 3–40 in Mikhail M. Bakhtin, *The Dialogic Imagination: Four Essays*. Translated by Caryl Emerson and Michael Holquist. Austin, Tex.: University of Texas Press, 1981.
Bal, Mieke. *Loving Yusuf: Conceptual Travels from Present to Past*. Chicago: University of Chicago Press, 2008.
Bamberger, Ludwig. *Joh. Conrad Seekatz. Ein deutscher Maler des achtzehnten Jahrhunderts*. Heidelberg: Winter, 1916.
Baron, Hans. *The Crisis of the Early Italian Renaissance: Civic Humanism and Republican Liberty in an Age of Classicism and Tyranny*. Revised one-volume edn. Princeton, N.J.: Princeton University Press, 1966.
Bartlet, M. Elizabeth C. *Etienne-Nicolas Méhul and Opera: Source and Archival Studies of Lyric Theatre during the French Revolution, Consulate and Empire*. 2 vols. Heilbronn: Musik-Edition Lucie Galland, 1999.
Battestin, Martin. *The Moral Basis of Fielding's Art: A Study of Joseph Andrews*. Middletown, Conn.: Wesleyan University Press, 1959.
——— and Ruthe R. Battestin. *Henry Fielding: A Life*. London: Routledge, 1989.
Beckermann, Bernard. *Theatrical Presentation: Performer, Audience and Act*. New York: Routledge, 1990.
Beebee, Thomas O. *Clarissa on the Continent*. University Park: Pennsylvania State University Press, 1990.
Benedict, Barbara M. *Framing Feeling: Sentiment and Style in English Prose Fiction, 1745–1800*. New York: AMS Press, 1994.
Béranger, Jean. "Pour une enquête européenne du ministériat au XVIIe siècle." *Annales* 29 (1974): 166–92.
Bercegol, Fabienne. "De la grâce au grotesque. Genèse de la 'poétique du christianisme' dans l'oeuvre de Chateaubriand." Pages 47–58 in *Ethique et littérature, XIXe–XXe siècle*. Edited by Eléonore Roy-Reverzy and Gisèle Séginger. Strasbourg: Presses Universitaires de Strasbourg, 2000.

Bergengruen, Maximilian. *Nachfolge Christi – Nachahmung der Natur. Himmlische und natürliche Magie bei Paracelsus, im Paracelsismus und in der Barockliteratur.* Hamburg: Meiner, 2007.
Best, Thomas W. *Macropedius.* Twayne's World Author Series. New York: Twayne Publishers, 1972.
Besterman, Theodore. *Voltaire.* 3rd edn. Oxford: Blackwell, 1976.
Blankert, Albert, ed. *Rembrandt: A Genius and his Impact.* Melbourne: National Gallery of Victoria, 1997.
Bocian, Martin. *Lexikon der biblischen Personen.* Stuttgart: Kröner, 1989.
Bode, Wilhelm. *Goethes Leben.* 9 vols. Berlin: Mittler, 1920–1927.
Bottigheimer, Ruth B. *The Bible for Children: From the Age of Gutenberg to the Present.* New Haven, Conn.: Yale University Press, 1996.
Brauneis, Walther. "Das Frontispiz im Alberti-Libretto von 1791 als Schlüssel zu Mozarts Zauberflöte." *Mitteilungen der Internationalen Stiftung Mozarteum* (1993): 49–59.
Breuer, Dieter. "Grimmelshausens politische Argumentation." *Daphnis* 5 (1976): 303–32.
Breyl, Jutta. "Assenat und Isis – eine poetologische Kontroverse in Bild und Text." Pages 719–39 in *Künste und Natur in Diskursen der Frühen Neuzeit.* Edited by Hartmut Laufhütte. Wiesbaden: Harrassowitz, 2000.
Brottier, Laurence. "Joseph le politique: de l'anonymat du héros dans la traité philonienne *De Josepho* à sa mise en scène à l'époque moderne." *Revue des études juives* 162 (2003): 43–68.
Brush, Craig B. *Montaigne and Bayle: Variations on the Theme of Skepticism.* The Hague: Nijhoff, 1966.
Castle, Terry. *Masquerade and Civilization: The Carnivalesque in Eighteenth-Century English Culture and Fiction.* London: Methuen, 1986.
Catastini, Alessandro. "Le testimonianze di Manetone e la Storia di Giuseppe (Genesi 37–50)." *Henoch* 17 (1995): 279–300.
———. "Ancora sulla datazione della Storia di Giuseppe (Genesi 37–50)." *Henoch* 20 (1998): 208–24.
Champion, Justin A.I. *The Pillars of Priestcraft Shaken: The Church of England and its Enemies, 1660–1730.* Cambridge: Cambridge University Press, 1992.
Chartier, Roger. *The Order of Books.* Translated by Lydia G. Cochrane. Cambridge: Polity Press, 1994.
Clark, Kenneth. *The Nude: A Study in Ideal Form.* Princeton, N.J.: Princeton University Press, 1972.
Clery, Emma J. *The Feminization Debate in Eighteenth-Century England.* Basingstoke: Palgrave Macmillan, 2004.
Conti, Vittorio. "The Mechanisation of Virtue: Republican Rituals in Italian Political Thought in the Sixteenth and Seventeenth Centuries." Vol. 2, pages 73–83 in *Republicanism: A Shared European Heritage.* Edited by Martin van Gelderen and Quentin Skinner. 2 vols. Cambridge: Cambridge University Press, 2002.
Courtines, Léo Pierre. *Bayle's Relations with England and the English.* New York: Columbia University Press, 1938.
Craveri, Benedetta. *Madame du Deffand and Her World.* Translated by Teresa Waugh. London: Halban, 2002.
Curtius, Ernst Robert. *Europäische Literatur und lateinisches Mittelalter.* 8th edn. Berne: Francke, 1973.
David, Alun. "The Story of Semiramis: An Oriental Tale in Elizabeth Rome's *The History of Joseph.*" *Women's Writing* 4 (1997): 91–101.
Devaux, Michael. "Bayle, Pierre (1647–1706)." Pages 102–4 in *Dictionnaire général de Voltaire.* Edited by Raymond Trousson and Jeroom Vercuysse. Paris: Honoré Champion, 2003.
Diebner, Bernd-Jörg. "Le Roman de Joseph, ou Israël en Egypte: un midrash post-exilique de la Tora." Pages 55–71 in *Le Livre de traverse. De l'exégèse biblique à l'anthropologie.* Edited by Olivier Abel et al. Paris: Cerf, 1992.
Dixon, Thomas. *From Passions to Emotions: The Creation of a Secular Psychological Category.* Cambridge: Cambridge University Press, 2003.

Donner, Herbert. "Der Redaktor. Überlegungen zum vorkritischen Umgang mit der Heiligen Schrift." Pages 259–85 in Herbert Donner, *Aufsätze zum Alten Testament*. Berlin: De Gruyter, 1994.
Doody, Margaret Anne. *The True Story of the Novel*. London: Fontana Press, 1997.
Douglas, Mary. *Natural Symbols*. 2nd edn. Harmondsworth: Penguin, 1973.
Droste, Heiko. "Patrioten ausländischer Herkunft. Zum Patriotismus in Schweden im 17. Jahrhundert." Pages 309–34 in *Patria und Patrioten vor dem Patriotismus. Pflichten, Rechte, Glauben und Rekonfigurationen europäischer Gemeinwesen im 17. Jahrhundert*. Edited by Robert von Friedeburg. Wiesbaden: Harrassowitz, 2005.
Dupont-Ferrier, Gustave. *Du Collège de Clermont au lycée Louis-Le-Grand (1563–1920)*. 3 vols. Paris: E. de Boccard, 1921–1925.
Dürbeck, Gabriele. *Einbildungskraft und Aufklärung*. Tübingen: Niemeyer, 1998.
Ebeling, Florian. *Das Geheimnis des Hermes Trismegistos. Geschichte des Hermetismus von der Antike bis zur Neuzeit*. Munich: Beck, 2005.
Ellis, J. Edward. *Paul and Ancient Views of Sexual Desire*. London: T & T Clark, 2007.
Emmerling, Ernst. *Johann Conrad Seekatz, 1719–1768. Ein Maler aus der Zeit des jungen Goethe*. Landau: Pfälzische Verlagsanstalt, 1991.
Engels, Hans-Werner. "Zu Leben und Werk von Johann Friedrich Ernst Albrecht (1752–1814)." Vol. 5, pages 645–79 in *Europa in der Frühen Neuzeit*. Edited by Erich Donnert. 7 vols. Cologne: Böhlau, 1997–2003.
Engelsing, Rolf. *Der Bürger als Leser. Lesergeschichte in Deutschland 1500–1800*. Stuttgart: Metzler, 1974.
Erffa, Hans-Martin von. *Ikonologie der Genesis*. 2 vols. Munich: Deutscher Kunstverlag, 1989–1995.
Evans, R.J.W. "The Court: A Protean Institution and an Elusive Subject." Pages 481–91 in *Princes, Patronage, and the Nobility: The Court at the Beginning of the Modern Age, c. 1450–1650*. Edited by Ronald G. Asch and Adolf H. Birke. Oxford: Oxford University Press, 1991.
Eyffinger, Arthur. "The Fourth Man: Stoic Tradition in Grotian Drama." *Grotiana*. New Series 22/23 (2001/2002): 117–56.
Feeß, Kurt. *Claude Genest. Sein Leben und seine Werke*. Strasbourg: Trübner, 1912.
Fisch, Harold. "Biblical 'Imitation' in *Joseph Andrews*." Pages 31–42 in *Biblical Patterns in Modern Literature*. Edited by David H. Hirsch and Nehama Aschkenasy. Chico, Cal.: Scholars Press, 1984.
Fischer, Bernd-Jürgen. *Handbuch zu Thomas Manns "Josephsromanen"*. Tübingen: Francke, 2002.
Forbes, Duncan. *Hume's Philosophical Politics*. Cambridge: Cambridge University Press, 1975.
Forster, Edward M. *Aspects of the Novel*. Edited by Oliver Stallybrass. London: Penguin, 1990.
Frenzel, Elisabeth. *Stoffe der Weltliteratur*. 10th edn. Stuttgart: Kröner, 2005.
Fumaroli, Marc. *Chateaubriand. Poésie et terreur*. Paris: Fallois, 2003.
Garber, Klaus. "Zur Statuskonkurrenz von Adel und gelehrtem Bürgertum im theoretischen Schrifttum des 17. Jahrhunderts." *Daphnis* 11 (1982): 115–43.
Gemünden, Petra von. "La Culture des passions à l'époque du Nouveau Testament." *Etudes théologiques et religieuses* 70 (1995): 335–48.
Gera, Dov. *Judaea and Mediterranean Politics 219 to 161 BCE*. Leiden: Brill, 1998.
Goedeke, Karl. *Grundriss zur Geschichte der deutschen Dichtung aus den Quellen*. 2nd edn. 18 vols. Dresden: L. Ehlermann, 1884–1957 (vols 1–13); Berlin: Akademie Verlag, 1959–1998 (vols 14–18).
Goethe-Wörterbuch. Edited by Berlin-Brandenburgische Akademie der Wissenschaften et al. Vol. 1—. Stuttgart: Kohlhammer, 1978—.
Grab, Werner. *Demokratische Strömungen in Hamburg und Schleswig-Holstein zur Zeit der ersten französischen Republik*. Hamburg: Hans Christians Verlag, 1966.
Grabbe, Lester L. *Judaism from Cyrus to Hadrian*. Minneapolis, Minn.: Fortress, 1992.
Grell, Alfred. *Goethe als Operndirektor*. Bregenz: Eugen Russ Verlag, 1949.
Grell, Chantal. *L'Histoire entre érudition et philosophie. Etude sur la connaissance historique à l'âge des Lumières*. Paris: Presses Universitaires de France, 1993.

———. *Le Dix-huitième Siècle et l'antiquité en France, 1680-1789*. 2 vols. Oxford: Voltaire Foundation, 1995.
Grimm, Reinhold. *Fielding's Tom Jones and the European Novel since Antiquity*. Frankfurt: Peter Lang, 2005.
Grotefend, H. *Der Königsleutnant Graf Thoranc in Frankfurt am Main: Aktenstücke über die Besetzung der Stadt durch die Franzosen, 1759-1762*. Frankfurt: Völcker, 1904.
Grottanelli, Cristiano. *Kings and Prophets*. Oxford: Oxford University Press, 1999. Pages 147-71: "Biblical Narrative and the Ancient Novel."
Haitsma Mulier, Eco O.G. *The Myth of Venice and Dutch Republican Thought in the Seventeenth Century*. Assen: Van Gorcum, 1980.
Hartman, Mary S. *The Household and the Making of History: A Subversive View of the Western Past*, Cambridge: Cambridge University Press, 2004.
Heiss, Gernot. "Die Liebe des Fürsten zur Geometrie. Adelserziehung und die Wertschätzung der höfischen Gesellschaft für Symmetrie und Regelmäβigkeit." Pages 101-19 in *Barock. Neue Sichtweisen einer Epoche*. Edited by Peter J. Burgard. Vienna: Böhlau, 2001.
Hengel, Martin. *Judaism and Hellenism: Studies in their Encounter in Palestine during the Early Hellenistic Period*. 2 vols. Eugene, Oreg.: Wipf & Stock, 2003.
Hesse, Carla. "Print Culture in the Enlightenment." Pages 366-80 in *The Enlightenment World*. Edited by Martin Fitzpatrick et al. London: Routledge, 2004.
Hillgarth, Jocelyn N. *The Spanish Kingdoms 1250-1516*. 2 vols. Oxford: Clarendon Press, 1976-1978.
Hirzel, Rudolf. *Plutarch*. Leipzig: Dieterich, 1912.
Horst, Pieter W. van der. *Chaeremon: Egyptian Priest and Stoic Philosopher*. Leiden: Brill, 1987.
Hunter, J. Paul. *Before Novels: The Cultural Context of Eighteenth-Century English Fiction*. New York: Norton, 1990.
Hunter, Michael, and David Wootton, eds. *Atheism from the Reformation to the Enlightenment*. Oxford: Clarendon Press, 1992. Pages 13-54: David Wootton, "New Histories of Atheism"; pages 255-72: David Berman, "Disclaimers as Offence Mechanisms in Charles Blount and John Toland."
Ingen, Ferdinand van. *Philipp von Zesen*. Stuttgart: Metzler, 1970.
———. "Grimmelshausen's *Keuscher Joseph* und sein Leser." *Simpliciana* 10 (1988): 405-20.
Israel, Jonathan I. *The Dutch Republic: Its Rise, Greatness, and Fall, 1477-1806*. Oxford: Clarendon Press, 1995.
———. *Radical Enlightenment: Philosophy and the Making of Modernity 1650-1750*. Oxford: Oxford University Press, 2001.
———. *Enlightenment Contested: Philosophy, Modernity, and the Emancipation of Man 1670-1752*. Oxford: Oxford University Press, 2006.
Jauss, Hans Robert. *Aesthetic Experience and Literary Hermeneutics*. Translated by Michael Shaw. Minneapolis, Minn.: University of Minnesota Press, 1982. Pages 152-88: "Interaction Patterns of Identification with the Hero."
Jedin, Hubert. "Laientheologie im Zeitalter der Glaubensspaltung: Der Konzilsarzt Fracastoro." *Trierer theologische Zeitschrift* 64 (1953): 11-24.
Joannidès, A. *La Comédie-française du 1680 à 1900: Dictionnaire général des pièces et des auteurs*. Geneva: Slatkine, 1970.
Johnson, Sara Raup. *Historical Fictions and Hellenistic Jewish Identity*. Berkeley: University of California Press, 2004.
Kaiser, Michael and Andreas Pecar. "Reichsfürsten und ihre Favoriten." Pages 9-19 in *Der zweite Mann im Staat*. Edited by Michael Kaiser et al. Berlin: Duncker & Humblot, 2003.
Katz, Eve. "Marmontel and the Voice of Experience." *Studies on Voltaire and the Eighteenth Century* 76 (1970): 233-59.
Katz, Jacob. *Jews and Freemasons in Europe, 1723-1939*. Cambridge, Mass.: Harvard University Press, 1970.

Kee, Howard C. "The Ethical Dimensions of the Testaments of the XII as a Clue to Provenance." *New Testament Studies* 24 (1978): 259–70.
Kempkens, Klaus. *Joseph und Aeneas. Untersuchungen zum "Joseph" des Girolamo Fracastoro, einem Bibelepos Italiens aus dem 16. Jahrhundert.* PhD dissertation. Bonn: Rheinische Friedrich-Wilhelms-Universität, 1972.
Koebner, Richard. "Despot and Despotism: Vicissitudes of a Political Term." *Journal of the Warburg and Courtauld Institutes* 14 (1951): 275–302.
Kölsch, Gerhard. *Johann Georg Trautmann (1713–1769). Leben und Werk.* Frankfurt: Peter Lang, 1999.
Konstan, David. *Sexual Symmetry: Love in the Ancient Novel and Related Genres.* Princeton, N.J.: Princeton University Press, 1994.
Korey, Michael. *The Geometry of Power – The Power of Geometry: Mathematical Instruments and Princely Mechanical Devices around 1600.* Munich: Deutscher Kunstverlag, 2007.
Koselleck, Reinhart. *Kritik und Krise. Ein Beitrag zur Pathogenese der bürgerlichen Welt*, Freiburg: Alber, 1959.
———. *Futures Past. On the Semantics of Historical Time.* Translated by Keith Tribe. Cambridge, Mass.: MIT Press, 1985. Pages 21–38: "Historia magistra vitae: The Dissolution of the Topos into the Perspective of a Modernized Historical Process."
Kozul, Mladen. "La Séduction critique: la lecture du roman entre la théologie et le libertinage." Pages 161–83 in *Des Sens au sens. Littérature et morale de Molière à Voltaire.* Edited by Jacques Wagner. Leuven: Peeters, 2007.
Kreuzer, Helmut. "Gefährliche Lesesucht? Bemerkungen zur politischen Lektürekritik im ausgehenden 18. Jahrhundert." Pages 62–75 in *Leser und Lesen im 18. Jahrhundert.* By Rainer Gruenter et al. Heidelberg: Winter, 1977.
Kullmann, Dorothea. *Description. Theorie und Praxis der Beschreibung im französischen Roman von Chateaubriand bis Zola.* Heidelberg: Winter, 2004.
Kunz, Andreas. "Ägypten in der Perspektive Israels am Beispiel der Josephsgeschichte (Gen 37–50)." *Biblische Zeitschrift* 47 (2003): 206–29.
Laforge, Danielle. "Theorien über Hof, Staat und Gesellschaft in Philipp von Zesens *Adriatischer Rosemund.*" *Daphnis* 11 (1982): 253–76.
Lang, Bernhard. "Buchreligion." Vol. 2, pages 143–65 in *Handbuch religionswissenschaftlicher Grundbegriffe.* Edited by Hubert Cancik et al. 5 vols. Stuttgart: Kohlhammer, 1988–2001.
———. *Sacred Games: A History of Christian Worship.* London: Yale University Press, 1997.
——— and Colleen McDannell. *Heaven: A History.* 2nd edn. New Haven, Conn.: Yale University Press, 2001.
———. *The Hebrew God: Portrait of an Ancient Deity.* New Haven, Conn.: Yale University Press, 2002.
———. "Joseph the Diviner: Careers of a Biblical Hero." Pages 93–109 in idem, *Hebrew Life and Literature: Selected Essays.* Farnham: Ashgate, 2008.
Latapie, Sophie. "Enseigner l'histoire sainte à la manière des précepteurs catholiques." *Revue d'histoire littéraire de la France* 107 (2007): 559–70.
Lenski, Gerhard. *Power and Privilege: A Theory of Social Stratification.* New York: McGraw-Hill, 1966.
Levine, Joseph M. *The Battle of the Books: History and Literature in the Augustan Age.* Ithaca, NY: Cornell University Press, 1991.
Lizé, Emile. "Voltaire et Les sermons de m. Yorick." *Studies on Voltaire and the Eighteenth Century* 215 (1982): 99–100.
Lüthi, Max. "Märchen und Sage." Pages 22–48 in idem, *Volksmärchen und Volkssage: Zwei Grundformen erzählender Dichtung.* 2nd edn. Berne: Francke, 1966.
———. "The Fairy-Tale Hero." Pages 135–46 in idem, *Once upon a Time: On the Nature of Fairy Tales.* Translated by Lee Chadeayne and Paul Gottwald. Bloomington: Indiana University Press, 1976.

Lynch, James J. *Henry Fielding and the Heliodoran Novel*. Rutherford, N.J.: Fairleigh Dickinson University Press, 1968.
McDannell, Colleen. *The Christian Home in Victorian America, 1840–1900*. Bloomington: Indiana University Press, 1986.
McLeish, Kenneth. "Dido, Aeneas, and the Concept of *pietas*." Pages 134–41 in *Virgil*. Edited by Ian McAuslan and Peter Walcot. Oxford: Oxford University Press, 1990.
Mandt, Hella. "Tyrannis, Despotie." Vol. 6, pages 651–706 in *Geschichtliche Grundbegriffe*. Edited by Otto Brunner et al. 8 vols. Stuttgart: Klett-Cotta, 1972–1997.
Martens, Wolfgang. "Zur Figur eines edlen Juden im Aufklärungsroman vor Lessing." Pages 65–77 in *Begegnung von Deutschen und Juden in der Geistesgeschichte des 18. Jahrhunderts*. Edited by Jakob Katz and Karl Heinrich Rengstorf. Tübingen: Niemeyer, 1994.
——. *Der patriotische Minister. Fürstendiener in der Literatur der Aufklärungszeit*. Weimar: Böhlau, 1996.
Meid, Volker. "Nachwort des Herausgebers." Pages 1*–54* in Philipp von Zesen, *Assenat 1670*. Edited by Volker Meid. Tübingen: Niemeyer, 1967.
Meinecke, Friedrich. *Machiavellism: The Doctrine of Raison d'Etat and its Place in Modern History*. Translated by Douglas Scott. London: Routledge & Kegan Paul, 1962.
Meinhold, Arndt. "Die Gattung der Josephsgeschichte und des Estherbuches: Diaspora-Novelle." *Zeitschrift für die alttestamentliche Wissenschaft* 87 (1975): 306–24; 88 (1976): 72–93.
Meldrum, Tim. *Domestic Service and Gender, 1660–1750: Life and Work in the London Household*. Harlow: Pearson Education, 2000.
Mentz, Steve. *Romance for Sale in Early Modern England: The Rise of Prose Fiction*. Aldershot: Ashgate, 2006.
Mentzel, Elisabeth. *Wolfgang und Cornelia Goethes Lehrer. Ein Beitrag zu Goethes Entwicklungsgeschichte*. Leipzig: R. Voigtländer, 1909.
Meyer, Stephen C. *Carl Maria von Weber and the Search for a German Opera*. Bloomington: Indiana University Press, 2003.
Modrzejewski, Joseph Mélèze. *The Jews of Egypt. From Rameses II to Emperor Hadrian*. Edinburgh: T. & T. Clark, 1995.
Moore, Cornelia Niekus. "Gottseliges Bezeugen und frommer Lebenswandel: Das Exempelbuch als pietistische Kinderlektüre." Pages 131–42 in *Das Kind in Pietismus und Aufklärung*. Edited by Josef H. Neumann et al. Tübingen: Niemeyer, 2000.
Moos, Peter von. *Geschichte als Topik. Das rhetorische Exemplum von der Antike zur Neuzeit*. Hildesheim: Olms, 1988.
Mumford, Lewis. *The City in History: Its Origins, its Transformations, and its Prospects*. Harmondsworth: Penguin, 1973.
Nellen, Henk. *Hugo de Groot. Een leven in strijd om de vrede, 1583–1645*. Amsterdam: Uitgeverij Balans, 2007.
Newmark, Catherine. *Passion – Affekt – Gefühl. Philosophische Theorien der Emotionen zwischen Aristoteles und Kant*. Hamburg: Meiner, 2008.
Niehoff, Maren R. "New Garments for Biblical Joseph." Pages 33–56 in *Biblical Interpretation: History, Context, and Reality*. Edited by Christine Helmer. Atlanta, Ga.: Society of Biblical Literature, 2005.
Nokes, G.D. *A History of the Crime of Blasphemy*. London: Sweet & Maxwell, 1928.
Norton, David. *A History of the Bible as Literature*. 2 vols. Cambridge: Cambridge University Press, 1993.
Nussbaum, Martha C. *The Therapy of Desire: Theory and Practice in Hellenistic Ethics*. Princeton, N.J.: Princeton University Press, 1994.
Oeftering, Michael. *Heliodor und seine Bedeutung für die Litteratur*. Berlin: Felber, 1901.
Ong, Walter J. *Orality and Literacy: The Technologizing of the Word*. London: Methuen, 1982.
Ort, Claus-Michael. "Affektenlehre." Pages 124–39 in *Die Literatur des 17. Jahrhunderts*. Edited by Albert Meier. Hansers Sozialgeschichte der deutschen Literatur vom 16. Jahrhundert bis zur Gegenwart, vol. 2. Munich: Hanser, 1999.

Parente, James A. *Religious Drama and the Humanist Tradition: Christian Theater in Germany and the Netherlands, 1500–1680.* Leiden: Brill, 1987.
Pearson, Roger. *The Fables of Reason: A Study of Voltaire's Contes Philosophiques.* Oxford: Clarendon Press, 1993.
Pech, Klaus-Ulrich. "Beispielgeschichten. Anmerkungen zu einem Prototyp der Kinder- und Jugendliteratur." Pages 78–118 in *Aufklärung und Kinderbuch. Studien zur Kinder- und Jugendliteratur des 18. Jahrhunderts.* Edited by Dagmar Grenz. Pinneberg: Raecke, 1984.
Pervo, Richard I. "The Testament of Joseph and Greek Romance." Pages 15–28 in *Studies on the Testament of Joseph.* Edited by George W.E. Nickelsburg. Missoula, Mont.: Scholars Press, 1975.
Peter-Perret, Sybille. *Biblische Geschichten für die Jugend erzählt. Eine Studie zur religiösen Kinder- und Jugendliteratur des 18. Jahrhunderts.* Essen: Westarp Wissenschaften, 1991.
Pigler, A. *Barockthemen. Eine Auswahl von Verzeichnissen zur Ikonographie des 17. und 18. Jahrhunderts.* 2nd enlarged edition. 3 vols. Budapest: Akadémiai Kiadó, 1974.
Pintard, René. "Autour de *Cinna* et *Polyeucte.* Nouveaux problèmes de chronologie et de critique cornéliennes." *Revue d'histoire littéraire de la France* 64 (1964): 377–413.
Pocock, John G.A. *The Machiavellian Moment: Florentine Political Thought and the Atlantic Republican Tradition.* Princeton, N.J.: Princeton University Press, 1975.
———. *Barbarism and Religion.* 2 vols. Cambridge: Cambridge University Press, 1999. Volume 2: *Narratives of Civil Government.*
Pomeau, René, ed. *Voltaire en son temps. Nouvelle édition.* 2 vols. Paris: Fayard, 1995.
Potter, Tiffany. *Honest Sins: Georgian Libertinism and the Plays and Novels of Henry Fielding.* Montreal: McGill-Queen's University Press, 1999.
Prak, Maarten. "The Carrot and the Stick: Social Control and Poor Relief in the Dutch Republic, Sixteenth to Eighteenth Centuries." Pages 149–66 in *Institutions, Instruments and Agents of Social Control and Discipline in Early Modern Europe.* Edited by Heinz Schilling. Frankfurt: Klostermann, 1999.
Premare, Alfred-Louis de. *Joseph et Muhammad. Le chapitre 12 du Coran.* Aix-en-Provence: Publications de l'Université de Provence, 1989.
Prescott, Sarah. *Women, Authorship and Literary Culture, 1690–1740.* Houndmills: Palgrave Macmillan, 2003.
Preyat, Fabrice. "Maître des divertissements ou trouble-fête? Charles-Claude Genest et le Petit Concile à la cour de la duchesse du Maine." Pages 137–54 in *La Duchesse du Maine (1676–1753). Une mécène à la croisée des arts et des siècles.* Edited by Fabrice Preyat (Etudes sur le 18e siècle 31). Brussels: Editions de l'Université de Bruxelles, 2003.
———. *Le Petit Concile de Bossuet et la christianisation des moeurs et des pratiques littéraires sous Louis XIV.* Berlin: Lit Verlag, 2007.
Raabe, Paul. "Goethe und Bogatzky – eine Marginalie." Pages 1–11 in *Goethe und der Pietismus.* Edited by Hans-Georg Kemper and Hans Schneider. Tübingen: Niemeyer, 2001.
Rang, Brita. "An Unidentified Source of John Locke's *Some Thoughts Concerning Education.*" *Pedagogy, Culture and Society* 9 (2001): 249–77.
Redford, Donald B. *A Study of the Biblical Story of Joseph (Genesis 37–50).* Leiden: Brill, 1970.
Richetti, John J. "Mrs Elizabeth Rowe: The Novel as Polemic." *Publications of the Modern Language Association of America* 82 (1967): 522–29.
Rist, John M. *Stoic Philosophy.* Cambridge: Cambridge University Press, 1969.
Roeck, Bernd. *Civic Culture and Everyday Life in Early Modern Germany.* Leiden: Brill, 2006.
Röhrich, Lutz. *Märchen und Wirklichkeit.* 2nd edn. Wiesbaden: Steiner, 1964.
Rojahn-Deyk, Barbara. *Henry Fielding. Untersuchungen zu Wesen und Funktion der Ironie in seiner frühen Prosa.* Nürnberg: Hans Carl, 1973.
Römer, Thomas. "La Narration, une subversion: l'histoire de Joseph (Gn 37–50) et les romans de la diaspora." Pages 15–27 in *Narrativity and Biblical and Related Texts.* Edited by George J. Booke and Jean-Daniel Kaestli. Leuven: Peeters, 2000.

Rosen-Zvi, Ishay. "Bilha the Temptress: *The Testament of Reuben* and *The Birth of Sexuality*." *Jewish Quarterly Review* 96 (2006): 65–94.
Schama, Simon. *The Embarrassment of Riches: An Interpretation of Dutch Culture in the Golden Age*. London: Fontana Press, 1991.
———. *Landscape and Memory*. London: HarperCollins, 1995.
———. *Rembrandt's Eyes*. New York: Knopf, 1999.
Schiffmann, Gustav A. *Die Entstehung der Rittergrade in der Freimaurerei um die Mitte des XVIII. Jahrhunderts*. Leipzig: Bruno Zechel, 1882.
Schneider, Ferdinand Josef. *Die Freimaurerei und ihr Einfluss auf die geistige Kultur in Deutschland am Ende des XVIII. Jahrhunderts*. Prague: 1909.
Schnitzer, Manuel. *Goethes Josephsbilder – Goethes Josephsdichtung*. Hamburg: W. Gente, 1921.
Schubart, Martin. *François de Théas Comte de Thoranc. Goethes Königsleutnant*. Munich: Bruckmann, 1896.
Schulz, Dieter. *Studien zur Verführungsszene im englischen Roman (1660–1760)*. Marburg: Mauersberger, 1968.
Schwarzbach, Bertram E. *Voltaire's Old Testament Criticism*. Geneva: Droz, 1971.
——— and A.W. Fairbairn. "History and Structure of Our *Traité des trois imposteurs*." Pages 75–129 in *Heterodoxy, Spinozism, and Free Thought in Early Eighteenth-Century Europe*. Edited by Silvia Berti et al. Dordrecht: Kluwer, 1996.
Schweitzer, Albert. *The Quest of the Historical Jesus*. Edited by John Bowden. London: SCM Press, 2000.
Scott, H.M. "The Rise of the First Minister in Eighteenth-Century Europe." Pages 21–52 in *History and Biography: Essays in Honour of Derek Beales*. Edited by T.C.W. Blanning and David Cannadine. Cambridge: Cambridge University Press, 1996.
Shackleton, Robert. *Essays on Montesquieu and on the Enlightenment*. Edited by David Gilson and Martin Smith. Oxford: Voltaire Foundation, 1988.
Simon, Renée. *Nicolas Fréret, académicien*. Studies on Voltaire and the Eighteenth Century, vol. 17. Geneva: Institut et Musée Voltaire, 1961.
Singer, Herbert. "Joseph in Ägypten. Zur Erzählkunst des 17. und 18. Jahrhunderts." *Euphorion* 48 (1954): 249–79.
Skinner, Quentin. "Machiavelli's *Discorsi* and the Pre-Humanist Origins of Republican Ideas." Pages 121–41 in *Machiavelli and Republicanism*. Edited by Gisela Bock et al. Cambridge: Cambridge University Press, 1990.
Smits-Veldt, Mieke B. "Die Kanzel des Bürgers: Theater und Schauspiel im Amsterdam des 17. Jahrhunderts." Pages 136–52 in *Amsterdam 1585–1672. Morgenröte des Kapitalismus*. Edited by Bernd Wilczek and Jos van Waterschoot. Bühl-Moos: Elster Verlag, 1993.
Soggin, J. Alberto. *Das Buch Genesis. Kommentar*. Darmstadt: Wissenschaftliche Buchgesellschaft, 1997.
Sommerville, C. John. "The Distinction between Indoctrination and Education in England, 1549–1719." *Journal of the History of Ideas* 44 (1983): 387–406.
Speyer, Heinrich. *Die biblischen Erzählungen im Qoran*. Darmstadt: Wissenschaftliche Buchgesellschaft, 1961.
Stanzel, Franz K. "Telegony: Procreation from a Distance. An Ignored or Suppressed Motif in Literature." *Anglistik. Mitteilungen des deutschen Anglistenverbandes* 11 (2000): 1–15.
———. *Telegonie – Fernzeugung. Macht und Magie der Imagination*. Vienna: Böhlau, 2008.
Starbuck, Edwin D. *The Psychology of Religion*. London: Scott, 1899.
Starnes, Thomas C. *Christoph Martin Wieland. Leben und Werk*. 3 vols. Sigmaringen: Thorbecke, 1987.
Staves, Susan. *A Literary History of Women's Writing in Britain, 1660–1789*. Cambridge: Cambridge University Press, 2006.
Stecher, Henry F. *Elizabeth Singer Rowe, the Poetess of Frome: A Study in Eighteenth-Century English Pietism*. Berne: Herbert Lang, 1973.

Stern, M.S. "Muhammad and Joseph: A Study of Koranic Narrative." *Journal of Near Eastern Studies* 44 (1985): 193–204.
Stichel, Rainer. *Beiträge zur frühen Geschichte des Psalters und zur Wirkungsgeschichte der Psalmen.* Abhandlungen der nordrhein-westfälischen Akademie der Wissenschaften 116. Paderborn: Schöningh, 2007.
Stolleis, Michael. *Geschichte des öffentlichen Rechts in Deutschland. Erster Band: Reichspublizistik und Policeywissenschaft, 1600–1800.* Munich: Beck, 1988.
Straub, Kristina. *Domestic Affairs: Intimacy, Eroticism, and Violence between Servants and Masters in Eighteenth-Century Britain.* Baltimore, Md.: Johns Hopkins University Press, 2009.
Stüssel, Kerstin. *In Vertretung. Literarische Mitschriften von Bürokratie zwischen früher Neuzeit und Gegenwart.* Tübingen: Niemeyer, 2004.
Tapié, Victor-L. *France in the Age of Louis XIII and Richelieu.* Translated and edited by D. McN. Lockie. Cambridge: Cambridge University Press, 1984.
Taylor, Dick. "Joseph as Hero in Joseph Andrews." *Tulane Studies in English* 7 (1957): 91–109.
Thalmann, Marianne. *Der Trivialroman des 18. Jahrhunderts und der romantische Roman: Ein Beitrag zur Entwicklungsgeschichte der Geheimbundmystik.* Berlin: Ebering, 1923.
Thiel, Michael. *Johann Friedrich Ernst Albrecht (1752–1814), Arzt, medizinischer Volksschriftsteller, politischer Belletrist.* Bamberg: Schmacht, 1970.
Thompson, John L. "The Immoralities of the Patriarchs in the History of Exegesis: A Reappraisal of Calvin's Position." *Calvin Theological Journal* 26 (1991): 9–46.
Thomson, Erik. "France's Grotian Moment? Hugo Grotius and Cardinal Richelieu's Commercial Statecraft." *French History* 21 (2007): 377–94.
Till, Dietmar. *Das doppelte Erhabene. Eine Argumentationsfigur von der Antike bis zum Beginn des 19. Jahrhunderts.* Tübingen: Niemeyer, 2006.
Tolstoy, Leo. *What Is Art?.* Translated by Richard Pevear and Larissa Volokhonsky. London: Penguin, 1995.
Trapnell, William H. "Destiny in Voltaire's *Zadig* and *The Arabian Nights*." *Studies on Voltaire and the Eighteenth Century* 278 (1990): 147–71.
Turner, David M. "Adulterous Kisses and the Meanings of Familiarity in Early Modern Britain." Pages 80–97 in *The Kiss in History.* Edited by Karen Harvey. Manchester: Manchester University Press, 2005.
Turner, James Grantham. *Libertines and Radicals in Early Modern London: Sexuality, Politics, and Literary Culture, 1630–1685.* Cambridge: Cambridge University Press, 2002.
———. "The Erotics of the Novel." Pages 214–34 in *A Companion to the Eighteenth-Century English Novel and Culture.* Edited by Paula A. Backscheider and Catherine Ingrassia. Oxford: Blackwell, 2005.
Uglow, Jenny. *Hogarth: A Life and a World.* London: Faber & Faber, 1997.
Unger, Johan. *On Religious Experience: A Psychological Study.* Stockholm: Almqvist & Wiksell, 1976.
van den Berg, Jan. "English Deism and Germany: The Thomas Morgan Controversy." *Journal of Ecclesiastical History* 59 (2008): 48–61.
van der Schueren, Eric. "La Tragédie biblique à Sceaux: le Joseph de Charles-Claude Genest (1706)." Pages 209–29 in *La Duchesse du Maine (1676–1753). Une mécène à la croisée des arts et des siècles.* Edited by Fabrice Preyat (Etudes sur le 18e siècle 31). Brussels: Editions de l'Université de Bruxelles, 2003.
Verdi, Richard. *Bartholomeus Breenbergh (1598–1657): Joseph Distributing Corn in Egypt.* Birmingham: The Barber Institute of Fine Arts, 2004.
Vermij, Rienk H. "The English Deists and the *Traité*." Pages 241–54 in *Heterodoxy, Spinozism, and Free Thought in Early Eighteenth-Century Europe.* Edited by Silvia Berti et al. Dordrecht: Kluwer, 1996.
Vetter, Theodor. "J.J. Bodmer und die englische Litteratur." Pages 313–86 in *Johann Jakob Bodmer. Denkschrift zum CC. Geburtstag (19. Juli 1898).* By Theodor Vetter et al. Zurich: Müller, 1900.

Vollenhoven, Cornelis van. "Sophompaneas." Vol. 1, pages 231–45 in *Mr. C. van Vollenhoven's Verspreide Geschriften*. 3 vols. 's Gravenhage: Nijhoff, 1934–1935.

Walker, Robert G. "Rochester and the Issue of Deathbed Repentance in Restoration and Eighteenth-Century England." *South Atlantic Review* 47 (1982): 21–37.

Ward, Albert. *Book Production, Fiction, and the German Reading Public, 1740–1800*. Oxford: Clarendon Press, 1974. Pages 59–91: "The Growth of the Novel-reading Habit."

Watt, Ian. *The Rise of the Novel: Studies in Defoe, Richardson and Fielding*. London: Chatto & Windus, 1957.

Weigelt, Horst. *Johann Kaspar Lavater. Leben, Werk und Wirkung*. Göttingen: Vandenhoeck & Ruprecht, 1991.

Weil, Françoise. *Livres interdits, livres persécutés 1720–1770*. Oxford: Voltaire Foundation, 1999.

Weilen, Alexander von. *Der ägyptische Joseph im Drama des XVI. Jahrhunderts*. Vienna: Hölder, 1887.

Weintraut, Edward James. "Islands in an Archipelago: The German Dramatized Novel." *German Quarterly* 70 (1997): 376–94.

Weller, Emil. *Lexicon Pseudonymorum: Wörterbuch der Pseudonymen aller Zeiten und Völker*. 2nd edn. Regensburg: Coppenrath, 1886.

Welzig, Werner. "Einige Aspekte barocker Romanregister." Pages 562–70 in *Stadt – Schule – Universität – Buchwesen und die deutsche Literatur im 17. Jahrhundert*. Edited by Albrecht Schöne. Munich: Beck, 1976.

White, Hayden. *Metahistory: The Historical Imagination in Nineteenth-Century Europe*. Baltimore, Md.: Johns Hopkins University Press, 1973.

Widmann, Horst. "Der 'jugendbewegte Pestalozzi'. Porträt einer Jugendbewegung im Zürich des 18. Jahrhunderts." Pages 42–61 in *Pestalozzi im internationalen Gespräch*. Edited by Sylvia Springer. Zurich: Orell Füssli, 1990.

Wills, Lawrence M. *The Jewish Novel in the Ancient World*. Ithaca, NY: Cornell University Press, 1995.

Wimmer, Ruprecht. *Jesuitentheater. Didaktik und Fest – Das Exemplum des ägyptischen Joseph auf den deutschen Bühnen der Gesellschaft Jesu*. Frankfurt: Klostermann, 1982.

Witt, Ronald, John M. Najemi, Craig Kallendorf, and Werner Gundersheimer. "Hans Baron's Renaissance Humanism." *American Historical Review* 101 (1996): 107–44.

Wittmann, Reinhard. "Gibt es eine Leserevolution am Ende des 18. Jahrhunderts?". Pages 419–54 and 611–13 in *Die Welt des Lesens*. Edited by Roger Chartier and Guglielmo Cavallo. Frankfurt: Campus, 1999.

Wunder, Bernd. "Hof und Verwaltung im 17. Jahrhundert." *Daphnis* 11 (1982): 5–14.

Zagorin, Perez. *Rebels and Rulers, 1500–1660*. 2 vols. Cambridge: Cambridge University Press, 1982.

Index

Abraham
  ancestor of Joseph, 98, 216
  conveys wisdom to Egypt, 230, 240, 356 n.27
Adams, Abraham (fictional character), 7, 153, 155, 159–60, 170
Adams, John, 296
Addison, Joseph, 289
adultery
  in Joseph story, 46, 76, 131
  as mental act, 120, 131, 136
  not legally punishable, 116
  preaching against, 132
  in Western moral code, 116
  see also libertinism
Aeneid (Virgil), 46, 128–29, 212, 308
  birthday oracle, 212
  in Chateaubriand's reading list, 330–31
  Dido episode, 49–50, 128–29, 143, 147–49
  source for Fracastoro, 47, 49–50, 354 n.9
  in Voltaire's reading list, 307–08
Akhenaten, 15–16
Albrecht, Johann Friedrich Ernst, 228–46
  creates Masonic Joseph figure, 13, 232–38
  depends on Terrasson, 235–36
  as Freemason, 355 n.5
  and Jewish emancipation, 238–40
  see also Keusche Joseph, Der
Albrecht, Johann Georg, 90
Alfonso el Sabio, 42–44
Amsterdam, 192, 200–03
  art in, 106, 108, 200–02
  Joseph plays performed in, 13, 203
Andrews, Joseph (fictional character), *see Joseph Andrews*
angel, Joseph's guardian, 47, 48, 50, 124, 126, 129, 139, 144, 207

Annet, Peter, 268
Apuleius, 167
Arabian Nights, The, 41, 43, 87, 296, 301
  and Voltaire, 9, 273, 294, 301–02, 308, 310, 312
Aristotle, 4, 119, 250, 265
  as literary critic, 292–94, 302, 304, 325–26
Artapanus, 32–33, 53
Assenat (Zesen), 204–05
  critical reception of, 212–13
  illustrations in, 215, 217, 220, 222
  interpretation, 213–27
  as learned novel, 210–13
  plot summary, 205–10
  political message, 221–27
  sources, 212–13
  has a subject index, 211, 212
  theory of excess and restraint in, 213–21
astrology, 211
Astruc, Jean, 290, 293, 359 n.2
Augustine, 148, 331

Bahrdt, Karl Friedrich, 234–35
Baker, Daniel, 131–32
Bakhtin, Mikhail M., 149
Bamberger, Ludwig, 104–05
Baron, Hans, 191
Barrow, Isaac, 173–74
Baour-Lormian, Pierre, 334–35
Bauer, Georg Lorenz, 283–84
Baxter, Richard, 61
Bayle, Pierre, 251–53, 257, 278
Behn, Aphra, 126
Behrisch, Ernst Wolfgang, 95
Bible enfin expliquée, La (Voltaire), 276, 277–83, 302

bibles for children, 63, 66–67, 71, 76, 81, 86
  illustrations in, 77
Bildungsroman, 169
birthday oracle, *see* oracle
blasphemy, 258–59
Bochart, Samuel, 212
Bodin, Jean, 183
Bodmer, Johann Jakob, 119–20, 138–52
  critical interest in Mrs Rowe, 119, 138,
    141–44, 147, 149
  and Wieland, 141, 144–47, 149, 151
  writes Joseph epic, 119, 138–41
  see also Joseph und Zulika
Bogatzky, Karl Heinrich von, 94–96
Boileau, Nicolas, 324
Bossuet, Jacques-Bénigne, 250, 254, 270–71,
    277, 312, 330–32
Boswell, James, appreciates Joseph story,
    290, 291–92
Boulanger, Nicolas-Antoine, 278, 282
Breenbergh, Bartholomeus, 100, 106–08,
    111, 202
  illustrations 106, 201
Bunyan, John, 3, 62, 126, 131–32,
    170–71, 289
Burnet, Gilbert, 115–16, 134

Calmet, Augustin, 272–73, 276, 277
Calvin, John, 271
Calypso, 167–68
censorship, 357 n.9
  in Britain, 256–57, 259, 275, 278
  in France, 243, 282–83, 296, 308
Ceriziers, René de, 197, 290, 293–95
Cervantes, Miguel de, 51, 171, 289
Chandler, Samuel, defends Joseph's integrity
    against Morgan, 266, 268
Chapman, John, 266
chastity
  female, 116, 126, 133, 139, 155, 159,
    219–20
  male, 13, 37, 75, 123, 129, 132, 144,
    174–75, 177
Chateaubriand, François-René de, 317–35
  compares Homer and Bible, 319, 324–28
  influenced by Pope, 328
  inspired by Rollin, 320
  literary canon, 330–32
  and Voltaire, 294, 318, 328–30
  see also Génie du Christianisme
children
  education of, 57–64
  Joseph story told to, 59–60, 67–70, 75–76

  story of Joseph loved by, 61–62, 64,
    85–86
  see also education; bibles for children
China as model for the West, 251, 268, 272
Christ, Joseph as type of, 74, 150, 345 n.22
Christliches Handbüchlein für Kinder
    (Lavater), 66–83
  critical reception, 82
  frontispiece, 79
  Joseph story retold, 67–70
  moral instruction, 75–76
  pedagogical method, 77–83
  personal piety, 71–75
Cicero, 181–82, 191, 195, 332
Cinna, 197, 312–13
city, immorality of
  in Fielding, 154–55, 168–71, 176
  in Mrs Rowe, 135
Claudius, Matthias, 235
Clauer, Johann Balthasar David, 92
clemency
  in Ceriziers, 197, 295
  in Corneille, 196–97
  in Grotius, 182, 194–96
  in Montesquieu, 313
  in Seneca, 196–97
  in Voltaire, 15, 295, 312, 315
  see also forgiving others
Cobden, Edward, 132
Collenuccio, Pandolfo, 46
Comenius, Johann Amos, 331
conscience
  clear, 20, 68
  guilty, 19, 69, 75, 322
conte, 61, 300
conte philosophique, 15, 296, 300, 304,
    310, 329
Corneille, Pierre, 196–97, 306, 331
court
  Joseph story read or performed at, 12,
    77, 80
  Joseph story retold as parable of courtly
    life, 221–27
Cowley, Abraham, 151
Cudworth, Ralph, 233

Daniel in der Löwen-Grube (Moser),
    90–93, 99
Dante Alighieri, 331
deathbed repentance, *see* repentance
Deffand, Mme du, 296–97, 304–07, 309, 316
deism, 15, 73, 251, 253, 259–60, 357 n.13,
    359 n.52

and Church of England, 259
  religious creed of, 256
demonic forces (devils, evil angels) manipulating Potiphar's wife
  in Bodmer, 139–47
  in Fracastoro, 47–48
  in Mrs Rowe, 117, 123–24, 126
  in Romanos, 46
  in Testaments of the Twelve
    Patriarchs, 35
Dennis, John, 330, 361 n.1
Desdossat, Jacques-François La Baume, 150
desire
  distinct from love, 145
  element of love, 121
  therapy of, 117–18
  uncontrolled, 134
despotism originating with Joseph, 254, 258, 265, 267, 299
Diaspora novella, 24–28
Dichtung und Wahrheit (Goethe), 84–99
  report of destruction of juvenile writings, 95
Dickens, Charles, 51, 153
Dictionnaire philosophique (Voltaire), 276, 294, 296–313
  article "Joseph" translated, 297–99
Diderot, Denis
  on ancient Egypt, 243
  daughter of, 61
  editor of the Encyclopédie, 243, 313
  as literary critic, 289–90
  sentimentality of, 306, 313
Dido 49–50, 128–29, 143, 147–49
Diodorus Siculus, 44, 127, 190
Dodd, William, 3, 96, 331
Du Halde, Jean-Baptiste, 251
  see also China

education
  in early-modern Europe, 57–64
  responsibility of father for, 57–59, 62, 80
  role of mother in, 77–80
  use of Joseph story in, 59–61, 66, 85
  use of stories in, 57, 81
Egypt
  Abraham in, 230, 240, 365 n.27
  as another Dutch Republic, 189–92
  deities of, 110, 126, 182, 206, 209, 214, 227, 230
  fertility of, 110, 215, 261, 285
  Jewish Diaspora in, 24–25, 27–28, 32, 34–35

Joseph trained in wisdom of, 257, 283–84
  modern study of, 15, 211–12
  moral laxity in, 34
  Napoleon in, 334
  reformed by Joseph, 32, 189–90, 231, 261
  ruled by Hebrews, 254, 265
  ruled by priests, *see* priestcraft, priests
Eichendorff, Joseph von, 212–13
Encyclopédie (Diderot et al.), 243, 290, 313
Enlightenment
  and politics, 184, 244, 246, 249, 259
  study of history, 252
  undermines authority of religion, Bible, church, 243, 275, 282–83, 317–18, 329–30, 333
  view of history, 250
  see also Bayle; deism; *Homme aux quarante écus*; Voltaire
epic poetry
  as declining genre, 9, 46, 151–52, 289
  as the most noble genre, 127, 152
  novelised, 149–50
  theory of, 127, 142, 146–47, 149–50
Erasmus of Rotterdam, 7
essay, 299–300

Famine Stela, 285–86
Fénelon, 11, 235–36, 319, 331, 343 n.7
  Les Aventures de Télémaque, 66, 85, 90, 236, 296, 319, 347
  Dialogues sur l'éloquence, 319
  De l'Éducation des filles, 60, 66
Fielding, Henry, 7, 31, 153–76, 308
  on love, 120–21
  see also Joseph Andrews
Filmer, Robert, 250
Firdausi, 41
first minister in early-modern Europe, 180–81, 184, 192, 195, 197
  in Joseph story, 18–19, 180–81, 275
Fisch, Harold, 52
Fleury, Claude, 59, 319–20
folk-tale, 23, 29–30, 254, 277
Fontanes, Louis de, 317–18
forgiving others
  in biblical Joseph story, 21
  in Ceriziers, 197, 295
  in Grotius, 188, 194, 196–97
  in Steele, 292–93
  in Sterne, 293
  in Voltaire, 297, 299, 312–14
  see also clemency

388 INDEX

Forster, E.M., 149, 314
Fortuna (fate), 171, 310, 326
Foucault, Michel, 117
Fracastoro, Girolamo
   uses Virgil, 47, 49–50, 354 n.9
   writes Joseph epic, 47–50
Frederick the Great
   and Albrecht, 228, 245
   as deist, 256
   and Voltaire, 272, 316
freedom of religion in Grotius, 193
Freemasonry, 181, 232, 236–41
   initiation into, 236–38
   and Judaism, 239–40
French Revolution, 14, 88, 242, 250
   Albrecht and, 228
   Chateaubriand and, 317–18, 329, 333–34
   Lavater and, 12, 80
Fréret, Nicolas, 283

Galland, Antoine, 296, 301
Gellert, Christian Fürchtegott, 94–95, 238–39
General estoria (Alfonso el Sabio), 43–44
Genest, Charles-Claude, 315, 319, 363 n.66
Génie du Christianisme (Chateaubriand), 318–19, 332–33
   Joseph story in, 320–29
   Joseph story compared with Homer, 324–29
Goethe, Cornelia, 62, 84–86, 94–95
Goethe, Johann Caspar ("Councillor Goethe"), 84, 85, 87, 90, 92–93, 111
Goethe, Johann Wolfgang, 65–66, 73, 81, 153, 169, 256, 335, 363–64 n.68
   appreciates Méhul's Joseph, 99
   destroys his "Joseph", 95–96
   early interest in Joseph story, 84–111
   uses Moser's Daniel as model for writing a Joseph story, 90–92
   summarises biblical Joseph story in autobiography, 98
   and Trautmann's Joseph paintings, 85–86, 100, 104–05
   see also Dichtung und Wahrheit; "Neue Paris. Ein Knabenmärchen, Der"
Goethe Museum (Frankfurt), 84, 100, 108
Grimmelshausen, 204, 211–13, 216, 218
Grotius, Hugo, 181–82, 186–203
   as another Joseph?, 199–200
   and Richelieu, 192–97
   see also Sophompaneas

Halde, Jean-Baptiste Du, *see* Du Halde
Hall, Joseph, 74, 324
Händel, Georg Friedrich, 11
Heliodorus
   extols chastity, 174–75
   source for Fielding, 121, 157–59
   source for Grimmelshausen, 218
Hengel, Martin, 284–85
Henry, Matthew, 136, 256
Herder, Caroline 63
Herder, Johann Gottfried, 82, 97
Herodotus, 28, 189, 211, 225–26, 301
Hippolytus, 49, 129, 298, 302
Historia Aseneth, see Joseph and Aseneth
history, critical study of, 249–52
History of Joseph, The (Mrs Rowe)
   message, 129–37
   plot summary, 123–26
   sources, 127–29
   Sylvester as source, 128
   reviewed by Bodmer, 141–42
Hobbes, Thomas, 275
home as setting for biblical reading or instruction, 57–63, 77, 80
Homer
   Bodmer as German Homer, 148
   Calypso episode, 167–68
   on Chateaubriand's reading list, 331
   inferior to Joseph story, 297, 302, 304, 308, 311–12, 324–29
   Milton as Christian Homer, 127
   reflects same milieu as the Old Testament, 319
Homme aux quarante écus, L' (Voltaire), 8–9
Hort, Josiah, 290–91
Hübner, Johann, 63, 71, 75–76, 81
humanism, civic, 191
Hume, David, 184, 267, 307
Hunter, Paul, 6
Husbands, John, 291

iconic character, ceremony, presentation, 4–6, 340 n.6
intellectuals, 242–45, 259
intertext, 10, 160
Isis (goddess), 110, 126, 140, 144, 206, 210–11, 214–15, 219
Islamic Joseph traditions, 39–45

Jâmi, 41
Jaspers, Karl, 4
Jesuits, 12, 212, 243, 270, 314, 316
   Joseph in school theatre, 12, 314, 316

Jews, Judaism
    Diaspora Judaism in antiquity, 24–30
    Jewish emancipation, 238–40
    Jews in high office, 27–28, 34–35, 278
    Joseph in Jewish tradition, 31–39
    Joseph's Judaism contrasted with that of
        Moses, 28–30
Johnson, Samuel, 289
    against biblical epic poetry, 151
    on novels, 362 n.14
    on reading, 8
Joseph, negative image of
    in Albrecht, 245
    in Calvin, 271
    in Emilie du Châtelet, 272
    in John Adams, 269
    in Lord Shaftesbury, 253, 256–57
    in Morgan, 253–54, 258–68
    in Peter Annet, 268
    in Reimarus, 269
    in Voltaire, 275–76
Joseph Andrews (Fielding)
    echoes Heliodorus, 120, 157–59
    moral message, 172–76
    plot summary, 153–56
    scenes of seduction, 161–72
    sources, 157–61
Joseph and Aseneth (also called *Historia
    Aseneth, Story of Aseneth, The Marriage
    and Conversion of Aseneth*), 32, 37–38,
    52–53, 211
    plot summary, 37–38
Joseph as statesman
    in Albrecht, 184–85, 240–46
    in art, 105–11, 201
    in Artapanus, 32–33
    in the Bible, 27–28
    in Grotius, 181–82, 189–200
    in Morgan, 253–54, 265
    in Philo, 33–35, 180
    in Zesen, 184, 221–27
    see also first minister
Joseph story
    in art, 11, 84–86, 88, 100–11, 200–02,
        341 n.22
    in the Bible, 17–30
    calls for narrative elaboration, 52–54,
        60, 89
    date of, 23, 282, 285–86, 341 n.4,
        360 n.43
    as Diaspora novella, 24–28
    as fiction, 275, 276, 294, 301
    as folk-tale, 23, 29–30, 61, 254

as historical account, 213, 252–53, 256,
    265, 283–84
in historical criticism, 252–54, 257,
    261–69, 271–72, 276–86
in literary criticism, 290–95, 297–316,
    319–33
loved by children, 61, 62, 64, 85–86
as oral tale, 23, 24
as oriental tale, 254, 301–04
as philosophical tale, 310–14
plot summary, 17–21
in religious education, 11–12, 59–64,
    66–83, 257, 314–15
told to children, 59–60, 67–70, 75–76
Joseph und Zulika (Bodmer)
    characterisation of Joseph and Zulika,
        144–49
    as novelised epic, 149–52
    plot summary, 138–41
    sources, 141–44
Josephus, 27, 211, 234, 356 n.27
    on biblical Joseph, 292
    on Joseph, Jewish tax collector,
        278–82, 284
Judaism, *see* Jews
Justinus, Marcus Junianus, 257

Kant, Immanuel, 244
Keusche Joseph, Der (Albrecht)
    as historical novel, 233–38
    as Masonic novel, 232–33
    plot summary, 229–32
    as political story, 240–46
    as story of Jewish emancipation, 238–40
    Terrasson as source, 235–36
Kircher, Athanasius, 212
Klettenberg, Katharina von, 92
Klopstock, Friedrich Gottlieb, 90, 151,
    290, 323
Kölsch, Gerhard, 100
Konstan, David, 158, 175
Kunz, Andreas, 285
Küsell (Kysel), Melchior, 105, 108
Kyburz, Abraham, 86, 345 n.6

La Roche, Sophie von, 64
Lampo, Hubert, 16
Lavater, Johann Kaspar, 65–83
    lectures on Joseph to adults, 67, 73, 76
    writes on Joseph for children, 66–67,
        76, 77
    see also *Christliches Handbüchlein für
        Kinder*

Le Jay, Gabriel, 314–15
Lenski, Gerhard, 242
Lessing, Gotthold Ephraim, 238–39, 256
Letters Moral and Entertaining (Mrs Rowe), 134–37
libertinism, 13, 115–20, 126, 130–37, 150, 339
   teaches free love, 116
Lisbon earthquake, 311
literature, critical study of
   in the 18th century, 148–50, 289–95
   today, 50, 149, 336–339
Locke, John
   on Bible reading, 11, 61, 257
   as political theorist, 250, 258–59, 265–66
London, city of loose morals, 115, 120, 154–55, 168–73; cf. 135
Longinus, 324
love, patterns of
   chaste love (Heliodorus, Fielding), 120–21, 156, 174–75
   free love, libertinism (Rochester), 116, 175
   guilty, scrupulous love (Mrs Rowe), 135–36
   irresistible Eros, sensibility (Bodmer), 148, 150
   see also desire
Luisini, Francesco, 49
Lüthi, Max, 29–30

Machiavelli, Niccolò, 182
Maiden's Blush, The (Sylvester), 123, 128
Manetho, 264–65
Mann, Thomas, 16
masquerade, 131–32
Massillon, Jean-Baptiste, 331–32
Méhul, Etienne-Nicolas, 11, 99, 334–35
Meier, Joachim, 212–13
Mencius, 251, 268
Mencius Philalethes (Peter Annet), 268
Mendelssohn, Moses, 240
Miller, Hugh, 62
Milton, John, 75, 119, 123, 126–27, 131, 138, 150–51, 289, 330–31
   source of literary motifs, 147, 159
minister, first, *see* first minister
Montesquieu, 313, 331, 363 n.68
Moral Philosopher, The (Morgan)
   critical reception, 265–66
   Joseph historically explained, 264–65
   Joseph passages summarised, 261–64
   as political statement, 267–69

More, Thomas, 183, 184
Morgan, Thomas, 258–69
   and Locke, 259, 266, 357 n.14
   and Shaftesbury, 258
   and Shuckford, 264
   see also Moral Philosopher, The
Moritz, Karl Philipp von, 91–92, 362 n.4
Moser, Friedrich Carl Ludwig, 91–93, 99
Moses contrasted with Joseph, 28–29
Muhammad, 39–41
   identifies with Joseph, 40–41
Mumford, Lewis, 269
Murillo, Bartolomé Esteban, 102, 104

Napoleon, 318, 333–35
"Neue Paris. Ein Knabenmärchen, Der" (Goethe), 87–88
Newton, Isaac, 174
Noozeman van den Bergh, Adriana, 202–03
novel
   dramatised, 229
   emergence of, 9, 13, 149–52, 289
   Heliodor as model for the genre, 157–58
   historical, 181, 210–13, 233, 238, 281, 314
   novelisation of literature, 149–50
nurse as confidante
   in classical literature, 50, 127–29, 326
   in Joseph stories, 42, 47–48, 50, 53, 125, 129, 133, 140, 142, 146

oracle
   birthday oracle for Aseneth, 48–50, 205–06, 212, 226
   literary source of, 354 n.9

Paris
   Joseph plays performed in, 99, 314–15, 334–35
   salons in, 243, 289, 296–97, 304–5, 316, 334, 361 n.1
Pascal, Blaise, 130–31, 307, 331
Paw, Cornelis de, 233
Perrault, Charles, 314
Peter Comestor, 44
Phaedra (Seneca), 46, 49–50, 128–29, 146, 302
Philo of Alexandria, 33–35, 53–54, 167, 180
piety, personal, 71–75
poeta doctus, 50, 159, 161, 210–13
Pope, Alexander, 7, 119, 146, 290, 328
Potiphar's wife
   in art, 102–03, 202; cf. 162–66
   assimilated to Dido, 128, 147–49

assimilated to Phaedra, 128–29
  as Cyrene in Ceriziers, 197
  as Daluka in Albrecht, 235
  as Geertje Dircx in Rembrandt, 202
  as Iëmpsar/Jempsar in Fracastoro and Vondel, 47, 203
  as Lady Booby, Mrs Slipslop and Betty in Fielding, 154–55, 162
  more interesting character than Joseph, 41, 149
  as Sabrina in Mrs Rowe, 117, 119, 124–36
  as Sephira in Zesen, 206, 223, 355 n.26
  tries to seduce Joseph, 18
  unnamed in Bible and Qur'an, 18, 39
  as Zulayme in Alfonso el Sabio, 43
  as Zuleika in Islamic tradition, 39–42, 298
  as Zulika in Bodmer, 119–20, 138–52
  see also demonic forces; seduction
Pratt, Samuel, 127
priestcraft, priests (of Egypt and in the modern world), 265, 267–68, 283–84
  appreciated, 236, 244, 250
  criticised, 243, 253, 257, 262, 264, 268

Qur'an, 39–41

Racine, Jean, 289, 296, 302, 303, 306, 330–32
reading
  Bodmer's reading list, 152
  Chateaubriand's reading list, 331
  history of, 6–9, 228, 296, 355 n.1
  Lavater's reading list, 66
  Voltaire's reading list, 9, 307
recognition, scene of (*anagnôrisis*)
  in Chateaubriand, 322, 325–26, 332
  in literary theory, 292, 294, 302, 305
  in Rollin, 294–95
  in Voltaire, 294, 299, 302, 304
Reimarus, Hermann Samuel, 269, 359 n.52
Reiser, Anton (fictional character), 8
Rembrandt, 11, 102–03, 106–07, 200–02
Renan, Ernest, 28
repentance
  on deathbed, 126, 134
  of Joseph's brothers, 75
  of Potiphar's wife, 40–42, 53, 126, 134
république des lettres, 243, 252, 260
Richardson, Samuel, 153, 157, 159, 289, 296, 305–06
Richelieu, 180, 182, 184, 189, 192–97, 295, 356 n.42
Rivet, Frédéric, 59–60, 61

Rochester, John Wilmot, Earl of, 115–16, 126, 134
Rollin, Charles, 60, 290, 294–95, 316, 319–20, 327, 331
Romanos the Melodist, 45–46
Romanticism, 9, 138, 142, 318, 332–33
Rousseau, Jean-Jacques, 66, 150, 153, 256, 306
  on reading, 7
Rowe, Mrs Elizabeth Singer, 117–18, 123–37
  influenced by Pascal, 130–31
  see also History of Joseph, The; Letters Moral and Entertaining

Saint-Exupéry, Antoine de, 300
Saint-Pierre, Bernardin de, 306
salon, 243, 296–97
Saumaise, Claude, 301
Scarron, Paul, 3, 157, 160–62
Schiller, Friedrich, 228
Schubart, Martin, 100, 104–105, 345 n.3
Scott, Walter, 213, 314
Scudéry, Madeleine de, 137
Seckendorff, Veit Ludwig von, 183
seduction, attempt at,
  in the biblical Joseph story, 18
  in early-modern adaptations, 115–76
  told to children and adults, 76
  see also Potiphar's wife
Seekatz, Johann Conrad, 85, 86, 105
Semiramis, 124–25, 128, 132–33
Seneca
  on clemency, 194, 196–97
  on iconic characters, 340 n.6
  see also Phaedra
sensibility, 138, 146, 148–49
sexual morality in early-modern Europe, 115–22, 131–32, 134–37, 172–76
  see also desire; libertinism; Stoicism
sexuality, invention of, 117
Shakespeare, William, 96–97, 153, 289, 296, 306, 331
Shuckford, Samuel, 253, 264–65, 290
Simon, Richard, 359 n.2
simplicity
  of manners idealised, 50, 154, 170–71, 303, 321–22, 324, 326, 364 n. 5
  of style as literary ideal, 51, 82, 151, 309, 323, 326, 328
Sophompaneas (Grotius)
  critical of Richelieu, 193–97
  as lesson in statecraft, 189–97

performed in Amsterdam, 203
plot summary, 187–89
Spinoza, Baruch de, 73, 203, 273
Steele, Richard, 290, 292–93
Sterne, Laurence,
   on Joseph, 290, 293
   and Voltaire, 313
Stoicism
   clemency as Stoic virtue, 196–97, 293, 313
   constancy as Stoic virtue, 53
   impact on Judaism and Christianity, 37, 118
   Stoic teaching on sexual morality and passions, 37, 117–19, 121, 136, 146, 148
Story of Aseneth, see Joseph and Aseneth
sublime, the, 148, 300, 323–24, 328
Sulzer, Johann Georg, 148
Swift, Jonathan, 153, 307
Sylvester, Joshua, 50, 123, 128–29

Tasso, Torquato, 330–31
tears
   in Chateaubriand, 303, 320–27
   express admiration, 303, 322–23
   at moments of recognition, 70, 188, 292, 294–95, 304, 522
   as response to happy ending, 297, 322
   as response of reader, listener, audience, 64, 139, 148, 292, 297, 315, 362 n.4
   shed by Joseph, 303, 320, 324
   shed by Ulysses, 324–25
   in Voltaire, 297, 303–04, 315
telegony (shaping of human foetus by external factors)
   in Fielding's *Joseph Andrews*, 218
   in Heliodorus, 218
   in Zesen's *Assenat*, 216–18
Terrasson, Jean, author of *Sethos*, 235–36
Testaments of the Twelve Patriarchs, 32, 35–37, 39, 211–12
   influenced by Stoicism, 37, 53, 342 n.14
   plot summary, 35–36
theatre
   age of the, 153, 296, 306–7
   Joseph story on stage, 99, 203, 205, 314–16, 334–35; cf. 229
Thomasius, Christian, 13–14
Thoranc, François de Théas Comte de, 84–89, 104–05, 109, 111
   portrayed as Joseph, 111
   understood as Joseph by Goethe, 88
Thym, Johann Heinrich, 85–86
Toland, John, 256
Tolstoy, Leo, 50–51
Trautmann, Johann Georg, 84–86, 89, 100–11
Turell, Jane, 137
typology, *see* Christ
tyranny, *see* despotism

Uglow, Jenny, 116
Ussher, James, 253, 255, 264, 270–71

Vanini, Giulio-Cesare, 267
Venice, 191–92, 204
Vico, Giambattista, 359 n. 13
Vincent of Beauvais, 37
Virgil, *see Aeneid*
Voltaire (François Marie Arouet), 254, 270–86, 291, 294–316
   biblical critic, 272–74
   early encounter with Joseph story, 3 14–15
   historian of Joseph, 276–85
   literary canon, 9, 307
   literary critic of Joseph story, 297–314
   polemicist, 274–76
   see also La Bible enfin expliquée; Dictionnaire philosophique
Vondel, Joost van den, 202–03
Vossius, Isaac, 251

Warburton, William, 233, 250
Watts, Isaac, 118, 348 n.5
Wesley, Susanna, 61
Wieland, Christoph Martin
   and Bodmer, 141, 144–47, 149, 151
   and Sophie von La Roche, 64
Woolston, Thomas, 258

Xenophon, 27, 180, 319

Zadig (Voltaire), 301, 304, 310–12, 316
Zesen, Philipp von, 182–84, 204–27
   as *poeta doctus*, 210–13
   see also Assenat
Zurich
   home of Bodmer, 120, 144, 151
   home of Lavater, 12, 65, 73, 75